T0281492

Lecture Notes in Computer Science　14386

Founding Editors

Gerhard Goos
Juris Hartmanis

The series Lecture Notes in Computer Science (LNCS), including its subseries Lecture Notes in Artificial Intelligence (LNAI) and Lecture Notes in Bioinformatics (LNBI), has established itself as a medium for the publication of new developments in computer science and information technology research, teaching, and education.

LNCS enjoys close cooperation with the computer science R & D community, the series counts many renowned academics among its volume editors and paper authors, and collaborates with prestigious societies. Its mission is to serve this international community by providing an invaluable service, mainly focused on the publication of conference and workshop proceedings and postproceedings. LNCS commenced publication in 1973.

Zhifeng Bao · Renata Borovica-Gajic ·
Ruihong Qiu · Farhana Choudhury ·
Zhengyi Yang
Editors

Databases Theory and Applications

34th Australasian Database Conference, ADC 2023
Melbourne, VIC, Australia, November 1–3, 2023
Proceedings

 Springer

Editors
Zhifeng Bao
Royal Melbourne Institute of Technology
Melbourne, VIC, Australia

Renata Borovica-Gajic
The University of Melbourne
Melbourne, VIC, Australia

Ruihong Qiu
The University of Queensland
Brisbane, QLD, Australia

Farhana Choudhury
The University of Melbourne
Melbourne, VIC, Australia

Zhengyi Yang
The University of New South Wales
Sydney, NSW, Australia

ISSN 0302-9743 ISSN 1611-3349 (electronic)
Lecture Notes in Computer Science
ISBN 978-3-031-47842-0 ISBN 978-3-031-47843-7 (eBook)
https://doi.org/10.1007/978-3-031-47843-7

This Springer imprint is published by the registered company Springer Nature Switzerland AG
The registered company address is: Gewerbestrasse 11, 6330 Cham, Switzerland

Paper in this product is recyclable.

Preface

It is our pleasure to present to you the proceedings of the 34th Australasian Database Conference (ADC 2023), which took place in Melbourne, Australia. ADC is an annual international forum for sharing the latest research advancements and novel applications of database systems, data-driven applications, and data analytics between researchers and practitioners from around the globe, particularly Australia and New Zealand. The mission of ADC is to share novel research solutions to problems of today's information society that fulfill the needs of heterogeneous applications and environments and to identify new issues and directions for future research and development work. ADC seeks papers from academia and industry presenting research on all practical and theoretical aspects of advanced database theory and applications, as well as case studies and implementation experiences. All topics related to databases are of interest and within the scope of the conference. ADC gives researchers and practitioners a unique opportunity to share their perspectives with others interested in the various aspects of database systems.

As in previous years, the ADC 2023 Program Committee accepted papers considered as being of ADC quality without setting any predefined quota. The conference received 41 submissions and accepted 26 full research papers. Each paper was peer reviewed in full by three independent reviewers on average. A conscious decision was made to select the papers for which all reviews were positive and favorable. The Program Committee that selected the papers consisted of 52 members from around the globe, including Australia, China, and New Zealand, who were thorough and dedicated to the reviewing process.

We would like to thank all our colleagues who served on the Program Committee or acted as external reviewers. We would also like to thank all the authors who submitted their papers and the attendees. This conference is held for you, and we hope that with these proceedings, you can have an overview of this vibrant research community and its activities. We encourage you to make submissions to the next ADC conference and contribute to this community.

September 2023

Zhifeng Bao
Renata Borovica-Gajic
Ruihong Qiu
Farhana Choudhury
Zhengyi Yang

.

General Chairs' Welcome Message

On behalf of the organizers and Steering Committee for ADC 2023, I am honored to welcome you to the proceedings of the 34th Australasian Database Conference (ADC 2023). In Australia and New Zealand, ADC is the premier conference on research and applications of database systems, data-driven applications, and data analytics. Over the past decade, ADC has been held in Sydney (2022), Dunedin (2021), Melbourne (2020), Sydney (2019), Gold Coast (2018), Brisbane (2017), Sydney (2016), Melbourne (2015), Brisbane (2014), Adelaide (2013), and Melbourne (2012). This year, apart from a joint PhD workshop co-organized within the ADC conference, two new tracks have been introduced for the first time: the Encore track and the Shepherding track. To keep up with the latest important and relevant research in the community, we introduced the Encore Track to help disseminate interesting work in the field and foster interactions among researchers. In the Encore Track, researchers were welcome to submit an abstract, title, and author information of their recent publications at prestigious venues for encore presentation at ADC (part of ADC's PhD workshop). Specifically, submissions must have been published, in-press, or accepted for publication since 1 June, 2022 in other well-known scholarly conferences (including but not limited to SIGMOD, VLDB, ICDE, EDBT, KDD, and CIKM) or journals (including but not limited to IEEE TKDE, VLDB Journal, and ACM TODS). The authors of the accepted submissions were invited to present their work during the main conference via a poster session and a lightning talk session to enhance the interaction among research students. The Shepherding Track served as a novel venue for high-quality publications of research conducted by pre/early-PhDs and honours/master students. This track aimed to enrich the academic training and experience of junior students by selecting early-career researchers as shepherd mentors to provide actionable instructions on students' full research paper submissions. After going through one or more rounds of the shepherding process, if the submission's research contribution and quality met the expectation in quality, the submission was accepted into the main conference as a full research paper.

After careful consideration by the Program Committee, a total of 26 research papers were accepted for inclusion in the conference proceedings. We were very fortunate to have three keynote talks presented by world-leading researchers, Gao Cong from Nanyang Technological University, Geoff Webb from Monash University, and Ling Chen from the University of Technology Sydney. In addition, we are grateful to Tongliang Liu from the University of Sydney, Xin Yu and Zijian Wang from University of Queensland, Liang Zheng from Australian National University, Shirui Pan from Griffith University, Yang Cao from Hokkaido University, Bang Wu from CSIRO, and He Zhang from Monash University for their tutorials in the PhD workshop.

I wish to take this opportunity to thank all speakers, authors, and organizers. My special gratitude goes out to the Program Committee Co-chairs Zhifeng Bao and Renata Borovica-Gajic for their dedication in ensuring a high-quality program, all members of the Program Committee for their commitment to providing high-quality reviews,

Proceedings Co-chairs Farhana Murtaza Choudhury and Zhengyi Yang for their timely preparation of the conference proceedings, Local Chair Jianzhong Qi for his tremendous efforts in registration site setup and covering the conference logistics, Shepherding Track Chair Ruihong Qiu for his dedication in ensuring high-quality submission and shepherding, Encore Track Co-chairs Shixun Huang and Junhao Gan for their dedication in fostering the culture of learning from peers for PhD student training, PhD Workshop and Tutorial Chair Hui Luo for her efforts in coordinating tutorial speakers on data-centric AI that fall in the common interest between the database community and the machine learning community, Web Chair Yiyun Zhang for his tremendous efforts in website maintenance, Sponsorship Chair Shazia Sadiq for helping fund sponsorships of student travel grants, Publicity Co-chairs Kaiqi Zhao and Anh Dinh for their efforts in disseminating our call for papers and attracting submissions in different regions, and Local Co-chairs Aamir Cheema and Jianxin Li for their efforts in local organization. Without them, this year's ADC would not have been a success.

Melbourne is a multi-cultural city and ADC 2023 was held on the main campus of the University of Melbourne. We hope all contributors had a wonderful experience with the conference. We were pleased to welcome all participants of ADC 2023 to the conference, the campus, and the city.

Xiaofang Zhou
Gill Dobbie

Organization

General Chairs

Xiaofang Zhou   Hong Kong University of Science and
Technology, China
Gill Dobbie   University of Auckland, New Zealand

Program Chairs (Research Track)

Renata Borovica-Gajic   University of Melbourne, Australia
Zhifeng Bao   RMIT University, Australia

Program Chairs (Encore Track)

Junhao Gan   University of Melbourne, Australia
Shixun Huang   University of Wollongong, Australia

Program Chair (Shepherding Track)

Ruihong Qiu   University of Queensland, Australia

PhD Workshop and Tutorial Chair

Hui Luo   University of Wollongong, Australia

Publicity Chairs

Anh Dinh   Deakin University, Australia
Kaiqi Zhao   University of Auckland, New Zealand

Proceedings Chairs

Farhana Choudhury   University of Melbourne, Australia
Zhengyi Yang   University of New South Wales, Australia

Local Chairs

Jianzhong Qi   University of Melbourne, Australia
Muhammad Aamir Cheema   Monash University, Australia
Jianxin Li   Deakin University, Australia

Sponsorship Chair

Shazia Sadiq   University of Queensland, Australia

Web Chair

Yiyun Zhang   University of Queensland, Australia

Steering Committee Chair

Helen Huang   University of Queensland, Australia

Steering Committee

Hua Wang   Victoria University, Australia
Muhammad Aamir Cheema   Monash University, Australia
Sebastian Link   University of Auckland, Australia
Uwe Röhm   University of Sydney, Australia
Wenjie Zhang   University of New South Wales, Australia
Xiaofang Zhou   Hong Kong University of Science and
                               Technology, China
Xuemin Lin   Shanghai Jiao Tong University, China
Ying Zhang   University of Technology Sydney, Australia

Program Committee

Boyu Ruan	Hong Kong Unversity of Science and Technology, China
Chen Liu	RMIT University, Australia
Dan He	University of Queensland, Australia
Daokun Zhang	Monash University, Australia
David Tedjopurnomo	RMIT University, Australia
Dong Wen	University of New South Wales, Australia
Fengmei Jin	University of Queensland, Australia
Guangyan Huang	Deakin University, Australia
Hanzhi Wang	Renmin University of China, China
Hongxu Chen	Commonwealth Bank of Australia, Australia
Hua Wang	Victoria University, Australia
Janusz Getta	University of Wollongong, Australia
Jianfeng Qu	Soochow University, China
Jianzhong Qi	University of Melbourne, Australia
Jiaojiao Jiang	University of New South Wales, Australia
Jiayuan He	RMIT University, Australia
Jinli Cao	La Trobe University, Australia
Junhao Gan	University of Melbourne, Australia
Junhu Wang	Griffith University, Australia
Ke Deng	RMIT University, Australia
Lei Li	Hong Kong University of Science and Technology (Guangzhou), China
Lijun Chang	University of Sydney, Australia
Lu Chen	Swinburne University of Technology, Australia
Lu Qin	University of Technology Sydney, Australia
Lu Chen	Swinburne University of Technology, Australia
Miao Xu	University of Queensland, Australia
Muhammad Farhan	Australian National University, Australia
Muhammad Aamir Cheema	Monash University, Australia
Nur Al Hasan Haldar	University of Western Australia, Australia
Peiyu Yi	RMIT University, Australia
Pingfu Chao	Soochow University, China
Quoc Viet Hung Nguyen	Griffith University, Australia
Rui Zhou	Swinburne University of Technology, Australia
Ruihong Qiu	University of Queensland, Australia
Saiful Islam	University of Newcastle, Australia
Sebastian Link	University of Auckland, New Zealand
Sheng Wang	Wuhan University, China
Tarique Anwar	University of York, UK

Thanh Tam Nguyen	Griffith University, Australia
Tong Chen	University of Queensland, Australia
Weiqing Wang	Monash University, Australia
Wen Hua	Hong Kong Polytechnic University, China
Wenjie Zhang	University of New South Wales, Australia
Wentao Li	Hong Kong University of Science and Technology (Guangzhou), China
Xiangmin Zhou	RMIT University, Australia
Xiaoyang Wang	University of New South Wales, Australia
Xin Zheng	Monash University, Australia
Xin Cao	University of New South Wales, Australia
Ying Zhang	University of Technology Sydney, Australia
Yixin Liu	Monash University, Australia
Zhengyi Yang	University of New South Wales, Australia
Zhuo Zhang	University of Melbourne, Australia

Contents

Database Systems and Data Storage

Data Quality and Fairness for Graphs

Mining Complex Types of Data

kNN Join for Dynamic High-Dimensional Data: A Parallel Approach

Nimish Ukey[iD], Zhengyi Yang[✉][iD], Wenke Yang, Binghao Li, and Runze Li

The University of New South Wales, Sydney, NSW 2052, Australia
{n.ukey,zhengyi.yang,wenke.yang,binghao.li,runze.li1}@unsw.edu.au

Abstract. The k nearest neighbor (kNN) join operation is a fundamental task that combines two high-dimensional databases, enabling data points in the User dataset U to identify their k nearest neighbor points from the Item dataset I. This operation plays a crucial role in various domains, including knowledge discovery, data mining, similarity search applications, and scientific research. However, exact kNN search in high-dimensional spaces is computationally demanding, and existing sequential methods face challenges in handling large datasets. In this paper, we propose an efficient parallel solution for dynamic kNN join over high-dimensional data, leveraging the high-dimensional R tree (HDR Tree) for improved efficiency. Our solution harnesses the power of Simultaneous Multi-Threading (SMT) technologies and Single-Instruction-Multiple-Data (SIMD) instructions in modern CPUs for parallelisation. Importantly, our research is the first to introduce parallel computation for exact kNN join over high-dimensional data. Experimental results demonstrate that our proposed approach outperforms the sequential HDR Tree method by up to 1.2 times with a single thread. Moreover, our solution provides near-linear scalability as the number of threads increases.

Keywords: kNN join · high-dimensional data · parallel computing · SIMD

1 Introduction

The k nearest neighbor join operation is widely employed in various domains, such as knowledge discovery [2], data mining, recommender systems [9], multimedia databases [23], and spatial databases [2,20,23], showcasing its broad applicability and significance. It can also be utilised as a preprocessing step for classification or cluster analysis within machine learning. Its application can also be found in image and video retrieval [5,6]. However, due to its high computational cost [16], especially on high-dimensional (HD) datasets, performing kNN join becomes time-consuming. Several researchers have proposed novel algorithms to enhance kNN join performance [2,17,18,20–23,25]. Nevertheless, all these techniques are designed for execution on a single thread. With the increasing size and dimensionality of real-world datasets, there is a compelling need for parallel processing. Although some parallel approaches have been suggested for low-dimensional data [12,26], little work has addressed the challenge of handling

Z. Bao et al. (Eds.): ADC 2023, LNCS 14386, pp. 3–16, 2024.
https://doi.org/10.1007/978-3-031-47843-7_1

HD data in parallel. A recent survey [16] revealed that none have specifically considered parallel processing for such HD datasets, which is crucial given the exponential growth of data nowadays.

Our focus in this paper is on the multi-threaded parallel approach on a single machine. A multi-threaded parallel approach offers advantages [15] such as improved efficiency and speed due to reduced communication [13], simplicity in design, and shared memory for efficient data sharing [8]. Moreover, operating on a single machine renders the parallel approach more accessible and cost-effective, offering the benefits of improved data locality and minimising the need for costly data movement.

Motivation. The existing solutions [2,20,23,25] for the exact kNN join have significant limitations due to the 'curse of high dimensionality' [11,19]. More recent work [17,21] utilises an HDR Tree to unlock the possibilities for faster data processing and retrieval of kNN in high-dimensional space. In this paper, we also adopt the HDR tree in our parallel approach.

A naive parallel solution is to protect the HDR Tree by a global lock and run the kNN update for each affected user in parallel. However, we identify the following three main limitations of the naive solution.

1. *High Lock Contention.* The global lock on the HDR tree can result in huge lock contention, as multiple threads contend for exclusive access to shared resources, impeding scalability and responsiveness.
2. *Large System Overhead.* The number of affected users in each update can be large, and updating them one-by-one in parallel can lead to significant system and memory overhead.
3. *Underutilisation of SIMD.* Most modern CPU architectures support advanced Single-Instruction-Multiple-Data (SIMD) instructions, which enable intra-process parallelism. However, despite this capability, existing solutions for high-dimensional kNN join do not fully utilise SIMD instructions.

Our Solution and Contributions. In this paper, we present effective solutions to address the challenges mentioned earlier. Our solution harnesses the power of both Simultaneous Multi-Threading (SMT) technologies and Single-Instruction-Multiple-Data (SIMD) instructions in modern CPUs for parallelisation. We outline the contributions of this paper as follows.

1. *Fine-Grained Locking Mechanism.* To address the challenge of high lock contention in multi-threads, we propose a fine-grained locking mechanism that reduces lock contention. By synchronising access more granularly, our approach significantly eases lock contention, enhancing the overall performance.
2. *Asynchronous Chunk-based Processing.* In our approach, users are divided into smaller groups called chunks, which helps reduce conflicts when multiple threads access shared resources simultaneously. Each thread focuses on handling a specific chunk of users, minimizing the need for synchronisation or locking mechanisms. This way, we can reduce the system and memory overhead in parallel execution.

3. *SIMD-accelerated Distance Computation.* Our experiments show that over 50% of the CPU time is dedicated to distance computation in this task. Therefore, we accelerate distance computation by leveraging the advanced capabilities of modern SIMD architectures in our solution.
4. *Extensive Experimental Evaluation on Diverse Datasets.* To assess the scalability and effectiveness of the proposed approach, we conducted extensive experiments using datasets of different dimensionalities and settings. Experimental results show that our proposed approach outperformed the sequential HDR Tree by an average of 1.2 times and up to 2 times in a single thread. Additionally, in multi-thread performance, it provides near-linear scalability as the number of threads increases.

Paper Organisation. Sect. 2 defines the problem, provides preliminary definitions, and briefly summarises the HDR Tree. Section 3 reviews relevant literature. Section 4 discusses our proposed parallel computing techniques. We present our experimental analysis results in Sect. 5. Lastly, Sect. 6 summarises our findings and conclusions.

2 Background

This section presents the formal definitions of the kNN join, reverse kNN join, and dynamic kNN join operations. Furthermore, in Subsect. 2.2, we also discussed the HDR Tree. Throughout this paper, we will use 'User Dataset' and 'Item Dataset' to refer to the datasets U and I, respectively, in the context of kNN join operations.

2.1 Definitions

Definition 1 (kNN Join). *Let U and I be the two datasets, in d-dimensional space $\mathbb{R}^d$. Each record $u_i \in U(i_j \in I)$ represents a d-dimensional point, and the similarity distance between any two records is measured using the Euclidean distance, denoted as $d(u_i, i_j)$. The primary goal is to find the k nearest neighbors of a given point u_i from the dataset I, where k is a natural number greater than or equal to 1. Here, the kNN query returns the set, $kNN(u_i) \subset I$ that contains k closest point. Formally, the kNNJ can be denoted as:*

$$kNNJ(U, I) = \{(u_i, kNN(u_i))|u_i \in U \wedge kNN(u_i) \subset I\}.$$

Definition 2 (Reverse kNN Join). *Let U and I be the two datasets in d-dimensional space $\mathbb{R}^d$. Each record $u_i \in U(i_j \in I)$ represents a d-dimensional point, and the similarity distance between any two records is measured using the Euclidean distance, denoted as $d(u_i, i_j)$. The RkNNJ is the process of finding all points from the set U with point i_j as one of their kNN in the d-dimensional space. Here, $RkNN(i_j)$ refers to the set of reverse k nearest neighbors of i_j. Formally, RkNNJ can be denoted as:*

$$RkNNJ(U, I) = \{(i_j, RkNN(i_j))|i_j \in I \wedge RkNN(i_j) \subset U\{\forall u_i \in RkNN(i_j)$$
$$: u_i \in U \wedge i_j \in kNN(u_i)\}\}.$$

Definition 3 (Dynamic kNN Join). *Let U and I be the two datasets, in d-dimensional space $\mathbb{R}^d$. Each record $u_i \in U(i_j \in I)$, represents a d-dimensional point. The similarity distance between any two records is measured using the Euclidean distance, denoted as $d(u_i, i_j)$ and k is a positive natural number. Then, the dynamic kNN join is the ability to dynamically join the similar data points $DkNNJ(U, I) \subseteq U \times I$ in $\mathbb{R}^d$, which includes for every point of U its $k(1 \leq k \leq |I|)$ closest neighbours in $I : DkNNJ(U, I) = (u_i, i_j) : \forall u_i \in U, i_j \in kNN(I, u_i)$ and maintains (updates) the complete join result with every update operation, i.e., for insertion or deletion of any data item $i_j \in I$, finding the affected user set $u_a : RkNN(i_j) \mid i_j \in I \wedge RkNN(i_j) \subset U$ and updating the affected user set $kNN(I, u_a) \subseteq U \times I$.*

Problem Statement. For each user point u_i in the User Dataset U, represented as $U = \{u_1, u_2, \ldots, u_i\}$, we aim to find the k nearest neighbor items from the Item Dataset I. The Item Dataset is denoted as $I = \{i_1, i_2, \ldots, i_j\}$, and all points in both datasets are in a d-dimensional space.

The objective is to parallelly compute the kNN join for each user point in U and identify their kNNs from the item set I in the d-dimensional space. Furthermore, we also consider the problem of reverse kNN join, where for a query item point from I, we determine the user points that consider it one of their kNNs.

We explore parallel computation techniques for the kNN join algorithms to achieve efficient and scalable solutions. These techniques aim to harness the power of parallel processing to expedite the computation of kNN joins for large high-dimensional datasets, providing practical benefits in various applications, such as data mining, recommendation systems, and spatial databases.

2.2   HDR Tree

In [21], researchers propose a solution that includes a new index structure called HDR Tree, which supports efficient search for affected users. It utilises dimensionality reduction techniques such as clustering and PCA to improve search effectiveness. In the subsections, we briefly discuss the details of the HDR tree, including the use of PCA for dimensionality reduction, index structure, the construction process of the HDR Tree using clustering, and the search algorithm that prunes unnecessary branches during the search procedure.

PCA is a valuable technique for reducing dimensionality [3]. PCA can preserve specific properties, like maintaining the relative distances between points and making it easier to transform new points into the reduced space with the already calculated transformation matrix.

Index Structure. The HDR Tree structure is similar to the R-tree but operates on lower-dimensional data in non-leaf nodes. The user set U is reduced to multiple lower-dimensional spaces using PCA to achieve this. The tree's levels correspond to different data space dimensions, and the partitioning is achieved through clustering. The dimensionality increases monotonically from the root to the leaf nodes. Cluster information is stored in non-leaf nodes, while leaf nodes store the original user data without dimensionality reduction.

Construction. The construction of the HDR Tree proceeds top-down, involving the partitioning of the user set using clustering techniques. Leaf and non-leaf nodes are differentiated based on a user count threshold. The tree's height can be approximated as $L = [log_f N]$, where f represents the fanout. The dimensionality of each level is determined using eigenvalues derived from the PCA algorithm. In the construction procedure, when the level of a cluster surpasses L and its size exceeds a predetermined threshold (θ), we continue partitioning the cluster using the user set in its original full dimensionality. This implies that $d_l = d$ when $l > L$.

Search Algorithm. The search algorithm prunes unnecessary non-leaf nodes and focuses on the leaf nodes to find the affected users. It transforms the item into a lower-dimensional space using PCA; distances between the item and cluster is compared and pruned accordingly (i.e., $dist_{pca}(i, C_j) \geq maxdknn$). This method efficiently identifies affected users and takes advantage of the computational benefits of PCA.

3   Related Works

Centralised kNN Join Queries. The existing literature proposes different methods for kNN join queries in centralised systems. In [1,2], the authors introduced Multi-page Indexing (MuX), an R-tree-based method that organises input datasets into large-sized pages to reduce I/O costs. Additionally, they designed a secondary structure within pages to decrease computation costs. Xia et al. [20] presented Gorder (G-ordering), a grid partitioning-based approach for kNN join, that utilises Principal Component Analysis (PCA) to sort objects based on a proposed Grid Order. Objects nearby are assigned to the same grid to reduce CPU and I/O costs using a scheduled block-nested loop join. Yu et al. [23] proposed "iJoin", a B$^+$-tree based method for kNN join, which splits input datasets into partitions and employs B$^+$-trees with the iDistance technique [10,24] to answer kNN join efficiently.

Distributed kNN Join Queries. Recently, considerable interest has been shown in supporting kNN join over the MapReduce framework. In [26], researchers introduced a novel algorithm leveraging MapReduce for achieving efficient parallel kNN join operations on datasets with low dimensionality. The Hadoop Block Nested Loop Join (H-BNLJ) is a two-phase MapReduce approach for kNN join. In the first phase, the datasets R and S are partitioned into equal-sized blocks, and each reducer performs a block-nested loop kNN join between local blocks of R and S, producing n local kNNs for each record r in R. Each reducer emits the top-k global kNNs for each record r in R based on the sorted local kNNs in the second phase, which sorts and groups the results from the first phase by record ID.

Hadoop Block R-tree Join (H-BRJ) [26] is an improved version of H-BNLJ that utilises R-tree indices for the S-block in the reducer. This approach accelerates kNN searches, leading to faster join performance and reduced computational overhead. When dealing with high-dimensional data, the H-BNLJ method is ineffective since the number of partitions is directly proportional to the number of blocks in each input dataset. To enable parallel processing, the H-BRJ method requires replicating dataset blocks, thereby necessitating the creation of n copies for each block when n blocks are generated, resulting in n^2 divisions and additional communication overhead.

In [12] work, researchers developed the PGBJ kNN join algorithm that utilises Voronoi diagram-based partitioning and a grouping strategy. PGBJ can efficiently perform the kNN join by dividing the input datasets into groups and examining object pairs solely within each group. The algorithm also incorporates several pruning rules to effectively reduce shuffling and computation costs. In PGBJ, the replication procedure involves computing multiple Euclidean distances during the preprocessing phase, which leads to significant computational expenses. As a result, this method is inefficient when applied to high-dimensional datasets.

In these studies [7,8,14], researchers primarily concentrated on addressing the low-dimensional kNN-join problem. Thus, we do not delve into further details about those approaches. Our focus in this paper is on exploring work related to high-dimensional kNN join techniques for parallel computing.

4   Proposed Work

In this section, we present our parallel approaches for the kNN join algorithm tailored for high-dimensional datasets.

Our solution consists of three main functions: `initialiseUsers`, `updateUsers`, and `computeDist`. Each function serves a distinct purpose in our approach to efficiently compute kNN join in HD space. In the `initialiseUsers` function, we will initialise the kNN list for all users in the user set. Considering the example that we set up 50,000 users and compute kNNs for each of them when the sliding window size is 200,000, the straightforward method requires at least 200,000 distance calculations to find the kNN for just one user (i.e., 10 billion computations in total). This will lead to massive computation, not to mention that kNN computations are computationally expensive. To tackle this, we employ a chunk-based approach to partition the initial users into chunks and compute all chunks in parallel. By doing so, we can lower redundant kNN computations and reduce system overhead. In the `updateUsers` function, for updates like adding/removing items, we identify affected users and update their recommendation lists. New items are added and ranked, while expired ones are removed. Fewer than k neighbors can lead to list recomputation. To ease the lock contention during parallel updating, we employ fine-grained locking and asynchronous mechanism in this function. Lastly, for computing kNN recommendations, we rely on the Euclidean distance metric. In leaf nodes of the HDR Tree, where data is in their original high-dimensional form, calculating distances incurs a substantial cost. For example, with a 128-dimensional dataset, finding the distance between two points requires 384 operations: 128 subtractions, 128 multiplications, 127 additions, and 1 square root. As dimensionality increases, the cost of distance calculations also grows. In our approach, we further optimise the approach by exploiting parallel operations by SIMD on modern architectures for faster distance calculations in the `computeDist` function.

Considering constraints imposed by page limitations, we focus on the key functions of computing the kNN join algorithm for HD datasets. We have identified the most computationally intensive tasks through thorough analysis: user initialisation, user update operation and distance computation for finding kNN.

Taking into account these findings, we have devised a highly efficient and optimised solution for these critical functions. Our proposed approach aims to minimise CPU computation requirements and maximise performance. By addressing the challenges posed by lock contention, overhead, limited workload balancing, and underutilisation of SIMD instructions, our solution significantly improves computational efficiency and overall execution time.

4.1   Chunk-Based User Initialisation

The computation of the kNN join query for a large HD dataset is optimised through chunk-based user initialisation and parallel processing. The dataset is divided into smaller chunks, and multiple threads work concurrently on these chunks, effectively distributing workload and using available CPU resources more efficiently. This parallelisation significantly accelerates the initialisation process, making it well-suited for handling large datasets in HD spaces. Additionally, load balancing ensures that each thread gets a fair share of work, preventing any underutilisation or overload of CPU resources. The real-time progress updates provide insights into the processing speed, reducing latency between starting and completing the initialisation. Overall, the approach enhances the efficiency of HDR Tree construction and subsequent operations, making it particularly beneficial for computationally intensive tasks with large-scale HD datasets.

Load balancing is essential for achieving optimal performance in parallel computing as it evenly distributes the workload among processing resources. In our work, we have employed a traditional load-balancing approach due to the nature of the workload and the absence of significant variations. The workload is divided into equal-sized chunks based on the number of available threads. Since the workload size is known and remains relatively stable, this static load-balancing approach works efficiently without requiring other complex load-balancing techniques. Efficient load balancing ensures effective utilisation of each resource, thereby improving overall system performance.

In Algorithm 1, line 1 leverages the available hardware concurrency to distribute the workload across multiple threads. The subsequent loop, i.e., lines 3 to 5, launches n asynchronous tasks, with each task assigned to a separate thread. These tasks invoke the UsersParallel() function, passing i and n as parameters. The resulting userInitialisationTasks are stored in the $userInitialisationTasks$ vector. Finally, in lines 6 and 7, the function waits for each $task$ in the $userInitialisationTasks$ vector to complete.

Algorithm 1. initialiseUsers()

Require: Users set
Ensure: The Initialisation of Users in Parallel
1: $n \leftarrow$ number of hardware threads
2: $userInitialisationTasks \leftarrow$ empty vector to store asynchronous tasks
3: **for** $i \leftarrow 0$ to $n - 1$ **do**:
4:     $task \leftarrow async(UsersParallel, i, n)$;
5:     $userInitialisationTasks.append(task)$

6: **for** $task$ in $userInitialisationTasks$ **do**:
7:     $wait$ for $task$ to complete

1: $UsersParallel(o, n)$ ▷ Function call
2: **for** $i \leftarrow o$ to size of Users step n **do**
3:     $Users[i].computeKNN(slidingWindow)$;

4.2   Fine-Grained Locking Update

This technique is designed to optimise data updates in multi-threaded systems. In concurrent applications, efficient management of shared data structures is critical to avoid data races and ensure thread safety. Fine-grained locking, which divides the shared data into smaller units with individual locks, offers a promising solution to minimise contention and improve parallelism. This approach aims to update a collection of affected users in parallel using multiple threads while leveraging the advantages of fine-grained locking. By distributing the workload evenly and allowing concurrent access to specific data elements, the Parallel Fine-Grained Locking Update Approach enhances performance and scalability, making it well-suited for modern multi-core processors.

In Algorithm 2, lines 1–3 determine and set the number of available hardware threads. Additionally, the algorithm calculates the size of each chunk and creates a vector of parallelUpdateTasks for each thread. Line 4 initialises a vector of mutexes, with one mutex for each user in Rp. In lines 5–16, the algorithm launches threads to process each chunk concurrently. Each thread acquires a lock for the specific user it updates, ensuring exclusive access. Once the update is complete, the thread releases the lock. Finally, lines 17–18 utilise parallelUpdateTasks and synchronisation to ensure all threads complete their tasks before proceeding.

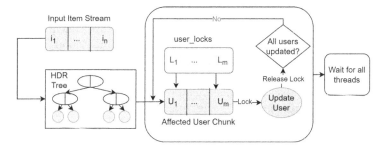

Fig. 1. Fine-Grained Locking Mechanism for parallel updates

Algorithm 2. updateUsers(I, m)

Require: Item I, Update mode m
Ensure: Updated affected user's (Rp) recommendation list (Rl)
 1: $num\_threads \leftarrow$ number of available threads
 2: $chunk\_size \leftarrow$ (size of $Rp + num\_threads - 1)/num\_threads$
 3: $parallelUpdateTasks \leftarrow$ empty vector to store asynchronous update tasks
 4: $user\_locks \leftarrow$ empty vector of mutexes, size $=$ size of Rp
 5: **for** $i \leftarrow 0$ to $num\_threads - 1$ **do**:
 6:     $start \leftarrow i * chunk\_size$
 7:     $end \leftarrow min(start + chunk\_size,$ size of $Rp)$
 8:     $parallelUpdateTasks.push\_back(async$ function()
 9:     **for** $j \leftarrow start$ to $end - 1$ **do**:
10:         $lock(user\_locks[j])$
11:         $u \leftarrow Rp[j]$
12:         $u.update(I, m)$
13:         **if** $u.Rl < k$ **then**
14:             $u.computeKNN(slidingWindow)$;
15:         $unlock(item\_locks[j])$
16:     end function)
17: **for** each $task$ in $parallelUpdateTasks$ **do**:
18:     $wait()$ for $task$ to complete

Figure 1 shows the workflow of the Fine-Grained Locking Mechanism for parallel updates. We use the HDR Tree to find affected users Rp efficiently. The number of threads and chunk size are calculated for balanced parallel processing. Fine-grained locking is implemented with a vector of $user\_locks$, ensuring exclusive access to each User during updates. Threads process their assigned Users, acquire locks, update data, and release locks afterwards. After all threads complete their updates, the function waits for their completion. This approach enhances performance, scalability and effectively utilises multi-core processors.

4.3 SIMD-Enabled Distance Computation

Efficiently processing high-dimensional datasets is crucial for achieving optimal performance. One commonly employed technique to enhance performance is the use of SIMD instructions. It allows parallel processing of multiple data elements using a single instruction, thereby exploiting data-level parallelism. Advanced Vector Extensions (AVX) is a specific implementation of SIMD, available on modern processors, that provides wider registers and additional instructions for even greater parallelism. Our work utilises AVX2 instructions to compute the Euclidean distance between two vectors.

Our analysis indicates that kNN computation utilises approximately 60% of CPU resources, with 50% dedicated to distance computation within the function. To enhance the efficiency of kNN and reduce computational time, our objective is to leverage the parallelism offered by modern processors. Traditional

Algorithm 3. computeDist(I,D)

Require: Item I, User center D
Ensure: Compute Euclidean Distance
 1: $aData \leftarrow$ pointer to the data array of I
 2: $bData \leftarrow$ pointer to the data array of center
 3: $diff \leftarrow$ AVX register initialized to zero
 4: $sum \leftarrow$ AVX register initialized to zero
 5: **for** $i \leftarrow 0$ to $128 - 1$ step 8 **do**:
 6:     $a \leftarrow$ load 8 elements from $aData[i]$ into AVX register
 7:     $b \leftarrow$ load 8 elements from $bData[i]$ into AVX register
 8:     $diff \leftarrow a - b$
 9:     $diff \leftarrow diff * diff$
10:     $sum \leftarrow sum + diff$
11: $hsum1 \leftarrow$ add the lower 128 bits of sum with the higher 128 bits of sum
12: $hsum2 \leftarrow$ move the higher and lower 64 bits of hsum1
13: $hsum3 \leftarrow hsum1 + hsum2$
14: $hsum4 \leftarrow$ add the scalar sum of hsum3 with the shuffled sum of hsum3
15: $sumResult \leftarrow$ store hsum4 as a scalar
16: $D \leftarrow sqrt(sumResult)$

---

sequential approaches for distance computation are computationally expensive due to the iterative nature of the calculation. Therefore, we explore using SIMD instructions, specifically the AVX instruction set, to significantly improve performance. SIMD AVX instructions allow parallel processing of multiple data elements, enabling simultaneous computations and efficient vector operations, resulting in significant speedup for operations involving large high-dimensional datasets. By employing SIMD AVX2 support, the algorithm achieves enhanced computational efficiency compared to an HDR Tree and a parallel locking-based approach.

The Algorithm 3 begins by extracting the data pointers $aData$ and $bData$ from the Item data point and the *center* vector, respectively (lines 1–2). Within the loop (lines 5–10), AVX instructions load eight elements from $aData$ and $bData$ into AVX registers, enabling simultaneous computation. The algorithm calculates the element-wise difference between the two vectors and squares these differences, accumulating the squared values in the *sum* register. Following the loop (lines 11–14), the algorithm performs a horizontal summation of the eight floats within the sum register, resulting in a single sum value. Subsequently, the algorithm extracts the sum value from the horizontal sum operation (line 15). Finally, the square root of the sum is computed using the *sqrt* function, and the resulting value is stored in the reference variable D.

5 Experiments

In this section, we conducted an experimental analysis and presented the results. All experiments were performed on a computer with an Intel Core i7-10700

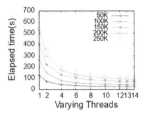 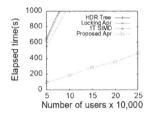 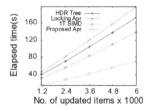

Fig. 2. Varying the num-   **Fig. 3.** Varying the num-   **Fig. 4.** Vary number of upd-
ber of Threads   ber of users   ated items

2.90 GHz processor, octa-core, and 16 GB RAM, running the Windows 10 Pro
operating system. We compared our proposed parallel approach with the Sequential HDR Tree approach, Parallel HDR Tree with standard locking mechanism,
and Parallel approach using single-threaded SIMD. Most experiments were conducted on the 128-dimensional NUS-WIDE Image DataSet [4], which consists of
269,648 records from the Flickr dataset. To evaluate the performance of our proposed approach in high-dimensional scenarios, we also performed experiments on
64, 75, 144 and 225-dimensional datasets [4]. To simulate a continuous stream
of items, we created a sliding window W with a default size of 200,000 and randomly selected 50,000 users. In our experiments, we set the default values of k
(the number of nearest neighbors) to 10, fanout (the number of child nodes per
internal node) to 5, and θ (threshold) to 7. We varied the number of threads in
our experiment Fig. 2 and found that the most optimal performance was achieved
with 13 threads. Therefore, unless otherwise specified, we used this value as the
default parameter throughout the experiments. We compare our work with the
following baseline algorithms:

1. *HDR Tree.* The HDR Tree [21] approach is used to identify affected users
   resulting from update operations, as described in Sect. 2.2.
2. *Parallel Locking Approach.* We implemented the standard locking parallel
   method on the HDR Tree in this approach. However, due to higher locking
   contention, its performance was often inferior to the HDR sequential approach.
3. *Parallel Single-threaded SIMD Approach.* To assess the impact of using SIMD
   instructions in a parallel approach, we also considered it a baseline approach.
   We compared this SIMD single-threaded parallel implementation with our
   proposed system.

Exp-1: Varying Threads. Figure 2 shows the near-linear scalability as the
number of threads increases. We varied the number of threads from 1 to 14 to
evaluate their impact on performance. When varying the number of users from
50,000 to 250,000, the proposed approach with threads increases demonstrates
the effectiveness of our proposed approach and highlights the significant performance gains achieved by utilising multiple threads in the context of user size
variations.

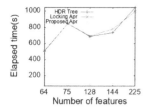 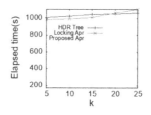 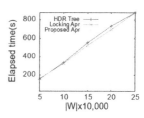

Fig. 5. Vary no. of features   **Fig. 6.** Vary number of k **Fig. 7.** Vary number of W

Exp-2: Varying the Number of Users. In our experiment Fig. 3, we varied user numbers from 50k to 250k. We noticed longer elapsed times with more users, so we set a time limit of 1000 s. Baseline methods are unable to complete within the time limit, even for 50k users. However, our method stays under 500 s, even at 250k users.

Exp-3: Varying the Number of Updated Items. In this experiment, we aimed to investigate the impact of the number of updated items on the performance of different approaches. We varied the number of updated items from 1,200 to 6,000 and compared the results across baseline approaches. Figure 4 illustrates the cost of searching the affected items for each approach. All approaches increase in cost linearly with the number of items updated. However, the proposed parallel approach consistently outperformed the baseline approaches.

Exp-4: Varying the Number of Features. To evaluate the performance of our approaches on different datasets, we conducted experiments using the NUS-WIDE Real-World Image DataSets [4] of various dimensions. The dimensions ranged from 64 to 225. As shown in Fig. 5, the elapsed time increases with the dimensionality. This can be attributed to the increased time required for distance computation. Remarkably, our proposed approaches consistently outperformed existing methods, as depicted in Fig. 5. The superiority of our approaches becomes even more pronounced as the dimensionality of the dataset increases.

Exp-5: Varying k. In Fig. 6, it is evident that increasing the value of k leads to a corresponding increase in $maxdknn$ (Maximum distance between $dknn$). As a result, more users are affected, which in turn causes a longer elapsed time for all the approaches. However, when considering the 225-dimensional dataset [4], the proposed parallel approach demonstrates a notable performance improvement compared to the baseline approaches. Specifically, it achieves a sixfold enhancement, indicating a substantial advancement in terms of efficiency.

Exp-6: Varying $|W|$. Figure 7 demonstrates that as the sliding window size increases from 50,000 to 250,000, the elapsed time for all the methods also increases. Additionally, the cost of searching for affected users decreases as $|W|$ rises, primarily due to a decrease in the average number of affected users. The increase in recalculation costs is the dominant factor contributing to the upward trend in the curves. However, despite this increase, the proposed approach outperforms the other methods by nearly eight times.

6 Conclusion

In this paper, we propose an approach to efficiently compute the kNN join over a high-dimensional dataset using a parallel computing approach and SIMD instructions. To address issues of high lock contention, larger system overhead, and underutilisation of SIMD instructions in modern CPUs, we develop an efficient parallel solution for dynamic kNN join over high-dimensional data. Our solution employs a fine-grained locking mechanism and asynchronous chunk-based processing while utilising the SIMD instructions for distance computation. The results of our experiments demonstrate a significant performance improvement over the sequential HDR Tree method and near-linear scalability. For future work, we will investigate further optimisations for non-uniform memory access (NUMA) architecture and study efficient distributed solutions for dynamic high-dimensional kNN join.

References

1. Böhm, C., Krebs, F.: Supporting KDD applications by the k-nearest neighbor join. In: Mařík, V., Retschitzegger, W., Štěpánková, O. (eds.) DEXA 2003. LNCS, vol. 2736, pp. 504–516. Springer, Heidelberg (2003). https://doi.org/10.1007/978-3-540-45227-0_50
2. Böhm, C., Krebs, F.: The k-nearest neighbour join: turbo charging the KDD process. Knowl. Inf. Syst. **6**(6), 728–749 (2004)
3. Chakrabarti, K., Mehrotra, S.: Local dimensionality reduction: a new approach to indexing high dimensional spaces. In: VLDB Conference (2000)
4. Chua, T.S., Tang, J., Hong, R., Li, H., Luo, Z., Zheng, Y.: NUS-WIDE: a real-world web image database from national university of Singapore. In: Proceedings of the ACM International Conference on Image and Video Retrieval, pp. 1–9 (2009)
5. Ferhatosmanoglu, H., Tuncel, E., Agrawal, D., El Abbadi, A.: Approximate nearest neighbor searching in multimedia databases. In: Proceedings 17th International Conference on Data Engineering, pp. 503–511. IEEE (2001)
6. Giacinto, G.: A nearest-neighbor approach to relevance feedback in content based image retrieval. In: Proceedings of the 6th ACM International Conference on Image and Video Retrieval, pp. 456–463 (2007)
7. Gowanlock, M.: KNN-joins using a hybrid approach: exploiting CPU/GPU workload characteristics. In: Proceedings of the 12th Workshop on General Purpose Processing Using GPUs, pp. 33–42 (2019)
8. Gowanlock, M.: Hybrid KNN-join: parallel nearest neighbor searches exploiting CPU and GPU architectural features. J. Parallel Distrib. Comput. **149**, 119–137 (2021)
9. Hu, Y., Yang, C., Zhan, P., Zhao, J., Li, Y., Li, X.: Efficient continuous KNN join processing for real-time recommendation. Pers. Ubiquit. Comput. **25**, 1001–1011 (2021)
10. Jagadish, H.V., Ooi, B.C., Tan, K.L., Yu, C., Zhang, R.: iDistance: an adaptive b+-tree based indexing method for nearest neighbor search. ACM Trans. Database Syst. (TODS) **30**(2), 364–397 (2005)
11. Kouiroukidis, N., Evangelidis, G.: The effects of dimensionality curse in high dimensional KNN search. In: 2011 15th Panhellenic Conference on Informatics, pp. 41–45. IEEE (2011)

12. Lu, W., Shen, Y., Chen, S., Ooi, B.C.: Efficient processing of k nearest neighbor joins using MapReduce. arXiv preprint arXiv:1207.0141 (2012)
13. McSherry, F., Isard, M., Murray, D.G.: Scalability! But at what {COST}? In: 15th Workshop on Hot Topics in Operating Systems (HotOS XV) (2015)
14. Shahvarani, A., Jacobsen, H.A.: Distributed stream KNN join. In: Proceedings of the 2021 International Conference on Management of Data, pp. 1597–1609 (2021)
15. Tanenbaum, A.S.: Distributed systems principles and paradigms (2007)
16. Ukey, N., Yang, Z., Li, B., Zhang, G., Hu, Y., Zhang, W.: Survey on exact kNN queries over high-dimensional data space. Sensors **23**(2), 629 (2023)
17. Ukey, N., Yang, Z., Zhang, G., Liu, B., Li, B., Zhang, W.: Efficient kNN join over dynamic high-dimensional data. In: Hua, W., Wang, H., Li, L. (eds.) ADC 2022. LNCS, vol. 13459, pp. 63–75. Springer, Cham (2022). https://doi.org/10.1007/978-3-031-15512-3_5
18. Wang, J., Lin, L., Huang, T., Wang, J., He, Z.: Efficient k-nearest neighbor join algorithms for high dimensional sparse data. arXiv preprint arXiv:1011.2807 (2010)
19. Weber, R., Schek, H.J., Blott, S.: A quantitative analysis and performance study for similarity-search methods in high-dimensional spaces. In: VLDB, vol. 98, pp. 194–205 (1998)
20. Xia, C., Lu, H., Ooi, B.C., Hu, J.: GORDER: an efficient method for KNN join processing. In: Proceedings of the Thirtieth International Conference on Very Large Data Bases, vol. 30, pp. 756–767 (2004)
21. Yang, C., Yu, X., Liu, Y.: Continuous KNN join processing for real-time recommendation. In: 2014 IEEE International Conference on Data Mining, pp. 640–649. IEEE (2014)
22. Yao, B., Li, F., Kumar, P.: K nearest neighbor queries and kNN-joins in large relational databases (almost) for free. In: 2010 IEEE 26th International Conference on Data Engineering (ICDE 2010), pp. 4–15. IEEE (2010)
23. Yu, C., Cui, B., Wang, S., Su, J.: Efficient index-based KNN join processing for high-dimensional data. Inf. Softw. Technol. **49**(4), 332–344 (2007)
24. Yu, C., Ooi, B.C., Tan, K.L., Jagadish, H.: Indexing the distance: an efficient method to KNN processing. In: VLDB, vol. 1, pp. 421–430 (2001)
25. Yu, C., Zhang, R., Huang, Y., Xiong, H.: High-dimensional kNN joins with incremental updates. GeoInformatica **14**(1), 55–82 (2010)
26. Zhang, C., Li, F., Jestes, J.: Efficient parallel kNN joins for large data in MapReduce. In: Proceedings of the 15th International Conference on Extending Database Technology, pp. 38–49 (2012)

Take a Close Look at the Optimization of Deep Kernels for Non-parametric Two-Sample Tests

Xunye Tian$^{(\boxtimes)}$ and Feng Liu

The University of Melbourne, Parkville, VIC 3052, Australia
1030953664@qq.com

Abstract. The *maximum mean discrepancy* (MMD) test with deep kernel is a powerful method to distinguish whether two samples are drawn from the same distribution. Recent studies aim to maximize the test power of MMD test to find the best deep kernel for testing, where the test power is the *ratio* of MMD value and MMD's asymptotic variance. However, in this paper, we find that direct maximization of the test power sometimes leads to an unreasonable case that MMD value is very small but the test power is large. In this case, the testing performance is not satisfactory. Thus we propose two main methods to simultaneously maximize the test power and the MMD value with deep kernel by combining the methods from non-smooth optimization and the methods from Pareto optimization. Experiments verify the effectiveness of two methods on two benchmark datasets in the field of two-sample testing.

Keywords: Two-sample test · Deep kernel · Optimization · Pareto optimization

1 Introduction

The classical parametric two-sample test is one of the hypothesis test to test whether the means of two sample populations were equal if the variance of them were assumed to be equal. However, due to the classical parametric two-sample test's limitations that assumptions of normality and homoscedasticity could not be met or known, nonparametric tests, i.e. *Kolmogorov-Smirnov* (K-S) test were introduced [10,15]. The K-S test was designed for one-dimensional and continuous data with assumptions that two samples which were compared should be independent. In recent years, a more powerful alternative to traditional nonparametric two-sample test was developed, called kernel two-sample test or *maximum mean discrepancy* (MMD) test, in order to meet the growing needs for more flexible and powerful tool for comparing the distributions of two independent samples, particularly when dealing with high-dimensional or complex data structure [7,11].

The kernel MMD test uses kernel methods to implicitly map the data to a high-dimensional data space, enabling the test to capture complex relationships

Supported by organization The University of Melbourne.

Z. Bao et al. (Eds.): ADC 2023, LNCS 14386, pp. 17–29, 2024.
https://doi.org/10.1007/978-3-031-47843-7_2

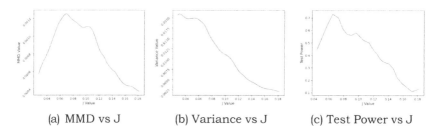

(a) MMD vs J   (b) Variance vs J   (c) Test Power vs J

Fig. 1. In the training process of deep neural network on Higgs dataset when sample size is 4000, (a) and (b) shows that the value of J will be maximized by decreasing MMD and extremely decreasing the variance in the process of training neural network. The testing test power in (c) shows that the performance of model is not acceptable if MMD value in training is quite small, even though the value of J is high enough in training.

and dependencies in the data. A kernel function $k(x, y)$, which measures the similarities between data points x and y, is used in the MMD test. Commonly used kernel functions are characteristic and translation-invariant, including the Gaussian (RBF) kernel and the Laplace kernel [4]. However, several limitations of these characteristic kernels can be discovered, particularly when facing samples from complex distributions. All translation-invariant kernels can be represented in a way of $k(x, y) = f(x - y)$ [6], which means that the value of the kernel depends only on the difference of data points x and y and a small number of fixed hyperparameters in the kernel method, like **euclidean distance** $\|x - y\|$ and the **length-scale** l in RBF kernel [17]. In contrast to the consistent behaviour of simple kernel on all the data through the space, deep kernel, which is parameterized by deep neural networks, is capable of adapting their structure to a specific task and data at hand [17]. The deep kernel is defined as

$$k_\omega(x, y) = [(1 - \epsilon)\kappa(\phi_\omega(x), \phi_\omega(y)) + \epsilon]q(x, y), \tag{1}$$

where ϕ_ω represents the deep neural networks with parameters ω to extract features of samples, while κ and q denotes a simple kernel and a characteristic kernel, respectively. This deep kernel method, implemented by Liu et al. [12], can work well for the problems that distinguish distributions with complex structures, e.g., a mixture of multimodal Blob dataset, and MNIST dataset.

Although the choice of the deep kernel is powerful, the objective function J in the deep neural network training process has a drawback that will lead to an irrationality when performing the test. We aim to maximize the objective function

$$\hat{J}_\lambda(S_\mathbb{P}, S_\mathbb{Q}; k) := \frac{\widehat{\mathrm{MMD}}_u^2(S_\mathbb{P}, S_\mathbb{Q}; k)}{\hat{\sigma}_{\mathcal{H}_1, \lambda}(S_\mathbb{P}, S_\mathbb{Q}; k)} \tag{2}$$

to maximize the test power, where $S_\mathbb{P}$ and $S_\mathbb{Q}$ are two samples drawn from distributions $\mathbb{P}$ and $\mathbb{Q}$, $\widehat{\mathrm{MMD}}_u^2(S_\mathbb{P}, S_\mathbb{Q}; k)$ is the unbiased estimator of MMD value between these two samples under a deep kernel k, and $\hat{\sigma}_{\mathcal{H}_1, \lambda}(S_\mathbb{P}, S_\mathbb{Q}; k)$

is the estimator of standard deviation of MMD estimator under the alternative hypothesis $\mathcal{H}_1 : \mathbb{P} \neq \mathbb{Q}$ and the regularization parameter λ. From Fig. 1a and 1b, we could see that during the training of deep neural network, the model will maximize the objective function by highly decreasing the numerator and extremely decreasing the denominator.

A small improvement in the value of J will lead to a extreme decrease in the MMD value in later epochs of training. However, we expect the test statistic MMD to be large if the distributions are distinct, In this situation, even though the value of test power in training is high enough, it cannot have the ability to distinguish two distributions when testing (so-called overfitting). In Fig. 1c, we can see that the testing test power is indeed lower than expected, even though the value of J reaches a high level in the training. Thus, in this paper, our target is to explore the issues within the optimization procedures of MMD and step further to optimize the objective function $\hat{J}$, so that there is a balance between the MMD and testing test power.

2 Preliminary

In order to alleviate the stringent assumptions inherent in traditional parametric two-sample tests, numerous statisticians introduced the concept of non-parametric two-sample tests. This notion culminated in the development of the K-S test by Kolmogorov and the Wilcoxon rank-sum test by Wilcoxon. Both represent paradigmatic examples of non-parametric two-sample tests. However, these conventional non-parametric tests are constrained by their requirements for low-dimensional data. As a response to this limitation, a new class of non-parametric statistical tests based on MMD has been proposed, with particular relevance to applications in the field of machine learning [5,7,9]. To comprehend the principles and functionality of the MMD two-sample test, it is prerequisite to revisit the fundamental concepts associated with this method.

2.1 Reproducing Kernel Hilbert Space

We will firstly introduce the *reproducing kernel Hilbert space* (RKHS), it is just a special kind of Hilbert space, which is a complete inner product space, that has the additional property of a reproducing kernel.

Definition 1 *(RKHS). Let $\mathcal{X}$ be a non-empty set and $\mathbb{R} - H$ be a Hilbert space over $\mathcal{X}$, i.e., a Hilbert space that consist of functions mapping $\mathcal{X} \times \mathcal{X} \to \mathbb{R}$. Then*

*(i) A function $k : \mathcal{X} \times \mathcal{X} \to \mathbb{R}$ is called a **reproducing kernel** if the function $k(\cdot, x) \in H, x \in \mathcal{X}$ holds the **reproducing property***

$$f(x) = \langle f, k(\cdot, x) \rangle,$$

for all $f \in H$ and all $x \in \mathcal{X}$.

*(ii) The space H is called **reproducing kernel Hilbert space (RKHS)** over*
$\mathcal{X}$ if for all $x \in \mathcal{X}$ the Dirac functional $\delta_x : H \to \mathbb{R}$ defined by

$$\delta_x(f) := f(x), \quad f \in H,$$

which is always continuous.

2.2   Maximum Mean Discrepancy

Now let us move back to MMD which is a kind of test statistic used to measure
the average distance between two probability distributions. It is achieved by
calculating the distance of two samples drawn from each distribution respectively
and utilize a universal kernel to map them into the RKHS. The original definition
on this test statistic are given as below

Definition 2 *[7]. Let $X \sim \mathbb{P}$ and $Y \sim \mathbb{Q}$ be the random variables that follow
distribution of $\mathbb{P}$ and $\mathbb{Q}$. $S_P = \{x_i\}_{i=1}^n \sim \mathbb{P}^n$ and $S_Q = \{y_j\}_{j=1}^m \sim \mathbb{Q}^m$ be
the two independent and identically distributed (i.i.d) samples drawn from the
distribution $\mathbb{P}$ and $\mathbb{Q}$, and $\mathcal{F}$ be a class of functions $f : \mathcal{X} \to \mathbb{R}$, the general form
of* MMD *can be defined as*

$$\text{MMD}[\mathcal{F}, \mathbb{P}, \mathbb{Q}] := \sup_{f \in \mathcal{F}} \left(E_{x \sim \mathbb{P}}[f(x)] - E_{y \sim \mathbb{Q}}[f(y)] \right), \tag{3}$$

and a biased estimator of the MMD *can be defined by replacing the population
expectations with the sample mean on $\mathbb{P}$ and $\mathbb{Q}$*

$$\widehat{\text{MMD}}_b[\mathcal{F}, \mathbb{P}, \mathbb{Q}] := \sup_{f \in \mathcal{F}} \left(\frac{1}{n} \sum_{i=1}^n f(x_i) - \frac{1}{m} \sum_{j=1}^m f(y_j) \right), \tag{4}$$

where $\sup_{f \in \mathcal{F}}$ *stands for supremum, a concept from real analysis, meaning that we
are looking for a function f that maximizes the expression inside the supremum:
the difference of expectations under the two distribution $\mathbb{P}$ and $\mathbb{Q}$.*

Thus we are attempting to find the function f that can best identify the
difference between $\mathbb{P}$ and $\mathbb{Q}$. Moreover, a MMD formula with its function class
$\mathcal{F}$ in a RKHS $\mathcal{H}$ can be established. Due to the properties of RKHS defined
before, we know that there is a Dirac function δ_x that can map function $f \in
\mathcal{H}$ to a feature space $f(x) \in \mathbb{R}$ is continuous and there is a feature mapping
$\boldsymbol{\Phi} : \mathcal{X} \to \mathbb{R}$ holding the reproducing property $f(x) = \langle f, \boldsymbol{\Phi}(x) \rangle_{\mathcal{H}}$, where we call
$\boldsymbol{\Phi}(x) = k(x, \cdot)$ the **canonical form**, $\boldsymbol{\Phi}$ the **canonical feature map** [16] and k
the kernel whose feature space is $\mathcal{H}$.

Then we define a $\mu_{\mathbb{P}} \in \mathcal{H}$ so that $E_{\mathbb{P}}[f(x)] = \langle f, \mu_{\mathbb{P}} \rangle_{\mathcal{F}}$ for all $f \in \mathcal{H}$, where
$\mu_{\mathbb{P}}$ gives the expectation of all RKHS functions on distribution $\mathbb{P}$, and we call
$\mu_{\mathbb{P}} := E_{x \sim \mathbb{P}}[k(x, \cdot)]$ and $\mu_{\mathbb{Q}} := E_{y \sim \mathbb{Q}}[k(y, \cdot)]$ the **mean embedding** (or **distribution embedding**) of distribution $\mathbb{P}$ and $\mathbb{Q}$ [7]. Let $x' \sim \mathbb{P}$ and $y' \sim \mathbb{Q}$ be
the independent random variables of x, y that follow the distribution $\mathbb{P}$ and $\mathbb{Q}$.

Then we can define the MMD by measuring the distance in $\mathcal{H}$ between mean embedding of distributions

$$
\begin{aligned}
\mathrm{MMD}^2[\mathcal{F}, \mathbb{P}, \mathbb{Q}] &= \left[\sup_{\|f\|_{\mathcal{H}} \leq 1} (E_{x \sim \mathbb{P}}[f(x)] - E_{y \sim \mathbb{Q}}[f(y)]) \right]^2 \\
&= \left[\sup_{\|f\|_{\mathcal{H}} \leq 1} \langle \mu_{\mathbb{P}} - \mu_{\mathbb{Q}}, f \rangle_{\mathcal{H}} \right]^2 \\
&= \|\mu_{\mathbb{P}} - \mu_{\mathbb{Q}}\|_{\mathcal{H}}^2 \\
&= \langle \mu_{\mathbb{P}} - \mu_{\mathbb{Q}}, \mu_{\mathbb{P}} - \mu_{\mathbb{Q}} \rangle_{\mathcal{H}} \\
&= \langle \mu_{\mathbb{P}}, \mu_{\mathbb{P}} \rangle + \langle \mu_{\mathbb{Q}}, \mu_{\mathbb{Q}} \rangle - 2 \langle \mu_{\mathbb{P}}, \mu_{\mathbb{Q}} \rangle \\
&= E_{x \sim \mathbb{P}}[\mu_{\mathbb{P}}(x)] + E_{y \sim \mathbb{Q}}[\mu_{\mathbb{Q}}(y)] - 2 E_{x \sim \mathbb{P}}[\mu_{\mathbb{Q}}(x)] \\
&= E_{x \sim \mathbb{P}} \langle \mu_{\mathbb{P}}, k(x, \cdot) \rangle + E_{y \sim \mathbb{Q}} \langle \mu_{\mathbb{Q}}, k(y, \cdot) \rangle - 2 E_{x \sim \mathbb{P}} \langle \mu_{\mathbb{Q}}, k(x, \cdot) \rangle \\
&= E_{x \sim \mathbb{P}} k(x, x') + E_{y \sim \mathbb{Q}} k(y, y') - 2 E_{x \sim \mathbb{P}, \mathbb{Q}} k(x, y),
\end{aligned}
$$

where the first two terms are called within distribution similarity and the last term is called cross-distribution similarity. Moreover, if $k(\cdot, \cdot)$ is a characteristic kernel, $\mu_{\mathbb{P}} = \mu_{\mathbb{Q}}$ infers $\mathbb{P} = \mathbb{Q}$, meaning that distribution $\mathbb{P}$ and $\mathbb{Q}$ are tested the same, and $\mathrm{MMD}^2[\mathcal{F}, \mathbb{P}, \mathbb{Q}] = 0 \Leftrightarrow \mathbb{P} = \mathbb{Q}$. Previously, we have already defined the biased estimator, so we will use the U-statistic to estimate MMD^2

$$
\begin{aligned}
\widehat{\mathrm{MMD}}_u^2[\mathcal{F}, S_{\mathbb{P}}, S_{\mathbb{Q}}] &= \frac{1}{n(n-1)} \sum_{i=1}^{n} \sum_{j \neq i}^{n} k(x_i, x_j) + \frac{1}{m(m-1)} \sum_{i=1}^{m} \sum_{j \neq i}^{m} k(y_i, y_j) \\
&\quad - \frac{2}{nm} \sum_{i=1}^{n} \sum_{j=1}^{m} k(x_i, y_j).
\end{aligned}
\tag{5}
$$

In our task, we assume $m = n$, so we can simplify the estimator by

$$
\widehat{\mathrm{MMD}}_u^2[\mathcal{F}, S_{\mathbb{P}}, S_{\mathbb{Q}}] = \frac{1}{n(n-1)} \sum_{i \neq j} H_{ij},
\tag{6}
$$

where $H_{ij} := k(x_i, x_j) + k(y_i, y_j) - k(x_i, y_j) - k(x_j, y_i)$. Note that the $\widehat{\mathrm{MMD}}_u^2$ may be negative since it removes the self-similarity term, which is H_{ii}. Thus

$$
\widehat{\mathrm{MMD}}_u^2 + \frac{1}{n(n-1)} \sum_{i=1}^{n} H_{ii} \geq 0,
$$

where H_{ii} is the same definition as above. Moreover, the unbiased estimator $\widehat{\mathrm{MMD}}_u^2$ does not have minimum variance, since it ignores the H_{ii} term. Overall, no matter what estimators are used, we expect the test statistics to be small if $\mathbb{P} = \mathbb{Q}$ and to be large if they are distinct.

2.3   Test Based on the Asymptotic Distribution of Unbiased MMD

Under $\mathcal{H}_0$, the distribution of $\widehat{\mathrm{MMD}}_u^2$ is shown below.

Theorem 1 [7]. *We assume $m = n$, so let $t = m+n = 2n = 2m$, $\lim_{m,n\to\infty} n/t \to \rho_x = \frac{1}{2}$ and $\lim_{m,n\to\infty} m/t \to \rho_y := 1 - \rho_x = 1 - \frac{1}{2} = \frac{1}{2}$. Then under the null hypothesis $\mathcal{H}_0$, the asymptotic distribution of $\widehat{\mathrm{MMD}}_u^2$ can be defined by*

$$t\widehat{\mathrm{MMD}}_u^2[\mathcal{F}, S_\mathbb{P}, S_\mathbb{Q}] \xrightarrow{d} \sum_i^\infty \sigma_i \left[(\rho_x^{-1/2} a_i - \rho_y^{-1/2} b_i)^2 - (\rho_x \rho_y)^{-1} \right], \qquad (7)$$

where $a_i \sim \mathcal{N}(0,1)$ and $b_i \sim \mathcal{N}(0,1)$, $\xrightarrow{d}$ is the convergence in distribution, and σ_i is the eigenvalues of $\mathbb{P}$-covariance operator of the centered kernel [12]. Moreover, due to the same number of samples that are drawn, we can simplify the general form of $t\widehat{\mathrm{MMD}}_u^2[\mathcal{F}, S_\mathbb{P}, S_\mathbb{Q}]$ in Eq. 7 to a form of $n\widehat{\mathrm{MMD}}_u^2[\mathcal{F}, S_\mathbb{P}, S_\mathbb{Q}]$ [12]. Let $Z_i \sim \mathcal{N}(0,2)$. Then we have

$$2n\widehat{\mathrm{MMD}}_u^2[\mathcal{F}, S_\mathbb{P}, S_\mathbb{Q}] \xrightarrow{d} \sum_i^\infty \sigma_i \left[\left(\frac{1}{2}^{-1/2} a_i - \frac{1}{2}^{-1/2} b_i \right)^2 - (\frac{1}{2}\frac{1}{2})^{-1} \right],$$

which results in

$$2n\widehat{\mathrm{MMD}}_u^2[\mathcal{F}, S_\mathbb{P}, S_\mathbb{Q}] \xrightarrow{d} \sum_i^\infty \sigma_i \left[\left(\sqrt{2} Z_i \right)^2 - 4 \right]$$

$$n\widehat{\mathrm{MMD}}_u^2[\mathcal{F}, S_\mathbb{P}, S_\mathbb{Q}] \xrightarrow{d} \sum_i^\infty \sigma_i \left[Z_i^2 - 2 \right]. \qquad (8)$$

Corollary 1. *Under the alternative hypothesis $\mathcal{H}_1$, where $\mathbb{P} \neq \mathbb{Q}$, and when $m = n$, the $\widehat{\mathrm{MMD}}_u^2$ converges in a Gaussian distribution where*

$$\sqrt{n} \left(\widehat{\mathrm{MMD}}_u^2 - \mathrm{MMD}_u^2 \right) \xrightarrow{d} \mathcal{N}(0, \sigma_{\mathcal{H}_1}^2) \qquad (9)$$

$$\sigma_{\mathcal{H}_1}^2 = 4 \left(E_i \left[E_j[H_{ij}]^2 \right] - E_{i,j}[H_{ij}]^2 \right),$$

where H_{ij} is the definition above [14].

When performing a test, we can use a permutation test instead of directly calculating the null distribution [12], since under $\mathcal{H}_0$, we assume both samples are drawn from the same distribution, we can repeatedly combine all observations into a single set, random reassign the data into two new groups and calculate the test statistics for these permuted groups. After performing the permutation test method, a rejection threshold, denoted as r, will be found.

2.4   Test Power

As the test power $(1 - \beta)$ often refers to the probability that our test is able to reject $\mathcal{H}_0$ when $\mathbb{P} \neq \mathbb{Q}$ under a specific drawing number n. According to the Eq. 9, let Φ be the standard normal *cumulative distribution function* (CDF), we have

$$\Pr_{\mathcal{H}_1}\left(n\widehat{\mathrm{MMD}}_u^2 > r\right) = \Phi\left(\frac{\sqrt{n}\,\mathrm{MMD}_u^2}{\sigma_{\mathcal{H}_1}} - \frac{r}{\sqrt{n}\,\sigma_{\mathcal{H}_1}}\right).$$

Since r, MMD and $\sigma_{\mathcal{H}_1}$ are all constants, while the sample size n is large enough, the test power will be dominated by the first term, our ultimate goal is to maximize the

$$J(\mathcal{F}, S_{\mathbb{P}}, S_{\mathbb{Q}}) := \mathrm{MMD}^2(\mathcal{F}, S_{\mathbb{P}}, S_{\mathbb{Q}})/\sigma_{\mathcal{H}_1}(\mathcal{F}, S_{\mathbb{P}}, S_{\mathbb{Q}}), \tag{10}$$

and we estimate it by

$$\hat{J}_\lambda(\mathcal{F}, S_{\mathbb{P}}, S_{\mathbb{Q}}) := \frac{\widehat{\mathrm{MMD}}_u^2(\mathcal{F}, S_{\mathbb{P}}, S_{\mathbb{Q}})}{\hat{\sigma}_{\mathcal{H}_1,\lambda}(\mathcal{F}, S_{\mathbb{P}}, S_{\mathbb{Q}})}, \tag{11}$$

where $\hat{\sigma}^2_{\mathcal{H}_1,\lambda}$ is a regularized biased estimator of $\sigma^2_{\mathcal{H}_1}$, defined by [12]

$$\frac{4}{n^3}\sum_{i=1}^{n}\left(\sum_{j=1}^{n}H_{ij}\right)^2 - \frac{4}{n^4}\left(\sum_{i=1}^{n}\sum_{j=1}^{m}H_{ij}\right)^2 + \lambda.$$

2.5   Choice of Kernel Method

For the kernel method we choose in our task, we use the deep kernel method mentioned in Eq. 1, repeated here:

$$k_\omega(x, y) = [(1 - \epsilon)\kappa(\phi_\omega(x), \phi_\omega(y)) + \epsilon]q(x, y),$$

where ϕ_ω is the deep neural network that extract features, κ is a Gaussian RBF kernel with a length-scale $l = \sigma_\omega$, q is also a Gaussian kernel with $l = \sigma_q$ and the ϵ is chosen between the range from 0 to 1 [12].

The reason why we do not choose the traditional simple RBF kernel as k is that most of the simple characteristic kernels are translation-invariant, meaning that the value of kernel depends only on the difference of data points x and y and a small number of fixed hyperparameters, like the length-scale l in the Gaussian kernel. However, deep kernels are parameterized by deep neural networks, so they are capable of adapting their structure to a specific task and data.

3   Motivation and Methods

In this section, we introduce our key motivation and propose two methods.

3.1   Motivation

In the previous experiments of directly maximizing the test power, we observe that sometimes even though the MMD value is quite small,pg the performance in the training process keeps improving by extremely decreasing the variance which is the denominator in Eq. 11. This phenomenon leads to an unsatisfactory result that the real testing test power in the permutation test is lower than the average result recorded in the previous work.

Thus, in order to balance the maximization of MMD value and the maximization of test power, we proposed two methods used in the optimization of our objective functions. They are based on the logarithm and Pareto optimization.

3.2 Logarithm of Test Power

In the code implementations, the loss function is defined by

$$L = -\hat{J} = -\frac{\widehat{\mathrm{MMD}}_u^2}{\hat{\sigma}_{\mathcal{H}_1, \lambda}}. \tag{12}$$

In the process of training deep neural network, there are several steps

1. **Initialization:** Initialize the weights w and bias b for each node, and initialize the hyperparameters, i.e., ϵ, σ required for the model.
2. **Forward Propagation:** The whole neural network takes input from training set and compute the output for each input. Inside the neural network, each layer will applies the set of weights to its input which has the same dimension, add bias, generate an output by an activation function and pass the output to the next layer until the **Output layer**.
3. **Loss Calculation:** In the neural network, there is a loss function which is to measure the difference between the prediction of neural network under the current values of parameters and the actual data. Thus the main objective of the training process of neural network is to **minimizing** the loss calculated. The smaller the loss is, meaning that the better the model predict the training data in the training process.
4. **Backpropagation:** This step is the key part of neural network, it enables each neuron in the network to learn from the loss of previous forward propagation. Using the chain rule from calculus, the network calculates the gradient of the loss function with respect to each weight and bias in the network. The gradient gives the direction of the steepest ascent in the loss function, but we want to minimize the loss, so we will move in the opposite direction, and the whole process is called **gradient-descent**.
5. **Update Parameters:** Each weight and bias is then updated in the opposite direction to the gradient. The size of the step taken is determined by the learning rate γ, a hyperparameter that must be set prior to training.
6. **Iteration:** Then move to the next iteration, and back to step 1 again, until the loss of the neural network converges to a specific value or the difference between loss of two consecutive iterations is small than a given threshold. However, neural network is prone to overfit the training data if the number of the iterations are chosen too large.

As discussed above, the neural network can maximizing the value of J by using the training data, with an objective

$$\min\left(\frac{\mathrm{MMD}_u^2}{-\hat{\sigma}_{\mathcal{H}_1,\lambda}}\right).$$

It is a traditional non-smooth optimization problem [8]. Through the inspiration from the method from [1], we take the logarithm on the objective function for optimization

$$L = \log(-\hat{J}) = \log(\hat{\sigma}_{\mathcal{H}_1,\lambda}) - \log(\widehat{\mathrm{MMD}}_u^2), \tag{13}$$

in order to improve the model's robustness and generalization.

3.3   Pareto Optimization in Objective Function

Before introducing the Pareto optimization, we firstly introduce two basic concepts in the field of Pareto Optimization.

Definition 3 *(Dominance). Solution x_1 dominates x_2 if x_1 is no worse than x_2 in all objectives and x_1 is strictly better than x_2 in at least one objective.*

In our problem, we have two objectives (or called **bi-objective optimization problem**), so we can state that a solution pair $(\mathrm{MMD}_{u1}^2, J_1)$ dominates another pair $(\mathrm{MMD}_{u2}^2, J_2)$ if both the value of MMD_{u1}^2 and J_1 are not smaller than MMD_{u2}^2 and J_2 and at lease one of the MMD_{u1}^2 and J_1 is greater than that of MMD_{u2}^2 and J_2.

However, not all solution pairs exist dominance between themselves. For example, in the Fig. 1a, before the elbow, all the solutions generated by next iteration of neural networks dominates the previous one, but after the elbow, we cannot directly claim that which solution is better, since when increment occurs in J, there is also a decrement in MMD^2. Thus we call the set of these solutions as **non-dominated solution set**, the boundary of all these points called **Pareto front**, and our goal is to find the optimized solution in the Pareto front.

The method we used is weighted-sum method which is a parametric scalarizing approach that can convert multi-objective function into a single-objective function, so we define our new objective function as

$$J^* = w_1 J + (1 - w_1)\mathrm{MMD}_u^2, \tag{14}$$

where J is the objective function defined in the previous work, and MMD_u^2 is the numerator used to derive J, w_1 is the weight of how much important the J value is compared to the MMD and the weight will be tuned by the neural network. This approach is one of the simplest solution of Pareto optimization problem. However, it performs well in our task, since two drawbacks of this method are all avoided in our problem. The first one is it is hard to select weight of objective. However, there are only two objectives in our problem, we can set one weight initially to be 0.5, and let neural network to find the best weight.

The best weight found by neural network varied across different datasets and different sample sizes, but in general, the weight is always greater than 0.5. It is reasonable, since we are focusing on maximizing test power without sacrificing MMD value too much. Then, the next problem of weight-sum method is that it cannot handle *non-convex front*, however, in our problem, our solution will never exists in the concave front, concave front means that there is always a solution that can increase test power highly with just little sacrificing in the MMD value in the later iterations, that is what we actually want. Therefore two drawbacks of weighted-sum method can be ignored in our problem.

4 Experiments and Results

We will introduce the details of experiments and results in each benchmarks in this section.

Baselines. We mainly perform 3 tests on the several datasets.

MMD-D: MMD test with a deep kernel which is proposed by Liu al. [12].

MMD-D-P: MMD test with a deep kernel which we apply pareto optimization on the objective function J.

MMD-D-L: MMD test with a deep kernel which we take logarithm on the objective function J.

Datasets. We use two benchmark datasets to verify the effectiveness of baselines and our methods.

Higgs Dataset [2]. Higgs dataset is one of the most challenged dataset for the deep kernel method, since the Test power converges to 1 when we increase the number of input data, denoted as n, to a huge number, while other datasets like synthetic datasets (Blob) or the image datasets MNIST [13] converges when $n = 40$ for Blob datasets and $n = 400$ for MNIST datasets, leading to a result that only minor improvement can be displayed. The result of average Test power in testing is reported in Table 1.

MNIST Dataset [13]. The MNIST dataset is a classical dataset that consist of a collection images of handwritten digits, from zero to nine. We compare the samples from true MNIST dataset and samples from fake MNIST dataset generated by adversarial network. The result of average Test power in testing for increasing number of samples is displayed in Table 2.

Implementation Details. Most of our implementation steps follow the Algorithm 1 described in [12], except that we replace the equation of $\hat{J}_\lambda(w)$ from original maximization of test power into Eq. 13 when using the method of Logarithm and into Eq. 14 when applying the Pareto optimization. Moreover, setting an initial weight $w_1 = 0.5$ in the experiment configuration phase is also additional when performing the Pareto optimization method.

Main Results. We could see that both optimization methods improve the test power performance, even though the increment is not so tremendous. Since the

Table 1. Higgs ($\alpha = 0.05$) datasets, result displayed in a form of average test power $\pm$ standard error for N samples drawn over 10 random trials. Results may differ between different random seeds, but trends will stay same. The highest column for each N will be bold highlighted.

N	MMD-D	MMD-D-P	MMD-D-L
2000	$0.164_{\pm 0.063}$	$0.197_{\pm 0.051}$	$\mathbf{0.261_{\pm 0.080}}$
4000	$0.358_{\pm 0.140}$	$0.368_{\pm 0.144}$	$\mathbf{0.394_{\pm 0.156}}$
8000	$0.927_{\pm 0.060}$	$0.948_{\pm 0.038}$	$\mathbf{0.971_{\pm 0.027}}$
9000	$0.970_{\pm 0.044}$	$\mathbf{0.986_{\pm 0.013}}$	$0.983_{\pm 0.019}$
10000	$0.989_{\pm 0.013}$	$\mathbf{0.993_{\pm 0.011}}$	$0.992_{\pm 0.012}$

Table 2. MNIST ($\alpha = 0.05$) datasets, result displayed in a form of average test power $\pm$ standard error for N samples drawn over 10 random trials. Results may differ between different random seeds, but trends will stay same. The highest column for each N will be bold highlighted.

N	MMD-D	MMD-D-P	MMD-D-L
200	$0.411_{\pm 0.159}$	$\mathbf{0.435_{\pm 0.178}}$	$0.430_{\pm 0.195}$
300	$0.725_{\pm 0.219}$	$0.757_{\pm 0.198}$	$\mathbf{0.794_{\pm 0.197}}$
400	$0.927_{\pm 0.060}$	$\mathbf{0.980_{\pm 0.032}}$	$0.973_{\pm 0.017}$
600	$\mathbf{1.000_{\pm 0.000}}$	$\mathbf{1.000_{\pm 0.000}}$	$\mathbf{1.000_{\pm 0.000}}$

MMD-D is already a method that can handle most of the two-sample test problem and outperforms than any other methods used in MMD test [12], combining it with our optimization methods is the *ice on the cake* study on the performance of test power. However, when looking at Fig. 2a and 2b, we could see that we indeed balance the MMD value and the J value. The value of J improves much without too much decrease in the MMD value, which result in a generality of the model.

Ablation Study. In this section, we analyze the impacts of our two optimization methods. For the Logarithm method, we could see that it improves the performance highly when the sample size is not large enough and the test power does not converge to 1. The reason why this happen is that when sample size is small, the model are prone to overfitting with the small set of training data, rather than fitting in a general model, the Logarithm on the test power function can mitigate the extreme decrease of the variance and generate better results. On the other hand, the Pareto optimization method aims to maximize both the MMD value and the test power, so it can have the best MMD value when it has the same test power as other methods. Thus, it can perform better when the sample size is large and most of the training test power converges to 1. In conclusion, both methods have effective improvement when the result of original method does not converge to 1.

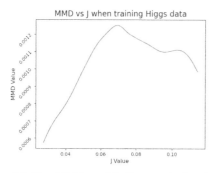
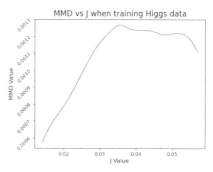

(a) The MMD vs J before optimization.   (b) The MMD vs J after optimization

Fig. 2.

5   Conclusions

Although the MMD test with deep kernel is a mature method in performing the two-sample test, it still has the trend to overfit the training data, which maximizing the training test statistics J by extremely decreasing the MMD value. Thus we propose two optimization methods to balance the MMD value and J value in the process of training deep kernel.

For future work, we will explore a few research directions based on this present study. In contemporary data science and machine learning research, the task of effectively discerning distributional discrepancies is gaining unprecedented significance. Both out-of-distribution data detection and adversarial data detection aim to justify that two hard-to-distinguish yet different data distributions indeed have large discrepancy [3,18]. It would be interesting to employ these optimized MMD test methods to solve such challenges.

References

1. An, N.T., Giles, D., Nam, N.M., Rector, R.B.: The log-exponential smoothing technique and Nesterov's accelerated gradient method for generalized Sylvester problems (2015)
2. Baldi, P., Sadowski, P., Whiteson, D.: Searching for exotic particles in high-energy physics with deep learning. Nat. Commun. **5**(1), 4308 (2014). https://doi.org/10.1038/ncomms5308
3. Fang, Z., Li, Y., Lu, J., Dong, J., Han, B., Liu, F.: Is out-of-distribution detection learnable? Adv. Neural. Inf. Process. Syst. **35**, 37199–37213 (2022)
4. Fukumizu, K., Gretton, A., Schölkopf, B., Sriperumbudur, B.K.: Characteristic kernels on groups and semigroups. In: Koller, D., Schuurmans, D., Bengio, Y., Bottou, L. (eds.) Advances in Neural Information Processing Systems, vol. 21. Curran Associates, Inc. (2008)
5. Gao, R., et al.: Maximum mean discrepancy test is aware of adversarial attacks. In: Meila, M., Zhang, T. (eds.) Proceedings of the 38th International Conference

on Machine Learning. Proceedings of Machine Learning Research, vol. 139, pp. 3564–3575. PMLR (2021). https://proceedings.mlr.press/v139/gao21b.html

6. Ghiasi-Shirazi, K., Safabakhsh, R., Shamsi, M.: Learning translation invariant kernels for classification. J. Mach. Learn. Res. **11**(45), 1353–1390 (2010). http://jmlr.org/papers/v11/ghiasi-shirazi10a.html

7. Gretton, A., Borgwardt, K.M., Rasch, M.J., Schölkopf, B., Smola, A.: A kernel two-sample test. J. Mach. Learn. Res. **13**(null), 723–773 (2012)

8. Herrmann, J.: A genetic algorithm for minimax optimization problems. In: Proceedings of the 1999 Congress on Evolutionary Computation-CEC99 (Cat. No. 99TH8406), vol. 2, pp. 1099–1103 (1999). https://doi.org/10.1109/CEC.1999.782545

9. Kirchler, M., Khorasani, S., Kloft, M., Lippert, C.: Two-sample testing using deep learning. In: Chiappa, S., Calandra, R. (eds.) Proceedings of the Twenty Third International Conference on Artificial Intelligence and Statistics. Proceedings of Machine Learning Research, vol. 108, pp. 1387–1398. PMLR (2020). https://proceedings.mlr.press/v108/kirchler20a.html

10. Kolmogorov, A.: Sulla determinazione empirica di una legge di distribuzione. G. Ist. Ital. Attuari **4**, 83–91 (1933). https://cir.nii.ac.jp/crid/1571135650766370304

11. Liu, F., Xu, W., Lu, J., Sutherland, D.J.: Meta two-sample testing: learning kernels for testing with limited data. Adv. Neural. Inf. Process. Syst. **34**, 5848–5860 (2021)

12. Liu, F., Xu, W., Lu, J., Zhang, G., Gretton, A., Sutherland, D.J.: Learning deep kernels for non-parametric two-sample tests (2021)

13. Radford, A., Metz, L., Chintala, S.: Unsupervised representation learning with deep convolutional generative adversarial networks (2016)

14. Serfling, R.J.: Approximation Theorems of Mathematical Statistics. Wiley, Hoboken (1980)

15. Smirnov, N.: Table for estimating the goodness of fit of empirical distributions. Ann. Math. Stat. **19**(2), 279–281 (1948). https://doi.org/10.1214/aoms/1177730256

16. Steinwart, I., Christmann, A.: Support Vector Machines. Springer, Heidelberg (2008). https://doi.org/10.1007/978-0-387-77242-4

17. Wilson, A.G., Hu, Z., Salakhutdinov, R., Xing, E.P.: Deep kernel learning (2015)

18. Zhang, S., et al.: Detecting adversarial data by probing multiple perturbations using expected perturbation score. arXiv preprint arXiv:2305.16035 (2023)

Probabilistic Reverse Top-k Query on Probabilistic Data

Trieu Minh Nhut Le[1] and Jinli Cao[2(✉)]

[1] Department of Computer Science and Information Technology, Sai Gon University, Ho Chi Minh City, Vietnam
nhuttrieu@gmail.com
[2] Department of Computer Science and Information Technology, School of Computing, Engineering and Mathematical Science, La Trobe University, Melbourne, Australia
j.cao@latrobe.edu.au

Abstract. Reverse top-k queries have received much attention from research communities. The result of reverse top-k queries is a set of objects, which had the k-most interest based on their objects' references. Moreover, answering the queries on probabilistic data has been studied in many applications. The most common problem with uncertain queries is how to calculate their probabilities. Currently, there are some proposed solutions for selecting answers to queries and calculating probabilistic values based on users' preferences. In this paper, we study answering reverse top-k queries on probabilistic data. Firstly, we propose a novel method to calculate probabilistic tuples based on the expected theory. Secondly, we present the advantages of our approach against the traditional approach. Furthermore, we upgrade the new algorithm using two techniques of R-tree and upper-lower bound. The experimental results illustrate the efficiency of the proposed algorithm compared to the traditional algorithms in terms of scalability.

Keywords: Reverse top-k query · user preferences · probabilistic data · uncertainty

1 Introduction

The reverse top-k query is one of the important tools for market analysis, decision-making, recommendation, and business intelligence in the marketplace. The reverse top-k queries return a set of the users' attention to objects based on their preferences [1–6]. The answer set of the reverse top-k query is used to analyze reliable and valuable customers for managers and projectors in their business domains. The highest-ranked answers of reverse top-k queries represent the most wanted users' preferences or customers' interested products [7–9].

Uncertainty occurs in many real-life applications, such as collecting data from inconsistent resources and noising environments [10, 11], and the results can be presented by probabilistic values [12–14]. Therefore, it is essential to study and identify their semantics on probabilistic data. Many studies focus on selecting reliable answers, such as top-k queries [12, 13, 15, 16], selecting the skyline queries on probabilistic data [14, 17–20] and nearest neighbor queries [21].

Z. Bao et al. (Eds.): ADC 2023, LNCS 14386, pp. 30–43, 2024.
https://doi.org/10.1007/978-3-031-47843-7_3

Table 1. Database of scores of different hotels' probability

hotel ID	rating	services	probability
t_1	50	40	0.8
t_2	70	90	0.6
t_3	20	120	0.5
t_4	60	140	0.4
t_5	90	50	0.7

Table 2. The users' preferences

user	w[rating]	w[services]
u_1	0.2	0.8
u_2	0.6	0.4
u_3	0.7	0.3

However, there has not been much research on the reverse top-k queries on probabilistic data. Earlier research on optimizing reverse top-k queries appeared in [2, 3]. A. Vlachou et al. [2] proposed the Branch-and-Bound for effectively answering the reverse top-k queries.

The significant problem of probabilistic data is how to deal with probability values in answers. It is crucial to have a new method of reverse top-k queries on probabilistic data in modern environments. The goal of this study is to select a reliable and meaningful answer set for the reverse top-k query.

We provide an example of five different hotels; each hotel was recorded in two dimensions for its rating and services. The attribute values range from 1 to150, representing scores as shown in Table 1. The higher score for an attribute indicates better quality and services at the hotel. For example, tuple t_1 presents the hotel's rating and services with scores of 50 and 40, respectively.

The user preferences of three users (u_1, u_2, u_3) in Table 2 show their weightings of interests in each attribute of hotels. That is, users expressed their preferences for each attribute of hotels with a weight (w_i). For example, user u_1 is more interested in the services (0.8) than the rating of hotels (0.2).

Managers need to analyze their business by evaluating customers' preferences. The technique of reverse top-k query can be used for decision support systems and business intelligence, as the result set provides information about their business potential market. Managers can adjust their improvement plans accordingly. In this example, Table 3 shows reverse top-2 answers. Hotel t_2 is interested in by one user (u_2). Hotel t_3 is interested in by one user (u_1) while hotel t_4 has attracted three users. The answers have not yet considered the probabilities (Table 4).

This paper investigates the reverse top-k queries with probabilistic data to obtain reliable results. The main contributions are as follows:

– Identifying problems and analyzing the semantics of the expected value for calculating probabilistic data.
– Introducing reverse top-k queries based on the expected theory along with some lemmas and theorems.
– Improving effectiveness of the algorithm for reverse top-k queries on probabilistic data.
– Conducting experiments to evaluate the effectiveness of the proposed approach.

Table 3. Result of reverse top-k queries of Table 1 and 2

user	w[rating]	w[stars]	score
t_2 - reverse top-2			
u_2	0.6	0.4	78
t_3 - reverse top-2			
u_1	0.2	0.8	100
t_4 - reverse top-2			
u_1	0.2	0.8	124
u_2	0.6	0.4	92
u_3	0.7	0.3	84
t_5 - reverse top-2			
u_3	0.7	0.3	78

Table 4. Scores of every user on hotels for selecting top-k

score	u_1	u_2	u_3
t_1	42	46	47
t_2	86	**78**	76
t_3	**100**	60	50
t_4	**124**	92	**84**
t_5	58	74	**78**

2 Preliminary Reverse Top-k Queries and Probabilistic Data

In this section, we present the basic concepts and definitions of top-k queries and reverse top-k queries.

2.1 Probabilistic Data

Generally, uncertain data can be presented as probabilistic database D, which is a finite set of tuples, where each tuple is associated with a probability value.

Definition 1. *(Probabilistic tuple): A probabilistic tuple includes a tuple (t_i) and a probability value (pr_i), which presents a likelihood of the tuple appearance in dataset D. The probability is presented as a new dimension in D ($0 \leq pr_i \leq 1$).*

Table 1 provides an example of a probabilistic dataset. For example, tuple t_1 (50, 40) has a probability likelihood of 0.8 to be true.

According to the probability theory, if $pr(t_i)$ is the likelihood of tuple t_i, else ($1 - pr(t_i)$) is the unlikelihood of t_i in the data.

2.2 Reverse Top-k Queries

Reverse top-k queries are a valuable tool in many applications. The answer set of the query is a set of users who are interested in the objects. This tool helps managers to create new services and identify their customer's behaviors [1–3, 5, 6].

Given a dataset D with n dimensions, a tuple is presented as $t_i = \{a_1, a_2,..., a_n\}$. A value in any dimension of a tuple $t_i(a_i)$ presents a feature/attribute of object t_i. A score function (f) is defined to calculate the overall score based on object scores and users' preferences, which is called the weight function:

$$f_u(t) = \sum_{i=1}^{n}(w_i \times a_i) \ (*)$$

where, $u_i = \{w_1, w_2, ..., w_m\}$ is users' preference, $w_i \geq 0$, w_i is users' preference evaluation, $i = \overline{(1..n)}$.

Definition 2. *(top-k): Given dataset D, the top-k answers of user's preference u_i are a set of k-best scores calculated by formula (*).*

$$Top_k = \left\{ \forall t, t' \in D; t \in TOP; t' \in \{D \backslash TOP\} : f(t) isbetterf(t') \right\}.$$

For example, the top-2 query of user u_2 is a set of hotels $\{t_2, t_4\}$ with top-2 best-scored tuples. That is, the set $\{t_2, t_4\}$ has the highest scores compared to all other tuples in Table 1.

Definition 3. *(Reverse top-k): Given dataset D and the set of users' preferences U, the answers of the reverse top-k query form a set RTop of top-k members.*

$$RTop_k(t_q) = \left\{ \forall u_i \in U : t_q \in Top_k(u_i), \forall t \in D \backslash Top_k(u_i), suchthatf_{u_i}(t_q) \geq f_{u_i}(t) \right\}.$$

where: $f_{u_i}(t_q)$ is the function score of a tuple t_q, and $f_{u_i}(t)$ is the function score of any tuple t in the set $D \backslash Top_k(D)$.

3   Reverse Top-k Query on Probabilistic Data Using Expected Value

3.1   Proposed the Expected Value on Probabilistic Data

The expected value in statistics is used to estimate probabilities with multivariate models to examine possible outcomes for a proposed prediction. It helps users determine whether they are taking an appropriate level of risk by giving the likely outcome of prediction. Taking the probability into data calculations, the expected value can provide more meaningful and realistic information. Therefore, this paper applied the expected value to calculate the user's score and modify the BBR algorithm [2] for a new algorithm called Probabilistic Branch and Bound Reverse (PBBR) algorithm. The novel PBBR algorithm can process reverse top-k queries in both certain data and probabilistic data.

Definition 4. *(Expected score): In probabilistic theory, the expected value is a generalization of the weighted average. The expected score of the discrete variables is the average value of probabilities in all possible worlds.*

Table 5. Expected scores of users selecting top-2

score	u_1	u_2	u_3
t_1	33.6	36.8	37.6
t_2	**51.6**	**46.8**	**45.6**
t_3	**50**	30	25
t_4	49.6	36.8	33.6
t_5	40.6	**51.8**	**54.6**

Table 6. Results of reverse top-k queries using expected score

user	w[Profit]	w[time]	Scores
t_2 - reverse top-2			
u_1	0.2	0.8	51.6
u_2	0.6	0.4	46.8
u_3	0.7	0.3	45.6
t_3 - reverse top-2			
u_1	0.2	0.8	50
t_5 - reverse top-2			
u_2	0.6	0.4	51.8
u_3	0.7	0.3	54.6

Using the expectation for probabilistic data, we obtain a new formula to calculate the score function:

$$f_e(t) = \sum_{i=1}^{n}(w_i \times a_i) \times pr \quad (**)$$

As an example, we select a probabilistic data $t_1(50, 40, 0.8)$ in Table 1 and a user preference data $u_1 = (0.2, 0.8)$ from Table 2. The score of t_1 attracting u_1 is calculated as follows:

$$Score(u_1, t_1) = (0.2 \times 50 + 0.8 \times 40) \times 0.8 = 33.6$$

3.2 The Reverse Top-k Query on Probabilistic Data Using the Expected Value

Based on definition of the reverse top-k queries and expected score theory, we calculated expected scores of all tuples shown in Table 5. The new result set for reverse top-k on probabilistic data is presented in Table 6.

Comparing the answer set of reverse top-k between non-probability and probability using the expected value, the obtained answer sets in Table 6 are more reliable than that in Table 3. The users of hotel t_4 has reduced from 3 to 0, and hotel t_5 has gained 2 users.

The expected score is introduced in the probabilistic theory which is more reliable and efficient than the past approaches. Therefore, utilizing the expected score for reverse top-k queries can get more reliable and accurate answers for recommendations and decision-making.

3.3 Theories Applying to Processing the Reverse Top-k on Probabilistic Data

We are proposing a novel algorithm using the expected score (**) to process reverse top-k queries on probabilistic data. The algorithm is updated to process data in both certain and uncertain values. When our proposed method is applied to process reverse top-k queries without probabilistic data, the answer set will be the same as BBR algorithm [2] if the default probability is assigned to 1.

a) Theories of eliminating and including rules

In this section, we present some definitions and theorems to support pruning rules in our algorithm. Given a user preference set V as a subset of U, we calculate the minimum and maximum expected scores of a tuple $t_p \in D$ based on the users' preference set $V = \{u_1, u_2, ..., u_o\}$. $u(w_1, w_2, ..., w_n) \in V \subseteq U$. The upper bound of V is $V_{up} = (max_{\forall u \in V}(w_{i_1}), max_{\forall u \in V}(w_{i_2}), ..., max_{\forall u \in V}(w_{i_n}))$, and the lower bound of V is $V_{low} = (min_{\forall u \in V}(w_{i_1}), min_{\forall u \in V}(w_{i_2}), ..., min_{\forall u \in V}(w_{i_n}))$. We have the following definitions:

Definition 5. *(lower bound of an expected score of tuple t_p): Given a probabilistic tuple $t_p \in D$ and a users' preference set $V \subseteq U$, the lower bound of the expected score of tuple t_p is:*

$$f^{V_{low}}(t_p) = \sum_{i=1}^{n}(min_{\forall u \in V}(w_i) \times a_{p_i}) \times pr_p$$

For example, with $V = \{u_1, u_2, u_3\}$, where $min(w_1) = 0.2$ and $min(w_2) = 0.3$ from Table 2, the lower bound of the expected score of tuple t_1 is calculated as follows.

$$f^{V_{low}}(t_1) = (0.2 \times 50 + 0.3 \times 40) \times 0.8 = 17.6$$

Definition 6. *(upper bound of expected score of tuple t_p): Given a probabilistic tuple $t_p \in D$ and a user's preference set $V \subseteq U$, the upper bound of the expected score of tuple t_p is calculated as follows:*

$$f^{V_{low}}(t_p) = \sum_{i=1}^{n}(max_{\forall u \in V}(w_i) \times a_{p_i}) \times pr_p$$

For example, $f^{V_{up}}(t_1) = (0.7 \times 50 + 0.8 \times 40) \times 0.8 = 53.6$

Lemma 1. *(expected score bound of t_p): Given a set of user's preference $V \subseteq U$, and a probabilistic tuple t_p, the expected score $f^u(t_p)$ of any $u \in V$ is between the lower bound $f^{V_{low}}(t_p)$ and the upper bound $f^{V_{up}}(t_p)$.*

$$\forall u \in V \subseteq U : f^{V_{low}}(t_p) \leq f^u(t_p) \leq f^{V_{up}}(t_p)$$

The proof was omitted due to the space limitation.

For example: the expected score u_1 is between the lower bound of 17.6 and the upper bound of 53.6: $17.6 \leq f^{u_1}(t_1) = (0.2 \times 50 + 0.8 \times 40) \times 0.8 = 33.6 \leq 53.6$.

The following lemma is expanding to the minimum and maximum scores of Bounding Rectangle (BR) based on user's preference set (V). The upper bound of BR is $t_{BR_{up}} = \{max_{\forall t \in BR}(a_{i_1}), ..., max_{\forall t \in BR}(a_{i_n}), max_{\forall t \in BR}(pr_i)\}$ in each attribute of dataset BR $\{t_1, t_2, ..., t_z\}\{t_1, t_2, ..., t_z\}$, and the lower bound of BR is $t_{BR_{low}} = \{min_{\forall t \in BR}(a_{i_1}), ..., min_{\forall t \in BR}(a_{i_n}), min_{\forall t \in BR}(pr_i)\}$ of each attribute of dataset BR $\{t_1, t_2, ..., t_z\}\{t_1, t_2, ..., t_z\}$. Then, we create lemma 2.

Lemma 2. *(expected score Bounding Rectangle BR ⊆ D):* Given a set of user's preference $V \subseteq U$ and an area $BR \subseteq D$, the expected score $f^{V_{up}}(t_p)$ of all probabilistic tuples $t_p \in BR \subseteq D$ is between the lower bound $f^{V_{low}}(BR_{low})$ and the upper bound $f^{V_{up}}(BR_{up})$. We have

$$\forall t_p \in BR, \forall u \in V : f^{V_{low}}(BR_{low}) \leq f^u(t_p) \leq f^{V_{up}}(BR_{up})$$

Definition 7. *(score domination):* Assuming a set of user's preference $V \subseteq U$, a set of probabilistic tuples $BR \subseteq D$, and a probabilistic tuple (t_q). If $f^{V_{low}}(t_q) > f^{V_{up}}(BR_{up})$, then we called t_q dominates BR based on V, being denoted $\left(t_q \prec_f^V BR \right)$.

Theorem 1. *(pruning rule):* Given a set of user's preference $V \subseteq U$, a probabilistic dataset D, and a reverse top-k query $RTOP_k(t_q)$. If k probabilistic tuples in D dominate t_q based on V, then user's set V can be safely pruned out of the answer set. There will be no users in V in the reverse top-k result set $RTOP_k(t_q)$.

Theorem 2. *(including answer set):* Given a set of user's preference $V \subseteq U$, a probabilistic dataset D, and a reverse top-k query $RTOP_k(t_q)$. If there is less than k probabilistic tuples (t_i) in D, based on V, which t_i dominates t_q, then all users in V can be inserted to the reverse top-k answer set $RTOP_k(t_q)$.

Theorems 1 and 2 have been proven that are omitted due to the space limitation.

3.4 The Proposed Probabilistic Branch-and-Bound Algorithm

Our proposed Probabilistic Branch and Bound Reverse top-k algorithm (PBBR) aims to select the users' preference set $(V \subset U)$ and dataset $(BR \subset D)$ using upper bound and lower bound. According to the Branch-Bound technique, the possible correlation between probabilistic tuples (t_q queries' tuple) and dataset (BR) based on users' preference set (V) is examined. This possible correlation is considered by the calculating expected score of probabilistic tuple t_q and the dataset which is a branch-bound rectangle (BR). The V and BR is in form of upper-bound and lower-bound to cover the set of uses' preference and dataset respectively. Moreover, all possible sets are stored in R-tree for further execution.

For example, Fig. 1 shows all possible sets of probabilistic data D stored in R-tree. Figure 2 shows the lower bound and upper bound of possible sets of probabilistic data (D) which is stored in the R-tree.

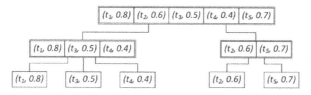

Fig. 1. R-Tree of dataset

Fig. 2. Upper bound and lower bound in Tree

The Probabilistic Branch and Bound Reverse top-k (PBBR-k) algorithm pseudocode is described as follows:

ALGORITHM 1: Probabilistic Branch and Bound Reverse top-k (PBBR) algorithm

Input: Probabilistic tuple $t_q(a_{q_1}, a_{q_2}, ..., a_{q_n}, pr_q)$, value k, probabilistic dataset D, a set of users' preferences U.

Output: Result set $PRTOP - k(t_q) = \{u_j, ..., u_l\}(j \leq l)$.

    // RtreeU is a tree structure containing set of user's preferences as branch and bound rectangle.

    // Get the first node in RtreeU and assign it to HeapU designed as a queue.

1   HeapU.enqueue(RtreeU.getRoot());

    // initial PRTOP-k is an empty set.

2   PRTOP-k(tq) ← {};

3   while (!heapU.isEmpty()) do

       // dequeue a node, which contains a bound rectangle covering user's preference tuples

4   V ← dequeue(heapU);

       // check the set V for including, excluding, or go further step ().

5   cTop CheckTOPk(D; V; tq; k);

6   // function CheckTOPk as presented in next section

      if (cT op == 1) then

         // add all tuples user's preference in rectangle

7   V in to the result.

8   PRTOP-k(tq) PRTOP-k(tq) [getSet(V);

      if (cT op == 0) then

9   // add children node in RtreeU a set' of user preference into HeapU.

10   heapU enqueue(RtreeU.getChildren());

    return RTOP-k(t$_q$);

Algorithm 1 PBBR is to process reverse top-k queries with probabilistic data. The Branch-and-Bound algorithm uses an R-tree to index the user's preferences. All nodes in R-tree are processed by using the queue structure in the R-tree with the Heap technique for descending order (line 1). The CheckTOP-k function is used to determine the users' preference set V whether it belongs to the answer set of top-k or not. The primary purpose of this function is to count the number of tuples in probabilistic dataset dominating t_q based on definition 7.

3.5 Evaluation the Queries Answers Using the Expected Value

In this section, we analyze the different result sets between our proposed method and the traditional reverse top-k method. Our proposed method proves to be more reliable than previous research. Traditional reverse top-k queries have ignored the probabilistic values in the probabilistic dataset to obtain the answer [2, 3].

Our proposed approach uses the expected value by multiplying score and probability together for processing reverse top-k queries on probabilistic data. It can be applied to certain data to obtain the same answer set as the traditional method. Therefore, our proposed approach is better than the traditional approaches.

4 Experiments

In this section, we implement our algorithms PBBR to demonstrate the advantages of our proposed method over the Branch and Bound Reverse Top-k algorithm (BBR) [3]. All experiments were executed in C# on a Windows 10 Operation System. The computer is configured with core i7 − 5500, 2.4 GHz CPU and 8 GB Random Access Memory.

4.1 Synthetic Data

We generated a three-dimensional dataset. The first two dimensions is assigned integer values in the range of [1K..10K] individually. The third dimension is assigned float value as a probability of tuple in the range of [0.001 to 0.999]. All random values are assigned using a uniform random distribution. Table 7 shows the default parameters used in our experiments.

4.2 Algorithm Setup

Two algorithms of BBR and PBBR were implemented for experiments. Both algorithms answer reverse top-k queries using the score function $f^u(t) = \sum_{i=1}^{2}(w_i \times a_i)$ for two dimensions.

- **Branch and Bound Reverse:** Answering reverse top-k queries without considering the probability values of the probabilistic data.
- **Probabilistic Branch and Bound Reverse:** Answering the reverse top-k queries using the probability values and the expected scores.

Table 7. Default parameters for the synthetic dataset

Parameter	Value
Maximum probability of tuples	[0.001, 0.999]
Number of dimensions	2
Value of k	20
Number of probabilistic tuples	10,000
Number of users' references	40,000

4.3   Measurement Metric

The metrics are used to measure the difference between the two algorithms:

- **Execution time by seconds:** This metric is used to compare the execution time differences between BBR and PBBR for various parameter settings.
- **Number of users' preferences in the result set:** This metric measures the number of users in the result set when comparing the BBR and PBBR approaches.

4.4   Experiment Results

The goal of this section is to analyze the distinct answer sets obtained from our approach and the traditional one. We detect the tuple's score (t_q) and probability (pr) to obtain the answer set based on their scores within the probabilistic data. Our experiments are divided into three parts. First, the different values of k are presented to observe different results. Second, the various quantities of users' preferences are applied to analyze different outcomes. Furthermore, the datasets with different numbers of probabilistic tuples are studied.

a. Identify the approximate probabilistic tuple based on scores and probability

In Fig. 3, the bar charts are presented to identify the attribute values of tuple t_q for analyzing the different results of BBR and PBBR processes. We detect the approximate tuple (t_q) and probability (pr) to prevent the empty results set. We are adjusting the values of each field based on their ranks (t_q) from 15 to 30 among the dataset as shown in Fig. 3a. It shows when the tuple t_q is ranked over 30 within the dataset, the result is empty. Therefore, we choose constant values of tuple (t_q) and ranked 20 within the dataset.

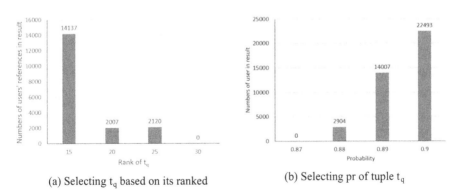

(a) Selecting t_q based on its ranked   (b) Selecting pr of tuple t_q

Fig. 3.   Selecting the probability tuple tq

b. The scalability of PBBR

Under the given circumstances, PBBR is superior to BBR in terms of scalability including the value of k, the number of users preference, and the number of probabilistic tuples. The difference in execution time typically ranges from a few seconds to a several hundred seconds. Furthermore, PBBR returns larger result sets of user preference than the usual BBR, and with the possibility of both methods returning the same user preferences.

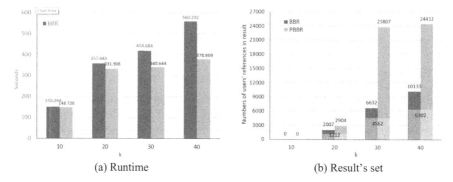

(a) Runtime   (b) Result's set

Fig. 4. The scalability of the value of k

In these experiments, one parameter from Table 7 is chosen in sequence for observation and the others are kept constant. We first analyze how the input value of k affects the runtime and results of the two methods. In Fig. 4a, the values of k increase the trend of runtimes keeping the same direction in both methods. The PBBR method is slightly faster than BBR.

In Fig. 4b, when we set k to 20, the number of users that PBBR return is 2904 while BBR is 2007, with both methods having 1212 users in common. The number of users obtained by PBBR method is greater than that by BBR method.

A variety quantities of user preferences can also impact the runtime and result sets. As shown in Fig. 5a, the runtime of BBR and PBBR is a few seconds difference if the number of user preferences is between 20k and 40k. However, if it reaches 60k or more, the difference exceeds 200 s. Figure 5b shows a steady growth of returned users. With the number of user preferences ranging from 20k to 80k, the number of returned users increases by about 1000 for BBR method and about 1400 for PBBR.

We also compare the performance of both methods concerning the number of probabilistic tuples. Figure 6a shows the number of tuples around 5k that only take 54.255 s by PBBR and 138.812 s by BBR to execute. In terms of users, 28582 users returned for PBBR and 27862 users for BBR. The execution time of BBR is over 1000 s if the number of probabilistic tuples is 15k or more in Fig. 6a. While, if the number of tuples reaches 20k, BBR returns an empty result set while PBBR returns only 75 users in Fig. 6b.

The runtime of processing PBBR is consistently faster than that of BBR. The reason is that we always choose the higher score in the better ranking. The upper bound of the expected score is lower than the upper bound of the origin score, so the execution of PBBR will be pruned earlier than the BBR. Therefore, PBBR runtime is faster than BBR.

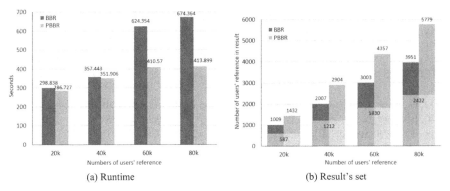

(a) Runtime   (b) Result's set

Fig. 5. The scalability of the number of users' preference

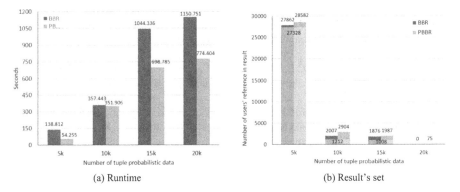

(a) Runtime   (b) Result's set

Fig. 6. The scalability of the number of probabilistic tuples

5 Conclusion

In this paper, we have addressed the problem of reverse top-k queries on probabilistic data. Initially, we identified the challenges associated with answering reverse top-k queries through practical examples. Subsequently, we introduced the concept of the expected value based on probabilistic theory, which fulfills users' requirements when dealing with probabilistic data. We computed the probabilities and scores of data as expected scores for each user. For the expected value theory, we proposed a novel method to answer reverse top-k queries on probabilistic data and extended the algorithm based on branch bound to process the expected scores of probabilistic data in handling reverse top-k queries. Furthermore, our experimental results demonstrate that our proposed method provides more meaningful results compared to traditional approaches.

Currently, the reverse top-k queries have been applied in many applications in decision support systems, recommendation systems, data analysis, business intelligence, data mining etc. In the future, the research of reverse top-k queries will be analyzed and extended to the processing of big data, distributed data, and uncertain data for recommendation systems. The new study will be focused on algorithm optimization and applications of the semantics answers for selecting queries on probabilistic data. This is a very interesting area for further investigation.

References

1. Li, G., Chen, Q., Zheng, B., Zhao, X.: Reverse top-k query on uncertain preference. In: Cai, Y., Ishikawa, Y., Xu, J. (eds.) Web and Big Data (APWeb-WAIM 2018). LNCS, vol. 10988, pp. 350–358. Springer, Cham (2018). https://doi.org/10.1007/978-3-319-96893-3_26
2. Vlachou, A., Doulkeridis, C., Nørvåg, K., Kotidis, Y.: Branch-and-bound algorithm for reverse top-k queries. In: Proceedings of the 2013 ACM SIGMOD international conference on management of data, pp. 481–492 (2013)
3. Vlachou, A., Doulkeridis, C., Kotidis, Y., Nørvåg, K.: Reverse top-k queries. In: 2010 IEEE 26th International Conference on Data Engineering (ICDE 2010), pp. 365–376. IEEE (2010)
4. Xiao, G., Li, K., Zhou, X., Li, K.: Efficient monochromatic and bichromatic probabilistic reverse top-k query processing for uncertain big data. J. Comput. Syst. Sci. **89**, 92–113 (2017)
5. Vlachou, A., Doulkeridis, C., Kotidis, Y., Norvag, K.: Monochromatic and bichromatic reverse top-k queries. IEEE Trans. Knowl. Data Eng. **23**(8), 1215–1229 (2011)
6. Jin, C., Zhang, R., Kang, Q., Zhang, Z., Zhou, A.: Probabilistic reverse top-k queries. In: Bhowmick, S.S., Dyreson, C.E., Jensen, C.S., Lee, M.L., Muliantara, A., Thalheim, B. (eds.) Database Systems for Advanced Applications, pp. 406–419. Springer International Publishing, Cham (2014)
7. Le, T.M.N., Cao, J., He, Z.: Top-k best probability queries and semantics ranking properties on probabilistic databases. Data Knowl. Eng. **88**, 248–266 (2013)
8. Suciu, D.: Probabilistic databases for all. In: Proceedings of the 39th ACM SIGMOD-SIGACT-SIGAI Symposium on Principles of Database Systems, pp. 19–31 (2020)
9. Zhang, W., Lin, X., Pei, J., Zhang, Y.: Managing uncertain data: probabilistic approaches. In: 2008 The Ninth International Conference on Web-Age Information Management, pp. 405–412. IEEE (2008)
10. Cheng, R., Kalashnikov, D.V., Prabhakar, S.: Evaluating probabilistic queries over imprecise data. In: Proceedings of the 2003 ACM SIGMOD International Conference on Management of Data, pp. 551–562 (2003)
11. Aggarwal, C.C., Philip, S.Y.: A survey of uncertain data algorithms and applications. IEEE Trans. Knowl. Data Eng. **21**(5), 609–623 (2008)
12. Hua, M., Pei, J., Zhang, W., Lin, X.: Ranking queries on uncertain data: a probabilistic threshold approach. In: Proceedings of the 2008 ACM SIGMOD International Conference on Management of Data, pp. 673–686 (2008)
13. Cormode, G., Li, F., Yi, K.: Semantics of ranking queries for probabilistic data and expected ranks. In: 2009 IEEE 25th International Conference on Data Engineering, pp. 305–316. IEEE (2009)
14. Atallah, M.J., Qi, Y.: Computing all skyline probabilities for uncertain data. In: Proceedings of the Twenty-Eighth ACM SIGMOD-SIGACT-SIGART Symposium on Principles of Database Systems, pp. 279–287 (2009)
15. Carmeli, N., Grohe, M., Lindner, P., Standke, C.: Tuple-independent representations of infinite probabilistic databases. In: Proceedings of the 40th ACM SIGMOD-SIGACT-SIGAI Symposium on Principles of Database Systems, pp. 388–401 (2021)
16. Zhang, X., Chomicki, J.: Semantics and evaluation of top-k queries in probabilistic databases. Distrib. Parallel Databases **26**(1), 67–126 (2009)
17. Liu, X., Yang, D., Ye, M., Lee, W.: U-skyline: a new skyline query for uncertain databases. IEEE Trans. Knowl. Data Eng. **25**(4), 945–960 (2013)

18. Pei, J., Jiang, B., Lin, X., Yuan, Y.: Probabilistic skylines on uncertain data. In: Proceedings of the 33rd International Conference on Very Large Data Bases, pp. 15–26 (2007)
19. Bartolini, I., Ciaccia, P., Patella, M.: Domination in the probabilistic world: computing skylines for arbitrary correlations and ranking semantics. ACM Trans. Database Syst. **39**(2), 1–45 (2014)
20. Le, T.M.N., Cao, J., He, Z.: Answering skyline queries on probabilistic data using the dominance of probabilistic skyline tuples. Inf. Sci. **340–341**, 58–85 (2016)
21. Lian, X., Chen, L.: Shooting top-k stars in uncertain databases. VLDB J. **20**(6), 819–840 (2011)

Optimizing Taxi Route Planning Based on Taxi Trajectory Data Analysis

Xinyi Yang[✉], Zhi Chen, and Yadan Luo

School of Electrical Engineering and Computer Science,
The University of Queensland, St Lucia 4067, Australia
`xinyi.yang4@uq.net.au`, {`zhi.chen`,`y.luo`}`@uq.edu.au`

Abstract. In daily life, taxis have become one of the most common and convenient ways of public transportation. With the advancement of positioning and mobility technologies, a large amount of taxi trajectory data has been collected, providing valuable data resources for urban planning, traffic management, and personalized route recommendations. However, these huge datasets also pose computational and processing challenges. This study uses the annual taxi trajectory data of Porto City obtained from the Kaggle platform, containing more than 1.7 million records, to study data query and analysis in a big data environment. We focus on comparing the efficiency and overhead of two spatial index structures, K-d tree and R-tree, in handling such large-scale datasets. Experimental results show that the K-d tree has a time-efficiency advantage in K-nearest neighbours query tasks, while the R-tree performs better in complex spatial query tasks. These findings provide important references for taxi route planning and other big data applications, especially in scenarios requiring efficient and accurate data retrieval.

Keywords: taxi trajectory data · K-nearest neighbours · Python · PostgreSQL · R-tree · K-d tree · route planning

1 Introduction

Daily commuting and travel necessitate the use of transportation, and taxis have emerged as one of the most common and convenient ways of public transport. Advances in positioning and mobile technologies have enabled the collection of large amounts of taxi trajectory data, which encapsulate the historical route selection experiences of taxi drivers. However, such large-scale data brings obvious computational challenges, which affect the efficiency of data processing and increase costs. Therefore, how to improve data processing efficiency and reduce overhead has become a critical issue in multiple application areas such as urban planning, traffic management, and personalized route recommendation.

In this paper, we extract an extensive dataset from Kaggle, an online platform for data mining and prediction competitions. The dataset obtains the trajectories for all 442 taxis operating in the city of Porto, Portugal, collected over an entire year (from July 1, 2013, to June 30, 2014). This huge dataset, comprising over 1.7 million entries, poses challenges to processing efficiency and overhead regardless of the algorithms or methods employed.

To efficiently handle such a large dataset and overcome the computational challenges they present, we have employed two index-based data structures known for their efficiency in handling large datasets: R-tree and K-d tree. Additionally, we have implemented iterative algorithms for processing the dataset. These algorithms serve to compare the performance of the R-tree and K-d tree in order to understand the impact of different data structures on efficiency and cost in specific application environments.

Through a series of detailed experiments, we delve deeply into the performance of K-d tree and R-tree spatial index structures in processing large-scale taxi trajectory datasets. Our findings indicate that the K-d tree offers superior time efficiency for tasks like K-nearest neighbours queries. On the other hand, R-tree shows better performance when dealing with more complex query tasks, such as finding data sets with the same starting and ending points. Although its time performance under this particular query is relatively slow, it is more flexible and efficient in handling queries with complex spatial queries.

These experimental results have important guiding significance for selecting appropriate data structures for efficient taxi route planning and other big data applications. Especially in application scenarios that require fast and accurate data retrieval and analysis, it is very useful to understand the respective advantages and limitations of the K-d tree and R-tree.

2   Related Work

R-tree is a tree data structure, which was first proposed by Antonin Guttman in 1984 [1]. The main purpose of R-tree is to store spatial data, such as geographic location information. Its main advantage is the ability to quickly perform spatial queries, such as finding all points within an area. Over time, many variants of R-tree have also been proposed, including R*-tree [2], R+-tree [3] and X-tree [4] etc.

As noted by Fèvre, Zgaya-Biau, Mathieu et al. in their 2023 study, R-tree shows remarkable effectiveness in the taxi-sharing problem. Compared with traditional, more empirical spatial indexing methods, R-tree provides a more dynamic and flexible way to organize and explore spaces, especially when dealing with complex multi-hop row-sharing problems [5].

K-d tree is a binary tree data structure that was first proposed by Jon Louis Bentley in 1975 [6]. The main purpose of the K-d tree is to store multidimensional data. Its main advantage is the ability to quickly perform nearest neighbours queries, such as finding the k closest points to a given point. Over time, many variants of k-d trees have also been proposed, including bd-tree [7], vp-tree [8], and M-tree [9] etc.

Among them, Pedro H.E. Becker et al. mentioned in their paper published in 2023 about optimizing the K-d tree (K-d Bonsai) to implement compress-point clouds to reduce data movement during radius search execution, thereby improving its performance and energy efficiency. In this paper, the K-d tree mainly implements "radius search", that is, finding all points within a certain distance r from a certain query point q. This operation is very important in aspects such as vehicle positioning optimization. This point of view is also similar to K-nearest neighbours because both involve finding other points closest to a given point in multi-dimensional space [10].

3   Task Definition

3.1   Preliminary Concepts and Comparisons of R Trees and K-d Tree

The R-tree is a dynamic index structure designed to facilitate spatial searches and queries. Figure 1 shows a simple diagram of how it works. It hierarchically organises data, which enables quick retrieval of spatial objects intersecting with a specified query range. The core idea of the R-tree lies in its ability to divide spatial objects into different rectangular regions, typically characterised as the Minimum Bounding Rectangle (MBR). These rectangular areas are then systematically organised into a multi-layered tree structure [11].

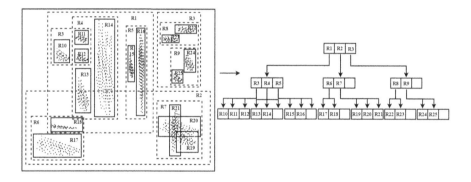

Fig. 1. A simple example diagram explains how R-tree works in 2-dimensional space

The K-d tree is a data structure designed for managing multidimensional data, an essential tool for executing spatial searches and range queries. It recursively divides the data space into a binary tree structure through partitioning. Figure 2 shows a simple diagram of how it works. The core idea behind the K-d tree is the division of the data space into binary space partitions. This division is accomplished by selecting one dimension from the data points to serve as the partitioning axis at each level of the tree [12].

R-tree and K-d tree are both used for spatial data but differ in key ways. First, the R-tree is better for high-dimensional data and complex shapes(such as rectangles and polygons), while the K-d tree performs better on low-dimensional data and is typically only used for memory points. Second, the R-tree is more

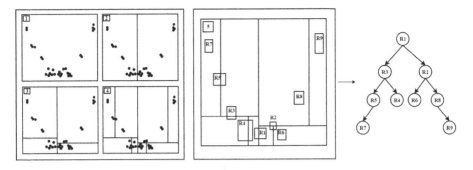

Fig. 2. A simple example diagram explains how K-d-tree works in 2-dimensional space

suitable for data sets that require frequent updates due to its dynamic nature, while the K-d tree is more suitable for static data sets. In addition, R-trees generally require more storage space and computation time to maintain their minimum boundary rectangle (MBRs), while k-d trees are generally more efficient in terms of space utilization and computation speed. These differences are crucial for choosing the right data structure for specific tasks and queries in this paper.

3.2   Indexing and Query

In order to analyse the driver's trip selection and derive insights from the results, it is necessary to design relevant queries. In Fig. 3, the overall query process for data is shown, and the data query at each stage corresponds to its response. Its ultimate purpose is to provide sufficient and correct data for path comparison for subsequent experiments.

Spatial Boundaries. Before executing these queries, two types of spatial boundaries are set:

1. **Bounding Box:** A rectangle that encloses all points in the line string, with sides parallel to the coordinate axes. Its coordinates (x_i, y_i) and (x_a, y_a) represent the lower-left and upper-right corners respectively. The bounding box is mainly used for spatial queries and visualization.
2. **Minimum Bounding Rectangle:** Unlike the bounding box, the sides of this rectangle are not necessarily parallel to the coordinate axes. This rectangle is computed using the `minimum_rotated_rectangle` method from the Shapely library, based on the Rotating Calipers Algorithm [13].

Query Algorithms. We evaluate the time and memory costs of three different query methods:

1. **Iterative Algorithm:** This basic approach involves traversing all geometric objects to find the ones that meet given conditions.
2. **K-d Tree Algorithm:** Effective in speeding up the query process, especially for tasks like finding K-nearest neighbours.
3. **R-tree Algorithm:** Useful for more complex queries, like identifying trips with identical start and endpoints.

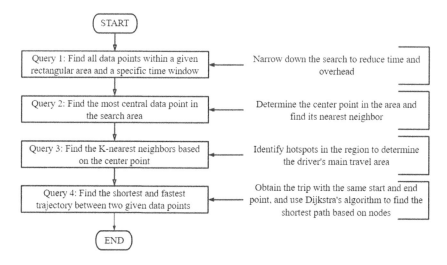

Fig. 3. There are four data queries, which are conducted in the corresponding order. Each query has a corresponding purpose.

3.3   Query Process

The query process comprises the following steps:

1. Query 1: Perform an initial spatial query to filter data points within a pre-defined area and time window.
2. Query 2: Calculate the central of the filtered data points.
3. Query 3: Find the K-nearest neighbours to the central.
4. Query 4: Identify trips in the dataset that have identical start and endpoints.

The above content is the basic framework of our analysis. In the next section, we delve into these aspects in more detail, providing a comprehensive explanation of the algorithm used, and its implementation details.

4   Methodology

In this section, the focus is on dissecting techniques for spatial data analysis through three distinctive approaches: Iterative Methods (I), R-tree Spatial Indexing (R), and k-d tree Spatial Indexing (KD). These approaches are evaluated using four spatial queries to provide insight into their data processing capabilities.

The notations used in this section include A for the search area, T for the time window, D for the dataset, F_d for the filtered dataset where is in A and T, C is the central point of A, K_n for the K-nearest neighbours where n is the number of K-nearest neighbours, and G_d for the count of each start-end coordinate pair of trips. The trip($trip$)'s start and end coordinates are represented by $trip_s$ and $trip_e$, respectively.

4.1   Four Types of Spatial Queries

In Query 1 (Fig. 3), after constraining the A and the T, the task is to identify all data points that meet these criteria. This forms the foundational step of spatial data analysis and employs spatial indexing using R-tree or K-d tree to accelerate the query. The mathematical representation for this part is (p_i is data point, t_i is the "TIMESTAMP" of p_i):

$$\text{Output} = \{p_i \mid p_i \in A \text{ and } t_1 \leq t_i \leq t_2\}$$

In Query 2 (Fig. 3), upon acquiring F_d after Query 1, the next step is to identify C of this area. To achieve this, the Euclidean distance algorithm($\text{dist}(C, p_i)$) is applied to compute the distance from each point to C and subsequently identify the closest one. The mathematical representation for distance is:

$$C = \arg \min_{p_i \in A} \text{dist}(C, p_i)$$

After identifying the central point C in Query 2, Query 3 (Fig. 3) aims to find K_n to C. The Euclidean distance algorithm is employed to measure the distance between C and the centroids of each geometric object in F_d. These distances are then stored and sorted in a Priority Queue (PQ). and the top n elements are extracted to form K_n [14].

The sorting algorithm uses a lambda function to prioritize the second element of each tuple $(index_{ji}, distance_{ji})$. The list is then sorted in ascending order based on this distance, and finally, the sorting operation rearranges the list into $distance_{ji} \leq distance_{ji+1}$.

In Query 4 (Fig. 3), the objective is to find all trips where $trip_s$ and $trip_e$ are the same and to group them together. This is implemented by grouping each trip with the same $trip_s$ and $trip_e$ in G_d.

For all four queries, we also calculate time cost and memory consumption to compare the efficiency of different spatial indexing methods which will be further analyzed in the subsequent experimental section.

Algorithm 1: The pseudocode for R-tree, k-d tree, and Iterative Algorithms in four queries

---

Input: S, T, D, R, KD
Output: F_d, C, K_n, G_d

1 **Query 1:**
2 **foreach** *geom in D* **do**
3   **Insert** *geom* **into** R **or** KD
4   **if** *geom within S and T* **then**
5   Append *geom* to F_d

6 **return** F_d

7 **Query 2:**
8 **foreach** *p in F_d* **do**
9   **Insert** *p* **into** R **or** KD
10   Calculate $d \leftarrow \text{dist}(C, p)$ `// where d is distance to center of S`
11   **if** $d < MinD$ **then**
12   Update C and $MinD$

13 **return** C

14 **Query 3:**
15 Initialize Priority Queue PQ
16 **foreach** *p in D* **do**
17   **Insert** *p* **into** R **or** KD
18   Calculate $d \leftarrow \text{dist}(C, p)$
19   Update PQ with d

20 **return** K_n from PQ

21 **Query 4:**
22 **foreach** *trip in D* **do**
23   **Insert trip_start, trip_end into** R **or** KD
24   **if** *(trip_start, trip_end) is not in G_d* **then**
       `// Check if this combination of start and end points already`
       `   exists in `G_d
25       $G_d[\text{trip\_start}, \text{trip\_end}]$
       `// Add t to the appropriate group in `G_d
26   Append t to $G_d[\text{trip\_start}, \text{trip\_end}]$

27 **return** G_d

---

5 Experiments

5.1 Data Explanation

Taxi Trajectory Data is from ECML/PKDD 15: Taxi Trip Time Prediction (III) Competition. It has provided an accurate dataset describing a complete year (from 01/07/2013 to 30/06/2014) of the trajectories for all the 442 taxis running in the city of Porto, Portugal. These taxis operate through a taxi dispatch centre, using mobile data terminals installed in the vehicles. It contains a total of 9 columns, and the main focus of the data during the experiment mainly includes the following contents:

- TRIP_ID & TAXI_ID: Each ID corresponds to a trip. And a unique identifier for the taxi driver that performed each trip.
- TIMESTAMP: Unix Timestamp (seconds). It identifies the trip's start time.
- POYLINE: The data includes GPS coordinates (WGS84 format) recorded every 15 min to track a taxi's route. The driving time can be estimated as $(n-1) \times 15$ minutes, where n is the total number of data points.

5.2   Data Cleaning and Analysis

When obtaining the data, we need to analyse the data and process the data. Table 1 shows that most of the customers choose to take a taxi at a designated (The top of CALL_TYPE is B). And all recorded taxi travel times are on week-days/Saturdays and not holidays/special days (The top of DAY_TYPE is A). Also, there are 5901 taxi trip records where "POLYLINE" is null, and these belong to missing data that need to be deleted.

Table 1. Classification of characteristic data condition.

	CALL_TYPE	DAY_TYPE	POLYLINE
unique	3	1	1703650
top	B	A	–
freq	817881	1710670	5901

After deleting missing data and processing duplicate "TRIP_ID", the timestamps are processed into a human-readable form for visualisation. And according to the "year", "month" and "day" to observe the changes in the itinerary, there is no special result. Therefore, time stamps will not be analysed too much in subsequent studies.

The attributes "TAXI_ID", "TIMESTAMP", "POLYLINE", "POLY_IEN" and "TRIP_TIME" are reserved for later data analysis and query. Among them, "POLYLINE_LEN" is the path length obtained by calculating the number of coordinate points in the "POLYLINE" column, and "TRIP_TIME" is to calculate the travel time of each path according to the polyline length attribute, and the calculation formula is $("POLYLINE\_LENGTH" - 1) \times 15$.

5.3   Data Query

All the experimental results were obtained by implementing the iterative algorithm, R-tree algorithm and K-d tree algorithm. Table 2 presents the recorded results of the first four queries, illustrating the time cost and memory consumption of the implemented algorithms for each query. If query speed is the main concern, then the K-d tree algorithm may be the best choice. On the other hand, if memory consumption is more critical, then the R-tree algorithm might be a better fit [1]. Although the Iterative algorithm performs poorly in some queries, it may still have certain advantages in handling simpler queries and smaller data sizes.

Table 2. This is about the time cost and memory cost of the four queries mentioned in Fig. 3. Each of these queries uses a different algorithm. (The results are taken from two decimal places).

Algorithms	Cost	Query 4	Query 1	Query 2	Query 3
Iterative	Time (s)	115.8831	0.4388	0.3959	0.1924
	Memory (MB)	5275.7851	2022.2695	2134.7382	2135.7187
K-d tree	Time (s)	283.4735	0.4807	0.4609	0.0009
	Memory (MB)	3117.3984	1996.7968	2098.4921	2098.5000
R-tree	Time (s)	393.6257	0.0698	0.4797	0.8447
	Memory (MB)	2928.3515	2084.5390	2235.9257	2241.6445

Query 4 (Fig. 3) is about finding all datasets that start and end at the same point. In terms of time cost, the Iterative algorithm performed the best. This is because the Iterative algorithm takes advantage of the Shapely library and avoids the use of complex index structures through data preprocessing and optimized query operations, resulting in lower time costs during the query process. In contrast, the K-d tree and the R-tree are spatial index structures [6]. Although they can speed up queries, their performance is relatively slow in this specific query. In terms of memory cost, the Iterative algorithm uses the most memory. In this query, the Iterative algorithm needs to save temporary results and information of a large number of data points, resulting in high memory usage.

Query 3 (Fig. 3) is about finding the k-nearest neighbours based on the centre point. In terms of time cost, the K-d tree performs the best among the three. This is due to the fact that the K-d tree is an efficient data structure that allows for quick localization of nearest neighbours, whereas the Iterative and R-tree algorithms involve more traversals and calculations, leading to comparatively higher time costs.

In order to find out whether the results obtained by the query algorithm used were correct, We used Python to connect with PostgreSQL and performed a comparison of the time cost between the database queries and the implemented algorithms.

The above queries are implemented using Python and PostgreSQL respectively. Table 3 shows that PostgreSQL can be used to know the travel of the current query areas more intuitively and clearly. In Python, for the convenience of the query, the travel is saved in the form of nodes. Different query algorithms are used for searching.

Table 3. PostgreSQL (SLQ) vs Python (Iterative) (Time cost)

Algorithms	Cost	Query 4	Query 1	Query 2	Query 3
Python	Time (s)	115.8831	0.4388	0.3959	0.1924
PostgreSQL	Time (s)	46.5773	49.9321	0.8549	0.8088

Figure 4 shows the results of extracting geometric objects within the specified search area and meeting the time range conditions by filtering the given data set in terms of space and time. Use the Shapely library to manipulate geometric objects, compute bounding boxes and minimum bounding rectangles, and do spatial relationships and temporal filtering. Finally, it outputs the number of eligible geometries and records code execution time and memory usage.

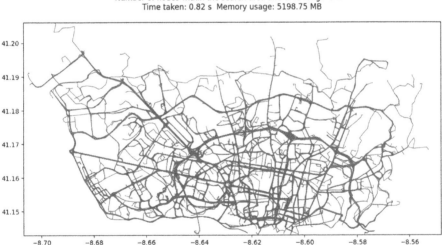

Fig. 4. The above image is visualized using Python based on the results of Query 1 in Fig. 3. It can be seen how densely distributed the route planning is.

What is implemented in Fig. 5 is to use PostgreSQL to find all data points within a given rectangular area and within a certain time window. Using WGS84, the time between 2014-6-24 14:00:00–15:00:00 is used as the time window. Since pgAdmin4 has added support for the geometry type, it has excellent GIS data

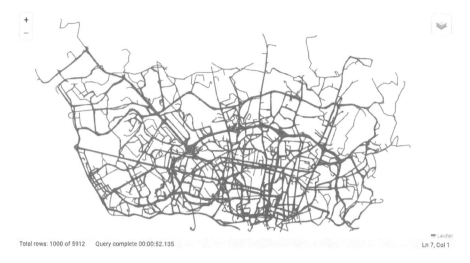

Total rows: 1000 of 5912   Query complete 00:00:52.135

Ln 7, Col 1

Fig. 5. Using PostgreSQL database system, the same effect as in Fig. 4 (get the result of Query 1 (Fig. 3)) is achieved and visualised through a basic SQL statement query.

visualization effects. Therefore, during the implementation of the query, the visualization results of pgAdmin4 will be compared with the Python visualization results to ensure the rationality of the Python visualization effects.

In the collected data, the information about the distance is displayed in the form of coordinate points, so when querying data in PostgreSQL, the coordinates of the limited rectangular area need to be processed. Use the spatial functions provided by PostGIS as filter conditions. It filters the data to include only records where the "geom" column falls within a specified envelope (bounding box) with the given coordinates and spatial reference system (SRID 4326).

6   Conclusions

This paper conducts a comprehensive experimental analysis of taxi route planning using robust data sets, focusing on basic attributes such as "TRIP ID & taxi ID", "TIMESTAMP" and "POLYLINE". It evaluates the performance of iterative, R-tree, and K-d tree algorithms, revealing that K-d trees excel in query speed, especially in finding K nearest neighbours, while r trees are more efficient in memory consumption. These insights are further enriched by comparisons with PostgreSQL, providing a nuanced understanding of algorithmic applicability to different optimization criteria in spatial data [15]

References

1. Guttman, A.: R-trees: a dynamic index structure for spatial searching. In: Proceedings of the 1984 ACM SIGMOD International Conference on Management of Data, pp. 47–57 (1984)
2. Beckmann, N., Kriegel, H.-P., Schneider, R., Seeger, B.: The R*-tree: an efficient and robust access method for points and rectangles. In: Proceedings of the 1990 ACM SIGMOD International Conference on Management of Data, pp. 322–331 (1990)
3. Sellis, T., Roussopoulos, N., Faloutsos, C.: The R+-tree: a dynamic index for multi-dimensional objects (1987)
4. Berchtold, S., Keim, D.A., Kriegel, H.-P.: The X-tree: an index structure for high-dimensional data. In: Very Large Data-Bases, pp. 28–39 (1996)
5. Fèvre, C., Zgaya-Biau, H., Mathieu, P., Hammadi, S.: Preferential optimization of multi-hop dynamic ridesharing based on R-trees and multi-agent systems. Transp. Res. Rec. 03611981231187530 (2023)
6. Bentley, J.L.: K-D trees for semidynamic point sets. In: Proceedings of the Sixth Annual Symposium on Computational Geometry, pp. 187–197 (1990)
7. James, D.L., Pai, D.K.: BD-tree: output-sensitive collision detection for reduced deformable models. In: ACM SIGGRAPH 2004 Papers, pp. 393–398 (2004)
8. Yianilos, P.N.: Data structures and algorithms for nearest neighbor search in general metric spaces. Soda **93**(194), 311–21 (1993)
9. Ciaccia, P., Patella, M., Zezula, P., et al.: M-tree: an efficient access method for similarity search in metric spaces. In: VLDB, vol. 97, pp. 426–435. Citeseer (1997)
10. Becker, P.H.E., Arnau, J.-M., González, A.: KD bonsai: ISA-extensions to compress KD trees for autonomous driving tasks. In: Proceedings of the 50th Annual International Symposium on Computer Architecture, pp. 1–13 (2023)
11. Hadjieleftheriou, M., Manolopoulos, Y., Theodoridis, Y., Tsotras, V.J.: R-trees: a dynamic index structure for spatial searching. Encycl. GIS 1805–1817 (2017)
12. Gill, S., Hooda, M.: The design perspective of the structures based on k-d tree. In: Rathore, V.S., Dey, N., Piuri, V., Babo, R., Polkowski, Z., Tavares, J.M.R.S. (eds.) Rising Threats in Expert Applications and Solutions. AISC, vol. 1187, pp. 515–524. Springer, Singapore (2021). https://doi.org/10.1007/978-981-15-6014-9_61
13. Toussaint, G.T.: Solving geometric problems with the rotating calipers. In: Proceedings of the IEEE Melecon, vol. 83, no. 83, p. A10 (1983)
14. Roussopoulos, N., Kelley, S., Vincent, F.: Nearest neighbor queries. In: Proceedings of the 1995 ACM SIGMOD International Conference on Management of Data, pp. 71–79 (1995)
15. Zhou, Z.-H.: Ensemble Methods: Foundations and Algorithms. CRC Press, Boca Raton (2012)

Natural Language Processing and Text Analysis

Learning Implicit Sentiment for Explainable Review-Based Recommendation

Ningning Sun[1], Yue Kou[1(✉)], Xiangmin Zhou[2], Derong Shen[1], Dong Li[3], and Tiezheng Nie[1]

[1] Northeastern University, Shenyang 110004, Liaoning, China
`2101789@stu.neu.edu.cn`, `{kouyue,shenderong,nietiezheng}@cse.neu.edu.cn`
[2] RMIT University, Melbourne, VIC 3000, Australia
`xiangmin.zhou@rmit.edu.au`
[3] Liaoning University, Shenyang 110036, Liaoning, China
`dongli@lnu.edu.cn`

Abstract. Users can publish reviews to express their detailed feelings about the items. Positive and negative sentiments about various aspects of an item co-existing in the same review may cause confusion in recommendations and generate inappropriate explanations. However, most current explainable recommendation methods fail to capture users' implicit sentiment behind the reviews. In this paper, we propose a novel Implicit Sentiment learning model for Explainable review-based Recommendation, named ISER, which learns users' implicit sentiments from reviews and explores them to generate recommendations with more fine-grained explanations. Specifically, we first propose a novel representation learning to model users/items based on the implicit sentiment behind the reviews. Then we propose two implicit sentiment fusion strategies for rating prediction and explanation generation respectively. Finally, we propose a multi-task learning framework to jointly optimize the rating prediction task and the explanation generation task, which improves the recommendation quality in a mutual promotion manner. The experiments demonstrate the effectiveness and efficiency of our proposed model compared to the baseline models.

Keywords: Explainable recommendation · Implicit sentiment learning · Fusion strategy · Multi-task learning

1 Introduction

Nowadays, most e-commerce and online review sites like Amazon and Yelp allow users to write reviews about movies, electronics, books, restaurants, etc.

This work was supported by the National Natural Science Foundation of China under Grant Nos. 62072084, 62172082 and 62072086, the Science and Technology Program Major Project of Liaoning Province of China under Grant No. 2022JH1/10400009, the Natural Science Foundation of Liaoning Province of China under Grant No.2022-MS-171, the Science Research Fund of Liaoning Province of China under Grant No. LJKZ0094.

The reviews are used to express users' opinions and detailed feelings about items, which contain rich information about both user preferences (e.g. user concerns) and different aspects of items (e.g. appearance, quality, size, price, and color). They are of great reference value for those who are going to make a purchase decision. Researchers have shown that such information is quite beneficial in generating more accurate recommendations and more reliable explanations [4,21]. The wide applications have demanded explainable review-based recommendation.

In fact, positive and negative sentiments about various aspects of an item usually co-exist in the same review. Figure 1 shows two reviews written by the same user after purchasing two different phones. Both of them contain the user's rich feelings and experiences. From the first review, we know that the user may be interested in aspects such as 'size', 'screen', 'battery', and 'price'. Also, the user prefers to buy cheaper phones. The second review shows that despite the negative sentiment expressed by the user about the 'price', the user is still satisfied with the phone due to the strong appeal of its other aspects. In reality, if some aspect of an item exceeds the user's expectations, the user might be willing to overlook other weak aspects of the item and buy it. A user's implicit sentiment, influenced by both positive and negative sentiments, will determine his/her final decision. Thus, capturing users' implicit sentiment from reviews is vital for generating recommendations and explanations.

Fig. 1. An example of two reviews written by the same user.

We study the problem of explainable review-based recommendation. Given a user u, an item i, and their respective historical reviews, we aim to predict the relevance ratings between u and i, and generate the corresponding explanation. For explainable review-based recommendation, three key issues need to be addressed. First, we need to design a representation learning that deeply captures users' implicit sentiment. Different users focus on different aspects when facing different items. And the aspects in the textual review are not equally important to act on users' implicit sentiment. For example, users may pay more attention to special effects when choosing sci-fi movies, and to plot when choosing comedy movies. A good model should be able to capture the users' implicit sentiment for high-quality recommendation. Then, we need to design a novel model for generating the recommendation with explanations that well reflects the users' implicit sentiment. The implicit sentiment can be captured from both the users' historical reviews and the items' historical reviews, and these two parts of implicit sentiment need to be fused to guide rating prediction and explanation generation simultaneously. A better model should be able to adopt an appropriate sentiment fusion strategy according to the characteristics of each task. Finally, we need to build a multi-task learning framework to jointly optimize the rating prediction task and the explanation generation task. A good model should be able to improve the recommendation quality in a mutual promotion manner.

A number of explainable review-based recommendation models have emerged. Some approaches leverage aspect extraction tools to extract aspect words from reviews, and use aspect words and ratings as labels to train the model [7,18,22]. But extracting aspects relying on external tools may lead to heavy costs for computation. Some approaches leverage deep learning techniques to learn the aspects of users and items [10,20]. However, they only extract aspect words from reviews which fail to capture users' implicit sentiment behind the review. In this paper, we propose a novel Implicit Sentiment learning model for Explainable review-based Recommendation, named ISER, which learns users' implicit sentiments from reviews and explores them to generate recommendations with more fine-grained explanations. We summarise our contributions as follows.

- We propose a novel representation learning to model users/items based on the implicit sentiment behind the reviews. With this model, users'/items' implicit aspects can be captured and integrated to represent users/items.
- We propose two implicit sentiment fusion strategies for rating prediction and explanation generation respectively. For rating prediction, we employ an MLP-based sentiment fusion strategy to match the sentiment implied in user reviews and item reviews respectively. For explanation generation, we adopt a GRU-based sentiment fusion strategy which utilizes a decoder with an attention fusion layer to generate fine-grained explanations.
- We propose a multi-task learning framework to jointly optimize the rating prediction task and the explanation generation task, which improves the recommendation quality in a mutual promotion manner.
- We conduct comprehensive experiments on three publicly accessible datasets to compare and evaluate the effectiveness of our proposed ISER model.

2   Related Work

In this section, we will review related research on review-based rating prediction and aspect-based explainable recommendation.

2.1   Review-Based Rating Prediction

User reviews express the item-related feelings, with varying informativeness. These reviews enable personalized recommendations by capturing the intricate user-item interaction for generating the text description for the recommended items [17]. Reviews have been used to extract the contextual factors of items or users for recommendation [11–13]. Some approaches use topic modeling to learn latent topic factors from reviews [1,3]. For example, A3NCF [3] employs Latent Dirichlet Allocation (LDA) to extract topic distributions for both users and items. Later, inspired by significant advances in deep NLP, such as Att2Seq [5], some approaches use neural networks as automatic feature extractors to parse relevant sets of historical reviews [6]. Additionally, attention-based approaches have been developed [14,19]. For example, NRCMA [14] encodes user and item through mutual attention modules, which facilitates the information exchange between reviews and ratings.

2.2 Aspect-Based Explainable Recommendation

As users express diverse feelings in reviews across various aspects, capturing aspect information is crucial for improving the explainability of recommendation [3]. U-ARM [16] utilizes the unsupervised neural network model ABAE to learn aspect-aware representations for each sentence in the reviews. PETER [8] uses the Transformer for rating prediction and explanation generation. Its inputs include users, items and the extracted item attributes. A2CF [2] infers each user's current demand on specific item attributes, and then recommends items that have advantages in these attributes to the user. SEER [7] synthesizes the explanations by selecting snippets from reviews while optimizing for the representativeness and coherence. It expands candidate selection to all aspect-relevant sentences by incorporating opinion contextualization for sentiment compatibility.

However, most existing approaches only extract aspect words from reviews, which fail to capture users' implicit sentiment behind reviews. Obviously, such recommendation results and explanations are less convincing. Our model learns users' implicit sentiments from reviews and leverages them to generate recommendations with more fine-grained explanations.

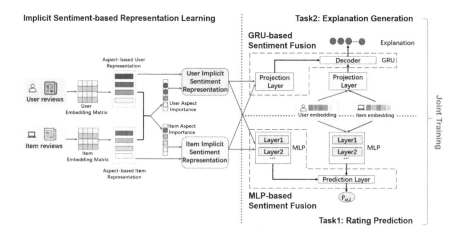

Fig. 2. Overall framework of ISER.

3   ISER: The Proposed Model

In this work, we propose a novel Implicit Sentiment learning model for Explainable review-based Recommendation, named ISER, which learns users' implicit sentiments from reviews and explores them to generate recommendations with more fine-grained explanations. The overall framework of the ISER is shown in Fig. 2. We will detail its components in this section.

3.1   Preliminaries

Suppose we have a set of items $\mathcal{I}$, a set of users $\mathcal{U}$, and corpus of ratings $\mathcal{R}$ and reviews $\mathcal{D}$. We represent each user-item interaction as a tuple $(u, i, r_{u,i}, d_{u,i})$ where $r_{u,i}$ and $d_{u,i}$ respectively denote the rating and review text of user u for item i. We use P_u and Q_i to represent the aspect-based representations of user u and item i respectively. Also, β_u and β_i respectively represent the aspect importance for user u and item i. The model's target is to provide users recommendations and personalized explanations based on implicit sentiments learned from reviews.

3.2   Implicit Sentiment-Based Representation Learning

The previous methods mostly ignore the fact that different users focus on different aspects when facing different items. Additionally, the aspects in the review are not equally important in influencing users' implicit sentiment. Therefore, merely extracting aspects directly from reviews is insufficient. In this subsection, we will capture the implicit user-item interaction from user/item reviews to learn implicit sentiment representation. Since the principle is the same for both users and items, we will describe this process based on a specific user u in the following discussion.

Let $\boldsymbol{D}_u$ indicate the processed user document. We transform $\boldsymbol{D}_u$ into the user embedding matrix by an embedding function:

$$f : D_u \rightarrow M_u \in R^{n \times d} \tag{1}$$

where n is the number of words in $\boldsymbol{D}_u$, and d is the number of dimensions for each word embedding vector. This embedding can be any pre-trained embeddings such as *Glove* or *word2vec*.

For all aspects defined, our goal is to derive a set of aspect-based user representations $P_u = \{p_{u,a} \mid a \in \mathcal{A}\}$. Thus, for an aspect a, an aspect-specific mapping matrix $W_a \in R^{d \times h_1}$ is first used to assist in constructing the aspect-specific word representation. More formally,

$$M_{u,a}[i] = M_u[i]W_a \tag{2}$$

where $M_u[i]$ is the initial d-dimensional word embedding for the i-th word in the user embedding matrix M_u. Finally, a tensor in $R^{K \times n \times h_1}$ dimensions can be obtained. K is the number of aspects defined, and each aspect a is represented as an embedding vector $v_a \in R^l$, where l is the length of the embedding vector.

The importance of the i-th word in the document depends on both the word itself and its surrounding words. So we construct the local context window $Z_{u,a,i} = M_{u,a}[i - l/(2h1)]; \ldots; M_{u,a}[i]; \ldots; M_{u,a}[i + l/(2h1)]$. Then, we calculate the attention vector of document word i on user u for aspect a as follows:

$$\text{Score}_{u,a}[i] = \text{softmax}\left(v_a\left(Z_{u,a,i}\right)^T\right) \tag{3}$$

Then, we construct aspect-aware user representation, which is derived from the following weighted sum:

$$p_{u,a} = \sum_{i=1}^{n}\left(\text{Score}_{u,a}[i]M_{u,a}[i]\right) \tag{4}$$

where $p_{u,a}$ is the aspect-based user representation for user u and aspect a. Similarly, the aspect-based item representation $q_{i,a}$ for item i and aspect a can be obtained, following Eqs. 1 to 4. By combining all aspects, we can derive the aspect-based representation $P_u \in R^{K \times h_1}$ for user u and the aspect-based representation $Q_i \in R^{K \times h_1}$ for item i.

In order to obtain the importance of each aspect for user/item representations, the aspect importance is learned:

$$Aff = \text{ReLU}\left(P_u W_s Q_i^T\right) \tag{5}$$

$$H_u = \text{ReLU}\left(P_u W_x + Aff^T\left(Q_i W_y\right)\right), \beta_u = \text{softmax}\left(H_u v_x\right) \tag{6}$$

$$H_i = \text{ReLU}\left(Q_i W_y + Aff\left(P_u W_x\right)\right), \beta_i = \text{softmax}\left(H_i v_y\right) \tag{7}$$

where $Aff \in R^{K \times K}$ is an aspect-level affinity matrix and $W_s \in R^{h_1 \times h_1}$ is a learnable weight matrix. W_x, $W_y \in R^{h_1 \times h_2}$ and v_x, $v_y \in R^{h_2}$ are the learnable parameters. β_u, $\beta_i \in R^K$ are the estimated aspect importance over the set of K aspects for user u and item i respectively.

Finally, we construct the implicit sentiment representation based on the aspect-based representation and the aspect importance:

$$IP_u = \beta_u^T P_u \tag{8}$$

$$IQ_i = \beta_i^T Q_i \tag{9}$$

where IP_u and $IQ_i \in R^{h_1}$ are the final implicit sentiment representations for user u and item i respectively, which will be used for implicit sentiment fusion.

3.3   Implicit Sentiment Fusion

Rating prediction and explanation generation have different purposes, so using the same fusion strategy for them is not ideal. In this section, we propose two specific implicit sentiment fusion strategies. For rating prediction, we employ an

MLP-based sentiment fusion strategy to align user and item review sentiments. For explanation generation, we use a GRU-based sentiment fusion strategy with an attention-based decoder to generate fine-grained explanations.

MLP-Based Sentiment Fusion for Rating Prediction. We adopt an MLP-based sentiment fusion strategy to fuse the implicit sentiment representations and predict the user u's rating $\hat{r}_{u,i}$ on the item i. We leverage MLP to fuse the implicit sentiment representations of users and items for rating prediction.

More specifically, we employ an MLP with L hidden layers to match the sentiment implied in user reviews and item reviews respectively. This fusion process can be formulated as follows:

$$h_{u,i}^{asp} = MLP_1\left([IP_u, IQ_i]\right) \tag{10}$$

where $[IP_u, IQ_i]$ is the concatenated user and item implicit sentiment vector.

As for users and items' latent embedding, they are concatenated and fed into another MLP. The process is shown as follows:

$$h_{u,i} = MLP_2([u, v]) \tag{11}$$

where $[u, v]$ represents the concatenated vector of user and item embedding vector. Here, MLP_2 represents the L-layer multi-layer perceptron and has a similar structure to MLP_1. For l-th layer of MLP_2, it can be formulated as follows:

$$h_l = \sigma\left(W_l h_{l-1} + b_l\right), \quad h_0 = [u, i] \tag{12}$$

where W_l and b_l are trainable parameters. $\sigma(\cdot)$ is the sigmoid activation function. h_{l-1} is the hidden state of the $(l\text{-}1)$-th layer and h_0 is the initial hidden state.

Finally, we integrate the encoded vectors for rating prediction. Here, we leverage the linear transformer to predict the final rating of user u to item i, which can be formulated as follows:

$$\hat{r}_{u,i} = W_r\left(h_{u,i} + h_{u,i}^{asp}\right) + b_u + b_i + b \tag{13}$$

where W_r is the transfer matrix in the rating prediction. b_u, b_i and b are the biases of user, item, and global average rating, respectively.

GRU-Based Sentiment Fusion for Explanation Generation. In Sect. 3.2, We have learned the user/item implicit sentiment representation. Here we adopt a GRU-based sentiment fusion strategy which utilizes a decoder with an attention fusion layer to generate fine-grained explanations.

The user/item embedding and user/item implicit sentiment representation are concatenated and fed into a projection layer with a *tanh* activation function separately. The outputs are calculated as follows:

$$u_U = \tanh\left(W_u[u, i] + b_U\right), v_V = \tanh\left(W_v\left[IP_u, IQ_i\right] + b_V\right) \tag{14}$$

where $W_u \in R^{d_h \times 2m}$, $W_v \in R^{d_h \times 2K}$, $b_U \in R^{d_h}$ and $b_V \in R^{d_h}$ are learnable parameters. m is the dimension of user/item embedding. d_h is the dimension of the hidden state of the GRU structure in decoder. *tanh* is the activation function.

We use a decoder with an attention fusion layer to generate sequences, incorporating aspect information. Given the start token, this two-layer GRU decoder is used to predict the target word. The encoded vector u_U and v_V are used to formulate the initial hidden state $h_0^g = u_U + v_V$. The hidden states of other time steps can be calculated by recurrently feeding the word representation w_t of the t-th input:

$$h_t^g = GRU\left(w_t, h_{t-1}^g\right) \tag{15}$$

where h_{t-1}^g is the $(t-1)$-th hidden state of the GRU. To fully exploit the projection layer information, we apply an attention mechanism to summarize the contribution of user/item latent information for word prediction and jointly determine the final word distribution. It can be expressed as follows:

$$
\begin{aligned}
\alpha_t^u &= \exp\left(\tanh\left(W_\alpha\left[u, h_t^g\right] + b_\alpha\right)\right)/Z \\
\alpha_t^i &= \exp\left(\tanh\left(W_\alpha\left[i, h_t^g\right] + b_\alpha\right)\right)/Z \\
a_t^g &= \alpha_t^u u + \alpha_t^i i
\end{aligned}
\tag{16}
$$

where $W_\alpha \in R^{1 \times (d_h + m)}$ and $b_\alpha \in R$ are learnable parameters. Z is the normalization term. Next, we also apply an attention mechanism to summarize the contribution of user and item implicit sentiment information for word prediction. The process is similar to the above and can be expressed as follows:

$$
\begin{aligned}
\gamma_t^u &= \exp\left(\tanh\left(W_\gamma\left[IP_u, h_t^g\right] + b_\gamma\right)\right)/Z' \\
\gamma_t^i &= \exp\left(\tanh\left(W_\gamma\left[IQ_i, h_t^g\right] + b_\gamma\right)\right)/Z' \\
b_t^g &= \gamma_t^u IP_u + \gamma_t^i IQ_i
\end{aligned}
\tag{17}
$$

where $W_\gamma \in R^{1 \times (d_n + m)}$ and $b_\gamma \in R$ are learnable parameters. Z' is the normalization term. b_t^g is a probability vector used to bias each aspect at time-step t.

Summing up the above two attention scores, the predicted word probability at time step t is as follows:

$$
\begin{aligned}
P_v\left(w_t\right) &= \tanh\left(W\left[h_t^g, a_t^g\right]\right) + b_v \\
P\left(w_t\right) &= P_v\left(w_t\right) + b_t^g \mathbb{1}_{w_t \in A_k}
\end{aligned}
\tag{18}
$$

where w_t is the target word at time-step t, A_k denotes all words belonging to aspect k, and $\mathbb{1}_{w_t \in A_k}$ is a binary variable indicating whether w_t belongs to A_k.

3.4 Multi-task Joint Optimization

In this subsection, we optimize the rating prediction task and the explanation generation task together to form end-to-end training. The loss function is composed of two parts. We adopt the Mean Squared Error (MSE) as the rating prediction task's loss function and the Negative Log-Likelihood (NLL) as the explanation generation task's loss function. Their calculation process is as follows:

$$\mathcal{L}_r = \frac{1}{|\Omega|} \sum_{(u,i) \in \Omega} \left(r_{u,i} - \hat{r}_{u,i}\right)^2 \tag{19}$$

$$\mathcal{L}_g = -\frac{1}{|\Omega|} \sum_{(u,i)\in\Omega} \sum_{w_t\in g_{u,i}} \log\left(\text{softmax}\left(P\left(w_t\right)\right)\right) \tag{20}$$

where $\mathcal{L}_r$ is the rating prediction loss and $\mathcal{L}_g$ is the explanation text generation loss. $r_{u,i}$ and $\hat{r}_{u,i}$ denote the ground truth and the predicted rating, respectively. $g_{u,i} = \{w_1, w_2, ..., w_{|g|}\}$ is the ground-truth explanation for the user u and the item i, Ω is the training dataset.

To this end, we integrate the rating prediction task and the explanation generation task into a multi-task learning framework. Its objective function is as follows:

$$\mathcal{J} = \min\left(\lambda_r \mathcal{L}_r + \lambda_g \mathcal{L}_g\right) \tag{21}$$

where λ_r and λ_g are proportions of each module in the total task. The whole framework can be trained by using back-propagation in an end-to-end paradigm.

4   Experiments

4.1   Experimental Settings

Datasets. We select three publicly accessible datasets from the Amazon Product Review dataset. The information of datasets is summarized in Table 1.

Table 1. The Statistics of Datasets.

Dataset	#Users	#Items	#Reviews
Pet Supplies	19853	8510	157836
Video Games	24301	10672	231780
Baby	19444	7049	160792

Evaluation Metrics. We consider evaluation metrics from two perspectives. For the rating prediction task, we use Mean Absolute Error (MAE) and Root Mean Square Error (RMSE) as evaluation metrics. For the explanation generation task, we employ BLEU-1, BLEU-4, ROUGE-1-F, and ROUGE-L-F as metrics. More specifically, BLEU [15] is used to evaluate how many generated words appear in real reviews. ROUGE [9] is used to evaluate how many real words appear in generated reviews.

Parameter Settings. ISER is trained by minimizing the loss in Eq. 21. We apply the Adam optimizer, where the batch size and learning rate are searched in [32, 64, 128, 256, 512] and [0.0005, 0.001, 0.005, 0.01, 0.05], respectively. We search λ_r and λ_g from [1e-5, 1e-4, ..., 1e+3]. We set the number of aspects to 15 and the number of layers in MLP to 3.

4.2   Performance Evaluation

Baselines. We compare ISER with four baseline models:

Table 2. The experimental results for rating prediction.

	Pet Supplies		Video Games		Baby	
	MAE	RMSE	MAE	RMSE	MAE	RMSE
A3NCF	0.8990	1.1417	0.8260	1.0694	0.8303	1.0826
MRG	0.8743	1.1055	0.8079	1.0478	0.8253	1.0807
U-ARM	<u>0.8701</u>	<u>1.1032</u>	**0.7915**	**1.0393**	<u>0.8182</u>	<u>1.0617</u>
ISER	**0.8623**	**1.1001**	<u>0.8074</u>	<u>1.0476</u>	**0.8148**	**1.0592**

- **A3NCF** [3]: It develops a novel topic model to extract both user and item features from reviews and adopts an aspect-aware rating prediction method based on an adaptive aspect attention modeling design.
- **MRG** [17]: It is a multi-task model for both review generation and rating prediction, using an MLP module to capture the complex user-item interaction for explanation generation.
- **Att2Seq** [5]: It utilizes an MLP to encode three key attributes: user, item, and rating, and incorporates a two-layer LSTM for decoding these encoded representations in order to generate a textual review.
- **U-ARM** [16]: It is a multi-task model for both review generation and rating prediction. It leverages an advanced unsupervised neural aspect extraction model to learn the aspect-aware representation for each review sentence.

Table 3. The experimental results for explanation generation.

	Pet Supplies			
	BLEU-1	BLEU-4	ROUGE-1-F	ROUGE-L-F
Att2Seq	0.2395	0.0056	0.2735	0.1928
MRG	0.2402	0.0058	0.2753	0.1938
U-ARM	0.2608	0.0089	0.3009	0.2083
ISER	**0.2633**	**0.0092**	**0.3014**	**0.2093**
	Video Games			
	BLEU-1	BLEU-4	ROUGE-1-F	ROUGE-L-F
Att2Seq	0.2553	0.0087	0.2918	0.2058
MRG	0.2581	0.0082	0.2951	0.2088
U-ARM	0.2650	0.0101	0.3081	0.2163
ISER	**0.2728**	**0.0106**	**0.3125**	**0.2202**
	Baby			
	BLEU-1	BLEU-4	ROUGE-1-F	ROUGE-L-F
Att2Seq	0.2481	0.0057	0.2810	0.1977
MRG	0.2562	0.0062	0.2891	0.1993
U-ARM	0.2656	0.0101	0.3072	0.2105
ISER	**0.2717**	**0.0105**	**0.3098**	**0.2169**

Rating Prediction. For the rating prediction task, we use three models for comparative evaluation. The overall performance of the proposed ISER and baseline models is presented in Table 2. It is obvious that in most cases, our model outperforms all baseline methods in terms of MAE and RMSE metrics on all datasets. Specifically, the performance of our model outperforms other baselines for Pet Supplies and Baby datasets. Even for the Video Games dataset, our model performs better than most baselines (A3NCF and MRG) except for U-ARM. We believe that the improved performance of ISER validates its effectiveness on the rating prediction, and ISER can help the rating prediction task to make more accurate recommendations.

Explanation Generation. As a multi-task model, our model ISER handles not only the rating prediction problem, but also the explanation generating problem, which can encourage users to accept the recommendation result. For the explanation generation task, we also compared our proposed ISER model with three models. Table 3 presents the overall performance of our model and the baseline models. The results demonstrate that our model consistently outperforms the baseline models, indicating its ability to fully explore implicit user sentiments and contribute to generating higher quality explanations.

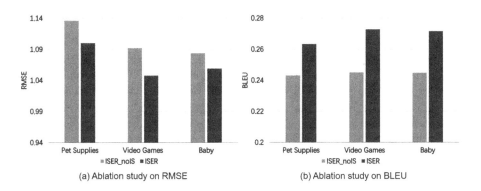

Fig. 3. The experimental results for ablation study.

Ablation Study. Although ISER performed well overall, it is worth studying whether our implicit sentiment-based representation learning effectively works in extracting user implicit sentiments and whether these sentiments improve performance in both rating prediction and explanation generation. Therefore, we conducted an ablation study to explore this issue by comparing it with a variant model, ISER_noIS, which does not consider the implicit sentiment representation of users/items based on reviews. The results of ablation experiments are shown in Fig. 3. The results reveal that the performance is worse in ISER_noIS. These findings demonstrate that learning implicit sentiment-based representation can improve rating prediction accuracy and help generate higher quality explanations.

Table 4. Examples of the generated explanations.

Ground-truth	I sit down on my bed and play with the game all night. It is comfortable and the price is great. It work excellent on XP and vista without any driver
Att2Seq	I love this game. It works well
MRG	I love this video game. It's very attractive to me, it runs well
U-ARM	The game is amazing. I love the price and the performance on XP and vista
ISER	I have been playing it for a few hours. I have to say I like the smoothness of it on XP and vista and it has a great price
Ground-truth	God of War is one of the best games to be released in recent times. From graphics/environment to gameplay, to story, this game is about as well rounded as you will find
Att2Seq	I have to say I love this game. It is a sensational game
MRG	I love God of War. It is the best game. I love the graphics
U-ARM	God of War is the best game and it is well made in graphics and story. It works well
ISER	God of War is the most well-made game in recent. It does well in graphics and story. I love the gameplay

Case Study. In this section, we will provide a demonstration of the effectiveness of our model in generating explanation texts. Table 4 shows some examples of explanations generated by baselines and our model for the Video Games dataset. We also display the real reviews to reveal her/his interest. From Table 4, we can see that the explanations generated by our model align seamlessly with the sentiments expressed in real reviews. Moreover, the generated content maintains a high relevance to the context at hand. Compared with the baseline models, our model can better capture users' implicit sentiments and generate more fine-grained explanations.

5   Conclusions

In this paper, we propose a novel Implicit Sentiment learning model for Explainable review-based Recommendation, named ISER, which learns users' implicit sentiments from reviews and explores them to generate recommendations with more fine-grained explanations. It learns implicit sentiment representations to express the implicit sentiments in review-based recommendations, and then adopts two implicit aspects fusion strategies for rating prediction and explanation generation respectively. It utilizes a multi-task learning framework to jointly optimize the above two tasks. Extensive experiments on three real-world datasets demonstrate the superiority of our proposed model. For future work, we will further improve our model by considering the consistency of the sentiment polarity between the predicted ratings and the generated explanations.

References

1. Bao, Y., Fang, H., Zhang, J.: TopicMF: simultaneously exploiting ratings and reviews for recommendation. In: Proceedings of the Twenty-Eighth AAAI Conference on Artificial Intelligence, 27–31 July 2014, Québec City, Québec, Canada, pp. 2–8. AAAI Press (2014)
2. Chen, T., Yin, H., Ye, G., Huang, Z., Wang, Y., Wang, M.: Try this instead: personalized and interpretable substitute recommendation. In: Proceedings of the 43rd International ACM SIGIR Conference on Research and Development in Information Retrieval, SIGIR 2020, Virtual Event, China, 25–30 July 2020, pp. 891–900. ACM (2020)
3. Cheng, Z., Ding, Y., He, X., Zhu, L., Song, X., Kankanhalli, M.S.: A^3NCF: an adaptive aspect attention model for rating prediction. In: Proceedings of the Twenty-Seventh International Joint Conference on Artificial Intelligence, IJCAI 2018, 13–19 July 2018, Stockholm, Sweden, pp. 3748–3754. Ijcai.org (2018)
4. Chin, J.Y., Zhao, K., Joty, S.R., Cong, G.: ANR: aspect-based neural recommender. In: Proceedings of the 27th ACM International Conference on Information and Knowledge Management, CIKM 2018, Torino, Italy, 22–26 October 2018, pp. 147–156. ACM (2018)
5. Dong, L., Huang, S., Wei, F., Lapata, M., Zhou, M., Xu, K.: Learning to generate product reviews from attributes. In: Proceedings of the 15th Conference of the European Chapter of the Association for Computational Linguistics, EACL 2017, Valencia, Spain, 3–7 April 2017, Volume 1: Long Papers, pp. 623–632. Association for Computational Linguistics (2017)
6. Hada, D.V., M, V., Shevade, S.K.: ReXPlug: explainable recommendation using plug-and-play language model. In: SIGIR 2021: The 44th International ACM SIGIR Conference on Research and Development in Information Retrieval, Virtual Event, Canada, 11–15 July 2021, pp. 81–91. ACM (2021)
7. Le, T., Lauw, H.W.: Synthesizing aspect-driven recommendation explanations from reviews. In: Proceedings of the Twenty-Ninth International Joint Conference on Artificial Intelligence, IJCAI 2020, pp. 2427–2434. Ijcai.org (2020)
8. Li, L., Zhang, Y., Chen, L.: Personalized transformer for explainable recommendation. In: Proceedings of the 59th Annual Meeting of the Association for Computational Linguistics and the 11th International Joint Conference on Natural Language Processing, ACL/IJCNLP 2021, (Volume 1: Long Papers), Virtual Event, 1–6 August 2021, pp. 4947–4957. Association for Computational Linguistics (2021)
9. Lin, C.Y.: ROUGE: a package for automatic evaluation of summaries. In: Text Summarization Branches Out, pp. 74–81. ACL (2004)
10. Liu, H., Wang, W., Xu, H., Peng, Q., Jiao, P.: Neural unified review recommendation with cross attention. In: Proceedings of the 43rd International ACM SIGIR Conference on Research and Development in Information Retrieval, SIGIR 2020, Virtual Event, China, 25–30 July 2020, pp. 1789–1792. ACM (2020)
11. Lumbantoruan, R., Zhou, X., Ren, Y.: Declarative user-item profiling based context-aware recommendation. In: Yang, X., Wang, C.-D., Islam, M.S., Zhang, Z. (eds.) ADMA 2020. LNCS (LNAI), vol. 12447, pp. 413–427. Springer, Cham (2020). https://doi.org/10.1007/978-3-030-65390-3_32
12. Lumbantoruan, R., Zhou, X., Ren, Y., Bao, Z.: D-CARS: a declarative context-aware recommender system. In: IEEE International Conference on Data Mining, ICDM 2018, Singapore, 17–20 November 2018, pp. 1152–1157. IEEE Computer Society (2018)

13. Lumbantoruan, R., Zhou, X., Ren, Y., Chen, L.: I-CARS: an interactive context-aware recommender system. In: 2019 IEEE International Conference on Data Mining, ICDM 2019, Beijing, China, 8–11 November 2019, pp. 1240–1245. IEEE (2019)
14. Luo, S., Lu, X., Wu, J., Yuan, J.: Review-aware neural recommendation with cross-modality mutual attention. In: CIKM 2021: The 30th ACM International Conference on Information and Knowledge Management, Virtual Event, Queensland, Australia, 1–5 November 2021, pp. 3293–3297. ACM (2021)
15. Papineni, K., Roukos, S., Ward, T., Zhu, W.: BLEU: a method for automatic evaluation of machine translation. In: Proceedings of the 40th Annual Meeting of the Association for Computational Linguistics, 6–12 July 2002, Philadelphia, PA, USA, pp. 311–318. ACL (2002)
16. Sun, P., Wu, L., Zhang, K., Su, Y., Wang, M.: An unsupervised aspect-aware recommendation model with explanation text generation. ACM Trans. Inf. Syst. **40**(3), 63:1–63:29 (2022)
17. Truong, Q., Lauw, H.W.: Multimodal review generation for recommender systems. In: The World Wide Web Conference, WWW 2019, San Francisco, CA, USA, 13–17 May 2019, pp. 1864–1874. ACM (2019)
18. Wang, N., Wang, H., Jia, Y., Yin, Y.: Explainable recommendation via multi-task learning in opinionated text data. In: The 41st International ACM SIGIR Conference on Research & Development in Information Retrieval, SIGIR 2018, Ann Arbor, MI, USA, 08–12 July 2018, pp. 165–174. ACM (2018)
19. Wang, P., Cai, R., Wang, H.: Graph-based extractive explainer for recommendations. In: WWW 2022: The ACM Web Conference 2022, Virtual Event, Lyon, France, 25–29 April 2022, pp. 2163–2171. ACM (2022)
20. Zhang, T., Sun, C., Cheng, Z., Dong, X.: AENAR: an aspect-aware explainable neural attentional recommender model for rating predication. Expert Syst. Appl. **198**, 116717 (2022)
21. Zhang, Y., Chen, X.: Explainable recommendation: a survey and new perspectives. Found. Trends Inf. Retr. **14**(1), 1–101 (2020)
22. Zhang, Y., Lai, G.: Explicit factor models for explainable recommendation based on phrase-level sentiment analysis. In: SIGIR 2014, pp. 83–92. ACM (2014)

Balanced and Explainable Social Media Analysis for Public Health with Large Language Models

Yan Jiang$^{(\boxtimes)}$, Ruihong Qiu, Yi Zhang, and Peng-Fei Zhang

The University of Queensland, Brisbane, Australia
{yan.jiang,r.qiu,y.zhang4,pengfei.zhang}@uq.edu.au

Abstract. As social media becomes increasingly popular, more and more public health activities emerge, which is worth noting for pandemic monitoring and government decision-making. Current techniques for public health analysis involve popular models such as BERT and large language models (LLMs). Although recent progress in LLMs has shown a strong ability to comprehend knowledge by being fine-tuned on specific domain datasets, the costs of training an in-domain LLM for every specific public health task are especially expensive. Furthermore, such kinds of in-domain datasets from social media are generally highly imbalanced, which will hinder the efficiency of LLMs tuning. To tackle these challenges, the data imbalance issue can be overcome by sophisticated data augmentation methods for social media datasets. In addition, the ability of the LLMs can be effectively utilised by prompting the model properly. In light of the above discussion, in this paper, a novel ALEX framework is proposed for social media analysis on public health. Specifically, an augmentation pipeline is developed to resolve the data imbalance issue. Furthermore, an LLMs explanation mechanism is proposed by prompting an LLM with the predicted results from BERT models. Extensive experiments conducted on three tasks at the Social Media Mining for Health 2023 (SMM4H) competition with the first ranking in two tasks demonstrate the superior performance of the proposed ALEX method. Our code has been released in https://github.com/YanJiangJerry/ALEX.

Keywords: Public Health · Social Media · Text Classification

1 Introduction

Social media mining with natural language processing (NLP) techniques has great potential in analysing public health information [3]. For example, mining social media posts about vaccines can indicate the vaccine acceptance rate, and analysing public opinions towards healthcare can influence government policies [2].

Despite that there are abundant health-related datasets on social media, their value in assisting public health analysis has been largely untapped [4]. Current techniques for public health analysis generally involve various transformer-based models, such as BERT [6] and LLMs [9,25,26,35,39,42,45]. With a strong ability

Z. Bao et al. (Eds.): ADC 2023, LNCS 14386, pp. 73–86, 2024.
https://doi.org/10.1007/978-3-031-47843-7_6

for text processing, such models can effectively extract valuable information from social media for various kinds of tasks such as text classification.

Although existing techniques have shown remarkable performance on some of the tasks, they often encounter problems when classifying public health information on social media. Firstly, the extremely large parameter sizes and high computational requirements for adopting LLMs in specific public health areas will increase their training difficulty, while smaller models such as BERT usually have limited input token size which may also make training difficult to include all the information. Secondly, imbalanced data also poses a significant challenge for current techniques, which may lead to biased predictions [12]. Lastly, in the social media datasets, it is common to witness a significant variation in the importance of different categories. For instance, when analysing social anxiety diagnosis, the positively diagnosed cases would hold greater analytical value than the others. Existing systems do not fully consider the above problems, therefore, the performance of public health analysis will be seriously limited.

In order to address the aforementioned problems, an effective method for public health text classification is urgently needed. In this paper, firstly, a complete data augmentation pipeline and a weighted loss fine-tuning are employed to address the imbalance problem in social media. Secondly, to reduce the computational cost of LLMs training and solve BERT's limited token size problem, an explanation and correction mechanism based on LLMs inference is introduced. Specifically, the predicted labels from BERT and the original text are prompted together for an LLM to examine by taking the given predicted labels to find the existence of evidence in the text thus explaining whether the given labels are correct or not. Such an innovative approach successfully incorporates the language generation capabilities of LLMs into text classification tasks, thus enhancing the credibility and performance of the results. This framework is named by **A**ugmentation and **L**arge language model methods for **EX**plainable (ALEX) social media analysis on public health. The main contributions can be summarised as follows:

- A balanced training pipeline is proposed by data augmentation and weighted-loss fine-tuning to address the class and importance imbalance problems.
- An LLMs-based method is proposed to conduct post-evaluation on the predicted results, which successfully leverages LLMs' ability without training.
- The ALEX model achieves number one in two text classification tasks (Task 2 and Task 4) in the SMM4H 2023 competition and a top result in Task 1.

2   Related Work

2.1   Text Classification

Text classification refers to classifying given sequences into predefined groups. Prior studies have highlighted the performance of recurrent models [17,32, 41] and attention mechanisms [36] for developing text representation [16]. Building upon those ideas, extensive research has substantiated the effectiveness of employing pre-trained models [27] such as BERT [7] and OpenAI

GPT [5, 25, 28, 29] on text classification. The BERT model is a multi-layer bidirectional Transformer [6] that has been proven to achieve state-of-the-art performance across a wide range of NLP applications [34]. After the advent of BERT, RoBERTa [18] is proposed to resolve BERT's undertrained problem. ALBERT is invented to reduce the computational resources of BERT [13]. DistilBERT, a distilled version of BERT, showed that it is possible to reduce the size of a BERT model by 40 percent [31]. The combination of BERT with other architectures such as BERT-CNN [30], BERT-RCNN [11], and BERT-BiLSTM [8] are also been proved to be capable to improve the classification accuracy for social media analysis.

In addition to structural improvement, BERT can also be fine-tuned on different domain-specific datasets. BERTweet is the first open-source pre-trained language model designed for English Tweets [24]. Similarly, TwHIN-BERT [44], Camembert [21] and Flaubert [14] have also achieved significant performance improvements for text classification in specific domains.

2.2 Large Language Models

LLMs are pre-trained on large corpus and exhibit a strong ability to generate coherent text. GPT-1 [29] is the first LLM to follow the transformer architecture [36] based on the decoder in 2017. Based on it, GPT-2 enlarges the parameter size to 1.5B and begins to learn downstream tasks without explicit training [29]. GPT-3 continues to scale the number of parameters to 175B with few shot learning [5]. Such strong models can be applied for inference without any gradient updates. Meanwhile, GPT-3.5 (ChatGPT) is invented to train on up-to-date datasets. In March 2023, OpenAI released the development of GPT-4 [25], a multimodal LLM capable of accepting both image and text inputs. Researchers have suggested the potential utility of LLMs in health fields [33]. For example, in disease surveillance tasks, such models can be employed by analysing large volumes of social media data to provide insights for detecting and monitoring disease outbreaks [43].

3   Preliminaries: Task Definition

For all three tasks, the problem can be framed as text classifications with binary classification for Task 1 and 4 and three-class classification for Task 2. For each task, given a set of social media post texts $\{x_1, ..., x_n\} \subseteq \mathcal{X}$ and the corresponding labels $\{y_1, ..., y_n\} \subseteq \mathcal{Y}$, the objective is to develop a model that can effectively classify the input social media texts. For all the following equations, bold lowercase letters denote vectors, lowercase letters denote scalars or strings and uppercase letters denote all the other functions.

4   Methodology

In this section, the ALEX method is divided into several components as Fig. 1 shows. Firstly, balanced training involves augmentation is employed to solve the imbalance problem. Secondly, fine-tuning with the weighted loss is conducted on BERT. Lastly, an LLM is applied to explain and correct the labels.

Fig. 1. Overall framework of ALEX method. Firstly, the social media posts are augmented to fine-tune the BERT models. The labels are then predicted by BERT. After combining the labels with their original posts and constructing a complete prompt by adding instructions and examples, LLMs can take the prompt to explain and identify those incorrectly predicted labels from BERT.

4.1 Augmentation and Resampling

For text classification in social media, data imbalance problems may significantly influence the models' performance. The TextAttack [22], which is a well-developed framework designed for adversarial attacks, data augmentation, and adversarial training, is chosen to enrich the number of the minority class because it can automatically incorporate adversarial attacks to enhance the robustness of data augmentation with just a few lines of code. After data augmentation, oversampling and undersampling are also introduced to make the number of each class exactly the same as Eq. 1 shown:

$$\mathbf{x}' = \text{Resample}(\text{Aug}(\mathbf{x})), \tag{1}$$

where $\mathbf{x}' \in \mathbb{R}^n$ denotes the augmented text. Aug is the TextAttack augmentation and Resample denotes oversampling and undersampling methods.

4.2 Social Media Text Encoding

After getting the balanced dataset, those texts will be encoded by BERT to get better embeddings for text classification as Eq. 2 shows. The BERT's output sequence can be divided into segments with the first token being [CLS], which is the special classification token for predicting the labels' probability.

$$\mathbf{e} = \text{BERT}(\mathbf{x}'), \tag{2}$$

where $\mathbf{e} \in \mathbb{R}^d$ represent the embedding of the [CLS] token while d represents its dimension. To employ the BERT's embedding for text classification, a straightforward approach is adding an additional classifier as Eq. 3 shows:

$$\hat{y} = \text{argmax}(\text{Classifier}(\mathbf{e})), \tag{3}$$

where $\hat{y} \in \mathbb{R}$ is the label predicted by BERT. The output from the classifier represents the probability of each label, then the argmax function will extract the index that has the max probability, which will be the predicted label.

4.3 Weighted Loss

In social media analysis for public health, there is usually a tendency to place importance on specific classes in text classification. For example, while analysing the number of COVID cases, the F1 score for the positive class holds greater analytical values compared to the negative class. To address this issue, the weighted binary cross-entropy loss will be adopted, which allows for the loss weight adjustments on different labels based on their importance. Such importance can be manually decided based on the task objectives. In this way, we can ensure the model assigns more emphasis to a specific label during the training process. Based on the importance, the loss weight λ can be introduced, which will be integrated into binary cross-entropy loss as Eq. 4 shows:

$$\ell = -\frac{1}{n} \sum_{i=1}^{n} \lambda y \log(\hat{y}) + (1 - y)\log(1 - \hat{y}). \tag{4}$$

4.4 LLM Explanation and Corrections at Inference Time

To overcome the limited input size of BERT and enhance its performance, LLMs will be introduced to further correct the prediction using their powerful language modelling ability. Firstly, the predicted label from BERT will be concatenated with the original text. Secondly, the processed text will be combined with the labelling rules and manually created instructions for each task with a few representative examples to form a complete prompt for LLMs' few-shot prompting as Fig. 2 shows:

By constructing BERT's prediction into a prompt, LLMs can seek logical proofs for the label within the original input. If LLMs successfully find supporting evidence in the original text that aligns with the given label, it will return "True" with a concise provable explanation that can

You are a highly intelligent and accurate social anxiety explainable system. You are given a text with a label in the end, your job is to take the label in the end and identify whether it is true or false according to the following rules:
1. Users explicitly report having a diagnosis of SAD.
Examples: "I've been diagnosed with SA"
2...(provided by the competition)
Here are some examples:
1. Input: I've had SAD, Label: 0
Output: False, because the user explicitly said he has SA. So should be Label 1 but the given label is 0.
2...(more examples create manually)
Your output should only be True or False with reasoning sentences that can show the proof step by step within 30 words. You should return True for most uncertain cases and be careful to return False.
Input: I get SA... Label: 0

| LLMs | Output: F, because... | Correct to Label: 1 | Final output: Label: 1 |

Fig. 2. LLM explanation and correction. The prompt includes instructions (orange), labelling rules (grey), examples (blue), and the input text concatenated with its wrong label predicted by BERT in red. The LLMs successfully identified the label as False therefore the label will be corrected to the final correct label in green. (Color figure online)

explain the reason. However, if LLMs fail to identify any compelling evidence that could support the given label or find the opposite proofs that can overturn the given label, it will return "False" and will use the Chain of Thought (CoT) [37] idea to give a step-by-step explanation for why it considers the label is incorrect as Eq. 5 shows:

$$\text{exp} = \text{LLMs}(\text{Prompt}(x, \hat{y})), \tag{5}$$

where exp refers to the explanation including the judgments of whether LLMs think the label is true with the step-by-step proof. Prompt represents the prompt construction including the concatenation of the original text with the BERT predicted label, adding labelling rules with manually created instructions, and a few examples.

Finally, to utilise the LLMs' explanation, a correction mechanism is designed. For cases when LLMs return "True" in the explanation, the original labels from BERT will remain. For cases when the LLM returns "False", there are two options. Firstly, if the number of "False" cases is relatively small, the manual review can be achievable to assess the LLMs' explanation. If the evidence is compelling, the label will be corrected to the others. Such a method will largely reduce the manual cost compared with the fully manual labelling method by leveraging the LLMs' language comprehension ability to screen out suspicious samples in advance. The second option is directly modifying the "False" label to the other label which will minimise the manual efforts. For binary text classification tasks, the "False" label can be directly converted to the other label. For the three-class text classification task, the "False" label can be converted to the majority label.

5   Experiments

5.1   Experimental Setup

Datasets. This study employed three public health-related social media datasets provided by the SMM4H 2023 workshop. For **Task 1**, the dataset involves 600,000 English-language tweets excluding retweets by Twitter streaming API[1]. Such tweets are selected based on the presence of keywords indicating COVID-19 testing, diagnosis, or hospitalisation [1]. Similarly, the dataset for **Task 2** is also a Twitter dataset that is labelled by three sentiments associated with therapies: negative, neutral, and positive. Lastly, the dataset for **Task 4** is extracted from the Reddit platform[2] and is divided into Label 0 for negative social anxiety cases and Label 1 for positive cases. The statistics of SMM4H competition are shown in Table 1. In this paper, only the validation set is evaluated since the competition only provides labels for the validation set instead of the testing set.

---

[1] https://developer.twitter.com/en/docs/twitter-api.
[2] https://www.reddit.com/.

Table 1. Statistics of the public health datasets from SMM4H 2023.

Dataset	Classes	Type	Average	Max	Train	Validate	Test
Task 1	2	COVID Diagnosis	38.1	106	7600	400	10000
Task 2	3	Sentiment Analysis	32.7	100	3009	753	4887
Task 4	2	Social Anxiety Analysis	235.2	2000	6090	680	1347

Metrics. Popular evaluation metrics such as precision, recall, and F1 score are used. For Task 1 and Task 4, only the F1 score for Label 1 is evaluated. For Task 2, the micro-averaged F1 score is evaluated as required by the SMM4H competition which is the same as the accuracy. Therefore, in all the experiments, the F1 score for Label 1 and the accuracy are observed. For the baseline experiment, the macro average F1 score is also evaluated to show the imbalanced problem effect.

Implementation. Firstly, the TextAttack will be implemented to augment the number of minority class samples. Then, the training set will be resampled which will make the number of each label balanced. For the fine-tuning, the implementation is based on the Transformers open-source library [38]. For hyperparameters optimisation, the batch size from the range {4, 8, 16} is tested and the AdamW optimiser [19] is implemented with a learning rate choosing from $2e-5$ to $1e-4$. To mitigate overfitting problems, the weight decay from {0.001, 0.005, 0.01} is used. The number of warm-up steps is set to zero and the experiments are conducted with the number of epochs within the range of {2, 4, 6, 8, 10, 12, 16, 20}. The loss weight λ is chosen from the range of {1, 1.5, 2, 2.5, 5}. For the baseline models, the batch size 8, learning rate 2e-5, weighted loss 0.1, and epoch 6 are used except for the XLNet model which uses batch size 4 due to the hardware limitations. For XLNet which has a larger token length, the inputs will not be truncated. However, for BERT-related models, the input will be head truncated [34] to be within 512 tokens for the large model and 128 tokens for the base model.

In Task 4, BERTweet-Large experiments indicate that a learning rate of $2e-5$, a batch size of 16, a weight decay of 0.005, and epochs of 6 will lead to the highest F1 scores for Label 1. For other tasks, weight decay of 0.01 and epoch 3 will be adopted as over-training may hinder the models' performance. For the LLMs part, GPT-3.5 is employed from OpenAI[3] to explain and correct the BERT's prediction as discussed in Sect. 4.4. For Task 1 and Task 4, the "False" Label 1 sample will be automatically converted to Label 0. While for Task 2, the "False" Label 0 predictions will be converted to the majority class Label 1.

Baselines. The following baselines are chosen for comparison:

- **BERT** [6] is the original baseline for all text classification Tasks which is pre-trained on the general corpus. Both base and large models are tested.

---

[3] https://openai.com/.

Table 2. Overall model performance.

Model	Task 1			Task 2			Task 4		
	F1	Accuracy	M-Avg	F1	Accuracy	M-Avg	F1	Accuracy	M-Avg
BERT-B	82.25	93.15	93.74	83.33	71.24	58.94	79.75	84.15	83.37
BERT-L	85.75	95.02	93.79	80.44	69.30	64.92	81.17	85.74	84.85
RoBERTa-B	91.84	92.77	91.01	77.33	70.07	66.45	81.86	87.13	85.87
RoBERTa-L	92.71	94.97	93.56	81.35	74.45	71.07	44.52	72.74	63.22
XLNet-B	3.04	64.56	51.47	84.82	76.28	76.87	78.92	82.73	82.14
XLNet-L	0.0	64.33	50.37	85.00	75.74	76.78	84.89	89.18	87.66
BERTweet-B	88.31	93.67	92.82	79.97	72.44	68.37	80.77	83.49	82.93
BERTweet-L	91.22	95.57	93.61	85.61	73.67	77.49	85.42	87.01	85.38
CT-BERT (v2)	93.11	95.62	94.47	85.02	76.43	77.81	61.93	70.29	68.78
ALEX-B (ours)	90.77	92.04	91.25	82.20	73.00	71.19	83.39	88.25	87.15
ALEX-L (ours)	**94.97**	**96.71**	**95.84**	**89.13**	**77.84**	**79.57**	**88.17**	**89.84**	**88.26**

- **RoBERTa** [18] is a compact and efficient version of the BERT, and it is designed for fast and resource-friendly NLP Tasks.
- **XLNet** [40] is a highly effective language model that leverages the Transformer-XL architecture with both autoregressive and permutation-based training. It allows for larger token size input than BERT.
- **BERTweet** [24] is a baseline for text classification Tasks on social media datasets like Twitter. Both the BERTweet-base and BERTweet-large models are experimented with.
- **CT-BERT (v2)** [23][4] is a BERT-Large model and it has been fine-tuned on more COVID Twitter datasets than CT-BERT (v1). As CT-BERT does not involve the base model, only the large model is evaluated.

In overall comparison, the "-B" indicates the base models with the "-L" denotes the large models. In all following experiments, only BERTweet-Large is used for ALEX-Large in Task 2 and Task 4 as well as CT-BERT (v2) is used for Task 1.

5.2   Overall Performance

The overall performance of baseline methods on the validation set is presented in Table 2. The first finding is that the original BERT models may outperform large models such as XLNet, which may owing to the serious impact of the imbalanced datasets in Task 1. Generally, for BERT-related models, the large model may outperform the base model. However, XLNet-Large underperforms XLNet-Base and gets a zero score for Label 1's F1 score in Task 1 which may related to the complexity of the model. Although XLNet models get generally low performance on Task 1 compared to other methods, their accuracy and macro-average F1 for Task 2 and Task 4 are remarkable. For RoBERTa, experiment results show that it can get better results compared to BERT on Task 1 and Task 4. However, for the base model, RoBERTa underperforms BERT in Task 2.

---

[4] https://huggingface.co/digitalepidemiologylab/covid-twitter-bert-v2.

Generally, in Task 1 and Task 4 where Label 1 is the minority class, the F1 score for Label 1 is observed to be lower than the overall macro F1 score, while for Task 2 where Label 1 is the majority class, the F1 score for Label 1 is observed to be higher than the overall macro F1 score. It is noticeable to see that BERTweet-Large model performances are generally better than others on the F1 score for Label 1 in Task 2 and Task 4. Moreover, for Task 1, CT-BERT (v2) gets the highest F1 score for Label 1 compared to all other baselines. Our ALEX-Large method outperforms all other methods in three tasks as it integrates balanced training and LLMs correction.

5.3 Ablation Study

In order to validate the effectiveness of ALEX's method, an ablation study is conducted. As shown in Table 3, firstly, for all the tasks, the effectiveness of balanced training ("Bal") is verified by observing improvements in the balanced training compared to baseline methods that use imbalanced training.

Table 3. Ablation study for the ALEX method.

Bal	LLMs	Task 1		Task 2		Task 4	
		F1	Acc	F1	Acc	F1	Acc
✗	✗	93.11	95.62	85.61	73.67	85.42	87.01
✓	✗	**94.97**	**96.71**	86.17	74.34	86.64	87.94
✓	✓	93.24	95.11	**89.13**	**77.84**	**88.17**	**89.84**

Another component of ALEX is the LLMs explanation and correction "LLMs". As GPT-3.5 is a language model and our objective is to leverage its language understanding ability to explain and correct the predictions, we do not test its performance directly on the text classification tasks. To simplify the process, the GPT-3.5 is constrained to only explain and correct Label 1's samples from BERT's prediction which aims to improve Label 1's precision. For Task 2, GPT-3.5 is constrained to only verify Label 0 predictions and correct them to the majority class which is Label 1. Experiment results reveal that GPT-3.5's explanation and correction can improve Task 2 and Task 4 Label 1's F1 scores from about 86 to above 88 compared to the results after balanced training.

However, as for Task 1, because the F1 score for Label 1 after balanced training has already achieved a high score of about 95, GPT-3.5 struggles to further identify the few false positive predictions from BERT output, thus resulting in decreased performance compared to the results that use balanced training only. The possible reasons will be analysed from two aspects which are the prompts effect in Sect. 5.5 and the LLMs hallucinations impact in Sect. 5.5. Therefore, only the balanced training method from ALEX is used in Task 1.

5.4 Strategies for Balanced Training

In this study, the effects of different methods for balanced training are compared. In the table, "Focal" refers to fine-tuning BERT with focal loss while "Weighted" means fine-tuning solely using weighted loss. "Aug" refers to data augmentation and "Balanced" refers to the combination of augmentation and weighted loss fine-tuning. The loss weight is set to 2 for Task 1 and Task 4. For Task 2, the weight for each class is set to be 2:1:2 according to experiment results.

Table 4. Strategies for balanced training.

Balanced Methods	Task 1		Task 2		Task 4	
	F1	Acc	F1	Acc	F1	Acc
Aug	93.31	95.98	85.98	74.11	85.65	87.34
Focal	91.04	93.05	77.93	68.45	82.91	84.74
Weighted	94.81	**97.14**	85.39	73.10	85.47	86.07
Balanced	**94.97**	96.71	**86.17**	**74.34**	**86.64**	**87.94**

As shown in Table 4, it is noticeable to see that focal loss fine-tuning without augmentation will lead to decreased performance on all three tasks while weighted loss fine-tuning may increase the F1 score and accuracy for Task 1. However, the improvement for Task 2 and Task 4 is not obvious only with the weighted loss fine-tuning. After combining the augmentation with weighted loss fine-tuning, the balanced training method can produce superior performance in all three Tasks, leading to a visible improvement for Task 2 and Task 4. Visualisation for the effectiveness of the balanced training is shown in Sect. 5.4.

Visualisation of Embeddings. To validate the effectiveness of the balanced training in ALEX, the [CLS] token embeddings of the baseline method are visualised to compare with the [CLS] embeddings after the augmentation with weighted-loss fine-tuning "(Balanced)" using t-SNE [20].

As shown in Fig. 3, it is obvious that for Task 2 and Task 4, the balanced training can successfully separate different labels' texts in different colours as the plot on the right shows. However, for Task 1, although the balanced training can also separate classes well, the effectiveness is not significant as the baseline model can also get high accuracy. Therefore, for text classification tasks that suffer from low accuracy or have low inter-class distance between each class, the balanced training method in ALEX can be proven to be effective for such public health-related problems.

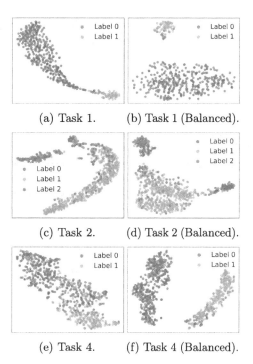

(a) Task 1.   (b) Task 1 (Balanced).

(c) Task 2.   (d) Task 2 (Balanced).

(e) Task 4.   (f) Task 4 (Balanced).

Fig. 3. Embeddings visualisations. The class separation using balanced training on the right-hand side is more clear.

5.5 Effectiveness of LLMs Explanation and Correction

In this section, the effectiveness and limitations of using LLMs for explanation and correction are analysed. Firstly, the effect of different prompts is examined by comparing a relevant prompt with an irrelevant prompt. Secondly, the effect of two strategies for the LLMs hallucinations phenomena [10] is evaluated.

Case Study for Prompts. The prompt design has a significant effect on LLMs. A relevant prompt "Rel" can guide LLMs to better comprehend the task thus enhancing experimental performance. Conversely, an irrelevant prompt "Irr" may mislead LLMs which may result in erroneous corrections. In this experiment, the effect of two prompt designs is compared. The relevant prompt guides LLMs to correct the classification results, while the irrelevant prompt misguides LLMs to interpret the task as a regression task.

In Table 5, the results indicate a significant decrease in performance

Table 5. Case study for prompts.

Task	Different Prompts		F1	Acc
1	Irr	...regression results... ...for COVID posts... ...give reasons...	53.39	59.71
	Rel	...classification... ...for COVID posts... ...step by step	**93.24**	**95.11**
2	Irr	...regression results... ...for sentiment... ...give reasons...	61.93	47.58
	Rel	...classification... ...for sentiment... ...step by step	**89.13**	**77.84**
4	Irr	...regression results... ...for social anxiety... ...give reasons...	55.34	61.77
	Rel	...classification... ...for social anxiety... ...step by step	**88.17**	**89.84**

when using the irrelevant prompt which is even worse than the baseline method. Conversely, when using an appropriate prompt, the F1 score and accuracy improve by around two percent in Task 1 and Task 4. It is worth noting that even if using a relevant prompt in Task 1, the performance will still decrease compared to the previous results. Such phenomenon will be further investigated in Sect. 5.5.

A Study for LLMs Hallucinations. Previous experiments have indicated that GPT-3.5 exhibits balderdash when determining the correctness of labels, which may be owed to the LLMs hallucinations [10] which refers to a phenomenon that LLMs generate responses that are actually incorrect or nonsensical. Experiments show that, in Task 1, even if GPT-3.5 successfully finds the context related to COVID and the given label is correct, it may still produce balderdash like "1 = 1 is False" thus return a false assertion as Fig. 4 shows.

Therefore, an investigation is conducted for potential causes behind LLM hallucinations. By observing those "False" assertion cases, it is evidently possible to find that the cause may be due to the repetitive presence of information such as "COVID" in the previous contexts. Similarly, researchers also found that LLMs may develop biases in their knowledge retention from the previous input, thus leading to Hallucinations [15]. For example, when the preceding input indicates the presence of COVID and is labelled as 0, the GPT-3.5 is more likely to carry

Table 6. Strategies for LLMs hallucinations.

Correction	Task 1		Task 2		Task 4	
	F1	Acc	F1	Acc	F1	Acc
All	87.76	89.33	75.89	71.94	79.11	81.32
Constrained	**93.24**	**95.11**	**89.13**	**77.84**	**88.17**	**89.84**

this knowledge over to the subsequent input disregarding its real label. A solution is to constrain the input within a certain label to mitigate the impact of this problem as discussed in Sect. 5.5.

Strategies for Preventing LLMs Hallucinations. As shown in Table 6, directly incorporating all BERT predictions to GPT-3.5 will lead to a decreased performance. In Task 1 and Task 4, GPT-3.5 is observed to tend to classify social media posts as positive class regardless of the facts. Therefore, it may misjudge the true negative class that is predicted from BERT thus leading to decreased performance.

A possible strategy to mitigate the LLM hallucination impact is constraining it to only verify the correctness of Label 1 predictions in Task 1 and Task 4 as well as the Label 0 predictions in Task 2. Results show that in this way, GPT-3.5 can reliably enhance the F1 score of Label 1 in Task 4 as well as the accuracy in Task 2. However, for Task 1, as the balanced training Label 1's F1 score has already reached a high value of about 95, it is challenging for GPT-3.5 to discover more true positive cases. There are also many other strategies for solving LLM hallucinations like using advanced LLMs such as GPT-4 and inventing more powerful prompts to instruct LLMs for better task comprehension and language generation.

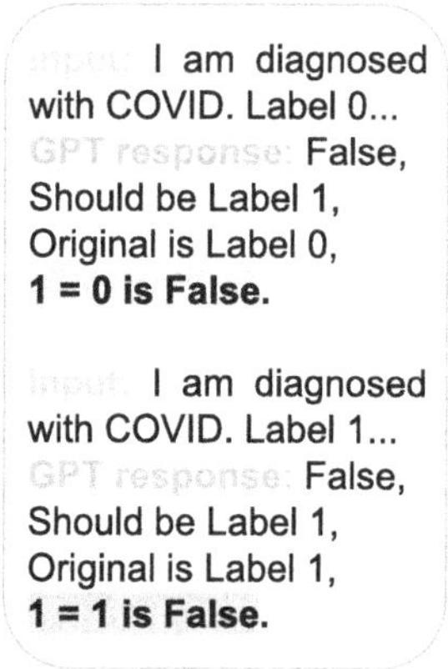

Input: I am diagnosed with COVID. Label 0...
GPT response: False,
Should be Label 1,
Original is Label 0,
1 = 0 is False.

Input: I am diagnosed with COVID. Label 1...
GPT response: False,
Should be Label 1,
Original is Label 1,
1 = 1 is False.

Fig. 4. LLMs Hallucinations examples. The green colour denotes correct responses while the red colour denotes incorrect responses. It is obvious that the LLM generates wrong explanations for the second input. (Color figure online)

6   Conclusion

In this paper, we focus on the promising area of analysing social media datasets for public health. To solve the imbalance problem existing in current methods, a framework involving balanced training is introduced. Moreover, the LLMs explanation and correction method is proposed to solve the limited token size problems and improve the performance of BERT. The remarkable competition results from the SMM4H 2023 competition have proven the effectiveness of our ALEX method on social media analysis for public health.

Acknowledgements. The work is supported by Developing a proof-of-concept self-contact tracing app to support epidemiological investigations and outbreak response (Australia-Korea Joint Research Projects - ATSE Tech Bridge Grant).

References

1. Klein, A.Z., Kunatharaju, S., O'Connor, K., Gonzalez-Hernandez, G.: Automatically identifying self-reports of COVID-19 diagnosis on Twitter: an annotated data set, deep neural network classifiers, and a large-scale cohort. J. Med. Internet Res. **25**, e46484 (2023)
2. Al-Dmour, H., Masa'deh, R., Salman, A., Abuhashesh, M., Al-Dmour, R.: Influence of social media platforms on public health protection against the COVID-19 pandemic via the mediating effects of public health awareness and behavioral changes: integrated model. J. Med. Internet Res. **22**(8), e19996 (2020)
3. Al-Garadi, M.A., Yang, Y.C., Sarker, A.: The role of natural language processing during the COVID-19 pandemic: health applications, opportunities, and challenges. In: Healthcare. MDPI (2022)
4. Bacelar-Nicolau, L.: The still untapped potential of social media for health promotion: the WHO example. In: PDH (2019)
5. Brown, T.B., et al.: Language models are few-shot learners. CoRR abs/2005.14165 (2020)
6. Devlin, J., Chang, M., Lee, K., Toutanova, K.: BERT: pre-training of deep bidirectional transformers for language understanding. CoRR abs/1810.04805 (2018)
7. Devlin, J., Chang, M., Lee, K., Toutanova, K.: BERT: pre-training of deep bidirectional transformers for language understanding. In: NAACL-HLT (2019)
8. Ge, H., Zheng, S., Wang, Q.: Based BERT-BiLSTM-ATT model of commodity commentary on the emotional tendency analysis. In: BDAI (2021)
9. Hoffmann, J., et al.: Training compute-optimal large language models. CoRR abs/2203.15556 (2022)
10. Ji, Z., et al.: Survey of hallucination in natural language generation. ACM **55**(12), 248:1–248:38 (2023)
11. Kaur, K., Kaur, P.: BERT-RCNN: an automatic classification of app reviews using transfer learning based RCNN deep model (2023)
12. Kumar, P., Bhatnagar, R., Gaur, K., Bhatnagar, A.: Classification of imbalanced data: review of methods and applications. In: IOP (2021)
13. Lan, Z., Chen, M., Goodman, S., Gimpel, K., Sharma, P., Soricut, R.: ALBERT: a lite BERT for self-supervised learning of language representations. In: ICLR (2020)
14. Le, H., et al.: FlauBERT: unsupervised language model pre-training for French. In: LREC (2020)
15. Lee, K., et al.: Deduplicating training data makes language models better. In: ACL (2022)
16. Liu, N., et al.: Text representation: from vector to tensor. In: ICDM (2005)
17. Liu, P., Qiu, X., Huang, X.: Recurrent neural network for text classification with multi-task learning. In: IJCAI (2016)
18. Liu, Y., et al.: RoBERTa: a robustly optimized BERT pretraining approach. CoRR abs/1907.11692 (2019)
19. Loshchilov, I., Hutter, F.: Decoupled weight decay regularization. In: ICLR (2019)
20. van der Maaten, L., Hinton, G.: Visualizing data using t-SNE. J. Mach. Learn. Res. **9**, 2579–2605 (2008)

21. Martin, L., et al.: CamemBERT: a tasty French language model. In: ACL (2020)
22. Morris, J.X., Lifland, E., Yoo, J.Y., Grigsby, J., Jin, D., Qi, Y.: TextAttack: a framework for adversarial attacks, data augmentation, and adversarial training in NLP. In: EMNLP (2020)
23. Müller, M., Salathé, M., Kummervold, P.E.: COVID-Twitter-BERT: a natural language processing model to analyse COVID-19 content on Twitter. CoRR abs/2005.07503 (2020)
24. Nguyen, D.Q., Vu, T., Nguyen, A.T.: BERTweet: a pre-trained language model for English Tweets. In: EMNLP (2020)
25. OpenAI: GPT-4 technical report. CoRR abs/2303.08774 (2023)
26. Ouyang, L., et al.: Training language models to follow instructions with human feedback. CoRR abs/2203.02155 (2022)
27. Qiu, X., Sun, T., Xu, Y., Shao, Y., Dai, N., Huang, X.: Pre-trained models for natural language processing: a survey. CoRR abs/2003.08271 (2020)
28. Radford, A., Narasimhan, K., Salimans, T., Sutskever, I., et al.: Improving language understanding by generative pre-training. OpenAI (2018)
29. Radford, A., Wu, J., Child, R., Luan, D., Amodei, D., Sutskever, I., et al.: Language models are unsupervised multitask learners. OpenAI Blog 1(8), 9 (2019)
30. Safaya, A., Abdullatif, M., Yuret, D.: KUISAIL at SemEval-2020 task 12: BERT-CNN for offensive speech identification in social media. In: SemEval (2020)
31. Sanh, V., Debut, L., Chaumond, J., Wolf, T.: DistilBERT, a distilled version of BERT: smaller, faster, cheaper and lighter. CoRR abs/1910.01108 (2019)
32. Seo, M.J., Min, S., Farhadi, A., Hajishirzi, H.: Neural speed reading via Skim-RNN. In: ICLR (2018)
33. Singhal, K., et al.: Large language models encode clinical knowledge. CoRR abs/2212.13138 (2022)
34. Sun, C., Qiu, X., Xu, Y., Huang, X.: How to fine-tune BERT for text classification? In: CCL (2019)
35. Touvron, H., et al.: LLaMA: open and efficient foundation language models. CoRR abs/2302.13971 (2023)
36. Vaswani, A., et al.: Attention is all you need. CoRR abs/1706.03762 (2017)
37. Wei, J., et al.: Chain-of-thought prompting elicits reasoning in large language models. In: NeurIPS (2022)
38. Wolf, T., et al.: HuggingFace's transformers: state-of-the-art natural language processing. CoRR abs/1910.03771 (2019)
39. Wu, D., et al.: U2++: unified two-pass bidirectional end-to-end model for speech recognition. CoRR abs/2106.05642 (2021)
40. Yang, Z., Dai, Z., Yang, Y., Carbonell, J.G., Salakhutdinov, R., Le, Q.V.: XLNet: generalized autoregressive pretraining for language understanding. CoRR abs/1906.08237 (2019)
41. Yogatama, D., Dyer, C., Ling, W., Blunsom, P.: Generative and discriminative text classification with recurrent neural networks. CoRR abs/1703.01898 (2017)
42. Zeng, A., et al.: GLM-130B: an open bilingual pre-trained model. CoRR abs/2210.02414 (2022)
43. Zeng, D., Cao, Z., Neill, D.B.: Artificial intelligence-enabled public health surveillance-from local detection to global epidemic monitoring and control. In: AIM (2021)
44. Zhang, X., et al.: TwHIN-BERT: a socially-enriched pre-trained language model for multilingual tweet representations. CoRR abs/2209.07562 (2022)
45. Zhao, W.X., et al.: A survey of large language models. CoRR abs/2303.18223 (2023)

Prompt-Based Effective Input Reformulation for Legal Case Retrieval

Yanran Tang[✉], Ruihong Qiu, and Xue Li

The University of Queensland, Brisbane, Australia
{yanran.tang,r.qiu}@uq.edu.au, xueli@eecs.uq.edu.au

Abstract. Legal case retrieval plays an important role for legal practitioners to effectively retrieve relevant cases given a query case. Most existing neural legal case retrieval models directly encode the whole legal text of a case to generate a case representation, which is then utilised to conduct a nearest neighbour search for retrieval. Although these straightforward methods have achieved improvement over conventional statistical methods in retrieval accuracy, two significant challenges are identified in this paper: (1) Legal feature alignment: the usage of the whole case text as the input will generally incorporate redundant and noisy information because, from the legal perspective, the determining factor of relevant cases is the alignment of key legal features instead of whole text matching; (2) Legal context preservation: furthermore, since the existing text encoding models usually have an input length limit shorter than the case, the whole case text needs to be truncated or divided into paragraphs, which leads to the loss of the global context of legal information. In this paper, a novel legal case retrieval framework, PromptCase, is proposed to tackle these challenges. Firstly, *legal facts* and *legal issues* are identified and formally defined as the key features facilitating legal case retrieval based on a thorough study of the definition of relevant cases from a legal perspective. Secondly, with the determining legal features, a prompt-based encoding scheme is designed to conduct an effective encoding with language models. Extensive zero-shot experiments have been conducted on two benchmark datasets in legal case retrieval, which demonstrate the superior retrieval effectiveness of the proposed PromptCase. The code has been released on https://github.com/yanran-tang/PromptCase.

Keywords: Legal case retrieval · Information retrieval

1 Introduction

Legal case retrieval (LCR) aims to retrieve relevant cases given a query case, which is important for legal practitioners in the world's two major legal systems, common law and civil law. From a legal perspective, the precedents are the historical cases that are similar to a given case in two determining aspects, legal facts and legal issues. In common law system, the judicial reasons of a judgement are critically based on the relevant cases, which is also called "the

Z. Bao et al. (Eds.): ADC 2023, LNCS 14386, pp. 87–100, 2024.
https://doi.org/10.1007/978-3-031-47843-7_7

doctrine of precedents" [13]. While in civil law system, although the judgement is not necessarily to be based on previously relevant cases, judges and lawyers are still strongly suggested to obtain legal information from these relevant cases[1]. Nowadays, the methods of LCR can be generally divided into two branches, statistical retrieval models [14,26,31] that measure the term frequency similarity between cases and neural LCR models [1,2,6,8,9,16,17,20,28,32,35–37,40] that encode the case into a representation to conduct nearest neighbour search.

Recently, neural LCR models have greatly attracted the research focus for the outstanding text representation ability. Generally, BERT-based legal case retrieval models use the whole text of a case to obtain the representation of the case, which directly determines the retrieval quality and accuracy with the case similarity calculation afterwards [1,8,9,36,37]. Due to the input length limit of BERT-based models, e.g., 512 tokens [11], a case is typically too long to be directly fed into these models with more than 5,000 words in a case. Therefore, most of these methods rely on truncating the case text to a suitable length [16] or dividing the whole text into smaller segments to process the input text [32].

Although these models have achieved competitive progress compared to traditional statistical models in LCR, there are still two challenges remaining: (1) Legal feature alignment: using the whole case text as the input for case representation generation [9,37] will incorporate redundant and noisy information, because from legal perspective, the determining factor of relevant cases is the alignment of legal features instead of whole text matching. When legal practitioners are retrieving relevant cases, they are actually finding "precedents", which refer to a court decision in an earlier case with legal facts and legal issues similar to the current case[2]. Therefore, similar legal facts and legal issues are the key to retrieving relevant cases considering legal theory. (2) Legal context preservation: furthermore, the whole case text is usually truncated [16] or divided into paragraphs [32] due to the input length limit of BERT-based models, which is ineffective in capturing the legal context information. A legal case generally contains more than 5,000 words (in certain situations, easily exceeding 50,000 words), which is much longer than the 512-token input limit for BERT [11], 16k-token for Longformer [7], or 8k-token for ChatGPT [25]. Thus, passively truncating or dividing the case will lead to a significant loss of decisive legal features and case global view among the legal context information.

In light of the above observations, a novel LCR framework called PromptCase is proposed in this paper to tackle these challenges. Firstly, the input representation with two determining legal features, legal facts and legal issues, are proposed to effectively obtain representative legal information in cases instead of using the entire case. According to the formal legal document writing requirements, the format of a case text is well structured so that *legal facts* and *legal issues* can be effectively extracted from the case with sufficient processing steps. Secondly, in order to effectively encode the extracted legal features, a novel prompt-based encoding scheme is proposed to encode these features with language models.

---

[1] https://www.court.gov.cn/zixun-xiangqing-243981.html.
[2] https://www.uscourts.gov/glossary.

Empirical experiments are conducted on two benchmark datasets, LeCaRD [21] and COLIEE [12], which shows that the specific legal features proposed in this paper can represent the legal case more precisely to make a good representation for neural LCR models and effectively improve the performance of neural LCR models. The main contributions of this paper are summarised as follows:

– A PromptCase model is proposed for effective legal case retrieval by tackling the legal feature alignment and legal context preservation challenges.
– Two determining legal features, *legal facts* and *legal issues* are identified and extracted from legal cases with adequate processing procedures.
– A prompt-based encoding scheme is derived to effectively encode the extracted legal features for the widely used language models.
– Extensive experiments conducted on two benchmark datasets demonstrate the state-of-the-art performance of the PromptCase framework.

2 Related Work

2.1 Legal Case Retrieval

LCR is a special type of IR. The methods of IR can be generally divided into two branches, statistical methods [14,26,31] and neural network methods [15,24,27, 30]. Similarly, in LCR there are the same two branches. Statistical models include TF-IDF [14], BM25 [31] and LMIR [26], which rely on the term frequency and inverse document frequency of words to determine the similarity between cases. Neural LCR models rely on encoding the case using the language models [10,11, 19,23]. With the increasing amount of online legal information and users' legal information needs, many neural LCR models [1,2,6,8,9,16,17,20,28,32,33,35–37,39] are conducted to bridge the information gap by capturing domain-specific and personal needs. Law2Vec [9] is a legal language model that pre-trains on a large legal corpus. Lawformer [37] focuses on combining three types of attention mechanisms to get the context of long legal cases. BERT-PLI [32] calculates the similarity between two paragraphs of cases text to tackle the lengthy problem of legal cases. SAILER [16] is a pre-trained language model that selects the reasoning, decision and fact sections in the cases to train the encoder and uses the fact section to be the input of the encoder to get the case representation.

2.2 Input Reformulation in Neural Legal Case Retrieval

Input reformulation plays an important role in neural LCR because a case is hard to fit into the model directly due to the length limit [3–5,16,34,38]. Askari et al. [5] and LeiBi [4] both propose to combine lexical and neural network methods to get a summary of a legal case as the case representation. LEVEN [38] utilises the frequency of legal events to reformulate the case input. Both CL4LJP [40] and QAjudge [42] intuitively reformulate the case input with only the fact instead of the whole case. IOT-Match [39] reformulates the case input based on legal rationales. BERT-PLI [32] divides the case input into the paragraph-level interaction between query and candidate cases. Liu et al. [17,18] proposes to use the conversational search paradigm to reformulate the query case.

3 Preliminary

3.1 Task Definition

In legal case retrieval, given a query case q, and a set of n candidate cases, denoted as $\mathcal{D} = \{d_1, d_2, ..., d_n\}$, the task is to retrieve a set of relevant cases $\mathcal{D}^* = \{d_i^* | d_i^* \in \mathcal{D} \wedge relevant(d_i^*, q)\}$ from $\mathcal{D}$, where $relevant(d_i^*, q)$ denotes that d_i^* is a relevant case of the query case q. From a legal perspective, the relevant cases are called precedents, which are the historical cases with legal facts and legal issues similar to the given query case. Specifically, given a query case, the relevant cases in COLIEE2023 dataset are the cases referred by the query case. While in LeCaRD dataset, cases having similar key facts and key circumstances to the query case are labelled as relevant cases by legal experts.

3.2 Input Reformulation in Neural Legal Case Retrieval

Existing neural LCR models generally use the full case as the input to the model with different input reformulation methods to deal with the overly long cases.

BERT-PLI [32] reformulates the case input into the paragraph-level interaction vector between the query and candidate cases as below:

$$\mathbf{e}_{(q_i,d_j)} = \text{BERT}([\text{CLS}]; q_i; [\text{SEP}]; d_j; [\text{SEP}]), \tag{1}$$

where ";" denotes the concatenation function, and [CLS] and [SEP] are two special tokens for BERT to denote the input's beginning and separation. q_i and d_j are the i-th paragraph and j-th paragraph of case q and d.

SAILER [16] uses the fact section of cases as the input of a finetuned BERT:

$$\mathbf{e}_q = \text{BERT}([\text{CLS}]; q_{(\text{fact})}; [\text{SEP}]), \quad \mathbf{e}_d = \text{BERT}([\text{CLS}]; d_{(\text{fact})}; [\text{SEP}]), \tag{2}$$

where $q_{(\text{fact})}$ and $d_{(\text{fact})}$ are the fact of the query case and the document case respectively. The fact is assumed to be located in the most front and if the length of the fact is longer than 512 tokens, the first 512 tokens of the case will be used.

BM25Inject [3] concatenates the BM25 score of the query case and the document case into the input of BERT-based cross-encoder:

$$s_{(q,d)} = \text{BERT}([\text{CLS}]; q; [\text{SEP}]; s_{\text{BM25}_{(q,d)}}; [\text{SEP}]; d; [\text{SEP}]), \tag{3}$$

where $s_{\text{BM25}_{(q,d)}}$ is the BM25 score scalar of the query case q and the candidate d and the final semantic similarity is $s_{(q,d)}$.

4 Method

In this section, the PromptCase framework will be introduced. In Sect. 4.1, two determining legal features are extracted. A prompt-based method utilising these legal features will be detailed in Sect. 4.2. The measurement of case similarity will be introduced in Sect. 4.3. The overview of PromptCase is shown in Fig. 1.

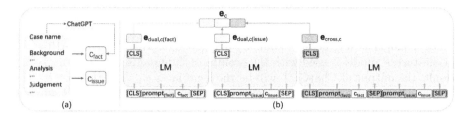

Fig. 1. The framework of PromptCase. LM means a language model, e.g., BERT. The final output of the [CLS] token is the representation embedding of a legal fact, a legal issue or a case. (a) The process of legal facts and legal issues extraction. When legal facts are not explicitly available, ChatGPT is applied to generate a case summary as legal facts. (b) Dual and cross encoding with prompt of a case.

Lafond v. Muskeg Lake Cree Na3on (2008), 330 F.T.R. 60 (FC)

Background
On February 13, 2006, the applicant was elected as a councillor to the MLCN Band Council
for a term of three years. The respondent Band is located in the province of Saskatchewan...

Analysis
Does this Court have jurisdiction over the present application? In order to determine the jurisdiction of the Federal Court in this matter, it is imperative to...
Indeed this was recognized by the Federal Court of Appeal in FRAGMENT_SUPPRESSED,
where it held that FRAGMENT_SUPPRESSED. I agree that the Chief does have inherent...

Order
For these reasons, the application for judicial review of Chief Ledoux's decision will be
allowed.

(a) COLIEE dataset (common law)

李月航容留他人吸毒一案 (Case name)

案件基本情况 (Background)
长乐市人民检察院指控：1、2017年9月25日22时许，被告人李月航在其租住的长乐市某街道某村某公寓房间内，容留王某吸食甲基苯丙胺（俗称"冰毒"）。2、2017年10月19日晚，被告人李月航在其租住的长乐市某街道某村某公寓房间内，容留王某...**经审理查明**：1、2017年9月25日22时许，被告人李月航在其租住的长...

裁判分析过程 (Analysis)
本院认为，被告人李月航多次为他人吸食毒品提供场所，其行为已构成容留他人吸毒罪。长乐市人民检察院指控的罪名成立，应依法追究被告人李月航的刑事责任。被告人李月航因涉嫌吸毒被公安机关抓获，主动向公安机关供述了尚未被掌握的其容留他人吸毒的犯罪事实，视为自动投案，系自首，依法可从轻处罚；被告人李月航被公安...

判决结果 (Judgement)
被告人李月航犯容留他人吸毒罪，判处拘役五个月，并处罚金人民币三千元。

(b) LeCaRD dataset (civil law)

Fig. 2. Example of case documents

4.1 Extraction of Legal Facts and Legal Issues

This section describes the extraction of legal facts and legal issues from cases as shown in Fig. 1(a) to overcome the legal feature alignment challenge. For common law (COLIEE dataset) or civil law (LeCaRD dataset) respectively, a case often has a relatively fixed writing style, which includes four basic parts as in Fig. 2. The first part is the case name with basic information about the case. The second part is the "Background" of the case demonstrating detailed information about the case. The third part is "Analysis" describing the reasons why the judges make the final decision. The final part called "Order" or "Judgement", is the judgement of the case. Such a clear and general structure of legal cases provides access to locate and extract legal facts and legal issues from extremely long cases.

Legal Facts. Legal fact is a fundamental part that describes the "who, when, what, where and why" in legal cases. Firstly, in the COLIEE2023 dataset, the detailed process of a case is generally written in the background part, which is often more than thousands of words that will exceed the input limit of BERT-based models. In order to get an abstract yet accurate legal facts of cases, the ChatGPT [25] is used to get the summary of legal facts. The ChatGPT API with "gpt-3.5-turbo" model is used with the prompt of "Summarise in 50 words: ". As a result, the output of ChatGPT will be the legal facts $c_{(\text{fact})}$ of the case c.

Secondly, in LeCaRD, the fact section is a separate and brief part that can be found in "Background", beginning with a description of "After the trial, it was found out that: " in Chinese (the bold Chinese words "经审理查明:" in the "Background" part in Fig. 2(b)). Thus, in LeCaRD, the legal facts $c_{(\text{fact})}$ of the case c are extracted directly based on the understanding of a legal case.

Legal Issues. The definition of "issue" in legal domain is "a critical feature that focuses on the dispute points between the parties in the case."[3] In case documents of common law, the legal issues are located in the "Analysis" part, which is given by the judges to settle the disputes between the parties with legal reasons. To have convincing reasons, the judges will list the relevant precedents' facts, issues or judgements in this part to support the judges' opinions. Specifically, as shown in Fig. 2(a), there are words replaced by placeholders with special terms in cases of the COLIEE2023 dataset, such as "FRAGMENT_SUPPRESSED". The original words for these placeholders are the case name of a precedent. These placeholders are for the task of legal case retrieval, which is to find the precedents being referred in the placeholder. Thus, for the COLIEE dataset, all of the sentences with placeholders will be selected as the legal issues $c_{(\text{issue})}$ of the case c.

Compared to common law, the judges in the civil law system often make their judgements according to the legal articles written in the acts while the judges of the common law system have the compulsory responsibility to refer the precedents to support their final decisions. And there is also no specific part for settling legal issues in the cases of civil law. After a thorough study of the cases from LeCaRD dataset under the civil law system, it is found that legal issues often appear in the case as the name of charges, such as "murder". Therefore, the names of charges in Chinese criminal law are collected and saved as a list of charges. For every case (queries and candidates) in LeCaRD, the full text of a case will be used to find the charges that appear both in the case and the list of charges. Finally, all of the found charges are the legal issues $c_{(\text{issue})}$ of the case c.

4.2 Prompt-Based Case Encoding

After extracting legal facts and legal issues, a prompt-based case encoding method is developed in this section to tackle the legal context preservation challenge.

Prompt Template. With the recent advances of prompt, the capability of prompting a language model is impressive in understanding the context information of a task. To enable the language models to capture the global context

---

[3] https://www.uscourts.gov/glossary.

of legal information, the prompt templates of "Legal facts:" ("法律事实:" in Chinese) and "Legal issues:" ("法律纠纷:" in Chinese) will be added to the beginning of the legal facts and legal issues texts and fed into the language model together. For every legal case in COLIEE2023 and LeCaRD datasets, the prompt template is formulated as below:

$$\text{prompt}_{(\text{fact})} = \text{"Legal facts:"}, \quad \text{prompt}_{(\text{issue})} = \text{"Legal issues:"}. \tag{4}$$

Dual Encoding with Prompt. To avoid the undesired cross-effect between legal facts and legal issues, the legal facts with prompt and legal issues with prompt will be fed into the BERT-based encoder separately to get the individual legal facts embedding $\mathbf{e}_{\text{dual},c_{(\text{fact})}}$ and legal issues embedding $\mathbf{e}_{\text{dual},c_{(\text{issue})}}$. The encoding process can be denoted as the following equations:

$$\begin{aligned} \mathbf{e}_{\text{dual},c_{(\text{fact})}} &= \text{LM}([\text{CLS}]; \text{prompt}_{(\text{fact})}; c_{(\text{fact})}; [\text{SEP}]), \\ \mathbf{e}_{\text{dual},c_{(\text{issue})}} &= \text{LM}([\text{CLS}]; \text{prompt}_{(\text{issue})}; c_{(\text{issue})}; [\text{SEP}]), \end{aligned} \tag{5}$$

where $\mathbf{e}_{\text{dual},c_{(\text{fact})}}$ and $\mathbf{e}_{\text{dual},c_{(\text{issue})}}$ are both the embedding of the final hidden state of the [CLS] token of the language model (LM), e.g., BERT.

Cross Encoding with Prompt. On the contrary, to obtain the deeper interactions between legal facts and legal issues, the cross encoding method is also being conducted as the following equations:

$$\mathbf{e}_{\text{cross},c} = \text{LM}([\text{CLS}]; \text{prompt}_{(\text{fact})}; c_{(\text{fact})}; [\text{SEP}]; \text{prompt}_{(\text{issue})}; c_{(\text{issue})}; [\text{SEP}]). \tag{6}$$

where $\mathbf{e}_{\text{cross},c}$ is the output embedding of the [CLS] token of LM.

Case Representation To obtain both the original and interaction information of legal facts and legal issues, the case representation will be the concatenation of the $\mathbf{e}_{\text{dual},c_{(\text{fact})}}$, $\mathbf{e}_{\text{dual},c_{(\text{issue})}}$, and $\mathbf{e}_{\text{cross},c}$ as the following equations:

$$\mathbf{e}_c = \mathbf{e}_{\text{dual},c_{(\text{fact})}}; \mathbf{e}_{\text{dual},c_{(\text{issue})}}; \mathbf{e}_{\text{cross},c}. \tag{7}$$

4.3 Case Similarity

Similar to traditional IR tasks, the dot product (denoted as $(\cdot)$) is used to measure the semantic similarity between two cases. Given the case representation $\mathbf{e}_q$ and $\mathbf{e}_d$ of case q and candidate case d generated by PromptCase, the similarity score $s_{(q,d)}$ is calculated as:

$$s_{(q,d)} = \mathbf{e}_q \cdot \mathbf{e}_d. \tag{8}$$

5   Experiments

5.1   Setup

Datasets. To evaluate the proposed PromptCase, the experiments are conducted on the following LCR datasets with summarised statistics in Table 1.

Table 1. Statistics of LeCaRD and COLIEE2023 datasets.

Datasets	LeCaRD	COLIEE2023
Language	Chinese	English
Avg. length/case	8,275	5,566
Largest length of cases	99,163	61,965
Avg. relevant cases/query	10.33	2.69

LeCaRD [21]. LeCaRD is a legal case retrieval dataset, where the cases are from the supreme court of China, a civil law system country. It contains 107 queries and over 43,000 candidate cases. For each query, there is a candidate pool of 100 cases. The evaluation of LeCaRD is based on the binary golden label for a more restrict requirement[4].

COLIEE2023 [12][5]. COLIEE2023 is a dataset from Competition on Legal Information Extraction/Entailment (COLIEE) 2023, where cases are from the federal court of Canada with common law system. Given a query case, relevant cases are retrieved from the entire candidate pool. To avoid the data leakage problem of pre-trained models, only the testing set of COLIEE2023 is used.

Metrics. For both datasets, precision (P), recall (R), Micro F1 (Mi-F1), Macro F1 (Ma-F1), Mean Reciprocal Rank (MRR), Mean Average Precision (MAP) and normalized discounted cumulative gain (NDCG) are used. For both LeCaRD and COLIEE2023 datasets, top 5 ranking results are evaluated by following previous methods [12,16,21]. All metrics are the higher the better.

Baselines. The following baselines are chosen for comparison:

- **BM25** [31] is a statistical retrieval model using the term frequency and inverse document frequency, which is still a strong baseline.
- **BERT** [11] is a strong bi-directional transformer encoder in language tasks. For LeCaRD in Chinese, the "uer/sbert-base-chinese-nli" [41] model is used, while for COLIEE2023 in English, the "bert-base-uncased" [11] model is used.
- **Lawformer** [37] is pre-trained on Chinese legal corpus and focuses on long documents processing.
- **LEGAL-BERT** [8] is pre-trained on a large English legal corpus and achieves state-of-the-art results in different legal understanding tasks.
- **MonoT5** [23] is a pre-trained sequence-to-sequence model focuses on document ranking task using the powerful T5 model [29].
- **SAILER** [16] is a structure-aware pre-trained model that achieves state-of-the-art performance on both datasets. Two-stage usage of SAILER with BM25 is evaluated as well.

---

[4] https://github.com/myx666/LeCaRD#golden_labelsjson.
[5] https://sites.ualberta.ca/~rabelo/COLIEE2023/.

BERT-PLI [32] is not compared since its paragraph-level interaction is not applicable to legal facts and legal issues. BM25Inject [3] is not compared because its cross encoding between cases is not extendable in our scenario.

Implementation. The French text in COLIEE2023 is removed. The two-stage method is based on the top 10 retrieved cases by BM25 model. All experiments are in a zero-shot manner without training, except that the SAILER model for COLIEE2023 is pre-trained on the COLIEE2023 training set. The experiment of BM25 model with PromptCase reformulated input utilises the original text, legal facts, legal issues and prompt together.

5.2   Overall Performance

In this section, the PromptCase is evaluated by being integrated into the baselines. The results are presented in Table 2 for LeCaRD and Table 3 for COLIEE2023.

Overall, the PromptCase can steadily improve the performances of all baselines by a large margin. With the state-of-the-art pre-trained SAILER model in legal domain, PromptCase significantly boosts the retrieval performance for both one and two stage manners with a proper reformulation of case input. For the traditional method BM25, the performance of using PromptCase is better than with the whole case as input. The improved performance shows that the reformulated input can capture the determining legal features with proper emphasis on the term frequency without being biased by the long and noisy case texts. For the pretrained BERT with full case as input, the performances on both datasets are worse than BM25 and SAILER. However, BERT+PromptCase outperforms BM25+PromptCase and the SAILER baseline model on LeCaRD, which indicates that BERT is a semantic LM that can better understand and represent a case using legal features semantics. While the term frequency cannot fully take advantage of the semantics in legal facts and legal issues, which also limits

Table 2. Overall performance on LeCaRD (%).

Methods	LeCaRD@5						
	P@5	R@5	Mi-F1	Ma-F1	MRR@5	MAP	NDCG@5
BM25	40.0	19.2	26.0	30.5	58.3	48.5	45.9
+PromptCase	41.3	19.9	26.8	31.7	60.6	58.8	65.2
BERT	38.7	18.6	25.1	26.7	57.4	54.3	61.0
+PromptCase	46.2	22.2	30.0	35.4	64.4	61.2	67.9
Lawformer	29.0	13.9	18.8	19.5	43.6	41.9	48.2
+PromptCase	38.9	18.7	25.3	30.7	62.0	59.7	64.0
SAILER	46.7	22.5	30.4	37.1	67.9	65.4	70.1
+PromptCase	51.6	24.8	33.5	43.0	71.1	67.6	74.2
Two-stage SAILER	47.8	23.0	31.1	36.1	67.3	64.4	70.6
+PromptCase	51.0	24.6	33.2	38.7	70.7	67.9	73.5

Table 3. Overall performance on COLIEE (%).

Methods	COLIEE2023						
	P@5	R@5	Mi-F1	Ma-F1	MRR@5	MAP	NDCG@5
BM25	16.5	30.6	21.4	22.2	23.1	20.4	23.7
+PromptCase	17.0	31.5	22.1	23.0	24.2	21.6	24.4
BERT	2.07	3.84	2.69	2.57	5.51	5.48	6.25
+PromptCase	2.38	4.42	3.10	3.02	6.33	6.25	7.21
LEGAL-BERT	4.64	8.61	6.03	6.03	11.4	11.3	13.6
+PromptCase	4.83	8.96	6.28	6.44	13.4	13.4	15.5
MonoT5	0.38	0.70	0.49	0.47	1.17	1.33	0.61
+PromptCase	0.56	1.05	0.73	0.72	1.63	1.43	0.89
SAILER	12.8	23.7	16.6	17.0	25.9	25.3	29.3
+PromptCase	16.0	29.7	20.8	21.5	32.7	32.0	36.2
Two-stage SAILER	19.6	32.6	24.5	23.5	37.3	36.1	40.8
+PromptCase	21.8	36.3	27.2	26.5	39.9	38.7	44.0

Table 4. Ablation study. Leg-Feat denotes legal features. (%)

Prompt	Leg-Feat	LeCaRD							COLIEE2023						
		P@5	R@5	Mi-F1	Ma-F1	MRR@5	MAP	NDCG@5	P@5	R@5	Mi-F1	Ma-F1	MRR@5	MAP	NDCG@5
✗	✗	46.7	22.5	30.4	37.1	67.9	65.4	70.1	12.8	23.7	16.6	17.0	25.9	25.3	29.3
✓	✗	46.5	22.4	30.2	36.9	68.6	65.8	70.5	12.8	23.7	16.6	17.0	25.4	24.8	28.5
✗	✓	52.0	25.0	33.8	43.3	69.4	66.2	72.9	15.9	29.5	20.6	21.3	32.6	31.5	35.8
✓	✓	51.6	24.8	33.5	43.0	71.1	67.6	74.2	16.0	29.7	20.8	21.5	32.7	32.0	36.2

the performance of two-stage SAILER on LeCaRD with or without Prompt-Case compared with one-stage SAILER. Lawformer and LEGAL-BERT are two neural LCR models pre-trained on Chinese and English respectively, whose performances are improved significantly with PromptCase. The performance of MonoT5 is the worst in COLIEE2023 dataset, possibly because MonoT5 is pre-trained for text-to-text tasks different from retrieval tasks. Comparing the results on these two datasets, the improvement with PromptCase on LeCaRD is more obvious than on COLIEE2023. The possible reason is the different definitions of relevance in these datasets. For LeCaRD, the relevant cases are defined by legal experts, which is easier for models to identify. While for COLIEE2023, the relevant cases are referred cases by the query case, which are a subset of all relevant cases and not a golden label for relevance, leading to an inferior performance.

5.3 Ablation Study

The ablation study is conducted to verify the effectiveness of the two main components of PromptCase, the legal features and the prompt encoding scheme. The SAILER [16] model is used as the base model in these experiments since SAILER is a state-of-the-art pre-trained model with English and Chinese on both datasets. Specifically, the prompt templates of the experiment without legal features are reformulated as "Legal facts and legal issues:" in English and "法律事实和法律纠纷:" in Chinese for COLIEE2023 and LeCaRD respectively.

As shown in Table 4, the reformulated input with prompt and legal features can significantly improve the performance compared with other variants for both datasets. The legal features alone can largely increase the retrieval performance. While only using prompt encoding, the performance is not improved since there is no specific legal feature used with the prompt.

5.4 Effectiveness of Legal Features

To verify the effectiveness of legal features, experiments are conducted using SAILER with: no legal features, only legal facts, only legal issues and both legal facts and legal issues. For no legal features, the second result in Table 4 is reused.

As shown in Table 5, the reformulated input with both legal facts and legal issues achieves the best performance in the effectiveness of legal features experiments, which indicates the challenge of legal feature alignment is well resovled. For LeCaRD, the performance of only using legal facts is better than only using

Table 5. Effectiveness of legal facts (Facts) and legal issues (Issues). (%)

Facts	Issues	LeCaRD							COLIEE2023						
		P@5	R@5	Mi-F1	Ma-F1	MRR@5	MAP	NDCG@5	P@5	R@5	Mi-F1	Ma-F1	MRR@5	MAP	NDCG@5
✗	✗	43.0	20.7	27.9	34.0	63.5	51.7	51.7	12.8	23.7	16.6	17.0	25.4	24.8	28.5
✓	✗	47.3	22.8	30.7	37.4	66.8	63.6	70.1	12.7	23.5	16.5	17.2	24.7	24.3	27.7
✗	✓	41.3	19.9	26.8	32.9	57.6	54.7	61.7	13.4	24.8	17.4	17.8	29.1	28.3	31.8
✓	✓	51.6	24.8	33.5	43.0	71.1	67.6	74.2	16.0	29.7	20.8	21.5	32.7	32.0	36.2

Table 6. Effectiveness of different prompts. Instructive (IT): **A**: "Legal facts:/Legal issues:"; **B**: "The following is legal facts:/The following is legal issues:";**C**: "The judge think:"; Misleading (ML): **D**: "This case is related to $<randomly sample one issue>:"; **E**: "Legal facts of this case is $<randomly sample one issue>:/Legal issues of this case is $<randomly sample one issue>:"; Irrelevant (IR): **F**: "Let's look:"; **G**: "ADC is a database conference:" and **NA**: no prompt is used.

		LeCaRD							COLIEE2023						
		P@5	R@5	Mi-F1	Ma-F1	MRR@5	MAP	NDCG@5	P@5	R@5	Mi-F1	Ma-F1	MRR@5	MAP	NDCG@5
	NA	52.0	25.0	33.8	43.3	69.4	66.2	72.9	15.9	29.5	20.6	21.3	32.6	31.5	35.8
IT	A	51.6	24.8	33.5	43.0	71.1	67.6	74.2	16.0	29.7	20.8	21.5	32.7	32.0	36.2
	B	51.4	24.7	33.3	42.7	71.0	67.4	74.0	15.9	29.5	20.6	21.4	32.8	32.0	36.0
	C	51.8	24.9	33.6	43.5	70.1	67.9	74.1	15.7	29.1	20.4	21.1	32.0	31.3	35.8
ML	D	42.8	20.6	27.8	30.8	58.1	56.0	62.7	14.5	26.9	18.8	19.6	28.7	27.8	31.9
	E	42.6	20.5	27.7	29.7	60.0	56.8	62.7	15.1	28.1	19.6	20.5	29.5	29.0	33.4
IR	F	51.4	24.7	33.4	42.9	69.3	66.5	72.9	15.6	29.0	20.3	21.1	32.4	31.4	35.8
	G	51.6	24.8	33.5	42.6	69.9	67.6	73.7	15.2	28.2	19.7	20.5	32.1	31.2	35.3

legal issues, while it is opposite in COLIEE2023 that only using legal issues is better than only using legal facts. This opposite phenomenon also appears in the experiments of ablation study. The different performances of datasets could be due to the different case structures in different legal systems, which may cause the different focuses of prompt and legal features.

5.5 Effectiveness of Prompt

In this experiment, the effectiveness of Prompt is investigated with different prompt templates using SAILER. The prompt templates are widely chosen from instructive, misleading and irrelevant categories, which are detailed in Table 6.

As shown in Table 6, seven different prompt templates are selected to evaluate the effectiveness of prompts, which can be classified into three categories: instructive (correct legal prompts), misleading (wrongful legal prompts) and irrelevant (correct non-legal prompts). The performances of the experiments indicate that instructive prompts can improve performance by giving correct and informative indications of the global view of legal context. On the contrary, misleading prompts negatively impact the case retrieval accuracy. Compared with the other categories of prompts, irrelevant prompts slightly hurts the performance by adding irrelevant noisy information to the input.

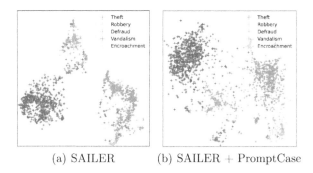

(a) SAILER   (b) SAILER + PromptCase

Fig. 3. Visulisation of case encodings with and without PromptCase for LeCaRD.

5.6   Visualisation Analysis

To further prove the effectiveness of PromptCase input reformulation method, t-SNE [22] is used to visualise cases embeddings with and without PromptCase. Cases from five legally similar and difficult to distinguish charges of LeCaRD are selected to visualise in Fig. 3, including *theft, robbery, defraud, vandalism,* and *encroachment*. All selected case embeddings are generated by the zero-shot SAILER model. As shown in Fig. 3(a), case embeddings generated by SAILER are classified into three clusters. Moreover, vandalism cases are wrongfully classified as robbery cases and encroachment cases are wrongfully classified as defraud cases. Compared with SAILER, adding PromptCase (as shown in Fig. 3(b)) makes cases embeddings evenly distributed as five clusters corresponding to five charges, which indicates the powerful discriminative ability and the ability to learn legal context information of PromptCase framework.

6   Conclusion

This paper identifies the challenges in the existing LCR models about legal feature alignment and legal context preservation. To tackle these challenges, a novel legal case retrieval framework called PromptCase is introduced. In PromptCase, **legal facts** and **legal issues** are effectively extracted from the original case, which is further encoded with a prompt-based schema to generate an informative case representation. Extensive experiments are conducted on two benchmark datasets, which successfully demonstrate the superiority of PromptCase by achieving the best performance compared with state-of-the-art baselines.

Acknowledgements. The work is supported by Australian Research Council CE200100025.

References

1. Abolghasemi, A., Verberne, S., Azzopardi, L.: Improving BERT-based query-by-document retrieval with multi-task optimization. In: Hagen, M., et al. (eds.) ECIR 2022. LNCS, vol. 13186, pp. 3–12. Springer, Cham (2022). https://doi.org/10.1007/978-3-030-99739-7_1

2. Althammer, S., Askari, A., Verberne, S., Hanbury, A.: DoSSIER@COLIEE 2021: leveraging dense retrieval and summarization-based re-ranking for case law retrieval. CoRR abs/2108.03937 (2021)
3. Askari, A., Abolghasemi, A., Pasi, G., Kraaij, W., Verberne, S.: Injecting the BM25 score as text improves BERT-based re-rankers. In: Kamps, J., et al. (eds.) ECIR 2023. LNCS, vol. 13980, pp. 66–83. Springer, Cham (2023). https://doi.org/10.1007/978-3-031-28244-7_5
4. Askari, A., Peikos, G., Pasi, G., Verberne, S.: LeiBi@COLIEE 2022: aggregating tuned lexical models with a cluster-driven BERT-based model for case law retrieval. CoRR abs/2205.13351 (2022)
5. Askari, A., Verberne, S.: Combining lexical and neural retrieval with longformer-based summarization for effective case law retrieval. In: DESIRES. CEUR (2021)
6. Askari, A., Verberne, S., Abolghasemi, A., Kraaij, W., Pasi, G.: Retrieval for extremely long queries and documents with RPRS: a highly efficient and effective transformer-based re-ranker. CoRR abs/2303.01200 (2023)
7. Beltagy, I., Peters, M.E., Cohan, A.: Longformer: the long-document transformer. CoRR abs/2004.05150 (2020)
8. Chalkidis, I., Fergadiotis, M., Malakasiotis, P., Aletras, N., Androutsopoulos, I.: LEGAL-BERT: the muppets straight out of law school. CoRR abs/2010.02559 (2020)
9. Chalkidis, I., Kampas, D.: Deep learning in law: early adaptation and legal word embeddings trained on large corpora. Artif. Intell. Law **27**(2), 171–198 (2019). https://doi.org/10.1007/s10506-018-9238-9
10. Dai, Z., Callan, J.: Context-aware sentence/passage term importance estimation for first stage retrieval. CoRR abs/1910.10687 (2019)
11. Devlin, J., Chang, M., Lee, K., Toutanova, K.: BERT: pre-training of deep bidirectional transformers for language understanding. In: NAACL-HLT (2019)
12. Goebel, R., et al.: Competition on legal information extraction/entailment (COLIEE) (2023)
13. Harris, B.: Final appellate courts overruling their own "wrong" precedents: the ongoing search for principle. Law Q. Rev. **118**(7), 408–427 (2002)
14. Jones, K.S.: A statistical interpretation of term specificity and its application in retrieval. J. Documentation **60**(5), 493–502 (2004)
15. Khattab, O., Zaharia, M.: ColBERT: efficient and effective passage search via contextualized late interaction over BERT. In: SIGIR (2020)
16. Li, H., et al.: SAILER: structure-aware pre-trained language model for legal case retrieval. CoRR abs/2304.11370 (2023)
17. Liu, B., et al.: Investigating conversational agent action in legal case retrieval. In: Kamps, J., et al. (eds.) ECIR 2023. LNCS, vol. 13980, pp. 622–635. Springer, Cham (2023). https://doi.org/10.1007/978-3-031-28244-7_39
18. Liu, B., et al.: Query generation and buffer mechanism: towards a better conversational agent for legal case retrieval. Inf. Process. Manag. **59**(5), 103051 (2022)
19. Liu, Y., et al.: RoBERTa: a robustly optimized BERT pretraining approach. CoRR abs/1907.11692 (2019)
20. Ma, Y., et al.: Incorporating retrieval information into the truncation of ranking lists for better legal search. In: SIGIR (2022)
21. Ma, Y., et al.: LeCaRD: a legal case retrieval dataset for Chinese law system. In: SIGIR (2021)
22. van der Maaten, L., Hinton, G.: Visualizing data using t-SNE. J. Mach. Learn. Res. **9**, 2579–2605 (2008)

23. Nogueira, R., Jiang, Z., Pradeep, R., Lin, J.: Document ranking with a pretrained sequence-to-sequence model. In: EMNLP (2020)

24. Nogueira, R.F., Yang, W., Lin, J., Cho, K.: Document expansion by query prediction. CoRR abs/1904.08375 (2019)

25. OpenAI: GPT-3.5-turbo (2021). https://openai.com/

26. Ponte, J.M., Croft, W.B.: A language modeling approach to information retrieval. In: SIGIR (2017)

27. Qiao, Y., Xiong, C., Liu, Z., Liu, Z.: Understanding the behaviors of BERT in ranking. CoRR abs/1904.07531 (2019)

28. Rabelo, J., Kim, M., Goebel, R.: Semantic-based classification of relevant case law. In: Takama, Y., Yada, K., Satoh, K., Arai, S. (eds.) JSAI-isAI 2022. LNAI, vol. 13859, pp. 84–95. Springer, Cham (2022). https://doi.org/10.1007/978-3-031-29168-5_6

29. Raffel, C., et al.: Exploring the limits of transfer learning with a unified text-to-text transformer. J. Mach. Learn. Res. **21**(1), 5485–5551 (2020)

30. Reimers, N., Gurevych, I.: Sentence-BERT: sentence embeddings using Siamese BERT-networks. In: EMNLP-IJCNLP (2019)

31. Robertson, S.E., Walker, S.: Some simple effective approximations to the 2-Poisson model for probabilistic weighted retrieval. In: Croft, B.W., van Rijsbergen, C.J. (eds.) SIGIR 1994, pp. 232–241. Springer, London (1994). https://doi.org/10.1007/978-1-4471-2099-5_24

32. Shao, Y., et al.: BERT-PLI: modeling paragraph-level interactions for legal case retrieval. In: IJCAI (2020)

33. Sun, Z., Xu, J., Zhang, X., Dong, Z., Wen, J.: Law article-enhanced legal case matching: a model-agnostic causal learning approach. CoRR abs/2210.11012 (2022)

34. Tran, V.D., Nguyen, M.L., Satoh, K.: Building legal case retrieval systems with lexical matching and summarization using a pre-trained phrase scoring model. In: ICAIL (2019)

35. Vuong, T., Nguyen, H., Nguyen, T., Nguyen, H., Nguyen, T., Nguyen, H.: NOWJ at COLIEE 2023 - multi-task and ensemble approaches in legal information processing. CoRR abs/2306.04903 (2023)

36. Wang, Z.: Legal element-oriented modeling with multi-view contrastive learning for legal case retrieval. In: IJCNN (2022)

37. Xiao, C., Hu, X., Liu, Z., Tu, C., Sun, M.: Lawformer: a pre-trained language model for Chinese legal long documents. AI Open **2**, 79–84 (2021)

38. Yao, F., et al.: LEVEN: a large-scale Chinese legal event detection dataset. In: ACL (2022)

39. Yu, W., Sun, Z., Xu, J., Dong, Z., Chen, X., Xu, H., Wen, J.: Explainable legal case matching via inverse optimal transport-based rationale extraction. In: SIGIR (2022)

40. Zhang, H., Dou, Z., Zhu, Y., Wen, J.R.: Contrastive learning for legal judgment prediction. ACM Trans. Inf. Syst. **41**(4), 25 (2023)

41. Zhao, Z., et al.: UER: an open-source toolkit for pre-training models. In: EMNLP-IJCNLP (2019)

42. Zhong, H., Wang, Y., Tu, C., Zhang, T., Liu, Z., Sun, M.: Iteratively questioning and answering for interpretable legal judgment prediction. In: AAAI (2020)

Surveying the Landscape: Compound Methods for Aspect-Based Sentiment Analysis

Marwah Alharbi⬤, Jiao Yin(✉)⬤, and Hua Wang⬤

Institute for Sustainable Industries and Liveable Cities, Victoria University,
Melbourne, VIC 3011, Australia
marwah.alharbi@live.vu.edu.au, {jiao.yin,hua.wang}@vu.edu.au

Abstract. Aspect-based sentiment Analysis (ABSA) has emerged as a
critical research area in natural language processing, facilitating a deeper
understanding of user opinions and sentiments expressed in text. This
review article comprehensively surveys the landscape of deep learning
approaches in ABSA, focusing on triplet and quadruplet ABSA. We delve
into the significance of ABSA in diverse domains and present an overview
of the critical components and challenges associated with compound
ABSA tasks. The review analyzes state-of-the-art models, encompassing pipeline-based and generative-based solutions. Comparative analysis
demonstrates the advantages and limitations of these approaches, including their performance, generalizability, and efficiency. Additionally, we
explore the domains and datasets used in ABSA research and highlight
the crucial factors contributing to ABSA task solutions' effectiveness.
This comprehensive review highlights current challenges and fosters further advancements in compound ABSA tasks.

Keywords: Aspect-Based Sentiment Analysis · Deep Learning · User
Generated Content

1 Introduction

In today's digital age, consumers rely heavily on online reviews before purchasing. With millions of users sharing opinions and experiences on platforms like
Twitter, Facebook, and Instagram, it becomes challenging for businesses to analyze all the data manually [18,30]. User-generated content (UGC) has attracted
the attention of researchers in recent years due to its potential to provide information on consumer behaviour [10]. UGC is content created by end users without
a direct link to financial gain or commercial interest, usually on an online platform and shared with others through social media or websites [19]. The ubiquity

We would like to express our sincere gratitude to the Saudi Arabian Cultural Mission in
Australia and the Ministry of Education (Saudi Arabia) for their unwavering support
and financial assistance, which made this work possible.

Z. Bao et al. (Eds.): ADC 2023, LNCS 14386, pp. 101–115, 2024.
https://doi.org/10.1007/978-3-031-47843-7_8

of UGC has steadily grown since the emergence of social media networks and websites that enable users to share their experiences and opinions [28]. UGC can provide valuable insights into customer sentiment, preferences, and loyalty in an increasingly crowded marketplace [33]. This explosive growth in UGC has created an unprecedented opportunity for Sentiment Analysis (SA) research, which analyses text data to discover its underlying emotional tone and sentiment [18].

Sentiment analysis (SA), also known as opinion mining, is a computational approach that uses natural language processing, text analysis, and machine learning techniques to determine the sentiment expressed in a text [26]. The main goal of SA is to identify and quantify the sentiment polarity of the text, whether it is positive, negative, neutral, or sometimes more nuanced emotions like joy, sadness, or anger. SA finds wide applications in various domains, including social media monitoring, customer feedback analysis, market research, and brand reputation management. By automating the sentiment analysis process, businesses and organizations can gain valuable insights into public opinions, identify trends, and make data-driven decisions to enhance customer satisfaction and improve their products or services [3,42]. SA is a vital area of research and development as it plays a crucial role in understanding and harnessing the power of sentiments expressed in textual data [4].

Aspect-Based Sentiment Analysis (ABSA) a natural language processing technique used to identify and analyze the text beyond simple sentiment analysis by breaking down reviews into specific aspects or features of a product or service [4], which allows businesses to gain deeper insights into what customers like or dislike about different aspects of their offerings. Unlike sentiment analysis, ABSA provides fine-grained insights by examining sentiments toward specific aspects within the text [4]. For instance, while sentiment analysis might classify an entire review as positive, ABSA can distinguish positive sentiment towards the service but negative sentiment towards the price, offering a more nuanced understanding of opinions and enhancing decision-making processes. The use of ABSA in UGC offers several advantages as a research method for market research, including data availability, efficient data collection, and non-intrusive analysis, overcoming limitations of traditional analysis methods like surveys or focus groups in understanding customer preferences in detail [19]. Therefore, utilizing UGC to conduct ABSA towards products and services can efficiently provide a more accurate analysis [42]. Its objective is to delve deeper into user opinions by identifying and extracting sentiments at the aspect level.

The traditional ABSA framework comprises two essential tasks: aspect extraction and aspect-level sentiment classification [37]. However, as the field has evolved, two additional tasks have emerged: category classification and opinion extraction [7]. To illustrate these tasks, consider the review sentence shown in Fig. 1: "The hotel staff is exceptional, but the gym equipment needs renovation." The corresponding ABSA consists of four tasks, divided into two categories [7]: extraction problem (aspect extraction and opinion extraction) and classification problem (category classification and sentiment classification). These four tasks are further explained below.

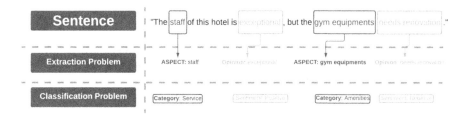

Fig. 1. A review with example of four tasks In ABSA

Aspect Extraction involves identifying and extracting specific aspects or features of a product or service that are mentioned in customer reviews or feedback [40]. Through aspect extraction, we can gain insights into what people are talking about and what attributes they associate with certain products, services, or experiences. It helps create structured data by breaking unstructured text into specific aspects, making quantifying and analysing the sentiments associated with each aspect easier.

Category Classification involves assigning various aspects or elements to predefined categories or classes [40]. The category Classification method allows for efficient organization and information grouping based on shared characteristics or attributes. Employing category classification creates a clear and structured system where data can be easily analyzed, compared, and understood. The process of category classification typically requires defining the criteria or parameters that determine the placement of items into specific categories. Once the categories are established, each aspect or element is examined and assigned to the appropriate category.

Opinion Extraction is crucial in sentiment analysis as it is pivotal in identifying and extracting opinions or sentiments expressed towards specific aspects or features of a given entity or topic [40]. Opinion extraction involves a comprehensive analysis of textual data to determine the sentiments associated with various aspects. By delving into the text, opinion extraction algorithms strive to pinpoint the specific words or phrases that express thoughts or feelings.

Sentiment Classification is a process that aims to determine the sentiment expressed towards specific aspects or features of a product, service, or entity [40]. The goal of sentiment classification is to identify the sentiment polarity associated with each aspect mentioned in a given text and determine whether the sentiment expressed towards each aspect is positive, negative, or neutral.

Before we delve into the different types of aspect-based sentiment analysis (ABSA) tasks, it's important to recognize the complexity of identifying implicit and explicit aspects and opinions within the text. Aspects, which represent the entities or features being evaluated, can be either explicitly mentioned in the text or implicitly conveyed, requiring context for interpretation [31]. Similarly, opinions, reflecting sentiments or viewpoints, can be directly expressed through sentiment words or phrases or indirectly implied through nuanced language [17].

This distinction between implicit and explicit aspects and opinions poses challenges and opportunities for ABSA models to capture a comprehensive range of sentiments in the text. Understanding these implicit and explicit elements enhances the depth of sentiment analysis, providing a nuanced comprehension of attitudes and emotions across various contexts. Many studies emphasize the significance of addressing implicit aspects, opinions, or both in ABSA due to their prevalence in product reviews [31]. According to the findings, a substantial portion, implicit aspects and opinions ranging from 35% to 45%, of the dataset contains either implicit aspects, implicit opinions, or both [7].

In the realm of ABSA studies, various approaches have been developed to address specific elements of ABSA, which is known as a single ABSA task (sometimes referred to as specific-task ABSA). Single ABSA task focuses on tackling particular aspects of sentiment analysis, like identifying aspects, classifying categories, extracting opinions, or determining sentiment [9]. Although these models can excel in their designated tasks, they might encounter challenges when dealing with the intricacies of real-world data, where various aspects are interconnected and carry more information than the task intended to extract [40]. A limitation of single ABSA task models lies in their reduced flexibility and adaptability to address diverse elements of sentiment analysis concurrently.

After extensive research on a single ABSA task, there has been a growing interest in compound tasks, which aim to identify more than one element simultaneously [13,29]. These tasks range from pair extraction to triplet extraction and, most recently, the Aspect Sentiment Quad Prediction (ASQP) task [40]. Fundamental triplet ABSA involves identifying three elements out of the four (aspect, category, opinion, and sentiment) in the text to determine sentiment, while quadruplet ABSA extracts all four elements for more nuanced sentiment analysis. Both approaches aim to extract and analyze sentiment associated with specific aspects of entities or products discussed in textual data. In particular, the pair extraction task involves predicting pairs of the four elements for each aspect in a review, such as {aspect, category}, {aspect, opinion}, and {aspect, sentiment}, providing a more fine-grained analysis of individual aspect sentiments. Building upon this, the triplet extraction task extends the scope by predicting one of the two target triplets: {aspect, sentiment, opinion} or {aspect, category, sentiment}, enabling a more comprehensive understanding of sentiments and their associated aspects. Further, to achieve the most comprehensive aspect-level sentiment structure, the ASQP task was introduced to predict all four sentiment elements in one shot. This compound task aims to capture the intricate relationships and dependencies among these elements, elevating the precision and depth of ABSA and paving the way for a more sophisticated understanding of sentiments expressed in complex review sentences.

Previous review articles have primarily focused on the background of ABSA, machine learning approaches, and single ABSA tasks with less focus on deep learning approaches on more complicated compound tasks such as triplet and quadruplet extraction [4,5,34,40]. This article emphasises the latest advancements in triplet and quadruplet deep learning techniques for ABSA. We focus on understanding the prevailing challenges in this domain, intending to offer valuable insights into these intricate ABSA tasks. Moreover, our work sets the stage for future directions in addressing their specific challenges.

The entirety of ABSA is encapsulated in Fig. 2, while the specific emphasis of this paper is illuminated in colour blue.

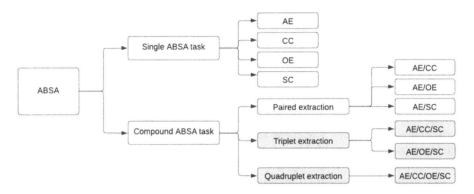

Fig. 2. Comprehensive Overview of Aspect-Based Sentiment Analysis (ABSA) with Focus Areas Highlighted in Blue (Color figure online)

This paper is organised as follows: Sect. 2 examines previous ABSA review articles. Section 3 explores state-of-the-art ABSA triplet and quadruplet approaches and conducts a comparative analysis. Section 4 presents domains and datasets focusing on products like laptops. Section 5 discusses challenges and future research directions in ABSA. Finally, Sect. 6 summarises key findings, acknowledges limitations, and emphasises the need for further research in ABSA triplet and quadruplet tasks.

2 Related Works

Numerous studies have been conducted in ABSA, focusing on sentiment extraction, classification, and analysis tasks. This section reviews and discusses the key research areas of relevant research studies.

The work [10] provides a comparative review of deep learning methods for three tasks of ABSA: opinion target extraction, aspect category detection, and sentiment polarity, highlighting their ability to capture syntactic and semantic features without extensive feature engineering. The study compared the results of studies conducted in deep neural networks (DNN), convolutional neural networks (CNN) [27], recurrent neural networks (RNN), recursive neural networks (RecNN), and hybrid models [12,32].

The paper [2] focused on aspect-oriented sentiment classification and discussed various approaches for aspect extraction, like frequency-based, syntax-based, supervised/unsupervised machine learning algorithms, and hybrid approaches. Another work [43] offers an overview of deep learning techniques for ABSA, presenting the ABSA two modelling processes: pipeline and generative. The article also highlighted several challenges that warrant consideration for future research directions. These challenges encompass implicit sentiment analysis, domain adaptation, multi-modal sentiment analysis, sentiment analysis in the context of Twitter, and the application of sentiment analysis in multilingual settings. These areas present complexities and unique characteristics that necessitate further investigation and innovation to advance the field of sentiment analysis.

This article [34] categorised aspect extraction methods in ABSA deep learning approaches for both implicit and explicit aspect extraction. It evaluated the effectiveness of these methods and emphasised the need for future research to achieve domain portability and independence. Zhang et al. Another work by Zhang et al. [40] presented a novel taxonomy for ABSA that categorises existing studies based on the key sentiment analysis elements, single or compound tasks. The taxonomy places particular emphasis on recent advancements in compound ABSA tasks.

Brauwers and Frasincar [5] reviewed a new classifying system for ABSA models, categorising them into three main types: knowledge-based, machine-learning methods, and hybrid models. The focus is on evaluating the performance of these models, with particular emphasis on considering aspect extraction and aggregation besides the classification in future models. [26] provided a similar system where studies are categorised into three categories: knowledge-based, statistical-based, and hybrid approaches, emphasising each study's benefits and gaps. Lastly, [8] provided an overview of significant corpora and their features concerning ABSA studies. It examines 65 publicly available ABSA datasets covering multiple domains and languages.

3   State-of-the-Art Compound ABSA Tasks Approaches

3.1   General Approaches for Compound ABSA Tasks

In the realm of ABSA models, where intricate relationships and dependencies greatly influence system performance, researchers have been exploring comprehensive strategies, such as pipelines and generative-based models, to address these challenges. These approaches aim to collectively model multiple sentiment analysis tasks, promoting better knowledge sharing and capitalizing on the interconnections between distinct aspects of sentiment analysis. By adopting a more unified framework, researchers have the potential to transcend the limitations posed by single ABSA task models, thereby attaining a more comprehensive comprehension of the sentiments conveyed within textual data. In the literature, three prominent approaches have surfaced to effectively manage triplet and quadrupled ABSA tasks: pipeline techniques, generative methods, and hybrid approaches. These methodologies hold promise in facilitating a more cohesive analysis of complex sentiment relationships, ultimately contributing to a more refined understanding of sentiments expressed in text.

The traditional pipeline approach has been commonly used in ABSA [7], where each task is executed sequentially. In this approach, aspect extraction is performed first, followed by a different sequence of classifying sentiment and category and extracting the opinion phrase. While the pipeline approach is straightforward and widely adopted, it has certain limitations. Since each task is tackled independently, errors made during aspect extraction can affect the downstream tasks, potentially leading to sub-optimal performance. Moreover, the pipeline approach may not fully capture the intricate relationships and dependencies between the tasks, hindering the overall coherence and accuracy of the ABSA model. To overcome the limitations of the pipeline approach and better exploit the relationships among different tasks, a new direction has emerged: generative-based ABSA.

The generative-based approach seeks to model different ABSA tasks jointly [1,20,38], allowing for a more comprehensive and interconnected analysis. By adopting this approach, the model can better capture the relationships between aspects, sentiments, and categories, enabling more effective information sharing and knowledge transfer across tasks. This holistic perspective can improve performance and efficiency in ABSA models, ultimately providing a more accurate and coherent understanding of sentiments and aspects in textual data. The generative-based ABSA opens up promising avenues for advancing the field and fostering innovative solutions for complex sentiment analysis tasks. However, it's important to note that the generative approach, while promising, can come with its challenges. For instance, the process of generating complex outputs can be time-consuming, leading to longer runtimes compared to the pipeline method.

Lastly, the hybrid approach simultaneously addresses subtasks [41], Aspect Category Detection (ACD), and Aspect Opinion Sentiment Co-Extraction (AOSC), leveraging the strengths of both approaches.

3.2 Triplet Task

Triplet ABSA represents a crucial advancement in sentiment analysis, encompassing two fundamental types: Aspect Sentiment Triplet Extraction (ASTE) and Aspect-Category-Sentiment Detection (ACSD), also known as Aspect-Category-Sentiment Analysis (ACSA). ASTE involves extracting aspect-opinion pairs and their corresponding sentiment polarities from text, providing a more comprehensive understanding of sentiments associated with specific aspects. On the other hand, ACSD extends the scope by detecting aspect-sentiment pairs and categorizing them into predefined aspect categories, adding an extra layer of depth to sentiment analysis [6]. In their pioneering work, Peng et al. (2020) [21] introduced the Aspect Sentiment Triplet Extraction (ASTE) task and presented a two-stage pipeline method to extract triplets effectively. In the first stage, they employed two sequence tagging models, one for extracting aspects with their associated sentiments and another for identifying opinion terms. Subsequently, in the second stage, a classifier was utilized to identify valid aspect-opinion pairs from the predicted aspects and opinions. This innovative approach enabled the construction of accurate triplet predictions, facilitating a more comprehensive

Table 1. Summary of triplet and quadrupled previous studies.

ABSA task	ABSA elements	Year	Study	Approach	Backbone method	Method	Dataset
Triplet	a, c, s	2020	[6]	Generative	BERT	Hierarchical Graph Convolutional Network (HGCN-BERT)	[23,24]
	a, o, s	2020	[21]	(two-stage) Pipeline	BLSTM+GCN	Peng-two-stage (Bidirectional Long Short Term Memory (BLSTM) Graph Convolutional Network (GCN))	[23,25]
	a, o, s a, c, s	2021	[39]	Generative	T5	GAS	[23–25]
	a, o, s	2021	[36]	Generative	BART	Span.Generation	[25]
	a, o, s	2021	[15]	(two-stage) Generative	BERT	Jing et al. BERT	[23–25]
	a, o, s	2023	[16]	Pipeline	BERT	Position-aware BERT-based Framework (PBF)	[23–25]
Quad	a, c, o, s	2021	[7]	Pipeline	BERT	Extract-Classify-ACOS	Original (Restaurant-ACOS, Laptop-ACOS)
		2021	[38]	Generative	T5	Sequenceto-sequence (S2S) - Paraphrase	[23,25]
		2022	[1]	Generative	T5	Tree generation	[6]
		2022	[20]	Generative	T5	Seq2Path	[23–25]
		2022	[22]	Generative	T5	GEN-NAT-SCL	[7]
		2023	[41]	Pipeline Generative	DeBERTaV3-base	Two subtasks One-ASQP	Original (en-Phone)
Multi-task	a, o, s a, c, s a, c, o, s	2022	[11]	Generative	T5	LEGO-ABSA	[23–25]

and precise analysis of aspect-based sentiments in text. In ABSA, the extraction of aspect categories holds significant importance due to the need for capturing sentiments associated with each aspect mentioned in a review sentence. Even if an aspect term is not explicitly present, having corresponding aspect categories enables identifying and analysing user sentiments directed towards specific aspects [6]. The aspect categories act as a framework for organizing and categorizing the various elements or attributes individuals express opinions about in their text. In a similar effort to Peng et al. [6, 21] aimed to address the triplet challenges with more focus on identifying sentiment polarities towards both explicit and implicit aspects of a text. While most research in ABSA focuses on explicit aspect terms, implicit aspects are often overlooked. To tackle this limitation, the authors of this work proposed aspect-category-based sentiment analysis, a novel approach involving joint aspect category extraction and category-oriented sentiment classification. They re-formalized the triplet task as a category-sentiment hierarchy prediction problem, introducing a hierarchy output structure. This structure allows for identifying multiple aspect categories in a text, followed by predicting sentiments for each category.

3.3 Quadruplet Task

The study conducted by Cai et al. [7] was the first to consider exploring the four elements of ABSA: the Aspect-Category-Opinion-Sentiment Quadruple Extraction task using deep learning approaches and followed by Zhang et al. (2021) [38]. Cai et al. employ a pipeline model with BERT (Bidirectional Encoder Representations from Transformers) as the backbone for their Extract-Classify-ACOS, while Zhang et al. utilize a generation-based Seq2Seq (Sequence-to-Sequence) model with T5 (Text-to-Text Transfer Transformer) as the backbone for their PARAPHRASE method. The two studies introduce new datasets, including Restaurant-ACOS and Laptop-ACOS, by Cai et al. Cai et al., and Rest15 and Rest16 derived from SemEval2015/2016 by Zhang et al., enabling annotations for ACOS quadrupled and implicit aspects and opinions. Comparing the performance of the two approaches, Zhang et al.'s method performs better due to the error propagation issue in the pipeline model. Error propagation is the phenomenon where inaccuracies or errors introduced at one stage or step of a process can have a cascading effect and impact subsequent stages or steps, ultimately leading to suboptimal or incorrect results [40]. Nevertheless, both studies successfully demonstrate the feasibility and effectiveness of the ACOS Quadruple Extraction task, showcasing its potential in handling implicit information in product reviews. Another study by Mao et al. [20] followed the direction of seq-to-seq by proposing seq2path (Sequence-to-Path) to generate sentiment tuples as paths of a tree that can represent "1-to-n" relations. A later study conducted by Zhou et al. [41] further supports the notion that generation-based methods (i.e., seq-to-seq and seq-to-path) outperform pipeline approaches in the Aspect-Category-Opinion-Sentiment (ACOS) Quadruple Extraction task. Their experiments on the Restaurant-ACOS and Laptop-ACOS datasets reported F1 scores of 44.61 and 35.80, respectively, for the Extract-Classify-ACOS pipeline method. In contrast, the Paraphrase generation-based approach achieved significantly higher F1 scores of 59.04 and 43.34 on the same datasets for seq-to-seq and 58.41 and 42.97, respectively, for seq-to-path. These results align with previous findings, emphasizing the superior performance of generation-based methods. The study by Zhou et al. reinforces the potential and efficacy of generation-based approaches in tackling the complexities of implicit information within product reviews. This study addressed the limitations of pipeline-based and generation-based methods in the Quad ABSA. To avoid error propagation commonly observed in pipeline approaches and overcome the slow training and inference issues of generation-based methods, they proposed a novel token-pair-based 2D (two-dimensional) matrix approach. Remarkably, their novel approach demonstrated noticeable performance, achieving results comparable to generation-based methods and outperforming traditional pipeline methods. Specifically, their base model achieved F1 scores of 59.78 and 41.37 on the Restaurant-ACOS and Laptop-ACOS datasets, respectively. We summarise previous studies of triplet and quadruplet tasks in Table 1.

4   Domains and Datasets

ABSA, datasets are paramount for advancing research. However, it is essential to acknowledge that a considerable portion of the available datasets revolves predominantly around two primary domains: electronic products, such as laptops and phones, and food and beverage, especially restaurants. These domains have garnered significant attention in ABSA research due to their relevance in real-world applications and the abundant availability of labelled data. The most commonly used source of datasets in ABSA compound tasks, such as ASTE, ACSD, and ACOS, is the SemEval corpus. Researchers often update the datasets to accommodate new additions and ensure their models cater to evolving sentiment analysis requirements. Referring to the Table 2 below, provides insights into the most frequently employed corpora in ABSA compound tasks.

Table 2. Summary of datasets used in previous studies of triplet and quadruplet extractions

Published	Article	Dataset	Type	Size	# Categories	Dataset source
2019	[35]	Bags	Product	3680	15	Original - Taobao
		Cosmetics		4293	16	
		Electronics		4094	10	
2019	[14]	MAMS - ASTA	Food & beverage	13854	4	Original - Citysearch
		MAMS - ACSA		8879	4	New York dataset
2020	[6]	Restaurant-15	Food & beverage	1674	30	[23]
		Laptop-15	Product	2041	198	
		Restaurant-16	Food & beverage	2260	30	[24]
		Laptop-16	Product	2609	198	
2020	[21]	14res	Food & beverage	2119	Not	SemEval 2014 [25]
		14lap	Product	1487	.	SemEval 2014 [25]
		15res	Food & beverage	1059	.	SemEval 2015 [23]
		16res	Food & beverage	1372	declared	SemEval 2016 [24]
2021	[38]	Rest15	Food & beverage	1580	Not	SemEval 2015 [23]
		Rest16		2124	declared	SemEval 2016 [24]
2021	[7]	Restaurant-ACOS	Food & beverage	2286	13	SemEval 2016 [24]
2021	[7]	Laptop-ACOS	Product	4076	121	Original - Amazon
2023	[41]	en-Phone	Product	7115	88	Original - E-commercial platforms

5   Challenges

Implicit Aspect/Opinion: The primary challenge in enabling current models to capture implicit sentiment lies in the insufficiency of ABSA datasets. With a limited number of labelled data, models struggle to discern comprehensive patterns of sentiment expressions and lack the capacity to incorporate essential commonsense knowledge necessary for accurate sentiment identification. This highlights the necessity of catering for implicit elements when developing new approaches and corpora to capture and analyze these implicit elements accurately, ultimately enhancing the overall effectiveness and comprehensiveness of sentiment analysis in product reviews.

Multiple Aspects: The observation from previous studies indicates that review sentences often contain multiple aspects and opinions [7]. Multiple aspects and opinions pose a challenge in effectively handling these intertwined elements [31]. To overcome this challenge, future research should focus on advancing sophisticated models capable of accurately extracting and analyzing implicit aspects and opinions, ultimately enhancing the precision and depth of ABSA.

Multi-media Sentiment Analysis: The current research in multimodal and cross-media sentiment analysis lacks a comprehensive exploration of effective integration of text, images, and videos to understand emotions across different modalities. To address this gap, future directions should prioritize the development of advanced models capable of processing and analyzing multimodal data. Investigating techniques for weighted scoring, complex emotion recognition, and intensity assessment across diverse data types will be pivotal in elevating the accuracy and depth of multimodal and cross-media sentiment analysis.

Multi-task: Previous ABSA research has identified a gap in accommodating multi-task training according to Gao et al. [11]. Their experiment showed that multi-task training improves performance by leveraging shared information among ABSA tasks. This suggests that training ABSA tasks together can outperform separate training. However, many generative models don't readily support multi-task training due to input and output limitations. This limitation hinders the full potential of multi-task learning, which could otherwise enhance the model's performance and efficiency by leveraging shared information and dependencies between tasks. To address this gap, future research should focus on developing novel generative architectures and frameworks that enable seamless multi-task training for ABSA by designing models capable of jointly handling multiple ABSA tasks. The competitive inference performance on multiple tasks through training on basic single tasks was an unexpected discovery. This finding highlights the potential of leveraging knowledge from more straightforward tasks to tackle more complex ones effectively.

Error Propagation: A critical limitation of current innovations in ABSA lies in addressing the challenges posed by pipeline-based and generation-based approaches. Pipeline-based methods often suffer from error propagation, where inaccuracies in one stage affect subsequent stages, leading to sub-optimal overall performance. On the other hand, while promising in capturing complex relationships, generation-based methods tend to be slow during training and inference, limiting their scalability and practicality [41]. Future research directions should focus on devising more efficient and accurate approaches that balance accuracy and efficiency, mitigating error propagation and improving training and inference speed to enhance the effectiveness of ABSA.

Domain and Corpus: The limitation of ABSA lies in the dominance of datasets centred around electronic products and food and beverage domains, potentially causing biases and limiting generalizability. Future research must prioritize diversifying datasets encompassing healthcare, finance, travel, hospitality, and other sectors to advance sentiment analysis. By incorporating varied domains, ABSA models can enhance robustness and adaptability, facilitating more accurate sentiment analysis across diverse real-world scenarios and user experiences. Generalizability, in particular, is a critical aspect to address as it ensures that ABSA models trained on specific domains can effectively perform across a wide range of industries, products, and services. This expansion of domain coverage will not only improve the reliability of ABSA models but also can lead to the development of more versatile and widely applicable solutions, ultimately benefiting various sectors and industries in understanding and responding to consumer feedback.

Cross-Domain: In current ABSA research, a notable gap exists in exploring task transfer performance under cross-domain settings. Challenges arise when annotations are not readily available for different tasks on the same corpus, making creating a unified annotation corpus challenging. To address this limitation and propel future research, further investigations should focus on developing robust transfer learning approaches that can effectively leverage knowledge from annotated data in related domains to enhance the performance of ABSA models in new and unseen domains. Exploring domain adaptation techniques and domain-specific pretraining methods can also contribute to bridging this gap and lead to more versatile and adaptable ABSA solutions.

Error Analysis: When creating a new model for ABSA, conducting multiple experiments is crucial, especially when multiple tasks involve identifying which tasks yield higher errors, impacting overall performance. Most of the published papers lack an error analysis section. [41] found that extracting aspects and opinions generally introduces larger errors than classifying categories and sentiments. Additionally, an imbalance in categories contributed to significant category errors in Laptop-ACOS [41]. Furthermore, the percentage of opinion errors exceeded aspect errors due to the variability in opinions, with implicit opinions posing additional challenges [38,41] Most likely, this is because the opinion term differs from the aspect term in that it is usually represented by a textual expression rather than a single word. Conducting a comprehensive error analysis section for future projects is crucial to self-evaluate the model critically. This analysis will help identify the specific challenges and weaknesses of the current models, leading to valuable insights for further improvements and creating new fields of research.

6   Conclusion

In conclusion, ABSA has emerged as a pivotal area in natural language processing, providing valuable insights into user opinions and sentiments expressed in text. This review article extensively explored deep learning approaches in ABSA, mainly focusing on triplet and quadruplet ABSA. We emphasized the significance of ABSA across diverse domains and discussed the key components and challenges of compound ABSA tasks. The analysis of state-of-the-art models, including pipeline-based and generative-based solutions, demonstrated their advantages and limitations. Moreover, exploring domains and datasets underscored the importance of dataset diversification for improved generalizability. By shedding light on current challenges, this comprehensive review aims to inspire further advancements in compound ABSA tasks, driving the progress of sentiment analysis and its application in real-world scenarios.

References

1. Bao, X., Zhongqing, W., Jiang, X., Xiao, R., Li, S.: Aspect-based sentiment analysis with opinion tree generation. In: Raedt, L.D. (ed.) Proceedings of the Thirty-First International Joint Conference on Artificial Intelligence, IJCAI-2022, pp. 4044–4050. International Joint Conferences on Artificial Intelligence Organization (2022). Main Track
2. Bhamare, B.R., Jeyanthi, P., Subhashini, R.: Aspect level sentiment analysis approaches. In: 2019 5th International Conference on Computing, Communication, Control and Automation (ICCUBEA), pp. 1–5 (2019)
3. Bi, S., Li, Z., Brown, M., Wang, L., Xu, Y.: Dynamic weighted and heat-map integrated scalable information path-planning algorithm. EAI Endorsed Trans. Scalable Inf. Syst. **10**(2), 1–11 (2022). https://eudl.eu/pdf/10.4108/eetsis.v9i5.1567
4. Birjali, M., Kasri, M., Beni-Hssane, A.: A comprehensive survey on sentiment analysis: approaches, challenges and trends. Knowl.-Based Syst. **226**, 107134 (2021)
5. Brauwers, G., Frasincar, F.: A survey on aspect-based sentiment classification. ACM Comput. Surv. **55**(4), 1–37 (2022)
6. Cai, H., Tu, Y., Zhou, X., Yu, J., Xia, R.: Aspect-category based sentiment analysis with hierarchical graph convolutional network. In: Proceedings of the 28th International Conference on Computational Linguistics, Barcelona, Spain, pp. 833–843. International Committee on Computational Linguistics (2020)
7. Cai, H., Xia, R., Yu, J.: Aspect-category-opinion-sentiment quadruple extraction with implicit aspects and opinions. In: Proceedings of the 59th Annual Meeting of the Association for Computational Linguistics and the 11th International Joint Conference on Natural Language Processing (Volume 1: Long Papers), pp. 340–350 (2021)
8. Chebolu, S.U.S., Dernoncourt, F., Lipka, N., Solorio, T.: Survey of aspect-based sentiment analysis datasets. arXiv preprint arXiv:2204.05232 (2022)
9. Chen, Y., Han, S., Chen, G., Yin, J., Wang, K.N., Cao, J.: A deep reinforcement learning-based wireless body area network offloading optimization strategy for healthcare services. Health Inf. Sci. Syst. **11**(1), 8 (2023). https://doi.org/10.1007/s13755-023-00212-3
10. Do, H.H., Prasad, P.W., Maag, A., Alsadoon, A.: Deep learning for aspect-based sentiment analysis: a comparative review. Expert Syst. Appl. **118**, 272–299 (2019)
11. Gao, T., et al.: LEGO-ABSA: a prompt-based task assemblable unified generative framework for multi-task aspect-based sentiment analysis. In: Proceedings of the 29th International Conference on Computational Linguistics, pp. 7002–7012 (2022)
12. Hong, W., et al.: Graph intelligence enhanced bi-channel insider threat detection. In: Yuan, X., Bai, G., Alcaraz, C., Majumdar, S. (eds.) NSS 2022. LNCS, vol. 13787, pp. 86–102. Springer, Cham (2022). https://doi.org/10.1007/978-3-031-23020-2_5
13. Hong, W., et al.: A graph empowered insider threat detection framework based on daily activities. ISA Trans. **141**, 84–92 (2023)
14. Jiang, Q., Chen, L., Xu, R., Ao, X., Yang, M.: A challenge dataset and effective models for aspect-based sentiment analysis. In: Proceedings of the 2019 Conference on Empirical Methods in Natural Language Processing and the 9th International Joint Conference on Natural Language Processing (EMNLP-IJCNLP), pp. 6280–6285 (2019)
15. Jing, H., Li, Z., Zhao, H., Jiang, S.: Seeking common but distinguishing difference, a joint aspect-based sentiment analysis model. In: Proceedings of the 2021

Conference on Empirical Methods in Natural Language Processing, Punta Cana, Dominican Republic, pp. 3910–3922. Association for Computational Linguistics (2021)

16. Li, Y., Wang, F., Zhong, S.H.: A more fine-grained aspect-sentiment-opinion triplet extraction task. Mathematics **11**(14), 3165 (2023)

17. Li, Z., Zou, Y., Zhang, C., Zhang, Q., Wei, Z.: Learning implicit sentiment in aspect-based sentiment analysis with supervised contrastive pre-training. In: Proceedings of the 2021 Conference on Empirical Methods in Natural Language Processing, Punta Cana, Dominican Republic, pp. 246–256. Association for Computational Linguistics (2021)

18. Liu, B.: Sentiment Analysis: Mining Opinions, Sentiments, and Emotions. Cambridge University Press, Cambridge (2015)

19. Lu, W., Stepchenkova, S.: User-generated content as a research mode in tourism and hospitality applications: topics, methods, and software. J. Hospitality Mark. Manag. **24**(2), 119–154 (2015)

20. Mao, Y., Shen, Y., Yang, J., Zhu, X., Cai, L.: Seq2Path: generating sentiment tuples as paths of a tree. In: Findings of the Association for Computational Linguistics: ACL 2022, Dublin, Ireland, pp. 2215–2225. Association for Computational Linguistics (2022)

21. Peng, H., Xu, L., Bing, L., Huang, F., Lu, W., Si, L.: Knowing what, how and why: a near complete solution for aspect-based sentiment analysis. In: Proceedings of the AAAI Conference on Artificial Intelligence, vol. 34, pp. 8600–8607 (2020)

22. Peper, J., Wang, L.: Generative aspect-based sentiment analysis with contrastive learning and expressive structure. In: Findings of the Association for Computational Linguistics: EMNLP 2022, Abu Dhabi, United Arab Emirates, pp. 6089–6095. Association for Computational Linguistics (2022)

23. Pontiki, M., Galanis, D., Papageorgiou, H., Manandhar, S., Androutsopoulos, I.: SemEval-2015 task 12: aspect based sentiment analysis. In: Proceedings of the 9th International Workshop on Semantic Evaluation (SemEval 2015), pp. 486–495 (2015)

24. Pontiki, M., et al.: SemEval-2016 task 5: aspect based sentiment analysis. In: ProWorkshop on Semantic Evaluation (SemEval-2016), pp. 19–30. Association for Computational Linguistics (2016)

25. Pontiki, M., Galanis, D., Pavlopoulos, J., Papageorgiou, H., Androutsopoulos, I., Manandhar, S.: SemEval-2014 task 4: aspect based sentiment analysis. In: Proceedings of the 8th International Workshop on Semantic Evaluation (SemEval 2014), Dublin, Ireland, pp. 27–35. Association for Computational Linguistics (2014)

26. Girija, V.R., Sudha, T.: A comparative review on approaches of aspect level sentiment analysis. In: 2023 Third International Conference on Artificial Intelligence and Smart Energy (ICAIS), pp. 770–777 (2023)

27. Sarki, R., Ahmed, K., Wang, H., Zhang, Y., Wang, K.: Convolutional neural network for multi-class classification of diabetic eye disease. EAI Endorsed Trans. Scalable Inf. Syst. **9**(4), e5–e5 (2022)

28. Shah, R., Zimmermann, R.: Multimodal Analysis of User-Generated Multimedia Content. Springer, Cham (2017). https://doi.org/10.1007/978-3-319-61807-4

29. Shaodong, H., Yingqun, C., Guihong, C., Yin, J., Wang, H., Cao, J.: Multi-step reinforcement learning-based offloading for vehicle edge computing. In: 2023 15th International Conference on Advanced Computational Intelligence (ICACI), pp. 1–8. IEEE (2023)

30. Singh, R., et al.: Antisocial behavior identification from twitter feeds using traditional machine learning algorithms and deep learning. EAI Endorsed Trans. Scalable Inf. Syst. **10**(4), e17–e17 (2023)

31. Soni, P.K., Rambola, R.: A survey on implicit aspect detection for sentiment analysis: terminology, issues, and scope. IEEE Access **10**, 63932–63957 (2022)

32. Tang, C., Cheng, Y., Yin, J.: An optimized algorithm of grid calibration in WSN node deployment based on the energy consumption distribution model. J. Inf. Comput. Sci. **9**(4), 1035–1042 (2012)

33. Timoshenko, A., Hauser, J.R.: Identifying customer needs from user-generated content. Mark. Sci. **38**(1), 1–20 (2019)

34. Truşcă, M.M., Frasincar, F.: Survey on aspect detection for aspect-based sentiment analysis. Artif. Intell. Rev. **56**(5), 3797–3846 (2023). https://doi.org/10.1007/s10462-022-10252-y

35. Wang, J., et al.: Aspect sentiment classification towards question-answering with reinforced bidirectional attention network. In: Proceedings of the 57th Annual Meeting of the Association for Computational Linguistics, pp. 3548–3557 (2019)

36. Yan, H., Dai, J., Ji, T., Qiu, X., Zhang, Z.: A unified generative framework for aspect-based sentiment analysis. In: Proceedings of the 59th Annual Meeting of the Association for Computational Linguistics and the 11th International Joint Conference on Natural Language Processing (Volume 1: Long Papers), pp. 2416–2429. Association for Computational Linguistics (2021)

37. Yin, J., You, M., Cao, J., Wang, H., Tang, M.J., Ge, Y.-F.: Data-driven hierarchical neural network modeling for high-pressure feedwater heater group. In: Borovica-Gajic, R., Qi, J., Wang, W. (eds.) ADC 2020. LNCS, vol. 12008, pp. 225–233. Springer, Cham (2020). https://doi.org/10.1007/978-3-030-39469-1_19

38. Zhang, W., Deng, Y., Li, X., Yuan, Y., Bing, L., Lam, W.: Aspect sentiment quad prediction as paraphrase generation. arXiv preprint arXiv:2110.00796 (2021)

39. Zhang, W., Li, X., Deng, Y., Bing, L., Lam, W.: Towards generative aspect based sentiment analysis. In: Proceedings of the 59th Annual Meeting of the Association for Computational Linguistics and the 11th International Joint Conference on Natural Language Processing (Volume 2: Short Papers), pp. 504–510 (2021)

40. Zhang, W., Li, X., Deng, Y., Bing, L., Lam, W.: A survey on aspect-based sentiment analysis: tasks, methods, and challenges. IEEE Trans. Knowl. Data Eng. **35**(11), 11019–11038 (2022)

41. Zhou, J., Yang, H., He, Y., Mou, H., Yang, J.: A unified one-step solution for aspect sentiment quad prediction. In: Findings of the Association for Computational Linguistics: ACL 2023, Toronto, Canada, pp. 12249–12265. Association for Computational Linguistics (2023)

42. Zhou, Y., Lin, Z., La, Y., Huang, J., Wang, X.: Analysis and design of power system transformer standard based on knowledge graph. EAI Endorsed Trans. Scalable Inf. Syst. **10**(2), 1–8 (2022). https://eudl.eu/pdf/10.4108/eetsis.v9i6.2642

43. Zhu, L., Xu, M., Bao, Y., Xu, Y., Kong, X.: Deep learning for aspect-based sentiment analysis: a review. PeerJ Comput. Sci. **8**, e1044 (2022)

Machine Learning and Computer Vision

Towards Reliable and Efficient Vegetation Segmentation for Australian Wheat Data Analysis

Bowen Yuan[✉][iD], Zijian Wang, and Xin Yu

The University of Queensland, Brisbane, Australia
bowen.yuan1@uqconnect.edu.au

Abstract. Automated crop data analysis plays an important role in modern Australian agriculture. As one of the key procedures of analysis, vegetation segmentation, which aims to predict pixel-level labels of vegetation images, has recently demonstrated advanced results on benchmark datasets. However, the promising results are built upon the assumption that the test data and the training data always follow an identical distribution. Due to the differences in vegetation species, country, or illumination conditions, such assumptions are commonly violated in the real-world scenario. As a pilot study, this work confirms the model pre-trained on worldwide vegetation data has a degradation issue when being applied to the Australian wheat data. Instead of conducting expensive pixel-level annotation of Australian wheat data, we propose a self-training strategy that incorporates confidence estimated pseudo-labeling of the wheat data in the training process to close the distribution gap. Meanwhile, to reduce the computational cost, we equip the lightweight transformer framework with a token clustering and reconstruction module. Extensive experimental results demonstrate that the proposed network can achieve 6.4% higher mIOU and 8.6% lower computational costs over the baseline methods.

1 Introduction

Recent years have witnessed a rapid development of precision agriculture [1,11, 43] in different countries. This trend leads to a strong demand for computer vision-driven automatic plant status monitoring and analysis [41,47,58]. As one of the fundamental techniques in computer vision that focuses on pixel-level prediction, semantic segmentation plays a key role in extracting crucial crop features (e.g., leaf area index, leaf spot disease, etc.) from plant images. Notably, Australia has taken a pioneering stance in facilitating semantic segmentation under different agricultural applications, such as monitoring crop quality [24], estimating crop yield [49], and enabling autonomous harvesting [29].

Traditional methods for vegetation segmentation primarily rely on vegetation indices [42,50], which may struggle to achieve satisfactory performance due to the high sensitivity to noise [38]. In contrast, deep learning techniques have emerged as effective tools for characterizing crop traits and demonstrated success in agricultural segmentation [43,51]. Deep learning excels for its ability to

Z. Bao et al. (Eds.): ADC 2023, LNCS 14386, pp. 119–135, 2024.
https://doi.org/10.1007/978-3-031-47843-7_9

handle abstract information rather than just events and its capability to automatically learn complex patterns and features from input images [12,70]. Neural networks including Convolutional Neural Network (CNN) [8,26,28,40] and state-of-art Transformer [11,67] architectures have shown the significant improvement in accuracy when compared to the conventional methods for agricultural segmentation.

While existing semantic segmentation for vegetation segmentation methods achieves promising performance, reliability, and efficiency are two major factors that hinder the application in the real-world scenario. In terms of reliability, most of the existing models experience significant performance degradation when apply to a new environment. The performance degradation is caused by the distributional shift between the training data and the new environment data. A straight-forward solution to mitigate such degradation is to annotate data of each new environment and fine-tune the trained model. However, the process of annotating datasets entails vast time and human effort, which even requires hours to annotate a single image in certain tasks. Moreover, from the computational efficiency perspective, there are many agriculture applications that require on-device computation. The current models often rely on heavy structures with a large number of parameters and floating-point operations (FLOPs), which makes real-time performance and resource constraint device deployment challenging.

Motivated by the aforementioned concerns on the existing vegetation segmentation methods, we propose a versatile approach that jointly considers the reliability and efficiency of the vegetation segmentation algorithm. Specifically, to address the reliability concern of the model applied in new environments, we proposed a self-training module, which utilizes a teacher network to generate pseudo-labels for target domain data. The student network is fine-tuned on the combination of the original source labels and pseudo-labeled target data. To reduce the computational overhead, we integrate model expediting layers on top of a lightweight semantic segmentation architecture. Specifically, a token clustering layer is applied to decrease the number of tokens for the high-resolution representations to reduce the computational complexity of the model, and a token reconstruction layer is used for increasing the number of tokens to rebuild the dimension of spatial representations. The model expediting layers can be seamlessly integrated into the trained model without the need for retraining the model.

Our work makes the following primary contributions:

- Recognizing the expensive cost of annotating large volumes of vegetation images, we propose adaptation segmentation method especially for crops, without requiring to label the samples.
- With the demand for computational efficiency and the practically deploying segmentation models on edge devices, we enhance the SegFormer models with token clustering and reconstruction techniques, with which we effectively reduce the computational complexity.
- We achieve the remarkable performance compared with baseline approaches even with model size reduced. The token cluster and reconstruction layers are directly applied to the blocks of light weight backbone of SegFormer to reduce

the FLOPs without the need for fine-tuning. It is notable that our expediting model shows practically the same mIOU score in comparison with the original model, the FLOPs are considerably reduced 8% from 100.2 GFLOPs to 92 GFLOPs.

2 Related Work

Ever since the advent of deep learning, convolutional neural network architecture-based neural networks have been the prevalent choice for semantic segmentation tasks [14], enabling pixel-level classification. Popular CNN-based segmentation models, for example, U-Net [54], FCN [35], DeepLab [4], have made important contributions to deep hierarchical representations with architecture extensions, leveraging the performance on various segmentation tasks. These extensions include attention mechanisms [9,69,74], that capture the feature interactions and representations, skip connections [15,21,54], that help gradient propagation and feature utilization, spatial pyramid pooling [4,5,76] for capturing multiple scales spatial information, and inception modules [63] that employs parallel convolutional layers with different filter sizes. While CNNs achieved impressive results, they are still sensitive to domain shifts [16,37,71] and adversarial noises [64], which results in limitations in generalization [2]. Recent researches [7,45,77] have shown that the transformers architecture, originally proposed for natural language processing tasks [69], are able to enhance the robustness to these attributes. Transformers enable to focus on relevant image regions with a self-attention mechanism [48]. SegFormer [72] is specifically designed for segmentation tasks, consisting of hierarchical transformer encoder, and output multi-scaled features, showing that transformers are more robust over CNN structured neural networks on the segmentation field.

Lightweight models have gained sufficient attention due to their efficient characteristics in segmentation tasks. CNN-based neural networks have been prominent in this field for their capability of learning features from receptive fields [44] and adaption to the predicted result [61]. MobileNet [19] employed depthwise separable convolutions [22,59] and generated two global hyper-parameters to trade-off between the computational cost and performance. EfficientNet [65] proposed a compound coefficient to uniformly scale the width, depth, and resolution to achieve a balance between accuracy and model size. To further mitigate the computational requirements of large-scale models, several techniques have been utilized to for size reduction. Recent researches extend the pruning ideas to vision transformers, such as searching for sub-structure from the original model [3], entangling the weights of different blocks [6], and multi-dimensional compression [18]. Another approach is TokenLearner [55] which utilizes a subset of tokens to generate a set of clustered tokens mostly adaptive to the input. Besides, patch merger [53] is a module that merges the patches or tokens [7] between two intermediate layers using an attention matrix [69], with a slight performance decrease. Token Pooling is a method to exploit redundant tokens and cluster them by a non-uniform down-sampling operator for transformers using algorithms such as K-Means or K-medoids to reduce the total number of tokens.

A recent study [30] introduces a novel approach that expedites visual transformer architectures [31,34,52] by applying token clustering using k-means and reconstruction by accomplishing the relations between high and low-resolution representations, between the layers without the need for fine-tuning.

Unsupervised domain adaptation is proposed to tackle the segmentation problems without seeing the test labels relied on labeled source domain [25]. Various approaches have been applied to handle UDA challenges. For instance, self-training utilize the unlabeled target domain data to assist domain adaptation [79], and consists of two main steps [33]: (1) generating pseudo-labels [27] in the target domain and (2) training the neural networks based on the pseudo-labels with target domain data. The pseudo labels can be computed both offline to repeat the self-training processes [57,73,78] and online such as prototypical pseudo label denoising [75] and consistency learning [60]. Adversarial learning is another UDA method that aims to align the feature distributions [17] between source and target domains in the GAN framework [10,13]. Other methods such as minimizing domain discrepancies [32] using techniques maximum mean discrepancy [56] or correlation alignment [62] are proposed in UDA.

3   Methodology

In this study, we propose a comprehensive methodology for resolving the Australian agricultural semantic segmentation tasks in unsupervised domain adaptation. Figure 1 provides an overview of out proposed method. Our method exploits three main components: (1) Self-Training that utilizes the target domain by pseudo-labels during the training. (2) the token clustering layer that compresses the feature representations to reduce the computational complexity. (3) the token reconstruction layer which restores high-resolution representations from clustered representations. We use the Segformer network architecture, with a lightweight encoder Mit-b0 and a robust context-aware decoder. The token clustering and reconstruction layers are integrated between the layers of the transformer blocks in order to reduce the model size.

In the domain adaptive vegetation segmentation, where only labels on source domains are available, the most direct way to obtain the predictive function is to perform fully supervised training on the source domain. For segmentation models that have softmax output, the loss function of the model can be formalized as follows:

$$\mathcal{L}_S^{(i)} = - \sum_{j=1}^{H \times W} \sum_{c=1}^{C} Y_S^{(i,j,c)} \log g_\theta(X_S^{(i)})^{(j,c)}, \tag{1}$$

where i, g_θ, $X_S^{(i)}$, Y_S, c denotes the ith sample, trained network, source domain image, corresponding label and classes.

3.1   Self-training for Unsupervised Domain Adaptation

While the baseline method could achieve a promising performance on the source domain, it ignores the unlabeled target samples in the training phase. This may

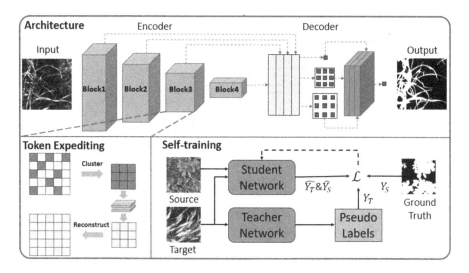

Fig. 1. (a) The structure of our model equipped with token expediting layers. The token clustering and reconstruction layers are applied in between the transformer layers for certain transformer blocks. (b) Token clustering uses K-Means to output super-pixels that has less size than original representation and reconstruction layers transforms the super-pixels back to high dimensional representation choosing the same neighboring positions. (c) The self-training process with the teacher network.

cause overfitting to the source domain and reduce performance on the target domain. To alleviate the overfitting to the source, we employ an online self-training strategy [66], where the network g_θ also learns from the target domain by exploiting a teacher network. Specifically, in addition to training the network on the source images, the teacher network h_ϕ is responsible for generating pseudo-labels for target domain images, and the pseudo-labels are treated as ground truth labels and are used for further training the network during the self-training process. In online self-training, the teacher network will not participate in gradient back-propagation, and the weights are computed by the exponential moving average of the weights of network g_θ after each training step to support prediction stability. Algorithm 1 shows the generic online UDA training process.

To further improve the performance, a quality confidence estimate is produced for each pseudo-label to represent the reliability in terms of the pseudo-label. We set a threshold τ to select a subset of pixels whose maximum softmax probabilities are higher than τ. Particularly, the confidence estimate is computed by:

$$q_T^{(i)} = \frac{\sum_{j=1}^{H \times W}[\max_{c'} h_\phi(X_T^{(i)})^{(j,c')} > \tau]}{H \cdot W}, \qquad (2)$$

where c' denotes classes.

Pseudo-labels and confidence estimates are together used to further train the network on the target domain:

$$\mathcal{L}_T^{(i)} = - \sum_{j=1}^{H \times W} \sum_{c=1}^{C} q_T^{(i)} p_T^{(i,j,c)} \log g_\theta(X_T^{(i)})^{(j,c)}. \tag{3}$$

Algorithm 1. The self-training process

Require: Source Sample S_S, Target Sample S_T, initialized network f_θ
Initialize teacher network h_Φ
  for $i = 1, 2, \ldots, N$ **do**
    Draw image X_S and label Y_S from S_S, X_T from S_T
    $\hat{Y}_S \leftarrow f_\theta(X_S)$ ▷ Generate prediction from f_θ
    $Y_T^{(i,j,c)} \leftarrow [c = \arg\max_{c'} h_\Phi(X_T^{(i)})^{(j,c')}]$
    $\hat{Y}_T = f_\theta(X_T)$
    $q_T^{(i)} = \frac{\sum_{j=1}^{H \times W} [\max_{c'} h_\Phi(X_T^{(i)})^{(j,c')} > \tau]}{H \cdot W}$ ▷ Get the confidence estimate of the
pseudo-label
    $\mathcal{L}_S^{(i)} = -\sum_{j=1}^{H \times W} \sum_{c=1}^{C} Y_S^{(i,j,c)} \log g_\theta(X_S^{(i)})^{(j,c)}$
    $\mathcal{L}_T^{(i)} = -\sum_{j=1}^{H \times W} \sum_{c=1}^{C} q_T^{(i)} p_T^{(i,j,c)} \log g_\theta(X_T^{(i)})^{(j,c)}$
    $\ell = \mathcal{L}_S + \mathcal{L}_T$
    Update weights of h_Φ by $\Phi_{t+1} \leftarrow \alpha \Phi_t + (1 - \alpha)\theta_t$
    Back propagate gradient descent to θ with $\nabla_\theta \ell$
  end for

3.2 Token Clustering and Reconstruction

Although the self-training strategy alleviates overfitting to the source domain, the computational cost is still prohibitive for edge devices to perform real-time segmentation. Towards this end, we equip our framework with a token clustering layer. The fundamental inspiration of the token clustering layer is based on the [23, 30], which utilizes the local K-means clustering. Firstly, we determine the initial super-pixel centers by applying adaptive average pooling over the high-resolution representations $\mathbf{Z}_\alpha$ from the α-th layer, resulting in $h \times w$ initial cluster center representations:

$$\mathbf{S}_\alpha = AAP(\mathbf{Z}_\alpha, (h \times w)), \tag{4}$$

where $AAP(\cdot)$ indicates the adaptive average pooling operator. Afterwards, we employ the iterative local clustering process that produces the output $\mathbf{S}_\alpha$ with size $h \times w$. The iterative local clustering consists of two steps:

(1) Expectation step: in this step, we compute the normalized similarity between each pixel and the surrounding super-pixel considering only λ neighbors.

$$\mathbf{Q}_{p,i} = \frac{\exp(-\|\mathbf{Z}_{\alpha,p} - \mathbf{S}_{\alpha,i}\|^2/\tau)}{\sum_{j=1}^{\lambda} \exp(-\|\mathbf{Z}_{\alpha,p} - \mathbf{S}_{\alpha,j}\|^2/\tau)}. \tag{5}$$

(2) Maximization step: this step computes the new super-pixel centers.

$$\mathbf{S}_{\alpha,i} = \sum_{p=1}^{N} \mathbf{Q}_{p,i} \mathbf{Z}_{\alpha,p}, \tag{6}$$

where τ is a temperature hyper-parameter.

The Expectation step and Maximization step are iterated for k times. The output S_α obtained from the token clustering layer is then subjected to β transformer layers instead of using the original Z_α, thus reduces the representation size, thereby reducing the computational complexity.

At the $\alpha+\beta$-th layer, the high-resolution representation $S_{\alpha+\beta}$ will be restored to the original shape representation $Z_{\alpha+\beta}$, by leveraging the similarity between the high-resolution representations and their corresponding low-resolution representations:

$$\mathbf{Z}_{\alpha+\beta,p} = \sum_{\mathbf{S}_{a,i} \in kNN(\mathbf{Z}_{\alpha,p})} \frac{\exp(-\|\mathbf{Z}_{\alpha,p} - \mathbf{S}_{\alpha,i}\|^2 / \tau)}{\sum_{j=1}^{\lambda} \exp(-\|\mathbf{Z}_{\alpha,p} - \mathbf{S}_{\alpha,j}\|^2 / \tau)} \mathbf{S}_{\alpha+\beta,i}. \tag{7}$$

3.3   Architecture

We select the Segformer [72] as the basic architecture of the network, which is equipped with Mix Transformer as the encoder and is tailored by semantic segmentation header. The Mix Transformer encoder of our model consists of four hierarchically structured transformer blocks, which output multi-scale feature representations. The input images are divided into small patches with size 4×4 before being applied to the transformers. To cope with the high feature resolution, sequence reduction is used in the self-attention blocks. To downsample to multi-scale feature representations, overlapping patch merging is implemented to keep dimension consistency. We choose the Mit-b0 which contains only two layers in each transformer block so as to achieve real-time segmentation. And the token clustering layer is applied after the first layer in the transformer block to reduce the representation size, and the token reconstruction layer is applied right after the second layer of the block to restore the representation to its original size.

Unlike the MLP decoder in Segformer, we utilize the context-aware decoder from DAFormer [20]. In contrast to only considering the context information from the bottleneck features, the decoder extracts the context features from different encoder levels that provide essential low-level information for high-resolution semantic segmentation. To overcome the various output dimensions from different transformer blocks, the context features from different transformer blocks are aligned using bilinearly upsampling and then concatenated together. Afterward, during the feature fusion process, multiple parallel 3×3 convolutions with different dilation rates are used to fuse the features, which is similar to the ASPP (Atrous Spatial Pyramid Pooling) approach [5] though without global average pooling and applying it to the bottleneck features.

4   Experiments

4.1   Experimental Setting

Given the labeled broader vegetation data (referred to as the source) and unlabeled Australian crop data (referred to as the target), the objective is to assess the performance of the model on the target. Therefore, we select all vegetation images from VegANN [39] except wheat crops images and Australia-based images (2,484 images) as the source data, and the Australian wheat images (500 images) are utilized as target data in this work. The VegAnn dataset is a collection of diverse vegetation images from 6 different datasets worldwide, where all Australian images only contain wheat crops. Each image in VegANN has 3 channels (*i.e.*, RGB) and has a resolution of 512×512 pixels with the corresponding annotations, where each pixel is either classified as vegetation or background.

4.2   Implementation Details

Network Architecture. To achieve the real-time segmentation equipped with lightweight networks, we choose the MiT-B0 encoder [72] that outputs feature representations with $C = [32, 64, 120, 256]$. The encoder uses the weights pretrained on ImageNet-1k. The MiT-B0 has 4 blocks of transformers with layer depth $[2, 2, 2, 2]$. For certain encoder blocks, the token clustering layer is applied after the first layer and the token reconstruction layer is applied following the second layer. We set $\lambda = 48$ and $\tau = 50$ in the clustering layer. For the decoder, we set channel size alignment to 256 and dilation rates to 1, 6, 12, and 18. The implementation is built upon the mmsegmentation framework.

Training Strategy. Following [20], we use the AdamW optimizer [36] with the base learning rate of 6×10^{-5} for encoder and 6×10^{-4} for decoder. The weight decay is set as 0.01 for both the encoder and decoder. We also utilize the learning rate warmup [20] with $\eta_{base} = 6 \times 10^{-5}$. We follow DACs [68] and use data augmentations including color jitter, Gaussian blur, and ClassMix [46] on the source domain images.

4.3   Quantitative Results

Distributional Difference Between Australian Wheat and Worldwide Vegetation Largely Affects the Model Performance. To evaluate how the distributional shift between the training and test dataset affects the model test performance, we conducted two sets of experiments: 1) No distributional shift. Various CNN and Transformer architectures are trained and tested using the Australian wheat dataset. 2) With distributional shift. The same models are subsequently trained on the images of diverse crop types excluding wheat crops and are applied directly to the Australian wheat dataset for evaluation. The segmentation results of two sets of experiments are shown in Table 1 and 2. In the table, we observe a performance discrepancy between the models trained exclusively on Australian wheat data and lacking wheat data. Upon training models on vegetation data where the domains are different from Australian wheat, the test mIOU reduces by around an absolute 6% across all architectures. The performance drop potentially arises from the limited generalizability of the models, where models tend to overfit the labeled training dataset, resulting in worse performance on the test dataset. Notably, the lightweight transformer-based encoder (i.e., MiT_b0) achieves similar performance to ResNet50, and outperforms other CNN lightweight models, indicating that the transformer structure has better generalization capabilities than CNNs in the vegetation segmentation tasks.

Table 1. Model performance comparison on no distribution shift task, where Australian wheat dataset is used for training and testing the models.

Model Name	Backbone	Training Data	Wheat Label	Test mIOU
Unet	Resnet50	AU Wheat	Yes	0.8378
Unet	Mobilenet_v2	AU Wheat	Yes	0.8282
Unet	Efficientnet_b0	AU Wheat	Yes	0.8255
MAnet	MiT_b0	AU Wheat	Yes	0.8513
Ours	MiT_b0	AU Wheat	Yes	**0.8953**

Table 2. Model performance comparison on distributional shift task, where training dataset consists of images representing different types of crops excluding the wheat.

Model Name	Backbone	Training Data	Wheat Label	Test mIOU
Unet	Resnet50	Worldwide Veg	No	0.7921
Unet	Mobilenet_v2	Worldwide Veg	No	0.7694
Unet	Efficientnet_b0	Worldwide Veg	No	0.7785
MAnet	MiT_b0	Worldwide Veg	No	0.7981
Ours	MiT_b0	Worldwide Veg	No	0.8168
Ours w. ST	MiT_b0	Worldwide Veg	No	**0.8336**
Ours w. ST+Exp	MiT_b0	Worldwide Veg	No	**0.8236**

Without Requiring Any Extra Label, Our Proposed Method Enhances the Reliability of the Model When Training and Test Distributions Are Different. Considering the performance degradation is primarily caused by the distributional difference between the training and test data, we investigate how well the proposed method can reduce the negative impact of distribution difference, under the label-scarcity scenario. Specifically, our proposed model is trained by leveraging the labeled worldwide vegetation data and unlabeled Australian Wheat data. Our model is built upon a more robust context-ware feature fusion decoder [20], in conjunction with a self-training module. In the no domain shift task, our model is merely trained on vegetation images excluding wheat crops, and is subsequently evaluated on unseen Australian wheat images.

As shown in Table 2, only using context-ware feature fusion decoder improves the performance from 79.81% to 81.68% mIOU. Furthermore, we observe an additional 2% performance increase when our model is trained with the self-training strategy. Our model defeats the previous best model equipped with the same MiT_b0 backbone. Compared with baseline methods, our proposed method is more reliable under the distributional difference scenario. Remarkably, our model narrows the performance gap between no distribution shift task and distribution shift task, and even achieves competitive performance with baseline models.

Table 3. Positional impact of expediting module on mit_b0 in domain adaptation task: Our model is trained in self-training strategy, and is embedded expediting layers during the evaluations. The numbers indicate the layer numbers of the expediting layers added to.

1	2	3	4	mIOU	GFlops
				0.83	100.28
✓				0.7460	74.37
	✓			0.7960	89.96
		✓		0.8133	92.07
			✓	**0.8250**	93.16
	✓	✓		0.7831	89.72
		✓	✓	0.8172	92
✓	✓	✓	✓	0.6580	**72.63**

Our Method Simultaneously Increases the Efficiency and Closes the Performance Gap. While our Transformer architecture model with 3M parameters in the encoder, has outperformed the heavy CNN model Resnet50 that has 23M encoder parameters, we investigate the prospect of further expediting the model and reducing the computational complexity in the distribution shift task. We integrate the token clustering and reconstruction layers between the layers of the MiT-B0 encoder during the evaluation. As the MiT-B0 encoder consists of two layers in each block, we insert the token clustering layer after the first layer and the reconstruction layer after the second layer. When the expediting layers are integrated into the 3rd and 4th blocks, our model achieves an 82.36% test mIOU score. Despite a marginal 1.2% performance drop compared to our model without expediting the module, it achieves a substantial 8.6% GFlops reduction, enhancing the efficiency in the prediction process. Gaining insights on the expediting module, it highlights that our method not only significantly mitigates the computational complexity, but also maintains strong performance comparable to the best model.

Various Sizes of Transformers. We assess the impact of different sizes of Transformers on the semantic segmentation performance, within the context of the self-training strategy. The MiT-B5 encoder has 4 blocks with depth [3, 6, 40, 3] producing feature representations with dimensions of $C = [32, 64, 120, 256]$, which is a large encoder with 81M parameters and is not feasible for real-time segmentation. In the distribution shift task, we conduct experiments using both models with encoder MiT-B5 and MiT-B0, while maintaining consistent network and environments settings.

Table 4 shows that the lightweight encoder MiT-B0 is expected a slight reduction in the test mIoU score compared to MiT-B5 (83.36% vs 85.13%). However, the minor performance difference comes with a significant reduction in model size and computational complexity. Specifically, MiT-B0 has a load of 100.28 GFlops which is merely $\frac{1}{3}$ of the 295.06 GFlops required by MiT-B5. Utilizing MiT-B0 makes the segmentation more efficient while still maintaining a satisfactory performance, enabling real-time segmentation on computational resources limited edge devices.

Comparison of Cluster Layer and Reconstruction Layer Applying to Different Blocks. To further understand how the positioning of expediting layers impacts UDA performance, we experiment applying expediting layers to different blocks of the Mix Transformer encoder. The summarized details are shown in the Table 3 under the same cluster and reconstruction layers hyperparameter settings, illustrating that when the expediting layers are applied to the last two blocks of the MiT-B0 encoder, the model achieves the best trade-off between computational complexity and segmentation accuracy. The expedited model achieves 82.36% mIOU while simultaneously reducing GFlops from 100.28 to 93.16. We also notice that embedding expediting layers into the first two blocks leads to a considerable performance drop, primarily attributed to substantial information loss during the feature representation clustering. The initial layers of neural network capture the low-level vegetation features, such as the shapes and edges of the leaves. Imprecise extraction of foundational features subsequently results in inaccurate high-level feature representation within subsequent blocks of the network, resulting in significant performance loss.

Table 4. The performance on DAFormers with different backbone sizes

Backbone	Test mIOU	GFlops	Encoder Params
MiT_b5	0.85	295.06	81M
MiT_b0	0.82	**100.28**	3M

4.4 Qualitative Results

Prediction Visualization. To show the effectiveness of our model that incorporates the self-training process and expediting layers in testing, we present a visualization of the predictions by our full model as well as the baseline model that does not use any technique to mitigate the distributional differences. The visualization results are demonstrated in Fig. 2. Notably, we can see that our

130   B. Yuan et al.

model produces more precise predictions than the baseline model, particularly in complex scenarios involving complex vegetation overlaps in images. In this case, our model exhibits accurate segmentation in identifying the background and vegetation, where the baseline model suffers to capture detailed outcomes.

Furthermore, our model effectively adapts to the distinct features of wheat crops. Our model and baseline achieve similar performance in segmenting green leaves in the wheat images, which is the common trait among vegetation types. However, in terms of the characteristics of wheat images that are unique to other crop types, such as the golden hue and special spike shapes of the wheat heads, our model produces more accurate segmentation, whereas the baseline model struggles in distinguishing background from wheat heads.

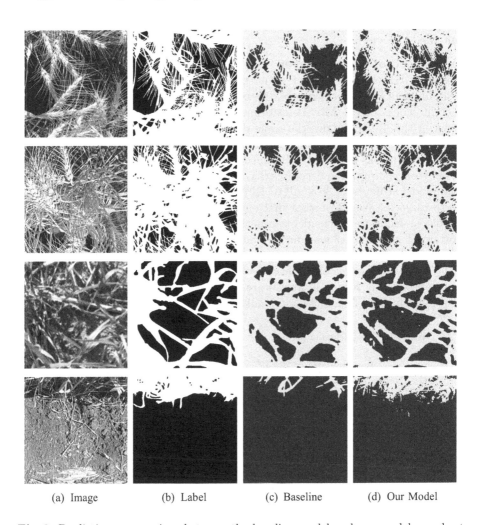

(a) Image   (b) Label   (c) Baseline   (d) Our Model

Fig. 2. Predictions comparison between the baseline model and our model on wheat images. (Color figure online)

5   Conclusion

This paper addresses the important problem of vegetation segmentation in Agriculture data analytic. Specifically, we present a lightweight semantic segmentation network to tackle the distributional difference problems in worldwide vegetation and Australian wheat under a label-scarce regime. We adopt the self-training strategy of producing reference pseudo-labels, supported by a context-aware decoder to enhance the generalization power. In addition, Our model integrates a Mix Transformer encoder equipped with a token clustering layer and reconstruction layer to expedite the model, without requiring fine-tuning. Devoid of the need for extra labels, our lightweight model represents a superior result compared to larger models, while significantly reducing computational complexity.

Acknowledgement. This work was partially supported by UoQ2003-011RTX (2020–2024).

References

1. Anand, T., Sinha, S., Mandal, M., Chamola, V., Yu, F.R.: AgriSegNet: deep aerial semantic segmentation framework for IoT-assisted precision agriculture. IEEE Sens. J. **21**(16), 17581–17590 (2021)
2. Bhojanapalli, S., Chakrabarti, A., Glasner, D., Li, D., Unterthiner, T., Veit, A.: Understanding robustness of transformers for image classification. In: Proceedings of the IEEE/CVF International Conference on Computer Vision, pp. 10231–10241 (2021)
3. Chavan, A., Shen, Z., Liu, Z., Liu, Z., Cheng, K.T., Xing, E.P.: Vision transformer slimming: multi-dimension searching in continuous optimization space. In: Proceedings of the IEEE/CVF Conference on Computer Vision and Pattern Recognition, pp. 4931–4941 (2022)
4. Chen, L.C., Papandreou, G., Kokkinos, I., Murphy, K., Yuille, A.L.: DeepLab: semantic image segmentation with deep convolutional nets, atrous convolution, and fully connected CRFs. IEEE Trans. Pattern Anal. Mach. Intell. **40**(4), 834–848 (2017)
5. Chen, L.-C., Zhu, Y., Papandreou, G., Schroff, F., Adam, H.: Encoder-decoder with atrous separable convolution for semantic image segmentation. In: Ferrari, V., Hebert, M., Sminchisescu, C., Weiss, Y. (eds.) ECCV 2018. LNCS, vol. 11211, pp. 833–851. Springer, Cham (2018). https://doi.org/10.1007/978-3-030-01234-2_49
6. Chen, M., Peng, H., Fu, J., Ling, H.: AutoFormer: searching transformers for visual recognition. In: Proceedings of the IEEE/CVF International Conference on Computer Vision, pp. 12270–12280 (2021)
7. Dosovitskiy, A., et al.: An image is worth 16×16 words: transformers for image recognition at scale. arXiv preprint arXiv:2010.11929 (2020)
8. Fawakherji, M., Youssef, A., Bloisi, D., Pretto, A., Nardi, D.: Crop and weeds classification for precision agriculture using context-independent pixel-wise segmentation. In: 2019 Third IEEE International Conference on Robotic Computing (IRC), pp. 146–152. IEEE (2019)
9. Fu, J., et al.: Dual attention network for scene segmentation. In: Proceedings of the IEEE/CVF Conference on Computer Vision and Pattern Recognition, pp. 3146–3154 (2019)

10. Ganin, Y., et al.: Domain-adversarial training of neural networks. J. Mach. Learn. Res. **17**(1), 2030–2096 (2016)
11. Goncalves, D.N., et al.: MTLSegFormer: multi-task learning with transformers for semantic segmentation in precision agriculture. In: Proceedings of the IEEE/CVF Conference on Computer Vision and Pattern Recognition, pp. 6289–6297 (2023)
12. Goodfellow, I., Bengio, Y., Courville, A.: Deep Learning. MIT Press, Cambridge (2016)
13. Goodfellow, I., et al.: Generative adversarial nets. In: Advances in Neural Information Processing Systems, vol. 27 (2014)
14. Guo, Y., Liu, Y., Georgiou, T., Lew, M.S.: A review of semantic segmentation using deep neural networks. Int. J. Multimed. Inf. Retrieval **7**, 87–93 (2018). https://doi.org/10.1007/s13735-017-0141-z
15. He, K., Zhang, X., Ren, S., Sun, J.: Deep residual learning for image recognition. In: Proceedings of the IEEE Conference on Computer Vision and Pattern Recognition, pp. 770–778 (2016)
16. Hendrycks, D., et al.: The many faces of robustness: a critical analysis of out-of-distribution generalization. In: Proceedings of the IEEE/CVF International Conference on Computer Vision, pp. 8340–8349 (2021)
17. Hoffman, J., Wang, D., Yu, F., Darrell, T.: FCNs in the wild: pixel-level adversarial and constraint-based adaptation (2016)
18. Hou, Z., Kung, S.Y.: Multi-dimensional model compression of vision transformer. In: 2022 IEEE International Conference on Multimedia and Expo (ICME), pp. 01–06. IEEE (2022)
19. Howard, A.G., et al.: MobileNets: efficient convolutional neural networks for mobile vision applications. arXiv preprint arXiv:1704.04861 (2017)
20. Hoyer, L., Dai, D., Van Gool, L.: DAFormer: improving network architectures and training strategies for domain-adaptive semantic segmentation. In: Proceedings of the IEEE/CVF Conference on Computer Vision and Pattern Recognition, pp. 9924–9935 (2022)
21. Huang, G., Liu, Z., Van Der Maaten, L., Weinberger, K.Q.: Densely connected convolutional networks. In: Proceedings of the IEEE Conference on Computer Vision and Pattern Recognition, pp. 4700–4708 (2017)
22. Ioffe, S., Szegedy, C.: Batch normalization: accelerating deep network training by reducing internal covariate shift. In: International Conference on Machine Learning, pp. 448–456. PMLR (2015)
23. Jampani, V., Sun, D., Liu, M.-Y., Yang, M.-H., Kautz, J.: Superpixel sampling networks. In: Ferrari, V., Hebert, M., Sminchisescu, C., Weiss, Y. (eds.) ECCV 2018. LNCS, vol. 11211, pp. 363–380. Springer, Cham (2018). https://doi.org/10.1007/978-3-030-01234-2_22
24. Korts, J.R., et al.: INVITA and AGFEML-monitoring and extending the value of NVT trials
25. Kouw, W.M., Loog, M.: An introduction to domain adaptation and transfer learning. arXiv preprint arXiv:1812.11806 (2018)
26. Kuwata, K., Shibasaki, R.: Estimating crop yields with deep learning and remotely sensed data. In: 2015 IEEE International Geoscience and Remote Sensing Symposium (IGARSS), pp. 858–861. IEEE (2015)
27. Lee, D.H., et al.: Pseudo-label: the simple and efficient semi-supervised learning method for deep neural networks. In: Workshop on Challenges in Representation Learning, ICML, Atlanta, vol. 3, p. 896 (2013)

28. Lee, J., Nazki, H., Baek, J., Hong, Y., Lee, M.: Artificial intelligence approach for tomato detection and mass estimation in precision agriculture. Sustainability **12**(21), 9138 (2020)

29. Lehnert, C., English, A., McCool, C., Tow, A.W., Perez, T.: Autonomous sweet pepper harvesting for protected cropping systems. IEEE Robot. Autom. Lett. **2**(2), 872–879 (2017)

30. Liang, W., et al.: Expediting large-scale vision transformer for dense prediction without fine-tuning. arXiv preprint arXiv:2210.01035 (2022)

31. Liang, Y., Ge, C., Tong, Z., Song, Y., Wang, J., Xie, P.: Not all patches are what you need: expediting vision transformers via token reorganizations. arXiv preprint arXiv:2202.07800 (2022)

32. Liu, X., Xing, F., Yang, C., El Fakhri, G., Woo, J.: Adapting off-the-shelf source segmenter for target medical image segmentation. In: de Bruijne, M., et al. (eds.) MICCAI 2021. LNCS, vol. 12902, pp. 549–559. Springer, Cham (2021). https://doi.org/10.1007/978-3-030-87196-3_51

33. Liu, X., et al.: Deep unsupervised domain adaptation: a review of recent advances and perspectives. APSIPA Trans. Sig. Inf. Process. **11**(1) (2022)

34. Liu, Z., et al.: Swin transformer: hierarchical vision transformer using shifted windows. In: Proceedings of the IEEE/CVF International Conference on Computer Vision, pp. 10012–10022 (2021)

35. Long, J., Shelhamer, E., Darrell, T.: Fully convolutional networks for semantic segmentation. In: Proceedings of the IEEE Conference on Computer Vision and Pattern Recognition, pp. 3431–3440 (2015)

36. Loshchilov, I., Hutter, F.: Decoupled weight decay regularization. arXiv preprint arXiv:1711.05101 (2017)

37. Luo, Y., Wang, Z., Chen, Z., Huang, Z., Baktashmotlagh, M.: Source-free progressive graph learning for open-set domain adaptation. IEEE Trans. Pattern Anal. Mach. Intell. **45**(9), 11240–11255 (2023)

38. Luo, Z., Yang, W., Yuan, Y., Gou, R., Li, X.: Semantic segmentation of agricultural images: a survey. Inf. Process. Agric. (2023)

39. Madec, S., et al.: VegAnn, vegetation annotation of multi-crop RGB images acquired under diverse conditions for segmentation. Sci. Data **10**(1), 302 (2023)

40. Marani, R., Milella, A., Petitti, A., Reina, G.: Deep neural networks for grape bunch segmentation in natural images from a consumer-grade camera. Precision Agric. **22**, 387–413 (2021). https://doi.org/10.1007/s11119-020-09736-0

41. Mavridou, E., Vrochidou, E., Papakostas, G.A., Pachidis, T., Kaburlasos, V.G.: Machine vision systems in precision agriculture for crop farming. J. Imaging **5**(12), 89 (2019)

42. Meyer, G.E., Neto, J.C.: Verification of color vegetation indices for automated crop imaging applications. Comput. Electron. Agric. **63**(2), 282–293 (2008)

43. Milioto, A., Lottes, P., Stachniss, C.: Real-time semantic segmentation of crop and weed for precision agriculture robots leveraging background knowledge in CNNs. In: 2018 IEEE International Conference on Robotics and Automation (ICRA), pp. 2229–2235. IEEE (2018)

44. Minaee, S., Boykov, Y., Porikli, F., Plaza, A., Kehtarnavaz, N., Terzopoulos, D.: Image segmentation using deep learning: a survey. IEEE Trans. Pattern Anal. Mach. Intell. **44**(7), 3523–3542 (2021)

45. Naseer, M.M., Ranasinghe, K., Khan, S.H., Hayat, M., Shahbaz Khan, F., Yang, M.H.: Intriguing properties of vision transformers. In: Advances in Neural Information Processing Systems, vol. 34, pp. 23296–23308 (2021)

46. Olsson, V., Tranheden, W., Pinto, J., Svensson, L.: ClassMix: segmentation-based data augmentation for semi-supervised learning. In: Proceedings of the IEEE/CVF Winter Conference on Applications of Computer Vision, pp. 1369–1378 (2021)
47. Ouhami, M., Hafiane, A., Es-Saady, Y., El Hajji, M., Canals, R.: Computer vision, IoT and data fusion for crop disease detection using machine learning: a survey and ongoing research. Remote Sens. **13**(13), 2486 (2021)
48. Paul, S., Chen, P.Y.: Vision transformers are robust learners. In: Proceedings of the AAAI Conference on Artificial Intelligence, vol. 36, pp. 2071–2081 (2022)
49. Payne, A.B., Walsh, K.B., Subedi, P., Jarvis, D.: Estimation of mango crop yield using image analysis-segmentation method. Comput. Electron. Agric. **91**, 57–64 (2013)
50. Phadikar, S., Goswami, J.: Vegetation indices based segmentation for automatic classification of brown spot and blast diseases of rice. In: 2016 3rd International Conference on Recent Advances in Information Technology (RAIT). pp. 284–289. IEEE (2016)
51. Rakhmatulin, I., Kamilaris, A., Andreasen, C.: Deep neural networks to detect weeds from crops in agricultural environments in real-time: a review. Remote Sens. **13**(21), 4486 (2021)
52. Rao, Y., Zhao, W., Liu, B., Lu, J., Zhou, J., Hsieh, C.J.: DynamicViT: efficient vision transformers with dynamic token sparsification. In: Advances in Neural Information Processing Systems, vol. 34, pp. 13937–13949 (2021)
53. Renggli, C., Pinto, A.S., Houlsby, N., Mustafa, B., Puigcerver, J., Riquelme, C.: Learning to merge tokens in vision transformers. arXiv preprint arXiv:2202.12015 (2022)
54. Ronneberger, O., Fischer, P., Brox, T.: U-Net: convolutional networks for biomedical image segmentation. In: Navab, N., Hornegger, J., Wells, W.M., Frangi, A.F. (eds.) MICCAI 2015. LNCS, vol. 9351, pp. 234–241. Springer, Cham (2015). https://doi.org/10.1007/978-3-319-24574-4_28
55. Ryoo, M., Piergiovanni, A., Arnab, A., Dehghani, M., Angelova, A.: TokenLearner: adaptive space-time tokenization for videos. In: Advances in Neural Information Processing Systems, vol. 34, pp. 12786–12797 (2021)
56. Saito, K., Watanabe, K., Ushiku, Y., Harada, T.: Maximum classifier discrepancy for unsupervised domain adaptation. In: Proceedings of the IEEE Conference on Computer Vision and Pattern Recognition, pp. 3723–3732 (2018)
57. Sakaridis, C., Dai, D., Hecker, S., Van Gool, L.: Model adaptation with synthetic and real data for semantic dense foggy scene understanding. In: Ferrari, V., Hebert, M., Sminchisescu, C., Weiss, Y. (eds.) ECCV 2018. LNCS, vol. 11217, pp. 707–724. Springer, Cham (2018). https://doi.org/10.1007/978-3-030-01261-8_42
58. Sharma, A., Jain, A., Gupta, P., Chowdary, V.: Machine learning applications for precision agriculture: a comprehensive review. IEEE Access **9**, 4843–4873 (2020)
59. Sifre, L., Mallat, S.: Rigid-motion scattering for texture classification. arXiv preprint arXiv:1403.1687 (2014)
60. Sohn, K., et al.: FixMatch: simplifying semi-supervised learning with consistency and confidence. In: Advances in Neural Information Processing Systems, vol. 33, pp. 596–608 (2020)
61. Sultana, F., Sufian, A., Dutta, P.: Evolution of image segmentation using deep convolutional neural network: a survey. Knowl.-Based Syst. **201**, 106062 (2020)
62. Sun, B., Feng, J., Saenko, K.: Return of frustratingly easy domain adaptation. In: Proceedings of the AAAI Conference on Artificial Intelligence, vol. 30 (2016)
63. Szegedy, C., et al.: Going deeper with convolutions. In: Proceedings of the IEEE Conference on Computer Vision and Pattern Recognition, pp. 1–9 (2015)

64. Szegedy, C., et al.: Intriguing properties of neural networks. arXiv preprint arXiv:1312.6199 (2013)
65. Tan, M., Le, Q.: EfficientNet: rethinking model scaling for convolutional neural networks. In: International Conference on Machine Learning, pp. 6105–6114. PMLR (2019)
66. Tarvainen, A., Valpola, H.: Mean teachers are better role models: weight-averaged consistency targets improve semi-supervised deep learning results. In: Advances in Neural Information Processing Systems, vol. 30 (2017)
67. Tavera, A., Arnaudo, E., Masone, C., Caputo, B.: Augmentation invariance and adaptive sampling in semantic segmentation of agricultural aerial images. In: Proceedings of the IEEE/CVF Conference on Computer Vision and Pattern Recognition, pp. 1656–1665 (2022)
68. Tranheden, W., Olsson, V., Pinto, J., Svensson, L.: DACS: domain adaptation via cross-domain mixed sampling. In: Proceedings of the IEEE/CVF Winter Conference on Applications of Computer Vision, pp. 1379–1389 (2021)
69. Vaswani, A., et al.: Attention is all you need. In: Advances in Neural Information Processing Systems, vol. 30 (2017)
70. Wang, W., Siau, K.: Artificial intelligence, machine learning, automation, robotics, future of work and future of humanity: a review and research agenda. J. Database Manag. (JDM) 30(1), 61–79 (2019)
71. Wang, Z., Luo, Y., Qiu, R., Huang, Z., Baktashmotlagh, M.: Learning to diversify for single domain generalization. In: Proceedings of the IEEE/CVF International Conference on Computer Vision, pp. 834–843 (2021)
72. Xie, E., Wang, W., Yu, Z., Anandkumar, A., Alvarez, J.M., Luo, P.: SegFormer: simple and efficient design for semantic segmentation with transformers. In: Advances in Neural Information Processing Systems, vol. 34, pp. 12077–12090 (2021)
73. Yang, Y., Soatto, S.: FDA: Fourier domain adaptation for semantic segmentation. In: Proceedings of the IEEE/CVF Conference on Computer Vision and Pattern Recognition, pp. 4085–4095 (2020)
74. Yuan, Y., Chen, X., Wang, J.: Object-contextual representations for semantic segmentation. In: Vedaldi, A., Bischof, H., Brox, T., Frahm, J.-M. (eds.) ECCV 2020. LNCS, vol. 12351, pp. 173–190. Springer, Cham (2020). https://doi.org/10.1007/978-3-030-58539-6_11
75. Zhang, P., Zhang, B., Zhang, T., Chen, D., Wang, Y., Wen, F.: Prototypical pseudo label denoising and target structure learning for domain adaptive semantic segmentation. In: Proceedings of the IEEE/CVF Conference on Computer Vision and Pattern Recognition, pp. 12414–12424 (2021)
76. Zhao, H., Shi, J., Qi, X., Wang, X., Jia, J.: Pyramid scene parsing network. In: Proceedings of the IEEE Conference on Computer Vision and Pattern Recognition, pp. 2881–2890 (2017)
77. Zhou, D., et al.: Understanding the robustness in vision transformers. In: International Conference on Machine Learning, pp. 27378–27394. PMLR (2022)
78. Zou, Y., Yu, Z., Vijaya Kumar, B.V.K., Wang, J.: Unsupervised domain adaptation for semantic segmentation via class-balanced self-training. In: Ferrari, V., Hebert, M., Sminchisescu, C., Weiss, Y. (eds.) ECCV 2018. LNCS, vol. 11207, pp. 297–313. Springer, Cham (2018). https://doi.org/10.1007/978-3-030-01219-9_18
79. Zou, Y., Yu, Z., Liu, X., Kumar, B., Wang, J.: Confidence regularized self-training. In: Proceedings of the IEEE/CVF International Conference on Computer Vision, pp. 5982–5991 (2019)

SMST: A Saliency Map to Scanpath Transformer

Xi Cao[1], Yong-Feng Ge[2], and Ying Lin[3(✉)]

[1] Department of Computer Science and Information Technology, La Trobe University, Melbourne 3086, Australia
[2] Institute for Sustainable Industries and Liveable Cities, Victoria University, Melbourne 3011, Australia
[3] Department of Psychology, Sun Yat-sen University, Guangzhou 510006, China
linying23@mail.sysu.edu.cn

Abstract. Regarding the virtual reality (VR) environment, scanpath prediction is critical for saving rendering resources and guiding content design due to its omnidirectional characteristic. However, only a few scanpath prediction models have been proposed, compared with the blossoming of saliency map prediction models. Focusing on scanpath prediction in the omnidirectional image area, this paper introduces a novel model that transforms the predicted saliency map into a potential scanpath, named saliency map to scanpath transformer (SMST). The model comprises three parts, filtering, clustering, and routing. Given a predicted saliency map in the VR environment, we first filter out mediocre areas and obtain the filtered saliency map. We then acquire a fixation set by clustering the filtered saliency map based on saliency distribution and taking the centers of the resulting clusters as potential fixation points. The fixation points are then connected, with the weights of the connections defined by the cylindrical distance and the primary visual feature of the original image. Based on the network composed of fully connected fixation points, the scanpath prediction model is converted to a routing problem, which aims to find the optimal route that reaches all the fixation points once and only once. We then propose a scanpath prediction model using an ant colony optimization algorithm. We evaluate the proposed model on multiple kinds of predicted saliency maps, and the prediction performance is promising.

Keywords: Virtual reality · Scanpath prediction · Evolutionary algorithm

1 Introduction

Understanding where people look holds a crucial role in improving human-computer interaction. The human visual system is an advanced sensory mechanism that receives visual stimuli in the surrounding environment and proactively obtains information from the world [26]. Eye movement is one of the most important representations of the visual system. It reflects the movement of the visual trajectory. In the field of human-computer interaction, analyzing human eye movement can reveal the user's interest. Through this, researchers are able to enhance the user experience by improving what and how to display the content [27].

Z. Bao et al. (Eds.): ADC 2023, LNCS 14386, pp. 136–149, 2024.
https://doi.org/10.1007/978-3-031-47843-7_10

There are two main representations of human attention on images, the saliency map and the scanpath [39]. While the saliency map embodies the saliency information of every pixel in the image, the scanpath comprises a temporal sequence of fixation points. The saliency map is a binary map that shows the degree of the user's interest in every pixel in the image. Through the saliency map, it can intuitively tell where users pay more attention. The scanpath is a route that shows the user's gaze position and sequence. It presents the moving path of the user's attention when viewing this image. Unlike the saliency map, scanpath gained less interest. However, with the development of virtual reality [41], human viewing content turned from flat to omnidirectional views. In omnidirectional contents, not all parts are within the user's field of view. Users need to move their heads to browse the entire omnidirectional content. Thus, areas of omnidirectional content are not equally exposed to users. In this case, it is critical to understand the movement path of human attention. For a particular scene, the content of an omnidirectional image or video is much larger than the flat media, which brings higher transmission time and rendering pressure. If we can predict the human's viewing path, we can transmit and render a part of the omnidirectional image or video in advance, thereby reducing the waste of resources and improving the efficiency of the virtual reality (VR) system. In addition, understanding the user's scanpath is helpful for improving the design of omnidirectional content, especially in the field of education and games, where content design has a decisive impact on the user experience.

Currently, there are not many scanpath prediction models. Previous models predict scanpath mainly through combining image features [28,37] and simulating the ground truth scanpath [25]. As for omnidirectional images, SaltiNet uses a deep neural network to generate scanpath [2]. However, this model does not utilize the existing information given by the saliency maps.

This paper directs to the scanpath prediction of omnidirectional images. Instead of developing a new prediction model, we take advantage of the existing saliency prediction models of omnidirectional images and develop a model to transform the predicted saliency map to the scanpath, named saliency map to scanpath transformer (SMST). The SMST can be generally used on saliency maps generated by any kind of model. In this paper, we choose two existing saliency prediction models and validate our model on their predicted saliency maps.

The rest of this paper is structured as follows. Section 2 gives a review of the previous research focused on scanpath prediction. Section 3 describes the research background of this paper. Section 4 presents the structure and details of our model, SMST. Section 5 presents a comparative experiment to evaluate the performance of our model. Section 6 concludes this paper.

2   Related Work

In previous studies, Cerf et al. [5] found that humans are more likely to see the content with meaningful semantic information. Their experiment showed that within the first two fixations of viewing, even when not instructed for viewing task, fixating on a face reaches a probability of over 80%, fixating on the text and the scrambled text is with a probability of over 65.1% and 57.9% respectively. With regard to the scanpath prediction, Wang et al. [37] proposed a scanpath simulating model on natural images. Their model firsts compute three multi-band filter response maps: reference sensory responses, fovea-periphery resolution discrepancy, and visual working memory. Then the three filter response maps are combined into multi-band residual filter response maps and calculate residual perceptual information for each location. Finally, the locations are connected with the maximal residual perceptual information to get the scanpath. Liu *et al.*'s model [28] was based on three main factors influencing human attention: low-level feature saliency, spatial position, and semantic content. They used YUV color values and Gabor features as low-level feature saliency, 2D Cauchy distribution to model the gaze shift, and Hidden Markov Model (HMM) with a Bag-of-Visual-Words descriptor of image regions to represent semantic content. Jiang *et al.* [25] proposed a method to predict the scanpath by learning from the ground truth data. They used least-squares policy iteration to learn a visual exploration pattern miming ground truth scanpaths. Assens *et al.* [2] proposed a deep neural network model, SaltiNet, to predict scanpath on omnidirectional images. Their model is based on temporal-aware saliency information, namely saliency volume. They used a trained model to generate the saliency volume and sample from the saliency volume to generate the scanpath.

3   Research Background

3.1 k-Means Clustering

k-means clustering is a popular unsupervised machine learning method to partition n data points into k clusters [40]. It can help identify the patterns within the data points by iteratively assigning data points to clusters based on their proximity to the cluster centroids. In the beginning, the k-means clustering method randomly selects k initial cluster centroids. Afterward, each data point is assigned to the nearest centroid according to the defined distance metric (e.g., Euclidean distance).

Once the initial procedure is finalized, the k-means cluster method enters an iterative process in which two operations are included, i.e., centroid update and data point assignment. In the former operation, the centroid of each cluster is calculated according to the mean value of all the data points assigned to the corresponding cluster. The updated value represents the center of the cluster. In the latter operation, each data point is reassigned to its nearest centroid. This process continues until the centroids do not show significant changes or the predefined iteration number or calculation time is reached.

By minimizing the within-cluster variance, the k-means method can help create compact and internally homogeneous clusters in which data points within each cluster are similar to each other. This optimization objective facilitates the discovery of patterns, structure, and relationships hidden in the data, enabling effective data analysis and efficient decision-making.

Due to its simplicity, scalability, and efficiency, the k-means method has been widely utilized in various scenarios [32] such as image segmentation, image compression, recommender system, and social network analysis.

3.2   Ant Colony Optimization

Ant colony optimization (ACO) is a kind of nature-inspired optimization method [1,13,20]. Recently, the nature-inspired optimization methods such as genetic

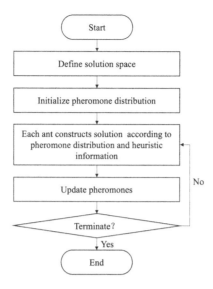

Fig. 1. A general process of ACO.

algorithm [18, 21, 29] and differential evolution [16, 17] have shown their advantages in efficiency, robustness, and scalability [15, 19, 36]. The ACO algorithm is designed based on the behavior of ant colony foraging. The ant leaves pheromones along the way of foraging. Pheromones are accumulated faster on shorter paths, and the ant is more likely to choose the path with high pheromone concentration. This positive feedback mechanism eventually makes the ants gather in the shortest path. ACO conducts optimization by simulating the positive feedback mechanism of ant colony foraging. The algorithm first initializes pheromones, setting all candidate solutions at the same level of pheromone concentration. Then, each ant constructs a solution according to pheromones and heuristic information. After that, pheromones will be decayed or enhanced to reduce the probability of the following ants selecting the components that have been selected before and increase the probability that the following ants selecting the components included in excellent solutions. The algorithm repeats the construction and the pheromone updating process until the optimization meets the termination requirement. Researchers have already developed a lot of models of ACO, such as Ant System [6, 9, 11], Elitist Ant System [6, 9, 11], Rank-based Ant System [4], MAX-MIN Ant System [33–35] and Ant Colony System (ACS) [8, 10, 14] and so forth.

The basic framework of different models is the same (as shown in Fig. 1); however, there are some differences in the implementation details of specific algorithms. In ACO, components with high pheromone concentration attract ants, so the following ants are more likely to select the components rather than explore others. ACS further enhances the relative importance of exploitation information to exploration information [3] through two ways: Firstly, ACS implements the elite strategy, that is, only pheromone concentration of components of the most optimal solution will be enhanced; Secondly, in ACS, ants select components according to the pseudo-random proportional

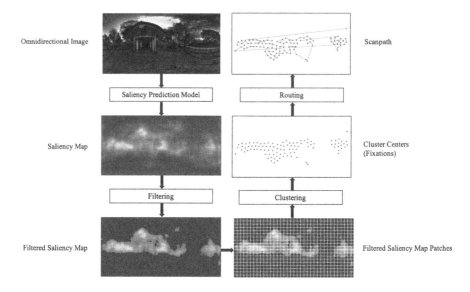

Fig. 2. The proposed scanpath prediction model: SMST.

rule, which means, there is a probability that ants directly select components with the best result in the comprehensive evaluation of pheromone and heuristic information [12]. ACS has been proved to be one of the best algorithms for solving classic combinatorial optimization problems – Traveling Salesman Problem [8].

4   Saliency Map to Scanpath Transformer

Figure 2 shows the framework of the proposed scanpath prediction model SMST. Giving an omnidirectional image, the saliency prediction model generates a saliency map composed of the corresponding saliency value for every pixel in the image. We implement three steps to transform a saliency map into a scanpath.

First, we filter the mediocre saliency pixel in the saliency map and set the saliency value of the mediocre pixel to zero. As shown in this figure, after the filtering process, some of the white pixels in the saliency map are colored blue since they are set as mediocre pixels according to the given threshold. After the filtering process is done, the scanpath prediction problem is simplified since fewer pixels are included in the following process.

Then, we cluster the filtered saliency map to get the fixation point set. As shown in this figure, after the clustering process, a number of centroids are generated. Each centroid in the given figure represents the data points around it. All these centroids represent all the focus points in the given saliency map.

Finally, the connection of fixation points is converted to a routing problem. Specifically, when connecting these fixation points, the order of connection directly affects the performance of the scanpath prediction. Therefore, we formulate this connection problem as an optimization problem, in which the optimization objective is to minimize the

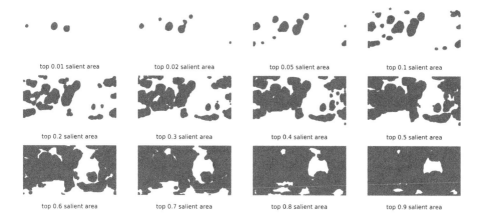

Fig. 3. Filtered saliency maps with different threshold percentile.

distance between all the contiguous points. As shown in this figure, with the help of the ACO algorithm, all the fixations are then connected as a scanpath. Note the weight of paths is defined based on two factors: a) the cylindrical distance between each pair of fixation in the fixation set, and b) the primary visual feature of the original image.

4.1 Filtering

In order to minimize the interference to cluster and concentrate the cluster centers in a more salient area, filtering the saliency map is necessary. Through the filter, a portion of the pixels become the salient superb pixel, and the rest become the salient mediocre pixel. The salient superb pixels will retain their saliency value, while the saliency value of the salient mediocre pixels will be set to zero. The proposed model defines the filter condition as the threshold percentile of saliency value. The pixels with a saliency value in the threshold percentile are the salient superb pixels, and those with saliency values lower than the threshold percentile are the salient mediocre pixels.

Filtered saliency maps with different threshold percentile of a sample image are shown in Fig. 3. If the threshold value is too low (e.g., 0.01, 0.02, 0.05), a very small number of pixels in the saliency map are chosen. Thus, a large part of the necessary pixel points in the scanpath are ignored, and the performance of the scanpath prediction will be affected. On the other hand, if the threshold value is too high (e.g., 0.7, 0.8, 0.9), almost all the pixels in the saliency map are chosen. Therefore, the computation complexity of the following process increases, and the performance of the scanpath prediction will be affected. Based on the above analysis, a proper threshold value in this process can help tackle the trade-off between pixel point inclusion and computational complexity. After multiple comparisons and verification, the threshold percentile is set as 0.2 in our model.

4.2   Clustering

The k-mean clustering method is utilized in this process to identify the fixation set. More specifically, we first cut the image into 2×2 pixel blocks. The weight of each block is defined as the sum of the saliency values of all the pixels in the block. Then we use weighted k-means to cluster the processed images and gain the cluster center. For each cluster center, we map it back to the pixel with the highest saliency value in its belonged block and take the pixel as the fixation point. The collection of fixation points is then used as the node set in the routing.

As mentioned in the above process, clustering is beneficial to decrease the computational complexity in the following routing process. Within each cluster, with the help of the clustering process, the pixel information is transferred into the centroids. In other words, the centroid of each cluster represents all the pixel points included. Therefore, instead of routing all the filtered pixels, we can focus on the centroids to produce the scanpath prediction result.

4.3   Routing

Through clustering, we get an unordered fixation set. For generating a scanpath, the fixations should be connected according to certain rules. Based on the network composed of fully connected fixation points, the connection within the fixation set is converted to a routing problem, which aims to find the optimal route that reaches all the nodes once and only once. We take the fixations as the nodes and set the weight for each path between pair of nodes depending on two components: the cylindrical distance and the visual attraction.

Although omnidirectional images are presented in terms of flat images in the normal environment, in the VR environment, they are end-to-end linked in longitude. Therefore, each pair of nodes are connected in two ways, as on the cylindrical surface. In addition, in the VR environment, users are free to browse the image towards the left or right, so the two paths are equally important. Considering these, we use the shorter of the two paths as one of the weight components, namely cylindrical distance.

The classic visual attention shift model depends on biological vision proposed by Itti *et al.* [23] is utilized as the visual attraction calculation. Itti's model is purely based on a bottom-up attention mechanism. The model predicts the attention shift through the images' orientation, intensity, and color information. Its effectiveness has gone through years of validation and is suitable as the representative of visual attraction here. Based on Itti's model, we calculate the conspicuity value of each fixation in the original image. Since the path is directed in the routing problem, we use the conspicuity value corresponding to the end node of the path as another weight component, named visual attraction.

The path's weight is inverse to the cylindrical distance and proportional to the visual attraction. The weight of each path is defined as

$$W = \frac{1}{D} \times I \tag{1}$$

where D denotes the cylindrical distance between the pair of nodes, and I denotes the visual attraction of the end nodes.

Encouraged by the outstanding performance of ACO on routing problems, we use the ACO algorithm to solve the routing problem over the fixation set. ACO algorithm conducts optimization by simulating the positive feedback mechanism of ant colony foraging [7]. It uses the heuristic information and pheromone to guide the routing optimization. The heuristic information is defined as path weight in our model. Pheromone represents the previous routing experience, and better paths accumulate more pheromones. The algorithm first initializes pheromones, setting all candidate solutions at the same level of pheromone concentration. Each candidate solution here indicates one kind of answer to the routing problem. Each ant in the ACO algorithm then constructs a solution according to pheromone and heuristic information. After that, pheromones will be decayed or enhanced to reduce the probability that the selected paths to be chosen by the following ants and increase the probability that the path included in promising solutions to be chosen by the following ants. The algorithm repeats the connection and pheromone update process until finding the optimal solution.

In the ACO algorithm, the number of ants is set as 100; the evaporation coefficient is set as 0.8; the values of α and β are set as 1.0 and 3.0, respectively; the maximum number of generation is set as 200.

Table 1. Comparison of predictive performance with the ground truth. Lower values are better.

Model	Datatype	Ground truth	SMST	Random
IIP	Head	0.16	**0.171**[†]	0.255
	Eye	0.198	**0.21**[†]	0.323
SAE	Head	0.16	**0.162**[†]	0.277
	Eye	0.198	**0.218**[†]	0.278

5   Experiment

SMST was evaluated on multiple types of predicted saliency maps. The performance is assessed and compared with ground truth and a random-based method.

5.1   Dataset

The test instances utilized in the following experiments are based on the Salient360! dataset provided by the University of Nantes [30,31]. The Salient360! dataset includes a number of omnidirectional images and videos as well as the eye-movement and head-movement ground truth scanpaths obtained from subjective experiments in the VR environment. The eye-movement ground truth scanpaths are derived from the head and eye movement data of subjective experiments, and the head-movement ground truth scanpaths are derived from the head movement data only. Dozens of eye-movement and head-movement ground truth scanpath are provided for each image. In the subjective experiment, users sit in a rolling chair free to rotate 360° and viewed the images wearing an Oculus Rift DK2 head-mounted display (HMD) equipped with a 60 Hz Sensomotoric Instruments eye-tracking camera. The Oculus Rift DK2 head-mounted display is weighed 440 g and offers a field of view of $95 \times 106°$. It has a resolution of 960×1080 per eye. In the experiment, users are instructed to freely explore each image for 25 s. Each user watched 60 images. For each image, all observers start viewing at the same position in the panorama.

In the following experiment, we utilize 50 omnidirectional images with the ground truth from the Salient360! dataset as the test instances to verify the performance of the proposed SMST.

5.2   Metric

The metric of scanpath prediction performance was first proposed by Jarodzka *et al.* [24]. The University of Nantes modified it to measure omnidirectional image scanpath prediction [22]. Jarodzka's method defines the scanpath as a series of geometric vectors, and it measures the similarity between temporally aligned scanpaths across multiple important features. The University of Nantes uses the equirectangular distance to replace Euclidean distance in the measurement to suit omnidirectional images. The modified Jarodzka's metric between the predicted scanpath and the ground truth scanpath represents the performance of the scanpath prediction model.

5.3   Saliency Maps

The experiment utilizes two kinds of saliency prediction models and four types of predicted saliency maps. Two kinds of saliency models are IIP and SAE. IIP was proposed by Zhang *et al.* [42] in 2018. They use a pre-trained feature-extracted 2D-CNN model and a feature-processed 3D-CNN model to predict saliency and a fusion network to combine the output of two streams and generate the saliency map. SAE was proposed by Xia *et al.* [38] in 2017. SAE uses a deep autoencoder-based C-S inference network to simulate the human visual perception process and obtain a unified reconstruction pattern of the image. Based on the unified network, SAE computes the saliency map according to the relation between saliency and reconstruction residual. Both IIP and SAE can predict head-movement saliency maps and eye-movement saliency maps. Therefore, we use these two models to generate four types of saliency maps, including IIP-predicted head-movement saliency map, IIP-predicted eye-movement saliency map, SAE-predicted head-movement saliency map, and SAE-predicted eye-movement saliency map. Based on these four types of saliency maps, four types of predicted scanpaths are generated separately through our model SMST. We use the scanpath metric to evaluate the performance of scanpaths. The result can be seen in Sect. 5.4.

5.4   Comparison

In this section, we compute the scanpath metric of four types of SMST predicted scanpath and a random-based method to do the comparative experiment.

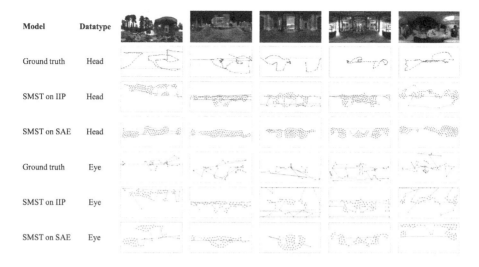

Fig. 4. Scanpaths sampled from ground truth or generated by different models.

Since dozens of ground truths derived from both eye movement and head movement of different subjects are provided for each image, we compute the scanpath metric within the ground truth data to obtain the predictive performance. Therefore, in the end, we compare the predictive performance of SMST with ground truth and the random-based method to validate the utility of our model.

Table 1 presents the comparative result of our model with the ground truth and random-based method. According to the comparative result, the proposed SMST model can produce better performance in all four combinations than the random-based method. Compared with the random-based method, the advantages of SMST in fixation set identification and connection are verified. With the help of the filtering and clustering processes, the potential points, including the surrounding pixel information, are selected. Afterward, according to each fixation point's location, all the fixation points are efficiently connected based on the ACO algorithm.

Besides, the saliency prediction model has a high impact on the predictive power of SMST. SMST on IIP shows a better predictive ability for eye-movement scanpath than SMST on SAE. For the head-movement scanpath, SMST on SAE has better performance. Therefore, SMST can base on different saliency prediction models according to different situations so as to exert the advantages of existing saliency prediction models.

Moreover, to investigate the advantage of SMST in a statistical sense, the Wilcoxon rank-sum test with a 0.05 level is utilized. In Table 1, the symbol † shows that the corresponding result is significantly better than the compared results. Overall, in all four combinations, the advantages of the proposed SMST model are significant.

Figure 4 shows an exhaustive comparison of different predicted scanpath and ground truth scanpath of sample images. With the help of the proposed SMST model, the fixation set is clearly identified and connected. When adopting different saliency models, different performance is shown. In the head-movement prediction scenario, the SAE with the SMST model shows better performance since more effective fixation points are selected and included in the predictive set. Similarly, in the eye-movement prediction scenario, the IIP with SMST model produces better performance since more effective fixation points are identified. Overall, the SMST model can fit both of these two saliency models, and the performance of the saliency model affects the prediction performance of the SMST model.

6   Conclusion

In this paper, we propose a novel scanpath prediction model for omnidirectional images. Instead of predicting the scanpath from the original image, the proposed model, based on the existing saliency prediction models, transform the predicted saliency map into the scanpath. Three steps are implemented to accomplish this process. First, we filter out mediocre areas of the predicted saliency map. Then, we cluster the filtered saliency map to obtain the collection of the cluster center and use it as the fixation set. The connection problem within the fixation set is then converted to a routing problem, which aims to find the optimal route that reaches all the fixations once and only once. Finally, we use the ant colony optimization algorithm to get the route within the fixation set, and the route is the scanpath we want. We have evaluated the proposed model on two kinds, four types of predicted saliency maps, and did a comparative experiment between our model and the random-based method. The result shows that our model is able to compete with the state-of-art scanpath prediction model. In addition, our model performance is affected by the choice of saliency prediction model.

Future research can use adaptive filters based on different saliency maps to obtain more accurate saliency features. Furthermore, we can see significant differences between the scanpaths of different observers. However, according to the results of our comparative experiments, the ground truth data shows the best predictive performance for the scanpath. Therefore, future research can customize the scanpath prediction for the users by combining the global scanpath feature with the users' custom trait.

References

1. Alvi, A.M., Siuly, S., Wang, H., Wang, K., Whittaker, F.: A deep learning based framework for diagnosis of mild cognitive impairment. Knowl.-Based Syst. **248**, 108815 (2022). https://doi.org/10.1016/j.knosys.2022.108815
2. Assens, M., i Nieto, X.G., McGuinness, K., OConnor, N.E.: SaltiNet: scan-path prediction on 360 degree images using saliency volumes. In: 2017 IEEE International Conference on Computer Vision Workshops (ICCVW). IEEE, October 2017. https://doi.org/10.1109/iccvw.2017.275
3. Bauer, A., Bullnheimer, B., Hartl, R., Strauss, C.: An ant colony optimization approach for the single machine total tardiness problem. In: Proceedings of the 1999 Congress on Evolutionary Computation-CEC99 (Cat. No. 99TH8406). IEEE, July 1999. https://doi.org/10.1109/cec.1999.782653
4. Bullnheimer, B.: A new rank based version of the ant system: a computational study. CEJOR **7**(1), 25–38 (1999)

5. Cerf, M., Frady, E.P., Koch, C.: Using semantic content as cues for better scanpath prediction. In: Proceedings of the 2008 Symposium on Eye Tracking Research & Applications - ETRA '08. ACM Press (2008). https://doi.org/10.1145/1344471.1344508
6. Dorigo, M.: Optimization, learning and natural algorithms. Ph.D. thesis, Politecnico di Milano (1992)
7. Dorigo, M., Caro, G.D.: Ant colony optimization: a new meta-heuristic. In: Proceedings of the 1999 Congress on Evolutionary Computation-CEC99 (Cat. No. 99TH8406). IEEE (1999). https://doi.org/10.1109/cec.1999.782657
8. Dorigo, M., Gambardella, L.: Ant colony system: a cooperative learning approach to the traveling salesman problem. IEEE Trans. Evol. Comput. 1(1), 53–66 (1997). https://doi.org/10.1109/4235.585892
9. Dorigo, M., Maniezzo, V., Colorni, A.: Ant system: optimization by a colony of cooperating agents. IEEE Trans. Syst. Man Cybern. Part B (Cybernetics) 26(1), 29–41 (1996). https://doi.org/10.1109/3477.484436
10. Dorigo, M., Gambardella, L.M.: Ant colonies for the travelling salesman problem. Biosystems 43(2), 73–81 (1997). https://doi.org/10.1016/s0303-2647(97)01708-5
11. Dorigo, M., Maniezzo, V., Colorni, A.: The ant system: An autocatalytic optimizing process (1991)
12. Dorigo, M., Stützle, T.: Ant colony optimization: overview and recent advances. In: Gendreau, M., Potvin, J.-Y. (eds.) Handbook of Metaheuristics. ISORMS, vol. 272, pp. 311–351. Springer, Cham (2019). https://doi.org/10.1007/978-3-319-91086-4_10
13. Du, J., Michalska, S., Subramani, S., Wang, H., Zhang, Y.: Neural attention with character embeddings for hay fever detection from twitter. Health Inf. Sci. Syst. 7(1) (2019). https://doi.org/10.1007/s13755-019-0084-2
14. Gambardella, L., Dorigo, M.: Solving symmetric and asymmetric TSPs by ant colonies. In: Proceedings of IEEE International Conference on Evolutionary Computation. IEEE, May 1996. https://doi.org/10.1109/icec.1996.542672
15. Ge, Y.F., Bertino, E., Wang, H., Cao, J., Zhang, Y.: Distributed cooperative coevolution of data publishing privacy and transparency. ACM Trans. Knowl. Discov. Data 18(1), 1–23 (2023). https://doi.org/10.1145/3613962
16. Ge, Y.F., Orlowska, M., Cao, J., Wang, H., Zhang, Y.: Knowledge transfer-based distributed differential evolution for dynamic database fragmentation. Knowl.-Based Syst. 229, 107325 (2021). https://doi.org/10.1016/j.knosys.2021.107325
17. Ge, Y.F., Orlowska, M., Cao, J., Wang, H., Zhang, Y.: MDDE: multitasking distributed differential evolution for privacy-preserving database fragmentation. VLDB J. 31(5), 957–975 (2022). https://doi.org/10.1007/s00778-021-00718-w
18. Ge, Y.F., et al.: Evolutionary dynamic database partitioning optimization for privacy and utility. IEEE Trans. Dependable Secure Comput. (2023). https://doi.org/10.1109/tdsc.2023.3302284
19. Ge, Y.F., Wang, H., Cao, J., Zhang, Y.: An information-driven genetic algorithm for privacy-preserving data publishing. In: Chbeir, R., Huang, H., Silvestri, F., Manolopoulos, Y., Zhang, Y. (eds.) Web Information Systems Engineering – WISE 2022. WISE 2022. LNCS, vol. 13724, pp. 340–354. Springer, Cham (2022). https://doi.org/10.1007/978-3-031-20891-1_24
20. Ge, Y.F., et al.: Distributed memetic algorithm for outsourced database fragmentation. IEEE Trans. Cybern. 51(10), 4808–4821 (2021). https://doi.org/10.1109/tcyb.2020.3027962
21. Ge, Y.F., et al.: DSGA: a distributed segment-based genetic algorithm for multi-objective outsourced database partitioning. Inf. Sci. 612, 864–886 (2022). https://doi.org/10.1016/j.ins.2022.09.003

22. Gutierrez, J., David, E.J., Coutrot, A., Silva, M.P.D., Callet, P.L.: Introducing UN salient360! benchmark: a platform for evaluating visual attention models for 360° contents. In: 2018 Tenth International Conference on Quality of Multimedia Experience (QoMEX). IEEE, May 2018. https://doi.org/10.1109/qomex.2018.8463369
23. Itti, L., Koch, C.: A saliency-based search mechanism for overt and covert shifts of visual attention. Vis. Res. **40**(10–12), 1489–1506 (2000). https://doi.org/10.1016/s0042-6989(99)00163-7
24. Jarodzka, H., Holmqvist, K., Nyström, M.: A vector-based, multidimensional scanpath similarity measure. In: Proceedings of the 2010 Symposium on Eye-Tracking Research & Applications - ETRA '10. ACM Press (2010). https://doi.org/10.1145/1743666.1743718
25. Jiang, M., Boix, X., Roig, G., Xu, J., Gool, L.V., Zhao, Q.: Learning to predict sequences of human visual fixations. IEEE Trans. Neural Netw. Learn. Syst. **27**(6), 1241–1252 (2016). https://doi.org/10.1109/tnnls.2015.2496306
26. Kietzmann, T.C., Spoerer, C.J., Sörensen, L.K.A., Cichy, R.M., Hauk, O., Kriegeskorte, N.: Recurrence is required to capture the representational dynamics of the human visual system. Proc. Natl. Acad. Sci. **116**(43), 21854–21863 (2019). https://doi.org/10.1073/pnas.1905544116
27. Kim, Y.M., Rhiu, I., Yun, M.H.: A systematic review of a virtual reality system from the perspective of user experience. Int. J. Hum.-Comput. Interact. **36**(10), 893–910 (2019). https://doi.org/10.1080/10447318.2019.1699746
28. Liu, H., Xu, D., Huang, Q., Li, W., Xu, M., Lin, S.: Semantically-based human scanpath estimation with HMMs. In: 2013 IEEE International Conference on Computer Vision. IEEE (2013). https://doi.org/10.1109/iccv.2013.401
29. Pang, X., Ge, Y.F., Wang, K.: Genetic algorithm for patient assignment optimization in cloud healthcare system. In: Traina, A., Wang, H., Zhang, Y., Siuly, S., Zhou, R., Chen, L. (eds.) Health Information Science. HIS 2022. LNCS, vol. 13705, pp. 197–208. Springer, Cham (2022). https://doi.org/10.1007/978-3-031-20627-6_19
30. Rai, Y., Callet, P.L., Guillotel, P.: Which saliency weighting for omni directional image quality assessment? In: 2017 Ninth International Conference on Quality of Multimedia Experience (QoMEX). IEEE, May 2017. https://doi.org/10.1109/qomex.2017.7965659
31. Rai, Y., Gutiérrez, J., Callet, P.L.: A dataset of head and eye movements for 360 degree images. In: Proceedings of the 8th ACM on Multimedia Systems Conference - MMSys'17. ACM Press (2017). https://doi.org/10.1145/3083187.3083218
32. Ran, X., Zhou, X., Lei, M., Tepsan, W., Deng, W.: A novel k-means clustering algorithm with a noise algorithm for capturing urban hotspots. Appl. Sci. **11**(23), 11202 (2021). https://doi.org/10.3390/app112311202
33. Stutzle, T., Hoos, H.: MAX-MIN ant system and local search for the traveling salesman problem. In: Proceedings of 1997 IEEE International Conference on Evolutionary Computation. IEEE, April 1997. https://doi.org/10.1109/icec.1997.592327
34. Stützle, T., Hoos, H.: Improvements on the ant-system: introducing the MAX-MIN ant system. In: Artificial Neural Nets and Genetic Algorithms, pp. 245–249. Springer, Vienna (1998). https://doi.org/10.1007/978-3-7091-6492-1_54
35. Stützle, T., Hoos, H.H.: MAX-MIN ant system. Futur. Gener. Comput. Syst. **16**(8), 889–914 (2000). https://doi.org/10.1016/s0167-739x(00)00043-1
36. Tawhid, M.N.A., Siuly, S., Wang, K., Wang, H.: Automatic and efficient framework for identifying multiple neurological disorders from EEG signals. IEEE Trans. Technol. Soc. **4**(1), 76–86 (2023). https://doi.org/10.1109/tts.2023.3239526
37. Wang, W., Chen, C., Wang, Y., Jiang, T., Fang, F., Yao, Y.: Simulating human saccadic scanpaths on natural images. In: CVPR 2011. IEEE, June 2011. https://doi.org/10.1109/cvpr.2011.5995423

38. Xia, C., Qi, F., Shi, G.: Bottom–up visual saliency estimation with deep autoencoder-based sparse reconstruction. IEEE Trans. Neural Netw. Learn. Syst. **27**(6), 1227–1240 (2016). https://doi.org/10.1109/tnnls.2015.2512898
39. Xiangjie Sui, Yuming Fang, H.Z.S.W.Z.W.: ScanDMM: a deep Markov model of Scanpath prediction for 360deg images. In: Proceedings of the IEEE/CVF Conference on Computer Vision and Pattern Recognition (CVPR), pp. 6989–6999 (2023)
40. Xie, H., et al.: Improving k-means clustering with enhanced firefly algorithms. Appl. Soft Comput. **84**, 105763 (2019). https://doi.org/10.1016/j.asoc.2019.105763
41. Xiong, J., Hsiang, E.L., He, Z., Zhan, T., Wu, S.T.: Augmented reality and virtual reality displays: emerging technologies and future perspectives. Light: Sci. Appl. **10**(1) (2021). https://doi.org/10.1038/s41377-021-00658-8
42. Zhang, K., Chen, Z.: Video saliency prediction based on spatial-temporal two-stream network. IEEE Trans. Circuits and Syst. Video Technol. 1 (2018). https://doi.org/10.1109/tcsvt.2018.2883305

Multi-level Storage Optimization for Intermediate Data in AI Model Training

Junfeng Fu[1], Yang Yang[1], Gang Hu[2], Xianqiang Luo[2], and Jie Shao[1(✉)]

[1] University of Electronic Science and Technology of China, Chengdu, China
{fujunfeng,yangyang_yy}@std.uestc.edu.cn, shaojie@uestc.edu.cn
[2] Huawei Data Storage, Huawei Technologies Co., Ltd., Chengdu, China
{hugang27,luoxianqiang}@huawei.com

Abstract. As Transformer-based large models become the mainstream of AI training, the development of hardware devices (e.g., GPUs) cannot keep up with the rapid increase of model scale. Although the development of various parallel training techniques enables models to be trained on multiple GPUs, it still requires high costs that most researchers cannot afford. The increase of the hardware threshold for AI model training has affected the application of deep learning. In fact, CPU memory and external disk memory can be used as cache, which can reduce the occupation of high-cost GPU memory. In this paper, we analyze two types of intermediate data used in AI model training and propose a multi-level intermediate data offloading policy for the training process. Firstly, we propose a dynamic management policy via warm-up to optimize GPU memory usage according to the characteristics of the AI training process. Secondly, we asynchronously offload the optimizer state data with a specified ratio to the HDD, which can further optimize CPU memory usage. We conduct experiments on the large pre-trained model GPT-2 to verify the effectiveness of our method, and the results indicate that the multi-level storage optimization of intermediate data can help to achieve a larger AI model training under constrained hardware resources.

Keywords: Heterogeneous training · Multi-level storage · Large models

1 Introduction

The birth of ChatGPT has caught the attention of people all over the world, which has driven the research boom of AI generated content. Such generative large models tend to be of enormous scale. Practically since the advent of Transformer [25], the scale of AI model training is getting larger as the number of model parameters has grown rapidly. For example, BERT [6], GPT [19] and ViT [7] are all milestones in the era of large model training. These large AI models

---

J. Fu and Y. Yang—These authors contributed equally to this work and should be considered co-first authors.

Z. Bao et al. (Eds.): ADC 2023, LNCS 14386, pp. 150–163, 2024.
https://doi.org/10.1007/978-3-031-47843-7_11

come with a great increase of calculation, which corresponds to the increase in hardware requirements. Taking the GPT series as an example, it only takes 2 years to develop from GPT-1 [19] to GPT-3 [4], but the number of parameters increased from 0.1 billion to 175 billion. During the same period, the GPU memory capacity of professional computing graphics cards from NVIDIA has only increased from 32GB of V100 to 80GB of A100. In AI model training, the increase of the demand for hardware resources has far exceeded the technical iteration of hardware, which is called the "memory wall".

To break the "memory wall", researchers in the distributed system field have proposed a series of parallel techniques for AI model training, resulting in more and more hardware resources being required for training. For example, the Huawei Pangu model [28] is trained on a large-scale cluster of 2,048 AI processors, which has far exceeded the resources available to most researchers. Besides, the increase in hardware use is not completely proportional to the improvement in AI model training capabilities. The scheduling and communication between computing units, and the high costs of the large-scale clusters are hard for AI model trainers to ignore, which leads that hardware scale cannot be infinitely increased. Therefore, it is of great significance to optimize the training of large AI models with a small scale of computing resources. For most devices, in addition to GPU memory, CPU memory and hard disks can be used to store data, which cost less. The main goal of memory optimization for intermediate data in AI model training is to offload the intermediate data that are currently not used in training to CPU memory or disks.

In AI model training, there are two main types of intermediate data, which are model data and non-model data. The model data consist of model parameters, gradients, and optimizer states. Additionally, the calculation of each operator in the AI model also generates intermediate tensors and temporary variables, which are called non-model data. There are three characteristics about the non-model data:

1. The calculation of the non-model data are usually encapsulated in the deep learning framework and are invisible to researchers.
2. The calculation of the non-model data usually depends on its built-in C/C++ library, and some specific numerical calculation algorithms are used for acceleration. Offloading such data will greatly affect computing efficiency.
3. In AI model training processes, once the intermediate data and temporary variables are calculated, they are quickly used as input data for the next operator. For a file system, they are hot data, and the migration of these intermediate data will cause frequent swap-in and swap-out.

These characteristics indicate that it is difficult and unnecessary to offload the non-model data during the AI model training.

However, the model data are different from the non-model data. The scale of the model data is related to the definition of the model and the optimizer, which is visible to us. Take the parameters of one layer in an AI model as an example. During trainings, after the forward propagation, they will not be used again until updating themselves in the back propagation. As cold data, model data can be offloaded to low-cost storage media, which is an effective cost-saving method.

While the model data and the non-model data compete for GPU memory resources at the same time, the storage space required for the non-model data changes dynamically during the whole AI training process. We turn to design an appropriate model data movement policy to dynamically offload according to the storage space required by the non-model data. In this paper, we propose a multi-level storage optimization for the intermediate data in AI model training, which uses low-cost hardware resources to train AI models heterogeneously. We collect the usage order of tensors in AI training through the first iteration, and design an efficient offloading policy called Dynamic Management (DM) policy, which releases GPU resources by offloading the intermediate model data. In addition, we offload the optimizer state from the CPU memory to the Hard Disk Drive (HDD) to relieve the pressure on the CPU memory. Overall, our contributions are as follows:

- We analyze the intermediate data in AI model training and investigate the difference between two main types of intermediate data, which are model data and non-model data.
- We propose a multi-level intermediate data offloading policy in AI model training. Our proposed policy contains the dynamic management policy via warm-up and the hard disk drive offloading, which effectively utilizes the CPU memory and HDD to relieve the pressure on the GPU memory.
- We conduct a series of experiments on GPT-2 with different parameter sizes and demonstrate the effectiveness of our proposed policy. Our policy achieves a $1.549\times$ speed-up on GPT-2-Large compared with the full offloading policy with an 86.7% proportion of intermediate data offloading. Besides, our policy achieves up to a $6\times$ batch size on GPT-2-Large compared with the non-offloading policy.

2   Related Work

There are two main technical roadmaps for large AI model training, which are parallel training and heterogeneous training. Parallel training aims to use multiple computing devices to work simultaneously to achieve large-scale model training, while heterogeneous training aims to utilize other resources such as memory to help achieve large-scale model training.

Parallel Training. *Data Parallelism (DP)* is the simplest and most commonly used parallelism. In this mode, each GPU trains only one mini-batch of data and updates model parameters globally. The core issue in DP is that each GPU needs to save a copy of parameters, which wastes much memory. In this work, we test our policy with a single GPU and two GPUs under data parallelism. *Model Parallelism (MP)* is also called tensor parallelism. MP aims to shard the matrix multiplication in one computing operation and put them to multiple GPUs for parallel computing. Different shard methods bring different tensor parallelism techniques. Currently, 1D [24], 2D [27], 2.5D [26] and 3D [3] tensor parallelism are available for AI model training. *Pipeline Parallelism (PP)* takes the characteristics of the AI model training process into account. Its core idea is to place different training phases on different GPUs to achieve parallelism. PP has "bubble overhead" [12], and Megatron-LM [24] and PipeDream [17] reduce the waste of computing resources and improve the efficiency.

Heterogeneous Training. Heterogeneous training is another effective way to solve the problem of insufficient GPU memory. Two works in Microsoft's Zero family, Zero-Offload [23] and Zero-Infinity [22], enable tensors to be offloaded to the CPU and Non-Volatile Memory express (NVMe) SSD during AI model training, respectively. TSPLIT [18] partitions the tensor into finer-grained units and memory management is designed based on this. In heterogeneous training, the selection of the offloading tensor and the offloading operations need to be considered. For offloading policies, SwapAdviser [11] uses genetic algorithms for heuristic search, and AutoTM [10] uses linear integer programming to search for the appropriate strategy. For offloading operations, PatrickStar [8] packs small tensors into a trunk to improve bandwidth utilization.

Other Training Strategies. In addition to the above two roadmaps, there are other ways to train large AI models. Lin et al. [14] use gradient accumulation, which means the data are segmented and sequentially input into the same device for serial computation, and the gradients are accumulated and updated together. Chen et al. [5] use activation checkpoints to recompute parts of the data so that they do not need to be saved. For the high-dimensional word embedding of large language models, Miao et al. [16] design the word embedding cache data exchange between the server and multiple clients to improve the communication efficiency of the distributed system in the training process.

3   Multi-level Intermediate Data Offloading Policy

We propose a multi-level intermediate data offloading policy, which effectively utilizes CPU memory and HDD to relieve the pressure on GPU memory. It contains two stages: dynamic management policy and HDD offloading. The first stage achieves a memory optimization from GPU memory to CPU memory and the second stage achieves a memory optimization from CPU memory to HDD.

3.1   Dynamic Management Policy via Warm-up

The model data and the non-model data compete for the same GPU memory resources, and the storage space required for the non-model data changes dynamically during the whole AI training process. Due to the invisibility and unsuitability of the non-model data, we convert the GPU memory optimization to an appropriate model data movement policy, which dynamically offloads the model data according to the storage space required by the non-model data. Therefore, we need to calculate the GPU memory occupation during the training process to achieve the dynamic memory management via warm-up. The dynamic management policy via warm-up can be divided into two steps, which are dynamic memory management and efficient offloading policy. The former is used for determining the total size of the model data to be offloaded, while the latter is used for selecting model data in each offloading operation.

Dynamic Memory Management. Different from common computation tasks, AI model training is a process of repeated computing flow with several epochs. In most cases, the dataset is too large to load all data in the model at once and is usually divided into several batches. Therefore, in an epoch of training, the computing flow is also a process of repeated iterations with different loaded data. Therefore, we only need to utilize one iteration as a warm-up phase to know the GPU memory occupation of the non-model data and the model data in the entire training process with the fixed batch size.

During the warm-up phase, we check the GPU memory occupation of the non-model data and the model data. Due to the unavailability of the non-model data, we cannot directly calculate their actual memory consumption. However, the model data are determined once the model is fixed, we can approximately estimate the GPU memory occupation of the non-model data by counting the maximum GPU memory occupation and the occupation of the model data in the current operation. The calculation of the GPU memory occupation of the non-model data can be written as:

$$V_{\text{nun\_model\_data}} = V_{\max} - \sum Volume\left(T_{\text{model\_data}}\right), \qquad (1)$$

where $V_{\text{nun\_model\_data}}$ and $V_{\max}$ represent GPU memory occupation of the non-model data and the maximum memory occupation during the entire computing process, respectively. $T_{\text{model\_data}}$ represents the model data tensor which can be offloaded. $Volume(\cdot)$ is used to calculate the memory occupation of the model data and it depends on both the number of the tensor elements and the precision of the floating-point number. Additionally, the usage sequence of the model data can also be recorded during the warm-up phase, which is used as a basis for the next efficient data offloading policy.

In the non-warm-up phase, the occupation of the model data in GPU memory can be dynamically offloaded based on the memory occupation of the non-model data in each computing process. When the memory requirement of the non-model data becomes large, we can offload more model data to ensure that the GPU can support a larger model. When the memory requirement of the non-model data becomes small, more model data can be retained in GPU memory to guarantee training speed. As shown in Fig. 1, compared with Zero-Offload [23], dynamic management of the model data can effectively improve the utilization of GPU memory resources and reduce unnecessary movement of intermediate data.

Efficient Offloading Policy. After capturing the GPU memory occupation from the dynamic memory management, the next step is to find an excellent intermediate data offloading policy, whose goal is to avoid frequent swaps of intermediate data similar to cache thrashing. In the field of cache replacement, Belady's [1] is the optimal cache eviction policy if the future cache accesses

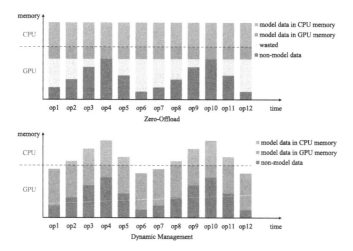

Fig. 1. The figure above shows static management of GPU memory in Zero-Offload. A large number of GPU memory resources are wasted, resulting in extra data migration. In the figure below, dynamic management effectively reduces this waste.

are known [15]. The usage sequence of the model data tensors is recorded in the warm-up phase, which provides conditions for using Belady's. However, Belady's is not the optimal policy for intermediate data offloading, because the size of the offloaded tensor is different. The size of memory released by a single tensor is not the same as the memory demanded, resulting in the number of tensors offloaded each time is not always 1. If the tensor size is not taken into account, unnecessary swaps will occur.

We design an intermediate data offloading policy similar to Belady's to avoid unnecessary swaps, which is shown in Algorithm 1. In lines 1–7, we obtain the index according to the usage order in the warm-up phase, which corresponds to when the tensor will be used in the future. In lines 8–17, each time we choose a tensor with the maximum index, which means it will not be used in the future or will be used at the latest. We repeat this operation until the total size of the tensors in the offloading queue reaches the required released GPU memory. This step is the same as Belady's, in which there is a problem. As shown in Fig. 2, when 12 MB of GPU memory needs to be released, Tensor 1 to Tensor 5 are put into the offloading queue in turn, but the total size of the 5 tensors in the queue is 15, which exceeds the expectations. To solve this problem, in lines 18–24, we traverse the offloading queue in reverse. If the offloading of a tensor is abandoned but the required released GPU memory can still be achieved, then we remove this tensor from the offloading queue. When the traversal is completed, tensors remaining in the queue will be offloaded from GPU memory to CPU memory.

3.2   Hard Disk Drive Offloading

The optimizer state is special in the model data offloading from GPU memory to CPU memory. Adam [13] is the most commonly used optimizer in AI

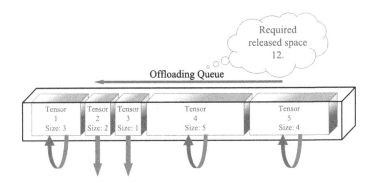

Fig. 2. Belady's policy will offload all tensors in the queue, but our approach keeps Tensor2 and Tensor3 in GPU memory, reducing unnecessary movement.

model training because it performs satisfactorily in most cases without extensively adjusting its hyperparameters. The calculations of Adam are as follows:

$$
\begin{cases}
m_t & = \beta_1 \cdot m_{t-1} + (1 - \beta_1) \cdot g_t, \\
v_t & = \beta_2 \cdot v_{t-1} + (1 - \beta_2) \cdot g_t^2, \\
\widehat{m}_t & = \frac{m_t}{1-\beta_1^t}, \\
\widehat{v}_t & = \frac{v_t}{1-\beta_2^t}, \\
\theta_t & = \theta_{t-1} - \alpha \cdot \frac{\widehat{m}_t}{\sqrt{\widehat{v}_t}+\epsilon}.
\end{cases}
\tag{2}
$$

In addition to momentum $\widehat{m}_t$ and variance $\widehat{v}_t$, Adam keeps copies of the parameters and gradients of the model. Generally, AI model training uses mixed precision. In this case, the memory space occupation of the optimizer state is 8× the model parameters [21]. Therefore, the offloading of the optimizer state can effectively reduce the CPU memory occupied by intermediate data. The transfer of the optimizer states between CPU memory and the HDD should minimize the impact on the dynamic management of the model data in GPU memory. To reduce unnecessary waiting, the optimizer states are offloaded by asynchronous writing, and it is reloaded from the HDD by asynchronous reading in the training process.

Despite cost limitations, we implemented HDD-based offloading of intermediate files. However, with the iterative upgrade of hardware, it is better for affordable organizations to use SATA or NVMe SSD as storage, which will effectively reduce the waiting time caused by data swaps.

4   Experiment

4.1   Experiment Configurations

Our multi-level intermediate data offloading policy aims to achieve larger-scale AI model training on limited hardware resources with an acceptable time waste,

---

Algorithm 1 Offloading policy in GPU memory

Input:

  hold_list: The model data tensor stored in GPU memory;

  compute_list: Tensor usage sequence obtained in the warm-up phase;

  demand: Capacity required for the non-model data in the next operation.

Output:

  offload_queue: The tensor that should be offloaded from GPU memory.

1: **for all** $tensor \in$ **hold_list do**
2:   **if** $tensor \in$ **compute_list then**
3:     $dict[tensor] =$ **compute_list**.$index(tensor)$
4:   **else**
5:     $dict[tensor] = +\infty$
6:   **end if**
7: **end for**
8: $dict.sort(by = values, descending = True)$
9: **offload_queue** $= [\ \ ]$
10: **for all** $tensor \in dict.keys()$ **do**
11:   **if** $avalable \geqslant$ **demand then**
12:     **break**
13:   **else**
14:     **offload_queue**.$append(tensor)$
15:     $avalable = avalable + tensor.size()$
16:   **end if**
17: **end for**
18: **offload_queue**.$reverse()$
19: **for all** $tensor \in$ **offload_queue do**
20:   **if** $avalable - tensor.size() \geqslant$ **demand then**
21:     **offload_queue**.$remove(tensor)$
22:     $avalable = avalable - tensor.size()$
23:   **end if**
24: **end for**
25: **return offload_queue**

---

and we chose GPT-2 [20] as the test model in our experiments. To evaluate the influence of the ratio between the model data and the non-model data on the offloading capacity, we use four different versions of GPT-2 models, and the details of these GPT-2 models are shown in Table 1.

All training processes in the experiments are constructed based on the Colossal-AI framework [2]. All experiments are conducted on a server with 64 GB of CPU memory, two NVIDIA GeForce RTX 3090 GPUs with 24 GB of GPU memory, and a 2 TB HDD.

The running time and memory occupation of the AI model training process in one epoch are the core measures in our experiments. We select a portion data of OpenWebText [9] as the training data to calculate the running time and memory occupation. Besides, batch size can be another important measure to demonstrate that our model can afford the larger AI model training.

Table 1. Architecture hyperparameters for model sizes of GPT-2.

Name	Layers	Heads	Hidden Size	Parameters
GPT-2-Small	12	12	768	124,475,904
GPT-2-Medium	24	8	1024	354,871,296
GPT-2-Large	36	12	1536	1,098,777,600
GPT-2-XL	48	16	1600	1,557,686,400

Table 2. The maximum batch size under different offloading strategies.

Number of GPUs: 1				
Policy	GPT-2-Small	GPT-2-Medium	GPT-2-Large	GPT-2-XL
GPU	33	29	4	out of memory
CPU	41	37	29	23
DM	40	36	25	18
Number of GPUs: 2				
Policy	GPT-2-Small	GPT-2-Medium	GPT-2-Large	GPT-2-XL
GPU	80	62	36	24
CPU	82	76	64	56
DM	82	76	60	52

4.2 Evaluation on GPU Memory Offloading

We use the following three strategies to evaluate the effectiveness of our proposed method:

– GPU: in this policy, all intermediate data are kept in GPU memory without any movement, which is the normal state of model training. It represents the fastest training speed and the highest GPU memory occupation.
– CPU: in this policy, all model data are offloaded to the CPU memory at each computing operation, which is the other extreme case. It represents the slowest training speed and the lowest GPU memory occupation.
– DM: Dynamic Management is our multi-level intermediate data offloading policy mentioned in Sect. 3.1 and it is a compromise between the first two policies. It achieves significant optimization for GPU memory by slightly reducing the training speed.

Training Scale. We collect the maximum batch size in AI model training that can be supported by the same GPU memory capacity under four model scales, as shown in Table 2. Batch size plays an important role in AI model training. If the batch size is too small, it is difficult for the AI model to converge, and it will take a long time to finish the training process. The space saved by offloading some intermediate data in GPU memory can be used to increase the batch size.

Table 3. The GPU memory usage (GB) under different offloading strategies.

Number of GPUs: 1				
Policy	GPT-2-Small	GPT-2-Medium	GPT-2-Large	GPT-2-XL
GPU	4.5	7.3	17.4	out of memory
CPU	3.8	3.2	3.1	5.7
DM	4.0	3.7	5.0	6.1
Number of GPUs: 2				
Policy	GPT-2-Small	GPT-2-Medium	GPT-2-Large	GPT-2-XL
GPU	2.3	3.7	8.8	12.0
CPU	1.7	1.6	2.9	3.3
DM	1.8	1.9	2.6	3.1

Table 4. The training time (min) in an epoch under different offloading strategies.

Number of GPUs: 1				
Policy	GPT-2-Small	GPT-2-Medium	GPT-2-Large	GPT-2-XL
GPU	2.9	5.5	11.7	out of memory
CPU	9.7	22.4	61.8	91.5
DM	6.5	15.2	39.9	56.4
Number of GPUs: 2				
Policy	GPT-2-Small	GPT-2-Medium	GPT-2-Large	GPT-2-XL
GPU	3.3	6.7	16.4	23.4
CPU	11.7	30.4	85.8	123.6
DM	9.5	23.3	66.0	95.2

As shown in Table 2, when the model becomes larger, the maximum batch size decreases rapidly, and even when the batch size is 1, there may be insufficient GPU memory for the GPU policy. However, the DM policy can achieve a 6× batch size of the GPU policy in GPT-2-Large model with the same size of GPU memory. In addition, some models that cannot be trained due to the large scale and insufficient GPU memory capacity can also be successfully trained under the DM policy, such as GPT-2-XL. Compared with the CPU policy, we also achieve an approximate optimization result for GPU memory. We also observe that when the scale of the trained model is small, the effect of the DM policy is not obvious. In this situation, the GPU memory resources are sufficient, and there is no need to exchange the time overhead for more GPU memory space by offloading intermediate data. In Table 2, we also investigate the performance of our method in the distributed system with two GPUs, which indicates the model is trained under data parallelism with Zero Redundancy Optimizer [21]. When using data parallelism with Zero Redundancy Optimizer, there is an increase in the maximum batch size because each GPU retains only a portion of the model data in memory. In this situation, the DM policy can still increase the maximum batch size under the current hardware resources, which means that GPU memory offloading can continue to improve the training scale of the AI model on the basis of parallel training.

Memory Occupation and Training Time. Furthermore, we investigate the GPU memory resource occupation and training time with an equal batch size in AI model training based on three different intermediate data offloading policies. Both situations using 1 and 2 GPUs for AI model training are considered. The GPU memory resource occupations are shown in Table 3 while the training time is shown in Table 4. From Table 3, we can find that in AI model training, GPU memory offloading and data parallelism with Zero Redundancy Optimizer can both reduce the memory occupation on each GPU. Moreover, they can be used simultaneously to free up GPU resources to a greater extent.

In Table 4, we find that when the same batch size is used, the training time under parallel training will be larger, which is the waiting cost caused by data communication between multiple computing devices. With the increase of the AI model scale, the waiting cost will take a larger proportion of the training time. As the model scale continues to increase, more GPUs will be added to the model training, resulting in longer time for communication and scheduling. This illustrates the necessity for an offloading policy to reduce the scale of computing resources for AI model training.

In order to better analyze the influence of different offloading policies on the training time and GPU memory resource occupations in AI model training, we chose two GPT-2 s with different model scales for the analysis, which are trained by single GPU with the same batch size. The results are shown in Fig. 3. The memory overhead in the training of GPT-2-Large based on our DM policy can be reduced to less than 1/3 of the GPU policy, and the space freed up by our policy reaches 86% of the CPU policy. Although the CPU policy requires the least space of GPU memory, it needs more than 5× training time compared with GPU policy, which cannot be tolerant. Our proposed DM policy reaches a 1.549× speed-up and greatly reduces the time overhead of training compared with the CPU policy. These results demonstrate that we reduce a lot of unnecessary intermediate data swaps. In GPT-2-Small, the difference between three policies is not obvious, which is due to the small scale of the model data. The larger the proportion of the model data in GPU memory, the more obvious the improvement brought by our method in AI model training.

4.3   Evaluation on CPU Memory Offloading

Figure 3 also shows the memory usage in the training process of two AI models under different policies. Less GPU memory usage means more CPU memory requirements. In our multi-level intermediate data offloading policy, offloading some intermediate data to the HDD can reduce the pressure on CPU memory, which achieves a lower cost of model training. In this policy, we offload the optimizer state to the HDD with an asynchronous style to avoid time waste.

We report the amount of disk writes, CPU memory usage, and training time in one epoch of model training under different offloading ratios, and the results are shown in Fig. 4.

As the offloading ratio of optimizer states increases, the CPU memory usage decreases and the disk write increases. We find that the training time does not increase proportionally with the increase of the offloading ratio, but increases sharply when the offloading ratio reaches a certain threshold. Because of the limited read/write speed of the HDD, high time-consuming intermediate data exchange affects the loading of the optimizer state.

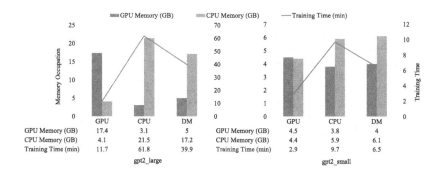

Fig. 3. Two figures show the memory usage and training time of GPT-2-Large and GPT-2-Small in one epoch of training, respectively. They are both trained on a single GPU with batch size set to 4.

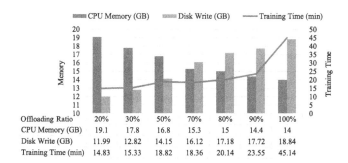

Fig. 4. The CPU memory usage, disk write and training time of GPT-2-Large in one epoch of training at different offloading ratios. The trainings are on a single GPU with batch size set to 24.

5 Conclusion

In this paper, from the perspective of multi-level storage, we train larger models with lower hardware costs. Facing the "memory wall" problem in AI training, we propose a multi-level intermediate data offloading policy. Our policy is a two-stage optimization for GPU memory, which are dynamic management (DM) policy and HDD offloading. The DM policy is an efficient intermediate file offloading policy according to the characteristics of different tensor sizes. At the same time, HDD offloading uses asynchronous reading and writing to offload the optimizer state to the hard disk, which alleviates the problem of high CPU memory usage caused. The experiments on GPT-2 models demonstrate that under the same hardware resources, our method can support the larger model training with an acceptable time waste.

References

1. Belady, L.A.: A study of replacement algorithms for virtual-storage computer. IBM Syst. J. **5**(2), 78–101 (1966)
2. Bian, Z., et al.: Colossal-AI: a unified deep learning system for large-scale parallel training. CoRR abs/2110.14883 (2021)
3. Bian, Z., Xu, Q., Wang, B., You, Y.: Maximizing parallelism in distributed training for huge neural networks. CoRR abs/2105.14450 (2021)
4. Brown, T.B., et al.: Language models are few-shot learners. In: Advances in Neural Information Processing Systems 33: Annual Conference on Neural Information Processing Systems, NeurIPS (2020)
5. Chen, T., Xu, B., Zhang, C., Guestrin, C.: Training deep nets with sublinear memory cost. CoRR abs/1604.06174 (2016)
6. Devlin, J., Chang, M., Lee, K., Toutanova, K.: BERT: pre-training of deep bidirectional transformers for language understanding. In: Proceedings of the 2019 Conference of the North American Chapter of the Association for Computational Linguistics: Human Language Technologies, NAACL-HLT 2019, vol. 1 (Long and Short Papers), pp. 4171–4186 (2019)
7. Dosovitskiy, A., et al.: An image is worth 16×16 words: transformers for image recognition at scale. In: 9th International Conference on Learning Representations, ICLR 2021 (2021)
8. Fang, J., et al.: Parallel training of pre-trained models via chunk-based dynamic memory management. IEEE Trans. Parallel Distrib. Syst. **34**(1), 304–315 (2023)
9. Gokaslan, A., Cohen, V., Pavlick, E., Tellex, S.: (2019). https://Skylion007.github.io/OpenWebTextCorpus
10. Hildebrand, M., Khan, J., Trika, S., Lowe-Power, J., Akella, V.: Autotm: automatic tensor movement in heterogeneous memory systems using integer linear programming. In: ASPLOS '20: Architectural Support for Programming Languages and Operating Systems, Lausanne, pp. 875–890 (2020)
11. Huang, C., Jin, G., Li, J.: Swapadvisor: pushing deep learning beyond the GPU memory limit via smart swapping. In: ASPLOS '20: Architectural Support for Programming Languages and Operating Systems, pp. 1341–1355 (2020)
12. Huang, Y., et al.: Efficient training of giant neural networks using pipeline parallelism. In: Advances in Neural Information Processing Systems 32: Annual Conference on Neural Information Processing Systems, NeurIPS 2019, pp. 103–112 (2019)
13. Kingma, D.P., Ba, J.: Adam: a method for stochastic optimization. In: 3rd International Conference on Learning Representations, ICLR 2015, Conference Track Proceedings (2015)

14. Lin, Y., Han, S., Mao, H., Wang, Y., Dally, B.: Deep gradient compression: reducing the communication bandwidth for distributed training. In: 6th International Conference on Learning Representations, ICLR 2018, Conference Track Proceedings (2018)
15. Liu, E.Z., Hashemi, M., Swersky, K., Ranganathan, P., Ahn, J.: An imitation learning approach for cache replacement. In: Proceedings of the 37th International Conference on Machine Learning, ICML 2020, pp. 6237–6247 (2020)
16. Miao, X., et al.: HET: scaling out huge embedding model training via cache-enabled distributed framework. Proc. VLDB Endow. **15**(2), 312–320 (2021)
17. Narayanan, D., et al.: Pipedream: generalized pipeline parallelism for DNN training. In: Proceedings of the 27th ACM Symposium on Operating Systems Principles, SOSP 2019, pp. 1–15 (2019)
18. Nie, X., Miao, X., Yang, Z., Cui, B.: TSPLIT: fine-grained GPU memory management for efficient DNN training via tensor splitting. In: 38th IEEE International Conference on Data Engineering, ICDE 2022, pp. 2615–2628 (2022)
19. Radford, A., Narasimhan, K., Salimans, T., Sutskever, I.: Improving language understanding by generative pre-training. OpenAI (2018)
20. Radford, A., Wu, J., Child, R., Luan, D., Amodei, D., Sutskever, I.: Language models are unsupervised multitask learners. OpenAI (2019)
21. Rajbhandari, S., Rasley, J., Ruwase, O., He, Y.: Zero: memory optimizations toward training trillion parameter models. In: Proceedings of the International Conference for High Performance Computing, Networking, Storage and Analysis, SC 2020, p. 20 (2020)
22. Rajbhandari, S., Ruwase, O., Rasley, J., Smith, S., He, Y.: Zero-infinity: breaking the GPU memory wall for extreme scale deep learning. In: International Conference for High Performance Computing, Networking, Storage and Analysis, SC 2021, p. 59 (2021)
23. Ren, J., et al.: Zero-offload: democratizing billion-scale model training. In: 2021 USENIX Annual Technical Conference, USENIX ATC 2021, pp. 551–564 (2021)
24. Shoeybi, M., Patwary, M., Puri, R., LeGresley, P., Casper, J., Catanzaro, B.: Megatron-LM: training multi-billion parameter language models using model parallelism. CoRR abs/1909.08053 (2019)
25. Vaswani, A., et al.: Attention is all you need. In: Advances in Neural Information Processing Systems 30: Annual Conference on Neural Information Processing Systems, NeurIPS 2017, pp. 5998–6008 (2017)
26. Wang, B., Xu, Q., Bian, Z., You, Y.: 2.5-dimensional distributed model training. CoRR abs/2105.14500 (2021)
27. Xu, Q., You, Y.: An efficient 2D method for training super-large deep learning models. In: IEEE International Parallel and Distributed Processing Symposium, IPDPS 2023, pp. 222–232 (2023)
28. Zeng, W., et al.: PanGu-α: large-scale autoregressive pretrained Chinese language models with auto-parallel computation. CoRR abs/2104.12369 (2021)

Enhancing Night-to-Day Image Translation with Semantic Prior and Reference Image Guidance

Junzhi Ning[1] and Mingming Gong[2(✉)]

[1] University of Sydney, Sydney, Australia
`jnin9950@uni.sydney.edu.au`
[2] University of Melbourne, Melbourne, Australia
`mingming.gong@unimelb.edu.au`

Abstract. Current unpaired image-to-image translation models deal with the datasets on unpaired domains effectively but face the challenge of mapping images from domains with scarce information to domains with abundant information due to the degradation of visibility and the loss of semantic information. To improve the quality of night-to-day translation further, we propose a novel image translation method named "RefN2D-Guide GAN" that utilizes reference images to improve the adaptability of the encoder within the generator through the feature matching loss. Moreover, we introduce a segmentation module to assist in preserving the semantic details of the generated images without the need for ground true annotations. The incorporation of the embedding consistency loss differentiates the roles of the encoder and decoder and facilitates the transfer of learned representation to both translation directions. Our experimental results show that our proposed method can effectively enhance the quality of night-to-day image translation on the night training set of the ACDC dataset and achieve higher mIoU on the translated images.

Keywords: Unpaired Image-to-Image Translation · Semantic Segmentation

1 Introduction

In the field of image translation, the primary objective is to develop an end-to-end model capable of converting images from one domain to another with the goals of preserving semantic details from the source domain and adapting the appearance in the target domain. In recent years, the paradigm of adversarial generative network [5] has enabled image translation applications [9,17,21] in areas such as super-resolution, style transfer, and image synthesis. To adopt more general scenarios and extend its applicability, the idea of unpaired image translation was proposed, which allows the conversion of images from the source to the target domain without the requirement of paired correspondences. One

Z. Bao et al. (Eds.): ADC 2023, LNCS 14386, pp. 164–182, 2024.
https://doi.org/10.1007/978-3-031-47843-7_12

of the research directions on unpaired image translation is to relieve the requirement of pair correspondence by establishing a distance measure that captures the difference through their source domain and the reconstructed image back to the original domain, namely Cycle Consistency Loss [26].

However, the methods [11,12,19,26] that use this cycle reconstruction cause a lack of control over the translated output, the emergence of unwanted artifacts, and the generation of unnatural representations within the target domain. Furthermore, the cycle consistency approach, while not requiring image or pixel-wise correspondence, may struggle to accurately depict the intricate structural details in the target domain. Such limitations could be particularly harmful when applying image translation in source and target domains where the contrast of the visual clues is sharp. Image translation from night-to-day directions is one such example in which the image translation quality in this setting has the need that not only realistically, but also correctly interpret the semantic details during the translation. In domains where illumination conditions significantly impact the quality and reliability of visual data, the ability to translate low-light, under-exposed images to their well-lit counterparts is crucial. To overcome inherent difficulties in image translation, most night-to-day image translation methods [10,13,16,25] augment their ability to extract details from low-light and under-exposed images by incorporating additional network structures and annotations. Nonetheless, it's imperative to highlight that these annotations might not always be conveniently accessible and often generate translation outcomes that lack the realism and accuracy required to depict actual scenes. An expedient solution presents itself in the utilization of additional data derived from images present in nearby locations, termed as "reference images". The acquisition of these reference images typically poses less of a challenge compared to procuring other forms of supplementary data.

The current methodology as presented by [13] necessitates additional elements, such as pixel-level semantic annotations, to optimize the conversion quality from the night-time to the daylight domain, which is infeasible in many translation scenarios. On the contrary, our approach negates the need for available pixel-level semantic annotations by integrating a pre-trained segmentation model capable of conducting on-the-fly pixel predictions for daylight images. Furthermore, the generators of the translation model for both directions, cultivated through this methodology, are connected to the converse path of image translation. The connection of this type is established via internal consistency constraints placed on embeddings being generated by the encoders from the translators. To reduce the chance of generating artificial visual elements in output image space that arise in transitioning from less detailed to more informative domains, our method makes use of visual cues derived from reference images. The reference images, procured from approximate Global Positioning System (GPS) coordinates under optimal lighting conditions, are subsequently mapped against each corresponding original image within the layers of the generator's encoder to extract pairs of feature maps. This permits the production of a more cohesive image generation, thereby improving the rendering of accurate semantic content from poorly lit and obscure areas.

Hence, our main contributions in this work are summarized as follows; First, we developed a novel model "RefN2D-Guide GAN" that leverages feature matching loss, utilizing reference images to facilitate the learning process of the encoder within the image translation model. Then we also introduced a segmentation module within the "RefN2D-Guide GAN" framework, which assists in retaining semantic detail throughout the translation process, eliminating the need for ground truth labels. Lastly, we employed an embedding consistency loss function in "RefN2D-Guide GAN" to differentiate the roles of the encoder and decoder in the image translation generator.

2   Related Work

Unpaired Image Translation. Unpaired Image Translation learns the bidirectional function of being able to map the image in the source domain into the target domain. CycleGan [26] utilizes the Cycle Consistency loss to enforce the conversion of images from the source domain to the target domain to be realistic and detailed by reducing the distance between the original images and the reconstructed images through the cycle reconstruction. Sequentially, the work of [12] enhances the resolution of the image translation by decoupling the stages of the translation in a multi-step manner. The methodology introduced by [11] employs an attention module and AdaLIN module to finely tune the geometric transformations in both texture and shape. This allows for a focused examination of critical regions within an image, a technique further expanded upon in subsequent research by [19] with their implementation of an attention mechanism. Later, the work in [6] constructs a constraint called SCC to alleviate the random changing pattern of color transformation during the image translation. The contrastive learning techniques discussed in [7,16] employ the contrastive learning framework to acquire more robust feature representations, thereby addressing image translation challenges. Nonetheless, existing methods of unpaired image-to-image translation grapple with problems associated with inaccuracies in visual interpretation and inconsistencies in the nuanced details of translated images. In the methodology we propose, we utilize reference images as aids to enhance the subtleties in detail and surmount the challenge of rendering high-precision details in the translated domains.

Night-to-Day Image Translation. Image translation methods dedicated to night-day conversion are designed to tackle the above problems. Prior work [10] extends the work from Tang et al. [19] with the aim of adapting the image translation under low light conditions by allocating local and global discriminators to discern subtle differences. ToDayGAN [1] leverages the pose estimation to identify semantic information on generated results under underexposed conditions. SPN2DGAN [13] explores the idea of supplying additional semantic masks to improve the translated image quality. ForkGan [25] introduces the alternative path of reconstruction beside the cycle reconstruction, improving the capability of invariant feature extraction for the encoder of the generator. However, current methods predominantly depend on supplementary network structures or extra annotations to enhance image quality in Night-to-Day scenarios, which may not always be practical for real-world implementation. Deploying our adaptive segmentation module reduces the need for ground-truth semantic annotations.

3   Methods

Notations. G and D denote the generators and discriminators of the image translation model, respectively. X_{name} refers to the dataset, with *"name"* indicating the specific dataset. $Seg_{subscript}$ represents the utilized segmentation model. $Enc_{generator}$ and $Dec_{generator}$ are notations for the encoder and decoder components of the generators in the image translation model.

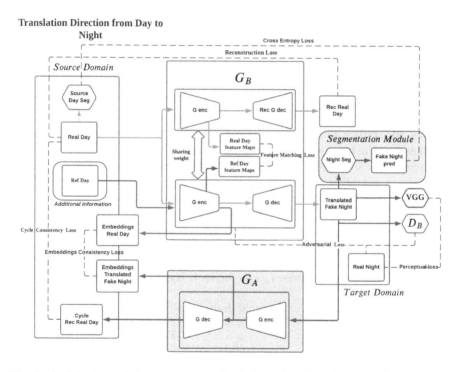

Fig. 1. Architecture of the proposed method: Direction from day to night domains.

Overview. Our training process consists of two distinct stages, a forward cycle and a backward cycle. In the transition from daytime to nighttime domains, depicted in Fig. 1, a copy of the segmentation model obtained from training on the source domain serves as the starting point for our segmentation module. The G_B generator processes the daytime domain image to produce a translated version. Concurrently, reference images are input into the generator G_B to obtain feature maps at intermediate layers for computing the feature matching loss. Given the same image, the embed-dings of the nighttime image and the trans-lated daytime image are extracted from the encoders of the generators G_B and G_A, respectively. The reverse translation direction is formulated similarly.

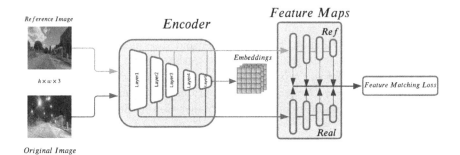

Fig. 2. The detailed architecture of Feature Matching Loss involves using 9 ResNet blocks as constituent elements of the encoder network. The output of each ResNet block serves as one feature map for both the original image and the reference image.

Feature Matching Loss. Feature maps of both reference and daytime images are aligned at the layer level to constrain the translation encoder of the genera-tor, learning feature representations from both the original and reference images. This aims to establish consistency in feature maps at each output layer level within an encoder of a generator. This main concept is visually illustrated in Fig. 2. Specifically, an encoder in the generators receives both the original image and its corresponding image as input images. Subsequently, the encoder net-work produces feature maps at the intermediate layers, and these feature maps obtained from the original and reference images are used to compute the normal-ized summation of channel-wise l_1 loss for each layer as $\mathcal{L}_{Fea}$. The formulation of this loss is defined as:

For the direction from the Daytime domain to the nighttime domain,

$$\mathcal{L}_{Fea}(G_B) = \sum_{(x,x_{ref})\in(X_{Day},X_{RefDay})} \sum_{l\in Layers} \frac{1}{HW}||\frac{Enc_{G_B}^l(x) - Enc_{G_B}^l(x_{ref})}{Mean(Enc_{G_B}^l(x))}||_2^2,$$

(1)

where $H \times W$ are two dimensions of the input image, and $Layers$ refer to a set of layers' index of the encoder network. $Enc_{G_B}^l$ refers to the lth layer of the feature map within the encoder of the network.

Semantic Loss. The translated daytime image subsequently passes through the segmentation module to produce semantic label predictions. Once the semantic labels are obtained from the segmentation module, semi-supervised learning is conducted using cross-entropy loss with the semantic predictions generated by the pre-trained model on the original daytime image. This property eliminates the need for source domain labels. In contrast to methods presented in [13], which require ground truth labels as a semantic prior, our approach only necessitates a segmentation model trained on a domain similar to the source domain. Mathematically, the semantic loss is expressed as a vectorized version:

$$\mathcal{L}_{Seg} = -\frac{1}{|X_{Day}|} \sum_{i=1}^{|X_{Day}|} \frac{1}{|H \times W|} \sum_{j \in C, x \in (X_{Day})i} p_i(x) log(\hat{p}_i(x)), \qquad (2)$$

where $|X_{Day}|$ denotes the size of the dataset in the source domain, i.e., the Daytime domain, C represents the class of labels in the dataset, $|H \times W|$ is the dimension of the input image, the segmentation model named as "*Source Day Seg*" illustrated in Fig. 1, remains fixed; its model parameters are not updated during image translation training process, yielding $p_i(x) = (Seg_{fixed}(x))_i$. Another segmentation model takes the translated image $G_B(X)$ as input and outputs the semantic label maps prediction, $\hat{p}_i(x) = [Seg(G_B(x))]_i$, with dimensions $|C| \times H \times W$. During the training phase, this segmentation model, Seg, is also trained, guided by the loss $\mathcal{L}_{Seg}$.

Embedding Consistency Loss. Bridging the embeddings produced by the encoders of the generators G_A and G_B promotes the similarity of the feature representation of both encoders in either translation direction shown in Fig. 2. The main principle of designing the loss for this ensures the correspondence of the original and translated images, reflecting in terms of feature representations produced by the encoders. The correspondence of the image and its translated image specifically refers to the consistency of the images that should reveal the same semantic details rather than their style outlined in different domains. To be more specific, we formulate the loss as follows.

For the images in the domain of Real Daytime,

$$\mathcal{L}_{Embeddings}(X_{Day}) = \frac{1}{|X_{Day}|} \sum_{i=1}^{|X_{Day}|} ||Enc_{G_B}(x_i) - Enc_{G_A}(G_B(x_i))||_F, \qquad (3)$$

where $Enc_{G_A}(\cdot)$ and $Enc_{G_B}(\cdot)$ are the feature embed-dings produced by the two encoders of the generators G_A and G_B in the image translation model and $||\cdot||_F$ is the Frobenius norm.

Additional Loss Functions. In the procedure of pixel-level correspondence establishment for image reconstruction, our method, taking inspiration from the approach delineated in [26], integrates a cycle consistency loss, $\mathcal{L}_{Cyc}(G_B, G_A)$. To facilitate the transformation between the source and target image domains, we incorporate an adversarial loss, $\mathcal{L}_{adv}$, within the architecture of a generative adversarial network. To ensure the preservation of the source domain's semantic details while mirroring the target domain's appearance in the shift from nighttime to daytime, we employ the perceptual loss, $\mathcal{L}_{per}$, and an edge loss, as detailed in [13]. For succinctness, we apply a commonly used l_1 reconstruction loss to improve boundary sensitivity, as described in [25].

Image Recovery Module. The Image Recovery module of the proposed method consists of two parts, one comes from the reconstruction loss and another part comes from the cycle consistency loss:

$$\mathcal{L}_{Recovery} = \lambda_{Cyc}\mathcal{L}_{Cyc} + \lambda_{Rec}\mathcal{L}_{Rec}, \tag{4}$$

where the values of λ_{Cyc} and λ_{Rec} are two parameters to control the weight of the losses $\mathcal{L}_{Cyc}$ and $\mathcal{L}_{Rec}$ in the objective function value.

Night-to-Day Image Translation Module. For the direction of Nighttime to Daytime, the translation module is composed of two parts for each direction of image translation.

$$\begin{aligned}\mathcal{L}_{Night \to Day} = &\lambda_{fea}\mathcal{L}_{fea}(G_A) + \lambda_{adv}\mathcal{L}_{adv}(G_A, D_A, X_{day}, X_{night}) \\ &+ \mathcal{L}_{per}(G_A, X_{night}, X_{day}) + \lambda_{Embeddings}\mathcal{L}_{Embeddings}(X_{Night}),\end{aligned} \tag{5}$$

where the values of λ_{fea}, $\lambda_{Embeddings}$, and λ_{adv} control the weight of loss components in the optimization of the model. Analogously, we define $\mathcal{L}_{Day \to Night}$, which implicates the reverse direction: transitioning from the daytime domain to the nighttime domain, notwithstanding the absence of the segmentation module.

Overall Objective Function. The final objective function of our proposed method is the combination of the modules introduced in the above sections. It can be written as:

$$\mathcal{L}_{Proposed\ Method} := \mathcal{L}_{Night \to Day} + \mathcal{L}_{Day \to Night} + \lambda_{Seg}\mathcal{L}_{Seg} + \mathcal{L}_{Recovery}. \tag{6}$$

4   Experimental Setup

4.1   Setup

Data-sets: ACDC [18] is the abbreviated name for Adverse Conditions Dataset with Correspondences, consisting of 4,006 images with fine-grained pixel-level annotations, divided into four subdomains representing adverse conditions. The images depict adverse conditions such as rain, fog, nighttime, and snow, and for each condition, a reference image of the same resolution is provided. These reference images are typically obtained by pairing nearby GPS locations of images in adverse conditions with those taken during daytime and under normal conditions. However, the reference images are not aligned at the pixel level, as illustrated in Fig. 3.

Fig. 3. Illustration of the collection process of ACDC

Evaluation Metrics

FID and KID stands for Fréchet Inception Distance [8] and kernel Inception Distance [2] are widely-used evaluation metrics for assessing the image quality of generated or translated images, particularly in the field of generative adversarial networks. The computation of FID and KID both involves comparing the similarity or distance between the distribution of real images and translated images by measuring the Fréchet Inception Distance between feature representations in the inception network and Maximum Mean Discrepancy using a kernel function called Radial Basis Kernel respectively. Generally, lower scores of KID and FID signify that the generated images are closer to the real image, implying a higher quality of image translation.

Mean Intersection-over-Union (mIoU) is an evaluation metric commonly used in the field of semantic segmentation computer vision tasks. mIoU quantifies the overlapping region of the predicted class labeled and the ground truth class labels, enabling a numerical way to measure the performance of the semantic segmentation model. To compute the IoU for one class label, it calculates the ratio of the interaction and union between the ground truth and the prediction class labels across all pixels of images in a dataset. Then, mean interaction over union is the average of Iou over all class labels.

Implementation Details. The implementation of the proposed work is built upon the works of SPN2D from [13] and CycleGAN from [26]. During the development of the proposed network, we make use of the code frameworks from [20,22], and [24]. To facilitate the training of the segmentation model used in our proposal, we also leverage the pre-trained semantic segmentation model trained on the Cityscapes dataset as an initialization for the segmentation module of our network. The training images are resized into a square dimension of 512×512 in order to pass through the network and are upsampled using bilinear interpolation to a resolution of 1920×1080 for evaluation. In terms of optimization, the Adam optimizer with beta parameters of 0.9 and 0.999 is adopted to optimize the components with a base learning rate of 0.0002, using the cosine annealing learning rate strategy throughout the training. During the testing stage of our experiments, we activate the trained generator to produce translated images from the nighttime domain to the daytime domain.

4.2   Results and Discussion

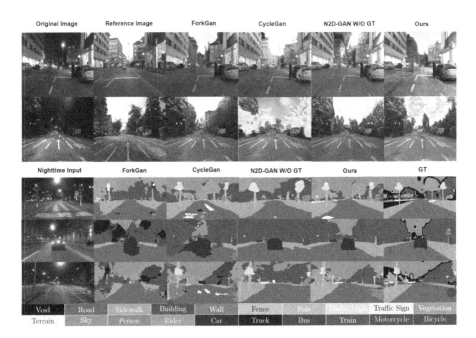

Fig. 4. Top: Experimental Results of Night-To-Day image Translation on ACDC night Val set. From left to right depict real-world nighttime images, the results of ForkGan, CycleGan, N2D GAN, Proposed Method. **Bottom**: Experimental Results of Night-To-Day Semantic Segmentation on ACDC night Train set Against the semantic predictions generated by the translated image obtained from the pre-trained RefineNet model on CityScapes. From left to right: real-world nighttime images, the results of ForkGan, CycleGan, N2D GAN, and Proposed Method. Ground truth semantic labels are in the last column.

Translation Methods Comparison. We compare our proposed RefN2D-Guide GAN method with previous methods used in night-to-day image translation settings, including CycleGAN [26], ForkGAN [25], and N2D-GAN[1] [14]. In particular, we examine three aspects of the methods using the metrics of KID, FID, and mIOU for assessing the image quality of translation and the capability of restoring semantic details. The experimental results of the three metrics are

---

[1] For the comparison in experiments, N2D-GAN employed has removed the segmentation module using the guidance of ground truth semantic labels.

shown in Table 1. The mIOU results obtained are the average mIOU over the pre-trained segmentation models of DeepLab [3], PSPNet [23], and Refinement [15], with detailed mIOU results in Table 2. Overall, thanks to the incorporation of the segmentation model, our proposed method shows an improvement of mIOU from 19.84% to 23.72% on the generated images compared to the N2D-GAN method. For other unpaired image translation methods, the improvement in mIOU metrics is even more significant.

At a more detailed level of the experimental results for the four image translation methods, our RefN2D-Guide GAN method is capable of performing night-to-day image translation by accurately maintaining the natural and clear-cut boundaries of semantic classes, effectively converting nighttime images to daytime style. This advantage is clearly demonstrated in Fig. 4. In the second row of the top part in Fig. 4, for other methods like CycleGAN, we can see that neighboring regions between the buildings and the sky are missing details in those areas. ForkGAN and CycleGAN methods fail to define the edge of the buildings and the sky, and the immediate transition from the building to the sky lacks visual details that are natural and realistic.

Table 1. Quantitative Comparison In Fid, Kid And Non-Ref Image Quality Metrics. mIOU results are the average of the semantic maps under the three methods: DeepLab, RefineNet, and PspNet.

Model	FID ↓	KID ↓	mIoU↑ (Train/Val)
CycleGAN	104.13	0.079 (0.002)	21.137/17.483
ForkGan	94.76	0.087 (0.002)	21.157/17.860
N2D-GAN	95.32	0.088 (0.003)	23.877/19.847
Our method	**74.10**	**0.056(0.002)**	**26.590/23.727**

To conduct a qualitative evaluation of semantic information preservation, we utilize three pre-trained segmentation models, derived from CityScapes, to generate semantic maps from images translated through four different image translation methods. The situation diverges for other classes, where numerous preceding image translation techniques tend to incur information loss for smaller, ambiguous classes that are common during the nighttime. These classes, due to the lack of a segmentation module, are prone to distortion during translation. Nevertheless, our proposed approach exhibits significant effectiveness in maintaining segmentation outcomes, as illustrated in Fig. 4. The semantic information supplied by the segmentation module augments the image translation process, leading to heightened restoration of semantic details in the image space as illustrated in Fig. 5. The mean Intersection over Union (mIOU) of semantic prediction sees an average increase of 5% compared to the results generated by the original nighttime images and exhibits a 2–4% improvement over the other two

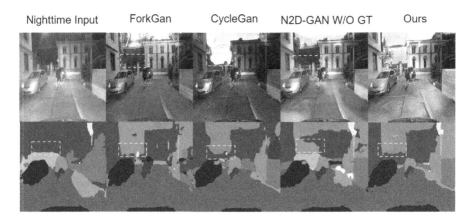

| Nighttime Input | ForkGan | CycleGan | N2D-GAN W/O GT | Ours |

Fig. 5. The experimental result of the night-to-day image translation on the ACDC night test set, compared against the semantic predictions generated by the pre-trained CityScapes model, are presented in this figure. From left to right, the images depict real-world nighttime images, the results of ForkGan, CycleGan, N2D GAN W/O GT, and the proposed method.

night-to-day image translation models. However, it is important to note that, akin to most image translation methods, the proposed method is not completely exempt from a slight loss of semantic information.

Table 2. The experimental results demonstrate the segmentation performance of pre-trained Cityscapes models on translated images produced by the four image translation approaches.

Translation Methods	Segmentation Model	Static Classes	Dynamic Classes	Background Classes	Urban Signage classes	mIoU(%)
Original Night Image	DeepLab	23.772	14.183	33.193	21.283	20.829
CycleGan		24.878	11.29	47.787	11.44	20.652
ForkGan		19.732	9.7775	47.922	15.4	19.307
N2D-GAN W/O GT		26.674	13.881	45.960	21.510	23.517
Proposed Method		**28.159**	**16.992**	**49.108**	**22.336**	**25.845**
Original Night Image	PspNet	20.504	**17.443**	35.747	**24.850**	22.308
CycleGan		23.652	9.206	49.817	11.153	19.727
ForkGan		18.724	9.460	52.845	14.125	19.485
N2D-GAN W/O GT		25.626	12.430	48.877	19.940	22.843
Proposed Method		**28.857**	14.643	**56.061**	22.182	**26.113**
Original Night Image	RefineNet	**30.987**	**22.561**	39.847	**23.363**	27.634
CycleGan		27.636	14.649	52.610	10.460	23.399
ForkGan		19.606	10.458	52.352	11.572	19.656
N2D-GAN W/O GT		28.278	16.224	49.307	19.837	25.190
Proposed Method		30.352	18.890	**52.867**	22.266	**27.804**

Ablation Study of the Proposed Method. The experimental results from the ablation study of our method are presented in Table 3. The baseline was established using the same settings as those applied in the CycleGAN method. Upon evaluating the experimental results, a consistent increase in the metrics scores (FID, KID, and mIOU) with each module addition to the baseline method is observed. The primary objective of the Reconstruction module was to enhance the encoder and decoder's roles within the generator to extract invariant features from the source domain. The desired outcome of this module was reflected by the mIOU score increase from 19.85% to 23.87% for the training set and from 19.85% to 22.11% on average. The module of the feature matching loss was to enrich the texture details on the target domains, specifically addressing the invisible regions in the nighttime images. As for the integration of the consistency embedding loss in our proposed method, our method enhances the homogeneity of feature representation produced by encoders in both directions when processing the same image during the cycle reconstruction in the image translation model. Lastly, the equipment of the segmentation module to the method further enhances the image quality of the translation from the nighttime to the daytime domain.

Table 3. Ablation Study of the Proposed method

Components				FID$_\downarrow$	KID$_\downarrow$	mIoU $\uparrow$(Train/Val)
$\mathcal{L}_{\text{Rec}}$	$\mathcal{L}_{\text{Fea}}$	$\mathcal{L}_{\text{Embeddings}}$	$\mathcal{L}_{\text{Seg}}$			
✗	✗	✗	✗	98.17	0.094 (0.003)	23.87/19.85
✓	✗	✗	✗	98.50	0.098 (0.003)	25.32/22.11
✓	✓	✗	✗	85.21	0.072 (0.002)	25.12/21.69
✓	✗	✓	✗	82.93	0.074 (0.003)	25.49/22.23
✓	✓	✓	✗	81.60	0.072 (0.002)	26.44/22.94
✓	✓	✓	✓	74.10	0.056 (0.002)	26.59/23.72

5 Conclusions

In this research, we introduce a novel unpaired image-to-image translation method, termed "RefN2D-Guide GAN". It improves and enhances the effectiveness of night-to-day image translation by utilizing reference images with the help of feature matching loss and the assistance of a segmentation module derived from a pre-existing segmentation model. The module does not depend on ground truth semantic labels, and it is capable of supporting fine-grained image translation in the context of night-to-day translation. An embedding consistency module reduces the distance of the feature representation on the same image during the process of the image translation generator. Our empirical analysis and results on the ACDC night dataset demonstrate enhancement in image quality in translation.

Acknowledgements. This project was carried out utilizing the high-performance computing resources provided by Artemis HPC [4] at the University of Sydney.

A   Appendix

A.1   Opposite Direction of Image Translation

See Fig. 6.

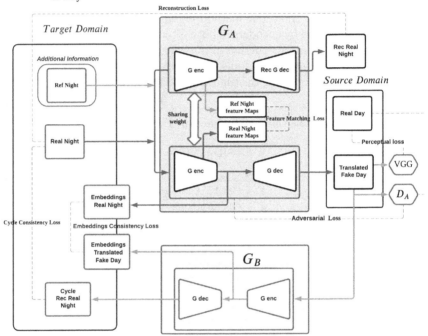

Fig. 6. Architecture of the proposed method: Direction from Night to Day domains.

A.2   Details on the Construction of the Training and Evaluation Data

For the evaluation stage of the image translation experiments, we evaluate our performance based on the translation task from the night condition of the ACDC dataset to the referring domains of three adverse conditions. We choose this image dataset as our primary evaluation benchmark for the following reasons:

- One of the key contributions of the proposed model is to leverage the reference images from the dataset. The ACDC dataset provides a set of reference images for each adverse condition, making the evaluation of our experimental results possible.
- ACDC contains a specific adverse domain dedicated to nighttime street views, with fine-grained pixel-level annotations for up to 400 images. This aligns with the proposed model's goal of translating from daytime to nighttime.

– The reference images of the three adverse conditions in the ACDC dataset, including rain, snow, and fog, can act as daytime domains, as reference images for each adverse condition are taken during daytime. The original images in the three adverse conditions can serve as reference images in the settings of image translation from nighttime to daytime, providing an abundant source of data to train a sufficiently accurate translation model for evaluation purposes.

The Table 4 presents the details of data used in the experiment for training and validation. For the Daytime domain, we leverage the reference images of the three adverse conditions (i.e., Rain, Snow, and Fog) in ACDC as the training images. This is possible because the reference images for these three conditions are all taken under normal weather conditions during the daytime. We swap the sets of Rain, Snow, and Fog images with their corresponding reference sets in ACDC, using them as the training set and reference set, respectively.

Table 4. Subsets of ACDC dataset used for the experiments and evaluation

Domains	Data-set	No.Train Images	No.Ref Images	No.Val Images
Nighttime	ACDC Night (Train)	400	400	106
	ACDC Night (Test)	500	500	
Daytime	ACDC Rain(Train)	400	400	106
	ACDC Snow(Train)	400	400	106
	ACDC Fog(Train)	400	400	106

A.3 Hyper Parameter Learning of λ_{Seg}

The strength of the coefficient in the final objective to control the importance of the segmentation module plays a role in determining the weight of accepting the useful guidance from this module. We explore the choices of λ_{Seg} over a range of 0.3 to 1. For the dataset of the ACDC nighttime domain, we found that our proposed method performs best on the interval between 0.3 and 0.7 and it has an average of 26.6816 mIoU for this chosen interval. In general, the performance is not significantly affected by the choices of λ_{seg}. Nonetheless, it is recommended to adjust this hyperparameter when applying it to disparate datasets (Table 5).

Table 5. Hyperparameter Study of different choices of λ_{Seg} of the proposed method evaluated on the three pre-trained City-Scapes segmentation models on ACDC train set.

Segmentation Models	$mIoU \uparrow$			
	$\lambda_{Seg} = 0.3$	$\lambda_{Seg} = 0.5$	$\lambda_{Seg} = 0.7$	$\lambda_{Seg} = 1.0$
DeepLab	25.165	25.55	25.545	25.843
PspNet	25.65	25.72	25.82	26.113
RefineNet	27.755	28.775	28.18	27.80
Average	26.196	**26.682**	26.515	26.58

A.4 Grouping the Classes for Better Visualization in Assessing the Segmentation Performance

Conducting Semantic Segmentation Evaluation (mIoU) on the translated images as opposed to the original images in the nighttime. This is to evaluate the model's ability to preserve semantic details and in-paint invisible and under-exposed regions of night-time images during the image translation from the nighttime domain to the target domain. Here, we group the class labels into four categories to better visualize the experimental results in Table 6.

Table 6. For a clearer visualization of the semantic results, we group the 19 semantic classes into ACDC into four broad categories.

Name of Class Groups	Classes	Number of Classes
Static Classes	Building, Wall, Fence, Vegetation, Terrain	5
Dynamic Classes	Person, Rider, Car, Truck, Bus, Train, Motorcycle, Bicycle	8
Background Classes	Sky, Road, Sidewalk	3
Urban Signage Classes	Pole, Light, Sign	3
Total Number of Class Labels		19

A.5 Table of the Notations and Symbols in the Proposed Method

Notations		Description
G_A	$\triangleq$	the image translation generator from the Nighttime Domain to Daytime Domain
G_B	$\triangleq$	the image translation generator from the Daytime Domain to the Nighttime Domain
D_A	$\triangleq$	the image discriminator to detect the Real Daytime image and the Fake "translated" Daytime image
D_B	$\triangleq$	the image discriminator to detect the Real Nighttime image and the Fake "translated" Nighttime image
X_{Night}	$\triangleq$	the nighttime domain
$X_{RefNight}$	$\triangleq$	the reference nighttime domain
$X_{RecNight}$	$\triangleq$	the reconstruction nighttime domain
$X_{CycleNight}$	$\triangleq$	the cycle consistency restoration nighttime domain
X_{Day}	$\triangleq$	the daytime domain
X_{RefDay}	$\triangleq$	the reference daytime domain
X_{RecDay}	$\triangleq$	the reconstruction daytime domain
$X_{CycleDay}$	$\triangleq$	the cycle consistency restoration daytime domain
$Seg_{Pretrained}$	$\triangleq$	the segmentation model that receives the input image from X_{Day}
Seg	$\triangleq$	the segmentation model that receives the input image from $G_B(X_{Night})$
$Enc_{G_{A/B}}$	$\triangleq$	the encoder of the generator G_A or G_B
$Dec_{G_{A/B}}$	$\triangleq$	the decoder of the generator G_A or G_B
$Dec_{G_{Rec\ A/B}}$	$\triangleq$	the reconstruction decoder of the generator G_A or G_B

A.6   The Code Skeleton of the Proposed Method

To illustrate the training procedure of our proposed method, we present the detailed pseudo codes in Algorithm 1 to implement this method for further inspection.

Algorithm 1. Pseudo Codes of RefN2D-Guide GAN

Input: $X_{Night}, X_{RefNight}, X_{RefDay}, X_{Day}, Seg_{pretrained}, f_{vgg}, epochs$
Initialize: $G_A^0, G_B^0, D_A^0, D_B^0$ and Seg^0 from $Seg_{pretrained}$
Output: G_A^k, G_B^k, Seg^k
for $k \leftarrow 1$ to $epochs$ do
    Forward Cycle: $Daytime \rightarrow Nigthtime \rightarrow Daytime$ ▷ **Step1A**
    $X_{FakeNight}, X_{RecDay}, F_{Day}^{GB}, F_{RefDay}^{GB}, E_{Day}^{GB} = G_B^k(X_{Day}, X_{RefDay})$
    $X_{CycDay}, E_{FakeNight}^{GA} = G_A^k(X_{FakeNight})$
    $P_{Day}^{Pred} = Seg_{pretrained}^k(X_{Day})$ and $P_{FakeNight}^{Pred} = Seg^k(X_{FakeNight})$
    Backward Cycle: $Nigthtime \rightarrow Daytime \rightarrow Nigthtime$ ▷ **Step1B**
    $X_{FakeDay}, X_{RecNight}, F_{Night}^{GA}, F_{RefNight}^{GB}, E_{Night}^{GA} = G_A^k(X_{Night}, X_{RefDay})$
    $X_{CycNight}, E_{FakeDay}^{GA} = G_B^k(X_{FakeDay})$
    Loss Computation ▷ **Step2**
    Compute the loss $\mathcal{L}_{Cyc}$ with $G_A^k, G_B^k, X_{Day}, X_{Night}, X_{CycNight}, X_{CycDay}$
    Compute the loss $\mathcal{L}_{Adv}$ with $G_A^k, G_B^k, D_A^k, D_B^k, X_{Day}, X_{Night}, X_{FakeNight}, X_{FakeDay}$
    Compute the loss $\mathcal{L}_{Rec}$ with $G_A^k, G_B^k, X_{Day}, X_{Night}, X_{RecDay}, X_{RecNight}$
    Compute the loss $\mathcal{L}_{Seg}$ with $Seg, P_{Day}^{Pred}, P_{FakeNight}^{Pred}$
    Compute the loss $\mathcal{L}_{Per}$ with $f_{vgg}, X_{Day}, X_{Night}, X_{FakeDay}, X_{FakeNight}$
    Compute the loss $\mathcal{L}_{Fea}$ with $F_{Day}^{GB}, F_{RefDay}^{GB}, F_{Night}^{GA}, F_{RefNight}^{GB}$
    Compute the loss $\mathcal{L}_{Embeddings}$ with $E_{FakeNight}^{GA}, E_{Night}^{GA}, E_{FakeDay}^{GA}$
    Sum up to obtain the total loss ▷ **Step 3**

$$L_{total\ Objective} = \lambda_{Cyc}\mathcal{L}_{Cyc} + \lambda_{adv}\mathcal{L}_{Adv} + \lambda_{Rec}\mathcal{L}_{Rec} + \lambda_{Seg}\mathcal{L}_{Seg}$$
$$+ \mathcal{L}_{Per} + \lambda_{Fea}\mathcal{L}_{Fea} + \lambda_{Embeddings}\mathcal{L}_{Embeddings}$$

    Update the models' parameters ▷ **Step 4**
    Update the parameters of $G_A^k, G_B^k, D_A^k, D_B^k, Seg^k$ with $L_{total\ Objective}$ using Adam
    to obtain $G_A^{k+1}, G_B^{k+1}, D_A^{k+1}, D_B^{k+1}, Seg^{k+1}$
end for

A.7   Limitations

Despite improvement in our model, we identify certain limitations that need to pay the attention for further improvement in future research:

- **Mitigating Unwanted Semantic In-Painting**
  We need to tackle the issue of unnecessary semantic in-painting in specific classes within the target domain, especially in vegetation. In scenarios where imbalanced classes are present, we have seen that the generator may erroneously interpret regions with low light conditions, which leads to in-painting inaccuracies in the translations. Although this is partially mitigated by semantic prediction it does exist in the proposed method. Specifically in our case, the semantic class of vegetation is being misinterpreted in the translated images where the image in the original domain does not have the visual clues in those regions.

– **Addressing Motion Blur and Glare**
Challenges related to motion blurring and glare elimination in night-to-day translation direction require addressing. Motion blurring is influenced by dataset choice and is common in datasets containing moving images. In our experiment, the ACDC datasets gathered from a car-mounted camera capturing street views, suffer from this problem and penalized the quality of image translation. In addition to motion blurring, glare from light sources is a significant hurdle to enhancing the existing image translation method from the nighttime domain to the daytime domain. As a primary research, direction involves improving the image translation method's capability to capture geometric and textural features, these issues can severely lead to inaccurate conversions of semantic details that do not actually exist in the daytime domain.

– **Semantic Detail Preservation Challenges**
It is essential to enhance the preservation of semantic details for smaller and dynamic objects. Without ground labels in our method, the mismatch between the source and target domains may cause semantic predictions to overlook these objects. For instance, a pre-trained semantic segmentation model, trained on a dataset similar to the source domains like the daytime domain in our problem settings, may fail to predict accurate semantic maps for distant objects or those with a small proportion. This limitation further restricts the guidance of semantic knowledge, which could otherwise improve the quality of image translation in our method.

– **Empirical Evaluation Challenges**
In the context of empirical investigation, our method's performance evaluation is limited due to the scarcity of datasets with the availability of reference images. For a more comprehensive performance assessment, it is critical to conduct empirical statistical analyses across a diverse range of datasets in night-to-day settings.

A.8   Future Directions

– **Improved Control of Semantic Prediction**
Due to the uncertainty of the semantic prediction produced by the segmentation module, attempts of adopting a mechanism to quantify the confidence of the semantic prediction should be designed dynamically to handle the adjustment of the weight for semantic loss in the final objective value. Specifically, computing the entropy of the semantic prediction into a concise quantity might be one of the possible approaches to serve as this purpose. This quantified confidence term could thereby used as an auxiliary instrument, bolstering the model's adaptability to varying semantic prediction scenarios.

Stop generating

– **Improving Reference Image Utilization**
The way to incorporate the reference images to extract useful information could be further improved. Instead of conditioning the outputs of the intermediate layers, considering the approach of using geometric matching could be more efficient in terms of utilizing the visual features present in the reference image. Particularly, existing methods of spatial alignment of two images can selectively surpass the regions that are mismatched, leading to more precisely pinpointing areas that are needed to pay attention to during the image translation.

References

1. Anoosheh, A., Sattler, T., Timofte, R., Pollefeys, M., Van Gool, L.: Night-to-day image translation for retrieval-based localization. In: 2019 International Conference on Robotics and Automation (ICRA), pp. 5958–5964. IEEE (2019)
2. Bińkowski, M., Sutherland, D.J., Arbel, M., Gretton, A.: Demystifying mmd gans. arXiv preprint arXiv:1801.01401 (2018)
3. Chen, L.C., Papandreou, G., Kokkinos, I., Murphy, K., Yuille, A.L.: DeepLab: semantic image segmentation with deep convolutional nets, Atrous convolution, and fully connected CRFs. IEEE Trans. Pattern Anal. Mach. Intell. **40**(4), 834–848 (2017)
4. Dar, H., Butterworth, N., Willet, C.E.: Sydney informatics hub: artemis training, October 2018. https://sydney-informatics-hub.github.io/training.artemis/, version 2018.10
5. Goodfellow, I., et al.: Generative adversarial networks. Commun. ACM **63**(11), 139–144 (2020)
6. Guo, J., Li, J., Fu, H., Gong, M., Zhang, K., Tao, D.: Alleviating semantics distortion in unsupervised low-level image-to-image translation via structure consistency constraint. In: Proceedings of the IEEE/CVF Conference on Computer Vision and Pattern Recognition, pp. 18249–18259 (2022)
7. Han, J., Shoeiby, M., Petersson, L., Armin, M.A.: Dual contrastive learning for unsupervised image-to-image translation. In: Proceedings of the IEEE/CVF Conference on Computer Vision and Pattern Recognition, pp. 746–755 (2021)
8. Heusel, M., Ramsauer, H., Unterthiner, T., Nessler, B., Hochreiter, S.: GANs trained by a two time-scale update rule converge to a local nash equilibrium. Adv. Neural Inf. Process. Syst. **30** (2017)
9. Isola, P., Zhu, J.Y., Zhou, T., Efros, A.A.: Image-to-image translation with conditional adversarial networks. In: Proceedings of the IEEE Conference on Computer Vision and Pattern Recognition, pp. 1125–1134 (2017)
10. Jiang, Y., et al.: EnlightenGAN: deep light enhancement without paired supervision. IEEE Trans. Image Process. **30**, 2340–2349 (2021)
11. Kim, J., Kim, M., Kang, H., Lee, K.: U-GAT-IT: unsupervised generative attentional networks with adaptive layer-instance normalization for image-to-image translation. arXiv preprint arXiv:1907.10830 (2019)
12. Li, M., Huang, H., Ma, L., Liu, W., Zhang, T., Jiang, Y.: Unsupervised image-to-image translation with stacked cycle-consistent adversarial networks. In: Proceedings of the European Conference on Computer Vision (ECCV), pp. 184–199 (2018)

13. Li, X., Guo, X.: SPN2D-GAN: semantic prior based night-to-day image-to-image translation. IEEE Trans. Multimed. (2022)
14. Li, X., Guo, X., Zhang, J.: N2D-GAN: a night-to-day image-to-image translator. In: 2022 IEEE International Conference on Multimedia and Expo (ICME), pp. 1–6. IEEE (2022)
15. Lin, G., Milan, A., Shen, C., Reid, I.: RefineNet: multi-path refinement networks for high-resolution semantic segmentation. In: Proceedings of the IEEE Conference on Computer Vision and Pattern Recognition, pp. 1925–1934 (2017)
16. Park, T., Efros, A.A., Zhang, R., Zhu, J.-Y.: Contrastive learning for unpaired image-to-image translation. In: Vedaldi, A., Bischof, H., Brox, T., Frahm, J.-M. (eds.) ECCV 2020. LNCS, vol. 12354, pp. 319–345. Springer, Cham (2020). https://doi.org/10.1007/978-3-030-58545-7_19
17. Park, T., Liu, M.Y., Wang, T.C., Zhu, J.Y.: Semantic image synthesis with spatially-adaptive normalization. In: Proceedings of the IEEE/CVF Conference on Computer Vision and Pattern Recognition, pp. 2337–2346 (2019)
18. Sakaridis, C., Dai, D., Van Gool, L.: ACDC: the adverse conditions dataset with correspondences for semantic driving scene understanding. In: Proceedings of the IEEE/CVF International Conference on Computer Vision, pp. 10765–10775 (2021)
19. Tang, H., Liu, H., Xu, D., Torr, P.H., Sebe, N.: Attentiongan: unpaired image-to-image translation using attention-guided generative adversarial networks. IEEE Trans. Neural Netw. Learn. Syst. (2021)
20. Tsai, Y.H., Hung, W.C., Schulter, S., Sohn, K., Yang, M.H., Chandraker, M.: Learning to adapt structured output space for semantic segmentation. In: Proceedings of the IEEE Conference on Computer Vision and Pattern Recognition, pp. 7472–7481 (2018)
21. Wang, X., et al.: Esrgan: enhanced super-resolution generative adversarial networks. In: Proceedings of the European Conference on Computer Vision (ECCV) Workshops (2018)
22. Wu, X., Wu, Z., Guo, H., Ju, L., Wang, S.: Dannet: a one-stage domain adaptation network for unsupervised nighttime semantic segmentation. In: Proceedings of the IEEE/CVF Conference on Computer Vision and Pattern Recognition, pp. 15769–15778 (2021)
23. Zhao, H., Shi, J., Qi, X., Wang, X., Jia, J.: Pyramid scene parsing network. In: Proceedings of the IEEE Conference on Computer Vision and Pattern Recognition, pp. 2881–2890 (2017)
24. Zheng, Z., Yang, Y.: Unsupervised scene adaptation with memory regularization in vivo. arXiv preprint arXiv:1912.11164 (2019)
25. Zheng, Z., Wu, Y., Han, X., Shi, J.: ForkGAN: seeing into the rainy night. In: Vedaldi, A., Bischof, H., Brox, T., Frahm, J.-M. (eds.) ECCV 2020. LNCS, vol. 12348, pp. 155–170. Springer, Cham (2020). https://doi.org/10.1007/978-3-030-58580-8_10
26. Zhu, J.Y., Park, T., Isola, P., Efros, A.A.: Unpaired image-to-image translation using cycle-consistent adversarial networks. In: Proceedings of the IEEE International Conference on Computer Vision, pp. 2223–2232 (2017)

Batch Level Distributed Training of LSTM with Infinity Norm Gradient Flow

Linzhe Cai[1]([✉]), Chen Liu[1], Xinghuo Yu[1], Chaojie Li[2], and Andrew Eberhard[3]

[1] School of Engineering, RMIT University, Melbourne, VIC 3000, Australia
s3548838@student.rmit.edu.au
[2] School of Electrical Engineering and Telecommunications,
University of New South Wales, Sydney, NSW 2052, Australia
[3] School of Science, RMIT University, Melbourne, VIC 3000, Australia

Abstract. The advent of the big data era has led to a substantial increase in available data for analysis and prediction, creating a need for effective utilization of this vast input to improve prediction quality. LSTM-based neural networks have demonstrated exceptional performance in tasks such as time series forecasting. However, the effectiveness of these models can be constrained by the limitations of GPU memory. Distributed computing has emerged as a promising solution to address the challenges posed by large-sample, long-sequence time series forecasting. This work develops a novel distributed training method for LSTM-based time series forecasting under big data scenario. Infinity norm gradient flow (INGF) is applied to speed up the convergence, acceleration techniques are designed to improve the utility rate of multiple GPUs. The study showcases significant insights into the performance of various distributed strategies and optimization techniques for batch level distributed training. As a result, we achieve an impressive tenfold increase in efficiency while making only a negligible sacrifice in accuracy.

Keywords: Large batch size · Time series forecasting · Long short term memory · Distributed training · GPU utility rate

1 Introduction

In the era of big data, the requirements of long sequence, large batch size, and large-scale data sample are attract more attention for time series forecasting [7,23]. As one of the most significant statistical analysis models that utilizes time series data to predict future trends, Auto Regressive Integrated Moving Average (ARIMA) [3] combines auto-regressive (AR), Integrated (I), and moving average (MA) components. These components individually capture the auto-correlation, trend, and seasonality characteristics of the time series data. The seamless integration of these components establishes ARIMA as the pinnacle in the realm of time series analysis. However, it has limited capability in capturing complex patterns, faces challenges in handling long-term dependencies, and is sensitive to outliers and noise, comparing with long short term memory (LSTM).

Z. Bao et al. (Eds.): ADC 2023, LNCS 14386, pp. 183–196, 2024.
https://doi.org/10.1007/978-3-031-47843-7_13

LSTM is a type of recurrent neural network (RNN) specifically designed to address the vanishing gradient problem, allowing it to capture long-term dependencies in the data [18]. This makes it particularly effective for time series with complex patterns and dependencies that span across multiple time steps. However, the LSTM-based training is time-consuming, even out of memory for some big data scenario.

To meet the requirements mentioned above, some techniques like parallel computing [27] and distributed training [11] have been mentioned more frequently. However, there has been less discussion on how to effectively utilize computing resources, enhance GPU utilization during distributed strategies specifically across various hardware architectures. This article primarily explores the allocation of computing resources and the cross-platform support when a specific distributed strategy is involved.

This article focuses on batch level distributed training, trying to explore enhanced cross-platform support to elevate TensorFlow compatibility across various hardware architectures. Contributions of this work are summarized below:

- Comprehensive comparison of different distributed training strategies under various combinations of acceleration and optimization techniques.
- In-depth study of algorithmic implementation of mixed precision, along with theoretical explanation for the adaptation of learning rates based on various optimization algorithms.
- Recommendations for implementing distributed time series forecasting using LSTM on x64 system with multiple GPUs.

The remainder of this paper is organized as follows. Section 2 reviews the related works about distributed training strategies. Section 3 elaborates our methodology of batch level distributed training with acceleration techniques and the algorithms. Section 4 illustrated the algorithm corresponding with the methodology mentioned above. Section 5 demonstrates the performance for different strategy under different acceleration techniques from the perspectives of running time and accuracy respectively, and Sect. 6 gives conclusion.

2   Related Works

2.1   Long Short Term Memory

LSTM first proposed by [19], which was further improved in 1999 by [16]. After introducing a forget gate, LSTM is allowed to discard some information when necessary, which enhancing LSTM's ability to process more complex data. The memory cell of LSTM neuron is regulated by three types of gates: input, output, and forget. The input gate manages the influx of fresh data into the memory cell. Simultaneously, the output gate oversees the outflow of information from the memory cell. Lastly, the forget gate determines the quantity of previously stored data that remains conserved in the memory cell. Numerous studies from various fields have confirmed LSTM's dominant position in the time series forecasting domain. [6] considers it in financial field, [28] uses LSTM to predict the petroleum production, [9] realizes COVID-19 transmission forecasting using LSTM networks. Due to the complex cell structure of LSTM, neural networks based on LSTM typically require a relatively longer training time. LSTM can benefits from parallel computation, allowing it to leverage GPUs and achieve a multiplicative increase in computation speed.

2.2 Paralleled LSTM

Parallel and distributed computing are both powerful technologies with distinct applications and advantages [24]. The choice between parallel and distributed computing depends on specific needs like the requirement for computational power, scalability, and resource availability [26]. Parallel computing [27] involves performing computational tasks simultaneously across multiple processors in a single computer, enhancing speed and efficiency. It's particularly useful in applications like complex simulations, scientific computations, and various analytical tasks. [29] introduces PyraMiD-LSTM rearranging computations in a pyramidal fashion, paving the way for enhanced parallelization, especially for 3D data. [2] uses LSTM layers to process sequential data and CNN layers for spectro-temporal features, implies a dual pathway where these networks can potentially be processed in parallel. [15] extends the application of parallel LSTMs and CNNs from classification to regression, and speeds up the training process. While parallel computing can mitigate the issue of slow training, memory limitation caused by hardware become another challenge in big data scenarios.

2.3 Distributed LSTM

Distributed computing [11] connects multiple computers across a network, allowing them to work together on large-scale computations and resource-sharing tasks. It offers scalability and redundancy, making it ideal for applications like cloud computing, edge computing, and software as a service. [19] introduces a Distributed Particle Filtering (DPF)-based training algorithm, which showed convergence to optimal LSTM coefficients under specific conditions. [14] combine Karhunen-Loève (KL) decomposition with multi-layer perceptions (MLP) and LSTMs, estimating the temperature distributions in nonlinear distributed parameter systems. [25] proposes a cloud-based distributed deep learning framework was introduced to detect and mitigate phishing, DDoS, and Botnet attacks. However, their researches conclusion only focus on accuracy, overlooking the convergence speed. [22] mentions that RNN-LSTM can efficiently compartmentalized the network into layers, reducing both the overhead at the fusion center and data transmission needs. The application field of reduced signaling overhead, delay, and improved the overall throughput is limited at wireless sensor network.

3   Batch Level Distributed Training

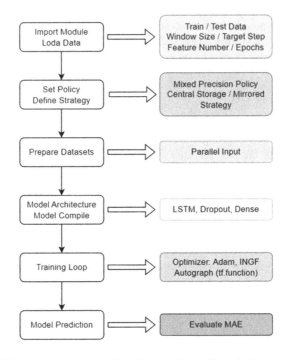

Fig. 1. Framework of Batch Level Distributed Training

Figure 1 illustrates the framework of our method. Two most popular batch level distributed training method, namely the mirrored strategy and central storage strategy to be discussed in Sect. 3.1, are implemented respectively. Mixed precision training, parallel input, and tf.function, to be discussed in Sect. 3.2, are used to accelerate distributed techniques through improving the utility rate of GPUs. Adam and INGF algorithms, to be discussed in Sect. 3.3, are used to comparing the performance of different distributed strategy under different combination of acceleration and optimization techniques.

3.1   Mirrored Strategy and Central Storage Strategy

Mirrored Strategy is a synchronous distributed training strategy that supports all-reduce algorithms. It creates one replica per device and uses efficient all-reduce algorithms to communicate variable updates across the devices. As the name implies, each device maintains a mirror of the model's variables. During training, it applies the same update to all replicas of each variable, keeping them in sync, which is typically used for training on multiple GPUs in one machine.

While it offers the benefits of redundancy and data availability, it increases storage costs and the complexity of data synchronization [13].

Central Storage Strategy is another type of synchronous training strategy. It keeps the variables on the CPU and replicates the computation to all local GPUs. If there is only one GPU, all variables and computations will be placed on that GPU. Central Storage Strategy is generally used in the situation where you have multiple GPUs and want to use the CPU for storing variables. while it provides centralized data management and consistency, single point of failure can lead to data unavailability [13].

3.2   Acceleration Techniques

In data-intensive machine learning tasks, data loading and preprocessing can often become a bottleneck in the overall training pipeline. Parallel input [8] is a technique used to overcome this issue by loading and preprocessing the next batch of data concurrently with the model training. This concurrent process minimizes the time the model spends idling, waiting for the next batch of data to be loaded and preprocessed, reducing the I/O cost significantly. This technique leverages multi-threading or multi-processing, depending on the specific implementation. It helps to make sure the GPU is not starved of data and keeps running at maximum efficiency.

Mixed precision training [21] is an approach that involves the use of both half-precision (FP16) and single-precision (FP32) floating-point numbers for computations. The basic idea is to use the lower precision FP16 for forward and backward propagation, which reduces memory consumption and increases computation efficiency. However, the reduced precision can lead to numerical instability and underflow problems. Therefore, certain computations, including weight updates, are still done using the higher precision FP32. In essence, mixed precision training strikes a balance between memory efficiency and numerical stability.

Tf.function [30] is a feature in TensorFlow that allows converting regular Python functions into TensorFlow graph execution functions. This process is also known as Autograph. In contrast to the default eager execution mode in TensorFlow, which executes operations line by line, graph execution compiles the entire function into a computational graph. The graph execution mode can automatically optimize the function, such as by merging operations, pruning unused nodes, and even distributing computations across devices if multiple GPUs/TPUs are available. These optimizations can lead to significant performance boosts, especially for large computations.

3.3   Adam and Infinity Norm Gradient Flow

Adam [20] is a widely-used optimization algorithm in deep learning that combines the benefits of two extensions of stochastic gradient descent: RMSProp (Root Mean Square Propagation) and Momentum. Adam leverages the concept of adaptive learning rates for individual parameters by using estimates of the first and second moments of gradients.

$$m_t = \beta_1 \cdot m_{t-1} + (1 - \beta_1) \cdot g_t \tag{1}$$

$$v_t = \beta_2 \cdot v_{t-1} + (1 - \beta_2) \cdot g_t^2 \tag{2}$$

$$\hat{m}_t = \frac{m_t}{1 - \beta_1^t} \tag{3}$$

$$\hat{v}_t = \frac{v_t}{1 - \beta_2^t} \tag{4}$$

$$\theta_t = \theta_{t-1} - \frac{\alpha}{\sqrt{\hat{v}_t} + \epsilon} \cdot \hat{m}_t \tag{5}$$

in this formula, m_t represents the first moment estimate, v_t represents the second moment estimate, g_t represents the gradient at time t, β_1 and β_2 are the exponential decay rates for the moment estimates, α is the learning rate, θ_t represents the parameters at time t, and ϵ is a small constant for numerical stability.

Infinity norm gradient flow (INGF) is a modified finite time convergence algorithm, proposed by [5]. According to the Equivalence of norms [10]: two finite dimensional linear normed spaces with the same dimension are algebraically isomorphic and topologically homeomorphic. A more precise relationship between different norms is obtained through Cauchy-Schwarz inequality and Hoder's inequality: for $p > r > 1$ on $\mathbb{R}^n$ [17],

$$\|x\|_p \leq \|x\|_r \leq n^{1/r - 1/p} \|x\|_p. \tag{6}$$

thus, modifying normal rescaled gradient descent through using infinity norm instead of Euclidean one, the convergence rate and robust are improved especially in deep neural networks.

$$\frac{dw}{dt} = -\frac{\nabla_w J}{\|\nabla_w J\|_\infty}. \tag{7}$$

in this formula, $\nabla_w J$ represents the gradient of weights with respect to Error J, while $\|\nabla_w J\|_\infty$ represents the infinity norm of batch of gradient used to rescaled the magnitude.

4   Distributed Training Algorithm

Our work represents a comprehensive comparison of different distributed training strategies under various combinations of acceleration and optimization techniques. This comparative analysis will be crucial in providing insights into selecting the most suitable combinations for different deep learning problems, leading to improved performance and efficiency in model training.

Algorithm 1. Batch Level Distributed Training

1: Set Mixed Precision Policy
2: Prepare dataset with, window_size, n_features, target_feature_idx, target_steps
3: Set Distribute Strategy
4: Set loss_fn with mean squared error
5: **for** epoch in range (Epochs) **do**
6:   Iterate over the train_dataset and run training step on each batch
7:   **for** {Parallel Input}batch in train_dataset **do**
8:     strategy.run {Packaged in tf.function}
9:   **end for**
10: **end for**
11: Calculate mean absolute error for all step prediction
12: Print running time and MAE

Algorithm 1 gives the batch level distributed training, and illustrates where acceleration techniques should be used. Initially, a mixed precision policy is set, facilitating the use of both single-precision (FP32) and half-precision (FP16) during training to expedite computation and decrease memory usage, given hardware compatibility. A distributed strategy is then established, directing how the training workload is divided and coordinated across multiple processing units such as GPUs or TPUs. The mean squared error (MSE) is used as the loss function. The main training loop iterates over a predetermined number of epochs, within each epoch, the algorithm traverses the training dataset in batches, running a training step on each batch using the "strategy.run" method, following the distributed strategy. This execution is wrapped within a TensorFlow function, enabling graph optimization for enhanced performance. Meanwhile, parallel input permits concurrent loading and preprocessing of the subsequent batch while processing the current one.

5   Numerical Experiments

To evaluate our proposed methods, New South Wales (NSW) electricity price [1] is chosen as the dataset, the time range is from 1st Jan, 2019 to 30th Sep, 2021, and the sample frequency is half hourly. Figure 2 demonstrates the batch level distribution under multiple GPUs for long sequences multi-step prediction.

As illustrate in Fig. 2, input length is 336, corresponding to one week time range, while the output length is 48, corresponding to one day period. We choose one layer LSTM with 256 cells, with a dropout layer (dropout rate = 0.25) and dense layer (neuron = 48) with ReLU [4] activation follows. To extend the effectiveness of the methodology under multiple feature conditions, we simultaneously incorporate electricity prices from Victoria (VIC), South Australia (SA), Tasmania (TAS), and Queensland (QLD) as only input feature vectors.

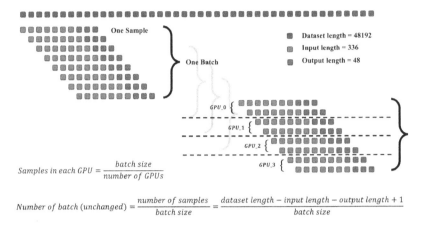

Fig. 2. Batch Level Distributed allocated to multiple GPUs

5.1 Central Storage Strategy

Case Study 1 compares the performance of the central storage strategy distribution method utilizing four combinations of acceleration techniques: standalone, with parallel input, with autograph, and with both parallel input and autograph. As the central storage strategy API in TensorFlow still under experimental stage, the mixed precision one is not supported.

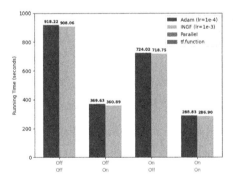

Fig. 3. Comparison of Central Storage

Figure 3 concludes the running time of Adam and INGF under central storage strategy with different acceleration techniques combination in the form of cylinder respectively. According to Fig. 3, the parallel input in data preprocessing stage can reduce by about 20% running time, while package distributed strategy into TensorFlow graph execution functions can reduce it to 40%. The combination of them can realize 3.125 times faster (32% running time) comparing with central storage strategy itself.

Figure 4 illustrates the MAE during the convergence process of both training and testing datasets respectively. The first letter in the label represent the parallel data, while the second letter represents the tf.function. X represents use the corresponding technique, while O represent negative.

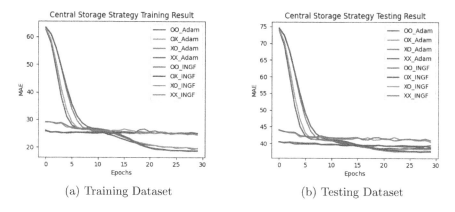

(a) Training Dataset   (b) Testing Dataset

Fig. 4. Central Storage Results

According to Fig. 4a, the training dataset convergence performance of INGF is better than Adam before 10 epochs, while after 12 epochs, Adam obtained smaller MAE. Additionally, with the parallel data acceleration technique, the MAE is slightly larger than the one without parallel data before 10 epochs for both Adam and INGF, while autograph almost has no effect on the accuracy on same epochs. According to Fig. 4b, the testing dataset convergence performance is worst than training one, but the trend are similar. While Adam and INGF can convergence to 20 and 24 MAE respectively in training, they convergence to 40 and 42 MAE in testing. Thus, the difference between Adam and INGF finial MAE is smaller.

5.2 Mirrored Strategy

Case Study 2 compares the performance of the mirrored strategy distribution method utilizing eight combinations of acceleration techniques: parallel input, mixed precision and with autograph. As the default NVDIA collective communication library (NCCL) is not supported in X64 system, we consider hierarchical copy to implement cross-device operations [31].

It is worth noting that the learning rate for the INGF algorithm under mixed precision training is adjusted to lr = 1e-7. This adjustment is necessary because mixed precision operations require both scaled gradients and scaled loss during optimizer calculations, and the scale factor is a 1e-4 magnitude value. Scaling the loss is intended to counterbalance the impact of scaled gradients on the learning rate. In the case of normal gradient descent algorithms like SGD and Adam, the scale factor for the loss does not affect the results. Regardless of the value of the scale factor, the outcomes remain unchanged. However, for the rescaled gradient descent (RGD) family of algorithms mentioned in [32], the scale factor of the loss is superfluous. This is due to the fact that the descent magnitude of the gradients in the RGD algorithm remains unchanged after all gradients under the same batch are multiplied by the same scale factor, as indicated by the norm in the denominator as shown in Eq. 7. Thus, to adjust the scaled loss to achieve similar convergence rate as traditional gradient descent methods, it requires a corresponding adjustment in the learning rate.

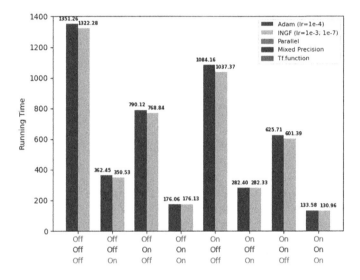

Fig. 5. Comparison of Mirrored Strategies

Figure 5 depicts the running time of Adam and INGF under mirrored strategy with different acceleration techniques combination respectively. According to Fig. 6, autograph given in green contributes the most to distributed acceleration (74%), followed by mixed precision given in purple (42%), while parallel input given in red contributes the least (22%) as shown in the second, third, and fifth bars respectively. Interestingly, when combining any two of these acceleration techniques, the improvement in computational effciency is slightly higher than the product of the individual improvements achieved by using each technique separately, which can be explained as the statistical error caused by the printing of the MAE for each epoch during iteration.

As a result, the combination of all three acceleration techniques can lead to a 10-fold increase in efficiency compared to using the mirrored strategy directly. Additionally, INGF consume 3% less time comparing with Adam. By monitoring the GPU utilization through nvidia-smi [12] command, it can be observed that when all three techniques are employed, the utilization of all four GPUs reaches

99%. Such a high level of computational resource utilization is quite rare in distributed computing based on the X64 system.

From Figs. 6 and 7, the MAE during the convergence process of both training and testing datasets using different combination of acceleration method under mirrored strategy are obtained. The first letter in the label represent the parallel data, while the second letter represents the mixed precision, and the third position represent the tf.function. Again, X represents the using of the corresponding technique, while O represents negative. As the convergence performance with or without the mixed precision has large difference, we separate them into different figures.

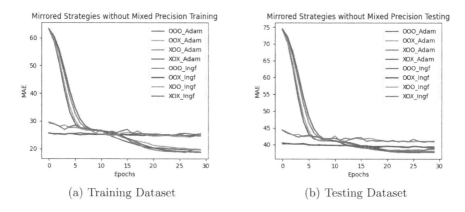

(a) Training Dataset   (b) Testing Dataset

Fig. 6. Mirrored Strategies without Mixed Precision

Figure 6 illustrates the mirrored strategies without mixed precision acceleration technique. Comparing with Fig. 4, performance for both training and testing datasets using the central storage and mirrored strategies are almost same from the perspective of convergence rate without mixed precision acceleration methods.

Figure 7 illustrates the mirrored strategies with mixed precision acceleration technique. According to Fig. 7a, the training dataset convergence performance of INGF is still better than Adam before 10 epochs with mixed precision method. However, Adam cannot continue convergence to a smaller MAE even we tried to reduce the learning rate as we did on INGF. Additionally, the initial value of MAE of INGF is relatively larger comparing with Fig. 6a, both can be explained as the trade off between accuracy and convergence rate after mixed precision technique involving. According to Fig. 7b, the testing dataset convergence performance is worst than training one, but the trend are similar. Again, Adam cannot continue convergence to a smaller MAE and the initial value of MAE of INGF is relatively larger comparing with Fig. 6b. Thus, the INGF should be considered as the priority algorithm when using all three acceleration techniques together during batch level distributed training under mirrored strategy.

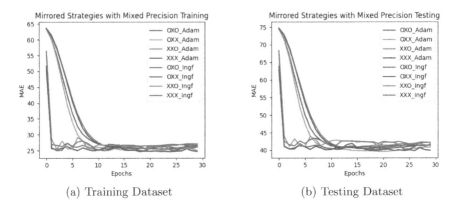

(a) Training Dataset   (b) Testing Dataset

Fig. 7. Mirrored Strategies with Mixed Precision

From the perspective of running time, acceleration effect of any combination strategies is even stronger than the product of their individual acceleration effects, and the perfect coupling led to an astonishing tenfold speedup. All three techniques are employed together, the utilization of all four GPUs reaches 99%, which is remarkable under X64 system based distributed computing.

From the perspective of accuracy, INGF has much better performance comparing with Adam, and the initial MAE of which is almost half. Within the first ten epochs, INGF can beat Adam, while Adam can be smaller after 10 epochs. After mixed precision method involving, the initial MAE of INGF is similar with Adam, but it still keep advantages from the second epoch, Adam cannot obtain smaller MAE after 10 epochs.

6   Conclusion

This study has provided significant insights into the performance of various distributed strategies and optimization techniques in the context of batch level distributed training. After integrating various acceleration techniques, the running time of distributed learning is reduced by 90%. At the start of training, INGF displayed advantages over Adam, yet as the training proceeded, Adam achieved a smaller MAE. However, with the introduction of mixed precision, the advantage Adam once held diminishes. Utilizing real-world datasets, our study emphasizes the importance of selecting appropriate algorithms and optimization techniques in achieving faster running times and higher GPU utilization while maintaining prediction accuracy.

References

1. Aggregated price and demand data (2023). https://aemo.com.au/en/energy-systems/electricity
2. Bae, S.H., Choi, I.K., Kim, N.S.: Acoustic scene classification using parallel combination of LSTM and CNN. In: DCASE, pp. 11–15 (2016)
3. Box, G.E., Jenkins, G.M., Reinsel, G.C., Ljung, G.M.: Time Series Analysis: Forecasting and Control. John Wiley & Sons, Hoboken (2015)
4. Brownlee, J.: A gentle introduction to the rectified linear unit (ReLU). Mach. Learn. Mastery **6** (2019)
5. Cai, L., Yu, X., Li, C., Eberhard, A., Nguyen, L.T., Doan, C.T.: Impact of mathematical norms on convergence of gradient descent algorithms for deep neural networks learning. In: Aziz, H., Correa, D., French, T. (eds.) AI 2022: Advances in Artificial Intelligence. AI 2022. LNCS, vol. 13728, pp. 131–144. Springer, Cham (2022). https://doi.org/10.1007/978-3-031-22695-3_10
6. Cao, J., Li, Z., Li, J.: Financial time series forecasting model based on CEEMDAN and LSTM. Phys. A **519**, 127–139 (2019)
7. Chen, Z., Ma, M., Li, T., Wang, H., Li, C.: Long sequence time-series forecasting with deep learning: a survey. Inf. Fusion **97**, 101819 (2023)
8. Cheng, H.T., et al.: Wide & deep learning for recommender systems. In: Proceedings of the 1st Workshop on Deep Learning for Recommender Systems, pp. 7–10 (2016)
9. Chimmula, V.K.R., Zhang, L.: Time series forecasting of COVID-19 transmission in Canada using LSTM networks. Chaos, Solitons Fractals **135**, 109864 (2020)
10. Conrad, K.: Equivalence of norms. Expository Paper, University of Connecticut, Storrs, heruntergeladen von, vol. 17, no. 2018 (2018)
11. Dean, J., et al.: Large scale distributed deep networks. Adv. Neural Inf. Process. Syst. **25** (2012)
12. developer, N.: System management interface SMI (2023). https://developer.nvidia.com/nvidia-system-management-interface
13. (2023). www.tensorflow.org/api_docs/python/tf/distribute/Strategy
14. Fan, Y., Xu, K., Wu, H., Zheng, Y., Tao, B.: Spatiotemporal modeling for nonlinear distributed thermal processes based on kl decomposition, MLP and LSTM network. IEEE Access **8**, 25111–25121 (2020)
15. Farsi, B., Amayri, M., Bouguila, N., Eicker, U.: On short-term load forecasting using machine learning techniques and a novel parallel deep LSTM-CNN approach. IEEE Access **9**, 31191–31212 (2021)
16. Gers, F.A., Schmidhuber, J., Cummins, F.: Learning to forget: Continual prediction with LSTM. Neural Comput. **12**(10), 2451–2471 (2000)
17. Golub, G.H., Van Loan, C.F.: Matrix Computations. JHU Press, Baltimore (2013)
18. Goodfellow, I., Bengio, Y., Courville, A.: Deep Learning. MIT Press, Cambridge (2016)
19. Hochreiter, S., Schmidhuber, J.: Long short-term memory. Neural Comput. **9**(8), 1735–1780 (1997)
20. Kingma, D.P., Ba, J.: Adam: a method for stochastic optimization. arXiv preprint arXiv:1412.6980 (2014)
21. Micikevicius, P., et al.: Mixed precision training. arXiv preprint arXiv:1710.03740 (2017)
22. Mohanty, S.N., Lydia, E.L., Elhoseny, M., Al Otaibi, M.M.G., Shankar, K.: Deep learning with LSTM based distributed data mining model for energy efficient wireless sensor networks. Phys. Commun. **40**, 101097 (2020)

23. Öztürk, M.M.: Hyperparameter optimization of a parallelized LSTM for time series prediction. Vietnam J. Comput. Sci. 1–26 (2023)

24. Pang, B., Nijkamp, E., Wu, Y.N.: Deep learning with tensorflow: a review. J. Educ. Behav. Stat. **45**(2), 227–248 (2020)

25. Parra, G.D.L.T., Rad, P., Choo, K.K.R., Beebe, N.: Detecting internet of things attacks using distributed deep learning. J. Netw. Comput. Appl. **163**, 102662 (2020)

26. Parallel vs. distributed computing: an overview (2022). blog.purestorage.com/purely-informational/parallel-vs-distributed-computing-an-overview/

27. Quinn, M.J.: Parallel Computing Theory and Practice. McGraw-Hill, Inc., New York (1994)

28. Sagheer, A., Kotb, M.: Time series forecasting of petroleum production using deep LSTM recurrent networks. Neurocomputing **323**, 203–213 (2019)

29. Stollenga, M.F., Byeon, W., Liwicki, M., Schmidhuber, J.: Parallel multi-dimensional LSTM, with application to fast biomedical volumetric image segmentation. Adv. Neural Inf. Process. Syst. **28** (2015)

30. Better performance with tf.function (2023). www.tensorflow.org/guide/function

31. Ueno, Y., Fukuda, K.: Technologies behind distributed deep learning: Allreduce (2018)

32. Wilson, A.C., Mackey, L., Wibisono, A.: Accelerating rescaled gradient descent: fast optimization of smooth functions. Adv. Neural Inf. Process. Syst. **32** (2019)

Database Systems and Data Storage

Health Status Assessment for HDDs Based on Bi-LSTM and N-Dimensional Similarity Metric

Bo Su[1], Xin Man[1], Hui Xu[1,2], Xiangmin Zhou[3], and Jie Shao[1(✉)]

[1] University of Electronic Science and Technology of China, Chengdu 611731, China
{subo,manxin}@std.uestc.edu.cn, {huixu.kim,shaojie}@uestc.edu.cn
[2] Intelligent Terminal Key Laboratory of Sichuan Province, Yibin 644000, China
[3] RMIT University, Melbourne, VIC 3000, Australia
xiangmin.zhou@rmit.edu.au

Abstract. In order to reduce the economic losses caused by hard disk failures, researchers have proposed various statistical and machine learning methods based on Self-Monitoring Analysis and Reporting Technology (SMART) attributes. Predicting hard drive health using SMART attributes, as proposed by previous methods, is effective for adopting different passive fault tolerance mechanisms in advance. Despite the effectiveness of these methods, there are still significant limitations. Specifically, these methods define health status according to the remaining time before it breaks down. However, they ignore changes in SMART features that reflect deteriorating disk health. In this paper, we propose an N-dimensional similarity metric to evaluate the health of HDDs, which acts on both SMART attributes and time-to-failure of HDDs. In addition, we use hypothesis test to eliminate abnormal data and propose a Bidirectional LSTM (Bi-LSTM) based model with weighted categorical cross-entropy loss. Experiments on the Backblaze and Baidu datasets show that our method obtains reasonably accurate health status assessments and outperforms previous methods. Code is available at https://github.com/su26225/HDD-Health-Status.

Keywords: Hard disk failure · SMART attributes · Health status assessment · Euclidean distance · Bi-LSTM

1 Introduction

In this era of cloud computing and big data, hard disk drives (HDDs) are the primary storage devices in current data centers. Despite their high reliability, the average age of HDDs is 52.4 months, and according to the data published by Backblaze [13], the Annual Failure Rate (AFR) of HDDs is gradually increasing. Therefore, data centers need to adopt some fault tolerance mechanisms to avoid serious losses caused by hard disk failures. There are two common fault tolerance mechanisms: passive fault tolerance mechanism [6,14] and active fault

Z. Bao et al. (Eds.): ADC 2023, LNCS 14386, pp. 199–212, 2024.
https://doi.org/10.1007/978-3-031-47843-7_14

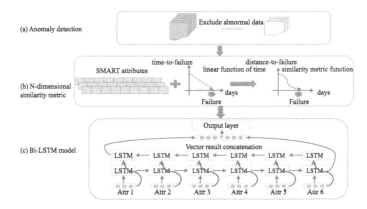

Fig. 1. The framework of our method. (a) represents the elimination of abnormal data caused by emergencies; (b) describes an N-dimensional similarity metric base on the Euclidean distance; (c) represents the structure of our method.

tolerance mechanism [19]. Passive fault tolerance usually uses backup and erasure codes to help data recover in a timely manner after corruption. Active fault tolerance predicts data corruption before it is damaged and adopts maintenance strategies to restore data in time. At present, some researchers combine the two mechanisms (i.e., passive fault tolerance mechanism and active fault tolerance mechanism) through disk scrubbing rate [11] and disk adaptive redundancy [12]. These researchers apply active fault prediction to real-world environments and guide the passive fault tolerance mechanisms.

In recent years, researchers have focused on building predictive models through statistical and machine-learning methods. These methods are effective in predicting two health status: either healthy or failure, treating the hard disk state as a binary classification. In order to design a more flexible fault tolerance mechanism, some researchers established a function linearly related to disk health and time. Taking the last moment as the failure state and the starting moment as the healthy state, a decreasing function is used to evaluate the current health degree of the disk. However, this method only considers the length of time-to-failure in a linear manner, while ignoring the correlation between changes in hard disk SMART attributes and health, especially in the process of gradual deterioration.

Considering that the health of HDDs will gradually deteriorate over time, their SMART attributes can reflect their health. In this paper, we propose an N-dimensional similarity metric based on the weighted Euclidean distance to assess the health of HDDs, as shown in Fig. 1. Furthermore, existing studies [8,19] do not consider filtering anomalies. Events such as power outages, natural disasters or human error can cause large numbers of disks to fail simultaneously and unusual changes in SMART parameters. Thus, it is important to distinguish between unexpected changes caused by anomalies and changes caused by deterioration.

Our contributions can be summarized as follows:

- We pay attention to relationships between changes in SMART features and disk health, and propose an N-dimensional similarity metric to quantity the health of HDDs, which acts on both SMART attributes and time-to-failure of HDDs.
- We use hypothesis test to eliminate abnormal data caused by emergencies and propose a Bi-LSTM based model for utilizing future information.
- To address issues due to data imbalance, we extend the weighted categorical cross-entropy loss function by emphasizing the loss of positive samples. Experiments on the Backblaze and Baidu datasets show that our method not only obtains reasonably accurate health status assessments but also outperforms previous prediction methods.

2 Related Work

There are two categories of existing work on disk health assessment: binary classification prediction and disk health prediction.

Binary Classification Prediction. This disk health assessment method evaluates HDDs using only two statuses: healthy or faulty. Hamerly and Elkan [8] use two Bayesian methods in statistics: naive Bayes and mixed expectation-maximization-trained naive Bayes models, experimenting on disks collected from Quantum Inc. (an equipment manufacturer). Murray et al. [16] conduct experiments with various statistical methods, especially their proposed method achieves 50% detection rate and 0% false alarms. Pang et al. [17] construct a Bayesian network and find that the average prediction accuracy for healthy and failed hard drives was 99.13% and 75.3%, respectively. However, these methods do not focus on long-term dependent properties of SMART attributes. Long Short-Term Memory (LSTM) is used for disk failure prediction due to its ability to solve the long-term backpropagation problem. Lima et al. [19] use LSTM for the long-term prediction of disk failures, which can achieve better results in long-term prediction. From the highly unorganized and class-imbalanced big data, Basak et al. [3] propose an LSTM model to predict the remaining useful life (RUL) of HDDs. Combining performance features, location features and SMART, Lu et al. [15] use the CNN-LSTM method to predict whether a hard drive will fail in the next 10 days. However, it is still inaccurate to describe disk health with only two category labels.

Disk Health Prediction. In practical scenarios, the health of HDDs gradually degrades, which is difficult to guide the passive fault tolerance mechanism of the disk. It would require more fine-grained metrics to measure disk health. Babu et al. [1] propose a deep Convolutional Neural Network (CNN) based regression approach, and Botezatu et al. [5] propose a SMART-based high-accuracy analysis pipeline to predict the RUL. Zhang et al. [21] propose an adversarial training based approach that uses manually defined disk health levels to judge the health of HDDs, which can solve the problem of overfitting. Bai et al. [2] propose an attention-based bidirectional LSTM with differential features extracted

(a) Time-to-failure based HDD health assessment

(b) N-dimensional similarity metric based HDD health assessment

Fig. 2. HDD health assessment methods. In (a), x_i denotes the days before the drive fails. In (b), wed denotes weighted Euclidean distances, and d_i denotes the N-dimensional similarity metric calculated by weighted Euclidean distances.

by manual feature engineering. Santo *et al.* [18] propose an LSTM-based model that uses an automatic policy to define the health degree of HDDs, as well as judge the health of HDDs according to time-to-failure (as shown in Fig. 2(a)). However, these methods ignore the relationship between changes in SMART attributes during deterioration and the health of HDDs. Therefore, we propose an N-dimensional similarity metric based method for hard disk health assessment (as shown in Fig. 2(b)). Meanwhile, we utilize the Bi-LSTM model, which is a type of recurrent neural network capable of leveraging both past and future information for prediction. To address issues arising from data imbalance, we extend the weighted categorical cross-entropy loss function by emphasizing the loss of positive samples.

3   Methodology

Although the hard disk is usually damaged gradually, it does not simply change linearly with time. Based on the time analysis method, changes in SMART attributes should be added to simulate the sequential dependence of HDD health over time. Therefore, we propose a method to estimate the health degree of hard drives by N-dimensional similarity. This method consists of three parts:

– Anomaly detection, in which abnormal data caused by accidents (e.g., power outages) are detected and eliminated;
– Quantifying disk health degree, in which the health of each hard drive in datasets is quantified as the similarity between the current state and the state at the time of failure;
– Health status computation, in which the health status is labeled using the decision tree algorithm.

3.1   Anomaly Detection

Failures caused by emergencies (e.g., power outages, disasters, or accidents) can easily exceed our tolerance for abnormal data. For this point, our study treats these emergencies as anomalies. According to the statistics of the Backblaze dataset, we screened the AFR data curve of the manufacturer HGST in recent years (as shown in Fig. 3), and AFR is calculated as follows:

$$AFR = \frac{fail_{drive}}{days_{drive}} * 365 * 100, \tag{1}$$

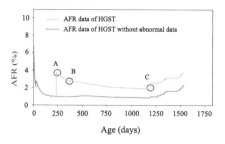

Fig. 3. Changes in Annual Failure Rate (AFR) collected from HGST [12]. Points A, B, and C correspond to three abnormal fault events, which should be excluded.

where AFR is calculated based on the number of failures in the past few days, $fail_{drive}$ is the number of disk failures in HDDs, and $days_{drive}$ is the number of running days.

We detect anomaly data based on the 3σ rule[1]. It refers to the assumption that a set of test data contains only random errors. Any data that falls outside this margin of error should be rejected. In the normal distribution probability formula, σ represents the standard deviation, μ represents the mean, and $f(x)$ represents the normal distribution function. Under the normal curve, the area within the horizontal axis interval $(\mu\text{-}n * \sigma, \mu\text{+}n * \sigma)$ is 68.26%, 95.44%, and 99.73% while n is 1, 2, and 3 respectively.

$$P|X - \mu| < n * \sigma = 2\phi(n) - 1. \tag{2}$$

It can be seen from the above that the probability of X falling outside $(\mu\text{-}3\sigma, \mu\text{+}3\sigma)$ is less than 3‰. Thus, those data beyond this range are outliers and should be excluded.

3.2 N-Dimensional Similarity Metric for HDD Health Quantization

Disk health is an important indicator to measure whether the disk can run normally. It is also of great significance to guide the operation of the passive fault tolerance mechanism. To improve the accuracy of the model, we define the health degree of each disk in the datasets according to the following two principles:

1. Most disks will gradually deteriorate as the number of failures increases. Previous health assessment strategies typically define the health state in terms of the time remaining before a disk fails. However, they ignored fluctuations in SMART attributes.
2. SMART attributes contain many properties (e.g., sector reallocation count, read and write error rate, and temperature), which can reflect the disk health. Furthermore, to deal with the overfitting problem caused by machine learning methods, we also take the time properties of the disk into account.

---

[1] https://en.wikipedia.org/wiki/68-95-99.7_rule.

Algorithm 1. HDD health degree algorithm

Input:
  SMART − attrs: SMART attributes of HDDs.
  Timetofail: Days before failure.
Output:
  DiskhealthDegree
1: *Initialization* : *DataCleaning, DataNormalization*
2: *attrs = concat(SMART − attrs, Timetofail)*
3: **for all** *dict* ∈ **data do**
4:    **if** *dict*[*Timetofail*] == **0 then**
5:       *base = dict*
6:    **end if**
7:    *attrs = dict*
8:    **while** *j < len(attrs)* **do**
9:       *dis ⇐ dis + W_j * (attrs[j] − base[j]) * *2*
10:       *j ⇐ j + 1*
11:    **end while**
12:    *Dis.append(sqrt(dis))*
13: **end for**
14: *DisToFailure ⇐ standard(Dis)*
15: **while** *i < len(Dis)* **do**
16:    *healthdegree ⇐ CLASS   of   DisToFailure*
17:    *i ⇐ i + 1*
18: **end while**
19: **return** *DiskHealthDegree*

To satisfy the above two conditions, we propose Algorithm 1 based on SMART attributes. Algorithm 1 introduces a time variable, takes the last time point n of the faulty disk as the origin, and obtains the Euclidean distance from each point at the recording time before the fault to point n. In lines 1–2, we initialize the input data, and concatenate SMART attributes and the time to failure. In lines 3–7, we select daily data from all data and assign the variable *attrs* at each time point to the concatenated attributes, and *base* represents the concatenated attributes of the failure time. In lines 8–12, we calculate the Euclidean distance according to the concatenated attributes. The formula is as follows:

$$DisToFailure(i) = \sqrt{\sum_{j=1}^{M} W_j * (x_{ij} - x_{nj})^2}, \tag{3}$$

where x_{ij} represents the j-th attribute of the disk in the i-th time (especially, x_{nj} represents the j-th attribute of the disk at the fault time), W_j represents the weight of each attribute, and M represents the number of features of each record. Compared with using Mahalanobis distance, our method gives a better representation of distance variation [10]. In lines 14–17, we use the calculated Euclidean distance as a quantified disk health value to compute the health status according to the decision tree algorithm (as detailed in Sect. 3.3).

3.3   Health Status Computation

After constructing the *DistoFailure* feature using weighted Euclidean distances (as shown in Algorithm 1), our next step is to label the dataset with health status using the decision tree algorithm. The Backblaze dataset contains

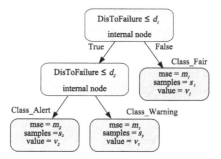

Fig. 4. Regression tree based disk health assessment (with the RawReadErrorRate feature). Leaf nodes represent three different health status of hard drives that will fail, namely Fair, Warning, and Alert. For each node, *mse* (mean squared error) measures branch quality, *samples* represents the number of samples for the node, and *value* is the average of all samples for the node.

year-long disk features, and the Baidu dataset contains disk features corresponding to 20 days before it breaks down. We choose the past 45 days and 20 days as prediction windows, respectively. We use a regression tree algorithm based on the feature RawReadErrorRate to identify the disk health status (as shown in Fig. 4). The decision tree is a classification and regression method that uses nodes and directed edges. Internal nodes represent attributes, while leaf nodes represent categories. Starting from the root node, we test the RawReadError-Rate feature of the sample and assign the sample to its child nodes based on the test result. We adopt a heuristic method to partition the feature space. Each partition examines the values of all features in the current set and selects the optimal one as the cut point according to the squared error minimization criterion:

$$\min_{j,s} \left[\min_{c_1} \sum_{x_i \in R_1(j,s)} (y_i - c_1)^2 + \min_{c_2} \sum_{x_i \in R_2(j,s)} (y_i - c_2)^2 \right], \tag{4}$$

where c_1 and c_2 are the fixed output values of the two divided regions, $\min_{c_1}$ and $\min_{c_2}$ refer to the optimal c_1 and c_2. The formula traverses the variable j, scans the segmentation point s for the fixed segmentation variable j, and selects the pair (j, s) that makes the above formula reach the minimum value. Then, the selected pair is used to divide the area and determine the corresponding output value.

4   Experimental Evaluation

4.1   Datasets

The Backblaze dataset [13] contains daily data collected from 29,878 consumer-grade disks manufactured by Seagate, with 795 failed disks and 29,083 healthy

Table 1. Selected attributes in SMART records.

SMART ID	Attributes	Information Gain Ratio
1	Raw Read Error Rate	0.6325
3	Spin Up Time	0.6307
5	Reallocated Sectors Count	0.6032
7	Seek Error Rate	0.4828
9	Power On Hours	0.6325
187	Reported Uncorrectable Errors	0.7433
189	High Fly Writes	0.7242
194	Temperature Celsius	0.6709
197	Current Pending Sector Count	0.7202
5	Raw Value of Reallocated Sectors Count	0.5192
197	Raw Value of Current Pending Sector Count	0.5192

disks. Each sample consists of information about timestamp, disk model, disk capacity and values for 90 SMART attributes. The Baidu dataset [18], collected on an hourly basis, contains 23,395 consumer-grade disks named ST31000524NS from the data center of Baidu Inc., with 22,962 healthy disks and only 433 disks in the failed class. Since some attributes do not change and even affect the correctness of our predictions, 11 attributes are handpicked as our experimental data (as shown in Table 1) based on the calculation of Information Gain Ratio (IGR). IGR measures the potential information generated by splitting the dataset on the attribute.

Based on data from these disks over the past 45 days and 20 days, the experiment classifies the health of the disks into four categories: Good, Fair, Warning, and Alert (as shown in Fig. 2). Each dataset is divided into the training set, validation set, and test set by the ratio of 70%, 15%, and 15%.

4.2   Implementation of Bi-LSTM Model

Our Bi-LSTM model comprises several layers. The first layer is a bidirectional LSTM layer with 128 units, followed by a dropout layer with a rate of 0.5. Subsequently, there is another bidirectional LSTM layer with 128 units that does not return sequences, followed by another dropout layer with the same rate. The final layer in the model is a dense layer with 4 units and a softmax activation function. This layer produces the predicted result of the model. The model is compiled using the Adam optimizer with a learning rate of 0.001 and the weighted categorical cross-entropy loss function.

As the majority of training samples in a batch are negative samples, representing the attributes of a healthy device, the gradients of negative samples overwhelm those of positive samples during the training process. Consequently, the derived model is highly confident in identifying negative samples due to the small ratio of positive samples. However, such high accuracy is meaningless as the

Table 2. Performance values for the Bi-LSTM models obtained by varying prediction window (days) and weights on the Backblaze dataset. Prediction window refers to the number of days of data collected prior to a hard drive failure. The weights $(W_1, ..., W_{j-1}, c)$ represent the values of W_j in Eq. (3). The best results are shown in bold.

Days	Weights	Accuracy	Precision	Recall	Macro-F1
20	$(W_1, ..., W_{j-1}, 0.5)$	97.68%	98.15%	87.67%	97.84%
20	$(W_1, ..., W_{j-1}, 0.1)$	97.36%	97.90%	85.37%	97.57%
20	$(W_1, ..., W_{j-1}, 0.05)$	97.45%	98.02%	85.95%	97.45%
30	$(W_1, ..., W_{j-1}, 0.5)$	97.26%	97.84%	83.70%	97.48%
30	$(W_1, ..., W_{j-1}, 0.1)$	98.05%	98.11%	86.95%	98.08%
30	$(W_1, ..., W_{j-1}, 0.05)$	98.81%	98.08%	91.46%	97.32%
45	$(W_1, ..., W_{j-1}, 0.5)$	98.21%	98.51%	90.46%	98.32%
45	$(W_1, ..., W_{j-1}, 0.1)$	**99.26%**	**99.28%**	**93.97%**	**99.27%**
45	$(W_1, ..., W_{j-1}, 0.05)$	98.80%	98.94%	93.57%	98.85%

model remains weak in predicting disk failures (positive samples). To address the issue of data imbalance, the loss function should allocate more loss (and thus more gradients) to the scarce positive samples. We introduce a loss function based on weighted classification as an extension of binary cross-entropy. The new loss is obtained by multiplying the basic binary cross-entropy by different coefficients, depending on whether the sample is positive or negative:

$$\text{Loss}(y, \hat{y}) = -\sum_{i=1}^{C} w_i y_i \log(\hat{y}_i), \tag{5}$$

where y is the true label of the sample, $\hat{y}$ is the predicted result of the model, C is the number of categories, and w_i is the weight of the i-th category.

4.3   Experimental Results

First, we conduct a parameter comparison experiment to determine the optimal combination of prediction window and weights. Specifically, Table 2 shows the results of the Bi-LSTM-based approach on the Backblaze dataset, demonstrating the performance using different sizes of prediction windows and weights. For the Backblaze dataset, the range of prediction window sizes is from 20 to 45 days. As expected, given the ability of Bi-LSTM to learn long-distance dependencies, the best results are obtained using a prediction window of 45 days. Additionally, when the weights for the 11 attributes and time are designed such that the feature weights are based on the information gain ratio and the weight for Timetofail is set to 0.05, the model achieves its best performance.

The ground-truth labels and prediction results of our trained Bi-LSTM model on the Backblaze dataset are shown in Fig. 5. The prediction quality of the

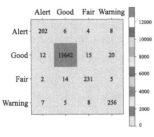
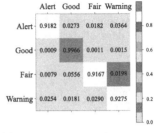

(a) Confusion matrix.   (b) Normalized confusion matrix.

Fig. 5. Confusion matrix for the Dis-Bi-LSTM model on the Backblaze Dataset. In (a), the values in each column represent the number of true data predicted to be that class, and in (b), the values in each column represent the probability of being predicted to be true data for that class. Numbers in the diagonal grid represent the number and probability of correct predictions.

Table 3. Model prediction quality on the Baidu dataset with each class. Recall computes metrics for each label and finds their average, weighted by the number of true instances of each label. Macro-F1 calculates the arithmetic mean for each category of F1 scores.

Metric	Alert	Good	Fair	Warning
Precision	83.47%	99.87%	85.77%	86.86%
Recall	94.09%	99.52%	93.25%	86.23%
Macro-F1	88.46%	99.69%	89.35%	86.55%

best model on the Baidu dataset (detailed by each class) is shown in Table 3. Confusion matrices present predictive performance data in an intuitive way and illustrate the data imbalance, with the majority of the data labeled as Good. This also leads to variations in the accuracy of the four labels. The model predictions reach the highest value in the class of Good with the largest sample size, and also achieve excellent results in other classes with smaller sample sizes, even if the mispredicted samples are still concentrated around the ground-truth labels.

We compare our method with previous work on the Backblaze dataset (as shown in Table 4), and with conventional methods and LSTM variants on the Baidu dataset (as shown in Table 5). Goodfellow et al. [7] propose a model based on an adversarial training method (Basic+AT). Zhang et al. [21] add adversarial training to all layers (LPAT-All). Santo et al. [18] propose an LSTM-based model (TA+LSTM) that combines temporal analysis and SMART attributes according to its time to failure. Comparisons with different models also demonstrate the effectiveness of our method. As shown in Table 5, we find that LSTM and other LSTM variants outperform Support Vector Machine (SVM) [4] and Gradient Boosting Decision Tree (GBDT) [20] in terms of comprehensive performance. LSTM is capable of capturing the temporal dependencies and long-term patterns

Table 4. Comparison of prediction results with previous work on the Backblaze dataset. Recall calculates the weighted average of the metrics for each class. The best results are shown in bold.

Model	Accuracy	Precision	Recall	Macro-F1
Basic+AT [7]	86.8%	81.8%	81.3%	81.5%
LPAT+All [21]	92.6%	89.3%	88.7%	88.9%
TA+LSTM [18]	98.5%	98.3%	98.3%	97.3%
Ours	**99.3%**	**99.3%**	**99.2%**	**99.3%**

Table 5. Comparison of prediction results with conventional methods and LSTM variants on the Baidu dataset. Recall calculates the unweighted average of the metrics for each class. The best results are shown in bold.

Model	Accuracy	Precision	Recall	Macro-F1
SVM [4]	87.6%	87.5%	74.8%	87.5%
GBDT [20]	95.1%	95.0%	62.6%	94.8%
Multi-LSTM	97.0%	97.8%	83.7%	97.5%
LSTM [9]	97.2%	97.3%	81.7%	97.3%
GRU-LSTM	97.8%	98.2%	87.8%	97.9%
CNN-LSTM	98.1%	98.4%	87.2%	98.2%
Ours	**99.0%**	**99.1%**	**94.7%**	**99.0%**

present in the data, while SVM and GBDT are based on static features and are unable to model sequential information. Multi-LSTM is a variant of LSTM that uses multiple LSTM layers stacked on top of each other to learn more complex relationships between the input data and the output. GRU-LSTM is a variant that combines the Gated Recurrent Unit (GRU) and LSTM architectures, with GRUs having a simpler structure with fewer gates. CNN-LSTM is a variant that combines CNN and LSTM, where CNN can be used to extract features from the input data before feeding it into LSTM. The experimental results demonstrate that the performance is robust across different model architectures. This robustness is attributed to the data imbalance, which allows the model to achieve good metrics even if it overfits to the features of the positive samples. Moreover, the CNN-LSTM and Bi-LSTM models, which have the ability to extract more features, outperform the other models.

We calculate the accuracy of different label categories separately. We randomly select faulty and good drives from the test set and evaluate them based on time-to-failure methods and similarity measures. In Table 6, we find that our method combining the N-dimensional Similarity Metric (NSM) and Weighted Categorical Cross-Entropy Loss (WCCL) has higher prediction accuracy than other methods. In summary, different models show only small differences in performance when predicting Good drives. Classifiers can easily identify healthy

Table 6. Ablation study results in accuracy on the Backblaze dataset. The Bi-LSTM model employs the time-to-failure method without the N-dimensional Similarity Metric (NSM) or Weighted Categorical Cross-entropy Loss (WCCL).

Model	Alert	Good	Fair	Warning
Bi-LSTM	76.79%	99.80%	85.38%	75.17%
+ NSM	82.28%	**99.91%**	83.57%	85.47%
+ WCCL	88.47%	99.81%	85.77%	86.86%
+ NSM and WCCL	**90.58%**	99.82%	**89.53%**	**88.58%**

Table 7. Ablation study results using FPR (False Positive Rate) and FNR (False Negative Rate) as the metrics on the Backblaze Dataset. The best results are in bold.

Model	FPR				FNR			
	Alert	Good	Fair	Warning	Alert	Good	Fair	Warning
Bi-LSTM	0.37%	3.61%	0.27%	0.51%	21.82%	0.39%	11.90%	21.01%
+ NSM	0.26%	4.55%	0.23%	0.27%	12.73%	0.39%	9.13%	13.41%
+ WCCL	0.32%	**1.60%**	0.33%	0.30%	**5.00%**	0.68%	**5.16%**	10.51%
+ NSM and WCCL	**0.15%**	3.34%	**0.19%**	**0.23%**	8.18%	**0.34%**	8.33%	**7.25%**

drives, but their accuracy drops significantly when identifying Warning and Alert drives, especially shortly before failure. It can be seen that the NSM component effectively improves the predictive accuracy of the model. At the same time, the WCCL component can effectively improve the accuracy of the remaining three labels while sacrificing some accuracy of the Good label, especially for the Alert label, where the accuracy is increased from 76.79% to 90.58%.

We extend the binary classification model metrics, i.e., FPR (False Positive Rate) and FNR (False Negative Rate), to our multi-class model. These metrics are computed separately for different models and different labels. As shown in Table 7, the addition of NSM and WCCL components can significantly reduce both FNR and FPR. At the same time, the accuracy of the Good label reached its highest value of 99.82%, which may cause the model to be over-sensitive, resulting in an increase in the false positive rate of the Good label. Overall, the evaluation results of HDD health demonstrate the effectiveness of the Bi-LSTM model based on N-dimensional similarity metric and weighted categorical cross-entropy loss, which performs significantly better than the time-to-failure model without these two components.

5   Conclusion

Modern HDDs have sensors that collect SMART attributes to monitor their health. In this paper, we use these attributes to assess HDD health. We remove abnormal data caused by emergencies from SMART, and use a weighted Euclidean distance to quantify the health degree of disks. Finally, we use the improved Bi-LSTM model with weighted categorical cross-entropy loss for HDD health status assessment. Our designed models and other methods are evaluated by extensive experiments in terms of accuracy, precision, recall, and Macro-F1 values. The results show that our proposed method outperforms other methods.

Acknowledgements. This work is supported by Open Fund of Intelligent Terminal Key Laboratory of Sichuan Province (No. SCTLAB-2007).

References

1. Sateesh Babu, G., Zhao, P., Li, X.-L.: Deep convolutional neural network based regression approach for estimation of remaining useful life. In: Navathe, S.B., Wu, W., Shekhar, S., Du, X., Wang, X.S., Xiong, H. (eds.) DASFAA 2016. LNCS, vol. 9642, pp. 214–228. Springer, Cham (2016). https://doi.org/10.1007/978-3-319-32025-0_14
2. Bai, A., Chen, M., Peng, S., Han, G., Yang, Z.: Attention-based bidirectional LSTM with differential features for disk RUL prediction. In: IEEE International Conference on Electronic Information and Communication Technology, ICEICT 2022, pp. 684–689 (2022)
3. Basak, S., Sengupta, S., Dubey, A.: Mechanisms for integrated feature normalization and remaining useful life estimation using LSTMs applied to hard-disks. In: IEEE International Conference on Smart Computing, SMARTCOMP 2019, pp. 208–216 (2019)
4. Boser, B.E., Guyon, I., Vapnik, V.: A training algorithm for optimal margin classifiers. In: Proceedings of the Fifth Annual ACM Conference on Computational Learning Theory, COLT 1992, pp. 144–152 (1992)
5. Botezatu, M.M., Giurgiu, I., Bogojeska, J., Wiesmann, D.: Predicting disk replacement towards reliable data centers. In: Proceedings of the 22nd ACM SIGKDD International Conference on Knowledge Discovery and Data Mining, pp. 39–48 (2016)
6. Dean, J., Ghemawat, S.: MapReduce: simplified data processing on large clusters. In: 6th Symposium on Operating System Design and Implementation (OSDI 2004), pp. 137–150 (2004)
7. Goodfellow, I.J., Shlens, J., Szegedy, C.: Explaining and harnessing adversarial examples. In: 3rd International Conference on Learning Representations, ICLR 2015, Conference Track Proceedings (2015)
8. Hamerly, G., Elkan, C.: Bayesian approaches to failure prediction for disk drives. In: Proceedings of the Eighteenth International Conference on Machine Learning (ICML 2001), pp. 202–209 (2001)
9. Hochreiter, S., Schmidhuber, J.: Long short-term memory. Neural Comput. **9**(8), 1735–1780 (1997)
10. Huang, S., Fu, S., Zhang, Q., Shi, W.: Characterizing disk failures with quantified disk degradation signatures: An early experience. In: 2015 IEEE International Symposium on Workload Characterization, IISWC 2015, pp. 150–159 (2015)
11. Jiang, T., Huang, P., Zhou, K.: Scrub unleveling: achieving high data reliability at low scrubbing cost. In: Design, Automation & Test in Europe Conference & Exhibition, DATE 2019, pp. 1403–1408 (2019)

12. Kadekodi, S., Rashmi, K.V., Ganger, G.R.: Cluster storage systems gotta have HeART: improving storage efficiency by exploiting disk-reliability heterogeneity. In: 17th USENIX Conference on File and Storage Technologies, FAST 2019, pp. 345–358 (2019)
13. Klein, A.: Backblaze drive stats for 2021. https://www.backblaze.com/blog/backblaze-drive-stats-for-2021/
14. Lakshman, A., Malik, P.: Cassandra: a decentralized structured storage system. ACM SIGOPS Oper. Syst. Rev. **44**(2), 35–40 (2010)
15. Lu, S., Luo, B., Patel, T., Yao, Y., Tiwari, D., Shi, W.: Making disk failure predictions smarter! In: 18th USENIX Conference on File and Storage Technologies, FAST 2020, pp. 151–167 (2020)
16. Murray, J.F., Hughes, G.F., Kreutz-Delgado, K.: Machine learning methods for predicting failures in hard drives: a multiple-instance application. J. Mach. Learn. Res. **6**, 783–816 (2005)
17. Pang, S., Jia, Y., Stones, R.J., Wang, G., Liu, X.: A combined Bayesian network method for predicting drive failure times from SMART attributes. In: 2016 International Joint Conference on Neural Networks, IJCNN 2016, pp. 4850–4856 (2016)
18. Santo, A.D., Galli, A., Gravina, M., Moscato, V., Sperlì, G.: Deep learning for HDD health assessment: an application based on LSTM. IEEE Trans. Comput. **71**(1), 69–80 (2022)
19. dos Santos Lima, F.D., Amaral, G.M.R., de Moura Leite, L.G., Gomes, J.P.P., de Castro Machado, J.: Predicting failures in hard drives with LSTM networks. In: 2017 Brazilian Conference on Intelligent Systems, BRACIS 2017, pp. 222–227 (2017)
20. Shi, Y., Li, J., Li, Z.: Gradient boosting with piece-wise linear regression trees. In: Proceedings of the Twenty-Eighth International Joint Conference on Artificial Intelligence, IJCAI 2019, pp. 3432–3438 (2019)
21. Zhang, J., Wang, J., He, L., Li, Z., Yu, P.S.: Layerwise perturbation-based adversarial training for hard drive health degree prediction. In: IEEE International Conference on Data Mining, ICDM 2018, pp. 1428–1433 (2018)

Why Query Plans Are Different: An Automatic Detection and Inference System

Hai Lan[1](✉)(iD), Yuanjia Zhang[2], Yu Dong[2], Dongxu Huang[2], Liu Tang[2], and Jian Zhang[2]

[1] RMIT University, Melbourne, VIC 3000, Australia
`hai.lan@student.rmit.edu.au`
[2] PingCAP, Sunnyvale, CA 94085, USA

Abstract. Preventing plan regression has always been a demanding task. SQL tuning advisor, e.g., index advisor, and optimizer testing tool are two common solutions. The former is proposed for database users to avoid a sub-optimal plan on a production system while the second tries to evaluate the optimizer before releasing a new version. However, both of them are uninformed for optimizer developers to quickly find the reason why a sub-optimal plan is generated for a query. Manual analysis is both labor-intensive and inefficient for large query plan and number of queries. To this end, we propose AutoDI, an <u>auto</u>matic <u>d</u>etection and <u>i</u>nference system to analyze why a sub-optimal plan is obtained. AutoDI consists of two main modules, *Difference Finder* and *Inference*. In *Difference Finder*, we introduce two types of signatures and design an efficient algorithm to detect the possible sub-optimal parts of the plan in a top-down manner. *Inference* has an extensible rule-action framework and takes the detected differences as the input to explore the possible reasons behind them. We test AutoDI with analytic workloads on a production database. Compared to developers, AutoDI can find the right reason in most cases with much less time. AutoDI has been deployed in TiDB to help optimizer developers analyze the plan regression cases.

1 Introduction

Motivation. Database vendors have been spending substantial resources on plan quality assurance. There are two common ways: 1) the first one is SQL tuning advisor [7,8], targeting database users. For example, Oracle provides the SQL Tuning Advisor [7], where users can submit one or more SQL statements as input to the advisor and receive advice, e.g., building indexes. However, it is uninformed for optimizer developers to quickly find the reason why such differences (performance change) come out. 2) The second is the optimizer testing [10,13,15], targeting the optimizer development team before releasing a new optimizer version. Most of these studies introduce a metric to assess the accuracy

---

Hai Lan: Hai Lan is the corresponding author.

Z. Bao et al. (Eds.): ADC 2023, LNCS 14386, pp. 213–226, 2024.
https://doi.org/10.1007/978-3-031-47843-7_15

of the optimizer. These metrics can be an early warning of an optimizer while they still lack feedback from a particular query.

A simple but important question is: *if we found that a worse plan was chosen for one query by the optimizer, what are the reasons behind that?* A reasonable analysis of this question can help database vendors improve their products. Two common cases can be found during the optimizer test:

Case 1: Different Cost Rank And Runtime Rank. For each query, a plan enumeration process will be called to find a set of plan candidates that are equivalent to the one generated in default. These plans will be costed and executed. After that, a plan regression will be found if a plan with a larger cost than the default one has a lower runtime.

Case 2: Regression In Different Optimizer Versions. The newly generated plan will be compared to the one from the last optimizer version. Similarly, a plan regression will be found if the runtime of the new plan is larger than the old one.

To answer the above question, a manual analysis has to be conducted by the optimizer development team at the moment. Such an analysis consists of two steps: 1) find the differences between two plans, 2) check out possible reasons with the corresponding collected data e.g., operators' cardinality, estimated cost, and running time. However, if the number of problematic queries or the plan tree is large, it is the *labor-intensive* work and is challenging for a developer to quickly find out the differences between two different plans and the reasons behind them.

Studied Problem. Motivated by this demanding need raised from the optimizer development team, we study the problem that how to automatically find out the reasons why two plans of one query are different. Formally, given two different plans of the same query, P_1 and P_2, P_1.cost $<$ P_2.cost while P_1.runtime $>$ P_2.runtime, report the differences between them and the reasons behind them.

Challenges. Building an automatic system to solve the problem above has three challenges: **C1.** To find out the parts (operator or subtree) of two plans with different implementations, they must have the same semantics. How to match the parts with the same semantics efficiently and how to make it work on the general case are challenging. **C2.** If multiple differences exist in two plans, the proposed method for inference can figure out which one is more important. **C3.** The proposed method should be *extensible*. With the development of an optimizer, new difference type, possible reasons, and operators could be introduced. The proposed methods must support the new features.

Our Contributions. We propose a system, called AutoDI, an <u>auto</u>matic <u>d</u>etection and <u>i</u>nference system to discover the reasons behind two different plans and overcome the aforementioned three challenges. AutoDI has been deployed in TiDB [11] to help optimizer developers analyze the plan regression cases. In this work, *detection* means finding the differences.

Preprocessing (Sect. 3.1). We introduce this module to regularize the plan pair, in order to facilitate *Difference Finder* part to find out the parts with same semantics and support the general cases. We introduce logical signature and physical signature to identify the equivalent (sub-)plans and preprocess the new added nodes during the optimization.

Difference Finder (Sect. 3.2). We design an algorithm to quickly locate where the two plans are different in a top-down manner, and it supports four types of difference as defined in Sect. 2.1.

Inference (Sect. 4). We introduce a rule-action framework, where each rule takes charge of one type of difference. A rule has several actions where each action is related to a possible reason. With this framework, we can easily extend *Inference* when new types of difference and new possible reasons come in. If multiple differences are presented in two plans, *Inference* will rank the differences and find out which one is crucial.

Evaluation (Sect. 5). We implement AutoDI and evaluate it on TiDB [11], an HTAP database system, with two analytic workloads, JOB [12] and TPC-H [9] to explore the efficiency and effectiveness of AutoDI. The experiments show that AutoDI can find the right reasons in most cases with much less time (Table 1).

Table 1. Summary of Notations

Symbol	Description
P	Execution plan of one query
n	A node in the execution plan
$n.ls$	Logical signature of node n
$n.ps$	Physical signature of node n
$n.cost$	Cost of node n
$n.card$	Cardinality of node n
$n.rt$	Running time of node n
$n.nt$	Type of node n
$n.op$	Implementation of node n
$n.left$	Left child of node n
$n.right$	Right child of node n
$n.pointer$	Pointer of node n
$n.level$	Depth of node n

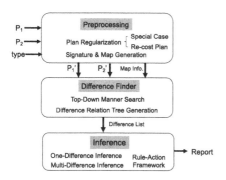

Fig. 1. Overview of AutoDI

2   Background and System Overview

2.1   Background

Existing Differences. After investigating several database systems [3,4,11], we find there are four typical types of differences: 1) different data access paths (*DADiff*), e.g., full table scan vs. index scan; 2) different operator implementations (*ImpDiff*), e.g., hash join vs. merge join; 3) different join orders (*JODiff*), e.g., $A \bowtie B \bowtie C$ vs. $A \bowtie C \bowtie B$; 4) different operator orders (*OODiff*), e.g., whether a union is under join. *OODiff* rarely occurs and is mainly determined by logical optimization.

Possible Reasons. We can classify the possible reasons into two categories: 1) code-level of the optimizer, which includes statistics model, cardinality estimation module, cost model, plan enumeration algorithm, and logical operator implementations; 2) the optimizer's input parameters, such as the used hint set and the built indexes. Most database systems have provided the idea of hint to specify the optimizer's behaviors by users.

2.2 System Overview

The overview of AutoDI is presented in Fig. 1, which consists of three modules: *Preprocessing* (Sect. 3.1), *Difference Finder* (Sect. 3.2), and *Inference* (Sect. 4).

Preprocessing. To locate the differences between two plans effectively and efficiently, we introduce the preprocessing module to regularize two plans and generate the nodes' signatures. We introduce two signature types to accelerate our detection process.

Difference Finder. This module adopts a top-down manner algorithm to find all possible differences between two plans. Currently, it supports all the differences defined in Sect. 2.1.

Inference. This module obtains the possible reasons behind the found differences. We introduce a rule-action framework to make it extensible, e.g., for a new difference. A difference type has a defined rule and a rule has several actions where each action is related to a possible reason. If multiple differences are in two plans, *Inference* will rank the found differences and find out the most crucial one. Finally, the obtained reasons will be reported to the developers.

3 Preprocessing and Difference Finder

3.1 Preprocessing

When finding the differences between two plans, we should make sure we compare the execution (sub-)plans with the same logical (sub-)plan. Thus, we introduce two signatures, logical signature and physical signature.

Logical Signature. The logical signature of the node n in a plan tree depicts the logical meaning of the plan with the node n as root, i.e., outputted rows. It contains the logical signature information of all operators under it. If two nodes have the same logical signature, their outputs must be the same. The details of logical signature information of different operators are in Table 2. We use the bag to represent the logical signature information, because the same operation can be executed multiple times, e.g., two tables can be joined multiple times.

Table 2. Operators' Logical and Physical Signature Information (Best Viewed In Color)

Operator	Logical (Physical) Signature
Hash/Index/Merge-Join	join type, table names, join conditions
TableScan	table name, predicates
IndexScan	index name, table name, predicates
Selection	attributes, predicates
Hash/Stream-Agg	agg. type, group attribute, agg. function
Sort	attributes, order type

Physical Signature. The physical signature of a node n records the execution plan with n as the root node. The details of physical signature information of different operators are similar to those of their logical signature. We use blue to label the contents that physical signatures add in Table 2. To depict the tree structure, we use Eq. 1 as the physical signature of node n, where $n.pi$ is the physical information of node n.

$$n.ps = (n.pi, (n.left.ps, n.right.ps)) \tag{1}$$

We generate the logical signatures and physical signatures of one plan in a bottom-up manner. We also build a signature map for the second plan of AutoDI input to quickly locate the node for a given logical signature.

Plan Regularization. In the proposed algorithms in *Difference Finder* and *Inference*, The input plan pairs have similar node types and count, and are comparable on cost. In reality, these two requirements may not be held. Thus, we introduce a plan regularization.

Special Case Handling. In a database, the 'Sort' node can be added with an enforced order property or implicitly implemented by other operators, e.g., 'Index Scan'. Similarly, to reduce the intermediate result size during query processing, database will add some operators near the data source, e.g., 'Aggregation', 'Limit' as a partial processing. For added nodes, we first detect the newly added nodes by traversing the plan tree and make the parent nodes of the added nodes 'absorb' them, i.e., recording the added node information in their parent nodes. To handle the case of an implicit 'Sort' node, we will record the order-related nodes that ensure some columns' values in order, e.g., 'Index Scan', which ensures the output is ordered in the indexed attributes. With order-related nodes, AutoDI can find the implicit 'Sort' implementation.

Plan Re-costing. If the plan regression happened in the different optimizer versions, the generated plans cannot be compared on cost directly because the cost model may be updated. In this case, we re-cost and run the plan from an old version in the new one and construct a new test pair. We do not re-cost the plan generated from a new version to an old one, because new features may be introduced but are not supported in an old version.

3.2 Difference Finder

A difference *diff* records the difference type (*diff.msg*), two nodes (*diff.n₁*, *diff.n₂*) where the difference is found, the difference level (*diff.level*), which is maximal value of $diff.n_1.level$ and $diff.n_2.level$.

With the plans annotated with logical signatures and physical signatures, *Difference Finder* tries to find the parts where the logical signature is the same while the physical signature is different. Its details are presented in Algorithm 1. It takes two different plans of the same query P_1, P_2, and the logical signature map M of P_2 as the inputs. Its output is a list of differences, and it is initialized as an empty list (line 1). The signature map M is used to find the node with a given logical signature, which helps us quickly locate the nodes with the same logical signature at different levels. We first get the root nodes of P_1 and P_2, denoted as

---

Algorithm 1: Find Differences (*FindDiff*)

Input: plan P_1, plan P_2, logical signature map M of P_2
Output: difference list R

1 $n_1 \leftarrow P_1.root; n_2 \leftarrow P_2.root; R \leftarrow \emptyset$;
2 **if** $n_1.ls = n_2.ls \land n_1.ps = n_2.ps$ **then**
3 $\quad$ | $\quad$ return R;
4 **if** $n_1.ls = n_2.ls \land n_1.ps \neq n_2.ps$ **then**
5 $\quad$ **if** $n_1.nt = n_2.nt \land n_1.op = n_2.op$ **then**
6 $\quad\quad$ | $\quad$ R.append(*FindDiff*($n_1.left, n_2.left, M$));
7 $\quad\quad$ | $\quad$ R.append(*FindDiff*($n_1.right, n_2.right, M$));
8 $\quad$ **if** $n_1.nt = n_2.nt \land n_1.op \neq n_2.op$ **then**
9 $\quad\quad$ **if** *implementations of* n_1, n_2 *are different* **then**
10 $\quad\quad\quad$ | $\quad$ R.add(<"ImpDiff", $n_1, n_2, max(n_1.level, n_2.level)$>);
11 $\quad\quad\quad$ | $\quad$ R.append(*FindDiff*($n_1.left, n_2.left, M$));
12 $\quad\quad\quad$ | $\quad$ R.append(*FindDiff*($n_1.right, n_2.right, M$));
13 $\quad\quad$ **if** *ls in children of* n_1 *and* n_2 *is different* **then**
14 $\quad\quad\quad$ | $\quad$ R.add(<"JODiff", $n_1, n_2, max(n_1.level, n_2.level)$>);
15 $\quad\quad\quad$ **foreach** *node* $n \in n_1.left$ **do**
16 $\quad\quad\quad\quad$ | $\quad$ $n' \leftarrow M(n)$;
17 $\quad\quad\quad\quad$ **if** $n' \neq null$ **then**
18 $\quad\quad\quad\quad\quad$ | $\quad$ R.append(*FindDiff*(n, n', M));
19 $\quad$ **if** $n_1.nt \neq n_2.nt$ **then**
20 $\quad\quad$ | $\quad$ R.add(<"OODiff", $n_1, n_2, max(n_1.level, n_2.level)$>);
21 $\quad\quad$ | $\quad$ same steps as line 15-18;
22 return R

---

n_1 and n_2 respectively (line 1). If the logical signatures and physical signatures of n_1 and n_2 are the same, the two (sub-)plans with n_1 and n_2 as roots must be the same, and an empty list is returned (line2-3). If the logical signatures of n_1 and n_2 are the same while the physical signatures are not, differences between two execution plans exists. We can divide it into three cases: 1) Node types and operators of n_1 and n_2 are the same and the differences exists in the sub-plans (line 5–6). We recursively call *FindDiff* on the subtrees. That two operators are equal (line 5) means their *implementations*, e.g., hash join or merge join, *parameters*, e.g., the joined tables and join condition, and the *children's logical signatures* must be same. 2) Node types are the same while the operators are not (line 8–18). First, we check whether the implementations of n_1 and n_2 are different. If that is true, we report *ImpDiff* case (line 10) and call *FindDiff* on the subtrees (line 11–12). Note that if the node type of n_1 (n_2) is the access operator on a table, we report *DADiff*. Then, we check whether the children's logical signatures of $n1$ and n_2 are the same. If not, we report *JODiff*. When meeting the *JODiff*, we cannot call *FindDiff* on the subtrees due the different logical signatures. Here, we traverse the nodes under n_1 and find whether one

```
Rule {                                  Rule4ImpDiff {
    /* rule id */                           ruleId: "ImpDiff"
    ruleId                                  actionList: {ce4imp, cm4imp}
    /* possible reasons to be checked */    actionFlag: {1, 1}
    actionList                          }
    /* reasoning flag, 0 or 1, if it is 1, the
corresponding action will be executed */    /* check cardinality estimation */
    actionFlag                          func ce4imp(node1, node2) {...}
}                                           /* check cost model */
                                        func cm4imp(node1, node2) {...}
```

Fig. 2. The Rule-Action Framework and an Example of ImpDiff

node with same logical signature in n_2 exists through M. If we find such a node n' for the node n, we call *FindDiff* on these two nodes (line 15–18). Note that, when finding n', we need to skip the nodes under the node n when traversing the sub-plan of n_1 in line 15 to avoid the redundant differences to be reported. 3) If the node types are different (line 19–21), we report the *OODiff* case and do the same work as lines 15–18, because the logical signatures of children are also different in this case.

4   Inference Framework

4.1   The Rule-Action Framework

To make *Inference* extensible with new difference types and reasons, we introduce a rule-action framework, which is shown in the left side of Fig. 2. Each difference type has a corresponding rule. In each rule, the *actionList* includes a list of actions for the possible reasons, and *actionFlag* is a 0/1 array. We execute the ith action if the ith value in *actionFlag* is 1. When a new difference type is introduced, we only need to define a new rule and implement its related actions. When a new possible reason for a difference type comes, we just need to add a new action in its *actionList* and set related item in *actionFlag*.

An example for *ImpDiff* is presented in the right side of Fig. 2. There are two actions, *ce4imp* and *cm4imp*, to check whether the reasons are inaccurate in cardinality estimation and cost model, respectively.

4.2   Inference

The inference process is shown in Algorithm 2. It takes the difference list R and crucial difference ratio α as input. It outputs possible reasons. If there is only one difference between two plans, we call the actions related to the difference (line 11–12). We also introduce the process for multiple differences (line 3–9).

Scope and Idea of Inference In this paper, we focus on cardinality estimation and cost model for the following reasons. 1) Our goal is to help optimizer developers find the shortage in optimizer implementation. 2) It is hard to measure whether a certain type of statistics is good. However, we can use the cardinality estimation as an indicator, since good statistics usually lead to a more accurate cardinality estimation. 3) The plan enumeration algorithm is also hard to

---

Algorithm 2: Inference
___
    Input: Difference list R, crucial difference ratio α
    Output: Possible reasons S
1 $S \leftarrow \emptyset$;
2 **if** $|R| > 1$ **then**
3      $diffs \leftarrow$ obtain the crucial differences in R under α;
4      $C \leftarrow sort\ diffs$;
5   **foreach** $diff \in C$ **do**
6         $r \leftarrow$ obtain the rule for $diff$;
7   **foreach** $a \in r.actionList$ **do**
8   **if** a's flag in $r.actionFlag$ is 1 **then**
9   S.add($a(diff.n_1,\ diff.n_2)$);

10    $R \leftarrow R - diffs$;
11 **foreach** $diff \in R$ **do**
12   same steps as line 6-9;
13 **return** S
___

Algorithm 3: Card. Estimation Check for $ImpDiff$ ($ce4imp$)
___
    Input: two difference nodes, n_1, n_2
    Output: A possible reason s
1 $s \leftarrow \emptyset$; set $isSameRoot$, $isSameLeft$, $isSameRight$;
2 **if** $isSameRoot$, $isSameLeft$, $isSameRight$ are $true$ **then**
3    $s \leftarrow$ "CardEst does not cause the diff";
4 **if** $not\ isSameRoot \wedge isSameLeft \wedge isSameRight$ **then**
5    $s \leftarrow$ report which one is worse;
6 **if** $not\ isSameLeft \vee not\ isSameRight$ **then**
7    $s \leftarrow$ "Children CardEst may cause the diff";
8 **return** s
___

analyze. However, the good news is that if the cost rank and the runtime rank are the same, we can infer that the reasons could be the enumeration algorithm, different index configurations, and used query hints.

When inferring the reasons, AutoDI first checks whether it is the problem in cardinality, and then checks the cost model. Here, we present $ImpDiff$ to explain.

Cardinality Estimation Check. The cardinality estimation of one node in the plan tree is also influenced by their children. Thus, we take the children cardinality estimation into consideration, as presented in Algorithm 3. $ce4imp$ takes the two nodes in a $ImpDiff$ as input. The $isSameRoot$, $isSameLeft$, and $isSameRight$ indicate whether the cardinality estimation of n_1 and n_2, their left children, and their right children are the same, respectively. _Case 1_, if they were both $true$, the different implementations of n_1 and n_2 are not caused by cardinality estimation (line 2–3). _Case 2_, if the children are the same, we report which one is worse (line 4–5). We compare them with *q-error* [12]. *Case 3*, any child that has a different cardinality estimation can lead to different cardinalities in n_1 and n_2, which should be checked first (line 6–7).

Cost Model Check. The estimated cost of a node n is the total cost of subtree with n as root. To analyze whether the cost model is accurate for two different nodes, we consider two aspects: 1) whether the cost model for current nodes is accurate; 2) whether the cost model for the subtree is accurate. We use *fr*, *fc*, and *fcn* to indicate whether the runtime of the subtree with n_1 as root is smaller than that with n_2 as root, whether the cost of that subtree with n_1 as the root is smaller that with n_2 as the root, and whether the cost of node n_1 is smaller than n_2, respectively. We analyze the reasons for cost model under the same three cases as cardinality estimation:

In *Case 1* and *Case 3*, we further check whether *fr* and fc are set with the same value (*true* or *false*). 1) If they have the same value, the estimated cost for the subtrees with n_1 and n_2 as the root is accurate. Then, we check values of *fr* and *fcn*. If they also have the same value, we report that this *ImpDiff* happens when the query hints are specified or there are different search spaces. If they have different values, we report the cost model is inaccurate and report which one is underestimated. 2) If *fr* and *fc* have different values, we first report cost model is inaccurate in ranking the cost of subtrees with n_1 and n_2 as the root. If the values of *fr* and *fcn* are the same, we report the children's cost is inaccurate. Otherwise, we report cost model is inaccurate at least in n_1 and n_2. In *Case 2*, we report that the cardinality estimation should be fixed first.

Inference of Multiple Differences. We analyze some plan regression cases and make two observations. 1) In most cases, there are several main differences, i.e., the runtime gap between the nodes in a difference is close to the runtime gap of two plans. 2) The nodes in the most crucial difference have a larger level than most nodes in other differences. Motivated by the above observations, we introduce a parameter α to define the crucial differences. Suppose two different plans of one query are P_1 and P_2, where $P_1.rt$ is smaller than $P_2.rt$. $P.rt$ indicates the runtime of plan P. A difference *diff* could be a crucial difference if $(diff.n_1.rt\text{-}diff.n_2.rt)$ is larger than $\alpha(P_1.rt\text{-}P_2.rt)$. We sort possible crucial differences in descending order of *diff.level* and use C to indicate the sorted set. A difference with the smaller rank in C has a larger probability as the most crucial difference. For each difference, we call the actions to obtain the reason. (line 3–9 in Algorithm 2)

5 Evaluation

Our evaluation aims to answer the following questions:
Q1: (i) Is AutoDI efficient at finding the possible differences between two different plans of the same query? (ii) Compared to developers, how well are the differences found by AutoDI?
Q2: (i) How efficient is AutoDI in discovering the reasons compared to the manual analysis? (ii) Whether the report of AutoDI is actionable for developers?

5.1   Experimental Setup

Testing Plan Pairs Generation. We use two analytic workloads, JOB [12] and TPC-H [9]. The scale of dataset is 1 in both workloads. We adopt Horoscope [2] to output the default plan generated by the optimizer and a plan with a lower runtime than the default as a test pair.

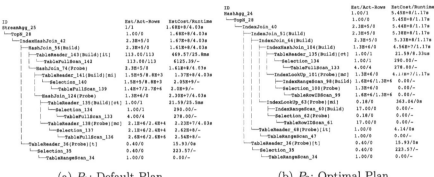

(a) P_1: Default Plan   (b) P_2: Optimal Plan

Fig. 3. Two Plans of JOB q5a

Implementation and Test Environment. We implement AutoDI with 2000+ lines of GO code and we put our source code in [1]. We evaluate AutoDI on TiDB [11], an HTAP database system. All experiments are conducted on a machine with 3.3 GHz Intel Core i7 and 16GB of RAM. We set the parameter α with 0.7 in *Inference* (See Sect. 4.2). Although we use TiDB in the experiments, the input of AutoDI is a plan pair, which can be generated from other database systems, e.g., PostgreSQL [4], as long as we implement a plan parser to transform the plan and collect the related data.

5.2   Difference Finder

Efficiency. We prepare five groups of queries from JOB and TPC-H, namely G1, G2, G3, G4, and G5, such that the default plan's node count in a group is as follows: G1=[1,16), G2=[16,31), G3=[31,46), G4=[46, 61), G5=[61, 76). For every query, we also randomly generate a different plan to construct a testing pair to verify the *Difference Finder*. We sample 3 test pairs from each group and ask the optimizer developers to find out the differences that can help them analyze the optimizer shortage. We report the average time in each group in Table 3: 1) With the increase of node count both strategies spend more time to find the possible differences, since more nodes are needed to be considered. 2) Compared to developers AutoDI takes much less time to find the differences.

Table 3. Efficiency of Difference Finder

	G1	G2	G3	G4	G5
AutoDI (μs)	191.2	277.6	393.7	668.9	943.2
Manual Processing (s)	46	102	121	132.0	158.3

Effectiveness. In our test setting, all queries in G1 and G5 can obtain the optimal plan in TiDB. We evaluate the effectiveness on queries with plan nodes larger than 15, i.e., G2-G4. We obtain 3 queries where the optimizer in TiDB generates the sub-optimal plan in default for each group. For each query, we obtain a better plan than the default one by enumerating the possible plans. We ask three optimizer developers to evaluate whether the differences found by AutoDI are good enough, i.e., whether they can find out the reasons based on the these differences. For all 9 queries, AutoDI has found right differences.

5.3   Inference

Here, we study the efficiency and effectiveness of *Inference* module to answer **Q2**. We use the same plan pairs in the effectiveness study of *Difference Finder*.

Table 4. Efficiency of Inference

	G2	G3	G4
AutoDI (μs)	345.8(302.3+43.5)	713.4(661.3+52.1)	874.3(805.0+69.3)
Manual Processing (s)	193.6	159.3	207.3

Efficiency. We compare the inference time used in AutoDI and manual analysis, and report the average time of queries in each group in Table 4. The time of manual process in Table 4 is the total time of the whole process. For AutoDI, we report the total time, the time used in finding differences only and in inference only. We observe that: 1) AutoDI is significantly faster than human in inference. 2) Combining with the time in Table 3, the process of *finding difference* is the main overhead in both AutoDI and human analysis.

Table 5. Reasons of Found Differences for *5a*

Diff. ID	Reasons
1	Cost model is not accurate at least at this diff
	P_1 (P_2) has been underestimated (overestimated)
2	With same rank in cost, card. estimation, and runtime, this can happen in P_1 with (1) user defined hints, (2) different index set
3	Children's card. are different, which may cause different cost in this diff
	Cost model is not accurate at least at this mode. P_1 is underestimated or P_2 is overestimated
4	Not support that the number of true returned rows is different
5	Children's card. are different, which may cause different cost in this diff
	Cost model is not accurate at least at this mode. P_1 is underestimated or P_2 is overestimated
6	Children's card. are different, which may cause different cost in this diff
	Cost model is not accurate at least at this mode. P_1 is underestimated or P_2 is overestimated
7	Children's card. are different, which may cause different cost in this diff
	Cost model is not accurate at least at this mode. P_1 is underestimated or P_2 is overestimated
8	Children's card. are different, which may cause different cost in this diff
	Cost model is not accurate at least at this mode. P_1 is underestimated or P_2 is overestimated
9	No report for this diff

Effectiveness. We ask three optimizer developers to evaluate whether the reasons generated by AutoDI are accurate enough. If the most crucial difference found by AutoDI and the given reasons in AutoDI are the same with developers, AutoDI gets 2 points. If the most crucial difference found by AutoDI is not the same with developers but it occurs in the non-crucial list of AutoDI, AutoDI gets 1 point. Otherwise, AutoDI gets 0 point. Overall, out of total 9 queries, 6 queries get 2 points and 3 queries get 1 point.

5.4   Case Study

We use the query JOB-*5a* as an example to compare compare AutoDI with the manual analysis from one expert. Figure 3 presents two different plans of *5a*, P_1, the default plan generated by TiDB's optimizer, and P_2, the optimal plan. We display the operator (*ID*), estimated row count (*EstRows*), actual row count (*ActRows*), estimated cost (EstCost), and runtime (*Runtime*).

Finding Differences. With AutoDI, 9 differences are found. Results are shown in Table 6. Column *Diff. Details* presents where the difference exists, i.e., the nodes have the same logical signature while their implementations are different. The expert finds four differences and we mark the differences found by the expert with a '•' in their id. The expert tries to find the root cause and some differences with small-level values will be skipped during the manual analysis.

Table 6. Differences between P_1 and P_2 of $5a$

Diff. ID	Diff. Type	Diff. Details(P_1,P_2)	Level	Runtime(P_1,P_2)
1•	*DADiff*	TableReader_138,IndexLookUp_101	7	$4.03\,s$,$1.17\,s$
2•	*DADiff*	TableReader_141,IndexLookUp_63	6	$4.03\,s$,$0ns$
3•	*ImpDiff*	HashJoin_124,IndexHashJoin_104	6	$4.03\,s$,$1.17\,s$
4	*JODiff*	HashJoin_124,IndexHashJoin_104	6	$4.03\,s$,$1.17\,s$
5•	*ImpDiff*	HashJoin_74,IndexJoin_64	5	$4.03\,s$,$1.17\,s$
6	*ImpDiff*	HashJoin_56,IndexJoin_51	4	$4.03\,s$,$1.17\,s$
7	*ImpDiff*	IndexHashJoin_42,IndexJoin_40	3	$4.03\,s$,$1.17\,s$
8	*ImpDiff*	StreamAgg_25,HashAgg_24	1	$4.03\,s$,$1.17\,s$
9	*DADiff*	TableReader_143,TableReader_48	5	$28.5ms$,$0ns$

Inference. We set the ratio of key difference as 0.7. The reasons reported by AutoDI are shown in Table 5. The root cause found by AutoDI is the first difference and its reason is the inaccuracy in the cost model. The expert reports the same root cause and the reason for that. Overall, the expert takes $335s$ to find the root cause and the reason behind it; in contrast, AutoDI only takes $284\mu s$. We further ask the expert to evaluate the reasons for other references in Table 5. Except for the fourth difference, other reasons are acceptable.

6   Related Work

Related User Tools. Many database vendors have their own tools for the database users to avoid plan regression [5–8,16] in a production system. For example, Oracle provides the SQL Tuning Advisor [7], where users can submit one or more SQL statements as input to the advisor and receive advice or recommendations for how to tune the statements, e.g., updating statistics, building indexes, along with a rationale and expected benefit. SQL Server has provided *Compare Showplan* [6] to help users analyze query plans in its management studio. Users can further click the operator to obtain detailed comparisons, e.g., cardinality of the operator, runtime.

Optimizer Analysis and Test. The study [12] digs into the impact of three optimizer modules, i.e., cardinality estimation, cost model, and plan enumeration algorithm on selecting an optimal plan. They find that errors in cardinality estimation are usually the reason for bad plans. The study [14] conducts a similar study and proposes a re-optimization method to improve the accuracy of cardinality estimation. In [10,13,15], the authors propose a new metric as an indicator of optimizer quality for a workload. All these metrics are based on the estimated cost rank and runtime rank of the possible plans.

7   Conclusion

In this paper, we propose AutoDI, to analyze plan regression. AutoDI first calls *Difference Finder* to detect the differences between two plans. After that, *Inference* sorts the differences according to the runtime and their levels, and then reasons the differences through the rule-action framework. Experiments have shown that AutoDI can find the right differences and reasons in most cases with much less time compared to developers.

References

1. Additional material. https://github.com/hailanwhu/AutoDI/
2. Horoscope. https://github.com/PingCAP-QE/horoscope
3. MySQL. https://dev.mysql.com/
4. PostgreSQL. https://www.postgresql.org/
5. SQL plan management. https://www.oracle.com/technetwork/database/bi-dataw arehousing/twp-sql-plan-mgmt-19c-5324207.pdf
6. SQL server compare showplan. https://docs.microsoft.com/en-us/sql/relational-databases/performance/compare-execution-plans?view=sql-server-ver15
7. SQL tuning advisor. https://docs.oracle.com/database/121/TGSQL/tgsql_sqltu ne.htm
8. SQL tuning advisor. https://docs.microsoft.com/en-us/sql/tools/dta/tutorial-database-engine-tuning-advisor?view=sql-server-ver15
9. TPC-H. http://www.tpc.org/tpch/
10. Gu, Z., Soliman, M.A., Waas, F.M.: Testing the accuracy of query optimizers. In: DBTest, p. 11 (2012)
11. Huang, D., et al.: TiDB: a raft-based HTAP database. Proc. VLDB Endow. **13**(12), 3072–3084 (2020)
12. Leis, V., Gubichev, A., Mirchev, A., Boncz, P.A., Kemper, A., Neumann, T.: How good are query optimizers, really? VLDB **9**(3), 204–215 (2015)
13. Li, Z., Papaemmanouil, O., Cherniack, M.: OptMark: a toolkit for benchmarking query optimizers. In: CIKM, pp. 2155–2160 (2016)
14. Perron, M., Shang, Z., Kraska, T., Stonebraker, M.: How i learned to stop worrying and love re-optimization. In: ICDE, pp. 1758–1761 (2019)
15. Waas, F.M., Giakoumakis, L., Zhang, S.: Plan space analysis: an early warning system to detect plan regressions in cost-based optimizers. In: DBTest, p. 2 (2011)
16. Ziauddin, M., Das, D., Su, H., Zhu, Y., Yagoub, K.: Optimizer plan change management: improved stability and performance in oracle 11g. PVLDB **1**(2), 1346–1355 (2008)

An Empirical Analysis of Just-in-Time Compilation in Modern Databases

Miao Ma[1], Zhengyi Yang[1(✉)] [iD], Kongzhang Hao[1], Liuyi Chen[1],
Chunling Wang[2], and Yi Jin[2]

[1] The University of New South Wales, Sydney, Australia
{miao.ma,zhengyi.yang,kongzhang.hao,liuyi.chen}@unsw.edu.au
[2] Data Principles (Beijing) Technology Co. Ltd, Beijing, China
{chunling.wang,yi.jin}@enmotech.com

Abstract. JIT (Just-in-Time) technology has garnered significant attention for improving the efficiency of database execution. It offers higher performance by eliminating interpretation overhead compared to traditional execution engines. LLVM serves as the primary JIT architecture, which was implemented in PostgreSQL since version 11. However, recent advancements in WASM-based databases, such as Mutable, present an alternative JIT approach. This approach minimizes the extensive engineering efforts associated with the execution engine and focuses on optimizing supported operators for lower latency and higher throughput. In this paper, we perform comprehensive experiments on these two representative open-source databases to gain deeper insights into the effectiveness of different JIT architectures.

Keywords: LLVM · WebAssembly · PostgreSQL · Mutable · JIT

1 Introduction

Databases are essential for storing, retrieving, and managing extensive data across industries like e-commerce, finance, healthcare, and logistics. The need for faster and more efficient data processing has led to research and innovation in enhancing database performance and optimizing resource use. An approach that has garnered significant interest is the incorporation of Just-in-Time (JIT) compilation into databases.

JIT compilation, a dynamic compilation approach, compiles code at run time just before execution, in contrast to Ahead-of-Time (AOT) compilation [1]. Early databases relied on AOT compilation result in limitations and significant overhead. JIT compilation, conversely, offers numerous advantages, including improved query execution speed, reduced memory usage, and adaptability to dynamic workloads. These advantages collectively enhance the query performance of JIT databases. Due to these benefits, there has been a recent surge in the development of JIT databases focused on enhancing query performance. They can be primarily categorized into two types: LLVM (Low Level Virtual Machine)-based and WASM (WebAssembly)-based databases.

Z. Bao et al. (Eds.): ADC 2023, LNCS 14386, pp. 227–240, 2024.
https://doi.org/10.1007/978-3-031-47843-7_16

LLVM-Based Databases. In LLVM-based databases, an intermediate representation (IR) is generated directly from the query execution plan, utilizing native LLVM or adapted LLVM. This IR is then compiled into machine code, undergoing effective optimization for faster compilation and improved query performance. Notably, examples like Hyper [2] and the open-source database PostgreSQL [3] demonstrate LLVM-based JIT adoption. As Hyper is not an open source database, we've chosen PostgreSQL as the representative database system for LLVM JIT. Starting from version 11, PostgreSQL introduced JIT support, enabling on-the-fly compilation of *expressions* within queries. These expressions are compiled into bytecode-based functions, replacing interpreted execution. This dynamic compilation generates optimized machine code tailored to the hardware architecture, enhancing query performance.

WASM-Based Databases. LLVM-based JIT databases outperform traditional databases but demand significant engineering efforts, including reengineering core compiler techniques. Given the evolving database landscape, continually reinventing JIT compilation in LLVM-based databases is costly and impractical. To tackle this challenge, WASM-based databases provide an alternative. They aim to reduce the extensive and complex engineering work associated with the execution engine. A notable example is Mutable [4], which introduces a novel query execution engine architecture. It employs WebAssembly as its intermediate representation (IR) and utilizes Google's V8 and Binaryen as its backend for compilation and execution. This leverages Binaryen's fully parallel code generation and optimization capabilities. Mutable's innovative approach eliminates the need for extensive reengineering of techniques developed by the compiler community over decades.

Aims and Contributions. This paper conducts a thorough comparative analysis of two significant JIT databases, PostgreSQL and Mutable. We analyze their JIT implementations, evaluate their strengths and weaknesses, and identify potential areas for future JIT research in databases. Our contributions include:

(A) Comprehensive Survey of JIT in Modern Databases. This study serves as a pioneering effort in surveying and comparing the performance of JIT compilation in contemporary open-source databases, with a particular emphasis on PostgreSQL and Mutable as prominent case studies. It stands as the first work to offer an in-depth analysis and comprehensive survey of well-established open-source JIT databases in modern database technology.

(B) Rigorous and Extensive Experimental Studies. To investigate the performance of JIT in databases, we conducted in-depth experimental studies. Our experiments encompassed various aspects, including the evaluation of aggregation performance, a comparative analysis of grouping calculations, the examination of expression evaluation, the compiling time, and the assessment of performance with increasing data volumes. By designing comprehensive experiments and employing representative datasets, we ensured accurate and reliable results.

(C) A Practical Guidance for JIT Compilation. This paper provides practical recommendations for JIT compilation grounded in empirical analysis and

extensive comparisons of JIT database implementations. These guidelines constitute a valuable reference for both practitioners and researchers aiming to leverage the advantages of JIT compilation. Furthermore, we offer insights and stimulate future advancements in JIT databases, highlighting potential domains for further exploration and enhancement.

Outline. Sect. 2 provides the background. Section 3 reviews the related works. Section 4 presents the details about JIT implementation in PostgreSQL and Mutable. Section 5 evaluates and analyzes the performance of PostgreSQL and Mutable. Section 6 discusses the future works and Sect. 7 concludes the paper.

2   Preliminary

In this section, we provide an overview of key concepts, including ahead-of-time compilation, just-in-time compilation, and the TPC-H Benchmark.

AOT Compilation. AOT (Ahead-Of-Time) compilation is commonly associated with programming languages like C and C++. In AOT, programs can execute without a run time environment and can directly link static or dynamic libraries to binary code. One advantage of AOT is to eliminate the need for the time and overhead associated with online compilation. This advantage is particularly beneficial for short-running programs with relatively flat method hotness curves [5]. AOT allows for code analysis and optimization without considering resource costs caused by ahead-of-time compilation. However, AOT typically lacks access to reliable profile data which is limiting its effectiveness. AOT also can not perform certain optimizations available in JIT, such as run time profile-guided optimization, pseudo-constant propagation, or indirect-virtual function inlining.

JIT Compilation. JIT compilation is a dynamic compilation technique that has gained significant attention in various domains. Unlike traditional AOT compilation, JIT compilation occurs at run time, generating optimized machine code just before it is executed. By fast compilation and dynamically optimizing code based on run time information, JIT compilation surpasses statically compiled or interpreted code in performance. It can the Intermediate language [6] code by translating to the native code repeatedly when it is supposed to be executed [7]. It has become an integral part of modern software systems especially in VM and web browsers. In the realm of database systems, JIT compilation holds promise for enhancing query execution performance.

TPC-H Benchmark. The TPC-H benchmark [8] is widely recognized for evaluating database system performance. It simulates real-world analytical scenarios with complex operations like multi-table joins and aggregations. Adhering to TPC-H guidelines ensures fair comparisons across systems. The evaluation focuses on metrics like query execution time and throughput, providing insights into query performance and concurrent workload handling. We use TPC-H to assess PostgreSQL and Mutable, aiming to understand JIT compilation's impact on complex query performance.

3   Related Work

LLVM. With the development of modern CPUs, the most widely used database execution framework of Volcano iterators [9] exposes the limitations of Cache inefficiency, CPU inefficiency, iterator overhead. In 2005, Hyper-Pipelining Query Execution proposes a vectorized model which can improve CPU execution efficiency. However, it also exposed two dangers including the significant fraction thereof and mispredicted branch [10]. In 2010, the paper [11] customized code generation to optimize it holistically by generating the hardware-specific source code. In 2011, [2] introduced dynamic compilation and parallel execution framework, highlighting the advantages of utilizing LLVM for generating cross-platform Intermediate Representation (IR) code. This approach exhibited rapid compilation and robust code optimization while ensuring compatibility with existing C++ code through features like function calls and direct memory access. Subsequently, numerous database systems which were inspired by HyPer [12] have adopted similar dynamic compilation techniques. In 2014, the concept of Morsel-driven parallelism [13] was introduced to address performance bottlenecks stemming from underutilized system resources when utilizing a single core. This concept involved dividing query execution data into morsels and implementing an operator pipeline with dynamic scheduling strategies. A morsel pipeline was treated as an independent task and executed by a worker in a thread pool. This approach enabled fine-grained dynamic adjustments, maximized throughput, and improved cache locality. In 2018, further optimization in compilation based on the Morsel-driven idea was explored [14]. This strategy entailed collecting statistical information during query execution, estimating compilation time based on the collected statistics, and dynamically switching to compilation mode. By allowing different query groups to employ distinct execution modes, more efficient query execution was achieved.

WASM. Recently, Mutable [15] offers an alternative JIT approach that could minimize the complex engineering work required by the execution engine, while it could also optimize supported operators to achieve lower latency and higher throughput. It utilizes V8 and Binaryen as the backend for compilation and execution. It takes advantage of Binaryen's fully parallel code generation and optimization capabilities which will maximize CPU utilization.PostgreSQL has also embraced JIT based on LLVM, but there is no performance comparison analysis conducted thus far between these two representative JIT architecture of LLVM and WebAssebly, namely PostgreSQL and Mutable.

Others. Various JIT compilers are utilized in different programming languages and platforms to enhance code execution efficiency. In the Python ecosystem, JIT compilers like PyPy, Numba, and Cython aim to optimize Python code execution, with Numba even offering the option to disable the Global Interpreter Lock (GIL) [16]. LuaJIT [17] is a trace-based JIT compiler designed for the Lua programming language, generating efficient code to boost Lua program execution. Meanwhile, in Java, Java Hotspot stands out as an efficient JIT compiler

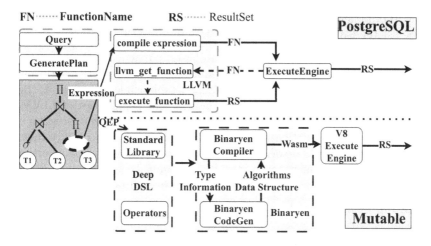

Fig. 1. The JIT architecture of Mutable and PostgreSQL

for the Java Virtual Machine (JVM). It identifies the frequently used methods and optimizes them into Java bytecode, with JDK-9 [18] introducing two compilers, *c1* and *c2*, to cater to different optimization needs. While *c1* prioritizes speed, *c2* applies an array of optimizations to produce high-quality code and optimize program execution [5].

4   JIT Implementations

In this section, we delve into the JIT implementation of both PostgreSQL and Mutable, and their architectures are illustrated in Fig. 1.

4.1   PostgreSQL

Starting from version 11, PostgreSQL introduces JIT compilation through an LLVM-based approach. The primary focus of JIT implementation centers on optimizing query *expressions*. This is achieved by incorporating the corresponding JIT provider, registered as an external dependency library, into PostgreSQL's execution engine. The default JIT provider in PostgreSQL is *llvmjit* [19]. However, PostgreSQL offers a JIT provider registration framework, enabling the replacement of JIT providers. This design accommodates the future development of provider libraries while ensuring the physical separation of provider code from the database execution engine. Once JIT is enabled, PostgreSQL initiates JIT for expressions. The process involves compiling the query's expressions into bytecode-based functions. These generated functions are seamlessly integrated into the evaluation function of *ExprState*, facilitating JIT incorporation into the existing execution framework without the need for modifications to the original SQL execution process.

The JIT implementation in PostgreSQL can be categorized into three main aspects: (1) JIT Compiled Expression, (2) Inlining, and (3) Optimization Passes.

JIT Compiled Expression. Modern databases, particularly those focused on online analytical processing (OLAP), frequently encounter CPU performance bottlenecks during expression calculations and table tuple scanning. To tackle these challenges, PostgreSQL harnesses the inherent capabilities of LLVM for accelerated expression operations. This encompasses optimizing expression evaluations and tuple deformation processes, which eliminate unnecessary function calls. Additionally, tuple deformation optimization involves the conversion of disk-based tuples into an in-memory state, reducing I/O costs and enhancing cache utilization, thereby significantly improving overall performance.

Inlining. In PostgreSQL, there are numerous redundant copies of general utility functions. Rewriting these functions is both impractical and undesirable. To address this, PostgreSQL utilizes inlining techniques, such as loop flattening [20], which could consolidate the nested loops into a single loop. This consolidation eliminates redundant jumps and unnecessary code branching during execution. Inlining effectively removes the overhead associated with function boundaries, significantly reducing code size and enhancing the overall efficiency of the database engine.

Optimization by Passes. In PostgreSQL, LLVM's passes are employed to further optimize the generated code in pipelines. Two core passes in LLVM are utilized: Analysis pass and Transform pass. The Analysis pass calculates statistical information of IR units, aiding in debugging and display. Conversely, the Transform pass modifies and optimizes IR into a simpler and equivalent form. For example, by analyzing the relationship of function calls using strongly connected components, optimization passes can eliminate redundant paths and code. Furthermore, the vectorization transform pass maximizes the utilization of vector registers. However, it's important to note that these passes come with associated costs. If their cost exceeds the execution cost of the query, they can potentially slow down the execution. To mitigate this issue, PostgreSQL employs a cost threshold to control the use of optimization passes.

4.2 Mutable

Mutable [4] is an experimental in-memory database designed to implement an alternative JIT architecture with the goals of improving throughput, reducing response time, and simplifying programming workloads. To achieve these objectives, Mutable adopts the WasmV8 architecture [4], which combines Binaryen and Google's V8 as the JIT backend. In the architecture of Mutable (Fig. 1), the Query Execution Plan (QEP) is fully compiled by the Binaryen compiler. Subsequently, Binaryen *CodeGen* generates WebAssembly code, which is then handed over to the embedded V8 engine for execution.

Fully Compiled QEP. Mutable adopts a fully compiled JIT approach as its backend execution engine. This allows for the implementation of operators in a deep Domain Specific Language (DSL) separately, resulting in a fully compiled Query Execution Plan (QEP). This approach provides a global view for optimizing instructions within the system. Additionally, Mutable utilizes an iterator architecture implemented through an inheritance framework, offering flexibility and abstraction structure which is similar to the Volcano iterator [21]. Operators can be effortlessly added to the framework by overriding the *(open()-next()-close())*execution functions, ensuring seamless integration into the execution framework.

Standard Library Implementations. WebAssembly lacks of a standard library [15]. To overcome this limitation, Mutable generates standard functions, like hash functions and item comparison functions, using a deeply embedded domain-specific language (deep DSL) [4]. This approach allows for fine-grained definition. However, it's important to note that Mutable produces monomorphic code that is specific to query execution in contrast to supporting the entire C standard library (LIBC) or Standard Template Library (STL).

Binaryen in WasmV8. WasmV8 utilizes Binaryen as the *CodeGen* framework to generate WebAssembly code. It employs WASM-specific optimizations and produces compacted data structures through various passes of optimization [22]. Binaryen also extracts morsel units for pre-compiled libraries in a pipeline. Additionally, it incorporates lazy compilation to decouple function dependencies in a global view, reducing the burden of building shaders. This approach allows for an early launch of the execution engine, which in turn reduces total execution time. Moreover, Binaryen achieves faster compilation by separating the tasks of work threads and allowing some worker threads to handle prediction instructions or independent tasks.

Adoptive Compilation in V8. Adaptive compilation in Mutable is facilitated by the V8 engine, which includes *TurboFan* and *Liftoff*. TurboFan utilizes a graph-based intermediate representation (IR) and implements various optimizations, including strength reduction, inlining, code motion, instruction combining, and sophisticated register allocation. It operates closely to machine code, bypassing several stages to achieve efficient performance [23]. In contrast, Liftoff serves as a baseline compiler specifically tailored for WebAssembly. Its primary objective is to minimize startup time for WASM-based applications by rapidly generating code [23]. In mutable, Liftoff is typically disabled by default, with an emphasis on alternative optimization strategies for JIT compilation.

5   Experimental Evaluation

Our aim is to evaluate and compare the performance of the JIT architectures in PostgreSQL and Mutable using the TPC-H benchmark. In order to isolate the effects of parallelism, we disabled parallel execution and enabled JIT in PostgreSQL by default. Due to the current limitations of WebAssembly's 32-bit addressing, we conducted our experiments using a TPC-H data scale of $1G$. As Mutable currently supports only a subset of TPC-H queries (Q1, Q3, Q6, Q12,

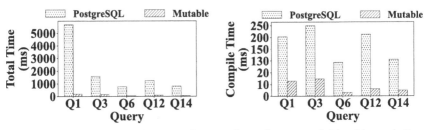

1 Execution time of Mutable and Post-greSQL in TPC-H 1G dataset

2 Compile time of Mutable and Post-greSQL in TPC-H 1G dataset

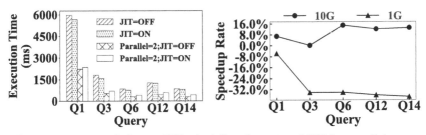

3 Execution time of PostgreSQL in TPC-H 1G dataset

4 Speedup rate of JIT for parallel execution in PostgreSQL

Fig. 2. Experiment Results

and Q14), we based our initial experiment on the performance of aggregation using Q1, analyzed grouping performance using Q3, and evaluated expression calculation performance using Q6, and overall performance using Q12 and Q14. Additionally, we compared the performance of JIT with and without parallel execution in PostgreSQL.

Environments. We utilized PostgreSQL 15.2, which has undergone extensive optimization for OrderBy and GroupBy operations. The default JIT provider is *llvm* [19], was employed for PostgreSQL JIT. For Mutable, we compiled a release version from version 0.17. We conduct our tests on Intel(R) Xeon(R) Gold 6342 CPU @ 2.80GHz server with two physical CPUs and 24 cores.

Compared Strategies. To ensure results accurate, each experiment was repeated five times, and the median value was obtained. To eliminate the disk I/O cost in PostgreSQL, we set the size of buffer pool to 10G and discard the first test result in PostgreSQL.

Exp-1: Overall Comparison. Figure 2.1 illustrates the performance comparison between PostgreSQL and Mutable based on the same query plan, where Mutable outperforms PostgreSQL in all queries, by an average of 16.11 times. The most significant difference is evident in Q1, where Mutable outperforms PostgreSQL by 27.75 times. We analyse the performance for each query in the following.

Q1. Q1 is distinguished by its CPU-intensive nature, involving eight aggregation functions [24]. Both Mutable and PostgreSQL employ an identical query plan for Q1, comprising TABLESCAN, HASHGROUP, and SORT operations. Despite both utilizing JIT compilation for generating aggregation functions, Mutable consistently outperforms PostgreSQL. This can be primarily attributed to three key optimizations within Mutable. Firstly, Mutable integrates the aggregation functions using Webassembly's DSL (Domain-Specific Language), enabling the database-specific optimized code in compiled Query Execution Plans (QEPs). Secondly, Mutable customizes the framework for aggregation code generation, reducing the generation of unnecessary code. Specifically, Mutable generates only the necessary functions for a given query, depending on the required aggregations. Thirdly, Mutable supports the full pipeline model of compiling SQL queries into executable code. This involves grouping the pipeline breaker [2], allowing the decomposition of jobs into several sub-processes. Each sub-process can execute efficiently, benefiting from improved cache locality.

Q3. Q3 involves a join of multiple tables with a large number of intermediate results, along with grouping, sorting, and aggregation operations. In Fig. 21 shows that Mutable outperforms PostgreSQL by a factor of 10.47 in Q3. The performance advantage of Mutable in this query is due to its JIT optimizations on Hash-based grouping. Typically, a HASHTABLE needs to generate complete instructions for all data types, resulting in potentially redundant instructions. Additionally, when collisions occur during the hash value lookup, it necessitates a minimum of n callbacks to resolve n keys [15]. In contrast, Mutable generates specialized HASHTABLE implementations for each query, with all hash table operations fully *inlined* into the query code [15]. This approach integrates a proprietary HASH algorithm directly into the compiled Query Execution Plans (QEPs) to reduce function calls. Mutable also fully inline comparison functions to minimize context switches, leading to improved query performance.

Q6. Q6 is a single table query operation with aggregate operations and sequential scans. From Fig. 21, Mutable outperforms PostgreSQL by 15.32 times, primarily because of the following factors. Firstly, Q6 extensively employs conjunctions in the *WHERE* condition and if-condition blocks [25]. These conjunctions can be optimized through branch prediction in JIT compilation by converting control dependence into data dependence, therefore enhancing performance [26]. In contrast to PostgreSQL, where expressions are delegated to LLVM in a serial manner, Mutable compiles all conjunction expressions together within a single filter operator. This allows for short-circuiting and constant folding optimizations to be applied, effectively trimming and optimizing expressions. In addition, Mutable also extends the type of unreachable code to perform code elimination when code becomes unreachable using the control flow graph to further optimize the code. This query demonstrates Mutable's performance improvement not only in complex queries but also in simpler ones.

Q12 & Q14. Q12 and Q14 both involve Join operations. Q12 includes general grouping, sorting, and aggregation operations, while Q14 is a simpler query with only join and aggregations. In both cases, Mutable outperforms PostgreSQL significantly, with improvements of 13.32 and 13.69 times, respectively. These queries underscore the advantages of Mutable in handling join, grouping, aggregation, and full Query Execution Plan (QEP) compilation, which jointly contribute to the overall performance improvement.

Exp-2: Compile Time. Figure 2.2 highlights a significant difference in compile times between PostgreSQL and Mutable across all test cases. Mutable has an average compile time of only 8.4ms, which outperforms PostgreSQL by 26 times. The shorter compilation time of Mutable is mainly attributed to Binaryen, which employs compact data structures during compilation and facilitates complete parallel compilation and optimization. Binaryen's efficiency is further enhanced by reusing existing memory blocks through its arena allocator for each WebAssembly module, reducing memory allocation costs and enhancing data cache utilization. Additionally, Binaryen implements an efficient in-place traversal of the abstract syntax tree (AST) during the compilation stage, considerably improving traversal speed.

Exp-3: Parallel Execution vs JIT. Figure 2.3 indicates the query execution time for PostgreSQL with JIT and parallel execution. It is evident that enabling JIT in PostgreSQL increases query performance by approximately 5% when parallel execution is turned off. However, when the number of threads is set to two in parallel execution, JIT has a negative impact on query performance. This is because of the significant overhead of serial compilation in PostgreSQL's JIT design, especially for small datasets or simple queries. Note that Mutable, which does not support parallel execution, was not included in this experiment.

Exp-4: Varying Datasets for Parallel Execution. For parallel execution, which is enabled by default in PostgreSQL 10 and later versions, we conducted additional testing of JIT across datasets of varying sizes. Figure 2.4 illustrates the speedup achieved by JIT in PostgreSQL in different datasets, specifically $1G$ and $10G$, each with two parallel workers. The results indicate that JIT in PostgreSQL has a negative impact on performance when using a $1G$ dataset. However, as the dataset size increases while the compilation time remains relatively stable, the proportion of compilation time within the query execution time gradually decreases. Consequently, JIT in PostgreSQL exhibits a positive effect in the $10G$ TPC-H dataset test. With the larger dataset, the improvement brought by JIT execution becomes more pronounced, and the benefits surpass the compilation overhead. These findings further corroborate the insights gained from Exp-3. Nevertheless, it is important to note that due to the inherent limitation of 32-bit addressing in WebAssembly, which restricts dataset sizes to under $4G$, we were unable to conduct tests on larger datasets using Mutable.

6   Discussions and Future Work

General Comparison. After conducting and analyzing various tests between the two databases, we have summarized their respective features in terms of

Table 1. The comparison of PostgreSQL and Mutable in JIT

	PostgreSQL	Mutable
Framework	LLVM	Webassembly V8
JIT Unit	Expression	QEP
Adaptive Execution	No	Yes
Debug Friendly	No	Yes
Maturity	Yes	No
Parallel Compilation	No	Yes

JIT compilation, as presented in Table 1. For the JIT framework, PostgreSQL opts for LLVM as the JIT provider, leveraging the advantages of mature LLVM technology and an active community. In contrast, Mutable utilizes the existing WebAssembly and V8 frameworks, complemented by a custom DSL to implement its JIT module.

JIT compilation in PostgreSQL primarily emphasizes compiling *expressions* rather than fully compiling QEPs which leads to significant limitations of JIT in PostgreSQL. Mutable enables the complete compilation of QEPs, allowing for comprehensive optimization, effective compiled code, rapid parallel code generation, and resource-friendly caching of compiled code. As a result, Mutable consistently achieves significantly better near-native execution speed compared to PostgreSQL.

Moreover, it is worth noting that PostgreSQL lacks support for adaptive execution [12], a feature that enables dynamic selection among different JIT modes. In contrast, Mutable utilizes V8 to implement adaptive execution, incorporating a tracing JIT compiler that can dynamically switch between JIT and interpreter modes. Meanwhile, PostgreSQL relies on a user-defined threshold to control optimization passes. This distinction highlights the flexibility and adaptability of Mutable's JIT framework.

In terms of debugging, JIT-compiled code can be highly optimized and challenging to correlate with the original source code, making visualization of the debugging process crucial. PostgreSQL often requires the use of external tools like LLDB [27] or GDB [28] to disassemble the code for analysis. However, Mutable offers a more user-friendly debugging experience by integrating with Chrome's DevTools. This integration allows for better visualization of debugging information encoded in the WebAssembly file, supports profiling of WebAssembly code, and facilitates memory inspection. These features provide Mutable with a significant advantage in terms of visual debugging and code analysis.

For parallel compilation, while LLVM 8.0 in PostgreSQL currently lacks parallel compilation capabilities, the V8 engine used in Mutable is capable of parallel compilation, giving Mutable an advantage in terms of compilation efficiency. An interesting future work could involve updating the LLVM version in PostgreSQL to a higher version that supports parallel compilation.

Future Work. We propose some future directions to further explore JIT technology and contribute to JIT in the database field.

- *Integrate WASM in PostgreSQL.* We plan to improve PostgreSQL's JIT performance by implementing WASM-based JIT. This involves starting with expression-level WASM JIT without altering the engine's structure. Upon successful validation, we will extend JIT compilation to encompass full QEPs. Additionally, we aim to enable adaptive execution in PostgreSQL by integrating the adaptive execution tracing compiler from V8 to dynamically adjust execution plans based on statistical information.
- *Expand Operators in Mutable.* Our second focus is on improving Mutable's JIT performance and debugging visibility. This includes iteratively optimizing JIT operator capabilities, integrating complex operators like SEMI-JOIN, WITH ROLLUP, and WINDOW functions. Priority will be given to enhancing CPU-intensive operators through strategic JIT function replacements. Our objectives also include improving observability and addressing concurrency architecture. Furthermore, we plan to gather runtime data during the JIT process to provide further optimization based on resource utilization, memory, threads, processing times, and more.
- *Harnessing Novel Hardware.* We aim to leverage WebAssembly's extended capabilities to address the 32-bit addressing constraint in Mutable, enabling performance evaluation with larger data sizes. Additionally, we will utilize the WebAssembly SIMD (Single Instruction Multiple Data) Extension [29,30] to facilitate intra-core parallelization, optimizing performance by consolidating aggregation primitives into a cohesive loop.
- *Expanded Practical Evaluation.* Our analysis will cover a broader spectrum, from single-core to multi-core scenarios, with datasets of varying size. We aim to include more JIT-enabled databases such as Hyper [31], Umbra [32], MonetDB [33], and others. Our goal is to distill and present prevalent performance patterns seen in SQL queries within the TPC-H benchmark. We will assess various operator implementations, considering both multithreaded and SIMD contexts. This comprehensive approach aims to provide insights into performance dynamics across different products and configurations.

7   Conclusion

In summary, the research focuses on analyzing the performance of two open-source databases: PostgreSQL and Mutable. These databases employ different JIT compilation approaches, namely LLVM and WebAssembly. PostgreSQL integrates LLVM-based JIT with mature optimizations and compatibility, allowing users to enable or disable JIT functionality as needed. While Mutable inherit the advantages of WebAssembly. In experiments, Mutable outperformed PostgreSQL significantly. This research enhances our understanding of JIT in databases, providing valuable insights for practitioners and researchers seeking to optimize database systems for improved performance.

Acknowledgements. Zhengyi Yang is supported by Enmotech Data AU. We would like thank the anonymous reviewers at ADC2023 Shepherding Track for their valuable insights and suggestions that significantly contributed to the paper's improvement.

References

1. McCarthy, J.: Recursive functions of symbolic expressions and their computation by machine. Commun. ACM **3**, 01 (1960)
2. Neumann, T.: Efficiently compiling efficient query plans for modern hardware. Proc. VLDB Endowment **4**(9), 539–550 (2011)
3. PostgreSQL. "Postgresql", 8 June 2023. https://www.postgresql.org/
4. M.O. "Github - mutable-org/mutable: a database system for research and fast prototyping", 7 June 2023. https://github.com/mutable-org/mutable/
5. Wade, A.W., Kulkarni, P.A., Jantz, M.R.: AOT vs. JIT: impact of profile data on code quality. In: ACM SIGPLAN Notices, vol. 52, pp. 1–10 (2017)
6. (Margaret Rouse, A. P.), "Intermediate language.techopedia", 16 Nov 2011. https://www.techopedia.com/definition/24290/intermediate-language-il-net
7. Metula, E.: Chapter 1 - introduction. In: Managed Code Rootkits (E. Metula, ed.), pp. 3–21. Syngress, Boston (2011)
8. (TPC-H Homepage. (n.d.)), TPC-H homepage. https://www.tpc.org/tpch/
9. Graefe, G.: Volcano-an extensible and parallel query evaluation system. IEEE Trans. Knowl. Data Eng. **6**, 120–135 (1994)
10. Boncz, P.A., Zukowski, M., Nes, N.: MonetDB/x100: hyper-pipelining query execution. In: 2nd Biennial Conference on Innovative Data Systems Research, CIDR 2005 (2005)
11. Krikellas, K., Viglas, S.D., Cintra, M.: Generating code for holistic query evaluation, pp. 613–624 (2010)
12. Muehlbauer, T.: HyPer: Hybrid OLTP&OLAP high-performance database system (n.d). https://hyper-db.de/
13. Leis, V., Boncz, P., Kemper, A., Neumann, T.: Morsel-driven parallelism: a NUMA-aware query evaluation framework for the many-core age. In: Proceedings of the 2014 ACM SIGMOD International Conference on Management of Data, pp. 743–754 (2014)
14. Kohn, A., Leis, V., Neumann, T.: Adaptive execution of compiled queries. In: 2018 IEEE 34th International Conference on Data Engineering (ICDE), pp. 197–208. IEEE (2018)
15. Haffner, I., Dittrich, J.: A simplified architecture for fast, adaptive compilation and execution of SQL queries. In: Proceedings of the EDTB (2023)
16. S., "Python JIT compilers". Accessed 21 June 2023
17. The LuaJIT Project. "The luajit project" (n.d.)
18. Cwi, T., Boncz, P.: Exploring query execution strategies for JIT, vectorization and SIMD (2017)
19. postgresql-llvmjit Fedora Packages. "Postgresql-llvmjit - fedora packages" (n.d.). https://packages.fedoraproject.org/pkgs/postgresql/postgresql-llvmjit/
20. Pop, S., Yazdani, R., Neill, Q.: Improving GCC's auto-vectorization with if-conversion and loop flattening for AMD's bulldozer processors. In: GCC Developers' Summit, p. 89 (2010)
21. Graefe, G.: Volcano/splminus/an extensible and parallel query evaluation system. IEEE Trans. Knowl. Data Eng. **6**(1), 120–135 (1994)

22. W. (n.d.) "binaryen/readme.md at main" (2017). https://github.com/WebAsse mbly/binaryen
23. Liftoff: a new baseline compiler for WebAssembly in V8, "Liftoff: A new baseline compiler for webassembly in v8 ··· v8" 20 August 2018. https://v8.dev/blog/liftoff
24. Boncz, P., Neumann, T., Erling, O.: TPC-H analyzed: Hidden messages and lessons learned from an influential benchmark, pp. 61–76 (2014)
25. Boncz, P., Neumann, T., Erling, O.: TPC-H analyzed: hidden messages and lessons learned from an influential benchmark. In: Nambiar, R., Poess, M. (eds.) TPCTC 2013. LNCS, vol. 8391, pp. 61–76. Springer, Cham (2014). https://doi.org/10.1007/978-3-319-04936-6_5
26. Quinoñes, E., Parcerisa, J.M., Gonzáilez, A.: Improving branch prediction and predicated execution in out-of-order processors, pp. 75–84 (2007)
27. LLDB, 4 Sept 2023. https://lldb.llvm.org/
28. GDB: The GNU Project Debugger (n.d.). https://www.sourceware.org/gdb/
29. W. (n.d.). "relaxed-simd/proposals/simd/simd.md at main · webassembly/relaxed-simd. github". https://github.com/WebAssembly/relaxed-simd/blob/main/proposals/simd/SIMD.md
30. Dreseler, M., Kossmann, J., Frohnhofen, J., Uflacker, M., Plattner, H.: Fused table scans: combining AVX-512 and JIT to double the performance of multi-predicate scans, pp. 102–109 (2018)
31. Kemper, A., Neumann, T.: Hyper: A hybrid OLTP&OLAP main memory database system based on virtual memory snapshots, pp. 195–206 (2011)
32. Kersten, T., Leis, V., Neumann, T.: Tidy tuples and flying start: fast compilation and fast execution of relational queries in umbra. VLDB J. **30**, 09 (2021)
33. Zukowski, M., Boncz, P., Nes, N., Héman, S.: MonetDB/x100 - a DBMS in the CPU cache. IEEE Data Eng. Bull. **28**, 17–22 (2005)

Relational Expressions for Data Transformation and Computation

David Robert Pratten$^{(\boxtimes)}$ ⓘ and Luke Mathieson ⓘ

University of Technology, Ultimo, NSW 2007, Australia
david.r.pratten@student.uts.edu.au, luke.mathieson@uts.edu.au

Abstract. Separate programming models for data transformation (declarative) and computation (procedural) impact programmer ergonomics, code reusability and database efficiency. To eliminate the necessity for two models or paradigms, we propose a small but high-leverage innovation, the introduction of complete relations into the relational database. Complete relations and the discipline of constraint programming, which concerns them, are founded on the same algebra as relational databases. We claim that by synthesising the relational database of Codd and Date, with the results of the constraint programming community, the relational model holistically offers programmers a single declarative paradigm for both data transformation and computation, reusable code with computations that are indifferent to what is input and what is output, and efficient applications with the query engine optimising and parallelising all levels of data transformation and computation.

Keywords: Relational Expressions · Constraint Programming

1 Introduction

Separate programming models for data transformation and computation impact programmer ergonomics, code reusability and database efficiency.

Concerning programmer ergonomics, when building business applications, programmers frequently switch between declarative SQL[1] code to transform data and then to a procedural programming language for the computation that encodes business logic and rules. Programmers' daily work is switching back and forth between these two paradigms.

With regard to reusability, data in a relational database sets a high bar not reached by procedural code. Once we have captured data in a set of relations, we have high confidence that we can use queries to answer arbitrary questions in the future. Procedural code does not have this ability. To illustrate this point, if we had procedural code that computed property sale stamp duty for the Australian Capital Territory (ACT) based on the sale price and multiple factors, we would

---

[1] SQL was chosen as an illustrative vehicle rather than Datalog, or some other relation expression language, due to its ubiquity.

Z. Bao et al. (Eds.): ADC 2023, LNCS 14386, pp. 241–255, 2024.
https://doi.org/10.1007/978-3-031-47843-7_17

be unlikely to be able to use that same code to compute the reverse query and tell us the possible sale prices if we knew the duty paid.

Finally, database procedural code imposes a performance penalty because query engines cannot introspect and optimise it. This issue is being addressed (after the fact) by efforts such as [10,16], and [34], which translate procedural code back into relational algebraic expressions including fixed-point operators.

To eliminate the necessity for two models or paradigms, we propose a small but high-leverage innovation, the introduction of complete relations into the relational database. A relation is complete if it has the value formed as the cross-product of all its attribute's domains.[2] Complete relations and the discipline of constraint programming, which concerns them, are founded on the same algebra as relational databases. Using a biological metaphor, complete relations may be likened to a stem cell, which, when coupled with a suitable predicate, may be specialised to become any computable relation. We introduce the term "sigma complete relation" to denote complete relations that have been specialised by the relational σ operator to capture a specific set of business rules and logic.

In this paper, we review related work that has previously explored the intersection of relational databases and constraint programming (Sect. 2). After demonstrating the relational database's and constraint programming's common foundations and crystalising the challenge that we are addressing (Sect. 3), we explore the core technical innovation of this paper, the sigma complete database relation (Sect. 4). We reproduce the results of a recent proof of concept by Salsa Digital for the OECD's Observatory of Public Sector Innovation using sigma complete relations, demonstrating single paradigm programming and the flexibility of querying sigma complete relations (Sect. 5).

2   Related Work

Constraint programming emerged as a generalisation of "inferential" and "deductive" approaches explored by the logic programming community [18]. In contrast, Codd carefully excluded such "inferential" and "deductive" systems from discussion in his seminal paper [5] on relational databases. Despite this separation at the foundation, in the relational database and constraint programming corpora, we find discussion of the connection of database relations with constraints and computation under three rubrics: Algorithmic Relations, Computed Relations, and Constraint Database. These prior works appear to be pushing toward the same intuition that underlies this paper.

Algorithmic Relations. In 1975 Hall, Hitchcock and Todd [15] introduced algorithmically represented relations as a complement to relations stored as a set of tuples. One of Hall, Hitchcock and Todd's motivations was the power of

---

[2] The related term "complete database" refers to a relational database where tuples are restricted to be drawn from the corresponding complete relation, i.e. NULL values are prohibited [23].

algorithmic relations to compute multi-directional queries being indifferent as to which attributes are input and which are output. They contributed the notion of a relation's "effectiveness". Effectiveness refers to the subset of grounded attributes for which the relation will define a complete set of tuples. For data relations, the effectiveness is always the powerset of attributes, meaning that if we ground none, any, or all attributes, then the data relation will yield all relevant tuples. For algorithmic relations, this is not assured. Hall, Hitchcock and Todd classified the subject of this paper as "pure predicate relations", however they appear unaware that these relations contain enough information for an evaluation engine to generate their extensions. No record of an implementation or further exploration of algorithmic relations has been found in the literature.

Computed Relations. Across the Atlantic, computed relations were separately described by David Maier and David Warren in 1981 [24] as a way of extending the standard relational theory of databases with more computation power. Maier and Warren motivated their proposal by considering the challenges of including arithmetic in the relational algebra and also use cases for posing reverse queries. Maier and Warren introduced the definitions and theorems to incorporate computed relations into the relational model, and their theory and algorithms fore-sage the comprehensive treatment that would subsequently be developed independently within the discipline of constraint programming. Maier and Warren showed how selection predicates and join conditions are vital context that enables a query engine to yield a listable (finite) extension from a computed relation. No record of an implementation or further exploration of computed relations has been found in the literature.

Constraint Database CD. The logic and constraint programming communities recognise the equivalence of first-order[3] constraint programming with relational algebra, see for example [19] and [21]. Bussche, one of the contributors to [22, p35] after consideration of related evaluation mechanisms, concluded that "the relational algebra serves as an effective constraint query language". Cai in [12, p173] discussed how to incorporate constraints within a relational database and reiterated the point made by Maier and Warren that it is vital for context to be shared from the relational expression with the constraint evaluation engine.

The practical outworking of this recognition has been in a model called "Constraint Database". Quoting Kuper, Libkin, and Paredaens [22, p7] "the basic idea of the constraint database model is to generalize the notion of a tuple in a relational database to a conjunction of constraints". In this model, linear or polynomial equations represent large or infinite sets compactly, which matches well to spatiotemporal applications [28].

---

[3] Constraint programming constructs outside of first-order logic are not considered in this paper as Relational Algebra is equivalent to Relational Calculus which can be expressed as formulas in first-order logic. [13, p241].

While sigma complete relations and CD constraint relations are clearly adjacent concepts, after reviewing Revesz's 2010 survey of the model [28], Table 1 summarises significant differences between them.

Table 1. Contrast of sigma complete relations with CD's constraint relations.

A sigma complete relation	A CD constraint relation
The relation is central to unifying the relational expression with constraint programming	The relation is aimed at compact representation and querying of segments and low order volumes
The focus is on complete relations, which may be infinite	The focus is on values that consist of infinite points
The complete relation may be constrained, as a whole relation, by a Boolean expression	Each tuple may contain a different constraint.
The complete relation can't hold any data belonging to any entity in the database	Each tuple may hold user data in addition to a constraint.
The relation is a constant value	The relation is subject to normal DML operations such as `INSERT`, `DELETE` and `UPDATE`

According to the Scopus database, publications on research into Constraint Databases, including proof of concept implementations, were most frequent for a decade from the mid-1990s. See [28] for a survey of this work.

3 Preliminaries and Problem Definition

The relational database and constraint programming communities' relative isolation is a historically contingent fact that belies their common foundation in the relational model. At the most fundamental level, the difference between the two communities is that one considers an empty data relation the starting point for work. In contrast, the other considers the complete relation the place to begin. The characteristic challenges being solved by each discipline have emerged naturally from their different starting points.

3.1 Database Relational Model

Along with data relations, today's relational databases have already incorporated aspects of computation. Following Date [6], the relational database model views a relation as a set of n typed attributes (constituting the relation's heading), along with a set of n-ary tuples (constituting the body).

In addition to a heading and a body, each data relation also has a predicate which represents the intended interpretation of the relation. The predicate is a natural language statement always true for the relation. An example of a predicate might be "Is one of our organisation's customers" for a relation called cust. Data relation values are empty until tuples are added by a relational expression or a Data Manipulation Language (DML) statement such as INSERT.

For partially enforcing a data relation's predicate, the SQL standard provides four integrity constraint types: PRIMARY KEY, UNIQUE, CHECK, and FOREIGN KEY [20]. For expressing computation, SQL adds features[4] beyond the relational algebra, including arithmetic expressions, derived attributes (a.k.a. generated columns) [9], table-valued functions, and stored procedures [14].

3.2 Constraint Programming

The Constraint Programming community has also adopted the relation as an abstraction; however, their starting place is the complete relation. Quoting Hooker's survey [17, p. 376], the parallels are immediate: "... a constraint can be viewed as a relation, i.e., a set of tuples belonging to the Cartesian product of the variable domains".

Following Marriott and Stuckey [26], Frisch and Stuckey [11], Stuckey and Tuck [32], and as embodied in the MiniZinc language, constraint programming views constraint relations as a set of arguments, each with their domain (type) and with a Boolean expression as a constraint over these arguments. When we ask, "What satisfies this constraint relation?" the answer is the constraint relation's extension, a set of solutions with zero, finite, or infinite cardinality. This foundation for constraint programming is sufficient to enable it to express arbitrary[5] computations in a declarative fashion. In contrast to data relations, constraint relations are always constant values.

For the benefit of relational database practitioners, who may not be familiar with constraint programming, here are two examples to illustrate these concepts. The first annotated example is written in the MiniZinc language [31]. It implements a business rule that says that all Australian states and territories should have different (one of three) colours when compared with each adjacent state. The code is based on the example in Sect. 2.1.1 of the MiniZinc Handbook[ibid].

```
int: number_of_colours = 3;
predicate colour_Australia(
    var 1..number_of_colours: wa, var 1..number_of_colours: nt,
    var 1..number_of_colours: sa, var 1..number_of_colours: qld,
    var 1..number_of_colours: nsw, var 1..number_of_colours: vic)
= let {
    constraint wa != nt;
    constraint wa != sa;
    constraint nt != sa;
    constraint nt != qld;  constraint sa != qld; constraint sa != nsw;
    constraint act != nsw; constraint sa != vic; constraint qld != nsw;
    constraint nsw != vic
} in true;
```

---

[4] Fixed-point operators [8] and string operators are not considered in the current work and are open questions for further investigation.

[5] Computations within the scope of the logical theories [2] embodied in the evaluation engine.

Table 2. Colouring Australian states and territories in three colours.

wa	nt	sa	qld	nsw	act	vic
3	2	1	3	2	1	3
3	2	1	3	2	3	3
2	3	1	2	3	1	2
2	3	1	2	3	2	2
3	1	2	3	1	2	3
3	1	2	3	1	3	3
1	3	2	1	3	1	1
1	3	2	1	3	2	1
2	1	3	2	1	2	2
2	1	3	2	1	3	2
1	2	3	1	2	1	1
1	2	3	1	2	3	1

When asked to supply all solutions, MiniZinc will respond with the twelve solutions shown in Table 2. Note that if we omitted the constraints, the extension of the constraint relation would have been the cross product of the attribute's domains i.e. the complete relation.

The second example implements the business rule for calculating Australian Goods and Services Tax (GST). The annotated `Australian_GST` constraint relation is of arity three. It captures the relationship between consumer `Price`, the Goods and Services Tax `GSTAmount`, and the price before applying the GST `ExGSTAmount`. This constraint relation is also written here in MiniZinc:

```
predicate Australian_GST(
    var float: Price,
    var float: ExGSTAmount,
    var float: GSTAmount) =
let {
    constraint Price/11 = GSTAmount;
    constraint ExGSTAmount = Price-GSTAmount;
    }
in true;
```

Note that even with the equation-like constraints in place, the `Australian_GST` constraint relation, while no longer complete, is of infinite cardinality.

3.3 The Database Relational Model and Constraint Programming

In this section, we will begin by clarifying terminology and then show their common foundations. In Table 3, cognate terms from the database relational model and those from constraint programming are shown along with the terms that will be used in the rest of this paper. Alternate terms found in the literature are included in italics.

Table 3. The relational model terminology used in the rest of this paper.

Term	Database Relational Model Cognates	Constraint Programming Cognates
Relation	Relation *or Table*	Predicate *or Constraint Relation*
Predicates	Predicate (natural language) Integrity constraints (Boolean expressions)	Constraints (Boolean expressions)
Heading	Heading *or Columns or Arguments*	Arguments, Variables or Parameters
Argument	A single Argument *or Column, Generated Column*	A single Argument, Variable or Parameter
Domain	Type *or Domain* of an argument	Domain *or Type* of an argument
Extension	Body *or Tuples or Rows*	Solutions *or Extension*
Tuple	Tuple *or Row*	Solution

After comparing the literature referenced above and after discounting purely linguistic distinctions, the commonalities, and some unique features, between the database relational model and constraint programming are summarised here:

- Both are based on the mathematical relation
- Their relations have a header with attributes, each with defined domains
- Their relations have predicates that describe the meaning of the relation. (For data relations, this is typically a natural language condition, whereas, for constraint programming, the predicate is explicit and computable).
- Their relations may be defined by their extensions. In SQL, using DML statements such as `INSERT`, `DELETE` and `UPDATE`. In MiniZinc's case, by providing a data file [31, 2.1.3].
- Both may be constants, however, constraint programming relations are always constant values.
- Both expression languages obey the relational algebra, including the familiar relational operators: π project, σ select, $\times$ cross-product, and the compositions of these operations such as $\bowtie$ join
- Both approaches are declarative, relying on an evaluation engine to take the declarative expression and construct an efficient evaluation strategy based on relational algebraic properties and heuristics. In MiniZinc's case, after applying algebraic transformations, solutions are found using a variety of back-end solvers. For example: Gecode, Chuffed, OR-Tools.

3.4   [Re]Uniting Two Worlds

We now finally arrive at a point where we can state the central problem and central thesis of this paper. Programmers have reaped only half the available benefits from the relational model. By adopting the relational database of Date and Codd, programmers gained independence [5] from providing a procedural access path to the data of interest and have been able to specify data transformations in a declarative fashion. The other potential benefit of the relational model is to free programmers from having to code computations and business rules procedurally, and this benefit remains to be realised.

We claim that by synthesising the relational database of Codd and Date, with the results of the constraint programming community, the relational model holistically offers programmers a *single declarative paradigm* for both data transformation and computation, *reusable code* with computations that are indifferent to what is input and what is output, and *efficient applications* with the query engine optimising and parallelising *all levels* of data transformation and computation.

4   Sigma Complete Relations

Formal Definition. Formally, a sigma complete relation S may be defined using relational algebra as:

$$S = \sigma P(Dom(a_1) \times Dom(a_2) \times ... \times Dom(a_N))$$

for predicate P and the domains $Dom()$ of the attributes $a_1, a_2, ...a_N$. Depending on the domains of attributes, the sigma complete relation may have a finite or infinite cardinality.

Illustrative Examples. Let's re-express the MiniZinc `Australian_GST` example to illustrate this. Firstly we look at the example through the idiom of SQL and, secondly, through the Tutorial-D [7] language of Date and Darwen. We may begin by letting the following form represent a complete relation with an arity of three:

```
COMPLETE(Price float, ExGSTAmount float, GSTAmount float)
```

As it stands, the COMPLETE(Price float, ExGSTAmount float, GSTAmount float) relation is infinite, so the following relation expression would *not* be listable.

```
SELECT * FROM COMPLETE(ExGSTAmount float, GSTAmount float, Price float);
```

We can now express the Australian GST rule as a specialisation of this complete relation. The required predicate is placed in the WHERE clause, noting, of course, that this is a Boolean expression, not a pair of assignment statements.

```
SELECT *
    FROM COMPLETE(Price float, ExGSTAmount float, GSTAmount float)
    WHERE GSTAmount = Price/11 AND ExGSTAmount = Price-GSTAmount;
```

If we supply further information by grounding (fixing) one of its attributes, the expression gives a listable extension. Here is an example GST calculation for Price = 110:

```
SELECT *
    FROM COMPLETE(Price float, ExGSTAmount float, GSTAmount float)
    WHERE GSTAmount = Price/11 AND ExGSTAmount = Price-GSTAmount
        AND Price = 110;
```

The single tuple result is shown in Table 4. For convenience and reuse, we can give the relation expression the name `Australian_GST` within our database:

```
CREATE VIEW Australian_GST AS
    SELECT *
        FROM COMPLETE((Price float, ExGSTAmount float, GSTAmount float)
        WHERE GSTAmount = Price/11 AND ExGSTAmount = Price-GSTAmount;
```

Table 4. Australian_GST relation expression result

Price	ExGSTAmount	GSTAmount
110	100	10

When evaluated, any of the following relation expressions will give the same result as above!

```
select * from Australian_GST where ExGSTAmount = 100;
select * from Australian_GST where GSTAmount = 10;
select * from Australian_GST where Price=110;
```

While less familiar to relational database practitioners, the constraint programming community will recognise the above as a straightforward application of satisfaction solving. The relation expression engine is **not** retrieving all rows of the infinite `Australian_GST` relation and then selecting the required tuple. Instead, predicate, or selection, push-down [33] is being used to strengthen the constraints on the sigma complete relation sufficiently to yield the required answer without search.

In recent[6] private correspondence on the topic of this article with C.J. Date and Hugh Darwen, they offered the following extension to their published Tutorial D syntax as a way of incorporating sigma complete relations in the database:

```
RELATION {Price float, ExGSTAmount float, GSTAmount float}
    WHERE GSTAmount = Price/11 AND ExGSTAmount = Price-GSTAmount
```

They noted that within Tutorial D, the sigma complete relation may appear as a database component by declaring it as a name constant, prefixing the above expression by `CONST AustralianGST`, giving:

```
CONST AustralianGST
    RELATION {Price float, ExGSTAmount float, GSTAmount float}
        WHERE GSTAmount = Price/11 AND ExGSTAmount = Price-GSTAmount
```

---

[6] by email 25 July 2023.

There are further worked examples available on GitHub including an Australian Capital Territory (ACT) Conveyance Duty sigma complete relation which encodes the multi-tiered and multi-variable contingent relationship between price and conveyancing duty in the Australian Capital Territory from July 1st, 2022. The single relation is equally able to answer the question "How much duty is chargeable for a property valued at \$1.2M?" and its inverse, "A property owner pays \$140,740 in conveyancing duty. What were the possible property prices?"

Implementation Considerations. To our knowledge, no one has yet built a holistic relation expression evaluation engine that operates over both data relations and complete relations. However, to use a botanical metaphor, building such an engine is likely to be akin to the grafting together of two stems rather than requiring radical replanting. The following observations support this:

- Sigma complete relations are subject to the same algebraic transformations already used in relational database engines. For example, sigma complete relations may be projected over a subset of their arguments.
- Optimisation techniques over data relations and complete relations are closely related. e.g. constraint propagation [3] is closely related, and may be identical to, the relational database optimiser's predicate push-down/migration strategy.
- Sigma complete relations have a well-defined ⋈ semantic close to, and possibly identical to, SQL:1999's LATERAL.

It is envisaged that the heuristics that guide expression simplification and optimisation will be where most of the effort will be. The first step in the implementation work will be to identify a harmonious minimum set of theories, domains, algorithms, and heuristics from relational databases and constraint programming languages.

Termination Considerations. Sigma complete relations may be of infinite cardinality, and this poses questions about the termination of the evaluation of relational expressions. In practice, it is found that the set of useful relational expressions over sigma complete relations correlates with expressions that provide just enough grounding in the expressions to enable the query engine to provide a useful (finite) extension. However, if a relation expression insufficiently constrains a sigma complete relation of infinite extent, its evaluation behaviour would be similar to SQL:1999, where a query will not terminate if a recursive common table expression fails to find a fixed point.

Due to the unavailability of a holistic relational expression evaluation engine, all the experiments in this paper have evaluated SQL relational queries over sigma complete relations defined by predicates in MiniZinc. They therefore are unable to fully test the single programming environment thesis of this paper. However, let's see what we can learn from evaluating this early prototype.

5   Experimental Study

This evaluation replicates the results of an internationally recognised proof of concept (PoC) and passes a comprehensive test suite with some advantages over the original implementation. An open-source project hosts all the code and instructions for repeating the evaluation using Docker.

Late in 2022, the OECD's Observatory of Public Sector Innovation published Salsa Digital's PoC "Delivering a personalized citizen experience using Rules as Code as a shared utility" [27]. The site "Interactive Q&A with COVID Rules for Workplaces" was coded using OpenFisca [1,30]. Salsa Digital host an interactive version of the PoC on their website [29].

Sigma complete relations were evaluated using the Jetisu Toolkit by David Pratten. While not ideal, to facilitate fast prototyping, this implementation used MiniZinc to code the sigma complete relation with its Boolean predicate. SQL is used for querying the relation.

Am I up to Date? The evaluation modelled rules for up-to-dateness of COVID vaccinations as a relation:

```
CREATE VIEW covid_vaccinations AS
    SELECT * FROM COMPLETE(age int,
                    recommended_doses int,
                    booster_doses int,
                    vaccine_doses intr,
                    immuno_compromised_disability bool,
                    months_since_last_dose_at_least int,
                    eligibility bool,
                    up_to_date bool
                    )
        WHERE <Boolean expression>;
```

The definition of the relation is 36 lines of MiniZinc code and may be found at github.com code link. Multiple relational expressions and their results may be found on this page: Australian COVID Vaccination eligibility and up-to-date (circa mid-2022).

Do I need COVID-19 vaccination for my workplace? The evaluation captured workplace-related rules across three Australian state jurisdictions: New South Wales, Victoria, and Western Australia with this relation:

```
CREATE VIEW covid_vaccinations_and_work AS
    SELECT * FROM COMPLETE(work_location work_location_enum,
                    work_sector work_sector_enum,
                    specialist_school bool,
                    aged_care_facility bool,
                    disability_worker_in_school bool,
                    private_home_only bool,
                    nsw_health_worker bool,
                    mandatory bool,
                    doses int
                    )
        WHERE <Boolean expression>;
```

The definition of the relation is 99 lines of MiniZinc code and may be found at github.com code link. The page Australian COVID Vaccinations and Work (circa mid-2022) shows how relation expressions may be used to ask inverse or abductive questions such as "What are the vaccination requirements for emergency service workers across the three jurisdictions?"

Interactive Q&A. As referenced above, the original PoC by Salsa Digital makes their Rules as Code model available to the public as a Question and Answer dialog. The Interactive Q&A with COVID Rules for Workplaces page shows how sigma complete relations support this use-case. The evaluation goes one step ahead of Salsa Digital's PoC here. The availability of the ruleset as a relation enables the code to automatically minimise the number of questions asked by ordering the questions based on which question, if asked next, will narrow the number of alternatives the fastest.

Evaluation Summary. The evaluation demonstrated that sigma complete relations can replicate PoC results created with a state-of-the-art tool, OpenFisca. The sigma complete relation passes all 103 cases of the PoC's test suite, replicates the Q&A ability and has the following advantages over the solution with OpenFisca:

- Automatic question sequencing based on the fastest path to an answer
- After discounting for OpenFisca's presentation level code, the code size for the sigma complete relations evaluation was an order of magnitude less than for OpenFisca. (36 vs 293 lines for `covid_vaccinations`, and 99 vs 520 lines for `covid_vaccinations_and_work`)
- Supports querying in the forward and reverse (abductive) directions.

6 Conclusion

This paper is an early report on using relational expressions for data transformation and computation, inviting feedback from researchers in both the relational database and constraint programming communities. We are in a line of researchers reaching for an intuition that is not yet fully revealed, and much remains to be explored and developed. As you have seen, this paper is an invitation to work towards a programmer experience where a declarative approach is used for all aspects of data transformation and computation. Where code is written once and used for many, as yet, un-thought-of queries. And where the execution engine has visibility of the whole computation stack and can optimise from top to bottom. The evaluation reported above suggests that this is a path worth following.

There are many questions surrounding sigma complete relations that recommend themselves for further study. One issue is to identify a minimum set of solving theories [2] that give programmers a good experience when utilising complete relations in the database. Research into relational algebraic languages is a vibrant field. New alternatives to SQL now include languages such as LINQ, PRQL, Malloy, Morel, EdgeDB, and Power Query's M formula language. A related question is to evaluate which relational expression language would be most approachable for an initial database implementation of sigma complete relations. The relational model is associated with concepts like normalisation, functional dependencies, candidate keys and primary keys. A question related to these concepts is how sigma complete relations increase the power of relational data modelling. And finally, what is the best way to extend the reported initial first-order results to cover aggregations (SQL `GROUP BY`) and predicates over aggregations (SQL `HAVING`) and then higher-order optimisation and combinatorial problems [25] and [4]?

Acknowledgements. Special thanks to Hugh Darwen without his encouragement and sharp insights, this paper would not have seen the light of day. And to the team behind MiniZinc for such a beautiful tool. Thanks to the management and staff of Salsa Digital for access to the Python code base behind their OECD Case Study.

Shepherding Process. Participation in the Shepherding Track resulted in the complete restructuring of this paper and the reorganisation and strengthening of Sect. 4 Sigma Complete Relations.

References

1. Agence Nationale de la Cohésion des Territoires: OpenFisca - Write rules as code. World Wide Web (2022). https://openfisca.org/en/
2. Barrett, C., Tinelli, C.: Satisfiability modulo theories. In: Clarke, E.M., Henzinger, T.A., Veith, H., Bloem, R. (eds.) Handbook of Model Checking, pp. 305–343. Springer, Cham (2018). https://doi.org/10.1007/978-3-319-10575-8_11
3. Bessiere, C.: Constraint propagation. In: Rossi, F., Beek, P.V., Walsh, T. (eds.) Handbook of Constraint Programming, vol. 2, chap. 3, pp. 29–83. Elsevier (2006). https://doi.org/10.1016/S1574-6526(06)80007-6
4. Brucato, M., Beltran, J.F., Abouzied, A., Meliou, A.: Scalable package queries in relational database systems. In: Proceedings of the VLDB Endowment, vol. 9 (2016). https://doi.org/10.14778/2904483.2904489
5. Codd, E.F.: A relational model of data for large shared data banks. Commun. ACM **13**(6) (1970). https://doi.org/10.1145/362384.362685
6. Date, C.J.: Database Design and Relational Theory: Normal Forms and All That Jazz (2019). https://doi.org/10.1007/978-1-4842-5540-7
7. Date, C.J., Darwen, H.: The Third Manifesto, 3rd edn. Addison-Wesley (2014). https://www.dcs.warwick.ac.uk/hugh/TTM/DTATRM.pdf
8. Eisenberg, A., Melton, J.: SQL:1999, formerly known as SQL3. SIGMOD Rec. (ACM Spec. Interest Group Manage. Data) **28**(1) (1999). https://doi.org/10.1145/309844.310075
9. Eisenberg, A., Melton, J., Kulkarni, K., Michels, J.E., Zemke, F.: SQL:2003 has been published. In: SIGMOD Record, vol. 33 (2004). https://doi.org/10.1145/974121.974142
10. Emani, K.V., Ramachandra, K., Bhattacharya, S., Sudarshan, S.: Extracting equivalent SQL from imperative code in database applications. In: Proceedings of the 2016 International Conference on Management of Data, pp. 1781–1796. ACM, New York (2016). https://doi.org/10.1145/2882903.2882926
11. Frisch, A.M., Stuckey, P.J.: The proper treatment of undefinedness in constraint languages. In: Gent, I.P. (ed.) CP 2009. LNCS, vol. 5732, pp. 367–382. Springer, Heidelberg (2009). https://doi.org/10.1007/978-3-642-04244-7_30

12. Cai, M.: Integrating constraint and relational database systems. In: Kuijpers, B., Revesz, P. (eds.) CDB 2004. LNCS, vol. 3074, pp. 173–180. Springer, Heidelberg (2004). https://doi.org/10.1007/978-3-540-25954-1_11
13. Garcia-Molina, H., Ullman, J.D., Widom, J.: Database Systems the Complete Book, 2nd edn. Pearson, Upper Saddle River (2009)
14. Gupta, S., Ramachandra, K.: Procedural extensions of SQL: understanding their usage in the wild. Proc. VLDB Endow. **14**, 1378–1391 (2021). https://doi.org/10.14778/3457390.3457402
15. Hall, P.A.V., Hitchcock, P., Todd, S.: An algebra of relations for machine computation. In: POPL 1975 (1975)
16. Hirn, D., Grust, T.: PL/SQL Without the PL. In: Proceedings of the ACM SIGMOD International Conference on Management of Data (2020). https://doi.org/10.1145/3318464.3384678
17. Hooker, J.: Integrated Methods for Optimization, 2nd edn. Springer, Cham (2012). https://doi.org/10.1007/978-1-4614-1900-6
18. Jaffar, J., Lassez, J.L.: Constraint logic programming. In: Proceedings of the 14th ACM SIGACT-SIGPLAN Symposium on Principles of Programming Languages, pp. 111–119. POPL 1987. Association for Computing Machinery, New York (1987). https://doi.org/10.1145/41625.41635
19. Kanellakis, P.C., Goldin, D.Q.: Constraint programming and database query languages. In: Hagiya, M., Mitchell, J.C. (eds.) TACS 1994. LNCS, vol. 789, pp. 96–120. Springer, Heidelberg (1994). https://doi.org/10.1007/3-540-57887-0_92
20. Kline, K., Obe, R.O., Hsu, L.S.: SQL in a Nutshell, 4th edn. O'Reilly, Sebastopol (2022)
21. Kolaitis, P.G.: Constraint satisfaction, databases, and logic. In: IJCAI International Joint Conference on Artificial Intelligence (2003)
22. Kuper, G., Libkin, L., Paredaens, J. (eds.): Constraint Databases. Springer, Heidelberg (2000). https://doi.org/10.1007/978-3-662-04031-7
23. Libkin, L.: SQL's three-valued logic and certain answers. ACM Trans. Database Syst. **41**(1), 1–28 (2016). https://doi.org/10.1145/2877206
24. Maier, D., Warren, D.S.: Incorporating computed relations in relational databases. In: Proceedings of the ACM SIGMOD International Conference on Management of Data (1981). https://doi.org/10.1145/582318.582345
25. Mancini, T., Flener, P., Pearson, J.K.: Combinatorial problem solving over relational databases. In: Proceedings of the 27th Annual ACM Symposium on Applied Computing, pp. 80–87. ACM, New York (2012). https://doi.org/10.1145/2245276.2245295
26. Marriott, K., Stuckey, P.J.: Programming with Constraints: An Introduction (1998)
27. Observatory of Public Sector Innovation: Delivering a personalized citizen experience using Rules as Code as a shared utility. https://oecd-opsi.org/innovations/rac-as-shared-utility/
28. Revesz, P.: Introduction to Databases - From Biological to Spatio-Temporal (2010)
29. Salsa Digital: Coronavirus (COVID-19) pandemic Australia - Rules as Code - Proof of Concept. https://nginx.main.openfisca-drupal.lagoon.salsa.hosting/about-proof-concept
30. Salsa Digital: What is OpenFisca? https://salsa.digital/insights/what-is-openfisca
31. Stuckey, P.J., Marriot, K., Tack, G.: The MiniZinc Handbook (2023). https://www.minizinc.org/doc-latest/en/index.html
32. Stuckey, P.J., Tack, G.: MiniZinc with functions. In: Gomes, C., Sellmann, M. (eds.) CPAIOR 2013. LNCS, vol. 7874, pp. 268–283. Springer, Heidelberg (2013). https://doi.org/10.1007/978-3-642-38171-3_18

33. Ullman, J.D.: Principles of database and knowledge-base systems, vol. I (1988). https://www.sti-innsbruck.at/sites/default/files/Knowledge-Representation-Search-and-Rules/principles-of-database-and-knowledge-base-systems-volume-1-1.pdf
34. Zhang, G., Mariano, B., Shen, X., Dillig, I.: Automated translation of functional big data queries to SQL. Proc. ACM Programm. Lang. **7**(OOPSLA1), 580–608 (2023). https://doi.org/10.1145/3586047

Data Quality and Fairness for Graphs

Discovering Graph Differential Dependencies

Yidi Zhang[1], Selasi Kwashie[2], Michael Bewong[3], Junwei Hu[1],
Arash Mahboubi[3], Xi Guo[1(✉)], and Zaiwen Feng[1(✉)]

[1] College of Informatics, Huazhong Agricultural University, Wuhan, Hubei, China
{xguo,zaiwen.feng}@mail.hzau.edu.cn
[2] AI and Cyber Futures Institute, Charles Sturt University, Bathurst, NSW,
Australia
[3] School of Computing, Mathematics and Engineering, Charles Sturt University,
Wagga Wagga, NSW, Australia

Abstract. Graph differential dependencies (GDDs) are a novel class
of integrity constraints in property graphs for capturing and expressing
the semantics of *difference* in graph data. They are more expressive,
and subsume other graph dependencies; and thus, are more useful for
addressing many real-world graph data quality/management problems.
In this paper, we study the *general discovery problem* for GDDs – the
task of finding a non-redundant and succinct set of GDDs that hold in
a given property graph. Indeed, we present characterisations of GDDs
based on their semantics, extend existing data structures, and device
pruning strategies to enable our proposed level-wise discovery algorithm,
GDDMiner, returns a *minimal cover* of valid GDDs efficiently. Further,
we perform experiments over three real-world graphs to demonstrate the
feasibility, scalability, and effectiveness of our solution.

Keywords: Graph differential dependency · Graph dependencies ·
Data dependencies · Dependency discovery

1 Introduction

The study of *graph dependencies* is receiving increasing research attention in
recent years due to the ubiquity of graph data and the usefulness of dependencies
for addressing various graph data quality as well as graph data management
problems (cf. [7,10,15,21]). *Graph differential dependencies* (GDDs) [15] are a
novel class of graph dependencies that encode the semantics of difference among
property values within topological patterns in a graph.

A graph differential dependency (GDD) σ over a graph G is a pair σ :
$(Q[\bar{z}], \Phi_L(X) \rightarrow \Phi_R(Y))$ – where $Q[\bar{z}]$ is a topological pattern (*a.k.a.* graph
pattern) in G serving as the "loose schema" (or scope) over which the differen-
tial dependency $\Phi_L(X) \rightarrow \Phi_R(Y)$ holds on the sets of attributes X, Y of $Q[\bar{z}]$.
Intuitively, σ states that for any *homomorphic match*, h, of $Q[\bar{z}]$ in G, if h satisfies the closeness constraint(s) specified by $\Phi_L(X)$, then it must also satisfy the
closeness constraint(s) in $\Phi_R(Y)$.

© The Author(s), under exclusive license to Springer Nature Switzerland AG 2024
Z. Bao et al. (Eds.): ADC 2023, LNCS 14386, pp. 259–272, 2024.
https://doi.org/10.1007/978-3-031-47843-7_18

Motivated by the growing literature on the usefulness of graph dependencies for entity linking and resolution (ELR) across relations and graphs [8,15,18], consistency and fact checking in (social media) networks [11,16], synthetic knowledge graph generation [12], etc., this paper studies the problem of mining/discovering GDDs in graphs. That is, the problem of finding a complete, non-redundant, and concise set of GDDs that hold in a given property graph.

To the best of our knowledge, the only GDD mining solution in existence is presented in [15]. However, the GDD discovery algorithm of [15] mines a subclass of GDD with fixed consequent constraints for ELR. That is, the proposed algorithm in [15] is essentially a *reduction algorithm* not a *general discovery algorithm*, hence, incapable of finding the full class of GDDs.

Thus, in this work, we propose and study the general GDD discovery problem, and present an efficient and effective solution for the task. Specifically, the main contributions of this paper are summarised as follows. First, we introduce, formulate, and formalise a general GDD discovery problem based on GDD semantics (cf. Sect. 3). Secondly, we propose a simple, yet efficient and effective discovery algorithm for finding a succinct and non-redundant set of *any* GDD that holds in a given property graph G. Indeed, we device various data structures and pruning strategies to ensure a fast and effective traversal of the huge search space of candidate GDDs. Further, to aid effective use of the discovered rules, we introduce a semantically meaningful ranking measure and present a ranking of the discovered GDDs (see Sect. 4). Finally, we perform extensive experiments on real-world graphs to show the feasibility, scalability, and effectiveness of our proposals (cf. Sect. 5).

Related Works. The problem of mining data dependencies is a well-studied subject in the relational data context (cf. [1,19,23] for review of works on the topic). Of particular note, are the works [5,13,14,22] on distance-based dependency discovery from relational data. However, none of these approaches can be applied to mine GDDs as they are semantically different.

The works in [9,17,24] on various graph dependency mining are relatively closer to ours: [9] considers graph functional dependency discovery (GFD); [17,24] propose graph entity dependency (GED) and approximate GED mining techniques respectively. However, GFDs and GEDs can be considered as special cases of GDDs where all distance thresholds are set to zero. Therefore, just like the approach in [15], these solutions are only capable of finding a limited/subclass of GDDs. We seek a more general GDD discovery solution in this work.

2   Preliminaries

This section presents relevant definitions used in the paper, following [10,15]. We use $\mathcal{A}, \mathcal{L}, \mathcal{C}$ to denote sets of *attributes, labels,* and *constants* respectively.

2.1   Property Graph, Graph Pattern, and Matching

We consider directed **property graph**, $G = (V, E, \lambda, \rho)$, where: a) V is a finite set of nodes; b) E is a finite set of edges, given by $E \subseteq V \times \lambda \times V$; c) λ is a function that assigns labels to node (resp. edge) from $\mathcal{L}$, e.g., $e = (u, l, v) \in E$ is an edge from node $u \in V$ to node $v \in V$, with label $\lambda(e) = l$; d) each node $v \in V$ has a label $\lambda(v)$ drawn from $\mathcal{L}$, and two key attributes id and eid, where id is the identity of the node, and eid is the identity of the real-world entity represented by the node (value often unknown/unavailable). Further, every node, v, has an associated list $\rho(v) = [(A_1, c_1), \cdots, (A_n, c_n)]$ of attribute-value pairs, where $c_i \in \mathcal{C}$ is a constant, $A_i \in \mathcal{A}$ is an attribute of v, written as $v.A_i = c_i$.

A **graph pattern**, denoted by $Q[\bar{z}]$, is a directed graph $Q[\bar{z}] = (V_Q, E_Q, \lambda_Q)$, where: (a) V_Q and E_Q represent the set of pattern nodes and pattern edges respectively; (b) λ_Q is a label function that assigns a label to each node $v \in V_Q$ and each edge $e \in E_Q$; and (c) $\bar{z}$ is the list of all nodes, called (pattern) variables in V_Q. All labels are drawn from $\mathcal{L}$, including the wildcard "*" as a special label. Two labels $l, l' \in \mathcal{L}$ are said to *match*, denoted $l \asymp l'$ iff: (a) $l = l'$; or (b) either l or l' is "*".

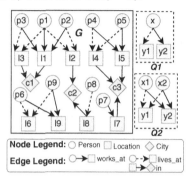

Fig. 1. A graph, G; and 4 graph patterns $Q_1 - Q_4$

Given a graph $G = (V, E, \lambda, \rho)$ and a graph pattern $Q[\bar{z}] = (V_Q, E_Q, \lambda_Q)$, a **match** of the graph pattern $Q[\bar{z}]$ in G is a homomorphism h from Q to G such that: (a) for each node $v \in V_Q$, there exists a node $h(v) \in G$ such that $\lambda_Q(v) \asymp \lambda(h(v))$; and (b) each edge $e = (u, l, v) \in E_Q$, there exists an edge $e' = (h(u), l', h(v))$ in G, such that $l \asymp l'$.

Given two graph patterns, $Q[\bar{z}] = (V_Q, E_Q, \lambda_Q)$ and $Q_1[\bar{z}_1] = (V_{Q_1}, E_{Q_1}, \lambda_{Q_1})$, we say $Q[\bar{z}]$ **subsumes** $Q_1[\bar{z}_1]$, denoted by $Q[\bar{z}] \sqsupseteq Q_1[\bar{z}_1]$, if $V_Q \supseteq V_{Q_1}$, $E_Q \supseteq E_{Q_1}$, and for each node $v_1 \in V_{Q_1}$ (resp. edge $e_1 \in E_{Q_1}$), we have $\lambda_{Q_1}(v_1) \asymp \lambda_Q(v), v \in V_Q$ (resp. $\lambda_{Q_1}(e_1) \asymp \lambda_Q(e), e \in E_Q$) and $\bar{z} \supseteq \bar{z}_1$.

We denote the set of all matches of $Q[\bar{z}]$ in G by $H(Q[\bar{z}], G)$. An example of a graph, graph patterns and their matches is illustrated in Example 1.

Example 1 (Graph, Graph Pattern and Matching). Figure 1 depicts a simple graph, G, (node properties are not shown); and two graph patterns. We illustrate the semantics of the graph patterns, and present their *matches* in G as follows:

- $Q_1[x, y_1, y_2]$ describes a **Person** node, x, with **lives_at** and **works_at** relationships with two **Location** nodes, y_1, y_2, respectively. The list of matches of pattern Q_1 in the example graph G is $H_1(x, y_1, y_2) = [\{p_3, l_3, l_1\}, \{p_1, l_3, l_1\}, \{p_1, l_2, l_1\}, \{p_2, l_2, l_1\}, \{p_4, l_4, l_5\}, \{p_5, l_4, l_5\}, \{p_6, l_6, l_9\}, \{p_9, l_6, l_9\}]$.
- $Q_2[x_1, x_2, y_1, y_2]$ specifies two **Person** nodes x_1, x_2, with the same **lives_at** and **works_at** relationships with two **Location** nodes y_1, y_2, respectively. Thus, the matches of Q_2 in G are $H_3(x_1, x_2, y_1, y_2) = [\{p_1, p_3, l_3, l_1\}, \{p_1, p_2, l_2, l_1\}, \{p_4, p_5, l_4, l_5\}, \{p_6, p_9, l_6, l_9\}]$.

Further, the following subsumption relation exist between the graph patterns in Fig. 1: $Q_2[x_1, x_2, y_1, y_2] \sqsupseteq Q_1[x, y_1, y_2]$. □

2.2   Graph Differential Dependency (GDD)

GDD Syntax. A *graph differential dependency* is a pair $\sigma : (Q[\bar{z}], \Phi_L(X) \to \Phi_R(Y))$, where: $Q[\bar{z}]$ is a graph pattern (*a.k.a.* the scope), and $\Phi_L(X) \to \Phi_R(Y)$ is called the dependency. $\Phi_L(X)$ and $\Phi_R(Y)$ are two (possibly empty) sets of distance constraints on the pattern variables $\bar{z}$. A distance constraint in $\Phi_L(X)$ and $\Phi_R(Y)$ on $\bar{z}$ is one of the following:

$$\delta_A(x.A, c) \le t_A; \quad \delta_{A_1 A_2}(x.A_1, x'.A_2) \le t_{A_1 A_2};$$
$$\delta_{\mathsf{eid}}(x.\mathsf{eid}, c_e) = 0; \quad \delta_{\mathsf{eid}}(x.\mathsf{eid}, x'.\mathsf{eid}) = 0;$$
$$\delta_{\equiv}(x.rela, c_r) = 0; \quad \delta_{\equiv}(x.rela, x'.rela) = 0;$$

where $x, x' \in \bar{z}$; A, A_1, A_2 are attributes in $\mathcal{A}$; c is a value of A; $\delta_{A_1 A_2}(x.A_1, x'.A_2)$ or $\delta_{A_1}(x, x')$, if $A_1 = A_2$ is a user specified distance function over values of A_1, A_2; $t_{A_1 A_2}$ is a threshold for $\delta_{A_1 A_2}(\cdot, \cdot)$; $\delta_{\mathsf{eid}}(\cdot, \cdot)$ (resp. $\delta_{\equiv}(\cdot, \cdot)$) is a function on eid (resp. relations), and returns 0 or 1. $\delta_{\mathsf{eid}}(x.\mathsf{eid}, c_e) = 0$ if the eid value of x is c_e, $\delta_{\mathsf{eid}}(x.\mathsf{eid}, x'.\mathsf{eid}) = 0$ if both x and x' have the same eid value, $\delta_{\equiv}(x.rela, c_r) = 0$ if x has a relation named **rela** and ended with the node c_r, $\delta_{\equiv}(x.rela, x'.rela) = 0$ if both x and x' have the relation named rela and ended with the same node.

The user-specified distance function $\delta_{A_1 A_2}(x.A_1, x'.A_2)$ is dependent on the types of A_1 and A_2. It can be an arithmetic operation of interval values, an edit distance of string values or the distance of two categorical values in a taxonomy, etc. The functions handle the wildcard value "*" for any domain by returning the 0 distance. We call $\Phi_L(X)$ and $\Phi_R(Y)$ the LHS and the RHS functions of the dependency respectively.

GDD Semantics. Given a GDD, $\sigma = (Q[\bar{z}], \Phi_L(X) \to \Phi_R(Y))$, and a match h of $Q[\bar{z}]$ in a graph G: h satisfies $\Phi_L(X)$, denoted by $h \vDash \Phi_L(X)$, if h satisfies every distance constraint in $\Phi_L(X)$; and $h \vDash \Phi_R(Y)$ is defined in the same way.

Let $H(Q[\bar{z}], G)$ be all the matches of $Q[\bar{z}]$ in G. We write $H(Q[\bar{z}], G) \vDash \sigma$, iff: for every $h \in H(Q[\bar{z}], G)$, if $h \vDash \Phi_L(X)$, then $h \vDash \Phi_R(Y)$ also. That is, G satisfies σ, denoted by $G \vDash \sigma$, if $H(Q[\bar{z}], G) \vDash \sigma$.

Let $sat(\Phi(X))$ denote the set of all matches in $H(Q[\bar{z}], G)$ that satisfy a constraint $\Phi(X)$ over $Q[\bar{z}]$. Then, Lemma 1 holds by the semantics of GDDs.

Lemma 1 (GDD satisfaction). *Given the matches $H(Q[\bar{z}], G)$ of $Q[\bar{z}]$ in G, $G \vDash \sigma = (Q[\bar{z}], \Phi_L(X) \to \Phi_R(Y))$ if and only if: $sat(\Phi_L(X)) \subseteq sat(\Phi_R(Y))$.* □

We illustrate the semantics of GDDs in Example 2 below.

Example 2 (GDD Semantics). Consider the GDD $\sigma_1 : (Q_2[x_1, x_2, y_1, y_2], \Phi_L(X) \to \Phi_R(Y))$, where $\Phi_L(X) = \{\delta_{\mathsf{name}}(x_1, x_2) \le 1, \delta_{\mathsf{dob}}(x_1, x_2) \le 2\}$ and $\Phi_R(Y) = \{\delta_{\mathsf{eid}}(x_1, x_2) = 0\}$. σ_1 states that for any two **Person** nodes x_1, x_2 that share the same living and working locations y_1, y_2 in G, if the distances between the **name** and **dob** attributes of x_1, x_2 as measured by the respective distance functions are within 1 and 2 respectively, then the nodes x_1, x_2 refer to the same real-world entity (i.e., $\delta_{\mathsf{eid}}(x_1, x_2) = 0$). Intuitively, σ_1 asserts that for any match of Q_2 in G, if the **Person** nodes have similar **name** and **dob** values, then they refer to the same person in the real-world. Thus, σ_1 is an example of entity linking rule. □

3   Problem Formulation

Given a property graph, G, the set of valid dependencies in G are often large, which affects their utility in downstream tasks. In this work, we are interested in finding a succinct set of GDDs in G. Thus, in the following, we present relevant definitions on our GDDs of interest, and present the formal problem definition.

Representative Graph Patterns. Recall, a GDD is a pair: $Q[\bar{z}]$, $\Phi_L(X) \rightarrow \Phi_R(Y)$. The graph pattern $Q[\bar{z}]$ of a GDD is the scope (i.e., "loose schema") over which the dependencies hold. Therefore, it is important to find "representative" graph patterns for the dependencies. We consider a graph pattern to be *representative* if it is *frequent* and *non-redundant*, as defined below.

Frequent Graph Pattern. Let the set $I = \{i_1, \cdots, i_m\}$ be the set of isomorphisms of a graph pattern $Q[\bar{z}]$ in a graph G, where $\bar{z} = x_1, \cdots, x_n$; and let $D(x_i) = \{i_1(x_i), \cdots, i_m(x_i)\}$ be the set of distinct nodes in G that map onto x_i via the isomorphisms. The *minimum image based support* [4] (MNI)[1] of $Q[\bar{z}]$ in G is defined as:

$$mni(Q[\bar{z}], G) = \min\{|D(x_i)|, \forall\ x_i \in z\}.$$

Thus, given a minimum MNI support, τ, we say a graph pattern $Q[\bar{z}]$ is **frequent** in G iff: $mni(Q[\bar{z}], G) \geq \tau$.

Example 3 (Frequent Graph Pattern). Consider the graph pattern $Q_2[x_1, x_2, y_1, y_2]$ and the graph G in Fig. 1. The isomorphisms of Q_2 in G are shown in Fig. 2 a). Specifically, $D(x_1) = \{p3, p2, p4, p6\}$, $D(x_2) = \{p1, p5, p9\}$, $D(y_1) = \{l3, l2, l8, l9\}$ and $D(y_2) = \{l1, l5, l9\}$. Thus, $mni(Q_2, G) = \min\{|D(x_1)|, |D(x_2)|, |D(y_1)|, |D(y_2)|\} = \min\{4, 3, 4, 3\}$. $\therefore$ $mni(Q_2, G) = 3$; and frequent if $\tau \leq 3$. □

Non-redundant Graph Patterns. Although the frequency of graph patterns is useful for eliminating non-persistent patterns, it is not sufficient. This is because a frequent graph patterns set often has redundancies. For example, in Fig. 2 b) is the set of frequent graph patterns in the example graph G (of Fig. 1) for $\tau = 3$. In this example, some of the redundancies include: $q0 \supset q1 \supset q4$; $q6 \supset q7 \supset q8$; etc. Hence, we are interested in frequent *and* non-redundant graph patterns.

   Given a minimum MNI support threshold τ, we say a graph pattern $Q[\bar{z}]$ in G is **non-redundant** iff: a) it is frequent, i.e., $mni(Q[\bar{z}], G) \geq \tau$; b) there exists no other pattern $Q_1[\bar{z}_1]$ where $Q_1[\bar{z}_1] \sqsupseteq Q[\bar{z}]$ in G such that $mni(Q[\bar{z}], G) = mni(Q_1[\bar{z}_1], G)$.

Example 4 (Non-redundant Graph Patterns). Given $\tau = 3$, all graph patterns in Fig. 2 b) are frequent. Graph patterns within the blue (i.e., $q10, q11$) and red (i.e., $q12$) boundaries have supports of 4 and 5 respectively, and every other pattern has a support of 3. Thus, it is easily verifiable that the non-redundant patterns are those with bold dotted line boundaries: $q0, q2, q6, q10, q11$, and $q12$.

---

[1] we adopt this graph pattern counting metric due to its anti-monotone property.

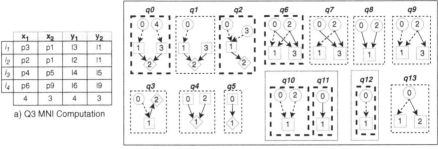

a) Q3 MNI Computation

b) Example Closed Frequent Patterns (in bold dotted lines) - MNI >=3

Fig. 2. Example of Representative Graph Patterns

We remark that the notion of non-redundant graph patterns is equivalent to that of *closed patterns* [3] in the frequent itemset mining literature.

Irreducible Dependencies. Without loss of generality, we consider GDDs with singleton RHSs, i.e., $\Phi_R(Y)$ has one and only one distance constraint.

The space of candidate GDDs is huge and complex as any number of distance constraints can be defined over attribute sets. Even more challenging, these constraints can interact. Let $\Phi(X_1), \Phi(X_2)$ be two sets of distance constraints over a given graph pattern $Q[\bar{z}]$.

The set $\Phi(X_1)$ is said to **subjugate** $\Phi(X_2)$, denoted by $\Phi(X_1) \succeq \Phi(X_2)$, iff.: (i) for every distance constraint $\delta_A(x.A, c) \leq t_A^{(1)}$, or $\delta_{A_1 A_2}(x.A_1, x'.A_2) \leq t_{A_1 A_2}^{(1)}$ in $\Phi(X_1)$, there exists $\delta_A(x.A, c) \leq t_A^{(2)}$, or $\delta_{A_1 A_2}(x.A_1, x'.A_2) \leq t_{A_1 A_2}^{(2)}$ in $\Phi(X_2)$, such that $t_A^{(1)} \geq t_A^{(2)}$, or $t_{A_1 A_2}^{(1)} \geq t_{A_1 A_2}^{(2)}$, respectively; and (ii) for every constraint $\delta_{\equiv/\text{eid}}(\cdot, \cdot) = 0$ in $\Phi(X_1)$ there exists $\delta_{\equiv/\text{eid}}(\cdot, \cdot) = 0$ in $\Phi(X_2)$ as well.

Intuitively, if $\Phi(X_1) \succeq \Phi(X_2)$, then for any match h of $Q[\bar{z}]$ in G that satisfies $\Phi(X_2)$, i.e., $h \vDash \Phi(X_2)$, it always satisfies $\Phi(X_1)$ too (i.e., $h \vDash \Phi(X_1)$).

Property 1 (Trivial GDD). For any two sets, $\Phi(X_1), \Phi(X_2)$, of constraints over $Q[\bar{z}]$, if $\Phi(X_1) \succeq \Phi(X_2)$, then GDD $(Q[\bar{z}], \Phi(X_2) \rightarrow \Phi(X_1))$ holds in G.   □

Consider a set Σ of GDDs and a single GDD σ. We say Σ *implies* σ, denoted by $\Sigma \vDash \sigma$ if and only if $\Sigma \vDash G$ implies $\sigma \vDash G$. We want Σ without any implied rules. It, thus, suffices to ensure any GDDs in Σ is *irreducible* as defined below.

Property 2 (Irreducible GDD). A GDD $\sigma : (Q[\bar{z}], \Phi_L(X) \rightarrow \Phi_R(Y)) \in \Sigma$, is said to be *irreducible* if and only if: a) any attribute $A \in \Phi_R(Y)$ does not exist in $\Phi_L(X)$; b) there does not exists another GDD $\sigma_1 : (Q_1[\bar{z}_1], \Phi_l(X_1) \rightarrow \Phi_r(Y_1)) \in \Sigma$ s.t.: (i) $Q_1[\bar{z}_1] \sqsupseteq Q[\bar{z}]$, (ii) $\Phi_l(X_1) \succeq \Phi_L(X)$, and (iii) $\Phi_R(Y) \succeq \Phi_r(Y_1)$.   □

We say a set Σ of GDDs is *minimal* iff: for any $\sigma \in \Sigma$, we have $\Sigma \not\equiv \Sigma \backslash \sigma$. That is, Σ contains no redundant GDD. Furthermore, a set Σ_c is a cover of Σ if: $\Sigma_c \subseteq \Sigma$ and $\Sigma_c \equiv \Sigma$.

Problem Definition. This paper studies the following GDD discovery problem.

Definition 1 (Discovery of GDDs). *Given a property graph, G, and a user-specified MNI threshold, τ: find a minimal cover set Σ_c of all irreducible GDDs that hold over τ-frequent and non-redundant graph patterns in G.*   □

4   The Proposed GDD Mining Approach

In this section, we introduce the proposed GDD mining solution, GDDMiner. It consists of three major tasks, viz: a) finding and matching representative graph patterns (in Sect. 4.1), b) mining distance dependencies over the matches of the graph patterns (in Sect. 4.2), and c) pruning and ranking the mined rules to produce a ranked minimal cover set (in Sect. 4.3). A sketch of the pseudo-code for the proposed three-phase solution is presented in Algorithm 1.

Algorithm 1: GDDMiner

Input: MNI thres. τ; dist. const. Δ (optional)
Output: Minimal cover Σ_c of GDDs
Data: Property graph, G

1 $\Sigma := \emptyset, \Sigma_c : \emptyset$

/* find representative graph patterns */

2 $\mathcal{Q} \leftarrow \mathsf{rGraMi}(G, \tau)$

/* mine GDDs over rep. graph patterns */

3 **for** $Q_i[\bar{z}_i] \in \mathcal{Q}$ **do**
4    $H(Q_i[\bar{z}_i], G) \leftarrow \mathsf{hMatches}(Q_i[\bar{z}_i], G)$
5    $\Sigma_i \leftarrow \mathsf{redGDDs}(H, \Delta)$
6    $\Sigma \leftarrow \Sigma \cup \Sigma_i$

/* prune implications   */

7 $\Sigma_c \leftarrow \mathsf{cover}(\Sigma)$
8 **return** Σ_c

4.1   Graph Pattern Mining and Matching

Mining representative graph patterns. Frequent subgraph mining (FSM) in a given graph G is a non-trivial, and well-studied problem. In this work, we extend the well-known *constraint satisfaction problem* (CSP) based FSM solution, GraMi [6] for the task of finding *frequent* and *non-redundant* graph patterns. For brevity and space constraints, we refer interested readers to [6] for the full details of the FSM solution.

Note that GraMi returns frequent graph patterns and *not* frequent non-redundant graph patterns. Thus, to achieve our goal, we extend the underlying data structure in GraMi, the *subgraph generation tree*, to enable the return of the frequency count associated with each frequent pattern. This adaptation allows us to effectively prune redundant frequent graph patterns based on the subsumption relation of graph patterns (see Sect. 2.1), with the same frequency as illustrated in Example 3 and 4. Given a minimum MNI threshold, τ, our extended FSM algorithm, rGraMi, returns the set $\mathcal{Q}$ of all representative graph patterns (cf. line 2 of Algorithm 1).

	x1: person			y1: location					x2: person			y2: location				
	id	Name (A1)	DOB (A2)	id	Type (A3)	Street Name (A4)	State (A5)	Zipcode (A6)	id	Name (A1)	DOB (A2)	id	Type (A3)	Street Name (A4)	State (A5)	Zipcode (A6)
h1	p1	William Johnson	1970.7.31	I3	Res	46 Adrian Ave	SA	5120	p3	Bill Johnson	7/31/70	I1	Comm	17 Tea Tree Gully	SA	5053
h2	p1	William Johnson	1970.7.31	I2	Res	28 Main Rd	NSW	2758	p2	Mary Smith	Jun. 1990	I1	Comm	17 Tea Tree Gully	SA	5053
h3	p4	Paul H. Colbert		I4	Com	93 High St	NSW	2000	p5	Colber, P.H.	25/12/89	I5	Com	93 High Street	NSW	2000
h4	p6	Tom Engel	1 Jun. 1956	I6		99 Mawson blvd	WA	6019	p9	Engel, Thomas	06/01/65	I9	Com	199 Main Road	WA	6000

Fig. 3. An example pseudo-table of matches of Q_2 in G

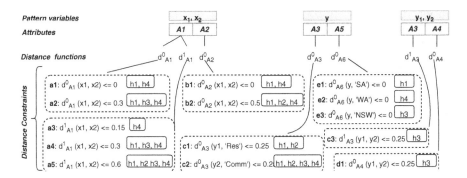

Fig. 4. Examples of distance constraints over matches of Q_2

Finding Homomorphic Matches of Graph Patterns. Given a representative graph pattern $Q[\bar{z}] \in \mathcal{Q}$, we find the set $H(Q[\bar{z}], G)$ of homomorphic matches of $Q[\bar{z}]$ in G using the efficient worst-case optimal join (WCOJ) based algorithm in [20] (i.e., line 4 of Algorithm 1). We generate a pseudo-relational table with the properties/attributes of the matches of the graph pattern. For example, Fig. 3 is an example of such a table over matches of the pattern Q_2 in G from our running example in Fig. 1.

4.2   Finding Valid GDDs over Graph Patterns

Pre-processing: Distance Functions and Thresholds. Given the set $H(Q[\bar{z}], G)$ of matches of $Q[\bar{z}]$ in G, various distance functions can be defined (with corresponding distance thresholds) over the attributes of the pattern variables based on domain knowledge. The domain knowledge may include which distance function(s) to define over specific pattern variable(s) as well as what thresholds of the distance functions are semantically meaningful. For instance, given the matches of Q_2 in Fig. 3, examples of possible distance functions and constraints are shown in Fig. 4. In exception of the name attribute, $A1$, each attribute has one normalised distance function with multiple constraints in Fig. 4. In particular, d^0_{A1} and d^1_{A1} measure phonetic and Sørensen-Dice distances of two name sets.

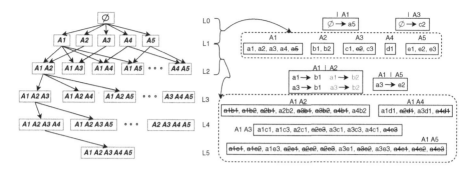

Fig. 5. Example of attribute lattice (left); and exemplar traversal & pruning of search space of candidate GDDs (right)

In this paper, we assume such domain knowledge exists, as an optional input Δ to Algorithm 1. However, in its absence, one can employ arbitrary distance functions with equidistant thresholds.

Search Space Construction and Traversal. Here, we discuss the search space of candidate GDDs. In principle, the space of possible GDDs is exponential to the number of distance constraints. Thus, we present data structures and strategies to enable effective and efficient search for valid GDDs.

We extend the attribute lattice [2] to model the GDD search space. The lattice is a level-wise directed graph with an empty-set attribute as the root node (at Level-0, $L0$). The first level, $L1$, consists of children nodes of $L0$ made up of all attributes of the pattern variables. Each attribute node $A_i \in L1$ is associated with a set of distance constraints defined over it. Nodes at subsequent levels are formed by combining two nodes from the previous level as follows. Let $n_{i \cdot j}, n_{i \cdot k}$ be the j-th and k-th nodes at level i respectively. $n_{i \cdot j}$ and $n_{i \cdot k}$ can be combined to form the node $n_{i+1 \cdot l}$ at level $i+1$ if and only if the size of the set union of the attribute sets $|n_{i \cdot j} \cup n_{i \cdot k}| = i + 1$. Further, $n_{i+1 \cdot l}$ is assigned the set union of distance constraints from $n_{i \cdot j}$ and $n_{i \cdot k}$, $\Phi(X)$, if the associated satisfaction set, $sat(\Phi(X))$, computed as the set intersection of the two parent satisfaction sets is non-empty. Then, edges directed from $n_{i \cdot j}$ and $n_{i \cdot k}$ to $n_{i+1 \cdot l}$. For example, Fig. 5 shows the attribute lattice (left) and associated distance constraint sets for levels $L1, L2$ (right) for our running example with 5 attributes $A1 - A5$. Note that, we only show all edges in levels $L0 - L2$ of the lattice for clarity.

We adopt a top-down left-right search strategy to traverse the lattice space.

Candidate GDD Generation and Validation. The construction of the lattice and generation of candidate GDDs is performed simultaneously in a level-wise fashion. Indeed, candidate GDDs are explored between two successive levels $Li, Li+1$ from top to down the lattice. All distance constraints at level Li form candidate LHS of the rule, whiles $Li + 1$ constraints are potential RHSs.

More specifically, for every directed edge between the node $n_{i \cdot j} \in Li$ and $n_{i+1 \cdot l} \in Li + 1$ we form and test candidate GDDs as follows. Let $\Phi_L(X), \Phi_R(Y)$

be sets of distance constraints in $n_{i \cdot j}$ and $n_{i+1 \cdot l}$ respectively. A candidate GDD is of the form: $\Phi_L(X) \rightarrow \Phi_R(A)$, where $A = Y \backslash X$, and $\Phi_R(A)$ a singleton distance constraint over A (this satisfies condition $a)$ of Property 2).

For efficiency of search, and in accordance with conditions $b) - (ii)$ and $b) - (iii)$ of Property 2, we consider LHS constraints of $n_{i \cdot j}$ in decreasing order of thresholds, and conversely, the RHS constraints in the increasing order. A candidate GDD $\Phi_L(X) \rightarrow \Phi_R(A)$ is validated via Lemma 1, i.e., iff: $sat(\Phi_L(X)) \subseteq sat(\Phi_R(Y))$. Further, we use the following pruning rule: if $\Phi_L(X) \rightarrow \Phi_R(Y)$, then $\Phi_R(Y)$ is excluded from candidate generation at the next level.

Example 5 (Finding valid GDDs). Consider the the set of distance constraints over attributes $A1 - A5$ of the pattern variables in Q_2 as shown in Fig. 4. The corresponding lattice for the search space of candidate GDDs is presented in Fig. 5. To find valid GDDs, we first evaluate candidates between levels $L0/L1$. Specifically, the only possible LHS constraint at $L0$ is $\Phi_L(X) = \{\emptyset\}$; and every distance constraint (on Y) at $L1$ is as a candidate RHS $\Phi_R(A) = \Phi_R(Y \backslash X)$. That is, the set of candidate GDDs on edge $\emptyset \rightarrow A1$ is $\{\emptyset \rightarrow a1, \emptyset \rightarrow a2, \cdots, \emptyset \rightarrow a5\}$, whereas for edge $\emptyset \rightarrow A2$ is $\{\emptyset \rightarrow b1, \emptyset \rightarrow b2\}$. And, similarly for other edges between $L0/L1$. Note that $sat(\emptyset) = \{h1, h2, h3, h4\}$, i.e., every match satisfies an empty-set constraint by definition. To validate the candidate GDDs on each edge between $L0/L1$, we test if $sat(\emptyset) \subseteq sat(w)$, where w is RHS constraint. Thus, the only valid rules are: $\emptyset \rightarrow a5$ and $\emptyset \rightarrow c2$ as shown in blue in Fig. 5. Consequently, constraints $a5, c2$ can be eliminated from forming nodes in level $L2$. Distance constraints of attribute sets at $L2$ are shown alongside the valid GDDs, and pruned constraints. We show all valid irreducible GDDs in blue, and valid but implied GDDs in red. □

4.3   Finding Cover and Ranking GDDs

Pruning Implied GDDs. So far, the set Σ of GDDs produced from the foregoing are irreducible *w.r.t.* a single pattern $Q[\bar{z}]$. That is, all conditions except the graph pattern interaction condition b)-(i) in Property 2 is satisfied by all GDDs in Σ. Therefore, we ensure general irreducibility of rules in Σ via the cover(Σ) function (in line 7 of Algorithm 1).

Note that Σ is a multi-set $\{\Sigma_1, \cdots, \Sigma_k\}$ of GDDs, where each $\Sigma_i \in \Sigma$ corresponds to a set of GDDs over a particular scope $Q_i[\bar{z}_i]$. Thus, we generate a minimal cover Σ_c of Σ by eliminating all implied GDDs due to pattern interactions in Σ through two simple steps. First, for any $\Sigma_i \in \Sigma$, the full set Σ_i is added to Σ_c if and only if no other Σ_j exists in Σ such that $Q_j[\bar{z}_j] \sqsupseteq Q_i[\bar{z}_i]$. Secondly, for any pair $\Sigma_i, \Sigma_j \in \Sigma$ such that $Q_i[\bar{z}_i] \sqsupseteq Q_j[\bar{z}_j]$: any GDD $\sigma' \in \Sigma_j$ is eliminated from Σ_j if there exists $\sigma \in \Sigma_i$ such that $LHS(\sigma) \succeq LHS(\sigma')$ and $RHS(\sigma') \succeq RHS(\sigma)$. This routine is repeated for all pairs Σ_i, Σ_j until no further changes occur, and the added to Σ_c.

Ranking GDDs. In practice, the minimal cover set of dependencies, albeit without any redundancies, is often still large. This makes using of the rules in downstream applications challenging. Thus, a measure to assess the quality of the rules is useful for the selection, and adoption of the discovered rules. We present an intuitive, easy to compute, and semantically meaningful interestingness measure for GDDs, inspired by the *lift* measure (from associations rule mining literature).

Recall, the lift of rule $R = A \rightarrow B$, is given as $lift(R) = \frac{conf(A \rightarrow B)}{conf(\emptyset \rightarrow B)}$, where $conf(x \rightarrow y)$ is the confidence (a.k.a conditional probability), given as $conf(x \rightarrow y) = \frac{P(x,y)}{P(x)}$. Simply, the lift of a rule R is quotient of the posterior and the prior confidence of the rule. A lift value near 1 indicates independence. A larger than 1 lift value indicates A has a positive effect on occurrence of B, and conversely, a less than 1 value show A has an adverse effect on B occurrence.

We define the *interestingness*, $\mathrm{intr}(\sigma)$, of a GDD σ as:

$$\mathrm{intr}(\sigma) = \frac{conf(Q[\bar{z}], \Phi_L(X) \rightarrow \Phi_R(Y))}{conf(Q[\bar{z}], \emptyset \rightarrow \Phi_R(Y))} = \frac{|H(Q[\bar{z}], G)|}{|sat(\Phi_R(Y))|}. \tag{1}$$

Note that, $conf(Q[\bar{z}], \Phi_L(X) \rightarrow \Phi_R(Y)) = 1$ for all valid GDDs, and $conf(Q[\bar{z}], \emptyset \rightarrow \Phi_R(Y)) = P(Y)$. Further, the quantity $|H(Q[\bar{z}, G])|$ is fixed for any $\sigma \in \Sigma$, thus, the only determinant of interestingness of any given GDD is the size of its satisfaction set $sat(\Phi_R(Y))$ – which relies on the strictness of the threshold(s) in $\Phi_R(Y)$. Essentially, GDDs with strict RHSs, hence, smaller $|sat(\Phi_R(Y))|$ are more interesting – consistent with GDD semantics.

5   Experiments

We present an empirical evaluation of our proposed GDD mining solution, GDDMiner, using three real-world graph data sets as described in Table 1. We defined several

Table 1. Summary of data sets

Graph	#Nodes (N)	#Edges (E)	#N Types	#E Types
DBLP	300K	800K	3	3
IMDB	300K	650K	5	8
YAGO4	380K	800K	7764	83

distance functions over node attributes of the graphs; and used up to three distance constraints per attribute with equi-distant thresholds. All implementations are conducted in Java, and the experiments run on a 2.20 GHz Intel Xeon processor computer with 128 GB memory running Linux OS.

Feasibility and Scalability of GDDMiner. Here, we demonstrate the feasibility and scalability of GDDMiner as follows. We set the MNI threshold, $\tau = 500$, to ensure the discovered scopes of the dependencies are persistent topological patterns in the data sets. For each dataset, we vary the number of attributes and the proportion of the matches of the pattern. The performance of GDDMiner over each dataset is presented in Fig. 6 a)–c). In general, the discovery time increases with number of attributes and the proportion of matches of the pattern (from 50% to 100%) in the graph.

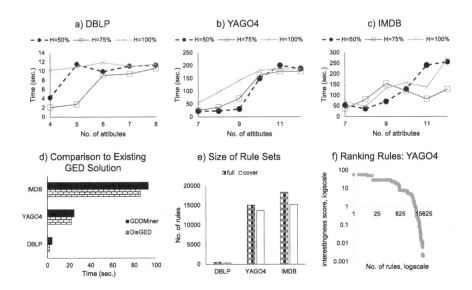

Fig. 6. Evaluation of GDDMiner on real-world graphs

Comparison to Existing Graph Dependency Miner. In this experiment, we set all distance thresholds to 0, to assess the performance of mining GEDs with our solution, compared to the GED mining technique in [17]. Figure 6 d) shows a close and comparable performance of the two algorithms on finding GEDs (i.e., 0-constraint GDDs) in all datasets. The DisGEDs algorithm [17] perform marginally better than ours, and a detailed analysis shows the advantage lies in the graph partitioning strategy used in [17] during the graph pattern mining stage. It is noteworthy that whereas our solution can be co-opted to find GEDs, DisGEDs [17] cannot be used to mine GDDs.

Discovered Rules. Figure 6 e) is a plot of the sizes of the irreducible and the minimal cover sets (i.e., Σ vs. Σ_c) found in the three graphs. It is clear that whilst further pruning of Σ to Σ_c (cf. Sect. 4.3) reduces that final set size, it is still quite large (especially for YAGO4 and IMDB). This shows the need for ranking the results for ease of use. Thus, we show the effectiveness of our interestingness measure (i.e., Eq. 1) for ranking the discovered rules in Fig. 6 f). Due to space constraints, we show only the case for the YAGO4 data as the same pattern is observed for all datasets. The scatter plot shows the ranking helps identify the most interesting GDDs easily. For example, the top 625 GDDs have at least an interestingness value of 10.

6   Conclusion

This paper introduces and studies the *general discovery problem* of GDDs. The proposed discovery algorithm, GDDMiner, leverages various properties of GDDs to search and prune the huge candidate space effectively. Empirical evaluations of GDDMiner on real-world graphs show its feasibility and scalability.

In the future, we shall study the simultaneous mining and matching of representative graph patterns, and automatic fine tuning of the thresholds of distance constraints, to boost the performance of GDDMiner in large graphs.

Acknowledgement. This research project was supported in part by the following grant schemes: the Innovation fund of Chinese Marine Defense Technology Innovation Center under Grant JJ-2021-722-04; the Fundamental Research Funds for the Chinese Central Universities under Grant 2662023XXPY004; the Inner Mongolia Key Scientific and Technological Project under Grant 2021SZD0099.

References

1. Abedjan, Z., Golab, L., Naumann, F.: Profiling relational data: a survey. VLDB J. **24**(4), 557–581 (2015). https://doi.org/10.1007/s00778-015-0389-y
2. Agrawal, R., Srikant, R., et al.: Fast algorithms for mining association rules. In: Proceedings of 20th International Conference on Very Large Data Bases, VLDB, vol. 1215, pp. 487–499. Santiago, Chile (1994)
3. Bastide, Y., Pasquier, N., Taouil, R., Stumme, G., Lakhal, L.: Mining minimal non-redundant association rules using frequent closed itemsets. In: Lloyd, J., et al. (eds.) CL 2000. LNCS (LNAI), vol. 1861, pp. 972–986. Springer, Heidelberg (2000). https://doi.org/10.1007/3-540-44957-4_65
4. Bringmann, B., Nijssen, S.: What is frequent in a single graph? In: Washio, T., Suzuki, E., Ting, K.M., Inokuchi, A. (eds.) PAKDD 2008. LNCS (LNAI), vol. 5012, pp. 858–863. Springer, Heidelberg (2008). https://doi.org/10.1007/978-3-540-68125-0_84
5. Caruccio, L., Deufemia, V., Polese, G.: Mining relaxed functional dependencies from data. Data Min. Knowl. Disc. **34**(2), 443–477 (2020)
6. Elseidy, M., Abdelhamid, E., Skiadopoulos, S., Kalnis, P.: Grami: frequent subgraph and pattern mining in a single large graph. Proc. VLDB Endowment **7**(7), 517–528 (2014)
7. Fan, W.: Big graphs: challenges and opportunities. Proc. VLDB Endowment **15**(12), 3782–3797 (2022)
8. Fan, W., Geng, L., Jin, R., Lu, P., Tugay, R., Yu, W.: Linking entities across relations and graphs. In: 2022 IEEE 38th International Conference on Data Engineering (ICDE), pp. 634–647. IEEE (2022)
9. Fan, W., Hu, C., Liu, X., Lu, P.: Discovering graph functional dependencies. ACM Trans. Database Syst. (TODS) **45**(3), 1–42 (2020)
10. Fan, W., Lu, P.: Dependencies for graphs. ACM Trans. Database Syst. (TODS) **44**(2), 1–40 (2019)
11. Fan, W., Lu, P., Tian, C., Zhou, J.: Deducing certain fixes to graphs. Proc. VLDB Endowment **12**(7), 752–765 (2019)
12. Feng, Z., et al.: A schema-driven synthetic knowledge graph generation approach with extended graph differential dependencies (gdd x s). IEEE Access **9**, 5609–5639 (2020)
13. Kwashie, S., Liu, J., Li, J., Ye, F.: Mining differential dependencies: a subspace clustering approach. In: Wang, H., Sharaf, M.A. (eds.) ADC 2014. LNCS, vol. 8506, pp. 50–61. Springer, Cham (2014). https://doi.org/10.1007/978-3-319-08608-8_5

14. Kwashie, S., Liu, J., Li, J., Ye, F.: Efficient discovery of differential dependencies through association rules mining. In: Sharaf, M.A., Cheema, M.A., Qi, J. (eds.) ADC 2015. LNCS, vol. 9093, pp. 3–15. Springer, Cham (2015). https://doi.org/10.1007/978-3-319-19548-3_1

15. Kwashie, S., Liu, L., Liu, J., Stumptner, M., Li, J., Yang, L.: Certus: an effective entity resolution approach with graph differential dependencies (GDDs). Proc. VLDB Endowment **12**(6), 653–666 (2019)

16. Lin, P., Song, Q., Wu, Y.: Fact checking in knowledge graphs with ontological subgraph patterns. Data Sci. Eng. **3**(4), 341–358 (2018)

17. Liu, D., et al.: An efficient approach for discovering graph entity dependencies (GEDs). arXiv preprint arXiv:2301.06264 (2023)

18. Liu, J., Kwashie, S., Li, J., Liu, L., Bewong, M.: Linking graph entities with multiplicity and provenance. In: 2nd International Workshop on EntitY REtrieval: EYRE 2019, pp. 1–7. Association for Computing Machinery (ACM) (2019)

19. Liu, J., Li, J., Liu, C., Chen, Y.: Discover dependencies from data-a review. IEEE Trans. Knowl. Data Eng. **24**(2), 251–264 (2010)

20. Mhedhbi, A., Salihoglu, S.: Optimizing subgraph queries by combining binary and worst-case optimal joins. Proc. VLDB Endowment, vol. 12. no. 11 (2019)

21. Song, Q., Lin, P., Ma, H., Wu, Y.: Explaining missing data in graphs: a constraint-based approach. In: 2021 IEEE 37th International Conference on Data Engineering (ICDE), pp. 1476–1487. IEEE (2021)

22. Song, S., Chen, L.: Differential dependencies: reasoning and discovery. ACM Trans. Database Syst. (TODS) **36**(3), 1–41 (2011)

23. Song, S., Gao, F., Huang, R., Wang, C.: Data dependencies extended for variety and veracity: a family tree. IEEE Trans. Knowl. Data Eng. **34**(10), 4717–4736 (2020)

24. Zhou, G., et al.: FASTAGEDS: fast approximate graph entity dependency discovery. arXiv preprint arXiv:2304.02323 (2023)

Maximum Fairness-Aware (k, r)-Core Identification in Large Graphs

Xingyu Tan[1], Chengyuan Guo[1], Xiaoyang Wang[1(✉)], Wenjie Zhang[1], and Chen Chen[2]

[1] The University of New South Wales, Sydney, Australia
{xingyu.tan,chengyuan.guo,xiaoyang.wang1,wenjie.zhang}@unsw.edu.au
[2] The University of Wollongong, Wollongong, Australia
chenc@uow.edu.au

Abstract. Cohesive subgraph mining is a fundamental problem in attributed graph analysis. The k-core model has been widely used in many studies to measure the cohesiveness of subgraphs. However, none of them considers the fairness of attributes in communities. To address this limitation, we propose a novel model, named fair (k, r)-core, to assess fairness equity within communities captured in attributed graphs. The model not only focuses on cohesive community structure but also eliminates vertices that contribute to unfairness. We prove that the problem of identifying the maximum fair (k, r)-core is NP-hard. To scale for large graphs, we introduce innovative pruning techniques and search methods. Comprehensive experiments are conducted on 6 real-world datasets to evaluate the efficiency and effectiveness of the proposed model and solutions.

Keywords: Community detection · k-core · fairness-aware

1 Introduction

Attributed graphs are widely used to model complex networks in real-world applications, where vertices or edges have attributed information. Cohesive graph identification is one of the fundamental tasks in graph analysis, and many models have been proposed in the literature to measure the cohesiveness of subgraphs, such as k-core [6,21], k-truss [5,20], and clique [4,17,18]. Among these models, k-core is one of the most widely used models and has various applications, including community detection, network visualization, and anomaly detection [2,3].

Motivation. Recently, the concept of fairness has been widely investigated in the field of data analysis [7,19]. Numerous existing studies reveal that there is certain discrimination against specific groups caused by machine learning models, such as gender and racial biases [1,23]. Although various effective solutions in data analysis fields have been proposed, such as group fairness and individual fairness [1,14,22], the fairness in graph data analysis is still under-explored.

© The Author(s), under exclusive license to Springer Nature Switzerland AG 2024
Z. Bao et al. (Eds.): ADC 2023, LNCS 14386, pp. 273–286, 2024.
https://doi.org/10.1007/978-3-031-47843-7_19

Existing studies on attributed graphs are majorly focusing on identifying communities that either exhibit a high correlation of attributes or satisfy particular attribute constraints [24]. None of them considers the fairness of attributes in resulting subgraphs while modeling k-core on attributed graphs.

Motivated by this, we propose a novel model named fair (k, r)-core by integrating the fairness constraint into the traditional k-core model. The fair (k, r)-core has various applications. For example, in a cooperation network, every vertex has an attribute that represents its study subject. The model can identify a core community where the number of each subject is exactly same or slightly different. It may be utilized to find research groups that not only collaborate closely but also have fair distributed research topics from various study disciplines to carry out a particular task.

In this paper, we focus on identifying maximum fairness-aware (k, r)-core on attributed graphs where each vertex has one attribute. A fair (k, r)-core is the maximal subgraphs that $i)$ each vertex in the fair (k, r)-core should have at least k neighbors, and $ii)$ the difference between the number of vertices with different attributes is not larger than the given r. This allows us to generate subgraphs that are not only dense but also diverse and inclusive. Notably, by adjusting the parameter r, users can modulate the fairness of results more flexibly. Different from the traditional k-core model, fair (k, r)-core in the attributed graphs is not unique. In this paper, we aim to find the maximum (k, r)-core, i.e., the one with the largest size, which usually preserves the dominant properties of the network.

Challenges and Contributions. The principal challenges of this problem are twofold. Firstly, we demonstrate that finding the maximum fair (k, r)-core is an NP-hard problem. Secondly, given the typically large size of real-world attributed networks, developing efficient detection methods and pruning strategies for scalability and faster processing is crucial. To the best of our knowledge, we are the first to propose and investigate the maximum fair (k, r)-core problem. Our main contributions are outlined below. First, we provide a formal definition of the fair (k, r)-core model and prove its NP-hardness. For scalability in large networks, novel pruning techniques and searching algorithms are introduced. Finally, comprehensive experiments as well as case study are conducted on real-world graphs to validate the efficiency and effectiveness of the proposed techniques and model.

Related Work. Attributed communities detection is one of the fundamental problems in graph data analysis and serves an important role in various applications [9,16]. In the attributed network, the communities are usually represented by cohesive subgraphs, utilized by various structure models. Among these models, the k-core model, originally proposed by Seidman et al., is widely employed [6,15]. For instance, [8] propose a CL-tree, an index structure, designed to efficiently support attributed community search. [12] introduce a 2-approximate query-based algorithm designed to mine subgraphs that are densely interconnected and centered around specific queries. [11] propose an embedding-based model designed to detect communities within attributed graphs. However, fewer studies consider the fairness of attributes while mining attributed communities. The concept of fairness-aware data mining has been extensively studied within the machine learning community. [19] propose various fairness constraint concepts suitable for different applications. [23] present a method for achieving guaranteed group fairness in ranking, ensuring that the proportion of protected elements in the ranking is not less than a predetermined threshold. [1] present a set of metrics to evaluate algorithmic fairness in the field of fairness in recommendation systems. In the field of graph data mining, [24] employ the fairness considerations in bicliques enumeration, and [13] utilizes it in the clique model. Unlike them, we consider the fairness of attributes in resulting communities while modeling k-core on attributed graphs, and our techniques markedly differ from those mentioned above.

2   Preliminaries

Consider an undirected and attributed graph $G = (V, E, A)$, where V is the set of vertices, E is the set of edges, and A is the set of attributes. For $\forall v \in G$, v has only one attribute from A. We denote the attribute value of v as $attr(v) \in A$. The cardinality of A is denoted by A_n, i.e., $A_n = |A|$. For simplicity, we also denote A as $A = \{a_i | 0 \leq i < A_n\}$, where each a_i symbolizes an individual attribute. The number of vertices with the same attribute $a_i \in A$ in G is denoted as $cnt_G(a_i) = |\{v \in V | attr(v) = a_i\}|$. Given a vertex v, the set of its neighbors in G is denoted as $N_G(v) = \{u \in V | (v, u) \in E\}$, and the degree of v in G is denoted as $d_G(v) = |N_G(v)|$. We define a subgraph $S = (V_S, E_S, A_S)$ of G such that $V_S \subseteq V$, $E_S \subseteq E$, and $A_S \subseteq A$.

Definition 1 (k-core). *Given a simple graph $G = (V, E)$, a positive integer k, and an induced subgraph $S \subseteq G$. S is a k-core of G, if it satisfies i) for any vertex $v \in V_S, d_S(v) \geq k$, and ii) S is maximal, i.e., any supergraph of S cannot be a k-core.*

In the literature, most research on k-core in attributed graphs primarily focuses on non-fairness-aware communities, i.e., does not consider the difference in the number of attributes, which may lead to unfair communities. As discussed, a fair community in attributed graphs should not only be densely interconnected but also incorporate the fairness constraint, that is, eliminating vertices that contribute to unfairness. Ignoring attribute fairness and only focusing on structure cohesiveness could result in subgraphs that lack diversity or exhibit biases towards particular attributes. In this paper, we utilize the k-core model to describe the cohesiveness of a subgraph. To achieve a fair community, we restrict the difference in the number of vertices with differing attributes to not exceed the given threshold r. When $r = 0$, the resulting subgraph represents a completely fair community. On the basis of the k-core model, we define the fair (k, r)-core as follows.

Definition 2 (Fair (k,r)-core). *Given an attributed undirected graph $G = (V, E, A)$, two positive integers k and r, and an induced subgraph $S \subseteq G$. S is a fair (k, r)-core of G, if it satisfies all the following constraints.*

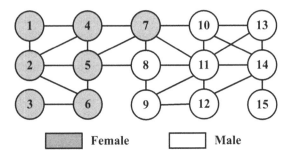

Fig. 1. Attributed Graph G

- *Degree: for $\forall v \in V_S$, $d_S(v) \geq k$.*
- *Fairness: for any two distinct attributes $a_i, a_j \in A$, the difference in the number of vertices with a_i and a_j in S is no larger than the threshold r, i.e., $|cnt_S(a_i) - cnt_S(a_j)| \leq r$.*
- *Maximal: any supergraph of S cannot be a fair (k,r)-core.*

In unattributed graphs, we can compute the k-core by iteratively removing the vertex that violates the degree constraint with time complexity with $O(m)$, where m represents the number of edges in the graph [10]. Besides, there exists a unique k-core subgraph for any given value of k for an unattributed graph. However, as shown in Theorem 1, multiple (k,r)-core subgraphs may exist in attributed graphs. In this paper, we are aiming to find the maximum (k,r)-core, i.e., the one with the largest vertices size.

Theorem 1. *Given an attributed graph $G = (V, E, A)$ and two positive integers k and r, there are multiple fair (k,r)-cores may existing in G.*

Proof. Consider the graph $G = (V, E, A)$ with $A = \{Male, Female\}$ in Fig. 1. Given $k = 3$ and $r = 1$, we can easily obtain a k-core S from the graph induced by $V_S = \{v_2, v_4, v_5, v_6, v_7, v_8, v_9, v_{10}, v_{11}, v_{12}, v_{13}, v_{14}\}$. However, S does not qualify as a fair (k,r)-core since it contains 5 vertices with the attribute $Female$ and 7 vertices with $Male$. By removing vertices with the attribute $Male$ from S, we can identify two distinct fair (k,r)-core subgraphs in G. These are the subgraph S_1 induced by $V_{S_1} = \{v_2, v_4, v_5, v_6, v_7, v_8, v_9, v_{10}, v_{11}, v_{12}, v_{14}\}$ with 5 vertices with $Female$ and 6 vertices with $Male$, and the subgraph S_2 induced by $V_{S_2} = \{v_2, v_4, v_5, v_6, v_7, v_8, v_{10}, v_{11}, v_{13}, v_{14}\}$ that involves 5 vertices with $Female$ and 5 vertices with $Male$. Therefore, the Theorem 1 holds.

Problem Statement. Given an attributed graph $G = (V, E, A)$ and two positive integers k and r, let F be the set of all fair (k,r)-cores in G. In this paper, we aim to develop efficient algorithms to identify the **maximum fair (k,r)-core** S^*, i.e., $|V_{S^*}| \geq |V_S|$ for any $S \in F$.

Problem Hardness. As shown in Theorem 2, the problem of maximum fair (k,r)-core identification is NP-hard.

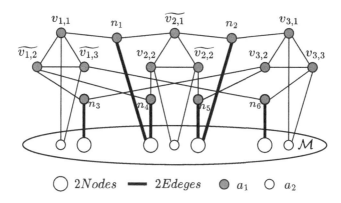

$\bigcirc$ 2Nodes   —— 2Edeges   ● a_1 ○ a_2

Fig. 2. Construction example for NP-hard proof, where $k = 3$, $b = 3$, $r = 0$. The attributed graph G is obtained from the 3-CNF formula $\psi = C_1 \wedge C_2 \wedge C_3$ with attributes set $\{a_1, a_2\}$, where $C_1 = (x_1 \vee \neg x_2 \vee \neg x_3)$, $C_2 = (\neg x_1 \vee x_2 \vee \neg x_2)$, $C_3 = (x_1 \vee x_2 \vee x_3)$.

Theorem 2. *Given an attributed graph $G = (V, E, A)$, two positive integers k and r, the maximum fair (k, r)-core identification is an NP-hard problem.*

Proof. When $k \geq 1$, we reduce the 3-CNF satisfiability problem, which is determining if a given boolean formula in 3-CNF can be satisfied, to our problem of finding the maximum fair k-core. Given a 3-CNF formula $\phi = C_1 \wedge C_2 \wedge \cdots \wedge C_b$, with b clauses, and each clause C_r containing three literals l_1^r, l_2^r and l_3^r. We construct an attributed graph G such that ϕ is satisfiable if and only if we can derive the maximum fair k-core from G. The construction procedure is as follows.

For each literal l_i^r, we create a vertex $v_{r,i}$ in G. We assign attributes a_1 to each vertex. We add a new co-neighbor vertex n_t between vertices $v_{r,i}$ and $v_{s,j}$ if the following conditions hold: (i) their corresponding literals are **complements**, that is, l_i^r is the negation of l_j^s, and (ii) $v_{r,i}$ and $v_{s,j}$ are in different triples, i.e., $r \neq s$. Suppose the set of co-neighbor vertices with attribute a_1 is denoted as $\mathcal{N}$, i.e., $\mathcal{N} = \{n_t | 1 \leq t \leq w \wedge attr(n_t) = a_1\}$. Besides, we construct a k-core $\mathcal{M}$ with $2b + w + r$ vertices and sign the attribute with a_2, i.e., $\mathcal{M} = \{m_t | 1 \leq t \leq (2b + w + r) \wedge attr(m_t) = a_2\}$. Then, we add $k - d_{G \backslash \mathcal{M}}(v)$ edges form each vertex v in $\mathcal{V} = \{v_{r,i} | 1 \leq r \leq b \wedge 1 \leq i \leq 3\}$ to $\mathcal{M}$ to make the degree of each vertex $v \in \mathcal{V}$ is $k + 1$. Meanwhile, adding $k - 1$ edges from each vertex $n_t \in \mathcal{N}$ to $\mathcal{M}$ to make its degree equals $k + 1$. Consequently, the construction is completed. Figure 2 is a construction example for $k = 3$, $b = 3$, and $r = 0$.

With the given construction, we guarantee the following property: (i) The removal of vertices in $\mathcal{V}$ and $\mathcal{N}$ will not alter $\mathcal{M}$; (ii) Eliminating v from $\mathcal{V}$ will only result in the removal of n_t, leaving other vertices unaffected; (iii) Vertex n_t will be deleted iff both its negation co-neighbors in $\mathcal{V}$ are also removed; (iv) The maximum fair k-cores correspond to the subgraphs formed by removing one vertex from each triangle in graph G. (v) To achieve the maximum fair k-core, it is sufficient to delete only one vertex from each triangle; otherwise, the resulting subgraph will not constitute a maximum fair k-core; (vi) Deleting all vertices in $\mathcal{V}$ will prevent the generated subgraph from being the maximum fair k-core. This outcome occurs because n_t will also be removed, reducing the size of the generated subgraph to less than $4b + 2w + r$.

Now, we show that this transformation of ϕ into G is a reduction. First, suppose that ϕ has a satisfying assignment. Then each clause C_r contains at least one literal l_i^r that is assigned 1, and each such literal corresponds to a vertex $v_{r,i}$. Picking one as 'true' literal from each clause yields a set V_d of b vertices. We claim that the subgraph induced by $\{V_G \backslash V_d\}$ is a maximum fair k-core. The degree constraint holds by construction, and the fairness constraint holds because there are no more differences between the number of vertices with different attributes.

Conversely, suppose that there exists a maximum fair k-core. Then we can find a set V_d containing one vertex from each triple. By construction, there will be a satisfying assignment to ϕ as each triple will contain at least one "true" corresponding to the vertices in V_d without fear of assigning "true" to both literal and its complement since V_d does not contain inconsistent literals. Otherwise, this subgraph is not the maximum fair k-core. Thus, each clause is satisfied, and ϕ is satisfied. Variables that do not correspond to any vertex in V_d could be set arbitrarily. Hence, the theorem holds.

3   Solution

Given the computational difficulty of the problem, we first present a greedy framework in this section, followed by various optimized techniques to accelerate the computation.

3.1   Greedy Framework

To find out the maximum fair (k, r)-core, one approach is to test different deletion sequences of vertices and select the one that results in the largest fair (k, r)-core. However, the enumeration space is vast. Due to the NP-hardness of this problem, in this paper, we utilize a greedy heuristic instead, which involves repeatedly eliminating the optimal vertex in each step and adjusting the graph according to the degree and fairness restrictions, until resulting in fair k-core subgraphs. The overall greedy process is illustrated in Algorithm 1.

The fairness difference constraint in the current graph G is defined in Line 2, and $Candidate(G)$ represents the set of candidate vertices marked for removal. Specifically, this includes vertices with attribute a_i, where the number of vertices associated with a_i is maximal. The overall search framework is outlined in Algorithm 1. Specific pruning and Fscore techniques can be added as mentioned. These additions serve to decrease the search space, manage the candidate vertices generation, and dictate the order in vertices deletion. In the sections as follow, we will detail the techniques needed to complete the algorithm. Within this greedy framework, we select the optimal vertex for removal and update the

---

Algorithm 1: Greedy Framework

Input: $G(V, E, A)$: attributed graph, k: degree constraint, r: fairness constraint

1 GraphReduction(G);
2 **while** $UnfairValue(G) = |cnt_G(a_i) - cnt_G(a_j)| > r,$ for $\forall a_i, a_j \in A$ **do**
3   **for** $v \in Candidate(G)$ **do**
4   **if** $UnfairValue(G) > UnfairValue(G \setminus v)$ **then**
5   calculate the Fscore(v);

6   select the optimal vertex v' based on its Fscore(v');
7   delete v' and maintain the G based on degree constraint;
8 **return** G;

---

graph G iteratively. In order to maintain the (k, r)-core of the result, other vertices may be excluded from the community due to degree and fairness constraints after each vertex deletion. Moreover, we only consider vertices that can decrease at least one UnfairValue(G).

3.2 Candidates Reduction and Score Function

Lemma 1. *Graph Structural Pruning (GSP)* *Given an attributed graph $G(V, E, A)$, the vertices of fair (k, r)-core of G must be contained in the vertices of the regular k-core of G.*

Proof. Let $C_k(G)$ denote the k-core of graph G. The subgraph $C_k(G)$ meets the degree constraints of the fair (k, r)-core and is maximal in nature. Consequently, any vertex belonging to the fair (k, r)-core must inherently be part of $C_k(G)$. Therefore, Lemma 1 holds.

Based on the Lemma 1, we can first shrink the search space to regular k-core $C_k(G)$ by iteratively removing all the vertices that do not satisfy the degree constraint until there are no more changes to the graph [25]. According to the Lemma 1, the problem of identifying the maximum fair (k, r)-core is equivalent to discovering a set of vertices $\mathcal{D}$ to be removed from $C_k(G)$, such that $C_k(G \setminus \mathcal{D})$ not only has largest vertices number but also satisfies the fairness constraint. Hence, we can diminish the search cost by confining the new candidate space, i.e., $Candidate(C_k(G)) = \{v \in V_{C_k(G)} | attr(v) = a_i \wedge |cnt_{C_k(G)}(a_i) - cnt_{C_k(G)}(a_j)| > r,$ for $\forall a_i, a_j \in A_{C_k(G)}\}$.

When a vertex v is eliminated, it may decrease the degree of its neighboring vertices and alter the overall fairness of the graph, leading to a set of vertices $\mathcal{F}$ being excluded from $C_k(G)$ due to degree and fairness constraints. We define the vertices set $\mathcal{F}$ as **followers** of v. Since we are aiming to identify the community with maximum size, the vertex with fewer followers is preferred to select in each iteration. Consequently, we formally define a score function as follows, named fairness-score, to facilitate this process.

Definition 3. (Fairness-score). *Given a regular k-core, $C_k(G)$. The fairness-score of a vertex $v \in V_{C_k(G)}$, denoted as $Fscore(v)$, is defined as the number of vertices in $C_k(G)$ removed after removing v from G, i.e.,*

$$Fscore(v) = |V_{C_k(G)}| - |V_{C_k(G \setminus \{v\})}| \tag{1}$$

To determine the set of followers of a vertex in a graph, we can examine its neighbors and eliminate the vertices based on the degree constraint. According to the definition, we should remove the optimal vertex with the minimal Fairness-score in each iteration. If a vertex has no followers, its Fscore is 1, which represents the minimum possible value.

3.3 Degree-Group Pruning

In Sect. 3.2, we optimize the searching cost trough limiting the candidate space and prioritizing the vertex with the smallest fairness-score for removal. To improve the efficiency further, we introduce the concept of the degree-group and explore its properties.

Definition 4. (degree-group). *Given the regular k-core $C_k(G)$, a subgraph g is a degree-group of $C_k(G)$, if i) for $\forall v \in g, d_g(v) = k$; ii)$g$ is a connected component.*

Lemma 2. *Given a degree-group g, the entire degree-group will be collapsed, if delete any vertex v from it. Since, $|V_g|$ is the lower bound of $Fscore(v)$.*

Proof. Based on the degree constraint, deleting any vertex will decrease the degree of its neighbors and the affected neighbors will be removed from $C_k(G)$. Since the vertices in g are interconnected, this process triggers a cascading effect where the degree of all other vertices is diminished by at least one. Ultimately, V_g will be eliminated from $C_k(G)$ and its vertices size represents a lower bound for $Fscore(v)$. Lemma 2 holds.

Our process for constructing degree-groups is detailed in Algorithm 2. Specifically, we only construct structures starting from the vertex in the candidate set (Line 2). Starting with an unvisited vertex v^* with the degree k (Line 3), we move on to its neighbors that share the same degree (Line 8). A degree-group formed from v^* is denoted as g_{v^*}. During traversal, all the connected vertices with the degree of k are added to group g_{v^*} (Lines 5–6). Then we initiate a new traversal from the next candidate vertex and expand it to generate a new degree-group within the graph.

According to Lemma 2, the degree-groups with the degree of k for candidate vertices can be constructed. To reduce the computation cost, the fairness-score of the entire group may be represented by calculating the score for any single vertex within the group. In following Lemma 3, we can further minimize the calculation cost for vertices that are part of distinct connected components.

Algorithm 2: Degree-group Construction

Input: $C_k(G)(V, E, A)$: k-core, k: degree constraint
Output: $\mathcal{G}$: degree-groups

1 $\mathcal{G} \leftarrow \{\}$; $visited \leftarrow \{\}$;
2 **for** $v^* \in Candidate(C_k(G))$ **do**
3   **if** $d_{C_k(G)}(v^*) = k \wedge v^* \notin visited$ **then**
4          $Q \leftarrow Q \cup \{v^*\}$; $visited \leftarrow visited \cup \{v^*\}$;
5   **while** $Q \neq \emptyset$ **do**
6          $v \leftarrow Q.pop()$; $g_{v^*} \leftarrow g_{v^*} \cup \{v\}$;
7   **for** $v_n \in N_{C_k(G)}(v)$ **do**
8   **if** $d_{C_k(G)}(v_n) = k \wedge v_n \notin visited$ **then**
9                  $Q \leftarrow Q \cup \{v_n\}$; $visited \leftarrow visited \cup \{v_n\}$;
10      $\mathcal{G} \leftarrow \mathcal{G} \cup \{g_{v^*}\}$;
11 **return** $\mathcal{G}$;

Lemma 3. *Consider the k-core $C_k(G)$ of G, which can be partitioned into a series of connected components denoted by $\{C_1, C_2, C_3, \ldots, C_i\}$. Removing a vertex v from a component C_i does not affect the fairness-score of vertices in any other component C_j, where $i \neq j$. Additionally, the vertex size of C_i serves as the upper bound for the fairness-score of all vertices $v \in V_{C_i}$.*

Proof. Given that C_i and C_j are disjoint, the elimination of any vertex from C_i has no impact on the degrees of vertices within C_j, where $i \neq j$. Moreover, the removal of any vertex from C_i could at most result in the entire component C_i being deleted from $C_k(G)$. Thus, Lemma 3 holds.

Based on Lemma 3, it is unnecessary to update the fairness-score for vertices contained within unaffected connected components, during the updating process after each deletion. Moreover, utilizing the upper and lower bounds established in the previous lemmas, allows us to bypass unpromising vertices readily.

3.4 FKC Algorithm

By incorporating the proposed pruning strategies and score function with greedy framework, we come up with the FKC algorithm. Given an attributed graph, we initially reduce the searching and candidate spaces according to Lemma 1. We then proceed to construct the degree-groups as delineated by Algorithm 2. Subsequently, we iteratively remove the vertex with the smallest fairness-score from the candidate set, while maintaining and updating the groups in accordance with the degree constraint based on Lemma 2–3. The algorithm terminates until the fairness constraint is satisfied.

Table 1. Statistics of the datasets

Dataset	Name	$n = |V|$	$m = |E|$	$degree_{max}$	Description
Slashdot1	**SL1**	77,358	468,554	2,537	Social network
Slashdot2	**SL2**	81,872	497,672	2,546	Social network
Epinions	**EP**	131,829	711,783	3,558	Social network
Facebook	**FB**	63,732	817,035	1,098	Social network
Themarker	**TM**	69,414	1,644,849	8,930	Social network
WikiTalk	**WT**	2,394,386	4,659,565	100,029	Communication network

4   Experiments

Algorithms. To the best of our knowledge, there is no existing work for the maximum fair (k, r)-core problem. In the experiments, we implement and evaluate the following algorithms.

- **Baseline.** In each iteration, we select a vertex with a vertex ID in increasing order from the candidate set $Candidate(C_k(G))$ by integrating Lemma 1.
- **FKC-.** This approach enhances the Baseline method by integrating the score function, as detailed in Sect. 3.2.
- **FKC.** This is our proposed optimized algorithm, as described in Sect. 3.4.

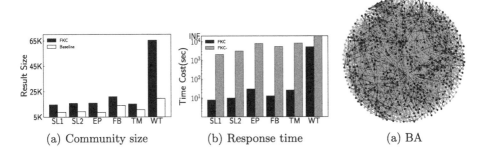

(a) Community size   (b) Response time   (a) BA

Fig. 3. Experiment results on all the datasets   **Fig. 4.** Case study

Datasets. We evaluated our algorithms on 6 real-world graphs. An overview of the datasets used in our experiments is provided in Table 1. WikiTalk represents a communication network, while Slashdot1, Slashdot2, Epinions, Facebook, and Themarker are all examples of social networks. The two Slashdot datasets are derived from the Slashdot platform, captured at distinct time periods. The datasets are public available[1]. Note that, all the datasets are non-attributed

---

[1] https://networkrepository.com/.

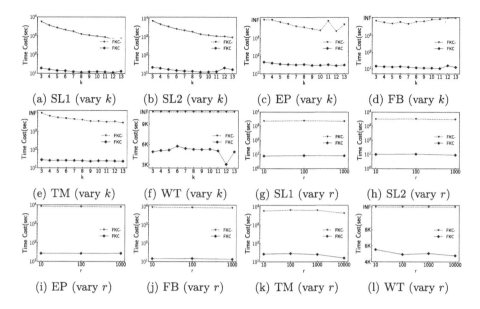

(a) SL1 (vary k)   (b) SL2 (vary k)   (c) EP (vary k)   (d) FB (vary k)

(e) TM (vary k)   (f) WT (vary k)   (g) SL1 (vary r)   (h) SL2 (vary r)

(i) EP (vary r)   (j) FB (vary r)   (k) TM (vary r)   (l) WT (vary r)

Fig. 5. Efficiency evaluation: response time when varying k and r

graphs, thus we randomly assign each vertex an attribute to generate attributed graphs for assessing the efficiency of our algorithms. All algorithms are implemented using C++. Since different datasets have various scales, the parameter r is set with varying integer values. For Themarker and WikiTalk, $r = 10^1, 10^2, 10^3$, and 10^4. For other datasets, $r = 10^1, 10^2$, and 10^3. The parameter k is chosen from the interval [3,13]. The default value for all datasets is $k = 5, r = 2$.

Efficiency Evaluation. To evaluate the efficiency of the proposed methods, we report the response time of FKC- and FKC on all the datasets. We denote the running time as **INF** if the algorithm cannot finish in 3 h. Figure 3(b) reports the response time for all the datasets. with the default setting. Additionally, we evaluate the efficiency when varying parameters k and r. The results, depicted in Figs. 5, clearly demonstrate that FKC significantly outperforms FKC- by a wide margin, with up to 800× speed up. This significant speed-up verifies the effectiveness of the pruning techniques employed. As k increases, the running time decrease for both algorithms, since the community size decreases correspondingly. It is also worth noting that, when k and the graph size are large, the FKC- method cannot finish in a reasonable time.

Effectiveness Evaluation. To evaluate the effectiveness of the proposed techniques, we first report the size of communities returned by the FKC algorithm compared with that of the Baseline algorithm. Figure 3(a) illustrates the outcomes across all datasets using the default configuration, while Fig. 6 indicates the results when varying parameters k and r. As observed, the FKC algorithm identifies significantly larger communities compared to the Baseline algorithm, owing to an effective node selection strategy. With an increase in the value of k,

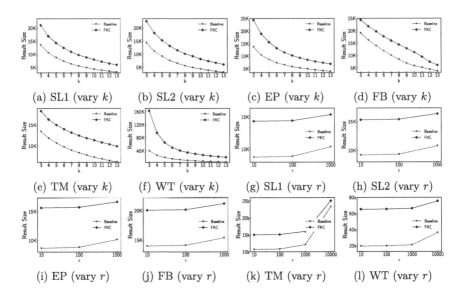

Fig. 6. Effectiveness evaluation: community size when varying k and r

the resulting community size diminishes, as a larger k imposes a more stringent cohesive structure constraint, thereby yielding smaller result communities. Similarly, as r increases, the size of the result increases, and the difference in the sizes of the result communities between Baseline and FKC diminishes. This is due to the fact that a larger r denotes a more relaxed fairness constraint, which consequently yields larger result communities.

Case Study. To further evaluate the advantages of our proposed model, we conduct a case study on Bitcoinalpha (see footnote 1) network (BA, $|E| = 14.1K$). As shown in Fig. 4, the whole graph is the k-core computed over the original graph. The subgraph induced by the vertices in blue is the maximum fair k-core. Whereas, the vertices in black is the unfair parts pruned by our algorithms. As observed, there are numerous unfair structures existing. Hence, disregarding the fairness of attributes is insufficient for accurately characterizing diverse communities and may lead to biases towards specific attributes.

5   Conclusion

In this paper, we conduct the first investigation into the problem of identifying core-based fair communities within attributed graphs and introducing a novel model, named fair k-core. We demonstrate that finding the maximum fair k-core is an NP-hard problem. To address this challenge, we have devised a greedy heuristic framework. To tackle this problem efficiently, score function and different pruning strategies are further proposed. Finally, we conduct extensive experiments over real-world attributed graphs to demonstrate the advantages of the proposed techniques.

References

1. Beutel, A., et al.: Fairness in recommendation ranking through pairwise comparisons. In: KDD, pp. 2212–2220 (2019)
2. Carmi, S., Church, B., Cohen, S., Havlin, S., Rutenberg, A.: A geographical k-core decomposition. EPL (Europhys. Lett.) **79**(2), 28005 (2007)
3. Chandola, V., Banerjee, A., Kumar, V.: Anomaly detection: a survey. ACM Comput. Surv. (CSUR) **41**(3), 1–58 (2009)
4. Chen, C., Wu, Y., Sun, R., Wang, X.: Maximum signed θ-clique identification in large signed graphs. IEEE Trans. Knowl. Data Eng. **35**, 1791–1802 (2021)
5. Chen, C., Zhang, M., Sun, R., Wang, X., Zhu, W., Wang, X.: Locating pivotal connections: the k-truss minimization and maximization problems. World Wide Web **25**(2), 899–926 (2022)
6. Chen, C., Zhu, Q., Sun, R., Wang, X., Wu, Y.: Edge manipulation approaches for k-core minimization: metrics and analytics. IEEE Trans. Knowl. Data Eng. **35**(1), 390–403 (2021)
7. Chierichetti, F., Kumar, R., Lattanzi, S., Vassilvitskii, S.: Fair clustering through fairlets. In: Advances in Neural Information Processing Systems, pp. 5029–5037 (2017)
8. Fang, Y., Cheng, C., Luo, S., Hu, J.: Effective community search for large attributed graphs. PVLDB (2016)
9. Khan, A., Golab, L., Kargar, M., Szlichta, J., Zihayat, M.: Compact group discovery in attributed graphs and social networks. Inf. Process. Manage. **57**(2), 102054 (2020)
10. Kong, Y.X., Shi, G.Y., Wu, R.J., Zhang, Y.C.: k-core: theories and applications. Phys. Rep. **832**, 1–32 (2019)
11. Li, Y., Sha, C., Huang, X., Zhang, Y.: Community detection in attributed graphs: an embedding approach. In: AAAI (2018)
12. Liu, Q., Zhu, Y., Zhao, M., Huang, X., Xu, J., Gao, Y.: VAC: vertex-centric attributed community search. In: ICDE, pp. 937–948 (2020)
13. Pan, M., Li, R.H., Zhang, Q., Dai, Y., Tian, Q., Wang, G.: Fairness-aware maximal clique enumeration. In: ICDE, pp. 259–271 (2022)
14. Sankar, G.S., Louis, A., Nasre, M., Nimbhorkar, P.: Matchings with group fairness constraints: online and offline algorithms. arXiv preprint arXiv:2105.09522 (2021)
15. Seidman, S.B.: Network structure and minimum degree. Soc. Netw. **5**(3), 269–287 (1983)
16. Sun, R., Chen, C., Wang, X., Wu, Y., Zhang, M., Liu, X.: The art of characterization in large networks: finding the critical attributes. World Wide Web **25**(2), 655–677 (2022)
17. Sun, R., Chen, C., Wang, X., Zhang, W., Zhang, Y., Lin, X.: Efficient maximum signed biclique identification. In: ICDE, pp. 1313–1325 (2023)
18. Sun, R., Wu, Y., Wang, X., Chen, C., Zhang, W., Lin, X.: Clique identification in signed graphs: a balance theory based model. IEEE Trans. Knowledge Data Eng. (2023)
19. Verma, S., Rubin, J.: Fairness definitions explained. In: Proceedings of the International Workshop on Software Fairness, pp. 1–7 (2018)
20. Wu, Y., Sun, R., Chen, C., Wang, X., Zhu, Q.: Maximum signed (k, r)-truss identification in signed networks. In: CIKM, pp. 3337–3340 (2020)
21. Wu, Y., Zhao, J., Sun, R., Chen, C., Wang, X.: Efficient personalized influential community search in large networks. Data Sci. Eng. **6**(3), 310–322 (2021)

22. Yao, S., Huang, B.: Beyond parity: fairness objectives for collaborative filtering. In: Advances in Neural Information Processing Systems, pp. 2921–2930 (2017)
23. Zehlike, M., Bonchi, F., Castillo, C., Hajian, S., Megahed, M., Baeza-Yates, R.: Fa* ir: A fair top-k ranking algorithm. In: CIKM, pp. 1569–1578 (2017)
24. Zhang, Q., Li, R.H., Pan, M., Dai, Y., Tian, Q., Wang, G.: Fairness-aware maximal clique in large graphs: concepts and algorithms. IEEE Trans. Knowl. Data Eng. **35**, 11368–11387 (2023)
25. Zhang, Y., Yu, J.X., Zhang, Y., Qin, L.: A fast order-based approach for core maintenance. In: ICDE, pp. 337–348 (2017)

IFGNN: An Individual Fairness Awareness Model for Missing Sensitive Information Graphs

Kejia Xu[1], Zeming Fei[2], Jianke Yu[2], Yu Kong[1], Xiaoyang Wang[1(✉)], and Wenjie Zhang[1]

[1] University of New South Wales, Sydney, NSW 2052, Australia
{kejia.xu,xiaoyang.wang1,wenjie.zhang}@unsw.edu.au,
yu.kong@student.unsw.edu.au
[2] University of Technology Sydney, Ultimo, NSW 2007, Australia
{zeming.fei,jianke.yu}@student.uts.edu.au

Abstract. Graph neural networks (GNNs) provide an approach for analyzing complicated graph data for node, edge, and graph-level prediction tasks. However, due to societal discrimination in real-world applications, the labels in datasets may have certain biases. This bias is magnified as GNNs iteratively obtain information from neighbourhoods through message passing and aggregation, generating unfair embeddings that implicitly affect the prediction results. In real-world datasets, missing sensitive attributes is common due to incomplete data collection and privacy concerns. However, research on the fairness of GNNs in incomplete graph data is limited and mainly focuses on group fairness. Addressing individual unfairness in GNNs when the sensitive attributes are missing remains unexplored. To solve this novel problem, we introduce a model named IFGNN, which leverages a GNN-based encoder and a decoder to generate node embeddings. Additionally, IFGNN adopts the Lipschitz condition to ensure individual fairness. Through comprehensive experiments on four real-world datasets compared with baseline models in node classification tasks, the results demonstrate that IFGNN can achieve individual fairness while maintaining high prediction accuracy.

Keywords: Individual fairness · Sensitive attribute · GNN

1 Introduction

Graph-structured data has been employed to represent real-world complex systems, such as social networks [32,33,36], financial networks [5,6], knowledge graphs [7], etc. GNNs have appeared as a solution for various downstream tasks, including node classification, link prediction, community detection, and graph search. GNNs provide an analytical approach to comprehend graph data [2,35]. For example, GNN-based recommender systems can personalize recommendations based on user preferences. The message-passing mechanism within GNNs

Z. Bao et al. (Eds.): ADC 2023, LNCS 14386, pp. 287–300, 2024.
https://doi.org/10.1007/978-3-031-47843-7_20

plays an important role in enabling its powerful learning ability, capturing and aggregating the graph structure and node attribute information to generate node embeddings [13].

However, the message-passing mechanism is prone to be influenced by sensitive attributes, resulting in biased representations for downstream tasks [1]. During the message-passing process, nodes incorporate neighbourhood information through diverse mechanisms, such as graph convolutional and attention mechanism [27,30]. Consequently, sensitive attributes (e.g., race, gender and age) from neighbour nodes are inherently included and amplified during the process, leading to bias within GNNs [3,28,37]. This bias becomes particularly concerning in high-risk decision-making and classification applications, as it can result in unfair implicit preferences towards privileged individuals, potentially leading to social discrimination [11,21,24]. For instance, if a particular age group has more positive labels in the dataset than other age groups, GNNs are inclined to produce positive predictions for individuals within that age group while ignoring the influence of other attributes.

To address the discrimination problem caused by sensitive attributes, researchers introduced the concepts of group fairness and individual fairness [24]. Group fairness ensures equal treatment across different demographic subgroups. For example, when considering different groups determined by race, the model should produce the same predictions for nodes within the same group [17]. On the other hand, individual fairness aims to mitigate the model's bias towards each individual and yield the same treatment to similar individuals [10,12]. Given that individual fairness imposes finer-grained constraints on the model, it is essential to consider how to minimize individual unfairness [34]. Particularly, when considering the missing sensitive attributes in graph data, individual fairness may be the only fairness criterion [37].

In many real-world applications, graphs usually suffer from missing information due to incomplete data collection and privacy concerns [4]. For instance, users may choose the 'prefer not to tell' option in social network applications, leading to missing sensitive attributes such as income and age. Existing research primarily falls into assuming that the graph data is complete without missing sensitive attributes or employing GNNs to predict the missing information [4,14,22]. FairGNN [9] is a notable model that utilizes an independent Graph Convolutional Networks (GCN) estimator to predict the limited missing sensitive attributes and subsequently evaluates the fairness of the node classification task. However, this approach of completing information may introduce noises and errors that significantly affect the model's accuracy and fairness [16,22]. While FairAC [14] mainly focuses on mitigating feature and topology-level unfairness by excluding sensitive features when the entire node attributes are missing. Although these two studies discuss the mitigation of GNNs fairness in an incomplete graph, they do not aim to solve the individual unfairness issue. Thus, they cannot be treated as baselines. To our best knowledge, no research has focused on individual fairness without constraining the number of missing sensitive attributes.

In this paper, our focus lies in ensuring the model's individual fairness while preserving the prediction accuracy without predicting the missing sensitive attributes, especially under various rates of missing sensitive attributes. To address this problem, we propose a novel GNN-based model named Individual Fairness Graph Neural Network (IFGNN). The IFGNN model incorporates the Lipschitz condition, a well-established and widely used mathematical approach for achieving individual fairness [18]. Unlike existing works, we introduce a GNN-based encoder and a decoder that obtain the latent neighbourhood information to generate node embeddings, thereby solving the issue of missing sensitive information.

Contributions. The main contributions of this paper are shown as follows.

- We present a novel problem of addressing individual unfairness and ensuring prediction performance for graph data with unlimited missing sensitive attributes.
- We propose a GNN-based encoder and a decoder with Lipschitz constraint model IFGNN, to solve the problem without predicting the missing information.
- Our proposed model outperforms baseline models regarding individual fairness and prediction accuracy on four real-world datasets.

Roadmap. The rest of the paper is organized as follows. In Sect. 2, we give a comprehensive overview of existing related work. In Sect. 3, we introduce the preliminaries and the formal problem definition. In Sect. 4, we present the details of our proposed model IFGNN. In Sect. 5, we conduct comparative experiments and the ablation study and conclude the paper in Sect. 6.

2   Related Work

In this section, we introduce the related works of fairness within graph data. Specifically, we introduce approaches dealing with incomplete graph data. Approaches to promote fairness can be categorized into three strategies: pre-processing, in-processing and post-processing. In the pre-processing phase, biased attributes within the original dataset are explicitly modified or fair node embeddings are directly introduced [8]. For instance, Rahman et al.'s Fairwalk framework [26] employs node2vec to generate fair node embeddings through a fairness-aware embedding method. In the in-processing phase, fairness is maintained by integrating fairness constraint objective functions into the model [39]. Zhang et al. proposed an adversarial learning framework [41], which balances the model's fairness by optimizing the prediction function while weakening the adversary function. The post-processing phase is processed after the model's execution, alleviating the discrimination found in the output embedding [17]. In the work of Masrour et al. [23], a dyadic-level fairness criterion was introduced, generating supplementary links to mitigate the problem of Internet users receiving excessively sensitive-attributes-dominated information.

These three strategies encompass both conventional and GNN-based approaches. Among conventional approaches, Zemel et al.'s framework [40] achieves bias-reduced data encoding by obfuscating non-sensitive attributes of individuals. Another conventional technique is the ifair framework [20], which maps personal attributes to low-rank representation while ensuring data integrity. In recent years, GNNs have experienced significant development [31,42,43]. A representative GNN-based technique is the GFairHint model [37], which generates fairness awareness graph data by determining if two nodes are similar and employs GNNs to generate fair node embeddings.

Inspired by the fairness research within non-graph data, introducing the Lipschitz condition as a fairness constraint is a common strategy in existing research [12]. A representative framework that employs Lipschitz conditions to solve fairness is InFoRM [18]. Furthermore, the GUIDE model [28], a GNN-based model that considers both individual and group fairness, achieves individual fairness in subgroups by minimizing the Lipschitz constant.

Fairness research within incomplete graphs remains limited. The most relevant to our work is the FairGNN mentioned above [9]. FairGNN uses a sensitive attribute estimator to predict the missing sensitive attributes and introduces it into adversarial learning to generate fair node embeddings [9]. However, FairGNN is only applicable when the number of missing sensitive attributes is limited, and it is designed to ensure group fairness instead of individual fairness [9]. It is worth considering that predicting sensitive attributes may not only affect the model performance but also violate privacy policies [16,22]. In contrast, our model effectively addresses the individual unfairness problem in incomplete graphs without having to know users' hidden sensitive attributes, and it remains unaffected by the number of missing sensitive attributes. Therefore, our proposed model has broader applicability for solving real-world problems.

3   Preliminaries

Let $\mathcal{G} = (\mathcal{V}, \mathcal{E}, \mathcal{X})$ denote an undirected attributed graph, where $\mathcal{V} = \{v_1, v_2, \ldots, v_N\}$ is the set of N nodes. For each node $v \in \mathcal{V}$, it is associated with a set of M attributes $\{x_v^1, x_v^2, \ldots, x_v^M\}$. Following the general setting, among the attributes, one attribute $x_s \in \{0, 1\}$ is considered as the sensitive attribute. We use $\mathcal{V}_S \subseteq \mathcal{V}$ to denote the set of nodes with the missing sensitive attribute. r_s is the missing proportion, which is the ratio of the number of nodes in $\mathcal{V}_S$ to that in $\mathcal{V}$. $\mathcal{E} \subseteq \mathcal{V} \times \mathcal{V}$ is the set of edges and $\mathcal{X} \in \mathbb{R}^{N \times M}$ is the node attribute matrix where M is the dimension of attributes. The value of the matrix $S \in \mathbb{R}^{N \times N}$ represents the cosine similarity between input feature vectors of pairs of nodes. $\mathcal{Y} = \{y_1, y_2, \ldots, y_N\}$ denotes the node labels where $y_N \in \{0, 1\}$.

Problem Statement. Given a graph $\mathcal{G} = (\mathcal{V}, \mathcal{E}, \mathcal{X})$ with the sensitive attribute x_s, which includes missing values, in this paper, we aim to learn a fair model f for node label prediction. It can be formulated as follows:

$$f(\mathcal{G}, x_s) \to \hat{\mathcal{Y}}. \tag{1}$$

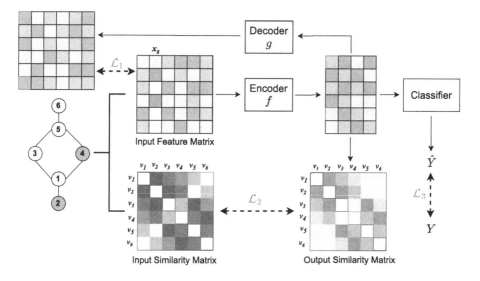

Fig. 1. The overview of the proposed IFGNN.

4 Proposed Model

We propose to solve the problem with a node representation learning model IFGNN. Figure 1 shows the general framework of our proposed model, which consists of a GNN-based encoder, a multi-layer perceptron (MLP) decoder, an individual fairness mechanism and a label classifier. The encoder generates node embeddings, while the decoder assists the encoder in learning more expressive node embeddings. The fairness mechanism addresses unfairness issues by minimizing the distance between the input pairwise similarity matrix and the output pairwise similarity matrix.

4.1 Encoder and Decoder

Figure 1 shows an example of an incomplete graph with missing sensitive attribute x_s. For demonstration, we intentionally set the rate of missing sensitive attributes r_s to 0.5. In the example graph, nodes v_3, v_5 and v_6 have missing sensitive attributes, while the sensitive attributes ($x_s \in \{0, 1\}$) of other nodes are represented by distinct colours. Intuitively, when there are missing node attributes, an estimator can be deployed to predict the missing information.

However, utilizing a GNN-based estimator for completing the node information might result in the amplification of error and noise in the subsequent operations (e.g., fairness-aware processing). To prevent this issue, it is imperative to leverage the characteristic of the message-passing mechanism in GNNs, which enables the information aggregation from neighbour nodes to generate node embeddings [38]. The missing sensitive information including the latent structural information will be implicitly compensated [16]. The GNN-based encoder

f takes the original informative node feature matrix denoted by $\mathcal{X} \in \mathbb{R}^{N \times M}$. For each node v, the embedding at the l-th layer will be:

$$h_v^l = Combine(h_v^{l-1}, Aggregate(h_u^l, \forall u \in \mathcal{N}(v))), \tag{2}$$

where h_v^l is the output embedding of node v at l-th layer and $\mathcal{N}(v)$ denotes the set of neighbour nodes of node v. The $Aggreagte(\cdot)$ operation iteratively aggregates and obtains the embeddings of neighbour nodes and the $Combine(.,.)$ operation combines the updated embedding of neighbour node u with the own embedding of node v from the previous layer.

The GNN-based encoder will generate the output embedding matrix H = $f(\mathcal{X})$, where $H \in \mathbb{R}^{N \times d}$. It is important to note that any model with GNN as a backbone, such as GCN and Graph Attention Networks (GAT), can be utilized as an encoder.

We employ the MLP with a nonlinear activation layer as the decoder g. The output of the decoder is defined as $\mathcal{X}' = g(H)$. $\mathcal{X}'$ is the reconstructed attribute matrix, where $\mathcal{X}' \in \mathbb{R}^{N \times M}$. The encoder and decoder are trained to minimize the following:

$$\mathcal{L}_1 = \frac{1}{N}(\mathcal{X}' - \mathcal{X})^2, \tag{3}$$

By minimizing the difference between $\mathcal{X}'$ and $\mathcal{X}$, the model is enabled to re-utilize the input feature matrix during the training process. The Eq. (3) not only helps the encoder obtain more representative node feature embeddings but also improves the overall training stability, thereby strengthening the robustness of the entire model.

4.2 Fairness Mechanism

To achieve individual fair node embeddings within the encoder, we adopted the Lipschitz condition. It is initially proposed by [12], indicating that any two similar individuals should receive the same outputs.

Definition 1. *Given any pair of nodes v_i and v_j, Lipschitz constraint ϵ_{ij} restricts the output distance between v_i and v_j by:*

$$D_{out}(f(v_i), f(v_j)) \leq \epsilon_{ij} \cdot D_{in}(v_i, v_j), \forall v_i, v_j \in \mathcal{V}, \tag{4}$$

where $D_{out}(.,.)$ denotes the output similarity distance of a pair of nodes, $D_{in}(.,.)$ denotes the input similarity distance.

The intention is that a model constrained by the Lipschitz condition will assign a smaller output similarity distance to any pair of nodes with a higher input similarity, aiming to treat similar node pairs equally, even in the existence of sensitive attributes. The Eq. (4) in Definition 1 can be written as follows:

$$D_{out}(f(v_i), f(v_j)) \cdot \frac{1}{D_{in}(v_i, v_j)} \leq \epsilon_{ij}, \forall v_i, v_j \in \mathcal{V}. \tag{5}$$

Given the input similarity distance of all node pairs, the sum of the total output similarity distance is minimized by minimizing the sum of ϵ_{ij} of all node pairs. Therefore, we propose to enhance the model's fairness awareness that minimizes:

$$\mathcal{L}_2 = \sum_{v_i \in \mathcal{V}} \sum_{v_j \in \mathcal{V}} \cos(\mathrm{H}[i,:], \mathrm{H}[j,:]) S[i:j], \tag{6}$$

where $\mathrm{H}[i,:]$ and $\mathrm{H}[j,:]$ is the encoder output node embeddings for node v_i and v_j, $S[i,j]$ is the corresponding similarity value in the input feature similarity matrix S, and $\cos(.,.)$ denotes the cosine similarity distance of the node pair. Note that any differentiable similarity metric can be used for similarity calculation. We employ cosine similarity for its efficiency in evaluation [25]. Training the encoder with the objective function $\mathcal{L}_2$, we can achieve the goal of tackling unfairness in the model, as it minimizes the sum of the Lipschitz constraint ϵ_{ij}.

4.3 Node Classifier

The node classifier consists of an MLP layer and a nonlinear activation layer. It takes the node attribute embedding matrix H as the input, which is generated by the encoder and mitigated unfairness by $\mathcal{L}_2$, to predict the node labels $\hat{y}$. The output of the MLP layer will be:

$$\hat{y}_v = \sigma(W h_v + b). \tag{7}$$

Here, we use binary cross-entropy with logits loss, which implicitly applies the nonlinear activation function, as the objective function for the classifier. It should be noted that the threshold τ should be set to obtain the label of each node. The objective function of the classifier is to minimize:

$$\mathcal{L}_3 = -[y_v \cdot log\hat{y}_v + (1 - y_v) \cdot log(1 - \hat{y}_v)], \tag{8}$$

where y_v is the label of node v and σ is the sigmoid function.

4.4 IFGNN Learning Objective

To train IFGNN, the final learning objective is to minimize:

$$\mathcal{L} = \lambda_1 \mathcal{L}_1 + \lambda_2 \mathcal{L}_2 + \lambda_3 \mathcal{L}_3, \tag{9}$$

where λ_1, λ_2 and λ_3 are hyperparameters and the sum of them is 1. Given that the $\mathcal{L}_3$ function is the primary loss function, while $\mathcal{L}_1$ and $\mathcal{L}_2$ are employed as auxiliary assurance for accuracy and individual fairness in the node classification task, we judiciously decrease the weights of $\mathcal{L}_1$ and $\mathcal{L}_2$ to mitigate the risk of overfitting without dampening the influence of $\mathcal{L}_3$.

By minimizing the overall objective function, IFGNN is optimized to generate node embeddings that capture the latent information with the missing sensitive attribute and deal with individual unfairness.

Table 1. Experiment results when the missing rate of the sensitive attribute is 0.3.

Dataset	Metrics	IFGNN	GCN	GAT	GraphSAGE
Credit	ACC($\uparrow$)	**0.7992**	0.7939	0.7772	0.7868
	AUC($\uparrow$)	0.7297	**0.7331**	0.6967	0.7077
	IUF ($\downarrow$)	**0.0043**	0.0600	0.0739	0.0443
German	ACC($\uparrow$)	**0.7360**	0.6760	0.7200	0.7000
	AUC($\uparrow$)	0.6674	0.6257	0.6569	**0.6753**
	IUF ($\downarrow$)	**0.0120**	0.0560	0.6398	0.0560
Income	ACC($\uparrow$)	**0.8325**	0.8122	0.7928	0.8214
	AUC($\uparrow$)	**0.8520**	0.7891	0.7778	0.8288
	IUF ($\downarrow$)	**0.0084**	0.0267	0.0302	0.0340
Recidivism	ACC($\uparrow$)	**0.7722**	0.7449	0.7315	0.7353
	AUC($\uparrow$)	**0.8692**	0.8328	0.8470	0.8231
	IUF ($\downarrow$)	**0.0182**	0.0481	0.0619	0.0612

5   Experiments

In this section, we conduct experiments on four real-world graph datasets to evaluate the performance of our proposed IFGNN. We aim to answer the following research questions:

- **RQ1** Compared to several baseline models, can the proposed IFGNN maintains the best individual fairness and prediction accuracy under different sensitive attribute missing rates?
- **RQ2** How well the GNN-based encoder and the encoder affect the prediction accuracy of the proposed IFGNN?
- **RQ3** Can the fairness mechanism help tackle individual unfairness in the IFGNN?

5.1   Experimental Setup

In our experimental setup, we implemented the random data split, taking 50% for the training set, 25% for the validation set, and the remaining 25% for the test set. We set the threshold $\tau = 0.5$. The proposed IFGNN is compared with three baseline models on datasets with different rates of the missing sensitive attribute. For each dataset, we set three missing rate values r_s as 0.3, 0.5 and 0.7, to simulate real-world scenarios where sensitive attributes are missing. We randomly select $|r_s N|$ nodes from the dataset and set the corresponding sensitive attribute value to –1. To reduce the training time for large datasets and demonstrate the utility of the fairness mechanism in addressing individual unfairness, we sampled only 20% of the nodes from the training set to participate in the process outlined in Eq. (6), such as the generation of node pair-wise similarity matrices.

Table 2. Experiment results when the missing rate of the sensitive attribute is 0.5.

Dataset	Metrics	IFGNN	GCN	GAT	GraphSAGE
Credit	ACC(↑)	**0.7992**	0.7904	0.7765	0.7856
	AUC(↑)	**0.7381**	0.7162	0.7057	0.7095
	IUF (↓)	**0.0031**	0.0372	0.0407	0.0425
German	ACC(↑)	**0.7280**	0.6680	0.7240	0.6720
	AUC(↑)	**0.6520**	0.6249	0.6398	0.6317
	IUF (↓)	**0.0180**	0.0600	0.0480	0.0520
Income	ACC(↑)	**0.8281**	0.8160	0.7976	0.8170
	AUC(↑)	**0.8511**	0.8265	0.7776	0.8274
	IUF (↓)	**0.0108**	0.0208	0.0240	0.0379
Recidivism	ACC(↑)	**0.7703**	0.7391	0.7052	0.7347
	AUC(↑)	0.8719	0.8564	**0.8812**	0.8275
	IUF (↓)	**0.0125**	0.0320	0.0521	0.0562

Datasets. The datasets including Credit Defaulter (Credit), German Credit (German), Income and Recidivism. The summaries of dataset details are presented as follows:

- Credit. The Credit dataset is comprised of 3,000 nodes, each representing individuals who are using credit card payments. There are 13 attributes for each node, including education level and other bills and payments-related features. The classification task is to predict whether an individual will choose to set a credit card as the default payment method for the next month, considering age as the sensitive attribute.
- German. The German dataset is constructed on 1,000 nodes, where each node represents individuals who are customers of a German bank. Individuals are described with the 30 attributes, such as employment statement, loan amounts and the number of loans. The gender attribute is considered a sensitive attribute. The classification task is to determine whether an individual is a creditworthy customer based on all attributes.
- Income. The Income dataset consists of 14,821 nodes, where each node represents a person with income. There are 14 attributes for each node, and we choose race as the sensitive attribute. Other attributes include working hours per week and work classes. The task is to predict if the income of an individual is over $50,000 annually.
- Recidivism. The Recidivism dataset has 18,876 nodes, each representing a defendant who got released on bail during 1990–2009 [21]. There are 18 attributes for each node, such as age, education level and marital status. The task is to determine if a defendant would receive bail based on all attributes of the defendant. The sensitive attribute used here is race.

Table 3. Experiment results when the missing rate of the sensitive attribute is 0.7.

Dataset	Metrics	IFGNN	GCN	GAT	GraphSAGE
Credit	ACC(↑)	**0.7992**	0.7904	0.7765	0.7648
	AUC(↑)	**0.7992**	0.7236	0.6775	0.7200
	IUF (↓)	**0.0023**	0.0312	0.0360	0.0275
German	ACC(↑)	0.7230	0.6960	**0.7360**	0.7040
	AUC(↑)	0.6498	0.6316	0.6515	**0.6746**
	IUF (↓)	**0.0080**	0.0480	0.0320	0.0440
Income	ACC(↑)	**0.8230**	0.8133	0.7955	0.8194
	AUC(↑)	**0.8468**	0.7902	0.7616	0.8177
	IUF (↓)	**0.0067**	0.0197	0.0189	0.0351
Recidivism	ACC(↑)	**0.7654**	0.7179	0.7004	0.7417
	AUC(↑)	**0.8716**	0.8424	0.8622	0.7926
	IUF (↓)	**0.0119**	0.0301	0.0403	0.0430

Evaluation Metrics. The model will be evaluated on utility (node classification performance) and individual fairness performance. The evaluation metrics are presented as follows.

- Utility. For evaluating the model's utility in node classification tasks, we employed widely used metrics: Accuracy (ACC) and AUCROC (AUC) scores.
- Individual fairness. An individual fairness awareness model should not be affected by the sensitive attribute and generate the same predictions for similar nodes, as highlighted by Dwork et al. [12]. Building upon this concept, we introduce a novel metric termed Individual Fairness (IUF), designed to measure individual fairness. In cases where the sensitive attribute is not considered, node predictions depend only on non-sensitive attributes. Consequently, the model should produce the same predictions for nodes with similar non-sensitive attributes. Therefore, when the sensitive attribute is considered, a model with individual fairness should yield predictions the same as those generated by the model that do not consider the sensitive attribute. IUF aims to quantify the inconsistency between predictions in these two cases. A lower IUF value implies enhanced individual fairness in the model.

Baseline. To our best knowledge, there is no research focusing on individual fairness in graph data with missing sensitive attributes, the proposed IFGNN is compared against three baseline models: GCN [19], GAT [29] and GraphSAGE [15].

5.2 Performances and Discussions

To solve **RQ1**, we conduct experiments under different r_s: 0.3, 0.5, and 0.7, to compare the performance of the proposed IFGNN with three baseline models.

The results of these experiments are presented in Table 1, 2, and 3. The results reveal that variations in r_s do not affect the effectiveness of the proposed IFGNN in maintaining individual fairness, as it consistently outperforms the baseline models significantly.

Moreover, the proposed IFGNN shows superior performance in terms of both ACC and AUC compared to the three baseline models in most cases. This observation indicates that the encoder and decoder enable the model to learn more representative node embeddings. It is worth noting that when the dataset contains a small number of nodes, such as the German dataset, the ACC and AUC of all the compared models are generally lower, including the proposed IFGNN. This can be attributed to the insufficient information in the dataset, which makes it a challenge for models to learn sufficient feature representations. However, the proposed decoder assists the encoder in enhancing feature learning, thereby leading to higher ACC and AUC for the proposed IFGNN compared to the baseline models. Although in rare cases, the three baseline models slightly outperform the proposed IFGNN in terms of ACC and AUC, they show severe individual discrimination at the same time. It indicates that the proposed IFGNN effectively addresses individual unfairness while maintaining satisfactory utility performance.

As for the baseline models, we observed that they do not show remarkable differences in terms of ACC and AUC. It implies that the aggregation processes among GCN, GAT and GraphSAGE do not significantly impact the utility performance in the node classification task. Therefore, the encoder in the proposed IFGNN can be replaced with any model using GNN as a backbone.

Table 4. Experiment results in the ablation study of IFGNN.

	Metrics	Credit	German	Income	Recidivism
IFGNN w/o $\mathcal{L}_1$	ACC (↑)	0.7756	0.7320	0.8200	0.7300
	AUC (↑)	0.7129	0.6352	0.8362	0.8326
	IUF (↓)	0.0131	0.0120	0.0121	0.0303
IFGNN w/o $\mathcal{L}_2$	ACC (↑)	0.7785	**0.7360**	0.8214	0.7196
	AUC (↑)	0.7131	0.6472	0.8392	0.8382
	IUF (↓)	0.0200	0.0160	0.0167	0.0476
IFGNN	ACC (↑)	**0.7992**	**0.7360**	**0.8325**	**0.7722**
	AUC (↑)	**0.7297**	**0.6674**	**0.8520**	**0.8692**
	IUF (↓)	**0.0043**	**0.0120**	**0.0084**	**0.0182**

5.3 Ablation Study

In this section, we aim to answer **RQ2** and **RQ3** on how the encoder, decoder and fairness mechanism affect the performance of IFGNN. In ablation experiments, we set the missing sensitive attribute rate to 0.3 for the four datasets. We explore the performance under two cases by excluding the objective functions: $\mathcal{L}_1$ and $\mathcal{L}_2$, respectively. These cases are denoted as IFGNN w/o $\mathcal{L}_1$ and IFGNN w/o $\mathcal{L}_2$. The results of the experiments are presented in Table 4.

When the IFGNN is without the learning objective function $\mathcal{L}_1$, the model does not employ the encoder and decoder to learn node feature embeddings for the node classification task. The ACC and AUC, which are used to evaluate the performance of the binary classification model, become unsatisfactory compared to the results of IFGNN w/o $\mathcal{L}_2$ and the IFGNN model. The encoder and decoder are employed to gather information from neighbourhoods, thereby alleviating the effect of missing sensitive attributes. The unsatisfactory prediction performance indicates that the IFGNN w/o $\mathcal{L}_1$ model loses the ability to obtain sufficient structure and node attribute information on the graph to generate representative node embeddings. In contrast, IFGNN achieves the highest utility performance with the help of $\mathcal{L}_1$.

When the IFGNN is without the learning objective function $\mathcal{L}_2$, the model does not under the constraint of the Lipschitz condition. As a result, the model can only produce biased results using the encoder, decoder, and node classifier, leading to higher IUF values compared to the results of IFGNN w/o $\mathcal{L}_1$ and the IFGNN model. While IFGNN consistently achieves the lowest IUF values across all four datasets. It indicates the superiority of our overall learning objective of IFGNN, which effectively enhances the model's individual fairness awareness.

6 Conclusion

In this paper, we study a novel problem of maintaining individual fairness while ensuring prediction performance in graph data with unlimited missing sensitive attributes. To solve this problem, we propose a novel model IFGNN which incorporates a GNN-based encoder and a decoder for learning node feature embeddings when the sensitive attribute is missing. To address the individual unfairness within IFGNN, we employ the Lipschitz condition that helps mitigate the discrimination caused by the sensitive attribute. We conduct extensive experiments on four real-world datasets to demonstrate that IFGNN outperforms the baseline models in terms of enhancing individual fairness awareness and prediction accuracy.

References

1. Agarwal, C., Lakkaraju, H., Zitnik, M.: Towards a unified framework for fair and stable graph representation learning. In: Uncertainty in Artificial Intelligence, pp. 2114–2124. PMLR (2021)
2. Awasthi, A., Garov, A.K., Sharma, M., Sinha, M.: GNN model based on node classification forecasting in social network. In: AISC, pp. 1039–1043 (2023)
3. Beutel, A., Chen, J., Zhao, Z., Chi, E.H.: Data decisions and theoretical implications when adversarially learning fair representations. arXiv preprint arXiv:1707.00075 (2017)

4. Chen, X., Chen, S., Yao, J., Zheng, H., Zhang, Y., Tsang, I.W.: Learning on attribute-missing graphs. IEEE Trans. Pattern Anal. Mach. Intell. **44**(2), 740–757 (2020)
5. Cheng, D., Chen, C., Wang, X., Xiang, S.: Efficient top-k vulnerable nodes detection in uncertain graphs. IEEE Trans. Knowl. Data Eng. (2021)
6. Cheng, D., Wang, X., Zhang, Y., Zhang, L.: Risk guarantee prediction in networked-loans. In: IJCAI (2020)
7. Cheng, D., Yang, F., Wang, X., Zhang, Y., Zhang, L.: Knowledge graph-based event embedding framework for financial quantitative investments. In: SIGIR, pp. 2221–2230 (2020)
8. Choudhary, M., Laclau, C., Largeron, C.: A survey on fairness for machine learning on graphs. arXiv preprint arXiv:2205.05396 (2022)
9. Dai, E., Wang, S.: Say no to the discrimination: learning fair graph neural networks with limited sensitive attribute information. In: WSDM, pp. 680–688 (2021)
10. Dong, Y., Kang, J., Tong, H., Li, J.: Individual fairness for graph neural networks: a ranking based approach. In: KDD, pp. 300–310 (2021)
11. Du, M., Yang, F., Zou, N., Hu, X.: Fairness in deep learning: a computational perspective. IEEE Intell. Syst. **36**(4), 25–34 (2020)
12. Dwork, C., Hardt, M., Pitassi, T., Reingold, O., Zemel, R.: Fairness through awareness. In: Proceedings of the 3rd Innovations in Theoretical Computer Science Conference, pp. 214–226 (2012)
13. Gilmer, J., Schoenholz, S.S., Riley, P.F., Vinyals, O., Dahl, G.E.: Neural message passing for quantum chemistry. In: International Conference on Machine Learning, pp. 1263–1272. PMLR (2017)
14. Guo, D., Chu, Z., Li, S.: Fair attribute completion on graph with missing attributes. arXiv preprint arXiv:2302.12977 (2023)
15. Hamilton, W., Ying, Z., Leskovec, J.: Inductive representation learning on large graphs. Adv. Neural Inf. Process. Syst. **30** (2017)
16. Hao, Y., Cao, X., Sheng, Y., Fang, Y., Wang, W.: KS-GNN: keywords search over incomplete graphs via graphs neural network. Adv. Neural Inf. Process. Syst. **34**, 1700–1712 (2021)
17. Hardt, M., Price, E., Srebro, N.: Equality of opportunity in supervised learning. Adv. Neural Inf. Process. Syst. **29** (2016)
18. Kang, J., He, J., Maciejewski, R., Tong, H.: Inform: individual fairness on graph mining. In: KDD, pp. 379–389 (2020)
19. Kipf, T.N., Welling, M.: Semi-supervised classification with graph convolutional networks. arXiv preprint arXiv:1609.02907 (2016)
20. Lahoti, P., Gummadi, K.P., Weikum, G.: iFair: learning individually fair data representations for algorithmic decision making. In: ICDE, pp. 1334–1345 (2019)
21. Loveland, D., Pan, J., Bhathena, A.F., Lu, Y.: Fairedit: preserving fairness in graph neural networks through greedy graph editing. arXiv preprint arXiv:2201.03681 (2022)
22. Mansoor, H., Ali, S., Alam, S., Khan, M.A., Hassan, U.U., Khan, I.: Impact of missing data imputation on the fairness and accuracy of graph node classifiers. In: IEEE International Conference on Big Data (Big Data), pp. 5988–5997 (2022)
23. Masrour, F., Wilson, T., Yan, H., Tan, P.N., Esfahanian, A.: Bursting the filter bubble: fairness-aware network link prediction. In: AAAI, vol. 34, pp. 841–848 (2020)
24. Mehrabi, N., Morstatter, F., Saxena, N., Lerman, K., Galstyan, A.: A survey on bias and fairness in machine learning. ACM Comput. Surv. (CSUR) **54**(6), 1–35 (2021)

25. Pieterse, J., Mocanu, D.C.: Evolving and understanding sparse deep neural networks using cosine similarity. arXiv preprint arXiv:1903.07138 (2019)
26. Rahman, T., Surma, B., Backes, M., Zhang, Y.: Fairwalk: towards fair graph embedding (2019)
27. Sarkar, D., Roy, S., Malakar, S., Sarkar, R.: A modified GNN architecture with enhanced aggregator and message passing functions. Eng. Appl. Artif. Intell. **122**, 106077 (2023)
28. Song, W., Dong, Y., Liu, N., Li, J.: GUIDE: group equality informed individual fairness in graph neural networks. In: KDD, pp. 1625–1634 (2022)
29. Veličković, P., Cucurull, G., Casanova, A., Romero, A., Lio, P., Bengio, Y.: Graph attention networks. arXiv preprint arXiv:1710.10903 (2017)
30. Velickovic, P., Cucurull, G., Casanova, A., Romero, A., Lio, P., Bengio, Y., et al.: Graph attention networks. Stat **1050**(20), 10–48550 (2017)
31. Wang, H., Yu, J., Wang, X., Chen, C., Zhang, W., Lin, X.: Neural similarity search on supergraph containment. IEEE Trans. Knowl. Data Eng. (2023)
32. Wang, X., Zhang, Y., Zhang, W., Lin, X.: Efficient distance-aware influence maximization in geo-social networks. IEEE Trans. Knowl. Data Eng. **29**(3), 599–612 (2016)
33. Wang, X., Zhang, Y., Zhang, W., Lin, X., Chen, C.: Bring order into the samples: a novel scalable method for influence maximization. IEEE Trans. Knowl. Data Eng. **29**(2), 243–256 (2016)
34. Wang, X., Gu, T., Bao, X., Chang, L., Li, L.: Individual fairness for local private graph neural network. Knowl.-Based Syst. **268**, 110490 (2023)
35. Wu, W., Li, B., Luo, C., Nejdl, W.: Hashing-accelerated graph neural networks for link prediction. In: Proceedings of the Web Conference 2021, pp. 2910–2920 (2021)
36. Wu, Y., Zhao, J., Sun, R., Chen, C., Wang, X.: Efficient personalized influential community search in large networks. Data Sci. Eng. **6**(3), 310–322 (2021)
37. Xu, P., Zhou, Y., An, B., Ai, W., Huang, F.: GFairHint: improving individual fairness for graph neural networks via fairness hint. arXiv preprint arXiv:2305.15622 (2023)
38. Yu, J., et al.: Group-based fraud detection network on e-commerce platforms. In: KDD, pp. 5463–5475 (2023)
39. Zafar, M.B., Valera, I., Rogriguez, M.G., Gummadi, K.P.: Fairness constraints: mechanisms for fair classification. In: Artificial Intelligence and Statistics, pp. 962–970. PMLR (2017)
40. Zemel, R., Wu, Y., Swersky, K., Pitassi, P.T., Dwork, C.: Learning fair representations. In: Proceedings of the 30th International Conference on Machine Learning, vol. 28, pp. 325–333 (2013)
41. Zhang, B.H., Lemoine, B., Mitchell, M.: Mitigating unwanted biases with adversarial learning. In: Proceedings of the 2018 AAAI/ACM Conference on AI, Ethics, and Society, pp. 335–340 (2018)
42. Zhang, X., Wang, H., Yu, J., Chen, C., Wang, X., Zhang, W.: Polarity-based graph neural network for sign prediction in signed bipartite graphs. World Wide Web **25**(2), 471–487 (2022). https://doi.org/10.1007/s11280-022-01015-4
43. Zhang, X., Wang, H., Yu, J., Chen, C., Wang, X., Zhang, W.: Bipartite graph capsule network. World Wide Web (WWW) **26**(1), 421–440 (2023)

Efficient Maximum Relative Fair Clique Computation in Attributed Graphs

Yufeng Zhang[1], Shiyuan Liu[1], Yanping Wu[2(✉)], Lu Qin[2], and Ying Zhang[2]

[1] Zhejiang Gongshang University, Hangzhou, China
[2] University of Technology Sydney, Sydney, Australia
Yanping.Wu@student.uts.edu.au, {Lu.Qin,Ying.Zhang}@uts.edu.au

Abstract. Cohesive subgraph mining is a fundamental problem in attributed graph analysis. However, the existing models on attributed graphs ignore the fairness of attributes. In this paper, we propose a novel model, called maximum relative fair clique, which integrates cohesiveness and fair resource allocation. Specifically, given an attributed graph G and a positive integer δ, a relative fair clique is a clique where the number of vertices with the most common attribute minus the number of vertices with the least amount of the common attribute should be no more than δ. We aim to find the maximum relative fair clique, which is the maximal one with the largest size. To solve this problem, we develop an algorithm, MRFCSearch, equipped with a novel heuristic algorithm and an efficient pruning technique. We evaluate the algorithm on four real-world graphs, demonstrating the performance of the proposed techniques.

1 Introduction

The problem of Maximum Clique Computation (MCC) in graph theory has gained significant interest in contemporary research due to its relevance in complex real-world networks like social networks [19–21], biological networks [5,23], road networks [22] and co-authorship networks [5]. As these networks grow, addressing issues like privacy and fairness becomes increasingly important.

Fairness has become a pivotal concern in various domains, including social network analysis, recommendation systems, and resource allocation [1,10]. Ensuring equitable resource allocation among groups with shared characteristics or interests is crucial. For example, in social networks, achieving a balanced gender distribution within cliques promotes fairness, and in healthcare interventions, selecting a fair group of patients enhances both fairness and study efficacy.

Motivated by these challenges, we introduce the novel concept of the Maximum Relative Fair Clique. This concept integrates clique size and fair resource allocation, aiming to maximize clique size while ensuring equitable resource distribution among members. This innovative concept finds applications across various domains, addressing fairness concerns in different real-world scenarios.

By integrating fairness into clique computation, our research strives to meet the growing demand for fairness in social networks and beyond. The goal is to

Z. Bao et al. (Eds.): ADC 2023, LNCS 14386, pp. 301–312, 2024.
https://doi.org/10.1007/978-3-031-47843-7_21

ensure fairer outcomes, promoting inclusivity and fairness in decision-making processes. This underscores the core motivation and significance of our research.

Applications. In social networks, it facilitates the identification of the largest clique community with equitable representation of both male and female members. This ensures a balanced gender distribution within the identified community, fostering inclusivity and fairness in social network analysis. In healthcare interventions, the concept assists researchers in selecting a representative and fair group of patients for clinical trials. By considering equitable distribution of attributes among the selected patients, biases are mitigated, and the fairness and efficacy of the study are enhanced.

Contributions. The main contributions of this paper are summarized as follows.

- To the best of our knowledge, we are the first to propose and investigate the maximum relative fair clique computation problem.
- Novel algorithms are proposed to solve the maximum relative fair clique computation problem. Pruning methods and searching algorithm are developed to scale for large graphs.
- Comprehensive experiments are conducted on four real-world datasets, which demonstrates the efficiency of the proposed techniques.

2 Preliminaries

Let $G = (V, E, A)$ be an undirected graph, where V and E denote the vertex set and edge set, respectively. We denote the number of vertices by $n = |V|$, and the number of edges by $m = |E|$. Each vertex $v \in V$ is associated with an attribute, which is represented by $v.val$. A is the set of attributes of all vertices in V, i.e., $A = \{v.val | v \in V\}$. Correspondingly, we define $A_n = |A|$ as the number of attributes in A. A subgraph $S = (V_S, E_S, A_S)$ is an induced subgraph of G, if $V_S \subseteq V$, $E_S \subseteq E$, and $A_S \subseteq A$. Given a subgraph S, the neighbors of $v \in V_S$ is denoted by $N(v, S) = \{u | (v, u) \in E_S\}$. For each attribute $a_i \in A_S$, we use $V(a_i, S)$ to denote the set of vertices associated with the attribute a_i in S. We use $V_{min}(A_S)$ and $V_{max}(A_S)$ to denote the set with smallest and largest size among $V(a_i, S)$ for all attributes $a_i \in A_S$. Based on the above concepts, we define the relative fair clique model as follows.

Definition 1 (Relative Fair Clique). *Given an attributed graph G and a positive integer δ, a subgraph S of G is a relative fair clique if i) S is a clique, i.e., each pair of vertices in S is adjacent; ii) S is relative fair, i.e., for all attributes in A_S, we have $|V_{max}(A_S)| - |V_{min}(A_S)| \leq \delta$.*

Given an attributed graph G and an integer δ, a relative fair clique S is maximal if there is no supergraph of S that is also a relative fair clique. The maximum relative fair clique of G is the maximal relative fair clique with the largest size, i.e., the one with the largest number of vertices.

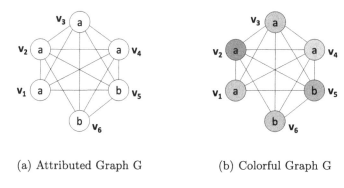

(a) Attributed Graph G   (b) Colorful Graph G

Fig. 1. Running examples

Problem Statement. Given an attributed graph G and an integer δ, in this paper, we aim to find the maximum relative fair clique from G.

Example 1. As shown in Fig. 1(a). The attribute value set is $A = \{a, b\}$. Suppose $\delta = 1$. There are four maximal relative fair cliques, $S_1 = \{v_1, v_2, v_5\}$, $S_2 = \{v_1, v_3, v_5\}$, $S_3 = \{v_1, v_4, v_5\}$, $S_4 = \{v_2, v_3, v_4, v_5, v_6\}$. The subgraph S_4 is the maximum relative fair clique because of its maximal number of vertices.

3 Solutions

In this section, a baseline method is first proposed. Then we develop two approaches: RFCMax method and a heuristic algorithm to get the upper and lower bound of maximum relative fair clique. Finally, to search the maximum relative fair clique, an exact algorithm MRFCSearch is proposed.

3.1 Baseline

In Algorithm 1, we extend the well-known Bron-Kerbosch algorithm [2] to obtain the maximum relative fair clique. It relies on two sets, denoted as R and P (line 1). R represents the current clique under construction, while P contains the vertices that can potentially be added to R for further expansion. The algorithm identifies that the clique formed by set R cannot be expanded any further when P becomes empty, signifying that all possible vertices have been considered. Then, we can get a maximum relative fair clique C by set R. If the size of C is larger than $|res|$, we can replace res with C (lines 4–6).

In our baseline method, we encounter computational challenges and the need to preserve the fairness criterion throughout the search. To tackle these obstacles, we develop two novel algorithms: a heuristic algorithm and MRFCSearch algorithm. These algorithms not only deliver precise outcomes but also exhibit substantial enhancements in computational efficiency.

Algorithm 1: BASELINE

    Input   : G : an attribute graph, δ : a positive integer
    Output : res : the maximum relative fair clique of G
1 $R \leftarrow \emptyset, P \leftarrow V$;
2 BRONKERBOSCH(R, P);

3 **Procedure** BRONKERBOSCH(R, P);
4 **if** P *is empty* **then**
5 | $C \leftarrow$ the maximum relative fair clique of R;
6 | **if** $|res| < |C|$ **then** $res \leftarrow C$;

7 **for each** *vertex* v *in* P **do**
8 | BRONKERBOSCH$(R \cup v, P \cap N(v))$;
9 | $P \leftarrow P \setminus v$;

3.2 RFCMax Calculate

We propose an innovative approach that considers vertex attributes to obtain more accurate upper bounds for the maximum relative fair clique. Traditional graph theory degeneracy orderings often overlook attribute information, leading to suboptimal results. By taking vertex attributes into account, our method provides a more precise estimation of the potential for vertices to form larger relative fair cliques. This improvement enhances the efficiency and effectiveness of the algorithm, leading to better performance in exploring the search space.

Definition 2 (Colorful degree). *Given an attributed graph $G = (V, E, A)$ and an attribute value $a \in A_{val}$. The colorful degree of vertex u based on a, denoted by $D_a(u, G)$, is the number of colors of u's neighbors whose attribute is a i.e., $D_a(u, G) = |\{color(v)|v \in N(u) \cup u, v.val = a\}|$.*

Example 2. As shown in the Fig. 1(b), the color on the vertices denotes their color value. The colorful degree of v_1 with attribute a is 4, while the colorful degree of v_3 with attribute a is 4.

    Certainly, in our graph G, each vertex u is associated with A_n colorful degrees, where A_n represents the number of distinct attribute values in the attribute set A_{val}. To be precise, we define $D_{min}(u, G)$ as the minimum colorful degree of vertex u, denoted as $D_{min}(u, G) = \min\{D_a(u, G)|a \in A_{val}\}$. In simpler terms, $D_{min}(u, G)$ corresponds to the smallest colorful degree among all the different attribute values that vertex u possesses.

Definition 3 (RFCMax). *Given an attributed graph $G = (V, E, A)$ and an attribute $a \in A_{val}$. The RFCMax of vertex u is the upper bound size of the maximum relative fair clique that contains u. The RFCMax of vertex u based on $D_a(u, G)$. i.e., $RFCMax_u = \sum_{a \in A} \min\{D_{min}(u, G) + \delta, D_a(u, G)\}$.*

Example 3. Reconsidering Fig. 1(b), the colorful degree of v_1 and v_2 are, $D_a(v_1) = 4, D_b(v_1) = 1, D_a(v_2) = 4$ and $D_b(v_2) = 2$. Suppose $\delta = 1$, $RFCMax$

of v_1 and v_2 is $min(D_{min}(v_1) + \delta, D_a(v_1)) + min(D_{min}(v_1) + \delta, D_b(v_1)) = 3$ and $min(D_{min}(v_2) + \delta, D_a(v_2)) + min(D_{min}(v_2)+\delta, D_b(v_2)) = 5$, respectively.

Algorithm 2: RFCMAXCALCULATE

Input   : G: an attribute graph, δ: a positive integer
Output : the $RFCMax$ value of each vertex
1 Color all vertices by invoking a degree-based greedy coloring algorithm;
2 **for** $u \in V$ **do**
3      $M_u(u.val, u.color)$++;
4      $D_{u.val}(u, G)$++;
5   **for** $v \in N(u)$ **do**
6   **if** $M_u(v.val, v.color) = 0$ **then** $D_{v.val}(u, G)$++;
7         $M_u(v.val, v.color)$++;
8      $D_{min}(u, G) \leftarrow min\{D_{a_i}(u, G) | a_i \in A_{val}\}$;
9      $RFCMax_u \leftarrow \sum_{a \in A} min\{D_{min}(u, G) + \delta, D_a(u, G)\}$;

We propose an innovative algorithm called RFCMaxCalculate, specifically designed to compute the $RFCMax$ value for each vertex, serving as an upper bound for the maximum relative fair clique. The pseudo-code for RFCMaxCalculate is presented in Algorithm 2. This algorithm determines the $RFCMax$ value for each vertex based on the attributes of its neighbors.

The key idea of our algorithm is to use a greedy coloring approach to minimize the number of colors while ensuring that adjacent vertices have distinct colors (line 1). By doing so, we can efficiently calculate the colorful degree of each vertex based on its attributes (lines 5–7). Subsequently, we identify the minimal colorful degree among the different attributes (line 8). Finally, we compute the $RFCMax$ value for each vertex, taking into account both its colorful degree and the minimal colorful degree (line 9). This approach allows us to estimate an upper bound for the maximum relative fair clique size for each vertex, considering both its attributes and overall colorful degree. As a result, the algorithm efficiently evaluates and compares the relative fairness among different cliques. The combination of greedy coloring and attribute-based analysis significantly improves the accuracy of the upper bound estimation and streamlines the subsequent search process for the maximum relative fair clique.

3.3   Heuristic Algorithm

In this section, a heuristic algorithm is proposed to compute a relative fair clique. This allows us to prune certain vertices based on their $RFCMax$ values, reducing the search space. Based on the proposed Lemma, we get a degeneracy ordering for each vertex, guiding the sequence of adding vertices to the maximum relative fair clique during the search.

Algorithm 3: HEURISTIC

Input   : G: an attribute graph, δ: a positive integer
Output : res : a relative fair clique
1 $res \leftarrow \emptyset$;
2 **for** $u \in V$ *in non-ascending RFCMax order* **do**
3 | **if** $RFCMax\_u \geq lb$ **then**
4 | | Let P be the neighbors whose $RFCMax \geq |res|$ of u;
5 | | Initialize Queue $C = \{\}$, Set $R = \{\}$;
6 | | **for each** $v \in P$ *in non-ascending order of RFCMax* **do**
7 | | | $C_{v.val}.push(v)$;
8 | | **while** *True* **do**
9 | | | **if** $|V_{max}(A_R)| - |V_{min}(A_R)| = \delta$ *Or* $C = \emptyset$ **then**
10 | | | | **break**;
11 | | | **for** *each* $a_i \in A_{val}$ **do**
12 | | | | **while** $R \cup C_{a_i}.front$ *isn't a clique* **do**
13 | | | | | $C_{a_i}.pop$;
14 | | | | Add v to R, $C_{a_i}.pop$;
15 | | **if** $|R| > |res|$ **then**
16 | | | $res \leftarrow R$;

Lemma 1. *The RFCMax value of a vertex directly correlates with its likelihood of being part of the maximum relative fair clique.*

Proof. The $RFCMax$ value assigned to a vertex v represents the upper bound on the size of a relative fair clique that includes v. A higher $RFCMax$ value implies a greater potential for a vertex to be included in larger relative fair cliques. Consequently, vertices with higher $RFCMax$ values are more likely to be part of the maximum relative fair clique, as they have the capacity to contribute significantly to its overall size.

The heuristic algorithm, outlined in Algorithm 3, constructs a relative fair clique by iteratively exploring the graph's vertices and greedily adding neighboring vertices that satisfy certain conditions. It aims to incrementally build a clique while considering the fairness constraint based on vertex attributes. The algorithm starts with an empty set R, representing the current relative fair clique (line 5). For each vertex, it traverses its neighbors and selects one vertex from each attribute group, ensuring only one vertex per group is added to R (lines 8–14). This process continues until no more vertices can be added. The algorithm incorporates a stopping condition, which involves checking if the difference is equal to δ and if the set C is empty (lines 9–10). This condition ensures that the algorithm stops when the relative fair clique satisfies the required fairness constraint and cannot be further expanded.

Algorithm 4: MRFCSEARCH

Input   : G: an attribute graph, δ: a positive integer
Output : res: the maximum relative fair clique of G
1 $R \leftarrow \emptyset, res \leftarrow \emptyset$;
2 Calculate $RFCMax$ values for all vertices;
3 $res \leftarrow$ **Heuristic**;
4 $S = (V_S, E_S, A_S) \leftarrow$ **Reduce Graph**;
5 Initialize an array B with $B(i) = false, 1 \leq i \leq |V_S|$;
6 **for each** $vertex\ v \in \hat{V}$ **do**
7 | **if** $B(v) = false$ **then**
8 | | $P \leftarrow$ ConnectedGraph(v, B);
9 | | SEARCH(R, P);

10 **Procedure** SEARCH(R, P);
11 **if** P *is empty* **then**
12 | $res \leftarrow R$;
13 | **return**;
14 $a_{\max} \leftarrow \arg\max_{a_i} |P_{a_i}|$;
15 **for each** $vertex\ v \in P$ **do**
16 | **if** $(v.val = a_{max}) \wedge (|V_{max}(A_R)| - |V_{min}(A_R)| = \delta)$ **then**
17 | | **continue**;
18 | $P \leftarrow P \setminus \{v\}; \hat{R} \leftarrow R \cup v; \hat{P} = \emptyset$;
19 | **for each** $u \in P$ **do**
20 | | **if** $u \in N(v, S)$ **then** $\hat{P} \leftarrow \hat{P} \cup u$;
21 | **if** $|\hat{R}| + |\hat{P}| \leq |res|$ **then continue**;
22 | calculate $RFCMax$ according to $\hat{R}$ and $\hat{P}$;
23 | **if** $RFCMax \leq |res|$ **then continue**;
24 | SEARCH$(\hat{R}, \hat{P})$;

3.4 MRFCSearch Algorithm

Our algorithm computes the $RFCMax$ values for each vertex in the graph (line 2). It then calculate a relative fair clique res, whose size is denoted as minimum size for the maximum relative fair clique (line 3). By eliminating vertices with $RFCMax$ values less than or equal to $|res|$ (line 4), the search space is efficiently reduced, focusing on potential candidates for the maximum relative fair clique. Next, we select a vertex v from the vertex set V. We perform a breadth-first search starting from v to obtain a connected subgraph that includes v (lines 6–9). We search for the maximum relative fair clique within this subgraph. In the search procedure, when P is empty, the set R is a relative fair clique whose size is larger than $|res|$, then we replace res with R (lines 11–12). We identify the attribute with the highest count of vertices, denoted as a_{max}, within set R (line 14). If the attribute value of a vertex v is equal to a_{max} and the difference between $V_{max}(A_R)$ and $V_{min}(A_R)$ is equal to δ, then we skip adding v to set R

to maintain the relative fair clique condition (lines 16–17). If v is added to R, we update the candidate set P to $\hat{P}$ by removing vertices that are not adjacent to v (lines 18–20). At this point, if the size of set $\hat{R}$ plus the size of set $\hat{P}$ is no more than $|res|$, we stop the search because we cannot obtain a larger relative fair clique from the remaining vertices in sets $\hat{R}$ and $\hat{P}$ (line 21). We also calculate the $RFCMax$ values for the vertices in sets $\hat{R}$ and $\hat{P}$. If the maximum $RFCMax$ value among these vertices is less than or equal to $|res|$, we halt the search as it indicates that the size of maximum relative fair clique formed by $\hat{R}$ and $\hat{P}$ cannot exceed $|res|$ (lines 22–24).

4   Experiments

Algorithms. Since there is no previous work for the proposed problem, we conduct experiments with the proposed algorithms. The baseline method is proposed in Sect. 3.1 for the maximum relative fair clique problem. The RFCMax method is proposed in Sect. 3.2 for tightening the upper bound of maximum relative fair clique. The heuristic algorithm is proposed in Sect. 3.3 for getting lower bound of maximum relative fair clique. The MRFCSearch is proposed in Sect. 3.4 for searching the maximum relative fair clique.

Datasets. We evaluate the algorithms on four real-world datasets, i.e., Douban (D1, 154.9K, 327.1K), Livejournal (D2, 4M, 27.9M), Pokec (D3, 1.6M, 22.3M), Dblp (D4, 425.9K, 1M). The two numbers following each dataset represent the number of vertices and edges, respectively. All of above datasets can be downloaded from Network Repository[1] and SNAP[2]. Note that the original datasets lack attribute information, each vertex is randomly assigned an attribute to create the attributed graphs [24].

Parameters and Workload. To evaluate the performances of proposed algorithms, we vary the maximum difference δ and the number of attributes values d. For all datasets, δ is chosen from the interval [3, 6] with a default value of $d = 2$. The parameter d is chosen from the interval [2, 5] with a default value of $delta = 3$. Unless explicitly specified otherwise, the remaining parameters assume their default values while varying a specific parameter.

All algorithms are implemented in C++11 with GNU GCC 7.5.0. Experiments are conducted on a PC with Intel(R) Xeon(R) Gold 5218R CPU @ 2.10 GHz and 256 GB RAM using Ubuntu 18.04 (64-bit).

4.1   Efficiency Testing

Evaluation of the MRFCSearch. In this experiment, we evaluate the MRFCSearch by comparing the time cost with varying δ and d. The results are depicted in Fig. 2. We can see that MRFCSearch outperforms the baseline algorithm in terms of computational speed. In Dblp and Livejournal, the baseline algorithm

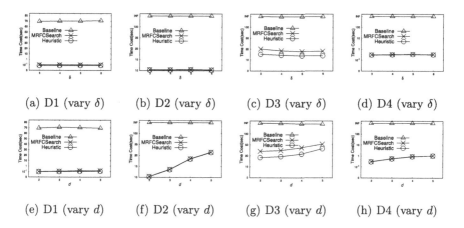

(a) D1 (vary δ)   (b) D2 (vary δ)   (c) D3 (vary δ)   (d) D4 (vary δ)

(e) D1 (vary d)   (f) D2 (vary d)   (g) D3 (vary d)   (h) D4 (vary d)

Fig. 2. Running time of the Baseline, Heuristic Algorithm and MRFCSearch Algorithm

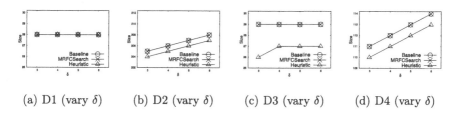

(a) D1 (vary δ)   (b) D2 (vary δ)   (c) D3 (vary δ)   (d) D4 (vary δ)

Fig. 3. The size of maximum relative fair clique with different algorithms

fails to search the maximum relative fair clique within a time limit of three hours, while MRFCSearch is able to efficiently compute the result. In dataset Dblp, the MRFCSearch only requires 0.5 s to get the maximum relative fair clique, which is at least 20,000 times faster than the baseline method. In addition, we can notice that the time cost increases with the increase of δ. When δ grows, the $RFCMax$ of each vertex either remains unchanged or increases. And if the lower bound of maximum relative fair clique which we obtain from the heuristic algorithm unchanged, the number of remaining vertices will increase because the number of vertices whose $RFCMax$ larger than the lower bound increases. This makes the search space larger and more time to find the result.

Evaluation of the Heuristic Algorithm. The heuristic algorithm is evaluated by comparing its time cost and correct rate, and results are shown in Fig. 2 and Fig. 3. As can be seen in Fig. 3, the heuristic algorithm provides a good approximation of the size of maximum relative fair clique. In the dataset Douban Fig. 3(a), the result got from heuristic is indeed the correct one. Heuristic also performs well in the datasets Dblp and Livejournal, the accuracy rate in these two datasets reaches an impressive 99%. In the other datasets, the result got from heuristic algorithm approaches the correct size. From Fig. 2, we observe that the heuristic algorithm generally has a lower time cost compared to the MRFCSearch

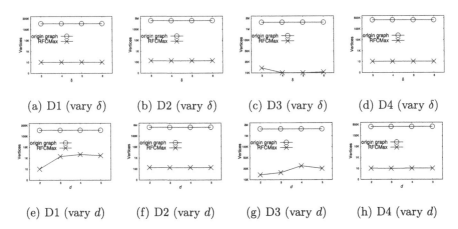

(a) D1 (vary δ)   (b) D2 (vary δ)   (c) D3 (vary δ)   (d) D4 (vary δ)

(e) D1 (vary d)   (f) D2 (vary d)   (g) D3 (vary d)   (h) D4 (vary d)

Fig. 4. The number of remaining vertices after remove vertices according to RFCMax

and baseline. Note that in the datasets where the heuristic algorithm performs well as MRFCSearch, the correct rate is also great, which means that the better heuristic algorithm performs, the faster MRFCSearch finds the result.

Evaluation of the RFCMax. The method of RFCMax can help us in the following scenes, i) help to calculate the upper bound of maximum relative fair clique, ii) help to prune search space. Moreover, we calculate the $RFCMax$ of each vertex in vertex set V in the time complexity $O(mn)$. In this experiment, we evaluate $RFCMax$ by comparing the remaining vertices. The results are depicted in Fig. 4. It is evident that RFCMax method results in the removal of a significant number of vertices. In datasets such as Dblp and Livejournal, the number of remaining vertices after applying the RFCMax-based vertex removal is close to the size of the maximum relative fair clique, with a difference of no more than 10 vertices. This reduction in the number of vertices allows for faster search of the maximum relative fair clique, as the search space is significantly reduced. Overall, the RFCMax method effectively reduces the size of the graph by removing vertices that are unlikely to be part of the maximum relative fair clique. This reduction in the search space enables faster computations and brings the time cost of the MRFCSearch algorithm closer to that of the heuristic algorithm, particularly in datasets where a large number of vertices are removed.

5 Related Work

Cohesive Subgraph Mining. Many researches are proposed to solve the maximum clique computation (MCC) problem, which can be divided into two categories, heuristic algorithm and exact algorithm. The heuristic algorithm depends on the degeneracy order [16,17]. Pattabiraman et al. [16] select the vertex with maximum degree in each turn to form the maximum clique. Rossi et al. [17] select the vertex with the maximum core number one by one to form the maximum clique. The exact algorithms adopt the *branch-&-bound* framework [4,15].

Chang [4] developed a new *branch-&-bound* with pruning techniques to solve MCC. Ostergard et al. [15] proposed a *branch-&-bound* algorithm with color degeneracy order. The alluring endeavor of enumerating all maximal cliques has captivated scholarly inquiry [3,11]. Recently, many studies

Attribute Graph Analysis. Notably, many scholars have delved into community detection and search in attributed graphs [8,9,13,18,24]. Fang et al. [8] revolve around identifying a subgraph where each vertex shares a common required attributes. Islam et al. [9] find the most influential communities from an attributed graph. Khan et al. [13] aims to find compact attributed groups in attributed graphs nodes are closely connected and each node contains as many query keywords as possible. Zhang et al. [24] enumerate fairness-aware maximal clique in attributed graph.

Research About Fairness. The pursuit of fairness can be classified into distinct realms. Group fairness mandates algorithms to refrain from discriminatory decisions based on specific individual characteristics [6]. Dai et al. [6] eliminate the bias of GNNs whilst maintaining high node classification accuracy by leveraging graph structures and limited sensitive information. Individual fairness embodies a more refined notion, scrutinizing fairness at a finer granularity than group fairness [7,12]. Kang et al. [12] presents the first principled study of Individual Fairness on graph Mining (InFoRM). Counterfactual fairness and degree-related fairness offer additional dimensions in the exploration of fairness concepts [14].

6   Conclusion

This study addresses the problem of computing the maximum relative fair clique in attributed graphs. We propose the concept of RFCMax as an upper bound estimator and develop an efficient heuristic algorithm to obtain lower bounds. Our approach demonstrates improved efficiency and accurate estimations for the maximum relative fair clique size in real-world scenarios.

References

1. Ali, J., Babaei, M., Chakraborty, A., Mirzasoleiman, B., Gummadi, K., Singla, A.: On the fairness of time-critical influence maximization in social networks. IEEE Trans. Knowl. Data Eng. (2021)
2. Bron, C., Kerbosch, J.: Algorithm 457: finding all cliques of an undirected graph. Commun. ACM **16**(9), 575–577 (1973)
3. Cazals, F., Karande, C.: A note on the problem of reporting maximal cliques. Theor. Comput. Sci. **407**(1–3), 564–568 (2008)
4. Chang, L.: Efficient maximum clique computation over large sparse graphs. In: Proceedings of the 25th ACM SIGKDD International Conference on Knowledge Discovery & Data Mining, pp. 529–538 (2019)
5. Chen, C., Wu, Y., Sun, R., Wang, X.: Maximum signed θ-clique identification in large signed graphs. IEEE Trans. Knowl. Data Eng. (2021)

6. Dai, E., Wang, S.: Say no to the discrimination: Learning fair graph neural networks with limited sensitive attribute information. In: Proceedings of the 14th ACM International Conference on Web Search and Data Mining, pp. 680–688 (2021)

7. Dong, Y., Kang, J., Tong, H., Li, J.: Individual fairness for graph neural networks: a ranking based approach. In: Proceedings of the 27th ACM SIGKDD Conference on Knowledge Discovery & Data Mining, pp. 300–310 (2021)

8. Fang, Y., Cheng, R., Luo, S., Hu, J.: Effective community search for large attributed graphs. Proc. VLDB Endow. 9(12), 1233–1244 (2016)

9. Islam, M.S., Ali, M.E., Kang, Y.B., Sellis, T., Choudhury, F.M., Roy, S.: Keyword aware influential community search in large attributed graphs. Inf. Syst. 104, 101914 (2022)

10. Jalali, Z.S., Chen, Q., Srikanta, S.M., Wang, W., Kim, M., Raghavan, H., Soundarajan, S.: Fairness of information flow in social networks. ACM Trans. Knowl. Discov. Data 17(6), 1–26 (2023)

11. Jin, Y., Xiong, B., He, K., Zhou, Y., Zhou, Y.: On fast enumeration of maximal cliques in large graphs. Expert Syst. Appl. 187, 115915 (2022)

12. Kang, J., He, J., Maciejewski, R., Tong, H.: Inform: individual fairness on graph mining. In: Proceedings of the 26th ACM SIGKDD International Conference on Knowledge Discovery & Data Mining, pp. 379–389 (2020)

13. Khan, A., Golab, L., Kargar, M., Szlichta, J., Zihayat, M.: Compact group discovery in attributed graphs and social networks. Inf. Process. Manag. 57(2), 102054 (2020)

14. Kusner, M.J., Loftus, J., Russell, C., Silva, R.: Counterfactual fairness. Adv. Neural Inf. Process. Syst. 30 (2017)

15. Östergård, P.R.: A fast algorithm for the maximum clique problem. Discret. Appl. Math. 120(1–3), 197–207 (2002)

16. Pattabiraman, B., Patwary, M.M.A., Gebremedhin, A.H., Liao, W.K., Choudhary, A.: Fast algorithms for the maximum clique problem on massive graphs with applications to overlapping community detection. Internet Math. 11(4–5), 421–448 (2015)

17. Rossi, R.A., Gleich, D.F., Gebremedhin, A.H.: Parallel maximum clique algorithms with applications to network analysis. SIAM J. Sci. Comput. 37(5), C589–C616 (2015)

18. Sun, R., Chen, C., Wang, X., Wu, Y., Zhang, M., Liu, X.: The art of characterization in large networks: finding the critical attributes. World Wide Web 25(2), 655–677 (2022)

19. Sun, R., Chen, C., Wang, X., Zhang, W., Zhang, Y., Lin, X.: Efficient maximum signed biclique identification. In: ICDE, pp. 1313–1325 (2023)

20. Sun, R., Wu, Y., Wang, X.: Diversified top-r community search in geo-social network: a k-truss based model. In: EDBT (2022)

21. Sun, R., Wu, Y., Wang, X., Chen, C., Zhang, W., Lin, X.: Clique identification in signed graphs: a balance theory based model. IEEE Trans. Knowl. Data Eng. (2023)

22. Wu, Y., Sun, R., Chen, C., Wang, X., Fu, X.: Efficiently answering minimum reachable label set queries in edge-labeled graphs. In: CIKM, pp. 4585–4589 (2022)

23. Wu, Y., Zhao, J., Sun, R., Chen, C., Wang, X.: Efficient personalized influential community search in large networks. Data Sci. Eng. 6(3), 310–322 (2021)

24. Zhang, Q., Li, R.H., Pan, M., Dai, Y., Tian, Q., Wang, G.: Fairness-aware maximal clique in large graphs: concepts and algorithms. IEEE Trans. Knowl. Data Eng. (2023)

Graph Mining and Graph Algorithms

Balanced Hop-Constrained Path Enumeration in Signed Directed Graphs

Zhiyang Tang[1], Jinghao Wang[1], Yanping Wu[2(✉)], Xiaoyang Wang[3], Lu Qin[2], and Ying Zhang[2]

[1] Zhejiang Gongshang University, Hangzhou, China
[2] University of Technology Sydney, Sydney, Australia
Yanping.Wu@student.uts.edu.au, {Lu.Qin,Ying.Zhang}@uts.edu.au
[3] The University of New South Wales, Sydney, Australia
xiaoyang.wang1@unsw.edu.au

Abstract. Hop-constrained path enumeration, which aims to output all the paths from two distinct vertices within the given hops, is one of the fundamental tasks in graph analysis. Previous works about this problem mainly focus on unsigned graphs. Nevertheless, with the ever-growing popularity of online social media, signed graphs with positive and negative edges are becoming increasingly ubiquitous and there is a paucity of balanced paths (i.e., paths with an even number of negative edges) enumeration which makes more sense according to balance theory. Motivated by this, in this paper, we propose a new problem, i.e., enumerate balanced paths with hop constraint (BPHC). A baseline method firstly is proposed by extending the DFS method. To further speed up the efficiency, we construct an almost-satisfy table to instantly correct unbalanced state during the search process. Based on the almost-satisfy table, we develop algorithm BMAS by combining the shortest path length in the process of table update and lookup. We conduct experiments on four real world networks to verify the performance of the proposed algorithms.

Keywords: Signed graph · Balanced paths · Path enumeration

1 Introduction

Graphs are widely used to represent the intricate relationships among diverse entities, including social networks [3,15,19], road networks [20,23], and protein-protein interaction networks [2,22]. A fundamental problem in graph analysis is to investigate the relations between two vertices and path enumeration is one of the classical problems. In many real-life applications, it is rather natural to impose a hop constraint k to path enumeration for the strength of the relation. Generally, given a source vertex s, a target vertex t and a hop constraint k, k-hop constrained path is the path from s to t within k hop. Previous works of k-hop constrained path enumeration problem mostly focus on unsigned graphs. However, with the ever-growing popularity of online social media, it is important

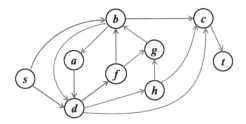

Fig. 1. An Example of Signed Directed Graph. (Color figure online)

to explicitly consider both positive and negative relationships between users hence the emergence of signed graphs [4,12,16]. In signed graphs, balance theory is widely used, which sums up the latent user relationships in signed graphs that a friend of my friend is my friend, an enemy of my friend is my enemy and an enemy of my enemy is my friend [6,13,21]. Due to the specific properties of the signed graphs, it is hard for users to properly specify the hop-constrained path.

To fill this gap, in this paper, we propose and investigate the problem of balanced paths enumeration with hop constraint. Specifically, given a signed graph G, two vertices s, $t \in V$ and an integer k, we say a path P from s to t is a balanced path with hop constraint (BPHC), iff i) P is k-hop constrained, i.e., $|P| \leq k$. ii) P is balanced, i.e., there is an even number of negative edges in P. We aim to enumerate all BPHCs from the source vertex s to the target vertex t.

Example 1. Figure 1 shows a signed directed graph with nine vertices, where the red (resp. blue) edges represent positive (resp. negative) edges. Given the source vertex s, the target vertex t and the hop constraint $k = 6$, we can obtain all BPHCs from s to t, that is, $\langle s, d, c, t \rangle$, $\langle s, b, d, h, c, t \rangle$, $\langle s, b, a, d, h, c, t \rangle$, $\langle s, d, h, g, b, c, t \rangle$.

Applications. Enumerating BPHCs can find many real-world applications.

– **Friends Recommendation.** To make a friend recommendation in recommendation systems, we only need to consider the possible level of positive interest. In other words, the more balanced paths exist, the stronger potential positive correlation between two users. In addition, two users are connected by multiple intermediate users and BPHC can easily realize the assignment of weights to paths of different lengths.
– **Precision Marketing.** User feedback in e-commerce can be positive or negative. We can consider users who give similar feedback on a product as friends and those who give the opposite feedback as enemies. Precision marketing can be achieved by finding potential users with highly positive relationships within the product's loyal user base.

Challenges. In the literature, path enumeration with hop constraint has a long history and many studies use various pruning techniques to complete performance optimization [9,11,17]. Moreover, some algorithms such as recursive expressions of the adjacency matrix, HP-index [1,8], or top-k shortest paths [5,7] all can greatly optimize the performance of this problem. When these methods run on signed graphs, they can no longer achieve special enumeration requirements or equivalent high performance by simply redefining constraints. First, original algorithms do not discriminate between positive and negative sign information, thus do not perform continuous sign statistics to determine the state of the current path. Furthermore, the emergence of negative edges continuously affects the state of the path and this influence has been dynamic throughout the enumeration process. When faced with the requirement of enumerating all balanced paths from s to t, if we just check the balanced or unbalanced state at the output of a path, it is bound to cause a lot of search waste. Therefore, how to deal with the availability of negative edges becomes a crucial factor.

Our Solutions. In this paper, we first propose a baseline method by combining the DFS strategy and the sign checking technique. To further improve the efficiency, we propose a novel table structure, called almost-satisfy table (AS-$Table$), which stores the almost-satisfy entries for certain vertices. Specifically, we denote an almost-satisfy entry of v_i as $(v_i, v_{i+1}, \ldots, v_j)$ which represents a path P from v_i to v_j and only the last edge of P is negative, i.e., (v_{j-1}, v_j) is negative and all the other edges of P are positive. Based on AS-$Table$, we develop a balance maintenance algorithm by AS-$Table$ (BMAS). BMAS calculates the length of the shortest path from each vertex to the target vertex in advance to judge whether a vertex can be processed (i.e., not exceed the hop constraint). Initially, AS-$Table$ is empty. When the search traverses a negative in-degree edge of vertex v and the almost-satisfy entries of v are not stored, AS-$Table$ is updated, i.e., construct the entries for v and store them in AS-$Table$. If the almost-satisfy entries of v have been stored, we look up AS-$Table$ and directly push the whole almost-satisfy entry to stack to be processed. The only negative edge in the last edge of the entry brings the path back to balance. Based on the table update and table lookup of AS-$Table$, BMAS can always maintain the balanced state of the path, and finally get BPHCs.

Contributions. The contribution of the paper can be summarized as follows.

- We are the first to propose and investigate the BPHC enumeration problem.
- We first design an almost-satisfy table (AS-$Table$) to store almost-satisfy entries. Based on AS-$Table$, we propose an efficient balance maintenance algorithm by AS-$Table$ (BMAS) in the process of table update and lookup.
- Comprehensive experiments are conducted on four networks to demonstrate the effectiveness and efficiency of our proposed model and techniques.

2   Problem Definition

We consider a directed signed graph $G = (V, E)$, where V and E are the sets of vertices and edges in G, respectively. Each edge $e \in E$ is associated with a label of either "+" or "−". An edge with the label "+" represents the positive relationship (e.g., like), and an edge with the label "−" represents the negative relationship (e.g., dislike) between the two vertices. Given a vertex $v \in V$, the set of its out-neighbor is defined as $N_{out}(v) = \{u \mid (v, u) \in E\}$, and the set of its

---

Algorithm 1: SC-DFS

    Input   : s : the source vertex, t : the target vertex, k : the hop constraint
    Output : P_k : balanced paths with k-hop constraint from s to t

1 $P_k \leftarrow \emptyset$;
2 EnumSC-DFS(s, 1, $\emptyset$);
3 **return** P_k;

4 **Procedure** EnumSC-DFS(v, $pSign$, S)
5 S.push(v);
6   **if** $v = t$ *and* $pSign = 1$ **then**
7 $\lfloor$ $P_k \leftarrow P_k \cup S$;

8   **else if** *len(S)* $< k$ **then**
9   **for each** *out-degree* $(w, sign)$ *of* v *where* $w \notin S$ **do**
10   **if** $sign = -$ **then**
11 $\lfloor$ $pSign = -pSign$;
12 $\lfloor$ EnumSC-DFS(w, $pSign$, S);

13 S.pop(v);

---

in-neighbor is defined as $N_{in}(v) = \{u \mid (u, v) \in E\}$. A path P in G from vertex v_0 to v_i can be described as a sequence $\langle v_0, v_1, \ldots, v_{i-1}, v_i \rangle$, where for any integer $0 \leq j \leq i-1$, $(v_j, v_{j+1}) \in E$. A simple path is a loop-free path without repeated vertices and edges. Path P is a k-hop constrained path if $|P| \leq k$, where $|P|$ is the number of edges in P and k is the hop constraint. Motivated by the concept of the balanced triangle that contains an odd number of positive edges [21], we say a path is balanced if there is an even number of negative edges inside.

Definition 1 (Balanced Path with Hop Constraint (BPHC)). *Given a signed graph G, two vertices s, $t \in V$ and an integer k, we say a path P from s to t is a balanced path with hop constraint, iff 1) P is k-hop constrained, i.e., $|P| \leq k$. 2) P is balanced, i.e., there is an even number of negative edges in P.*

Problem Statement. In this paper, we study the problem of balanced paths with hop constraint enumeration on a signed directed graph. Specifically, given a signed graph G, two vertices s, $t \in V$ and an integer k, we aim to develop efficient algorithms to enumerate all BPHCs from s to t.

3 Solutions

In this section, we first introduce a baseline method in Sect. 3.1. Then, we present a novel table structure in Sect. 3.2. Based on the concept of table, we further develop an optimized algorithm in Sect. 3.3.

3.1 Baseline Method

To solve our problem, a naive method is to enumerate all hop-constrained paths from the source vertex to the target vertex by adopting the DFS strategy and then skip all the unbalanced paths.

SC-DFS Algorithm. Details of our baseline method is illustrated in Algorithm 1. The input of the algorithm is the source vertex s, the target vertex t and the hop constraint k. The output is a set P_k of balanced paths with k-hop constraint from s to t. We first initialize P_k to be an empty set at Line 1 and invoke the procedure EnumSC-DFS at Line 2, which aims to recursively output BPHCs from s to t. The details of EnumSC-DFS are shown in Lines 4–13. We use v denote the current traversed vertex and we store all the traversed vertices into stack S, which is initialized $\emptyset$. We use $pSign = 1$ (resp. $pSign = -1$) denote the positive (resp. negative) state of the currently processing path. In each recursion, we first push the current vertex v into the stack S (Line 5). If $v = t$ and $pSign = 1$, S stores a new BPHC and we add it into P_k (Lines 6–7). Otherwise, if the current stack length is less than k, we search every out-degree neighbour w of v where $w \notin S$ at Line 9. When this out-degree edge is negative, $pSign$ becomes its negative value (Lines 10–11). Then, we invoke EnumSC-DFS to process vertex w and the new value of $pSign$ (Line 12). Finally, vertex v is popped after all recursions of v are returned (Line 13).

Theorem 1. *SC-DFS is an exponentially growing algorithm with $O(n^k)$ time, where n is the number of vertices in graph, k is the hop constraint.*

Proof. SC-DFS adopting the DFS strategy starts from the source vertex s with the search depth at most k. Therefore, the time complexity of SC-DFS is $O(n^k)$.

Limitations. Although SC-DFS can return all the BPHCs from the source vertex to the target vertex, it still faces efficiency issue. This is because that we can only know the state of the path when we traverse to the end of it, which means we still need to traverse all hop-constrained paths. This motivates us to design an efficient enumeration algorithm without failed search.

3.2   Almost-Satisfy Table (*AS-Table*)

Below we propose a novel almost-satisfy table (*AS-Table*), which is used in our algorithm. Before introducing that, we first present its storage contents, i.e., almost-satisfy entries. Then, we give a formal definition of *AS-Table*.

   An entry of a given vertex $v_i \in V$ is a $(k$-1)-hop constrained path $P = \langle v_i, v_{i+1}, \ldots, v_j \rangle$, which stores a path from v_i to v_j. We say an entry is a positive entry if all the edges of P is positive. Besides, an entry is an almost-satisfy entry if only the last edge of P is negative, i.e., (v_{j-1}, v_j) of P is negative and all the other edges are positive. We use B_p to denote the set of positive entries and U_p to denote the set of almost-satisfy entries, where p is the length of each entry.

Example 2. Considering the example in Fig. 1. Suppose $p = 1$. The set of positive entries of b is $B_1 = \{(b, c)\}$. The set of almost-satisfy entries of b is $U_1 = \{(b, d), (b, a)\}$.

   Based on the concept of the almost-satisfy entry, we formally give the definition of almost-satisfy table (*AS-Table*).

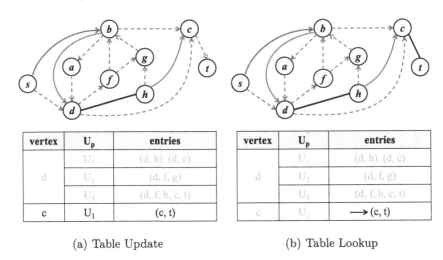

vertex	U_p	entries
	U_1	(d, h) (d, c)
d	U_2	(d, f, g)
	U_4	(d, f, b, c, t)
c	U_1	(c, t)

(a) Table Update

vertex	U_p	entries
	U_1	(d, h) (d, c)
d	U_2	(d, f, g)
	U_4	(d, f, b, c, t)
c	U_1	⟶ (c, t)

(b) Table Lookup

Fig. 2. A Balanced Path Output

Definition 2 (almost-satisfy table (AS-$Table$)). *Given a signed graph G and a hop constraint k, AS-$Table$ stores the sets of almost-satisfy entries U_p for each vertex from $W \subseteq V$, where $1 \le p \le k - 1$. For each vertex $v \in W$, we have $\exists u \in N_{in}(v)$ and (u, v) is negative, i.e., v has at least one negative in-degree.*

The table presented in Fig. 2 shows the specific structure of AS-$Table$. The role of AS-$Table$ is that when the search traverses a negative in-degree edge of vertex v to make the path unbalanced, we take out the corresponding U_p of v and add a whole almost-satisfy entry to the stack to bring the path back to balance. Therefore, AS-$Table$ has correctness in the output of a balanced path. Moreover, in fact, we push any unbalanced path of v to the stack can also effectively bring the path back to balance when all vertices in this pushed path do not touch any vertex in the stack. But to avoid redundant storage, we choose to store the almost-satisfy entries. We use Example 3 to demonstrate the completeness (i.e., ensure accurate enumeration results) of this type of storage.

Example 3. Reconsidering Fig. 1. When we traverse from s to d, we encounter a negative edge (b, d) and there is an unbalanced path $\langle d, h, c, t \rangle$ from d to t, which can form a BPHC with the previous path from s to d, i.e., $\langle s, b, d, h, c, t \rangle$. When d is traversed, we can obtain $(d, h) \in U_1$ for it and add it to the stack to bring the path back to balance. Then the search continues downward, the path falls into unbalance again after c is traversed. In this case, we push the almost-satisfy entry $(c, t) \in U_1$ for c to the stack and finally output this BPHC.

3.3   BMAS Algorithm

Based on AS-$Table$, we propose a balance maintenance algorithm (BMAS) to obtain exact enumeration results. In BMAS, we adopt the method proposed in [11] to obtain the shortest path length for each vertex in advance. By doing this,

---

Algorithm 2: Construct Almost-satisfy Entries(v, k)

Input   : v: the vertex to be built almost-satisfy entries, k: the hop constraint
Output : I_v: all the almost-satisfy entries of v

1   $B_0 \leftarrow \{(v)\}$, $U_0 \leftarrow \{(v)\}$;
2   **for** $i \leftarrow 1$ to k **do**
3      $B_i \leftarrow \emptyset$, $U_i \leftarrow \emptyset$;
4   **if** $B_{i-1} = \emptyset$ **then**
5   break;
6   **for each** $entry$ $N_{i-1} \in B_{i-1}$ **do**
7   **for each** $out\text{-}degree$ $(w, sign)$ of $N_{i-1}.back()$ $where$ $w \notin N_{i-1}$ **do**
8   **if** $len(N_{i-1}) + D_w < k$ **then**
9            $N_i \leftarrow N_{i-1}.push(w)$;
10   **if** $sign = +$ **then**
11             $B_i \leftarrow B_i \cup \{N_i\}$;
12   **else if** $sign = -$ **then**
13             $U_i \leftarrow U_i \cup \{N_i\}$;

14 **return** $I_v \leftarrow \{U_1, U_2...\}$

---

we can determine whether the current traversed vertex can be processed. Note that, in the following, we use D_w to denote the shortest path length from the vertex w to the target vertex t.

Table Update. *AS-Table* stores all the almost-satisfy entries for certain vertices. Initially the table is empty, if i) the search traverses a negative in-degree edge of vertex v and ii) the almost-satisfy entries of v are not stored, we do a table update, i.e., construct the almost-satisfy entries for v. In this process, the length of the current positive entry and the shortest path length D_w from the traversed vertex w to the target vertex t are jointly used as the conditions to determine whether w can form a new almost-satisfy entry for v.

The detailed process of the algorithm is shown in Algorithm 2. We first add $\{(v)\}$ into B_0 and U_0 (Line 1). Then we start to find the almost-satisfy entries within length $k - 1$ (Line 2). In fact, the almost-satisfy entries in U_i are formed by the positive entries in B_{i-1} with a hop negative out-degree. If B_{i-1} is empty, i.e., vertex v does not have any positive entry of length $i - 1$, we can end the search early (Lines 4–5). Otherwise, based on the last vertex of a positive entry in B_{i-1}, we recursively search its out-going neighbors and push them to B_i or U_i, respectively (Lines 6–13). The out-going neighbors that can be pushed to a positive entry in B_{i-1} and form a new almost-satisfy entry in U_i must satisfy $len(N_{i-1}) + D_w < k$. This means that this new almost-satisfy entry is likely to be a part of a hop-constrained s-t path. In the end, I_v as a summary set stores all the almost-satisfy entries of v with different length (Line 14).

Example 4. In Fig. 2(a), suppose the source vertex is s, the target vertex is t, the hop constraint $k = 6$ and the almost-entries of d have been stored in the

---

Algorithm 3: BMAS

    Input   : s : the source vertex, t : the target vertex, k : the hop constraint

    Output : P_k : balanced paths with k-hop constraint from s to t

1 $P_k \leftarrow \emptyset$;

2 BMAS$(s, \emptyset)$;

3 **return** P_k;

4 **Procedure** BMAS(v, S)

5 S.push(v);

6 **if** $v = t$ **then**

7   ⌊ $P_k \leftarrow P_k \cup S$;

8 **else if** $len(S) < k$ **then**

9   **for each** $out\text{-}degree$ $(w, sign)$ of v where $w \notin S$ and $len(S) + D_w < k$ **do**

10   **if** $sign = +$ **then**

11   ⌊ BMAS(w, S);

12   **else if** $sign = -$ **then**

13   **if** $I_w = \emptyset$ **then**

14   ⌊ Construct Almost-satisfy Entries(w, k);   /* Algorithm 2 */;

15   **for each** $N \in I_w$ where $len(S) + len(N) < k$ and $N \cap S = \emptyset$ **do**

16          $u \leftarrow N$.pop$()$;

17   S.push(N);

18   BMAS(u, S);

19   S.pop(N);

20 S.pop(v);

---

grey part of *AS-Table*. We use solid lines to denote path that is currently being processed and dotted lines to denote unprocessed paths. When we traverse from s to c, the negative edge (h, c) makes the path unbalanced and the almost-satisfy entries of c are not stored. Since c has only one negative out-degree edge, $B_1 = \emptyset$, $U_1 = \{(c, t)\}$. Because of $B_1 = \emptyset$, we end the search early. We store $U_1 = \{(c, t)\}$ for c in the table (i.e., the black part in *AS-Table*). Besides, we observe the almost-satisfy entries of d and find that the almost-satisfy entry $N = (d, f, b, a)$ is not in the table because when processing vertex a, $len(N) + D_a = 3 + 3 = 6$. This result is not smaller than $k = 6$ and is hence not saved.

Table Lookup. When the search traverses a negative in-degree edge of a vertex, we look up the table to see if the corresponding U_p of this vertex has been built before. If it does not exist, we invoke Algorithm 2 to do a table update. If it exists, we directly take out an almost-satisfy entry in U_p to correct the unbalanced state caused by the current traversed negative in-degree edge.

The detailed process is shown in Algorithm 3. We first initialize P_k to be an empty set at Line 1 and invoke the procedure BMAS at Line 2. The details of BMAS are shown in Lines 4–20. In each recursion, after pushing the current traversed vertex v to the stack S, if $v = t$, a new BPHC is added into P_k (Lines

Table 1. Statistics of Datasets

Dataset	$|V|$	$|E|$	$|E^+|$	$|E^-|$
Bitcoin	7,605	14,125	12,973	1,152
Epinion	82,144	500,481	382,915	117,566
Slashdot	131,828	711,210	592,592	118,618
Wiki	138,593	715,884	629,858	86,026

5–7). Otherwise, if $len(S) < k$ at Line 8, we will continue the search through the each neighbor w of v that $w \notin S$ and $len(S) + D_w < k$ at Line 9. This means that w may reach t under the hop constraint. If the edge (v, w) is positive, we perform recursion directly (Lines 10–11). If the edge (v, w) is negative, we look up the table and take out an almost-satisfy entry (Lines 12–19). If we have not previously constructed almost-satisfy entries for w, we call Algorithm 2 for table update (Lines 13–14). Otherwise, we push an entry $N \in I_w$ where $len(S) + len(N) < k$ to stack S to bring the path back to balance and then continue the recursion (Lines 15–18). When the recursion returns from Line 18, we pop the entire entry N directly from the stack S at Line 19. Finally, we pop up vertex v after all recursions of v are returned at Line 20. When recursions of each vertex are over, i.e., s is popped up the stack, P_k obtains all BPHCs.

Example 5. In Fig. 2(b), we start to look up the table caused by the negative edge (h, c). The only almost-satisfy entry (c, t) can be pushed to stack to rebalance the path (i.e., the black line in Fig. 2(b), and we get a BPHC, that is, $\langle s, b, d, h, c, t \rangle$. When looking up the table, this almost-satisfy entry (c, t) can be also exploited in another path like $\langle s, d, c \rangle$ and gets a BPHC, that is $\langle s, d, c, t \rangle$. This reusability shows the efficiency of BMAS.

Theorem 2. *BMAS takes $O(m\xi)$ time for each table update where ξ is the number of almost-satisfy entries. When BMAS performs only table lookup, the time complexity of getting BPHCs is $O(km\delta + m\delta')$ where m is the number of edges, δ is the number of hop-constrained paths, δ' is the number of BPHCs.*

Proof. BMAS will pre-run [11] to obtain the shortest path length for each vertex, and the time overhead of this part is $O(km\delta)$ where m is the number of edges, δ is the number of hop-constrained paths. In the early stages of the algorithm, we perform table update for a vertex to build its almost-satisfy entries. The output of each entry has $O(m)$ time and the total time is $O(m\xi)$ where ξ is the number of almost-satisfy entries. In the later stages of the algorithm, AS-Table store the complete almost-satisfy entries for each vertex in $W \subseteq V$. At this point, the output of each BPHC has $O(m)$ time and the total time complexity is $O(m\delta')$ where δ' is the number of BPHCs. Therefore, when AS-Table is complete, the time complexity of BMAS is $O(km\delta + m\delta')$.

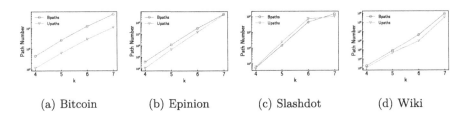

(a) Bitcoin   (b) Epinion   (c) Slashdot   (d) Wiki

Fig. 3. Path Number with Different k

4 Experiments

4.1 Experiment Setup

Algorithms. To the best of our knowledge, we are the first to propose the BPHC enumeration problem. In the experiment, we implement and evaluate the following algorithms. i) SC-DFS: baseline method proposed in Sect. 3.1; ii) BMAS: Algorithm 3 proposed in Sect. 3.3.

Datasets. We employ four real-world signed networks in our experiments, i.e., Bitcoin, Epinion, Slashdot and Wiki. Statistic details of these datasets are shown in Table 1. The proportion of negative edges is 8%, 23%, 17% and 12%, respectively. These datasets are obtained from SNAP[1], which are public available.

Parameter and Workload. To evaluate the performance of proposed techniques, we vary the parameters k from 4 to 7. Without loss of generality, we randomly generate 1,000 query pairs (s, t) on all datasets where s can reach t in k hops [11]. All algorithms are implemented in C++ with GNU GCC 7.4.0. Experiments are conducted on a PC with Intel Xeon 3.2GHz CPU and 32 GB RAM using Ubuntu 18.04 (64-bit).

4.2 Experiment Result

Exp-1: Number of BPHCs. To verify the significance of BPHC problem proposed in this paper, we report the average number of balanced paths and unbalanced paths with hop-constraint on all datasets by varying hop-constraint (k) values. The results are shown in Fig. 3. Statistically, only 10% of the vertices in Bitcoin are associated with negative edges, compared to 43%, 33%, and 30% in Epinion, Slashdot, and Wiki, respectively. Thus the number of balanced paths in Bitcoin is more than the number of unbalanced paths, while in the other three datasets the number of balanced and unbalanced paths is close. The statistical results of the number of BPHCs reflect the following conclusions. First of all, the average number of hop-constrained paths grows exponentially with k. Secondly, there are a considerable majority number of unbalanced paths in all hop-constrained paths. Therefore, it is necessary to design efficient algorithms for enumerating balanced hop-constrained paths.

---

[1] http://snap.stanford.edu.

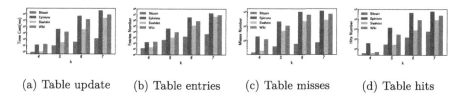

(a) Table update   (b) Table entries   (c) Table misses   (d) Table hits

Fig. 4. Metrics of negative weight path table

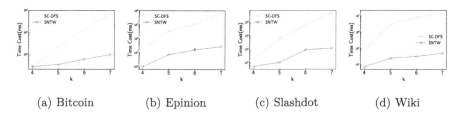

(a) Bitcoin   (b) Epinion   (c) Slashdot   (d) Wiki

Fig. 5. Average Response Time

Exp-2: Effectiveness Evaluation. Here we verify the effectiveness of *AS-Table*. Note that, we use hit to denote the situation that the vertex traversed by the negative in-neighbor and the almost-entries for this vertex are already exist. We use miss to denote the situation that there is no almost-entries for a vertex stored in our experiments. Figure 4(a) shows the average time of each (s, t) spent for table update on all datasets. According to Sect. 3.3, each vertex can cause at most one table update. As k increases, the more vertices are covered by the search, and thus the number of cases in which we perform table update becomes correspondingly large and grows in time consumption. In addition, we count the number of vertices in W for four datasets and their share in V are 7%, 39%, 28% and 26%, respectively. The statistic reflects the sign distribution in the datasets which has a direct impact on experimental result. As a result, Epinion has the largest time overhead for table update compared to other datasets, even though it is not the largest dataset. The comparisons and variations in the size of the almost-satisfy table presented in Fig. 4(b) similarly corroborate the time-consuming nature of the table update invoked to construct the almost-satisfy entries in the four datasets. Besides, almost-satisfy table are reusable. We count the total number of table misses and total number of table hits in the batch as shown in Fig. 4(c) and Fig. 4(d). When $k = 7$, Bitcoin has 98% hits, Epinions has 98% hits, Slashdot has 96% hits and Wiki has 97% hits.

Exp-3: Efficiency Evaluation. We vary k from 4 to 7 and compare the average response time of algorithm SC-DFS and BMAS on all datasets, as shown in Fig. 5. When k is very small, the time overhead of BMAS and SC-DFS is close. Because when we determine whether a vertex can be processed to the stack with $len(S) + len(N) < k$, the very small value of k makes it so that very few vertices satisfy this condition. The probability of repeatedly visiting a vertex is thus extremely small, and at this point BMAS fails to hit in the table lookup. As the coverage of the search increases as k increases, the table hits become more and more frequent. When $k = 7$, experiments on Bitcoin, Epinions, Slashdot and Wiki all have more than 95% hits. As shown in Fig. 5, BMAS outperforms SC-DFS by nearly three orders of magnitude in terms of time efficiency. BMAS is an accurate and efficient balanced hop-constrained path enumeration algorithm.

Summary. As demonstrated in the experiments, BMAS is significantly faster than SC-DFS. It achieves a characteristic reduction of the search space with a very high table hit rate in the later stages of the experiment to ensure that each output is a balanced path. At the same time, the pre-running barrier pruning technique ensures the hop constraint requirement. BMAS efficiently fulfils the two constraints of the BPHC problem.

5   Related Work

Signed Graph Analysis. Signed graph analysis is widely studied in the literature due to its numerous applications. In these works, they can be mainly divided into vertex-oriented tasks (e.g., community detection) [14], link-oriented tasks (e.g., links prediction) [10] and application-oriented tasks (e.g., recommendation system) [25]. [13] studies the maximum stable community detection problem and proposes a greedy framework. Sun et al. [14] study the maximal balanced signed biclique enumeration in signed bipartite graphs. For link-oriented tasks, Leskovec et al. [10] use balance theory for positive and negative links prediction. Signed graphs analysis has important value for practical applications. [18] provides a mathematical approach and proposes a model RecSSN to use both positive and negative connections for recommendation tasks. To our best knowledge, there is no existing work about path enumeration in signed graphs.

Path Enumeration on Unsigned Graph. Path enumeration is one of the fundamental tasks in graph analytics. Most of the existing methods adopt DFS strategy and use different pruning techniques to efficiently accomplish enumeration [11,17,24]. In [11], BC-DFS proposed by Peng et al. which allows exploration of some search branches that have no output first, but avoids exploring unpromising branches in the future. Additionally, a join-oriented algorithm, namely JOIN is also proposed by [11], which shares the computation of the partial paths and hence further significantly enhance the query response time than BC-DFS. Sun et al. [17] proposed PathEnum which adopts a single directional search-based join paradigm. It produces either none or only a portion of intermediate results. If we simply consider collecting the sign information in the signed graphs and use the traditional methods on unsigned graphs for path enumeration, it will inevitably cause a lot of search waste as demonstrated in the paper.

6   Conclusion

In this paper, we propose the BPHC problem, i.e., balanced paths enumeration with hop constraint, which combines the balance theory of signed graphs. To fulfill the requirement of enumerating balanced paths and avoid getting unbalanced paths, we construct an almost-satisfy table to instantly correct unbalanced state during the search process. To further speedup the search, algorithm BMAS combines the shortest path length to obtain all the balanced paths in the process of table update and lookup. We conduct experiments on four real world networks to verify the efficiency of the proposed algorithms.

References

1. Bernstein, A., Chechi, S.: Incremental topological sort and cycle detection in expected total time. In: SODA, pp. 21–34 (2018)
2. Chen, C., Wu, Y., Sun, R., Wang, X.: Maximum signed θ-clique identification in large signed graphs. IEEE Trans. Knowl. Data Eng. (2021)
3. Chen, S., Qian, H., Wu, Y., Chen, C., Wang, X.: Efficient adoption maximization in multi-layer social networks. In: ICDMW, pp. 56–60 (2019)
4. Derr, T., Ma, Y., Tang, J.: Signed graph convolutional networks. In: ICDM, pp. 929–934 (2018)
5. Gotthilf, Z., Lewenstein, M.: Improved algorithms for the k simple shortest paths and the replacement paths problems. Inf. Process. Lett. **109**(7), 352–355 (2009)
6. Harary, F.: On the notion of balance of a signed graph. Mich. Math. J. **2**(2), 143–146 (1953)
7. Hershberger, J., Maxel, M., Suri, S.: Finding the k shortest simple paths: a new algorithm and its implementation. TALG **3**(4) (2007)
8. Kumar, R., Calders, T.: 2SCENT: an efficient algorithm to enumerate all simple temporal cycles. PVLDB **11**(11), 1441–1453 (2018)
9. Lai, Z., Peng, Y., Yang, S., Lin, X., Zhang, W.: PEFP: efficient k-hop constrained ST simple path enumeration on FPGA. In: ICDE, pp. 1320–1331 (2021)
10. Leskovec, J., Huttenlocher, D., Kleinberg, J.: Predicting positive and negative links in online social networks. In: WWW, pp. 641–650 (2010)
11. Peng, Y., Zhang, Y., Lin, X., Zhang, W., Qin, L., Zhou, J.: Hop-constrained ST simple path enumeration: towards bridging theory and practice. PVLDB **13**(4), 463–476 (2019)
12. Sun, R., Chen, C., Wang, X., Zhang, W., Zhang, Y., Lin, X.: Efficient maximum signed biclique identification. In: ICDE, pp. 1313–1325 (2023)
13. Sun, R., Chen, C., Wang, X., Zhang, Y., Wang, X.: Stable community detection in signed social networks. IEEE Trans. Knowl. Data Eng. **34**(10), 5051–5055 (2020)
14. Sun, R., Wu, Y., Chen, C., Wang, X., Zhang, W., Lin, X.: Maximal balanced signed biclique enumeration in signed bipartite graphs. In: ICDE, pp. 1887–1899 (2022)
15. Sun, R., Wu, Y., Wang, X.: Diversified top-r community search in geo-social network: a k-truss based model. In: EDBT (2022)
16. Sun, R., Wu, Y., Wang, X., Chen, C., Zhang, W., Lin, X.: Clique identification in signed graphs: a balance theory based model. IEEE Trans. Knowl. Data Eng. (2023)
17. Sun, S., Chen, Y., He, B., Hooi, B.: Pathenum: towards real-time hop-constrained ST path enumeration. In: SIGMOD, pp. 1758–1770 (2021)
18. Tang, J., Aggarwal, C., Liu, H.: Recommendations in signed social networks. In: WWW, pp. 31–40 (2016)
19. Wang, X., Zhang, Y., Zhang, W., Lin, X., Chen, C.: Bring order into the samples: a novel scalable method for influence maximization. IEEE Trans. Knowl. Data Eng. **29**(2), 243–256 (2016)

20. Wu, Y., Sun, R., Chen, C., Wang, X., Fu, X.: Efficiently answering minimum reachable label set queries in edge-labeled graphs. In: CIKM, pp. 4585–4589 (2022)
21. Wu, Y., Sun, R., Chen, C., Wang, X., Zhu, Q.: Maximum signed (k, r)-truss identification in signed networks. In: CIKM, pp. 3337–3340 (2020)
22. Wu, Y., Zhao, J., Sun, R., Chen, C., Wang, X.: Efficient personalized influential community search in large networks. Data Sci. Eng. **6**(3), 310–322 (2021)
23. Zhang, C., Zhang, Y., Zhang, W., Lin, X., Cheema, M.A., Wang, X.: Diversified spatial keyword search on road networks. In: EDBT (2014)
24. Zhang, J., Yang, S., Ouyang, D., Zhang, F., Lin, X., Yuan, L.: Hop-constrained ST simple path enumeration on large dynamic graphs. In: ICDE, pp. 762–775 (2023)
25. Zhang, X., Wang, H., Yu, J., Chen, C., Wang, X., Zhang, W.: Polarity-based graph neural network for sign prediction in signed bipartite graphs. World Wide Web **25**(2), 471–487 (2022). https://doi.org/10.1007/s11280-022-01015-4

An Experimental Evaluation of Two Methods on Shortest Distance Queries over Small-World Graphs

Houyu Di and Junhu Wang[✉]

Griffith University, Gold Coast, Australia
j.wang@griffith.edu.au

Abstract. Efficient computation of shortest distances is a fundamental problem in graph databases. In this paper, we report our experimental evaluation and comparison of two state-of-the-art methods for exact distance computation over small-world graphs. Our experiment reveals some results that are not previously reported. These results provide insights on the pros and cons of each method, and on the possible directions these methods can be improved. They can also help us in choosing the right method for specific application scenarios.

1 Introduction

A shortest distance query asks for the minimum distance between a pair of vertices in a graph. Answering shortest distance queries is one of the fundamental problems in graph theory. To calculate the distance between a pair of vertices, we can use breadth-first search (BFS) for unweighted graphs or Dijkstra's algorithm for weighted graphs. However, these algorithms are too slow for large graphs since they may need to traverse the entire graph in the worst case. Distance queries can be answered instantly by creating an index that stores the shortest distances between all pairs of vertices in the graph. However, this is impractical because of its quadratic index size and index construction time. Therefore, extensive work has been done to design distance indexes to make a trade-off between query time and index size.

Over the last decade, many distance indexes have been built using hub-labeling [4], tree-decomposition [11], graph partitioning [8,12] and so on. Among them are *Core-Tree (CT) labeling* [10] and *Highway labeling (HL)* [7], two state-of-the-art methods designed for exact distance computation over small-world graphs. CT is based on tree decomposition and *pruned landmark labelling (PLL)* [5] and its variant PSL [9]. Compared with PLL, its index is much smaller and the query performance is only mildly slower for graphs that have the core-periphery structure. HL is a 3-hop hub-labeling method which computes an index using a small set of landmarks. Given any two vertices, it first computes a distance upper bound using the index, and then uses bi-directional traversal over the sparse graph (the graph after deleting the landmarks), in combination with the upper bound, to compute the distance. Although the HL index is usually small,

the query performance is quite good, and on some graphs it is even better than
PLL, as shown in the experiments of [7]. More details about CT and HL are
given in Sect. 3.

To the best of our knowledge, there has been no independent comparison
between CT and HL. This paper intends to fill in the gap by conducting experimental evaluations of CT and HL using some additional real-world graphs. First,
we conduct more detailed experiments on the index size, index construction time,
and query time for both CT and HL. The purpose of this experiment is to see
the relative contribution to these metrics of each component in the methods
(e.g., the relative time spent on computing the distance upper bound and on
bi-directional search in HL, and the relative size of core and tree indexes in CT).
Second, we compare CT and HL in terms of index size and query time under
different parameter settings. This experiment reveals some trends that are not
mentioned in the original papers. Third, we conduct experiments to see how the
distance affects the query time for both methods. We also provide a discussion
about possible ways to improve or combine these methods.

The rest of this paper is organized as follows. Section 2 provides the preliminary concepts. Section 3 provides a brief description of CT and HL. Section 4
reports our experimental results. Section 5 concludes the paper.

2   Preliminaries

Shortest Path and Shortest Distance. We consider simple undirected and
unweighted graphs in this paper. A graph $G(V, E)$ consists of a set of vertices
V and a set of edges $E \subseteq V \times V$ between the vertices. An edge from vertex u
to vertex v is denoted (u, v). Given two vertices s and t in graph G, a *path* from
s to t is a sequence of edges $(s, v_1), (v_1, v_2), \ldots, (v_{k-1}, v_k), (v_k, t)$. The *length* of
the path is the number of edges in the path. A *shortest path* from s to t is a path
from s to t which has the minimum length (among all paths from s to t), and
the *shortest distance* (or simply *the distance*) between s and t, denoted $d_G(s, t)$,
is the length of a shortest path from s to t in G. When the graph G is clear from
the context, we use $d(s, t)$ to represent $d_G(s, t)$. Note that for undirected graphs
$d(u, v) = d(v, u)$.

2-Hop Cover Labeling. Suppose $G(V, E)$ is a graph. In a 2-hop labeling, for
each vertex $u \in V$, we have a label $L(u)$ which is a set of $(vertex, distance)$ pairs
$(v, d(u, v))$, where v is a vertex in V, and $d(u, v)$ is the distance from u to v. In
other words, a 2-hop labeling L consists of a label $L(u)$ as described above for
every vertex $u \in V$. To compute the distance between two vertices s and t using
L, we can use the formula below:

$$d^L(s, t) = \min_v \{ d(s, v) + d(v, t) | (v, d(s, v)) \in L(s), (v, d(v, t)) \in L(t) \} \quad (1)$$

A 2-hop labeling is called a *2-hop cover* labeling if $d^L(s, t) = d(s, t)$ for every
pair of vertices $s, t \in V$, that is, the distance computed using Eq. (1) is the
correct distance between s and t.

Tree Decomposition. Let $G(V, E)$ be a graph. A tree decomposition of G is a tree T_G such that (1) every node in T_G is a set of vertices in G, and every vertex in G belongs to some of the tree nodes; (2) for every edge (u, v) in G, there is a tree node that contains both u and v; (3) for every vertex $v \in V$, the tree nodes that contain v form a connected subtree. For every node B in T_G, its *size* is defined to be the number of vertices in B. The maximum size of all nodes in T_G, minus 1, is called the *width* of T_G. The *treewith* of G is defined to be the smallest integer w such that no tree decomposition of G has a width smaller than w.

3 Core-Tree Index and Highway Cover Labeling

Core-Tree Index. As mentioned in Sect. 1, Core-Tree index (CT) [10] is based on tree decomposition and PLL (and its variant PSL). Specifically, given a graph G, it first uses the *minimum degree elimination (MDE)* algorithm [6] to create a tree decomposition T_G of G. The nodes in T_G, $N_1, \ldots, N_K$, are created one by one as a sequence. Then it uses an integer parameter d, called *bandwith*, to divide the nodes in T_G into two parts: let $\lambda(d)$ be the smallest integer in $[0, K]$ such that $|N_{\lambda(d)+1}| > d + 1$. Then the core part consists of the vertices in the nodes $N_{\lambda(d)+1}, \ldots, N_K$, and the *tree part* consists of the remaining nodes $N_1, \ldots, N_{\lambda(d)}$. It follows that the larger the value of d, the smaller the core. By way of construction, the core is a connected weighted graph, and the tree is a set of subtrees of T_G. Now a PLL index is built on the core, called the *core-index* (When d=0, the core is the same as G, and PSL is used to build the index), and a separate *tree-index* is built for the tree part. Query processing for $d(s, t)$ is done according to four different cases: both s and t are in the core, one of them is in the core, both of them are in the same tree, or they are in different trees.

The parameter d can be used to adjust the sizes of the core and the tree, hence the index size and query time. Generally, the larger the value d, the smaller the core part, hence it is expected that the core-index will be smaller. However, the query is expected to take longer time since the distance for fewer vertex pairs can be computed using the core-index. It is reported in [10] that setting $d = 100$ provides a good trade-off between index size and query time.

Highway Labeling. In highway labeling (HL) [7], a small set R of vertices in G is chosen as the *landmarks*. Then for each vertex $u \in V$, a set $L(u)$ of labels of the form $(v, (d(u, v)))$ is built, where v is a landmark in R. The HL labeling also satisfies *highway cover* property, which ensures that for any vertices $s, t \in V$, the length of the shortest paths from s to t that pass through any landmarks in R can be computed using the labels in L, if we pre-compute and store the distances between every pair of landmarks. Specifically, the following equation computes a value $d^L(s, t)$ which is equal to the length of the shortest path that pass through any landmarks in R; thus, $d^L(s, t)$ can serve as an upper bound of the distance between s and t.

$$d^L(s, t) = min_{u,v}\{d(s, u) + d(u, v) + d(v, t)|(u, d(s, u)) \in L(s), (v, d(v, t)) \in L(t)\}$$
$$(2)$$

To find the real distance $d(s,t)$, we first delete all the landmarks (and their incident edges) from G, resulting in a smaller and usually sparser graph, which is the induced subgraph of G using $V - R$, denoted $G[V - R]$. Then we conduct two-way traversal from both s and t, while also checking the upper bound in the process, so that we never need to go more than the upper bound number of hops in the traversal.

Obviously, the number of landmarks $|R|$ is an important parameter for both the label size and the query performance. It is expected that the more landmarks, the larger the label size, the tighter the upper bound, and the smaller the induced subgraph $G[V - R]$, hence the better the query performance. In [7], it is reported that setting $|R|$ to 40 to 50 achieves good trade-off between label size and query performance. The way the landmarks are chosen is also important. The default method is to choose vertices with the largest degrees.

4   Experiments

In this section, we report our experimental evaluation and comparison of the HL and CT methods. We first report experiments on each individual method. The purpose of these experiments is to assess their performance under different parameter settings that were not mentioned in the original papers or tested in detail. We then compare HL and CT in terms of index construction time, index size, and query speed, which has not been done before. Finally, we explore the influence of the shortest distances between vertices on the query times for the two methods because this was not done in the original papers.

4.1   Experimental Set Up

Table 1. Datasets

Name	Dataset	Type	n (M)	m (M)	size (MB)	Source
DBLP	DBLP	Social	0.41	1.04	13.9	[1]
YT	Youtube	Social	1.13	2.98	38.7	[1]
TG	Twitch Gamers	Social	0.16	6.79	86.2	[1]
LJ	LiveJournal	Social	3.90	34.00	501.6	[1]
OT	ORKUT	Social	3.00	106.30	1602.1	[2]
SW	SINAWEIBO	Social	21.00	261.00	4049.8	[2]
FS	FRIENDSTER	Social	65.60	1800.00	38720.8	[2]
ND	NotreDame	Web	0.42	1.50	20.1	[2]
BS	BERKSTAN	Web	0.68	7.60	107.3	[2]
BK	BAIDU-BAIKE	Web	2.10	17.90	235.3	[2]
UK2002	UK domain (2002)	Web	18.00	261.00	4326.9	[3]
UK2007	UK domain (2007)	Web	105.00	3301.00	58098.1	[3]
CW	CLUEWEB09	Web	1700.00	7800.00	147179.7	[2]

Datasets. The experiments are conducted on 6 web networks, and 7 social networks. The 13 datasets are downloaded from the Network Repository [2], the Stanford Large Network Dataset Collection [1], and The KONECT Project [3]. The number of edges in the graphs varies from 300 thousand to 8 billion. Table 1 provides a summary of the datasets.

Running Environment. All the experiments were conducted on a Linux server (Ubuntu 22.04, X64) with a 16-core, 32-thread AMD Epyc CPU and 512 GB of main memory. The source codes for both methods are kindly provided by the original authors, and they were implemented in C++. The C++ compiler was GNU GCC 11 with -O3-level optimization. We made some minor modifications to the source code to meet our experimental requirements. If the programs run out of memory during index construction, the result of the corresponding test will be marked "Fail". As for the parallelization technique, the openMP framework is adapted for the PSL method and the Core-Tree labeling method, while the concurrency support library (since C++11) is adopted for the HL method.

Parameters. Both HL and CT have parameters that must be set manually. The parameter for the HL method is the number of landmarks. The number of landmarks is also the number of threads during the index construction process. Our experiments on the HL method were conducted under HL(8) (which uses 8-bit representation of vertices in the labels), and the number of landmarks was set to 20, 32, 64, and 128. The parameter for CT is the bandwidth d. Bit-Parallel is a technique introduced in [5], which exploits bit-level parallelism. The CT method adopts it to support multi-threading, which generates an additional index called bp_index. We set the number of threads to 32 during our experiment. When comparing the performance of the two methods, we use HL(8) with 32 landmarks (i.e., HL-32) and CT-100 with $d = 100$ and 32 threads.

4.2 Experiment on Highway Labeling

Index Size and Index Construction Time. The HL index is composed of 3 parts: distances between landmarks, HL labels, and the sparser subgraph. The distances between landmarks are only a few KB at most in our experiments because the number of landmarks is small, so they can be ignored. The index size reported in this section are the HL label size only, as the size of the sparse subgraph is only slightly smaller than that of the original graph, due to the small number of landmarks used.

   The second and third columns of Table 2 show the index construction time and index size respectively on some of the larger datasets (results on the remaining data sets are omitted due to space limit). It can be seen that the label construction time and label size increase with the number of landmarks on all the tested datasets. As for the total query time, the overall trend is that the query time becomes shorter when the number of landmarks increases. This is as expected and consistent with the results in [7].

Query Time. The query time of the HL method consists of upper bound computation time using the HL labels, and bi-directional search time over the sparse

Table 2. Experimental Result of HL Under Different Number of Landmarks(NoL)

Dataset-NoL	Construction Time (sec)	Index Size (MB)	Upper Bound Query Time (μs)	Total Query Time (μs)
LJ-20	2.402	104	0.9	59.238
LJ-32	2.869	154	0.9	57.853
LJ-64	6.245	259	1.1	56.531
LJ-128	12.178	442	1.1	54.85
OT-20	3.1	71	1.0	139.2
OT-32	3.6	100	1.1	145.3
OT-64	7.6	161	1.3	131.6
OT-128	14.8	271	1.8	116.7
SW-20	37.1	520	1.0	289.2
SW-32	53.1	717	1.1	271.5
SW-64	113.5	1228	1.3	253.6
SW-128	225.9	2252	1.6	235.6
FS-20	111.7	2560	0.8	661.8
FS-32	138.5	3993	1.2	628.0
FS-64	288.9	7680	1.2	640.2
FS-128	573.6	15360	1.4	670.4
BK-20	1.2	43	1.0	23.7
BK-32	1.5	59	1.1	21.8
BK-64	3.4	95	1.3	12.8
BK-128	6.9	156	1.5	11.5
UK2007-20	29.5	1945	0.9	5834.7
UK2007-32	38.7	3584	1.1	5759.5
UK2007-64	84.3	6348	1.4	5513.6
UK2007-128	166.4	11264	1.8	5166.9

subgraph. For all the tested graphs, the former takes only a few microseconds at most. Most of the query time is spent on the graph search, and larger graphs requires more time. For example, the upper bound calculation time for LJ with 64 landmarks is about 1 μs, but the search time is 55 μs; For FS with 64 landmarks, the former is 2 μs and the latter is 638 μs. This suggests that to further improve the query performance, we should target the sparser subgraph. Also can be seen from Table 2 is that the total query time decreases when the number of landmarks increases. This is not surprising and it is also observed in [7].

Discussion. The HL labels can only be used to compute an upper bound of the shortest distance, and it must pre-compute and store the pairwise distances between all landmarks. Therefore, although it is said in the experiments of [7] that the index construction time and index size increase linearly with the number of landmarks, it is impractical to use a large landmark set, since otherwise computing and storing the pairwise distances among the landmarks will be too costly. Also, as shown in our experiment, computing the distance upper bound takes little time (due to the small sizes of the landmark set), while doing the bi-directional search over the induced subgraph $G[V - R]$ takes much longer time. One might think the induced subgraph $G[V - R]$ is smaller and hence building an PLL index on it will be faster and it will take less space than the PLL index on the original graph. We have tested this assumption with several real datasets. To our surprise, however, our experiments show the PLL size on $G[V - R]$ is actually larger than that on G unless we increase the size of R to more than $1/8$ of $|V|$. However, this large number of landmarks is impractical as discussed above. Another idea we tried is based on the observation that $G[V - R]$ is likely to be disconnected. So, we can compute the connected components (CCs) (which can be done rather quickly), and label each vertex in $V - R$ with its CC ID. Given two vertices, we can check whether their CC IDs are equal. If not, we can directly take the distance upper bound as the distance. Only when the two ver-tices are in the same CC will we need to conduct the bi-directional traversal. We conducted some experiments about it as well, unfortunately, the number of CCs is not big enough to make a big difference on the average query performance, after deleting only 40 to 64 landmarks for our datasets. Also, we found that the majority of vertices in the sparser graph are located in a single CC, while all the other CCs are very small, many of them contains just a single vertex.

4.3   Experiment on Core-Tree Labeling

Index Construction Time and Index Size. The index construction time of the CT method consists of four parts: bit-parallel index construction time (bp_time), core-tree decomposition time (decomposition_time), tree index con-struction time (tree_time), and core index construction time (core_time). Table 3 shows the relative lengths of these components for CT-100 on all the tested datasets. It can be observed that, for CT-100, the decomposition_time and tree_time are similar, both are much larger than bp_time. tree_time is larger than core_time on small graphs yet core_time is much larger than tree_time on large graphs. Similarly, the index size of CT consists of three parts as well: bp index (bp_size), tree index (tree_size), and core index size (core_size). The size of each component is shown in Table 4. It can be seen that, overall, for the small graphs the tree_size is larger than the core_size, but for the large graph the core_size is larger than the tree_size. This is not surprising because for the small graphs setting $d = 100$ will create a relatively small core compared with the large graphs.

The original authors tested the index size and query time with increasing band-width d, by setting d from 2 to 100, and the result suggested that the index size decreases with increasing d, and the margin gain (index size reduction) becomes very small when $d = 100$. We tested larger bandwidths on two data sets LJ and UK2002 by setting d to 200 and 300. Our experiments show that when d exceeds 100, the index sizes start to increase with increasing d, see Table 5.

Query Time. As for the query time, the results of our tests are the same as that of the original paper, it always increases with the increase of d.

Table 3. CT Index Construction Time (sec)

Datasets	bp_time	decomposition_time	tree_time	core_time
DBLP	0.065	0.8	1.277	0.814
YT	0.133	2.2	2.892	1.515
TG	0.169	1.4	1.794	4.409
LJ	1.754	33.3	39.443	1550.407
OT	3.876	39.0	44.502	14818.339
SW	11.077	77.2	86.704	1369.812
FS	92.969	659.4	Fail	Fail
ND	0.026	0.5	0.751	0.142
BS	0.08	2.0	3.081	0.564
BK	0.731	9.9	12.38	40.439
UK2002	2.946	70.0	95.924	413.927
UK2007	24.678	608.6	820.268	7303.592
CW	562.411	Fail	Fail	Fail

Table 4. CT Index Size (MB)

Datasets	bp_size	tree_size	core_size
DBLP	16.1	58.0	34.4
YT	48.7	105.1	35.0
TG	11.4	18.1	183.8
LJ	254.4	653.3	15288.3
OT	204.1	250.4	92914.4
SW	1541.8	926.8	6268.0
FS	4134.8	Fail	Fail
ND	9.7	39.6	1.1
BS	30.2	150.2	3.4
BK	116.2	209.1	790.1
UK2002	708.1	3038.3	6222.5
UK2007	4366.6	16878.6	90680.6
CW	45570.0	Fail	Fail

Table 5. Change of Index Size (MB) and Query Time (μs) with Bandwidth

Dataset	bp_size	core_size	tree_size	total index size	query time
lj-50	254.4	16668.2	318.5	17241.1	191.2
lj-100	254.4	15288.3	653.3	16196.0	255.1
lj-200	254.4	14513.8	1340.0	16108.2	308.4
lj-300	254.4	14212.9	2040.5	16507.8	331.2
uk2002-50	708.1	9780.2	1440.2	11928.5	148.9
uk2002-100	708.1	6222.5	3038.3	9968.9	210.6
uk2002-200	708.1	4351.3	6244.5	11303.9	291.5
uk2002-300	708.1	3544.1	9447.2	13699.4	326.8

4.4 Comparison of HL and CT

Index Construction Time. Figure 1 compares the index construction time of CT-100 and HL-32 with PSL as the baseline. PSL failed to construct indexes on FS, UK2007 and CW. CT-100 successfully completed the index construction process on 11 datasets, but it failed to generate tree indexes on FS and CW. While HL-32 constructed an index for each dataset. CT-100 is faster in index construction than PSL except on 4 graphs, and the results are consistent with [10]. As for HL-32, it not only succeeded on all graphs but is also significantly faster than CT-100 on each graph.

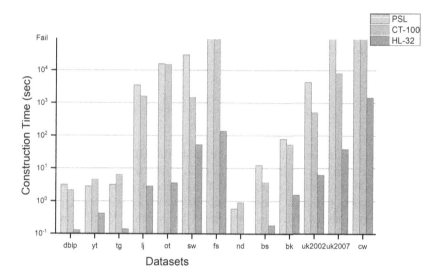

Fig. 1. The Comparison of Construction Time

Index Size. Figure 2 presents the comparison of the index size of PSL, CT-100 and HL-32. Compared to the baseline, CT-100 has a smaller index size on most datasets except ND and BS, and for most graphs, the index size of CT-100 is far smaller. For HL-32, as discussed before, when calculating the index size, the sparser subgraph size used for the bi-directional search also needs to be included, so we saved the subgraphs and observed their sizes. As shown in the Figure, the index size of HL-32 is smaller than CT-100 on every graph, and by large extent on most of the graphs.

Query Time. Figure 3 shows the comparison of the query time of the three methods. The baseline method PSL achieved the shortest query time on all the graphs except FS, UK2007 and CW because it failed to construct the indexes. For graphs under a billion edges, both methods can answer distance queries within 1 ms. On UK2007, CT-100 still achieved an average query time under 1 ms, while the time of HL-32 was near 10 ms. As for CW, HL-32 can successfully

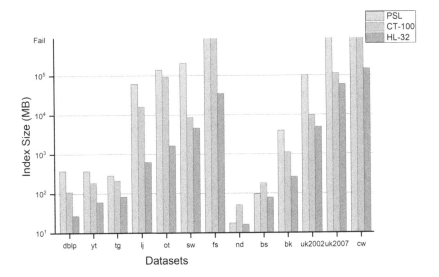

Fig. 2. The Comparison of Index Size

answer the queries in around 10 ms. Note that, the HL method requires extra initializing time for distance query operations in order to prepare a data structure for bi-directional traversal in memory, and the larger the graphs, the longer the initializing time, but it only needs to be initialized once for multiple queries. Hence, for single queries, HL may take much longer than the CT method, but for batch queries and online queries, the initializing time can be ignored.

The Influence of Distance on Query Time. To find out how the shortest distance affects the query time on both methods, we record the average query time under different distances on 4 datasets. This test hasn't been done before. Figure 4 and Fig. 5 show the trend. When the length of the shortest distance increase, the query time of the HL (HL-32) method shows a general uptrend on all 4 datasets. On datasets BK and OT, the query time grows relatively slowly with distance, but on UK2007 and SW, the query time increases rapidly. When looking at the CT-100 method, on datasets BK and OT, it has a similar trend to HL-32, but on UK2007, the growth curve is much flatter, which means the distance doesn't affect the query time much, and on SW, the query time does not exhibit monotonicity with the distance.

The experimental results show that the HL method is significantly better than the CT method in label construction time and index size, and it can construct the labels on graphs that the CT method cannot deal with, such as FS and CW. The HL method has faster query speed on some of the social networks than the CT method, e.g., TG, LJ and OT. But on most of the web graphs that the CT method can handle, CT is faster than HL. Although CT and HL have a longer query time than PSL, they still answer shortest distance queries in a reasonable time. The HL method is more distance-sensitive in query time than CT.

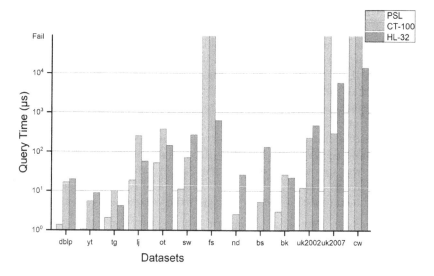

Fig. 3. The Comparison of Query Time

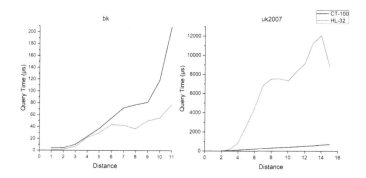

Fig. 4. The Relationship Between the Distance and Query Time (Web)

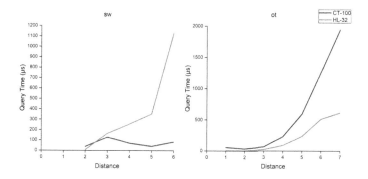

Fig. 5. The Relationship Between the Distance and Query Time (Social)

5   Conclusion

We conducted a detailed experimental evaluation of CT and HL, and compared their performance in index construction time, index size, and query time. We have observed that the HL method cannot use large landmark sets. However, even with a small number of landmarks, it can build an index to achieve quite good query performance on some very large graphs, while CT cannot handle such large graphs. However, on most large web graphs for which CT can successfully build an index, CT has much better query performance than HL.

We also observed the query time of HL is mostly contributed by the graph traversal over the sparser graph, while the upper bound computation is very fast. Also, over large graphs CT's tree index may become too large when d is too large. It would be interesting to see if and how these drawbacks can be overcome.

References

1. https://snap.stanford.edu/data
2. http://konect.cc/networks
3. https://networkrepository.com
4. Abraham, I., Delling, D., Goldberg, A.V., Werneck, R.F.: A hub-based labeling algorithm for shortest paths in road networks. In: SEA (2011)
5. Akiba, T., Iwata, Y., Yoshida, Y.: Fast exact shortest-path distance queries on large networks by pruned landmark labeling. In: SIGMOD, pp. 349–360 (2013)
6. Berry, A., Heggernes, P., Simonet, G.: The minimum degree heuristic and the minimal triangulation process. In: Bodlaender, H.L. (ed.) WG 2003. LNCS, vol. 2880, pp. 58–70. Springer, Heidelberg (2003). https://doi.org/10.1007/978-3-540-39890-5_6
7. Farhan, M., Wang, Q., Lin, Y., McKay, B.D.: A highly scalable labelling approach for exact distance queries in complex networks. In: EDBT, pp. 13–24 (2019)
8. Jing, N., Huang, Y.W., Rundensteiner, E.A.: Hierarchical encoded path views for path query processing: an optimal model and its performance evaluation. IEEE TKDE **10**(3), 409–432 (1998)
9. Li, W., Qiao, M., Qin, L., Zhang, Y., Chang, L., Lin, X.: Scaling distance labeling on small-world networks. In: SIGMOD, pp. 1060–1077 (2019)
10. Li, W., Qiao, M., Qin, L., Zhang, Y., Chang, L., Lin, X.: Scaling up distance labeling on graphs with core-periphery properties. In: SIGMOD, pp. 1367–1381 (2020)
11. Wei-Kleiner, F.: Tree decomposition-based indexing for efficient shortest path and nearest neighbors query answering on graphs. J. Comput. Syst. Sci. **82**(1), 23–44 (2016)
12. Zhong, R., Li, G., Tan, K.L., Zhou, L., Gong, Z.: G-tree: an efficient and scalable index for spatial search on road networks. IEEE TKDE **27**(8), 2175–2189 (2015)

Discovering Densest Subgraph over Heterogeneous Information Networks

Haozhe Yin[1], Kai Wang[2], Wenjie Zhang[1(✉)], Dong Wen[1], Xiaoyang Wang[1], and Ying Zhang[3]

[1] The University of New South Wales, Sydney, Australia
{wenjie.zhang,dong.wen,xiaoyang.wang1}@unsw.edu.au
[2] Antai College of Economics and Management,
Shanghai Jiao Tong University, Shanghai, China
w.kai@sjtu.edu.cn
[3] University of Technology Sydney, Ultimo, Australia
ying.zhang@uts.edu.au

Abstract. Densest Subgraph Discovery (DSD) is a fundamental and challenging problem in the field of graph mining in recent years. The DSD aims to determine, given a graph G, the subgraph with the maximum density according to the specified definition. The majority of current research focuses on identifying DSD in homogeneous information networks. Nevertheless, these techniques cannot be applied directly in Heterogeneous Information Networks (HINs) since the semantics of paths are not considered. This limits the application of these approaches in certain fields, as many graphs, e.g., the DBLP dataset, comprise of many types of edges. In order to remedy this research need, this paper proposes approaches for resolving the DSD issue over HINs.

By examining numerous linkage paths between two vertices, we characterize the relationship between two objects of the same type using the concept of meta-path. We further build two new HIN models and provide DSD techniques that perform well in large networks. In addition, comprehensive experiments on various HIN datasets demonstrate the effectiveness and efficiency of the proposed methods.

1 Introduction

In real-life scenarios, networks can be formed by different types of entities and relationships, and Heterogeneous Information Networks (HINs) is naturally used to depict such networks. As discussed in recent works [23,25,28], most traditional techniques for homogeneous information networks do not work well in HINs; hence, obtaining useful information from HINs is a crucial task of the data mining discipline. Figure 1(a) is an example of HIN.

In the literature, Densest Subgraph Discovery (DSD) is the problem of identifying a "dense" subgraph from graph G that has the highest density according to a specific density definition [5,6,10,24]. This paper focuses on the DSD problem over heterogeneous information networks. Given an HIN G and a specific type t for the vertex, we aim to find a set of vertices (a community), in which all the

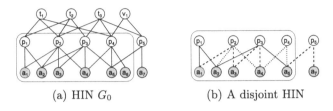

(a) HIN G_0 (b) A disjoint HIN

Fig. 1. Heterogeneous information networks.

target vertices are densely connected in G; the density of the community should be the largest among all feasible communities. To measure the density of HINs, existing studies evaluate density based on the ratio of target vertex pairs to the total number of target vertices. In this approach, a target vertex pair should be connected by one or more instances of meta-path, which is a sequence of links containing different types of vertices and edges. By using this definition, it is always possible to identify a community within the HIN that has the highest density among all possible communities.

Despite being able to obtain the densest subgraph using the aforementioned definition, there are still some issues with this procedure. Firstly, when the input networks are large-scale or the length of the meta-path is very long, searching for the densest subgraphs can be time-consuming and the size of the densest subgraph can be quite large, making it difficult to extract meaningful information from it. In addition, the definition only focuses on whether two vertices are connected without considering the routes of their connection which will result in the loss of important information. For instance, in Fig. 1(a) a_6 only publishes one paper, nonetheless, since a_6 has two co-authors a_4 and a_5, he or she will be grouped with the remaining authors in the densest graph (the part surrounded by the rectangle). Clearly, all the linkages for a_6 depend on the edge $a_6 \rightarrow p_4$, which results in a_6's weak engagement. To address this issue, we introduce the well-known concept of the disjoint path in the graph clustering field. Existing research measures the similarity between two vertices by the number of edge- or vertex-disjoint paths. Inspired by this concept, we introduce two metrics by using edge- and vertex-disjoint paths [7,27] which requires that each instance of meta-path between two vertices in the densest subgraph should be edge- or vertex-disjoint paths. Figure 1(b) demonstrate a disjoint HIN for Fig. 1(a) based on the meta-path 'APA'. Intuitively, the disjoint HIN is simpler than the original graph and the densest subgraph (the part surrounded by the rectangle) successfully filters out a_6 which has weak engagement.

Applications. (1) *Research group building*: For a research topic, researchers need to form a group in order to collaborate intensively. However, it is difficult to locate researchers, who can collaborate harmoniously together and are acquainted with respect to the research topic. To tackle this problem, we can detect the densest subgraph. (2) *Online marketing*: In certain E-commerce platforms, the dataset always consists of HINs. To precisely recommend the product or perform advertisements to the users, we can find the group in the dataset through the densest subgraph.

Related Work. (1) *Densest subgraph discovery*: There are two definitions for the densest subgraph of a graph: edge density subgraph (EDS) and h-clique densest subgraph (CDS). In this paper, our algorithms are based on the solution for EDS. The solution for EDS on evolving graphs is presented in [8], while Qin developed algorithms for finding the top-k locally densest subgraphs in [19]. These algorithms perform well for small graphs. However, as the graph size increases, exact algorithms for EDS become infeasible. Therefore, approximation algorithms have been developed in [1,4], and [17]. (2) *Disjoint path*: A disjoint path is an important part in graph clustering, which is helpful for the researcher to find a group with high cohesiveness. Based on the concept of k-component and k-block, in [7], the author developed clustering algorithms that aim to find a maximal subgraph such that each vertex in this subgraph should have k edge- or vertex-disjoint path. In [27], Zhang measure the similarity between two vertexes by using the disjoint path. In [21], the author uses the number of edges- or vertex disjoint path for each vertex to measure the similarity between two vertexes, and based on this value, clusters the graph into different groups.

Challenges. The primary challenges and solutions are listed as follows:

(1) *Connection between two vertices.* The connection between two vertices with the same type is no longer directly connected; hence, we employ the well-known concept of meta-path, which defines a path in HINs as a fixed sequence of edge type and vertex type. Consequently, meta-path can be regarded as a special type of path in HINs.

(2) *Definition for density.* The definition for edge-based density cannot be used in HINs, as the semantic meanings of each edge may vary, rendering the edge-based density useless. Based on the concept of meta-path, we modify the definition as the number of target vertices pairs over the number of target vertices.

(3) *Limitation of the existing algorithms.* The algorithms employed in existing studies are only applicable in homogeneous networks, as they do not account for the presence of multiple instances of meta-paths between two target vertices in HINs, nor do they consider the specific routes of these paths, which may result in weaker engagement. Furthermore, for the disjoint densest subgraphs, the algorithms should ensure that the paths within the final graph are disjoint from each other. As a result, proposing an approach for the DSD in HINs that incorporates the specific routes represents a nontrivial challenge.

Contributions. In summary, our primary contributions are:

(1) *Exact Algorithms.* We develop an exact algorithm for searching basic densest subgraphs in HINs.

(2) *Vertex and Edge Disjoint Based Models.* Based on the concept of the disjoint path, we propose two new models of HIN: global edge/vertex- disjoint HIN.

(3) *Advanced Optimizations.* For searching disjoint densest subgraphs in HINs, we design a exact algorithms with advanced optimizations which can decrease the computation time and lower the size of the final graphs.

(4) *Effectiveness and Efficiency.* We conducted comprehensive experiments on diverse datasets to demonstrate the effectiveness and efficiency of our proposed HIN densest subgraph algorithm. Additionally, we evaluated our disjoint edge-based and vertex-based algorithms aimed at enhancing performance.

2 Preliminaries

(See Table 1).

Table 1. Notations

Notations	Description
$\psi(v)(\phi(e))$	The vertex/edge type of a vertex v/edge e
l	Edge number of P/length of P
$Bdeg_G(v)$	Number of P-neighbors of v in G
$E/Vdeg_G(v)$	Number of P-neighbors of v connected by edge-/vertex- disjoint path instances in G
$B_k(B_{k,P})$	A basic (k,P)-core
$E_k(E_{k,P})$	A global edge-disjoint (k,P)-core
$V_k(V_{k,P})$	A global vertex-disjoint (k,P)-core
n_i	Number of vertex whose types match with i-th vertex in P

Definition 1. *(HIN [15,22]). An HIN is a directed graph $G = (V,E)$ with a vertex type mapping function $\psi : V \to A$ and an edge type mapping function $\phi : E \to R$, where each vertex $v \in V$ belongs to a vertex type $\psi(v) \in A$, and each edge $e \in E$ belongs to an edge type (also called relation) $\phi(e) \in R$.*

Definition 2. *(Meta-path [22]). A meta-path P is a path defined on an HIN, and is denoted in the form $A_1 A_2 \cdots A_{l+1}$ where l is the length of P, $A_i \in A$.*

We call a vertex as target vertex if it has the same type as the first vertex in P. A meta-path is a symmetric meta-path if the reverse path P' is the same as P. For example, meta-path $P_1=$(APA) is a symmetric meta-path, since the reverse path is still $P_1'=$(APA). We call a path $p = a_1 \to a_2 \cdots \to a_{l+1}$ path instance of P, if $\forall i$, the vertex a_i satisfy $\psi(a_i)=A_i$. For example in Fig. 1(a), $a_1 p_1 t_1 p_2 a_2$ is a path instance for $P_1=$(APTPA). Moreover, a vertex v_1 is P-neighbor of a vertex v_2 if they are connected by an instance of meta-path. v_1 is P-connected to a vertex v_2 if they are connected by a chain of vertices in which each vertex is P-neighbor of its adjacent vertex. In this paper, all the meta-path are symmetric, and we use the number of target vertices pairs that are connected by a valid path instance over the number of target vertices to measure the density. As aforementioned, directly searching the densest subgraph in HINs may obtain a graph that include some vertices which have weak engagement. Hence we impose a limitation on the path instances in the HINs to filter vertices. In detail, for a given meta-path P, two path instance P_1, P_2 of P which start from target vertex v are two edge-disjoint paths, if the i-th ($1 \leq i \leq l$) edges and $(l+1)$-th vertices of P_1, P_2 are different. Similarly, if the i-th ($2 \leq i \leq (l+1)$) vertices of P_1, P_2 are different, then P_1 P_2 are two vertex-disjoint paths.

Definition 3. *(Path instance set). Given an HIN $G = (V, E)$, a meta-path P, and the limitation of the path instance (basic/edge-disjoint/vertex-disjoint). Φ is a corresponding path instances set if $\forall$ P_1, P_2 $\in$ Φ so that P_1, P_2 are two basic/edge-disjoint/vertex-disjoint paths. We denote the basic/edge-disjoint/vertex-disjoint path instances set as $\Phi_B/\Phi_E/\Phi_V$ for distinction.*

Example 1. For the given HIN $G = (V, E)$ depicted in Fig. 1(a), the maximal basic path instance set Φ_B contains all the path instances of type 'APA'. However, when we restrict the paths to be edge-disjoint or vertex-disjoint, we will obtain a different path set Φ_E/Φ_V (as illustrated in Fig. 1(b)). Based on this set, the density of Fig. 1(b) is $\frac{7}{6}$ since there are 7 pairs of P-connected target vertices in Φ_E/Φ_V. Note that a_1 and a_4 cannot be considered as a P-connected vertex pair because the presence of the edge a_1p_2 in the path instance $a_1p_2a_3$ invalidates the path instance $a_1p_2a_4$.

Problem Statement. Given a HIN G, a symmetric meta-path P. Based on the limitation of the path instances (basic/edge-disjoint/vertex-disjoint), we aim to find the path set of the densest subgraph in G whose density is the highest among all the subgraphs. We use $\underline{B}$asic/$\underline{G}$lobal $\underline{E}$dge-disjoint/$\underline{G}$lobal $\underline{V}$ertex-disjoint - based $\underline{D}$ensest $\underline{S}$ubgraph (BDS/GEDS/GVDS) to describe the densest subgraph as well as its corresponding path set.

3   Basic Densest Subgraph Discovery in HINs

At present, the Goldberg's algorithm [11] is a well-established approach for identifying the densest subgraphs. The core concept of this algorithm is based on a parametric flow network. A flow network [14] is a directed graph $F = (V_F, E_F)$ that comprises a source node s, a sink node t, and some intermediate nodes. Each edge in the flow network has a capacity, and the flow on an edge cannot exceed the edge's capacity. The maximum flow of a flow network is equal to the capacity of its minimum st-cut, $\langle S, T \rangle$, which separates the node set V_F into two non-overlapping sets, S and T, where $s \in S$ and $t \in T$. By adjusting the flow network's parameter, Goldberg's algorithm iteratively estimates the maximum density value. In order to find the BDS, we modify Goldberg's algorithm so that it can adopt in HINs, we depict it in Algorithm 1.

Based on the 'Exact' algorithm, we can successfully obtain the BDS. However, as the magnitude of the HIN increase, the accumulation of path instances will escalate dramatically, rendering the "Exact" algorithm laborious. Evidently, to enhance the efficacy of the algorithm even further, streamlining the size of the flow network and minimizing iteration cycles is imperative.

Remove Invalid Vertices. In 'Exact', the algorithm builds the flow network based on the whole HIN, however, only a few target vertices are included in the BDS. Therefore, if we can prune some invalid vertices in advance, the computing time of the algorithm will be shortened. To achieve this, an important model called basic (k,P)-core is introduced as below:

Definition 4. *(Basic (k,P)-core). Given an HIN $G = (V, E)$, a meta-path P. A basic (k,P)-core B_k is a maximal Φ_B of G so that for all the target vertices $v \in \Phi_B$, $Bdeg_{B_k}(v) \geq k$.*

Lemma 1. *Given a HIN G, for any B_k in G, the range of its density ρ is:* $\frac{k}{2} \leq \rho$.

Algorithm 1: Exact

---

1 $G(V, E)$ ←Input graph, P ←Input Meta-path
2 collect all the vertices with target type into set S
3 $\Phi_B[]$ ← path instance set for each target vertex
4 initialize $l \leftarrow 0, u \leftarrow \underset{v \in S}{maxBdeg_G(v)}, D \leftarrow \emptyset$
5 initialize $Y \leftarrow |S|, X \leftarrow$ number of vertices pair in Φ_B
6 **while** $u - l \geq \frac{1}{Y^2}$ **do**
7     $\alpha \leftarrow \frac{l+u}{2}, V_F \leftarrow \{s\} \cup S \cup \{t\}$
8   **for each** *vertex $v \in S$* **do**
9   add an edge from $s \rightarrow v$ with capacity X
10   add an edge from $v \rightarrow t$ with capacity $X + 2\alpha - Bdeg_G(v)$
11   **for each** *path instance $(v, u) \in \Phi_B$* **do**
12   **if** *not exist edge (v, u)* **then**
13   add an edge from $v \rightarrow u$ with capacity 1
14   add an edge from $u \rightarrow v$ with capacity 1
15   Find minimum st-cut $\langle S, T \rangle$ from $F=(V_F, E_F)$
16   **if** $S=\{s\}$ **then**
17       $u \leftarrow \alpha$
18   **else**
19       $l \leftarrow \alpha, D \leftarrow S \setminus \{s\}$
20 **return** extract path from D based on Φ_B;

Proof. Suppose the number of target vertex in B_k is Y and the number of target vertex pairs that are P-connected is X. Each target vertex in B_k is contained in at least k path instances, and each path instance involves two target vertices. Hence, there at least $\frac{Yk}{2}$ path instances, the density is at least $\frac{k}{2}$.

Proposition 1. *Given a HIN G, a meta-path P, the B_k is unique for each value of k, if $B_{k+1} \neq \emptyset$ then $B_{k+1} \subseteq B_k$.*

For the BDS, we denote its density as ρ_{max}, based on the lemma below, we can locate it in $B_{\lceil \rho_{max} \rceil}$.

Lemma 2. *Removing a target vertex from the BDS will result in the removal of at least ρ_{max} target vertex pair from BDS.*

Proof. Suppose the number of target vertex pair that are removed is δ. Since the BDS has the largest density among all the subgraphs, so we have: $\frac{X}{Y} \geq \frac{X-\delta}{Y-1} \Rightarrow \delta \geq \frac{X}{Y} = \rho_{max}$. Hence the Lemma 2 hold.

Based on the Lemma 2, each target vertex should has at least k P-neighbors in BDS. Therefore, the BDS must be included in the $B_{\lceil \rho_{max} \rceil}$. However, generally we do not know the value of ρ_{max} in advance, so it is hard to locate BDS in the $B_{\lceil \rho_{max} \rceil}$ directly.

Lemma 3. *Given a HIN G, we denote the maximal core number as k_{max}. The BDS is contained in a B_k where $k = \lceil \frac{k_{max}}{2} \rceil$:*

Proof. Based on the Lemma 1, the density ρ of $B_{k_{max}}$ is no less than $\frac{k_{max}}{2}$, and ρ_{max} is the largest density among all the subgraphs, hence we have: $\frac{k_{max}}{2} \leq \rho \leq \rho_{max}$.

Combine this equation with Proposition 1, we can conclude that BDS $\subseteq B_{\lceil \rho_{max} \rceil} \subseteq B_{\lceil \frac{k_{max}}{2} \rceil}$, thus the lemma hold.

By Lemma 3, instead of locating the BDS in $B_{\lceil \rho_{max} \rceil}$, we can compute the value of k_{max} and then locate BDS in $B_{\lceil \frac{k_{max}}{2} \rceil}$. We can obtain the $B_{\lceil \frac{k_{max}}{2} \rceil}$ by modifying existing decomposition algorithms [2].

Adjust Initial Range. In 'Exact' algorithm, we set a guessing density α, and try to find a subgraph whose density is larger than α in a binary search manner. Apparently, the computing times for the minimum st-cut depend on the initial range of α. Based on the Lemma 3, we obtain the lower bound for ρ_{max} which is $\frac{k_{max}}{2}$. However, the upper bound $maxBdeg_G(v)$ is not tight enough, so we still need to reduce its value.

Lemma 4. *Given a HIN $G = (V, E)$, for the largest density ρ_{max} we have: $\rho_{max} \leq k_{max}$.*

Proof. Based on the Lemma 2, the BDS can be obtained in $B_{\lceil \rho_{max} \rceil}$. If $\rho_{max} > k_{max}$, which means we can find a larger basic core that contains the BDS. This contradicts the fact that k_{max} is the maximal core number. Hence, the lemma hold.

Equipped with the Lemma 3 and Lemma 4, we obtain a tighter range for the guessing density: $\frac{k_{max}}{2} \leq \rho_{max} \leq k_{max}$.

Locate Locally Densest Subgraphs. For a HIN, it may be divided into several components which are isolated from each other, we refer to the densest subgraphs for these components as the locally densest subgraphs. Apparently, the BDS contained in these locally densest subgraphs and the time required to search for the densest subgraph in multiple components will be shorter than the time required to search the entire graph.

Through these three improvements, we develop an optimized algorithm for searching BDS called 'BasicExact' and we depict it in Algorithm 2.

4   Disjoint Densest Subgraph Discovery in HINs

Algorithm 2: BasicExact

---

1 $G(V, E)$ ←Input graph, P ←Input Meta-path
2 Collect all the vertices with target type into set S
3 $D \leftarrow \emptyset, U \leftarrow \emptyset, l \leftarrow \frac{k_{max}}{2}, u \leftarrow k_{max}$
4 G' ←divide $B_{\lceil l \rceil}$ into several connected components
5 **for each** *connected component* $C(V_C, E_C) \in G'$ **do**
6   Find minimum st-cut for C where $\alpha = l$
7   **if** *exist* **then**
8   Remove vertices in C based on the minimum st-cut
9          $U \leftarrow$ run 'Exact' to find locally densest subgraphs in C using l and u as the bounds
10   **if** *density(U)= l* **then**
11   add U into D
12   **if** *density(U)> l* **then**
13         $D \leftarrow U$

14 **return** extract path from Φ_B based on D;

In this section, we introduce how to find a disjoint densest subgraph in HINs. We use GEDS as an example (for the algorithm to find GVDS, we only need to modify the requirement in the following algorithms from edge-disjoint to vertex-disjoint). To compute the GEDS in HINs, we first introduce some concepts:

Definition 5. *(Global edge (vertex) disjoint HIN). Given an HIN $G = (V, E)$, a meta-path P. If we can find a disjoint path instance set Φ_E (Φ_V) of G such that $\forall v \in V$ and $\forall e \in E$, v, $e \in \Phi_E$ (Φ_V). Then G is the Global Edge (Vertex) disjoint HIN, we denote it as GEHIN (GVHIN).*

Example 2. The HIN $G = (V, E)$ presented in Fig. 1(b) is a GEHIN/GVHIN based on the meta-path 'APA'. The Φ_E (Φ_V) consists of 7 disjoint paths (as indicated in the graph) which contain all the vertices and edges in G.

Definition 6. *(Global edge (vertex) disjoint (k,P)-core). Given an HIN $G = (V, E)$, a meta-path P. A global edge (vertex) disjoint (k,P)-core E_k (V_k) is a maximal Φ_E (Φ_V) in G so that for all the target vertices $v \in \Phi_E$ (Φ_V), $Edeg_{E_k}(v) \geq k$ ($Vdeg_{V_k}(v) \geq k$).*

Proposition 2. *Given a HIN G, a meta-path P, the E_k may not be unique for each value of k, if $E_{k+1} \neq \emptyset$ then we can always find a E_k so that $E_{k+1} \subseteq E_k$. This proposition also hold for V_k.*

Proposition 3. *Given a HIN G, a meta-path P, a number K, for any E_k, $E_k \subseteq B_k$. This proposition also hold for V_k.*

In pursuit of obtaining GEDS, there are three formidable obstacles that must be surmounted:

1. Finding E_k in HINs. Limited by the characteristic of edge-disjoint paths, choosing one path instance may result in the disconnection of another path instance. To address this issue, a feasible method based on Proposition 3 is that for a given value of k, we can first use the decomposition algorithm to find B_k, and then search for E_k within B_k to reduce computation time. So in this paper, we developed an algorithm called 'GlobalECore' to search the global edge-disjoint (k, P)-core.

Algorithm 3: GlobalECore

---

1 **Input** $\leftarrow G(V, E), P, k$
2 $B_k \leftarrow$ run decomposition algorithm
3 $N \leftarrow$ target vertices in B_k
4 $\Phi_E[] \leftarrow \emptyset, R \leftarrow \emptyset$
5 **for each** $v \in N$ **do**
6   initialize a set $\Phi'_E[v] = \emptyset$
7   **while** *true* **do**
8 $\Psi[(v, u)] \leftarrow$find a new path instance of P from v to u where $u \in N$
9   **if** $\Psi[(v, u)] = \emptyset$ **then**
10   break
11   **if** $\Psi[(v, u)]$ *contradict with* $\Phi_E[v]$ *or* $\Phi'_E[v]$ **then**
12   continue
13   **if** $\Psi[(u, v)]$ *contradict with* $\Phi_E[u]$ **then**
14   continue
15   add path $\Psi[(v, u)]$ into $\Phi'_E[v]$
16   **if** $|\Phi_E[v]| + |\Phi'_E[v]| < k$ **then**
17   add v into R
18   **else**
19   **for each** *path* $\Psi[(v, u)] \in \Phi'_E[v]$ **do**
20   add $\Psi[(v, u)]$ into $\Phi_E[v]$, add $\Psi[(u, v)]$ into $\Phi_E[u]$
21 **while** $|R| > 0$ **do**
22 $v \leftarrow$get a vertex from $R, N \leftarrow N\backslash\{v\}$
23 $H \leftarrow \{u|u \in N$ and $\exists\Psi[(u, v)] \in \Phi_E[u]\}$
24   **for each** $u \in H$ **do**
25   remove $\Psi[(u, v)]$ from $\Phi_E[u]$, repeat line 6-20 for vertex u
26 **return** Φ_E;

---

2. Tighter the initial density range. Due to the characteristics of disjoint paths, we cannot directly determine the lower bound of the density for the disjoint densest subgraph. To improve the algorithm's efficiency, we devise a new approach to locate the GEDS and narrow down the search range. Specifically, while we cannot directly locate the GEDS within an E_k, we can still increase the lower bound. We compute the density ρ of the GEHIN and use 'GlobalECore' to locate $E_{\lceil \rho \rceil}$. We repeat this process based on the density of $E_{\lceil \rho \rceil}$ until $\lceil \rho \rceil$ no longer changes. Without utilizing the minimum st-cut, this process can significantly increase the lower bound in a short time.

3. Dynamically adjusting the guessing density. During the minimum st-cut process, some new path instances become available as vertices that will not be part of the GEDS are iteratively removed. If Φ_E is adjusted after the minimum st-cut, some vertices that should not have been removed may be removed, leading to an inaccurate result. Therefore, we modify the algorithm by adding path instances during the minimum st-cut process. Since the Φ_E is changed, we update the upper bound based on the lemma below:

Lemma 5. *Given an edge-disjoint path set Φ_E, adding n new path instances in the set will result in the density of GEDS increase at most $n/\lceil \frac{1+\sqrt{1+8n}}{2} \rceil$. Note that this lemma also holds for vertex-disjoint path set.*

Proof. We use Y and X to denote the number of target vertices and the number of P-connected vertex pairs in the path set. Assume $\Phi_E^1 = (Y_1, X_1)$ is the path set for the original GEDS, $\Phi_E^2 = (Y_2, X_2)$ is the path set for the new GEDS after adding n new path instances. Besides, we use $\Phi_E^3 = (Y_2, X_2')$ to denote the original path set for Φ_E^2 before adding the new path instances. Clearly, we have: $\frac{X_2'}{Y_2} \leq \frac{X_1}{Y_1} \leq \frac{X_2}{Y_2}$. Suppose the difference between X_2 and X_2' is m ($m \leq n$), then the increment for the density is: $\frac{X_2}{Y_2} - \frac{X_1}{Y_1} \leq \frac{X_2}{Y_2} - \frac{X_2'}{Y_2} = \frac{m}{Y_2}$. For Y_2 target vertices, they can form at most $\frac{Y_2(Y_2-1)}{2}$ vertex pairs. Based on this fact, the range for Y_2 in terms of m is: $m \leq \frac{Y_2(Y_2-1)}{2} \Rightarrow Y_2 \geq \lceil \frac{1+\sqrt{1+8m}}{2} \rceil$. Eventually, the upper bound for the increment is: $\frac{m}{Y_2} \leq \frac{m}{\lceil \frac{1+\sqrt{1+8m}}{2} \rceil} \leq \frac{n}{\lceil \frac{1+\sqrt{1+8n}}{2} \rceil}$. Therefore, Lemma 5 hold.

First, using the methods mentioned earlier, we obtain the path set corresponding to the final $E_{\lceil \rho \rceil}$ (line 2). Then, based on the path set, we divide the graph into few disconnected subgraphs. For each component, we reexamine the $E_{\lceil lo \rceil}$ based on the current lower bound changes (lines 5–8). Additionally, we set the upper bound to the maximum value of k for the target vertices within the current component based on the original graph (line 9). Next, we search for the densest subgraph among them, dynamically adjusting the edges and the upper bound as the graph becomes smaller (lines 16–19). For each densest subgraph within each component, we compare it with the previously identified densest subgraph. If the density of the current subgraph is higher, we delete the previous subgraph and save the current subgraph. If the densities are equal, we save all the current subgraphs simultaneously (lines 20–24).

Algorithm 4: ImprovedED

---

1 **Input** $\leftarrow G(V,E), P$
2 $\Phi_E \leftarrow$ path set for the last $E_{\lceil \rho \rceil}$ as aforementioned
3 $R \leftarrow \emptyset, U \leftarrow \emptyset, lo \leftarrow \lceil \rho \rceil, k \leftarrow \lceil \rho \rceil, N \leftarrow$ disconnected components in Φ_E
4 **for each** *component's path set* $\Phi_E^i \in N$ **do**
5   **if** $lo > k$ **then**
6          $\lfloor \; \Phi_E^i \leftarrow \Phi_E^i \cap E_{\lceil lo \rceil}$
7   **if** $\Phi_E^i = \emptyset$ **then**
8          $\lfloor$ continue
9      $up \leftarrow k_{max}$ of the target vertices in this component
10     $\beta \leftarrow$ number of target vertex in Φ_E^i
11   **while** $up - lo > \frac{1}{\beta^2}$ **do**
12          $\alpha \leftarrow \frac{lo+up}{2}$
13          $\langle S, T \rangle \leftarrow$ minimum st-cut on Φ_E^i's flow network
14   **if** $S=\{s\}$ **then**
15             $\lfloor \; up \leftarrow \alpha$
16   **else**
17   remove vertices then add path instances on Φ_E^i
18             $n \leftarrow$ number of new path instances
19             $\lfloor \; up \leftarrow up + n / \lceil \frac{1+\sqrt{1+8n}}{2} \rceil, lo \leftarrow \alpha, U \leftarrow S \backslash \{s\}$
20     $T \leftarrow$ extract path from Φ_E^i based on U
21   **if** $\rho_T > \rho_R$ **then**
22          $\lfloor \; R \leftarrow T$
23   **if** $\rho_T = \rho_R$ **then**
24          $\lfloor$ add T into R
25 **return** R;

---

5 Experiments

5.1 Experiments Setup

Settings. Experiments are conducted on a Linux server with Intel Intel(R) Xeon(R) Platinum 8260L CPU 2.30HZ and 120 GB memory. The algorithms are implemented in Java, which follows the settings in [9].

Datasets. We use seven real networks to test the algorithms. The seven real networks used in the experiments have simple schema, except for DBPedia. The statistics, including the numbers of vertices, edges, vertex types, and edge types, for all the graphs are shown in Table 2.

Case Study: We utilize the DBPedia dataset to compare the three types of densest subgraphs - normal and two with edge/vertex disjoint constraints. BDS consists of 1284 vertices, with 42 being the target type, and takes 169.712 s to find. In contrast, GVDS contains 1256 vertices, with 30 being the target type, and takes only 0.347 s to find. GEDS contains 1260 vertices, with 31 being the target type, and takes 0.359 s. We utilize node graphs to visually demonstrate the differences between BDS and GVDS/GEDS, as shown in Fig. 2(a) and Fig. 2(b).

Table 2. The Statistics of the dataset

Name	n	m	VType	EType
MovieLens [12]	1,327	10,186	4	3
Amazon [13, 18]	6,568	209,746	5	4
LastFM [3, 20]	15,734	277,775	3	3
Foursquare [26]	43,199	405,476	5	4
DBLP [16]	682,819	1,951,209	4	3
IMDB	1,233,903	7,597,591	4	3
DBPedia	5,900,558	17,961,887	413	637

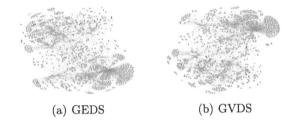

(a) GEDS   (b) GVDS

Fig. 2. Comparison between disjoint densest subgraph and basic densest subgraph

In the graphs, all the nodes together form the BDS; the blue nodes represent GVDS/GEDS, and the red nodes represent the filtered-out nodes. From the images, we observe that GVDS/GEDS preserves the majority of the nodes, and the filtered-out nodes have low participation. Additionally, by recovering all path instances in GVDS/GEDS, we obtained their respective normal densities, which are 9.667/9.742. In comparison to the density of BDS (11.143), the difference is not significant. Considering the run time, it is evident that using GVDS/GEDS to find communities is a highly effective approach.

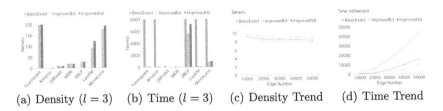

(a) Density ($l = 3$)   (b) Time ($l = 3$)   (c) Density Trend   (d) Time Trend

Fig. 3. Density and time for $l = 3$

Algorithm Comparison: We set the upper limit for the running time to be three hours. Figure 3(a) (b) shows the running time of three algorithms and their corresponding densities in seven graphs when the meta-path length is three. However, the 'BasicExact' algorithm exceeds the three-hour limit in some graphs, so we do not display the corresponding density for those cases. When the meta-path length is greater than three, we do not show the results for them as the running time for 'BasicExact' exceeded three hours in all graphs. For the convenience of contrasting the differences between disjoint densest subgraph and normal densest subgraph, the density of all disjoint densest subgraphs in Fig. 3 is calculated by reverting the target vertices from the final GEDS/GVDS to the normal graph and then computing their corresponding normal density. From Figure Fig. 3(a), we can observe that regardless of the density of the final densest subgraph, the densities obtained by 'ImprovedEd' and 'ImprovedVd' are always close to those obtained by the basic algorithm. Additionally, Figure Fig. 3(b) demonstrates that the time taken by these two algorithms is significantly less than the time taken by 'BasicExact'. By generating random datasets[1] we compare the effectiveness of disjoint and normal densest subgraph. Figure 3(c) and (d) demonstrate that as the dataset continues to grow, the density of GEDS/GVDS consistently approaches the density of the BDS, while the required time decreases. From the above data, we can observe that in the case of larger datasets, searching for a disjoint densest subgraph is clearly more advantageous.

6   Conclusion

We investigate the problem of densest subgraph discovering over HINs. And based on the concept of disjoint path, we developed a new model in HINs called global disjoint HINs, which make up the problem that finding basic densest subgraph in large HINs is time-consuming. The comprehensive experiments demonstrate that the disjoint densest subgraphs discovering algorithms can effectively search the GEDS/GVDS in HINs. Each target vertex in GEDS/GVDS still maintain close relation. Our comprehensive evaluations verify that GEDS/GVDS can be a good solution for community detection in large graphs.

References

1. Bahmani, B., Kumar, R., Vassilvitskii, S.: Densest subgraph in streaming and MapReduce. In: PVLDB, pp. 454–46 (2012)
2. Batagelj, V., Zaversnik, M.: An o(m) algorithm for cores decomposition of networks. arXiv preprint cs/0310049 (2003)
3. Cantador, I., Brusilovsky, P., Kuflik, T.: 2nd workshop on information heterogeneity and fusion in recommender systems (HetRec 2011). In: Proceedings of the 5th ACM Conference on Recommender Systems, RecSys 2011, New York, NY, USA (2011)
4. Charikar, M.: Greedy approximation algorithms for finding dense components in a graph. In: Jansen, K., Khuller, S. (eds.) APPROX 2000. LNCS, vol. 1913, pp. 84–95. Springer, Heidelberg (2000). https://doi.org/10.1007/3-540-44436-X_10

---

[1] https://www.cse.psu.edu/~kxm85/software/GTgraph/.

5. Chen, J., Saad, Y.: Dense subgraph extraction with application to community detection. TKDE **24**(7), 1216–1230 (2012)

6. Cohen, E., Halperin, E., Kaplan, H., Zwick, U.: Reachability and distance queries via 2-hop labels. SIAM J. Comput. **32**(5), 1338–1355 (2003)

7. Dongen, S.M.V.: Graph clustering by flow simulation. Ph.D. thesis, University of Utrecht (2000)

8. Epasto, A., Lattanzi, S., Sozio, M.: Efficient densest subgraph computation in evolving graphs. In: WWW, pp. 300–310 (2015)

9. Fang, Y., Yang, Y., Zhang, W., Lin, X., Ca, X.: Effective and efficient community search over large heterogeneous information networks. Proc. VLDB Endow. **13**(6), 854–867 (2020)

10. Fratkin, E., Naughton, B.T., Brutlag, D.L., Batzoglou, S.: MotifCut: regulatory motifs finding with maximum density subgraphs. Bioinformatics **22**(14), e150–e157 (2006)

11. Goldberg, A.V.: Finding a maximum density subgraph. UC Berkeley (1984)

12. Harper, F.M., Konstan, J.A.: The MovieLens datasets: history and context. ACM Trans. Interact. Intell. Syst. **5**, 19:1–19:19 (2015). https://doi.org/10.1145/2827872

13. He, R., McAuley, J.: Ups and downs: Modeling the visual evolution of fashion trends with one-class collaborative filtering. In: WWW (2016). https://cseweb.ucsd.edu/jmcauley/datasets.html#amazon_reviews

14. Heineman, G., Pollice, G., Selkow, S.: Network flow algorithms. Algorithms in a Nutshell (2008)

15. Huang, Z., Zheng, Y., Cheng, R., Sun, Y., Mamoulis, N., Li, X.: Meta structure: computing relevance in large heterogeneous information networks. In: KDD, pp. 1595–1604 (2016)

16. Schloss Dagstuhl - Leibniz Center for Informatics.: DBLP computer science bibliography (2019). http://dblp.uni-trier.de/xml

17. Khuller, S., Saha, B.: On finding dense subgraphs. In: Albers, S., Marchetti-Spaccamela, A., Matias, Y., Nikoletseas, S., Thomas, W. (eds.) ICALP 2009. LNCS, vol. 5555, pp. 597–608. Springer, Heidelberg (2009). https://doi.org/10.1007/978-3-642-02927-1_50

18. McAuley, J., Targett, C., Shi, J., van den Hengel, A.: Image-based recommendations on styles and substitutes. In: SIGIR (2015). https://cseweb.ucsd.edu/jmcauley/datasets.html#amazon_reviews

19. Qin, L., Li, R.H., Chang, L., Zhang, C.: Locally densest subgraph discover. In: KDD, pp. 965–974 (2015)

20. S. M. of Science Innovation, the Regional Government of Madrid: International Workshop on Information Heterogeneity and Fusion in Recommender Systems (2011). http://www.lastfm.com

21. Scott, J.: Social Network Analysis: A Handbook. Sage Publications (2000)

22. Sun, Y., Han, J., Yan, X., Yu, P.S., Wu, T.: PathSim: meta path-based top-k similarity search in heterogeneous information networks. PVLDB **4**(11), 992–1003 (2011)

23. Tang, J., Qu, M., Mei, Q.: Predictive text embedding through large-scale heterogeneous text networks. In: SIGKDD (2015)

24. Tsourakakis, C., Bonchi, F., Gionis, A., Gullo, F., Tsiarli, M.: Denser than the densest subgraph: extracting optimal quasi-cliques with quality guarantees. In: KDD, pp. 104–112 (2013)

25. Yan, Y., Wang, Q., Liu, L.: Latent influence based self-attention framework for heterogeneous network embedding. IEICE Trans. Inf. Syst. **105**, 1335–1339 (2022)

26. Yang, D., Zhang, D., Yu, Z., Yu, Z.: Fine-grained preference-aware location search leveraging crowdsourced digital footprints from LBSNs. In: ACM International Joint Conference on Pervasive and Ubiquitous Computing, pp. 8–12 (2013)
27. Zhang, B., Nie, T., Shen, D., Kou, Y., Yu, G., Zhou, Z.: A graph clustering algorithm for citation networks. In: Li, F., Shim, K., Zheng, K., Liu, G. (eds.) APWeb 2016. LNCS, vol. 9932, pp. 414–418. Springer, Cham (2016). https://doi.org/10.1007/978-3-319-45817-5_37
28. Zhang, X., Xie, H., Lui, J.C.S.: Improving bandit learning via heterogeneous information networks: algorithms and applications. ACM Trans. Knowl. Discov. Data 16, 1–25 (2022)

Influence Maximization Revisited

Yihan Geng, Kunyu Wang, Ziqi Liu, Michael Yu$^{(\boxtimes)}$, and Jeffrey Xu Yu

The Chinese University of Hong Kong, Sha Tin, Hong Kong SAR
{yhgeng,kunyuwang,zqliu}@link.cuhk.edu.hk,
mryu@cse.cuhk.edu.hk, yu@se.cuhk.edu.hk

Abstract. Influence Maximization (*IM*) has been extensively studied, which is to select a set of k seed users from a social network to maximize the expected number of influenced users in the social network. There are many approaches proposed under a cascade model to find such a single set of k seed users. Such a set being computed may not be unique, as it is most likely that there exist more than one set, $S_1, S_2, \cdots$, each of them leads to the same *IM*, given a social network exhibits rich symmetry as reported in the literature. In this paper, first, we study how to select a set of k seed users from a set of seed k' ($\geq k$) users which can be either a union of sets of seed users, $\mathbb{S} = \bigcup_i S_i$, where S_i is a set of k seed users, or simply a set of seed users of size k' ($\geq k$) being computed, based on cooperative game using Shapley value. Second, we develop a visualization system to explore the process of influence spreading from topological perspective, as *IM* only gives the expected number of influenced users without much information on how influence spreads in a large social network. We conduct experimental studies to confirm the effectiveness of the seed users selected in our approach.

Keywords: Automorphism · Influence Maximization · Visualization

1 Introduction

Influence Maximization (*IM*) is a problem to select k seed users from a social network to maximize the expected number of influenced users, and has been extensively studied over decades given the importance in real applications such as advertising, viral marketing, and product recommendations over social networks. In the literature, *IM* has been studied in many different setting. In [14], Huang *et al.* study *IM* in real-world closed social networks to recommend users a limited number of existing friends to help to propagate information. In [2], Bian *et al.* study budgeted *IM* where the total cost of the users selected is under a budget constraint. In [13], He and Kempe study robust *IM* to identify a set of k nodes who are influential for all given influence functions. In [21], Lin *et al.* study balanced *IM* to maximize influence where the attributes associated with nodes are balanced. In [29], Tang *et al.* study *IM* with the diversity of the influenced crows. Chen *et al.* in [3] study *IM* under the consideration that users are most likely to be influenced by the users if they share the similar interest. Tsaras

© The Author(s), under exclusive license to Springer Nature Switzerland AG 2024
Z. Bao et al. (Eds.): ADC 2023, LNCS 14386, pp. 356–370, 2024.
https://doi.org/10.1007/978-3-031-47843-7_25

et al. in [30] study *IM* to select seeds for each of multiple competing products in order to maximize the collective influence for all products. There are studies on location-aware *IM* [18,19,31,33]. Two recent surveys can be found in [1,20].

All the existing work focus on selecting a set of k seed users. As indicated in [23], a social network exhibits rich symmetry, and there is an efficient way to find graph automorphism for a given node or even subgraph existing in a graph [22]. It becomes possible to find a set of seed users S_2 that is different from the set of seed users, S_1, computed by *IM*. By graph automorphism, the two sets of S_1 and S_2 are identical, and they result in the same expected number of influenced users [22]. This motivates us to study a problem on how to select a set of k seed users from a union of such sets, $\mathbb{S} = \bigcup_i S_i$, if there are multiple seed sets, $S_1, S_2, \cdots$ in a social network G. The problem is related to an issue how to take the cooperation of seed users in influence spreading into consideration. In other words, *IM* maximizes the expected number of influenced users for k seed users, but does not pay attention on how the seeds collaboratively influence the others as a whole. It is likely that two seeds will influence two sets of users that have overlapping in a social network. In [25], Narayanam and Narahari study computing *IM* using Shapley value in cooperative game theory. That is, they map the process of influence spreading to the formation of coalitions in a cooperative game using Shapley value. Gaskó *et al.* in [6] also study Shapley value for *IM*. Zhang and Zhang [34] study *IM* from a game perspective, and propose a coordination game model, in which every individual makes its decision based on the benefit of coordination with its network neighbors. In this paper, different from [6,25], we study how to select k seed users from a set of seed users of size k' ($\geq k$) that is computed by any existing *IM* approach, using Shapley value [28,32]. In addition, we explore the process of influence spreading from topological perspective, as *IM* only gives a value that is the expected number of users being influenced without much information on how they influence in a large social network.

Our main contributions are summarized below.

- As there are possible multiple sets, $S_1, S_2, \cdots$ by *IM*, we study how to select nodes from the union of such set $\mathbb{S} = \bigcup_i S_i$ using Shapley value. Our approach can also be used to select k nodes from a set of seeds with k' ($\geq k$).
- We have developed a visualization system to visual how influence spreads in an interactive way. Our system assists users to investigate a single approach such as PMC [27], GAME [34], HIST [12], SUBSIM [12], SSA [26], and DSSA [26] under a cascade model (e.g., *IC*, *LT*), and compares two different approaches.
- We conduct experimental studies using four datasets to confirm that superiority of our approach of selecting nodes from a given set of seeds computed.

The paper is organized as follows. We give the preliminaries and the problem statement in Sect. 2, and discuss how to select nodes from a set of seeds selected in Sect. 3. We present our *IM* visualization system in Sect. 4, and discuss some related works in Sect. 5. We report our experimental studies in Sect. 6, and conclude the paper in Sect. 7.

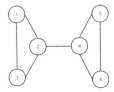

Fig. 1. An Example

2   Preliminaries

We model a social network as an undirected graph $G = (V, E)$, where V is a set of nodes and E is a set of edges. We denote n to be the number of vertices, and m the number of edges in G. For each node v, the degree of v is denoted as $d(v) = |N(v)|$, where $N(v)$ is the set of neighbors of v such that $N(v) = \{u | (u, v) \in E\}$. For each edge (u, v), there is a propagation probability $p_{u,v}$ associated with, which indicates how one node is influenced by the other via an edge.

In this paper, we study two cascade models for information propagation, namely, Independent Cascade (*IC*) [7,8] and Linear Threshold (*LT*) [10], where a node u, activated at the iteration i, has only one chance to activate its neighbors that have not yet been activated in the next iteration $i + 1$. The main difference between *IC* and *LT* is as follows. In *IC*, a node u at the i-th iteration activates $v \in N(u)$ with a probability $p_{u,v}$. In *LT*, there is an activation threshold λ_v associated with a node v in the range of $[0, 1]$, a node v can be possibly activated if the sum of its probability $p_{u,v}$ for $u \in N(v)$ that have been activated is greater than or equal to λ_v in an iteration.

The problem of *IM* (Influence Maximization) is to select a set of nodes S in $G = (V, E)$ of size k that maximizes the expected number of nodes activated by S, denoted by $\sigma(S)$. In the literature, the focus of *IM* is to find a single set of nodes, S, of size k that has the maximum influence. But, there are multiple sets that have the same maximum influence over the given graph G. In [22], Can *et al.* study how to identify all such sets if one single set of S has been computed by a cascade model based on graph automorphism. Here, for a given graph $G = (V, E)$, an automorphism is a bijective function $\gamma : V \mapsto V$ such that $(u, v) \in E$ iff $(\gamma(u), \gamma(v)) \in E$, and an automorphism can be represented as a product of disjoint cycles regarding permutation, where a disjoint cycle, $(v_1, v_2, \ldots, v_k)$, means $\gamma(v_i) = v_{i+1}$ for $1 \leq i \leq k - 1$ and $\gamma(v_k) = v_1$. Such an automorphism γ maps G to itself in a structure-preserving manner. As an example, for graph G in Fig. 1, an automorphism is $(1, 3)$, where we relabel 1 as 3, 3 as 1, and keep all others map to themselves. The resulting graph is isomorphism to the given graph itself. As indicated in this example, if 1 is selected in S, then 3 can be selected as well in another set S' to replace 1, suppose that all $p_{u,v}$ are identical.

Fig. 2. An Example

3   Node Selection in Influence Maximization

The possible existence of multiple sets, $\mathbb{S} = \{S_1, S_2, \cdots\}$, that have the same *IM* (e.g., $\sigma(S_i) = \sigma(S_j)$) for $|S_i| = |S_j| = k$, motivates us to study how to select nodes in $\bigcup_{S_i \in \mathbb{S}} S_i$. The issue is whether it is possible to select nodes in $\mathbb{S}$ that have a better chance to interact in a positive manner in influence maximization. In other words, two nodes, u and v, selected in the process of influence spreading, are better to influence different groups of nodes, or have less overlapping over the nodes they influence directly and indirectly. Figure 2 shows that there are two nodes, 698 and 857, in the given seed S that influence the same node during the process of influence spreading, which is difficult to predict.

We give some details on *IM*. The influence maximization to select a set of nodes of size k can be defined as the following optimization problem, for a given cascade model M over a social network $G = (V, E)$.

$$S^* = \underset{\substack{S \subseteq V \\ |S| \leq k}}{\operatorname{argmax}} \sigma(S) \tag{1}$$

Here, $\sigma(S)$ can be defined as

$$\sigma(S) = \int_X \sigma_X(S) dp \tag{2}$$

where X is the output of all coin flips on edges, and σ_X is the number of nodes that are reached from any node in S. In the literature, there are many approaches that approximately found a set with $\sigma(S) \geq (1 - 1/e)\sigma(S^*)$.

In this paper, we aim at selecting k nodes, S', in $\mathbb{S}$ while keeping the similar $\sigma(S') = \sigma(S_i)$ for $S_i \in \mathbb{S}$. This optimization problem is an integer programming problem with a NP-complete search complexity. We adopt greedy search to solve this problem. We follow the idea of gradient descent, and prune the seeds by eliminating the nodes with the least interaction with the community using Shapley value.

The Shapley value proposed in game theory provides us with a unique and unbiased approach to fairly allocate the total reward gained by all players in a game to each player [32]. Here, we consider a node represents a player in a game aiming to maximize its influence spread, and examine influence maximization from a different perspective.

Definition 1. *Let $\Omega = 1, 2, \ldots, n$ be the set of all players, and r be a reward function, which is a mapping function from $V \to R$, where R is a domain of real numbers. The Shapley value, denoted as $\phi(i|\Omega)$, unbiasedly measures the contribution of the i-th player to the total reward gained by all players in Ω, and is formulated as follows.*

$$\phi(i|\Omega) = \sum_{S \subseteq \Omega \setminus \{i\}} \frac{|S|!(n-|S|-1)!}{n!}(r(S \cup \{i\}) - r(S)) \qquad (3)$$

Some properties are given below [32].

- **Linearity:** Suppose that there are three games, $\aleph_1$, $\aleph_2$, and $\aleph_3$, such that $\forall S \subseteq \Omega, \aleph_1(S) = \aleph_2(S) + \aleph_3(S)$. Then the Shapley value for the player i in game $\aleph_1$ is the sum of Shapley values of the player i in other two games, *i.e.* $\phi^{\aleph_1}(i|\Omega) = \phi^{\aleph_2}(i|\Omega) + \phi^{\aleph_3}(i|\Omega)$. More precisely, in influence maximization, if we have two communities that do not have interaction where $\aleph_2$ and $\aleph_3$ are two spreading functions on the two communities respectively, then the Shapley value of $\aleph_1$ for the reward of the two communities has linear properties.
- **Dummy:** A player i is called a dummy player if $r(S\cup\{i\}) = r(S)+r(\{i\})$. A dummy player satisfies $\phi(i|\Omega) = r(\{i\}) - r(\emptyset)$. In influence maximization, a dummy player denotes an individual node that is far away from a community.
- **Symmetric:** Then Shapley values for two players, i and j, are the same, if $\forall S \subseteq \Omega \setminus \{i,j\}$, it satisfies $r(S \cup \{i\}) = r(S \cup \{j\})$.
- **Efficiency:** We have total reward that is attributed to each player: $\sum_i \phi(i|\Omega) = r(\Omega) - r(\emptyset)$. The summation of overall individual contributions can be the total spreading in the seed set.

Below, we treat $S_{ij} = \{i,j\}$ as a new player to replace i and j. In doing so, we remove the two players, i and j, from the set of all players S, and add the new player S_{ij} to the set of players. The Shapley value of S_{ij} is defined as the join contribution of i and j.

Definition 2. *Let $S_{ij} = \{i,j\}$, $\Omega' = \Omega \setminus \{i,j\} \cup S_{i,j}$, $\phi(S_{ij}|\Omega')$ is defined as the joint contribution of i and j with a reward function r.*

$$\phi(S_{ij}|\Omega') = \sum_{S \subseteq \Omega'} \frac{|S|!(n-|S|-2)!}{(n-1)!}[r(S \cup \{i,j\}) - r(S)] \qquad (4)$$

Next, we consider the interaction between the two players, i and j, denoted as I_{ij} [24].

Algorithm 1. NodeSelection $(G, \mathbb{S}, k)$

Input: a graph $G = (V, E)$, the seed Set $\mathbb{S}$, and k;
Output: a subset of $\mathbb{S}$ with max average interaction;
1: $\tilde{S} \leftarrow \mathbb{S}$;
2: **while** $|\tilde{S}| > k$ **do**
3:     Compute E_{ij} by Eq. (10);
4:     Find the smallest i that has less contribution to E_{ij};
5:     Remove i from $\tilde{S}$;
6: **end while**
7: Return $\tilde{S}$;

Definition 3. *Let* $S_{ij} = \{i, j\}$ *and* $\Omega' = \Omega \setminus \{i, j\} \cup S_{i,j}$, *the interaction between two players,* i *and* j, *denoted as* I_{ij}, *is defined as follows.*

$$I_{ij} = \phi(S_{ij}|\Omega') - [\phi(i|\Omega \setminus \{i\}) + \phi(j|\Omega \setminus \{j\})] \tag{5}$$

Here, $\phi(i|\Omega \setminus \{j\})$ denotes individual contribution of player i when player j is absent. We can formulate $\phi(i|\Omega \setminus \{j\})$ based on the definition of Shapley value.

$$\phi(i|\Omega \setminus \{j\}) = \sum_{S \subseteq \Omega \setminus \{i,j\}} \frac{|S|!(n - |S| - 2)!}{(n - 1)!}[r(S \cup \{i\}) - r(S)] \tag{6}$$

With the Efficiency property [28], we have

$$\sum_j \phi(j|\Omega \setminus \{i\}) = r(\Omega) - r(\{i\}) \tag{7}$$

The precise expression of I_{ij} can then be derived as follows.

$$I_{ij} = \sum_{S \subseteq \Omega \setminus \{i,j\}} \frac{|S|!(n - |S| - 2)!}{(n - 1)!}[r(S \cup \{i, j\})$$
$$- r(S \cup \{i\}) - r(S \cup \{j\}) + r(S)] \tag{8}$$

It is important to note that the positive I_{ij} means the cooperation is successful and yields positive interaction.

Given $\mathbb{S}$, we want to reduce its size, and select a subset, denoted as $\tilde{S}$, and want to eliminate the nodes in $\mathbb{S}$ that have large overlapping in the process of influence spreading. We give two objective functions. First, the resulting seed set, $\tilde{S}$, is expected to maintain a similar influence power as $\mathbb{S}$. To do so, we maximize $\sigma(\tilde{S})$. Second, we want every pair of players in $\tilde{S}$ contribute to the influence spreading with a high average interaction, where the interaction between the seeds can be formulated as $\sum_{i,j} I_{ij}$. The problem can be formulated as follows.

$$\text{Max}_{\tilde{S} \subseteq V} \ \sigma(\tilde{S}) + \frac{1}{(|\tilde{S}| - 1)^2} \sum_{i,j} I_{ij} \tag{9}$$

Alternatively, we can convert from summation to expectation by deriving from the probability we chose a player from the set of nodes is $1/(|\tilde{S}| - 1)$, and maximize the expectation as follows.

$$\text{Max}_{\tilde{S} \subseteq V} \; \sigma(\tilde{S}) + \lambda \mathbf{E}_{ij}(I_{ij}) \tag{10}$$

where λ is a regularization factor. Furthermore, given the interaction I_{ij} and reward function r, we have the following equation to reduce the computational cost.

$$\mathbf{E}_{ij}(I_{ij}) = \frac{1}{n-1} \mathbf{E}_i[r(\Omega) - r(\Omega \setminus \{i\}) - r(\{i\}) + r(\emptyset)] \tag{11}$$

This can be proved as follows.

$$\mathbf{E}_{ij}(I_{i,j}) = \mathbf{E}_{ij}\left[\sum_{S \subseteq \Omega \setminus \{i,j\}} \frac{|S|!(n - |S| - 2)!}{(n-1)!} (r(S \cup \{i,j\}) \right.$$

$$\left. - r(S \cup \{i\}) - r(S \cup \{j\}) + r(S)) \right]$$

$$= \mathbf{E}_{ij}\left[\phi(i|\Omega \setminus \{i\}) - \phi(j|\Omega \setminus \{i\}) \right]$$

$$= \frac{1}{n-1} \mathbf{E}_i\left[\sum_{j \in \Omega \setminus j} [\phi(i|\Omega \setminus \{i\}) - \phi(j|\Omega \setminus \{i\})] \right]$$

$$= \frac{1}{n-1} \mathbf{E}_i\left[r(\Omega) - r(\Omega \setminus \{i\}) - r(\{i\}) + r(\emptyset) \right] \tag{12}$$

The summation can be computed based on limited sample space. With Fubini'theorem, the integration is commutative, and with the definition of expectation, we can easily get this proof.

We give our algorithm NodeSelection in Algorithm 1. NodeSelection takes three inputs, the graph $G = (V, E)$, the set of seeds, $\mathbb{S}$, computed, and a threshold k to terminate the algorithm; and outputs a subset of $\mathbb{S}$, denoted as $\tilde{S}$, in which seeds have better interactions. It is worth mentioning that the NodeSelection algorithm can be used when $\mathbb{S}$ is computed by graph automorphism [22], and can be used in other settings. First, a user can select k' ($\geq k$) and then use NodeSelection to reduce it to k. Second, a user can also use NodeSelection to select more effective k seeds from the set of k' seeds.

4   An *IM* Visualization System

We have developed a client-server *IM* visualization system. At the client-side, there is a visualization module that renders graphs and provides ways for users to explore the graph interactively including the functions to visualize the process of influence spreading iteratively, the graph automorphism for nodes and subgraphs. In other words, given a node in G, it visualizes the nodes that are graph automorphic to the given node in G, given a subgraph that exists in G,

Fig. 3. The GUI of the Visualization System

it visualizes the subgraphs that are graph automorphic to the given subgraphs, which is called SSM (Symmetric Subgraph Matching), based on Auto-tree developed in [22]. At the server-side, it provides functions to maintain graphs, and compute graph automorphism, SSM, and *IM*. Figure 3 shows the system when it presents the statistics regarding the graph, such as degree distribution, density, and information about the selected node and its neighborhood.

We discuss the details on the rendering time of large graphs, which is the time between for a graph to be shown with ForceAtlas2 layout [15] in our system. The ForceAtlas2 layout turns structural proximities into visual proximities, and facilitates the efficient identification of clusters without specifying the positions of nodes in advance. We have developed three subsystems based on three existing frameworks. The first is with Cytoscape [5], a widely used software for complex network visualization. Cytoscape integrates various user interactive components and is highly compatible with Python modules. However, it can not efficiently handle large-scale graphics rendering with more than 500 nodes. The second is with Sigma (https://github.com/jacomyal/sigma.js), which is an emerging JavaScript library specifically optimized for massive graph rendering. Sigma can support up to approximately 100,000 edges. But there are minor lags when the graph is large in size. The third is with Cosmos (https://github.com/cosmograph-org/cosmos), which leverages GPU in layout processing and makes it highly efficient for large-scale network visualization tasks. Cosmos can support up to 800,000+ edges. Figure 4 shows the differences among Cytoscape, Sigma, and Cosmos when we visualize the Facebook dataset with 4,039 nodes and 88,234 edges. Cytoscape takes about 171 s to initialize the visualization module but fails to generate a readable layout; Sigma finalizes the initialization and optimizes the layout based on the ForceAtlas2 algorithm in 12.4 s; and Cosmos can be generated in 9 s.

For *IM*, our system visualizes newly activated nodes in each iteration with different colors, clearly highlighting the spread of influence across a network. We can observe whether there are large overlaps of influenced nodes for two influential seeds located at different areas, or whether there are significant speedups in spread given activation of certain nodes.

Our visualization system supports the following approaches, namely, PMC [27], GAME [34], HIST [12], SUBSIM [12], SSA [26], and DSSA [26]. In

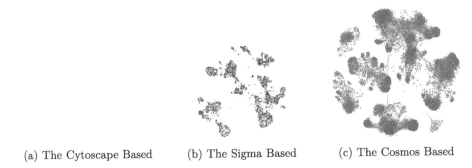

(a) The Cytoscape Based   (b) The Sigma Based   (c) The Cosmos Based

Fig. 4. Graph Visualization by Cytoscape, Sigma, and Cosmos

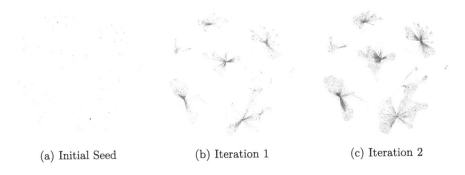

(a) Initial Seed   (b) Iteration 1   (c) Iteration 2

Fig. 5. Influence Propagation Process

Fig. 5, we show the initial seed nodes, the nodes influenced in the first and the second iterations, respectively, using the Facebook dataset (Table 1), where the nodes in different iterations are marked with different colors. In Fig. 6, we visualize the main difference between PMC and SUBSIM (*IC*) using the Facebook dataset. Figure 6(a) shows the summary of the iterations on the left, and the influence spreading by PMC and SUBSIM (*IC*) on the right in order. A user can select any node presented to visualize its neighbors and influence spreading in any iteration. PMC is likely to select the nodes with high degree initially, where SUBSIM (*LT*) does not. Figure 6(b) shows the influence spreading in the iteration 3, where PMC intends to spread over evenly whereas SUBSIM (*IC*) has its focuses. Figure 6(c) shows the eigenvector-centrality over iterations, where the bold line is for PMC and the blue line is for SUBSIM (*IC*). Our system can also show the other centrality (e.g., degree, pageRank). In Fig. 7, with the Facebook dataset, we visualize the main difference between PMC and SUBSIM (*LT*). Figure 7(a) shows the initial iteration, Fig. 7(b) shows how a node in Fig. 7(a) spreads in detail, and Fig. 7(c) shows the results in the iteration 3.

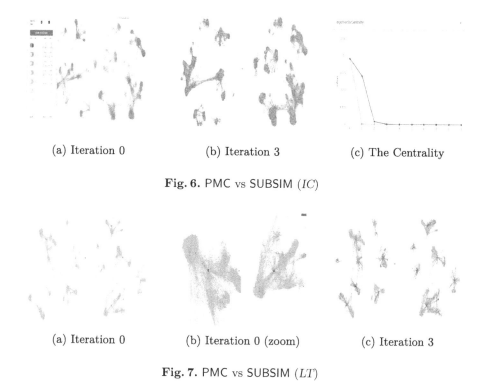

(a) Iteration 0   (b) Iteration 3   (c) The Centrality

Fig. 6. PMC vs SUBSIM (*IC*)

(a) Iteration 0   (b) Iteration 0 (zoom)   (c) Iteration 3

Fig. 7. PMC vs SUBSIM (*LT*)

5   Related Works

Kempe *et al.* [16] proved that finding the optimal solution for *IM* is NP-hard and proposed a greedy algorithm that provides approximation with guaranteed polynomial time. Leskovec *et al.* [17] leverages the submodular property of diffusion models and extends the greedy algorithm, reducing evaluation costs of spread and achieve high speed up. Goyal *et al.* [9] improved the efficiency of CELF algorithms [17]. The above methods could not fully address large-scale networks due to the high time complexity for simulating influence cascade. Ohsaka *et al.* developed a monte-carlo-simulation-based greedy method and pruned BFSs to reduce simulation costs and recalculation, which approximates the optimal solution with less time on large-scale networks [27]. Clark and Poovendran in [4] explored extensions of the *IC* model, the Dynamic Influence in Competitive Environments (DICE). Guo *et al.* in [11] presented a study on random reverse reachable (RR) set generation phase and proposed an efficient random RR set generation algorithm under *IC* model, and Nguyen *et al.* in [26] proposed two novel sampling frameworks for *IM*-based viral marketing problems, and improved the efficiency to handle billion-scale networks while providing the same approximation guarantee.

Table 1. Graph Dataset

Graph	Node	Edge	d_{max}	d_{avg}
Facebook	4,039	88,234	1045	43.69
Wiki-Vote	7,115	103,689	1,065	28.32
Gnutella	62,586	147,892	95	4.73
Epinions	75,879	405,740	3,044	10.69

Table 2. Influence Spreading

Model	k	Facebook	Wiki-vote	Epinion	Gnutell
PMC	10	3,048.5	3,461.7	18,031.4	2,680.8
	50	3,054.3	3,464.3	18,075.9	3,357.7
	100	3,078.5	3,470.8	18,157.8	3,672.4
NodeSelection	10	**3,051.2**	**3,470.2**	**18,077.4**	**2,691.6**
	50	**3,077.2**	**3,473.7**	**18,108.3**	**3,372.0**
	100	**3,086.0**	**3,473.5**	**18,177.8**	**3,727.3**
SSA	10	3,047.4	3,471.9	18,062.8	2,818.6
	50	3,062.1	3,483.3	18,094.4	3,087.9
	100	3086.0	3,516.3	18,146.1	3,664.0
NodeSelection	10	**3,053.3**	**3,475.9**	**1,8087.9**	**3,134.5**
	50	**3,080.4**	**3,490.4**	**1,8191.9**	**3,125.3**
	100	**3,094.4**	**3,522.7**	**1,8174.7**	**3,787.3**
DSSA	10	3,022.2	3,475.4	18,009.2	2,417.23
	50	3,043.2	3,483.4	18,051.8	3,107.4
	100	3,106.2	3,512.7	18,130.8	3,560.4
NodeSelection	10	**3,051.4**	**3,475.5**	**18,032.5**	**2,491.4**
	50	**3,096.2**	**3,494.4**	**18,084.0**	**3,141.6**
	100	**3,111.0**	**3,516.0**	**18,152.3**	**3,602.5**
SUBSIM	10	3,052.7	3,475.2	17,985.4	1,850.6
	50	3,062.9	3,490.8	17,999.2	2,806.9
	100	3,070.48	3,509.7	18,021.8	3,175.4
NodeSelection	10	**3,058.2**	**3,478.9**	**18,057.4**	**1,883.6**
	50	**3,071.4**	**3,511.7**	**18,108.3**	**2,808.7**
	100	**3,077.78**	**3,518.9**	**18,025.2**	**3,432.1**

6   Experiments

We conduct testing over four real-world graphs including three social networks (e.g. Facebook, Epinions, Wiki-Vote) and one peer-to-peer network (Gnutella). All datasets are obtained from SNAP(https://snap.stanford.edu/data/). The

Table 3. Interactions

Model	k	Facebook	Wiki-vote	Epinion	Gnutell
PMC	10	−24,472.0	−3,4704.4	−180,254.4	−6,025.8
	50	−135,994.2	−17,2792.0	−797,550.4	−25,919.0
	100	−260,434.0	−34,3298.4	−1,389,000.8	−49,288.6
NodeSelection	10	**−24,183.6**	−34,544.0	**−180,215.2**	**−5,823.2**
	50	**−135,588.8**	−170,163.1	**−588,814.6**	**−21,247.4**
	100	**−224,406.1**	−338,197.8	**−1,003,680.0**	**−46,601.4**
SSA	10	−27,040.4	−15,365.6	−1,443,93.5	−9,084.5
	50	−123,944.6	−68,062.2	−263,427.8	−33,739.4
	100	−249,248.2	−152,669.0	−4862,06.0	−51,468.2
NodeSelection	10	**−25,543.0**	**−9,744.6**	**−108,283.0**	**−8,179.5**
	50	**−123,843.7**	**−58,228.0**	**−183,753.8**	**−21,061.7**
	100	**−212,045.5**	**−127,705.7**	**−303,670.3**	**−42,959.6**
DSSA	10	−25,849.1	−15,229.6	−180,697.8	−7,881.7
	50	−135,614.6	−64,711.5	−400,330.9	−27,284.8
	100	−248,489.9	−144,419.7	−573,875.0	−43,518.2
NodeSelection	10	**−25,376.9**	**−10,337.4**	**−72,433.7**	**−7,568.8**
	50	**−121,807.4**	**−58,800.2**	**−394,094.3**	**−26,437.5**
	100	**−210,824.9**	**−144,241.8**	**−260,940.7**	**−42,989.4**
SUBSIM	10	−52,479.4	−15,336.1	−144,742.9	−6,025.8
	50	−131,352.2	−65,856.0	−758,381.2	−8,640.8
	100	−253,710.0	−151,106.0	−1,389,000.8	−25,091.7
NodeSelection	10	**−23,303.0**	−10,435.4	**−137,268.6**	**−5,823.2**
	50	**−129,179.2**	−65,730.3	**−744,175.2**	**−7,691.2**
	100	**−241,664.0**	−120,246.2	**−1,003,680.0**	**−22,407.0**

details are shown in Table 1. We set the influence probability of each node following uniform distribution $U(0, 0.2)$. We report our experimental studies for the following approaches, namely, PMC [27], SSA [26], DSSA [26], and SUBSIM [12].

To investigate the effect of interactions among the nodes in the set of seeds, we compare the result of PMC, SSA, DSSA, and SUBSIM using $k = 10, 50, 100$ over the four datasets. We conduct NodeSelection as follows. First, we use one of the approaches (e.g., PMC, SSA, DSSA, and SUBSIM) to compute IM with $k = 200$ for all datasets, and then we use NodeSelection to obtain $k = 10, 50, 100$. The expected numbers by IM and by NodeSelection are shown in Table 2. The better results are shown in bold. We can see that in the four real-world networks, NodeSelection outperforms the others which validates the superiority of our proposed algorithm. We also show the interactions based on Shapley values. We examine the performance of our NodeSelection in solving the optimization problem (Eq. (10)). Table 3 shows the average interaction of the respective seed set. As the graphs are connected, the seeds show interactions as negative values. The table shows that the resulting seed set by NodeSelection has a larger interaction than that of the others.

7   Conclusion

In this paper, we studied two issues. First, we proposed an NodeSelection algorithm to select a set of k seed users from a set of seed k' ($\geq k$) users being computed, based on cooperative game using Shapley value. As confirmed in our experimental studies using four large networks, our NodeSelection algorithm selects better k seed users from k' ($\geq k$) seed users using an algorithm than the k seed users computed by the same algorithm in terms of the expected number of influenced users. Second, we developed a visualization system to assist users to investigate how influence spreads for a single approach and how two different approaches behave under a cascade model from topological perspective.

Acknowledgement. This work is supported by the Research Grants Council of Hong Kong, No. 14202919 and No. 14205520.

References

1. Banerjee, S., Jenamani, M., Pratihar, D.K.: A survey on influence maximization in a social network. Knowl. Inf. Syst. **62**(9), 3417–3455 (2020)
2. Bian, S., Guo, Q., Wang, S., Yu, J.X.: Efficient algorithms for budgeted influence maximization on massive social networks. Proc. VLDB Endow. **13**(9), 1498–1510 (2020)
3. Chen, S., Fan, J., Li, G., Feng, J., Tan, K., Tang, J.: Online topic-aware influence maximization. Proc. VLDB Endow. **8**(6), 666–677 (2015)
4. Clark, A., Poovendran, R.: Maximizing influence in competitive environments: a game-theoretic approach. In: Baras, J.S., Katz, J., Altman, E. (eds.) GameSec 2011. LNCS, vol. 7037, pp. 151–162. Springer, Heidelberg (2011). https://doi.org/10.1007/978-3-642-25280-8_13
5. Franz, M., Lopes, C.T., Huck, G., Dong, Y., Sümer, S.O., Bader, G.D.: Cytoscape.js: a graph theory library for visualisation and analysis. Bioinformatics **32**(2), 309–311 (2016)
6. Gaskó, N., Suciu, M.A., Képes, T., Lung, R.I.: Shapley value and extremal optimization for the network influence maximization problem. In: 2019 21st International Symposium on Symbolic and Numeric Algorithms for Scientific Computing (SYNASC), pp. 182–189. IEEE (2019)
7. Goldenberg, J., Libai, B.: Using complex systems analysis to advance marketing theory development: modeling heterogeneity effects on new product growth through stochastic cellular automata. Acad. Market. Sci. Rev **9**, 01 (2001)
8. Goldenberg, J., Libai, B., Muller, E.: Talk of the network: a complex systems look at the underlying process of word-of-mouth. Mark. Lett. **12**, 211–223 (2001)

9. Goyal, A., Lu, W., Lakshmanan, L.V.: CELF++: optimizing the greedy algorithm for influence maximization in social networks. In: Proceedings of the 20th International Conference Companion on World Wide Web, WWW 2011, New York, NY, USA, pp. 47–48. Association for Computing Machinery (2011)

10. Granovetter, M.: Threshold models of collective behavior. Am. J. Sociol. **83**(6), 1420–1443 (1978)

11. Guo, Q., Wang, S., Wei, Z., Chen, M.: Influence maximization revisited: efficient reverse reachable set generation with bound tightened. In: Proceedings of the 2020 ACM SIGMOD International Conference on Management of Data, pp. 2167–2181 (2020)

12. Guo, Q., Wang, S., Wei, Z., Lin, W., Tang, J.: Influence maximization revisited: efficient sampling with bound tightened. ACM Trans. Database Syst. **47**(3), 12:1–12:45 (2022)

13. He, X., Kempe, D.: Robust influence maximization. In: Krishnapuram, B., Shah, M., Smola, A.J., Aggarwal, C.C., Shen, D., Rastogi, R. (eds.) Proceedings of the 22nd ACM SIGKDD International Conference on Knowledge Discovery and Data Mining, San Francisco, CA, USA, 13–17 August 2016, pp. 885–894. ACM (2016)

14. Huang, S., Lin, W., Bao, Z., Sun, J.: Influence maximization in real-world closed social networks. Proc. VLDB Endow. **16**(2), 180–192 (2022)

15. Jacomy, M., Venturini, T., Heymann, S., Bastian, M.: ForceAtlas2, a continuous graph layout algorithm for handy network visualization designed for the Gephi software. PLoS ONE **9**(6), e98679 (2014)

16. Kempe, D., Kleinberg, J., Tardos, É.: Maximizing the spread of influence through a social network. In: Proceedings of the ninth ACM SIGKDD International Conference on Knowledge Discovery and Data Mining, pp. 137–146 (2003)

17. Leskovec, J., Krause, A., Guestrin, C., Faloutsos, C., VanBriesen, J., Glance, N.: Cost-effective outbreak detection in networks. In: Proceedings of the 13th ACM SIGKDD International Conference on Knowledge Discovery and Data Mining, pp. 420–429 (2007)

18. Li, G., Chen, S., Feng, J., Tan, K., Li, W.: Efficient location-aware influence maximization. In: Dyreson, C.E., Li, F., Özsu, M.T. (eds.) International Conference on Management of Data, SIGMOD 2014, Snowbird, UT, USA, 22–27 June 2014, pp. 87–98. ACM (2014)

19. Li, J., Cai, T., Mian, A., Li, R., Sellis, T., Yu, J. X.: Holistic influence maximization for targeted advertisements in spatial social networks. In: 34th IEEE International Conference on Data Engineering, ICDE 2018, Paris, France, April 16–19, 2018, pp. 1340–1343. IEEE Computer Society (2018)

20. Li, Y., Fan, J., Wang, Y., Tan, K.: Influence maximization on social graphs: a survey. IEEE Trans. Knowl. Data Eng. **30**(10), 1852–1872 (2018)

21. Lin, M., Li, W., Lu, S.: Balanced influence maximization in attributed social network based on sampling. In: Caverlee, J., Hu, X.B., Lalmas, M., Wang, W. (eds.) WSDM 2020: The Thirteenth ACM International Conference on Web Search and Data Mining, Houston, TX, USA, 3–7 February 2020, pp. 375–383. ACM (2020)

22. Lu, C., Yu, J.X., Zhang, Z., Cheng, H.: Graph ISO/auto-morphism: a divide-&-conquer approach. In: Proceedings of the 2021 International Conference on Management of Data, SIGMOD 2021, New York, NY, USA, pp. 1195–1207. Association for Computing Machinery (2021)

23. MacArthur, B.D., Sánchez-García, R.J., Anderson, J.W.: On automorphism groups of networks. arXiv preprint arXiv:0705.3215 (2007)

24. Michel, G., Marc, R.: An axiomatic approach to the concept of interaction among players in cooperative games. Int. J. Game Theory (1999)

25. Narayanam, R., Narahari, Y.: A shapley value-based approach to discover influential nodes in social networks. IEEE Trans. Autom. Sci. Eng. **8**(1), 130–147 (2011)
26. Nguyen, H.T., Thai, M.T., Dinh, T.N.: Stop-and-stare: optimal sampling algorithms for viral marketing in billion-scale networks. In: Proceedings of the 2016 International Conference on Management of Data, pp. 695–710 (2016)
27. Ohsaka, N., Akiba, T., Yoshida, Y., Kawarabayashi, K.-I.: Fast and accurate influence maximization on large networks with pruned Monte-Carlo simulations. In: Proceedings of the AAAI Conference on Artificial Intelligence, vol. 28 (2014)
28. Shapley, L.S.: A value for n-person games. Contrib. Theory Games **28**, 307–317 (1953)
29. Tang, F., Liu, Q., Zhu, H., Chen, E., Zhu, F.: Diversified social influence maximization. In: Wu, X., Ester, M., Xu, G. (eds.) 2014 IEEE/ACM International Conference on Advances in Social Networks Analysis and Mining, ASONAM 2014, Beijing, China, 17–20 August 2014, pp. 455–459. IEEE Computer Society (2014)
30. Tsaras, D., Trimponias, G., Ntaflos, L., Papadias, D.: Collective influence maximization for multiple competing products with an awareness-to-influence model. Proc. VLDB Endow. **14**(7), 1124–1136 (2021)
31. Wang, X., Zhang, Y., Zhang, W., Lin, X.: Distance-aware influence maximization in geo-social network. In: 32nd IEEE International Conference on Data Engineering, ICDE 2016, Helsinki, Finland, 16–20 May 2016, pp. 1–12. IEEE Computer Society (2016)
32. Weber, R.J.: Probabilistic values for games. In: The Shapley Value. Essays in Honor of Lloyd S. Shapley, pp. 307–317 (1953)
33. Zhang, K., Zhou, J., Tao, D., Karras, P., Li, Q., Xiong, H.: Geodemographic influence maximization. In: Gupta, R., Liu, Y., Tang, J., Prakash, B.A. (eds.) KDD 2020: The 26th ACM SIGKDD Conference on Knowledge Discovery and Data Mining, Virtual Event, CA, USA, 23–27 August 2020, pp. 2764–2774. ACM (2020)
34. Zhang, Y., Zhang, Y.: Top-k influential nodes in social networks: a game perspective. In: Proceedings of the 40th International ACM SIGIR Conference on Research and Development in Information Retrieval, pp. 1029–1032 (2017)

On Directed Densest Subgraph Detection

Kai Yao$^{(\boxtimes)}$, Xin Yang, and Lijun Chang

The University of Sydney, Sydney, Australia
{kai.yao,lijun.chang}@sydney.edu.au, xyan5144@uni.sydney.edu.au

Abstract. The well-studied directed densest subgraph problem aims to find two (possibly overlapping) vertex subsets S^* and T^* in a given directed graph $G = (V, E)$ such that $\rho(S, T) = \frac{|E(S,T)|}{\sqrt{|S||T|}}$ is maximized; here $E(S, T)$ denotes the set of edges from vertices of S to T in G. This problem is polynomial-time solvable, and both exact algorithms and approximation algorithms have been proposed in the literature. However, the existing exact algorithms are time-consuming, while the existing approximation algorithms often yield trivial solutions that consist of the highest-degree vertex and its in-neighbors or out-neighbors. Moreover, there is nothing special about geometric mean that is adopted in the existing density measure for combining $\frac{|E(S,T)|}{|S|}$ and $\frac{|E(S,T)|}{|T|}$. In this paper, we explore alternative density measures and propose corresponding algorithms, for directed densest subgraph identification. Specifically, we introduce three density measures that combine $\frac{|E(S,T)|}{|S|}$ and $\frac{|E(S,T)|}{|T|}$ by harmonic mean, arithmetic mean, and minimum mean, respectively. Based on these density measures, we formulate the harmonic mean-based directed densest subgraph (HDDS) problem, the arithmetic mean-based directed densest subgraph (ADDS) problem, and the minimum mean-based directed densest subgraph (MDDS) problem. We then propose a 2-approximation algorithm for HDDS, a 2-approximation algorithm for ADDS, and a heuristic algorithm for MDDS; our HDDS and MDDS algorithms run in linear time to the input graph size. Extensive empirical studies on large real-world directed graphs show that our ADDS algorithm produces similar trivial results as the existing approximation algorithm, and our HDDS and MDDS algorithms generate nontrivial and much better solutions and scale to large graphs.

Keywords: Directed densest subgraph · Directed graphs

1 Introduction

Directed graphs are essential for modeling relationships in real-world contexts like social networks, information networks, and biological networks [1]. Recently, identifying the densest subgraph in a directed graph has gained substantial attention [2–6]. This problem finds applications in areas like fake follower detection [6], community detection [4], and graph compression [7]. Instead of returning a vertex subset (or vertex-induced subgraph) as done in densest subgraph identification over undirected graphs, densest subgraph identification over directed graphs typically returns two (possibly overlapping) vertex subsets S and T such that there are a lot of edges from S to T. Specifically, Kannan and Vinay [2] defined the density of $S, T \subseteq V$ as $\rho(S, T) = \frac{|E(S,T)|}{\sqrt{|S||T|}}$, where $E(S, T)$ is the set of edges from S to T in the input graph. The pair of vertex subsets S^* and T^* that maximizes $\rho(S^*, T^*)$ is referred to as the directed densest subgraph, which is polynomial-time computable. This density measure has been followed and used by all subsequent work on directed densest subgraph identification [2,6,8,9]. Both exact algorithms and approximation algorithms have been proposed in the literature. However, the existing exact algorithms are time-consuming due to lots of maximum flow computations and thus are not suitable for handling large graphs. Among the existing approximation algorithms, Core-Approx [6] is a state-of-the-art algorithm that achieves a good balance between the time complexity and the approximation ratio; specifically, Core-Approx computes a 2-approximate result in $O(\sqrt{m}(n+m))$ time, for a graph with n vertices and m edges. However, our empirical studies show that Core-Approx usually reports trivial solutions that consist of the highest-degree vertex and its in-neighbors or out-neighbors, due to the power-law degree distribution prevailing in real-world graphs. Such skewed and trivial solutions severely curtail the meaningful insights attainable through directed densest graph extraction.

In this paper, we aim to explore alternative density measures and propose corresponding algorithms, for directed densest subgraph identification. We observe that the density formulated by Kannan and Vinay [2] can be regarded as the *geometric mean* of $\frac{|E(S,T)|}{|S|}$ and $\frac{|E(S,T)|}{|T|}$ that measure the density for the S part and for the T part, respectively. There is nothing special about geometric mean, and we can use other mean measures instead. Thus, we introduce three novel density measures, namely the *harmonic mean-based density*, *arithmetic mean-based density*, and *minimum mean-based density* that, respectively, apply the harmonic mean, arithmetic mean, and minimum mean to $\frac{|E(S,T)|}{|S|}$ and $\frac{|E(S,T)|}{|T|}$. For each of these density measures, we formulate a distinct directed densest subgraph problem, whose objective is to identify S and T that maximize the corresponding density measure. This endeavor yields three specific problem instances: the harmonic mean-based directed densest subgraph (HDDS) problem, the arithmetic mean-based directed densest subgraph (ADDS) problem, and the minimum mean-based directed densest subgraph (MDDS) problem. To solve the HDDS problem, we establish the equivalence between the problem over directed graphs and the extensively studied densest subgraph problem over undirected graphs. Subsequently, existing exact and approximation algorithms for undirected densest subgraph identification can be directly applied. Regarding the ADDS problem, we propose a 2-approximation algorithm A-Approx that runs in $O(\sqrt{m}(n+m))$ time. For the MDDS problem, we propose a heuristic algorithm M-Approx that runs in $O(n+m)$ time.

Our main contributions are summarized as follows.

- We formulate three alternative density measures for directed densest subgraph identification (Sect. 2).

- We establish the equivalence between the HDDS problem and the extensively studied densest subgraph problem over undirected graphs (Sect. 3).
- We propose a 2-approximation algorithm A-Approx for the ADDS problem that runs in $O(\sqrt{m}(n + m))$ time (Sect. 4).
- We propose a heuristic algorithm M-Approx for the MDDS problem that runs in $O(n + m)$ time (Sect. 5).

We conduct extensive experiments on large real-world directed graphs to demonstrate the effectiveness and efficiency of our algorithms in Sect. 6. The results show that A-Approx produces similar trivial solutions as the existing algorithm Core-Approx, and our H-Approx and M-Approx algorithms generate nontrivial and much better solutions and scale to large graphs. Related works are discussed in Sect. 7. Proofs of all theorems and lemmas are omitted due to limit of space.

2 Preliminaries

Let $G = (V, E)$ represent a directed graph, where $n = |V|$ denotes the number of vertices and $m = |E|$ denotes the number of edges in the graph G. Given two (possibly overlapping) vertex subsets S and T, we use $E(S, T)$ to denote the set of all edges that connect vertices from set S to set T, formally defined as $E(S, T) = E \cap (S \times T)$. We use the term (S, T)-induced subgraph to refer to the subgraph of G that is induced by vertices S and T and edges $E(S, T)$. This subgraph is denoted as $G[S, T]$. We use $d_G^+(v)$ and $d_G^-(v)$ to denote v's out-degree and in-degree in G, respectively. Next, we present possible density measures for (S, T)-induced subgraphs of a directed graph by leveraging the combination of two components $\frac{|E(S,T)|}{|S|}$ and $\frac{|E(S,T)|}{|T|}$.

Definition 1 (Geometric Mean-based Density [2]). *Given a directed graph* $G = (V, E)$ *and two vertex sets* $S, T \subseteq V$, *the geometric mean-based density of the* (S, T)-*induced subgraph* $G[S, T]$ *is defined as:*

$$\rho_g(S, T) = \sqrt{\frac{|E(S,T)|}{|S|} \cdot \frac{|E(S,T)|}{|T|}} = \frac{|E(S,T)|}{\sqrt{|S||T|}}$$

Definition 2 (Harmonic Mean-based Density). *Given a directed graph* $G = (V, E)$ *and two vertex sets* $S, T \subseteq V$, *the harmonic mean-based density of the* (S, T)-*induced subgraph* $G[S, T]$ *is defined as:*

$$\rho_h(S, T) = \left(\frac{\left(\frac{|E(S,T)|}{|S|} \right)^{-1} + \left(\frac{|E(S,T)|}{|T|} \right)^{-1}}{2} \right)^{-1} = \frac{2|E(S,T)|}{|S| + |T|}$$

Definition 3 (Arithmetic Mean-based Density). *Given a directed graph* $G = (V, E)$ *and two vertex sets* $S, T \subseteq V$, *the arithmetic mean-based density of the* (S, T)-*induced subgraph* $G[S, T]$ *is defined as:*

$$\rho_a(S, T) = \frac{\frac{|E(S,T)|}{|S|} + \frac{|E(S,T)|}{|T|}}{2} = \frac{(|S| + |T|)|E(S,T)|}{2\,|S||T|}$$

Definition 4 (Minimum Mean-based Density). *Given a directed graph* $G = (V, E)$ *and two vertex sets* $S, T \subseteq V$, *the minimum mean-based density of the* (S, T)-*induced subgraph* $G[S, T]$ *is defined as:*

$$\rho_m(S, T) = \min \left\{ \frac{|E(S, T)|}{|S|}, \frac{|E(S, T)|}{|T|} \right\} = \frac{|E(S, T)|}{\max\{|S|, |T|\}}$$

Problem Definition: Given a directed graph $G = (V, E)$ and one of the above density measures, we aim to find the (S^*, T^*)-induced subgraph whose density is the highest among all the possible (S, T)-induced subgraphs of G.

Adopting different density measures leads to four specific problems: the geometric mean-based directed densest subgraph (GDDS) problem, the harmonic mean-based directed densest subgraph (HDDS) problem, the arithmetic mean-based directed densest subgraph (ADDS) problem, and the minimum mean-based directed densest subgraph (MDDS) problem. We use ρ_g^*, ρ_h^*, ρ_a^* and ρ_m^* to represent the density of the densest subgraph for the four problems, respectively.

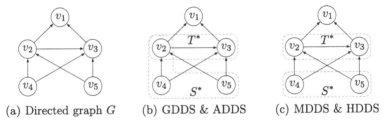

(a) Directed graph G (b) GDDS & ADDS   (c) MDDS & HDDS

Fig. 1. Illustration of different density measures

Example 1. Consider the directed graph G in Fig. 1(a). Both the GDDS and ADDS are the subgraph induced by $S^* = \{v_2, v_4, v_5\}$ and $T^* = \{v_2, v_3\}$, and $\rho_g^* = \frac{5}{\sqrt{2 \times 3}} = 2.04$ and $\rho_a^* = \frac{(2+3) \times 5}{2 \times 2 \times 3} = 2.08$ (see Fig. 1(b)). Both the MDDS and HDDS are the subgraph induced by $S^* = \{v_4, v_5\}$ and $T^* = \{v_2, v_3\}$, and $\rho_m^* = \frac{4}{\max\{2,2\}} = 2$ and $\rho_h^* = \frac{2 \times 4}{2+2} = 2$ (see Fig. 1(c)). Note that the subgraph induced by $S^* = \{v_2, v_4, v_5\}$ and $T^* = \{v_2, v_3\}$ also has the harmonic mean-based density of 2 and thus is also an HDDS.

Presently, the mainstream approach to capturing the directed densest subgraph is through the use of geometric mean-based density, with both exact and approximation algorithms being designed. In this paper, we initiate the study of directed densest subgraph identification for other alternative density measures. Approximation/heuristic algorithms are proposed in the following, while designing efficient exact algorithms is left as our future work.

3   Harmonic Mean-Based Directed Densest Subgraph

In this section, we demonstrate the equivalence between the HDDS problem over directed graphs and the extensively studied densest subgraph problem over undirected graphs [10]. Consequently, the existing exact and approximation algorithms for the densest subgraph problem over undirected graphs can be directly employed to tackle the HDDS problem.

Let us begin by discussing how to transform a directed graph $G = (V, E)$ into an undirected bipartite graph $G' = (V_1, V_2, E')$. We create two sets of vertices $V_1 = V_2 = V$. Note that, to distinguish the same vertex in V_1 and V_2, for each $v \in V_1$ we use v' to denote its counterpart in V_2. Then, for each directed edge (u, v) in G, we add an undirected edge to E' by linking $u \in V_1$ and $v' \in V_2$. This implies that for each vertex $u \in V$, its out-degree in G is equal to the degree of vertex u in G', and its in-degree in G is equal to the degree of vertex u' in G'. Furthermore, in the bipartite graph $G' = (V_1, V_2, E')$, the subgraph induced by $S \subseteq V_1$ and $T \subseteq V_2$ is denoted as $G'[S \cup T]$. With this transformation, we can now establish the following lemma, describing the connection between the HDDS problem over G and the densest subgraph problem over G'; note that, we will treat the undirected bipartite graph G' simply as an undirected graph, by ignoring its bipartiteness.

Lemma 1. *For a given directed graph $G = (V, E)$ and any two sets $S, T \subseteq V$, the harmonic mean-based density of $D = G[S, T]$ in the directed graph G is exactly twice the density of $H = G'[S \cup T]$ in the undirected graph G'.*

Algorithm 1: H-Approx

Input: A directed graph $G = (V, E)$
Output: A 2-approximate HDDS $G[S, T]$
1 Transform G to an undirected graph $G' = (V_1, V_2, E')$;
2 $(S, T) \leftarrow \mathsf{Approx}(G')$;
3 **return** $G[S, T]$;

Procedure $\mathsf{Approx}(G = (V_1, V_2, E))$
4 $S \leftarrow V_1, T \leftarrow V_2, \rho^* \leftarrow \frac{|E(V_1, V_2)|}{|V_1| + |V_2|}$;
5 **while** $G \neq \emptyset$ **do**
6 $\quad$ $u \leftarrow$ the vertex with the smallest degree in G;
7 $\quad$ **if** $u \in V_1$ **then** $V_1 \leftarrow V_1 \setminus \{u\}$;
8 $\quad$ **else** $V_2 \leftarrow V_2 \setminus \{u\}$;
9 $\quad$ **if** $\frac{|E(V_1, V_2)|}{|V_1| + |V_2|} > \rho^*$ **then**
10 $\quad\quad$ $S \leftarrow V_1, T \leftarrow V_2$;
11 $\quad\quad$ $\rho^* \leftarrow \frac{|E(V_1, V_2)|}{|V_1| + |V_2|}$;

12 **return** (S, T);

We propose to first compute the dense subgraph $H = G'[S \cup T]$ in G' using the state-of-the-art 2-approximation algorithm Approx [10], and then construct the directed dense subgraph $D = G[S, T]$ in G. As per Lemma 1, it is established that subgraph $D = G[S, T]$ achieves a 2-approximation ratio to the HDDS in G. The pseudo-code of our algorithm H-Approx is shown in Algorithm 1. Firstly, it transforms the directed graph $G = (V, E)$ to the undirected graph $G' = (V_1, V_2, E')$ (Line 1). Then, it invokes Approx to obtain the dense subgraph $G'[S \cup T]$ in G' (Line 2). Based on the returned S and T, it returns the subgraph $D = G[S, T]$ (Line 3). The procedure Approx uses S and T to record the best solution found so far, and ρ^* to record its density. Firstly, the best solution is initialized as the original graph (Line 4). Then, it iteratively deletes the smallest-degree vertex and its associated edges from the remaining graph (Lines 6–8). After deleting a vertex, it computes the density of the remaining graph and updates S, T, and ρ^* if necessary (Lines 9–11). Finally, it returns (S, T) such that $G[S \cup T]$ has the highest density among all the intermediate subgraphs (Line 12). The time complexity of H-Approx is $\mathcal{O}(n + m)$ by using the bin-sort technique [11].

4   Arithmetic Mean-Based Directed Densest Subgraph

In this section, we present a 2-approximation algorithm for the ADDS problem. Before delving into the details of the algorithm, we first introduce some concepts and prove some important properties that form the basis for our approach.

Definition 5 ((x, y)-core [6]). *Given a directed graph $G = (V, E)$, an (S, T)-induced subgraph $H = G[S, T]$ is called an (x, y)-core if it satisfies:*

(1) $\forall u \in S, d_H^+(u) \geq x$ and $\forall v \in T, d_H^-(v) \geq y$;
(2) $\nexists H'$ s.t. $H \subset H'$ and H' satisfies (1).

We call (x, y) the *core number pair* of the (x, y)-core, abbreviated as *cn-pair*. We call a cn-pair (x, x) as the maximum equal cn-pair, if x has the maximum value among all possible (x, x)-cores.

Definition 6 (Key cn-pair [6]). *Given a directed graph $G = (V, E)$ and its maximum equal cn-pair (γ, γ), the cn-pair of an (x, y)-core is a key cn-pair, if one of the following conditions is satisfied:*

(1) if $x \leq \gamma$, there is no (x, y')-core in G s.t. $y' > y$;
(2) if $y \leq \gamma$, there is no (x', y)-core in G s.t. $x' > x$.

Example 2. Consider the directed graph G in Fig. 1(a). The subgraph induced by $S = \{v_4, v_5\}$ and $T = \{v_2, v_3\}$ is a $(2, 2)$-core, and $(2, 2)$ is the maximum equal cn-pair in G. The subgraph induced by $S = \{v_2, v_4, v_5\}$ and $T = \{v_3\}$ is a $(1, 3)$-core, which is a key cn-pair.

Lemma 2. *Given a directed graph $G = (V, E)$ and its ADDS $D = G[S^*, T^*]$ with density ρ^*, let $\frac{|S^*|}{|T^*|} = a$, it satisfies the following properties:*

(1) For any subset $U_S \subset S^*$, removing U_S from S^* will result in the removal of at least $\frac{2\rho^*|U_S|}{(1+a)^2}$ edges from D;
(2) For any subset $U_T \subset T^*$, removing U_T from T^* will result in the removal of at least $\frac{2\rho^*|U_T|}{(1+\frac{1}{a})^2}$ edges from D.

Corollary 1. *Given a directed graph $G = (V, E)$ and its ADDS $D = G[S^*, T^*]$ with density ρ^*, let $\frac{|S^*|}{|T^*|} = a$, then D is contained in the $(\lceil \frac{2\rho^*}{(1+a)^2} \rceil, \lceil \frac{2\rho^*}{(1+\frac{1}{a})^2} \rceil)$-core.*

Lemma 3. *Given a directed graph $G = (V, E)$ and an (x, y)-core $H = G[S, T]$, we have that $\rho_a(S, T) \geq \frac{x+y}{2}$.*

Definition 7 (Max-sum cn-pair). *Given a directed graph $G = (V, E)$, a cn-pair (x, y) is called max-sum cn-pair, if $x+y$ achieves the maximum value among all the possible (x, y)-cores. We denote the max-sum cn-pair by (x^*, y^*).*

Lemma 4. *(x^*, y^*)-core is a 2-approximate solution to the arithmetic mean-based densest subgraph problem.*

Algorithm 2: A-Approx

Input: A directed graph $G = (V, E)$
Output: A 2-approximate ADDS $G[S, T]$, i.e., (x^*, y^*)-core
1   $x^* \leftarrow 0$, $y^* \leftarrow 0$;
2   Compute the maximum equal cn-pair (γ, γ) by the peeling algorithm [3];
3   **for** $x \leftarrow 1$ *to* γ **do**
4      $y \leftarrow \mathsf{MaxY}(G, x)$;
5   **if** $x + y > x^* + y^*$ **then** $x^* \leftarrow x$, $y^* \leftarrow y$;

6   **for** $y \leftarrow 1$ *to* γ **do**
7      $x \leftarrow \mathsf{MaxX}(G, y)$;
8   **if** $x + y > x^* + y^*$ **then** $x^* \leftarrow x$, $y^* \leftarrow y$;

9   **return** (x^*, y^*)-core;

  Procedure $\mathsf{MaxY}(G, x)$
10   $S \leftarrow V$, $T \leftarrow V$, $y_{max} \leftarrow 0$, $y \leftarrow x^* + y^* - x + 1$;
11   **if** $y > \arg\max_{u \in T} d_G^-(u)$ **then return** y_{max};
12   **while** $|E| > 0$ **do**
13   **while** $\exists u \in T$ *s.t.* $d_G^-(u) < y$ **do**
14          $E \leftarrow E \setminus \{(v, u) \mid v \in S\}$, $T \leftarrow T \setminus \{u\}$;
15   **while** $\exists v \in S$ *s.t.* $d_G^+(v) < x$ **do**
16              $E \leftarrow E \setminus \{(v, u) \mid u \in T\}$, $S \leftarrow S \setminus \{v\}$;

17   **if** $|E| > 0$ **then** $y_{max} \leftarrow y$;
18      $y \leftarrow y + 1$;

19   **return** y_{max};

  Procedure $\mathsf{MaxX}(G, y)$
20   Reuse lines 10-19 by interchanging u with v, S with T, x with y, and changing y_{max} to x_{max};

Next, we will introduce how to compute (x^*, y^*)-core efficiently. One straightforward approach is to compute all (x, y)-cores in G and return the one with the maximum $x + y$ value. The time complexity of this approach is $\mathcal{O}(n(n + m))$, since there are n possible values of x and it takes $\mathcal{O}(n + m)$ to compute all (x, y)-cores for each specific x. Based on the concepts of maximum equal cn-pair and key cn-pair, we propose a more efficient approach to compute (x^*, y^*)-core. As shown in our algorithm A-Approx (i.e., Algorithm 2), it firstly computes the maximum equal cn-pair (γ, γ) by using the peeling algorithm in [3], which iteratively peels vertices that have the minimum in-degrees or out-degrees (Line 2). Then, it enumerates x and y from 1 to γ to search all the key cn-pairs (Lines 3–8). Finally, the (x^*, y^*)-core is returned (Line 9).

Given an input x, the procedure MaxY computes the key cn-pair whose first element is x. In MaxY, it first initializes S, T, y_{max}, and y, where y is set to $x^* + y^* - x + 1$ (Line). Then, in the while loop, if there is vertex $u \in T$ with in-degree less than y, the algorithm deletes it (Lines 13–14). The deletion of u may make some vertices' out-degrees become less than x, so the algorithm deletes these vertices as well (Lines 15–16). After that, we update y_{max} and increase y by 1 (Lines 17–18). Finally, we get the maximum value of y. Similarly, we have a procedure MaxX to get the key cn-pair whose second element is a given y.

Theorem 1. *The time complexity of* A-Approx *(Algorithm 2) is* $\mathcal{O}(\sqrt{m}(n+m))$.

5   Minimum Mean-Based Directed Densest Subgraph

This section is dedicated to a theoretical analysis of the MDDS problem. Subsequently, leveraging the insights from this analysis, we proceed to devise an approximation algorithm tailored specifically for addressing this problem. Firstly, we have the following lemma.

Lemma 5. *Given a directed graph* $G = (V, E)$, *there exists an* (S^*, T^*)-*induced subgraph* $G[S^*, T^*]$ *with the highest minimum mean-based density and* $|S^*| = |T^*|$.

The above lemma highlights that the optimal solution for the MDDS problem exhibits an equal size of vertex sets S and T. Motivated by this insight, we endeavor to find a high-quality approximate solution by enforcing $|S| = |T|$. To achieve this, we introduce an approximation algorithm named M-Approx. The main idea is to maintain two vertex sets S and T, both of equal size, and iteratively remove the minimum out-degree vertex from S and the minimum in-degree vertex from T, until all vertices are removed. Throughout this process, we keep track of the minimum mean-based density of each intermediate (S, T)-induced subgraph and select the highest value as our final result.

The pseudo-code for M-Approx is presented in Algorithm 3. In this algorithm, S^* and T^* are used to store the current optimal solution found, and ρ^* records the corresponding density. Firstly, it initializes both S and T as V (Line 1) and regards the entire graph as the current optimal solution (Line 2). Then, it removes from S the vertex u that has the minimum out-degree and from T the vertex v that has the minimum in-degree (Lines 4–6). After removing u and v, it recomputes the minimum mean-based density of the remained (S, T)-induced subgraph and updates ρ^*, S^*, and T^* if necessary (Lines 7–8). It repeats the above step until S and T become empty. Finally, the algorithm returns the intermediate subgraph $G[S^*, T^*]$ with the highest density, as the desired approximation result (Line 9).

Algorithm 3: M-Approx

Input: A directed graph $G = (V, E)$
Output: A subgraph $G[S, T]$ with high minimum mean-based density
1 $S \leftarrow V, T \leftarrow V$;
2 $S^* \leftarrow S, T^* \leftarrow T, \rho^* \leftarrow \rho_m(S, T)$;
3 **while** $S \neq \emptyset$ and $T \neq \emptyset$ **do**
4       $u \leftarrow \arg\min_{u \in S} d^+_{G[S,T]}(u)$;
5       $v \leftarrow \arg\min_{v \in T} d^-_{G[S,T]}(v)$;
6       $S \leftarrow S \setminus \{u\}, T \leftarrow T \setminus \{v\}$;
7   **if** $\rho_m(S, T) > \rho^*$ **then**
8           $S^* \leftarrow S, T^* \leftarrow T, \rho^* \leftarrow \rho_m(S, T)$;

9 **return** $G[S^*, T^*]$;

Theorem 2. *The time complexity of* M-Approx *(Algorithm 3) is* $\mathcal{O}(n + m)$.

6 Experiments

In this section, we empirically evaluate the efficiency and effectiveness of our algorithms. We compare the following algorithms:

- H-Approx: Our approximation algorithm for the HDDS problem.
- A-Approx: Our approximation algorithm for the ADDS problem.
- M-Approx: Our approximation algorithm for the MDDS problem.
- Core-Approx: The approximation algorithm proposed in [6] for the GDDS problem.

All algorithms are implemented in C++ and compiled with g++ 7.5.0 with the -O3 flag.[1] All experiments are conducted on a machine with an Intel Core-i7 3.20 GHz CPU and 64 GB RAM running Ubuntu 18.04. The time cost is measured as the amount of wall-clock time elapsed during the program's execution.

Datasets. We evaluate our algorithms on 10 real-world directed graphs, which are publicly available on Konect[2]. The main characteristics of the tested graphs are summarized in Table 1, where d^+_{max}, d^-_{max} and γ represent the maximum out-degree, maximum in-degree and the maximum x value among all possible (x, x)-cores in the graph, respectively.

6.1 Effectiveness Evaluation of Different Models

In this experimental study, we analyze the sizes of sets S and T yielded by each algorithm in Table 2. Our observations reveal that, except on Enron and Baidu, both A-Approx and Core-Approx consistently generate identical outcomes across

---

[1] Our source codes are available at https://github.com/kyaocs/DDS.
[2] konect.cc.

Table 1. Statistics of datasets

Abbreviation	Dataset	$|V|$	$|E|$	d_{max}^+	d_{max}^-	γ	Category
TW	Twitter	23,370	33,101	238	57	10	Social
AD	Advogato	5,155	47,135	785	721	18	Social
EN	Enron	86,978	320,154	1,566	1,338	49	Communication
EP	Epinions	75,879	508,837	1,801	3,035	50	Social
AU	AskUbuntu	157,222	544,621	4,965	1,953	34	Communication
AM	Amazon	403,394	3,387,388	10	2,751	10	Trade
YT	YouTube	1,138,494	4,942,297	28,564	25,487	49	Social
WT	wikiTalk	2,394,385	5,021,410	100,022	3,311	96	Communication
BA	Baidu	2,140,198	17,632,190	2,477	97,848	59	Hyperlink
DB	DBpedia	18,268,991	136,537,566	8,105	612,308	132	Hyperlink

various datasets, and their outcomes frequently manifest as imbalanced in terms of the sizes of S and T. For instance, on DBpedia graph, both A-Approx and Core-Approx identify the $(1, 612308)$-core, i.e., $|S| = 612308$ and $|T| = 1$. This outcome can be attributed to the prevalence of the power-law degree distribution characteristic in real-world graphs. Consequently, a small number of vertices tend to exhibit exceptionally high out-degrees or in-degrees, leading to pronounced imbalances in the outcomes. Such skewed outcomes severely curtail the meaningful insights attainable through directed graph analysis. Interestingly, H-Approx exhibits superior equilibrium between the sizes of S and T. For instance, when applied to the DBpedia graph, H-Approx identifies a subgraph with $|S| = 1225$ and $|T| = 1298$. The outcomes produced by M-Approx invariably maintain an equitable balance between the sizes of S and T due to the inherent strict criteria in the algorithm's design.

Table 2. The sizes of S and T returned by each algorithm

	TW	AD	EN	EP	AU
H-Approx	$(16, 29)$	$(401, 386)$	$(626, 813)$	$(796, 631)$	$(287, 353)$
A-Approx	$(1, 238)$	$(1, 785)$	$(1, 1566)$	$(3035, 1)$	$(1, 4965)$
M-Approx	$(17, 17)$	$(387, 387)$	$(679, 679)$	$(697, 697)$	$(322, 322)$
Core-Approx	$(1, 238)$	$(1, 785)$	$(17, 158)$	$(3035, 1)$	$(1, 4965)$
	AM	YT	WT	BA	DB
H-Approx	$(243939, 143922)$	$(1875, 1937)$	$(1179, 1222)$	$(7170, 4059)$	$(1225, 1298)$
A-Approx	$(2751, 1)$	$(1, 28564)$	$(1, 100022)$	$(97848, 1)$	$(612308, 1)$
M-Approx	$(429, 429)$	$(1886, 1886)$	$(1197, 1197)$	$(5270, 5270)$	$(1248, 1248)$
Core-Approx	$(2751, 1)$	$(1, 28564)$	$(1, 100022)$	$(95762, 2)$	$(612308, 1)$

To get a deeper insight into different algorithms and measures, we evaluate the various densities associated with outcomes produced by different algorithms.

Table 3 presents the outcomes for the Epinions dataset. Notably, the densities of outcomes from H-Approx and M-Approx closely align (as evident in the second and fourth rows), which can be attributed to the similar or identical sizes of S and T derived by these algorithms. Conversely, the outcomes generated by A-Approx and Core-Approx showcase considerable density fluctuations across different measures. This fluctuation results from the imbalances in the sizes of S and T. For instance, the outcome produced by A-Approx displays an arithmetic mean-based density of 1518, whereas its harmonic mean-based density, minimum mean-based density, and geometric mean-based density are only 1.99, 1, and 55.09, respectively (as shown in the third row). A noteworthy observation is the higher geometric mean-based density exhibited by outcomes from H-Approx and M-Approx compared to those from Core-Approx. This discrepancy underscores the drawbacks stemming from imbalanced S and T distributions. We also conduct the comparison on YouTube, as shown in Table 4, where a similar phenomenon can be observed.

Table 3. Cross-comparison between different algorithms and measures on Epinions

	$(|S|,|T|,|E|)$	ρ_h	ρ_a	ρ_m	ρ_g
H-Approx	$(796, 631, 63718)$	89.30	90.51	80.05	89.91
A-Approx	$(3035, 1, 3035)$	1.99	1518	1	55.09
M-Approx	$(697, 697, 61724)$	88.56	88.56	88.56	88.56
Core-Approx	$(3035, 1, 3035)$	1.99	1518	1	55.09

Table 4. Cross-comparison between different algorithms and measures on YouTube

	$(|S|,|T|,|E|)$	ρ_h	ρ_a	ρ_m	ρ_g
H-Approx	$(1875, 1937, 168333)$	88.32	88.34	86.90	88.33
A-Approx	$(1, 28564, 28564)$	1.99	14282.5	1	169.01
M-Approx	$(1886, 1886, 166543)$	88.30	88.30	88.30	88.30
Core-Approx	$(1, 28564, 28564)$	1.99	14282.5	1	169.01

6.2   Efficiency Evaluation of Different Algorithms

In this experiment, we evaluate the efficiency of different algorithms on all datasets. As shown in Fig. 2, the running time of H-Approx and M-Approx are almost the same with each other on all datasets. For example, on YouTube, their running times are 0.45 s and 0.42 s, respectively. This alignment is congruent with their underlying theoretical time complexities, both characterized by $\mathcal{O}(n+m)$. A-Approx and Core-Approx are around one or two orders of magnitude slower than H-Approx and M-Approx. For example, on YouTube, the running times of A-Approx and Core-Approx are 5.97 s and 17 s, respectively. This is because A-Approx (resp. Core-Approx) needs to find the (x,y)-core that maximizes $x + y$ (resp. $x \times y$), which leads to the theoretical time complexity of $\mathcal{O}(\sqrt{m}(n+m))$.

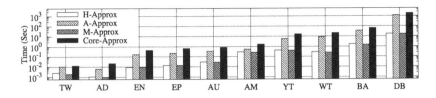

Fig. 2. Running time on all datasets

7 Related Work

Densest Subgraph Detection on Undirected Graphs. Goldberg [12] laid the groundwork for the problem of identifying the densest subgraph in undirected graphs. This problem seeks the subgraph with the highest edge-density among all subgraphs, where the edge-density of a graph $G = (V, E)$ is defined as $\frac{|E|}{|V|}$. Goldberg proposed an exact algorithm based on the max-flow technique. In [10], Charikar proposed a 2-approximation algorithm which takes linear time cost with regard to the graph size. Some variants of the densest subgraph detection problem are also studied, such as the k-clique densest subgraph detection [13–15], the locally densest subgraph detection [16,17], the size-bounded densest subgraph detection [18], and the (p, q)-biclique densest subgraph detection [19]. However, these approaches primarily address undirected graphs and are not directly applicable to the distinct problem formulations tackled in this study.

Densest Subgraph Detection on Directed Graphs. The directed version of the densest subgraph problem was introduced by Kannan and Vinay [2]. In [10], an exact algorithm was proposed by solving $\mathcal{O}(n^2)$ linear programmings. Later, another exact algorithm was proposed in [3] by extending the max-flow based technique. However, these exact algorithms are time-consuming and are not suitable for larger directed graphs. In [2], Kannan and Vinay proposed an $\mathcal{O}(\log n)$-approximation algorithm to compute the directed densest subgraph. In [10], Charikar designed a 2-approximation algorithm with a time complexity of $\mathcal{O}(n^2(n+m))$. Bahmani et al. [8] proposed a $2(1+\epsilon)$-approximation algorithm in the streaming model ($\epsilon > 0$). Recently, Ma et al. [6] proposed an 2-approximation algorithm with time complexity of $\mathcal{O}(\sqrt{m}(n + m))$. However, these algorithms are tailored to address the geometric mean-based directed densest subgraph problem, and their adaptation to the novel problem formulations addressed in this paper remains unexplored.

8 Conclusion

In this paper, we complemented the existing studies of directed densest subgraph identification by introducing three alternative density measures to capture the density between two vertex subsets S and T of a directed graph. Based on these density measures, we formulated three distinct directed densest subgraph problems, and proposed corresponding approximation/heuristic algorithms. Extensive experiments on real-world directed graphs demonstrated the effectiveness and efficiency of our techniques. One interesting direction of future work is to design exact algorithms for the formulated directed densest subgraph problems.

Acknowledgements. This work was partially supported by the Australian Research Council Funding of DP220103731.

References

1. Malliaros, F.D., Vazirgiannis, M.: Clustering and community detection in directed networks: a survey. Phys. Rep. **533**(4), 95–142 (2013)
2. Kannan, R., Vinay, V.: Analyzing the structure of large graphs. Universität Bonn. Institut für Ökonometrie und Operations Research (1999)
3. Khuller, S., Saha, B.: On finding dense subgraphs. In: Albers, S., Marchetti-Spaccamela, A., Matias, Y., Nikoletseas, S., Thomas, W. (eds.) ICALP 2009. LNCS, vol. 5555, pp. 597–608. Springer, Heidelberg (2009). https://doi.org/10.1007/978-3-642-02927-1_50
4. Yang, J., McAuley, J., Leskovec, J.: Detecting cohesive and 2-mode communities indirected and undirected networks. In: Proceedings of the 7th ACM International Conference on Web Search and Data Mining, pp. 323–332 (2014)
5. Sawlani, S., Wang, J.: Near-optimal fully dynamic densest subgraph. In: Proceedings of the 52nd Annual ACM SIGACT Symposium on Theory of Computing, pp. 181–193 (2020)
6. Ma, C., Fang, Y., Cheng, R., Lakshmanan, L.V.S., Zhang, W., Lin, X.: Efficient algorithms for densest subgraph discovery on large directed graphs. In: Proceedings of the 2020 ACM SIGMOD International Conference on Management of Data, SIGMOD 2020, New York, NY, USA, pp. 1051–1066. Association for Computing Machinery (2020)
7. Buehrer, G., Chellapilla, K.: A scalable pattern mining approach to web graph compression with communities. In: Proceedings of the 2008 International Conference on Web Search and Data Mining, pp. 95–106 (2008)
8. Bahmani, B., Kumar, R., Vassilvitskii, S.: Densest subgraph in streaming and mapreduce. Proc. VLDB Endow. **5**(5) (2012)
9. Gionis, A., Tsourakakis, C.E.: Dense subgraph discovery: KDD 2015 tutorial. In: Proceedings of the 21th ACM SIGKDD International Conference on Knowledge Discovery and Data Mining, KDD 2015, New York, NY, USA, pp. 2313–2314. Association for Computing Machinery (2015)
10. Charikar, M.: Greedy approximation algorithms for finding dense components in a graph. In: Jansen, K., Khuller, S. (eds.) APPROX 2000. LNCS, vol. 1913, pp. 84–95. Springer, Heidelberg (2000). https://doi.org/10.1007/3-540-44436-X_10
11. Batagelj, V., Zaversnik, M.: An o (m) algorithm for cores decomposition of networks. arXiv preprint cs/0310049 (2003)
12. Goldberg, A.V.: Finding a maximum density subgraph (1984)
13. Fang, Y., Yu, K., Cheng, R., Lakshmanan, L.V.S., Lin, X.: Efficient algorithms for densest subgraph discovery. Proc. VLDB Endow. **12**(11), 1719–1732 (2019)
14. Tsourakakis, C.: The k-clique densest subgraph problem. In: Proceedings of the 24th International Conference on World Wide Web, pp. 1122–1132 (2015)

15. Sun, B., Danisch, M., Chan, T.H.H., Sozio, M.: KClist++: a simple algorithm for finding k-clique densest subgraphs in large graphs. Proc. VLDB Endow. (PVLDB) (2020)

16. Qin, L., Li, R.-H., Chang, L., Zhang, C.: Locally densest subgraph discovery. In: Proceedings of the 21th ACM SIGKDD International Conference on Knowledge Discovery and Data Mining, pp. 965–974 (2015)

17. Trung, T.B., Chang, L., Long, N.T., Yao, K., Binh, H.T.T.: Verification-free approaches to efficient locally densest subgraph discovery. In: 2023 IEEE 39th International Conference on Data Engineering (ICDE), pp. 1–13. IEEE (2023)

18. Andersen, R., Chellapilla, K.: Finding dense subgraphs with size bounds. In: Avrachenkov, K., Donato, D., Litvak, N. (eds.) WAW 2009. LNCS, vol. 5427, pp. 25–37. Springer, Heidelberg (2009). https://doi.org/10.1007/978-3-540-95995-3_3

19. Mitzenmacher, M., Pachocki, J., Peng, R., Tsourakakis, C., Xu, S.C.: Scalable large near-clique detection in large-scale networks via sampling. In: Proceedings of the 21th ACM SIGKDD International Conference on Knowledge Discovery and Data Mining, pp. 815–824 (2015)

Author Index

Printed in the United States
by Baker & Taylor Publisher Services